Understanding
corporate strategy

Withdrawn

Understanding corporate strategy

John L. Thompson

University of Huddersfield

THOMSON
LEARNING

Australia   Canada   Mexico   Singapore   Spain   United Kingdom   United States

THOMSON

LEARNING

Understanding Corporate Strategy

Copyright © 2001 John L Thompson

The Thomson Learning logo is a registered trademark used herein under licence.

For more information, contact Thomson Learning,
Berkshire House, 168–173 High Holborn, London WC1V 7AA or visit us on the World Wide Web at:
http://www.thomsonlearning.co.uk

British Library Cataloguing-in-Publication Data
A catalogue record for this book is available from the British Library

ISBN 1-86152-755-1

Text design by Malcolm Harvey Young
Produced by Gray Publishing, Tunbridge Wells

Printed in Great Britain by The Alden Press, Oxford

Contents

Preface

About This Book

This book is about corporate strategy – the direction and specific strategies chosen by different organizations in their search for distinctiveness, competitiveness and success. It focuses on the analytical approach to studying the subject of strategy, examining the strategic change options available to organizations of various types and sizes, and providing a series of models and approaches for strategic decision making. There is, however, proper consideration of how changes typically happen in reality. Because competitive strategy is a fundamental component of corporate strategy for many organizations, this subject is also examined in some depth. To make the book complete, the final chapter introduces the topic of strategy implementation and change. Normally when we include a detailed treatment of strategy implementation and strategic change management we adopt the term 'strategic management' to describe the subject.

The book is designed for use by students who will become future managers and for managers in practice; after all, as we shall see, in some way or another '*all managers are strategy makers*'. It looks, therefore, at how managers become strategically aware of their company's position and potential opportunities for change and at how changes often happen in reality.

Corporate strategy and strategic management are concerned with the actions that organizations take to deal with the changes, opportunities, threats, challenges and surprises in their external and internal environments. Put simply, strategies are means to ends. We need to understand how organizations:

- determine desired outcomes
- understand the circumstances and events affecting these outcomes and the means of attaining them
- decide upon actions they intend to take
- implement these desired strategies through a series of tactical moves and changes
- evaluate progress and relative success.

These are the broad themes we address in this book.

Although derived from its 'big brother', John Thompson's *Strategic Management* (Thomson Learning, 1990, 1993, 1997 and 2001), this book is new and it contains the latest thinking and ideas on strategy. In recent years, the subject of corporate strategy has been developed and our understanding of certain aspects has changed. In addition, the 'world of business' has been transformed by the rapid growth of the Internet and the emergence of the new and entrepreneurial 'dot.com' organizations. Indeed, entrepreneurship as a subject has also increased in popularity and significance and it is not realistic to treat it as completely divorced from strategy as the two are very clearly related.

How To Use This book

Structure and content

The content follows the established Analysis, Evaluation, Implementation model and is structured in thirteen chapters.

Chapter 1 introduces corporate strategy and strategic management, explores the scope of the subject and explains the differences between prescribed (intended) strategy and emergent strategy. It also defines a number of key concepts and it has been designed to serve, in part, as a reference chapter for these important strategic ideas. It concludes by looking at strategy in different organizational contexts. The theme of Chapter 2 is mission and objectives – we look at issues of purpose and outcomes. Strategies, after all, are means to ends. Developing from this, Chapter 3 is an extensive treatment of strategic success. It incorporates a new, holistic model and explores the relevance of reputation. Financial measures are included as a supplement. Chapter 4 examines culture and values – culture is a vital element of our study as it determines how strategies and changes are both determined and implemented.

These four chapters thus address the following questions:

- How is the organization doing? Where is it doing well and where is it doing less well?
- Where is the organization going – and how might this have to be changed?

The next three chapters concentrate on environmental analysis, resources and competitiveness. We begin by looking at two distinct but clearly related approaches to strategy, opportunity-driven and resource-based strategic management. These chapters then include a number of tools and techniques which help us to understand the current competitive situation, strategic positioning and competitive advantage. We ask:

- Where are the future opportunities and threats for the organization?
- How might it capitalize on its strengths, competencies and capabilities and reduce any key weaknesses?
- How can its competitiveness be improved and strengthened?

Chapter 5 focuses on the environment, Chapter 6 on competition and competitive strategy and Chapter 8 on strategic resources.

Chapters 8–12 first describe and evaluate the different ways in which strategies are formulated and created. We discuss a number of valuable planning models and techniques (Chapter 9). We also look at both entrepreneurship and intrapreneurship in Chapters 8 and 10. There is then (in Chapter 11) a study of the various strategic alternatives which a firm might consider and (Chapter 12) the determinants of a good choice. Chapter 11 incorporates changes in both corporate and competitive strategies, and it deals with both growth and retrenchment issues. It also includes a section on international strategy. Chapter 12 has sections on strategic decision making and judgement.

We are therefore asking:

- How might the organization be developed in the future?
- How can its competitiveness be strengthened? – and assess
- How good is the organization's information management?
- What corporate strategic alternatives are available and worthy of serious consideration?
- What can, cannot, should and should not the organization do in the future?

The final chapter (Chapter 13) introduces the issues involved in strategy implementation. Organization structures, corporate management style and the complexities of managing change are included.

Differing Perspectives

It must be emphasized that no single approach, model or theory can explain the realities of strategic change in practice for all organizations; different organizations and managers will find certain approaches much more relevant to their circumstances and style. All approaches will have both supporters and critics. It is therefore important to study the various approaches within a sound intellectual framework so that they can be evaluated by students and other readers.

Students of business and management and practising managers must work out for themselves the intricacies and difficulties of managing organizations at the corporate level and of managing strategic change at all levels of the organization. It is no good being told how to be prescriptive when it is patently obvious that there is no universal model. Observations of practice in isolation are equally limited in their usefulness. However, an attempt to find explanations which can be utilized does make sense. Testing and evaluating reality against a theoretical framework helps this process.

Key features

Cases and examples

In addition to numerous references in the main text to organizations and events, every chapter opens with a carefully selected case study. Well-known organizations such as Marks and Spencer, McDonald's, Coca-Cola, Disney, Lego and Apple are all included. Two long cases are included at the end of the book to enable further consideration of the key issues we discuss. Amazon.com and C & J Clark ('Clarks shoes') have been deliberately selected as they are organizations with which most, if not all, readers will be familiar. The cases and examples relate to a wide variety of organization types and sizes – and they are international in their coverage. While the cases are designed to illustrate points in the main text, they are also intended to supplement your own experiences and reading. There are specific questions at the end of every chapter to help you to focus your thinking on the key issues. In addition, relevant website addresses are provided to enable easy follow-up.

Inevitably some of the cases will 'date' in the sense that the strategies and fortunes of the companies featured in the examples will change. Strategies have life cycles, and strategies which prove effective at certain times will not always remain so. Companies that fail to change their strategies at the right time are likely to experience declining fortunes. I have sometimes included questions at the ends of chapters which encourage you to research and analyse the subsequent fortunes of companies included as cases.

Additional case examples are also included on the accompanying website.

Boxes

There are three types of box used in the text and featured separately within the relevant chapter for special emphasis and easy reference:

 Key Concepts boxes define and explain significant concepts and contributions which underpin an understanding of strategic management.

Discussion boxes feature particular debates where there are differing opinions.

Strategy in Action boxes provide annotated applications of particular ideas and concepts.

Pause for thought. Short and pithy quotations from a variety of senior managers in the private and the public sectors are sprinkled throughout the text to illustrate a spectrum of opinions. These are useful for provoking class discussion and examination questions.

Figures

A comprehensive set of figures, which are either new or redrawn, illustrate and explain the issues covered in the text.

Chapter summary

There is an outline summary of the content and main points at the end of every chapter. This can help readers to check that they appreciate the main points and issues before they read on.

Questions and research projects

These are included at the end of each chapter. Some questions relate to the ideas contained in the text and the illustrative cases, and some are examples of the type that feature in non-case study examinations of this subject.

A number of research projects, both library and Internet based, are included to encourage you to develop your knowledge and understanding further. The library-based assignments assume access to a library in the UK; lecturers in other countries will be able to advise students on similar, more local, companies which can be substituted and researched. The website provides a 'gateway' of links to sites that are helpful in researching the Internet projects.

Comprehensive version

Understanding Corporate Strategy is ideal for those readers studying or teaching a one-semester strategy course focusing on the analytical aspects of strategic management. *Strategic Management (Thomson Learning,* 4th edition, 2001) provides a more comprehensive treatment of the subject. This book has 25 chapters and it:

- looks at strategic alternatives in far more depth
- examines key aspects of strategic leadership
- includes a chapter on business failure
- develops the study of strategy implementation and strategic change considerably.

Strategic Management has over 100 minicases and a comprehensive set of long cases at the end.

Website

An extensive accompanying website (accessible from http://www.thomson-learning.co.uk) provides a comprehensive set of additional resources for both students and lecturers. It includes additional material and examples about strategic management, links to companies and further information sources, guidance for lecturers and interactive resources for students. Full details are given in the following sections.

Advice for Lecturers

Teaching aims

The main purpose of the book is to help students who aim to become managers, and managers in practice, to:

- develop their strategic awareness
- increase their understanding of how the functional areas of management (in which they are most likely to work) contribute to strategic management and to strategic changes within organizations
- appreciate how proposed strategic changes are selected.

The content is broad and the treatment is both academic and practical, in order to provide value for practising managers as well as full- and part-time students. The subject matter included is taught in a wide variety of courses including undergraduate courses in business studies and related areas, MBA and other postgraduate master's degrees, post-experience management courses and courses for a number of professional qualifications. The subject can be entitled corporate strategy, strategic management, business policy, or business planning.

The material is relevant for all types of organization: large and small businesses, manufacturing and service organizations, and both the public and private sectors. The examples included relate to all of these. Although the topics discussed are broadly applicable, there are certain issues which are sector specific, and these are discussed individually.

Clearly some lecturers will opt to spend longer on some topics than others or possibly switch the order of the chapters marginally. Neither of these should present any problems and there are suggested course outlines provided on the website for different types of course.

The website

Lecturers who adopt this book for their course can gain access to the protected section of the accompanying website (contact your local Thomson Learning representative for access details), which includes:

- Suggested course structures for different levels and lengths of courses
- Learning outcomes for each chapter
- Lecture notes to accompany each chapter
- Guidance on using the Internet exercises with students
- Guidance on teaching using case studies
- Additional case studies
- Teaching notes for the long case studies with suggested answers to the case questions
- A test bank of questions containing over 100 exercises
- PowerPoint slides for each chapter

In addition, lecturers can obviously access all the material that is freely available to students (outlined below).

Advice for Students

Studying strategy

Corporate strategy is concerned with understanding, as well as choosing and implementing, the strategy or strategies that an organization follows. It is a complex process which can be considered from a number of different perspectives. For example, one can design prescriptive models based upon a series of logical stages which look at how to choose and implement strategies aimed at achieving some form of long-term success for the organization. This is a systematic approach designed to bring about optimum results. An alternative paradigm, or conceptual framework, is a systemic approach which concerns understanding what is happening in reality and thinking about how things might be improved. The emphasis is on learning about how strategic management is practised by looking at what organizations actually do and by examining the decisions they make and carry out.

In this book we consider both these perspectives, linking them together. While it is always useful to develop models which attempt to provide optimizing solutions, this approach is inadequate if it fails to explain reality. Strategic management and strategic change are dynamic, often the result of responses to environmental pressures, and frequently not the product of extensive deliberations involving all affected managers.

Managers should be aware of the issues and questions which must be addressed if changes in strategy are to be formulated and implemented effectively. At the same time they should be aware of the managerial and behavioural processes which take place within organizations in order that they can understand how changes actually come about.

Prescriptive models are in fact found quite frequently in business and management teaching. For example, there are models for rational decision making built around the clear recognition and definition of a problem and the careful and objective analysis and evaluation of the alternative solutions. There are economic models of various market structures showing how an organization can maximize profit. However, decision making invariably involves subjectivity and short cutting; and organizations do not always seek profit maximization as their top priority. Although organizations and individuals rarely follow these models slavishly – quite often they cannot, and sometimes they choose not to – this does not render them worthless. Far from it; they provide an excellent framework or yardstick for evaluating how people reach their decisions, what objectives are being pursued and how situations might be improved. The argument is that if managers observe what is happening and seek to explain it and evaluate it against some more ideal state then they will see ways of managing things more effectively. In this way managerial performance can be improved. Note the use of the expression 'more effectively'. For a whole variety of reasons situations cannot be managed 'perfectly'.

If you have personal experience of organizations, management and change (whether it is limited or extensive, broad or specialized) you should use this experience to complement the examples and cases described in the book. Ideally the experience and the cases will be used jointly to evaluate the theories and concepts discussed. There is no universal approach to the management of strategy and strategic change. You must establish for yourself what approaches and decisions are likely to prove most effective in particular circumstances, and why. This is a learning experience which can be enhanced

(a) by evaluating the theoretical and conceptual contributions of various authors
(b) by considering practical examples of what has proved successful and unsuccessful for organizations
(c) by examining these two aspects in combination to see which theories and concepts best help an understanding of reality.

Managers perform a number of activities, including planning and organizing the work of their subordinates, motivating them, controlling what happens and evaluating results. All managers are planners to some degree; and it is extremely useful if they can develop an ability to observe clearly what is really happening in organizations and reflect on how things might be improved. Kolb (1979) calls this the learning cycle, and it can be usefully applied to a study of strategic management and change. Students and managers build on their own experiences when they read about theories and concepts and think about case study examples. They should reflect upon all these experiences continually and seek to develop personal concepts which best explain for them what happens in practice.

Wherever appropriate they should experiment with, and test out, these concepts to establish how robust they are. This, of course, constitutes added experience for further reflection. In other words:

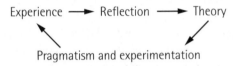

This approach is illustrated in more detail in Figure 1.

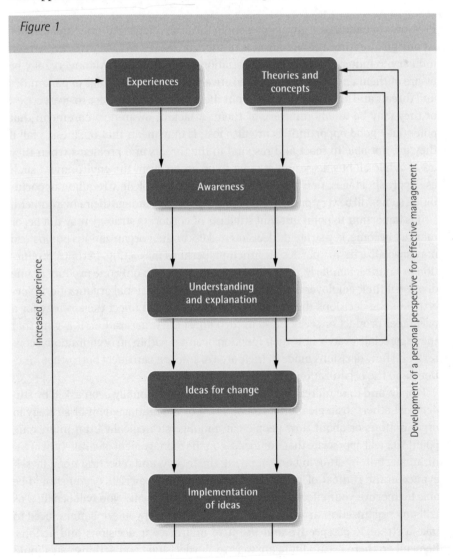

Figure 1

Experiences, theories and concepts generate awareness. This, with reflection, improves understanding. Constant evaluation helps to develop a personal perspective of effective management. This process is enhanced by trying out ideas which generate new experiences.

The manager's job is change. It is what we live with. It is what we are to create. If we cannot do that, then we are not good at the job. It is our basic job to have the nerve to keep changing and changing and changing again.

(Sir Peter Parker)

Pressures to change are always present in the form of opportunities and threats. At any point in time the significance of these pressures will vary markedly from industry to industry and from organization to organization. Managers may be aware of them and seek to respond positively; they may recognize opportunities and threats and choose to do little about them other than perhaps to avert crises; or they may be totally unaware of them. A lack of awareness can mean that potentially good opportunities are also lost; it may mean that businesses fail if they are not able to react and respond to the threats and problems when they arise. While all businesses must react to pressures from the environment such as supply shortages, new products from competitors or new retailing opportunities, some will be very proactive and thereby seek to manage their environment.

It is important to point out that students of corporate strategy may not be, or may not become, key strategic decision makers in their organizations but instead may specialize in one particular function, perhaps marketing, perhaps production or finance. Similarly, their experience may be with only one product or one division if their employer is a multiproduct or multidivisional organization. Nevertheless the decisions they make or contribute to can affect the strategy for a particular product or service and in turn affect the organization. It is vital that they appreciate exactly how their function operates within an organizational context, and how decisions made in their area of interest can affect both other functions and the organization as a whole.

Finally, and to reinforce this last point, I have occasionally been asked by students whether 'strategic management' is about the management of strategy in organizations or about how people can manage strategically – an interesting point! You will appreciate that our focus is on the management of strategy in organizations, but, by studying and applying the theory, and reflecting upon its relevance in the context of personal observations and experience, you should be able to improve your effectiveness as a manager. In essence you will benefit – as will any organization in which you work in – because you are better placed to take a strategic perspective and use it to inform your decisions and actions. Remember, there are no finite answers to the decisions and actions you should take. Organizations, and many of the problem issues they have to deal with, are complex and ill-defined. After all, if strategy was straightforward, the relative success rate of organizations of every type and size would be much greater than it is.

> *Experience is a wonderful thing, but not a useful one. When you are young, you don't trust others' experience – for if you do, this can paralyse you. When you get old, it is too late to use it – and you cannot transmit it for the reasons outlined.*
> (Jacques Calvet, Le President du Directoire, PSA Peugeot Citroën)

The website

Anybody studying with this book can use the accompanying website, which includes:

- revision notes
- links to general strategy sites and company homepages
- a '*gateway*' site of links to help readers research the projects suggested at the end of each chapter
- '*Want to know more?*' in-depth coverage of topics referenced from the text
- Further Reading suggestions
- updates to case studies
- interactive multiple choice quizzes to test your understanding of each chapter
- an online searchable glossary
- '*Words of Wisdom*' quotes from real managers.

Reference

Kolb, DA (1979) *Organizational Psychology*, Prentice Hall.

Introducing Strategy and Strategic Management

1

Introducing Strategy

The Strategic Management Process

Strategy Creation

Key Strategic Concerns

Strategic Management in Specific Contexts

Summary

Strategies are means to ends. All organizations, large and small, profit-seeking and not-for-profit, private and public sector, have a purpose, which may or may not be articulated in the form of a mission statement. Strategies relate to the pursuit of this purpose. Strategies must be created and implemented, and it is these issues which are addressed by our study of strategic management. This opening chapter begins by outlining how successful organizations manage their strategies, and what they achieve, before exploring the meaning of strategy in greater detail. It then continues by describing how the subject of strategic management has been developed in the past 30 years, before explaining the different ways that strategies are created. This is followed by an introduction to a number of important strategic concepts which affect strategy creation and implementation in every organization, and which crop up in many places throughout the book. This part of the chapter thus constitutes a valuable reference section if readers need to re-check the meaning of key strategic concepts. The chapter concludes with a brief consideration of the similarities and differences in strategic management in various types of organization.

Case Study 1: Marks and Spencer plc

Marks and Spencer (M&S) is a well-known and revered high-street retailer in the UK. The early growth of M&S was built around clothing, and its reputation owes much to the popularity of its underwear! It built a second reputation for foods, pioneering chilled fresh varieties. Always gradually, other ranges such as cosmetics, homewear, gifts and furniture have been added systematically. A home-delivery service for furniture has been expanded to include other items. Every shopping centre developer wants M&S to open a store, as they always attract customers.

The original foundations of the business lay with a young, Jewish immigrant and his Leeds market stall. Michael Marks had a poor grasp of English, a clear disadvantage for a trader in a noisy street market! Opportunistically, he turned his disadvantage into a strength. He had a sign on his stall: *Don't Ask The Price – It's a Penny*, and for a penny he provided the widest range and best-quality items he could find. This philosophy of *value for money* has pervaded through the generations and been sustained with innovation and change – but the focus on value has never been lost. The market stall led to a store, and then to stores on most high streets in Britain. The Spencer name came from Marks' first partner, an accountant. However the Marks family became related to the Sieff family through marriage and it is these two families who have dominated the business for most of its history. Indeed, Michael Sieff, who controlled the business though most of the middle years of the twentieth century, is regarded as a 'retail genius' and the person who established and cemented in place Marks and Spencer's high-street dominance.

The strategy of M&S then, is concerned with diversification of their product ranges within these broad product groups, but at the same time seeking to specialize where their own St Michael label could be used effectively. All M&S products have traditionally carried the M&S name and quite often the St Michael brand. At the beginning of the new millennium a decision has been made to reduce the emphasis on using the St Michael brand name and emphasize the company name more prominently. M&S seeks to innovate whilst upgrading and adding value to its existing ranges. Over the years, M&S has found that many of its long-established stores in town and city centres are simply too small. An expansion programme has therefore developed along several lines. Adjacent units have been acquired when practical and new larger stores created, especially in new out-of-town shopping centres; if land has been available, buildings have been extended; and new sales floors have been opened up by converting stockrooms and moving stock to outside warehouses. This brings its own logistics problems. Satellite stores – smaller branches some distance away from the main branch – have been opened in certain towns. These satellites typically carry complete ranges – it might be men's fashions, ladies' clothes or children's items. The choice depends on the square footage available and the local prospects for particular lines. In a similar vein, in towns considered too small to support a full branch, specialist stores, perhaps just for food, have been opened. The selection of products within the whole M&S range varies between stores.

Other strategic changes are:

- Constant improvements in displays, partly to present products better, and also to get more items into the stores. 'Sales per square foot' is a vital measure of success.
- Electronic point-of-sale (EPOS). Information technology has been harnessed to improve productivity and to enable M&S to respond more quickly to market changes, particularly relevant for fashion items. Thanks in part to technology, M&S staff costs as a percentage of their turnover are less than those of many competitors, but the quality of service has remained high.
- The development of support financial services, such as unit trusts, building upon the success of the M&S Chargecard, the third most popular credit card in the UK.
- International growth in, for example, France, Belgium, Canada, the USA and Hong Kong. The development has been gradual, with one of the objectives being to introduce new types of competition. Some mistakes have been made as part of the learning process, and sales in some countries have been disappointing, but the risks have been contained in order not to threaten the UK interests.

In the 1930s M&S pioneered a new form of inventory control when it designed perforated tags in two identical halves. Half was torn off at the point-of-sale, dropped in a box and then sent to the Baker Street (London) head office, where it was used to direct store replenishment. Over time this enabled M&S to introduce sophisticated replenishment from out-of-town warehouses and reduce the in-store stockrooms in favour of more direct selling space.

M&S possesses a number of identifiable strategic resources which have been instrumental in meeting customer key success factors, and thereby providing long-term profitable returns for shareholders. They include:

Physical resources	–	The wide range of value-for-money, own-brand products The sites and store displays
Intangible resources	–	Image and reputation Staff knowledge, expertise and commitment to service
Capabilities/processes	–	Supply-chain management.

While there have been, and continue to be, strategic changes, the fundamental principles or values of the business have remained constant. These are:

- high-quality, dependable products, styled conservatively and offering good value for money
- good relations with employees, customers, suppliers and other stakeholders
- simple operations
- comfortable stores
- financial prudence (most properties, for example, are freehold – they have not been sold and leased back to fund the expansion).

The foundation for the unique (St Michael) products and competitive prices is the M&S system of supply-chain relationships, a considerable proportion of these being with UK manufacturers for much of its history. In recent years M&S has, somewhat controversially, included more and more goods sourced overseas, sometimes for particular quality issues, but mostly for lower costs. In general, where they have been successful, the arrangements with suppliers have been long term and non-contractual. They are based on mutual trust and common understanding. M&S is actively involved in product specification, input management (to its suppliers), quality control and production scheduling. M&S is frequently the supplier's most important customer. Why has it worked so effectively? The M&S reputation for fair dealing – with its suppliers, customers and employees – has been seen as too valuable to put at risk.

But, at the end of the 1990s, this long-established business was suffering declines in sales and profits. Critics argued that too many product ranges were no longer the winners that people associated with the company, and its management needed strengthening at all levels. Interestingly, this setback occurred in the decade when the company had, for the first time in its history, a chief executive who was not a descendant of one of the Marks or Sieff families.This change had taken place in the mid-1980s.

Peter Drucker (1985) had earlier summarized M&S as 'probably more entrepreneurial and innovative than any other company is Western Europe these last fifty years . . . may have had a greater impact on the British economy, and even on British society, than any other change agent in Britain, and arguably more than government or laws'.

Was it conceivable that this visible and successful business was under real threat for the first time? One executive, Clara Freeman (2000), admitted that M&S 'lost the pace, lost the focus . . . no-one saw it coming. It was the classic management story – everything is going swimmingly and you don't tinker with a successful formula. After sales and profits declined, M&S put the magnifying lens on the business and asked what was wrong. Staff and customers told us that the quality was not as consistent as it used to be, and the service needs to be better than it is'.

In 1999 the current Chairman and Chief Executive, Richard Greenbury, announced he would retire early and, after a very visible and acrimonious internal wrangle, a new Chief Executive (Peter Salsbury) was appointed from inside the business. Later, a new Executive Chairman, Luc Van de Velde, previously the head of a major French supermarket chain, was recruited. Several ranges were quickly revamped and successful stock trials accelerated. M&S began to use more demographic and customer data to determine the product ranges for each store – previously stores of roughly the same size had carried similar ranges, regardless of their location. Sales did not pick up as rapidly as had been hoped, and rumours of possible take-over bids appeared in the press. Peter Salsbury has has also left the business.

References

Drucker, PF (1985) *Innovation and Entrepreneurship*, Heinemann.
Freeman, C (2000) Interview, *Management Today*, January.

QUESTIONS: Why do you think Marks and Spencer's fortunes changed as quickly as they did? How might such a decline have been avoided?

(If you are an M&S customer . . .) Did you notice many changes during 2000 and 2001?

Marks and Spencer   http://www.marks-and-spencer.co.uk

Introducing Strategy

At their simplest, strategies help to explain the things that managers and organizations do. These actions or activities are designed and carried out in order to fulfil certain designated purposes, some of them short term in nature, others longer term. The organization has a direction and broad purpose, which should always be clear, articulated and understood, and that sometimes will be summarized in the form of a mission statement. More specific milestones and targets (objectives) can help to guide specific actions and measure progress. Strategies, then, are means to ends. As we shall see, they are relevant to the organization as a whole, and for the individual businesses and/or functions which comprise the organization. They are created and changed in a variety of ways. They have, however, one common feature: they all have lifecycles and need changing, either marginally or dramatically, at certain times.

The need for all managers to be able to think strategically was stressed in the Preface, and the approach taken in this book concentrates on the development of strategic awareness. While strategic management incorporates major changes of direction for the whole business, such as diversification and growth overseas, it also involves smaller changes in strategies for individual products and services and in particular functions such as marketing and operations. Decisions by managers in relation to their particular areas of product or functional responsibility have a strategic impact and contribute to strategic change. To some extent all managers are strategy makers.

Strategic management is a complex and fascinating subject with straightforward underlying principles but no 'right answers'. Companies succeed if their strategies are appropriate for the circumstances they face, feasible in respect of their resources, skills and capabilities, and desirable to their important stakeholders: those individuals and groups, both internal and external, who have a stake in, and an influence over, the business. Simply, strategy is fundamentally about a fit between the organization's resources and the markets that it targets – plus, of course, the ability to sustain fit over time and in changing circumstances.

Companies fail when their strategies fail to meet the expectations of these stakeholders or produce outcomes which are undesirable to them. To succeed in the long term, companies must compete effectively and outperform their rivals in a dynamic, and often turbulent, environment. To accomplish this they must find suitable ways for creating and adding value for their customers. A culture of internal co-operation and customer orientation, together with a willingness to learn, adapt and change, is ideal. Alliances and good working relationships with suppliers, distributors and customers are often critically important as well.

While strategy is a complex topic, the underlying principles are essentially simple. There is, though, no 'one best way' of managing strategic change; and no single technique or model can provide either the right answer concerning what an organization should do, or superior and crystal-clear insight into a situation. Instead, managers should utilize the range of theories and concepts which are available, adapting them to meet their own situation and circumstances.

At the same time, a study of strategic changes in a variety of different organizations is valuable. An examination of outcomes, followed by an analysis of the decisions which led to these relative successes and failures, is rich in learning potential. Examples should not be confined to just one sector. Manufacturing and service businesses, the private and public sectors and not-for-profit organizations are all relevant.

Everyone who can make or influence decisions which impact on the strategic effectiveness of the business should have at least a basic understanding of the concepts and processes of strategy. The processes will often be informal, and the outcomes not documented clearly. But they still exist, and managing the processes effectively determines the organization's future.

Without this understanding, people often fail to appreciate the impact of their decisions and actions for other people within the business. They are less likely to be able to learn from observing and reflecting on the actions of others. They are also more likely to miss or misjudge new opportunities and growing threats in the organization's environment.

As a starting point, key terms used in this book are defined in Box 1.1 and examples of strategic change in a number of different organizations are illustrated in Box 1.2.

KEY CONCEPT – Box 1.1
Key Terms

Mission is the essential purpose of the organization, concerning particularly why it is in existence, the nature of the business(es) it is in, and the customers it seeks to serve and satisfy.

Objectives (or goals) are desired states or results linked to particular time-scales and concerning such things as size or type of organization, the nature and variety of the areas of interest and levels of success.

Strategies are means to ends, and these ends concern the purpose and objectives of the organization. They are the things that businesses do, the paths they follow, and the decisions they take, in order to reach certain points and levels of success.

KEY CONCEPT – Box 1.1 (Continued)

Tactics are the specific activities which deliver and implement the strategies in order to fulfil objectives and pursue the mission. Often short term, they can be changed frequently if necessary.

Strategic management is a process which needs to be understood more than it is a discipline which can be taught. It is the process by which organizations determine their purpose, objectives and desired levels of attainment; decide on actions for achieving these objectives in an appropriate time-scale, and frequently in a changing environment; implement the actions; and assess progress and results. Whenever and wherever necessary the actions may be changed or modified. The magnitude of these changes can be dramatic and revolutionary, or more gradual and evolutionary.

Strategic change concerns changes which take place over time to the strategies and objectives of the organization. Change can be gradual or evolutionary; or more dramatic, even revolutionary.

Strategic awareness is the understanding of managers within the organization about: (a) the strategies being followed by the organization and its competitors, (b) how the effectiveness of these strategies might be improved, and (c) the need for, and suitability of, opportunities for change.

Synergy is the term used for the added value or additional benefits which ideally accrue from the linkage or fusion of two businesses, or from increased co-operation either between different parts of the same organization or between a company and its suppliers, distributors and customers. Internal co-operation may represent linkages between either different divisions or different functions.

STRATEGY IN ACTION – Box 1.2

Examples of Strategy Changes

Lex Service Group, sizeable distributor of Rover, Rolls Royce and Volvo cars in the main, felt too dependent on one area of business and sought to find suitable diversification opportunities. Lex chose four- and five-star hotels in the UK and USA but later chose to sell them when the results were below those desired. This took place in the 1970s and 1980s, since when Lex entered and exited the distribution of electronics parts. More recently Lex has acquired related businesses to become the UK's largest car distribution and leasing company. In 1995 Lex bought Multipart, a distributor of commercial vehicle parts; and more recently it has acquired the roadside assistance business, the RAC.

Lex Service Group   http://www.lex.co.uk

WH Smith, desiring growth beyond the scope offered from its (then) current business lines (wholesaling and retailing newspapers and magazines, stationery, books and sounds), diversified into do-it-yourself with a chain of Do-It-All stores, introduced travel agencies into a number of its existing stores and acquired related interests in Canada and America. Travel was later divested, along with investments in cable television, to enable greater concentration on sounds, videos and consumer and office stationery. Important acquisitions included the Our Price

STRATEGY IN ACTION – Box 1.2 (Continued)

and Virgin music stores and the Waterstone's chain of specialist booksellers. Do-It-All became a joint venture with Boots, but it struggled to be profitable with strong competition from B & Q (owned by Kingfisher) and Texas, acquired by Sainsbury's in the mid-1990s. In 1996 WH Smith divested Do-It-All and its office stationery businesses. Later in the 1990s both Waterstone's and Our Price were also divested, and the book publisher, Hodder Headline, was acquired. These are all examples of corporate strategic change.

In October 1995 WH Smith, responding to the willingness of the leading supermarket chains to sell newspapers, magazines and a carefully selected range of books – with discounted prices for current bestsellers – began to discount books from a number of publishers. This was an important change of competitive strategy as, previously, Smiths had been a staunch supporter of the Net Book Agreement. This longstanding agreement between publishers and booksellers was designed to prevent intense price competition.

WH Smith   http://www.whsmith.co.uk

The Burton Group sold the last of its manufacturing interests in 1988. Once one of the leading men's clothing manufacturers in Europe the group, by a series of acquisitions and divestments, has become essentially a major retailer of fashion goods for both men and women. In recent years Burton acquired – and later divested – Debenham's.

Arcadia (Burton Group)   http://www.arcadia.co.uk

UK building societies, restrained by legislation until the mid-1980s, expanded their financial services to include current accounts with cheque books and cash-dispensing machines – to compete more aggressively with the high-street banks – and diversified into such linked activities as estate agencies and insurance. Mergers took place between, for example, the Halifax and Leeds Permanent societies and Abbey National and National & Provincial, to strengthen their positions as diversified financial institutions. Moreover, the largest ones (notably Abbey National and the Halifax) have given up their mutual status and become quoted companies.

In a quite different (and more evolutionary) way the decision by high-street banks to open on Saturdays for a limited range of services was strategic change. Here the banks were copying the building societies.

Abbey National   http://www.abbeynational.co.uk
Halifax   http://www.halifax.co.uk

National Bus Company was privatized during the mid-1980s, mostly by splitting it up into small local or regional companies which were bought out by their existing management teams. The sector has since become more concentrated as certain growth-orientated operators such as Stagecoach and First Bus (a name change from Badgerline) have bought out other smaller companies. One major challenge for these aggressive companies has been to try and avoid intervention from the UK regulatory authorities, concerned with competition in the industry. Having acquired a number of local bus franchises in the UK, Stagecoach has also expanded overseas and bought a minority shareholding (49%) in Virgin Rail.

Stagecoach   http://www.stagecoachholdings.com

There are a number of aspects to strategic management. First, the strategy itself, that is concerned with the establishment of a clear direction for the organization and for every business, product and service, and a means for getting there, and which requires the creation of strong competitive positions. Second, excellence in the implementation of strategies in order to yield effective performance. Third, creativity and innovation to ensure that the organization is responsive to pressures for change, and that strategies are improved and renewed. Four, the ability to manage strategic change, both continuous, gradual, incremental changes and more dramatic, discontinuous changes. Innovation and change concern the strategy process in an organization. Excellence and innovation should enable an organization to thrive and prosper in a dynamic, global environment, but in turn they depend on competencies in strategic awareness and learning. Organizations must understand the strategic value of the resources they employ and deploy, and how they can be used to satisfy the needs and expectations of customers and other stakeholders while outperforming competitors.

The strategic success in recent years of certain low-price, no-frills airlines, such as SouthWest Air (US), Ryanair and EasyJet (UK), shows that:

- newcomers can change an industry – by being creative, innovative and different
- new competitors can, and will, find ways of breaking down apparent barriers to entry
- companies need to find some clear and distinct competitive advantage, something which is both attractive to customers and profitable
- this advantage will come from what organizations do, their distinctive competencies and capabilities
- charismatic and visible strategic leaders often have a major impact on the choice and implementation of key strategies
- people are critically important if strategies are to be implemented effectively
- the Internet is becoming increasingly important, and
- business can be fun!

It is, however, also important to realize that in many organizations certain parts may be *world class* and highly profitable while other businesses are not. Good practices in the strong businesses can be discerned, transferred and learned, but this may not be enough. Some industries and competitive environments are simply less *friendly* and premium profits are unlikely. The real danger occurs if the weaker businesses threaten to bring down the strong ones which are forced to subsidize them. It is, of course, an irony that companies in real difficulty, possibly through strategic weaknesses, need to turn in an excellent performance if they are to survive.

Finally, it must be realized that past and current success is no guarantee of success in the future. Companies are not guaranteed, or entitled to, continued prosperity. They must adapt and change in a dynamic environment. Many fail to do this, for all sorts of reasons, and disappear. Some close down; others are acquired. Case Study 1, Marks and Spencer, provides a notable example of how a once outstanding company lost its way in the 1990s.

Strategic thinking

It is worth mentioning that strategic management is not something that many companies are thought to be very good at. For example, by measuring factors such as relative world and European market shares won by companies, investment expenditure, productivity and the proportion of revenue allocated for research and development, Britain has performed less well industrially than many of her major competitors in a number of key sectors over the past 40 years. A lack of marketing skills, low productivity, inadequate investment and poor management generally have all been identified as causes, but in many cases these have improved in recent years. Another important aspect is the general failure to assess properly how to compete best.

Caulkin (2000) argues that effective management is demonstrated when organizations 'get their strategy and their operations right at the same time', and that the mistakes made by British companies in recent years include:

- misguided strategic choices
- poor strategy implementation, especially in the case of merger and acquisition integration
- technical weaknesses – relative to the best companies in the world
- market complacency – and a consequent lack of innovation
- a failure to maximize the potential and contribution of people.

The flame of competition has changed from smokey yellow to intense white heat. For companies to survive and prosper they will have to have a vision, a mission and strategy. They will pursue the action arising from that strategy with entrepreneurial skill and total dedication and commitment to win.
Peter B Ellwood, Chief Executive, Lloyds TSB Group

Discussing the same theme, a few years ago Peter Beck, the Chairman of the British Strategic Planning Society during 1984–86, was critical of British companies as a whole:

> *Far too many companies either have no goals at all, other than cost reduction, or their boss hides them in his head. There's no hope for companies in Britain unless more top managements accept the need for a widely communicated set of clear objectives.*
>
> (Beck, 1987)

Many of Beck's points are still pertinent in Britain and elsewhere. Strategic clarity is absent, Beck argues, for essentially three reasons: the difficulties of forecasting in today's business environment (but difficulty is no excuse for not trying!); the lack of managerial competence in many companies; and, above all, the frequent absence of strong leadership from the top.

Part of the problem is the distinction between established views hostile towards the formal and elaborate strategic planning systems that were in vogue during the 1960s and 1970s, but which failed to work in many cases, and the idea of strategic thinking. It is perfectly possible for any organization to address a number of key questions about how well the company is doing, and why, and where it should seek to develop in the future, and how. It will be argued in this book that the most successful companies strategically are likely to be those that are aware of where they are and of what lies ahead, those that understand their environment and those that seek to achieve and maintain competitive advantage. By way of illustration the following points have been developed from a *Financial Times* article (Morrison and Lee, 1979).

Whatever their strategy, companies that are adept at strategic thinking seem to be distinguished from their less successful competitors by a common pattern of management practices. First, they identify more effectively than their competitors the key success factors inherent in the economics of each business. For example, in the airline industry, with its high fixed costs and relatively inflexible route allocations, a high load factor is critical to success. It is important, though, that high load factors are not at the expense of healthy sales of more expensive seats; and this requires skilful marketing.

Second, they segment their markets so as to gain decisive competitive advantage. The strategic thinker bases his or her market segmentation on competitive analysis and thus may separate segments according to the strengths and weaknesses of different competitors. This enables him or her to concentrate on segments where he or she can both maximize their own competitive advantage and avoid head-on competition with stronger competitors.

Third, successful companies base their strategies on the measurement and analysis of competitive advantage. Essential to this is a sound basis for assessing a company's advantages relative to its competitors.

Fourth, they anticipate their competitors' responses. Good strategic thinking also implies an understanding of how situations will change over time. Business strategy, like military strategy, is a matter of manoeuvring for superior position and anticipating how competitors will respond, and with what measure of success.

Fifth, they exploit more, or different, degrees of freedom than their competitors. They seek to stay ahead of their rivals by looking for new competitive opportunities. While innovation and constant improvement are essential, there are also potentially huge rewards for organizations which are first to reach the new *competitive high ground* by changing the currently practised *rules of competition*.

Finally, they give investment priority to businesses or areas that promise a competitive advantage.

Strategic success

In order to be successful, organizations must be strategically aware. They must understand how changes in their competitive environment – some of which they may have started and others to which they will have to react – are unfolding. The implied and simultaneous proactivity and reactivity require strong and appropriate resources which continue to ensure that the organization is able to meet the needs and expectations of its external stakeholders including customers, suppliers and shareholders. Employees are a key resource for delivering this satisfaction and also an important internal stakeholder.

The UK Department of Trade and Industry recently carried out research in an attempt to clarify the 'winning characteristics' of the most successful companies. The findings, published in 1995, are summarized in Table 1.1.

Table 1.1   Ingredients for strategic success

Characteristics	Requirements
The most successful UK companies are:	
Led by visionary, enthusiastic champions of change	Communicated vision
Able to use the potential of employees	Empowerment
in a customer-focused culture	Benchmarking good practice
in a flattened structure	Team working
Aware of customer needs and expectations	Awareness of key success factors
by constant learning and	Networking
innovating in response to competitive pressures	Competitor awareness
Constantly introducing new, differentiated products and services	Total quality management
because they understand their competitors	
because they are innovative and	
because they use strategic alliances to enable them to focus on core businesses	Supplier alliances
Able to exceed their customers' expectations with these new products and services	

Source: Competitiveness – How the Best UK Companies are Winning. Department of Trade and Industry, London, 1995.

Satisfying the changing needs of stakeholders in a dynamic environment demands flexibility and sound control measures. Employees should be empowered to make and carry out decisions, but, to be strategically effective, this must be within a clear and co-ordinated directed framework. Hamel and Prahalad (1989) use the term 'strategic intent' to describe this directional vision. Coca-Cola, for example, intend 'to put a Coke within arms' reach of every consumer in the world', while the growth of Canon in the photocopying market was driven by a desire to 'beat Xerox'. Taking up an earlier point, Canon successfully rewrote the rules of competition. Xerox had become the market leader with a strategy based on large, high-capability machines which organizations leased from them; Canon sold smaller machines designed for the individual office.

Later we will see how these three themes of environment, resources and organizational management and control can be synthesized into a useful model.

Functional, competitive and corporate strategies

Figure 1.1 summarizes three distinct, but interrelated and interdependent, levels of strategy – corporate (the whole organization), competitive (the distinct strategy

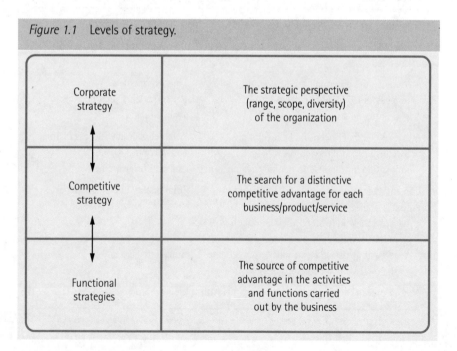

Figure 1.1   Levels of strategy.

Corporate strategy	The strategic perspective (range, scope, diversity) of the organization
Competitive strategy	The search for a distinctive competitive advantage for each business/product/service
Functional strategies	The source of competitive advantage in the activities and functions carried out by the business

for each constituent business, product or service in the organization) and functional (the activities which underpin the competitive strategies).

Simply, most organizations choose to produce one or more related or unrelated products or services for one or more markets or market segments. Consequently, the organization itself should be structured to encompass this range of product markets or service markets. As the number and diversity of products increase the structure is likely to be centred on divisions which are sometimes referred to as strategic business units (SBUs). Such SBUs are responsible individually for developing, manufacturing and marketing their own product or group of products. Each SBU will therefore have a strategy, which Porter (1980) calls a competitive strategy. Competitive strategy is concerned with 'creating and maintaining a competitive advantage in each and every area of business' (Porter, 1980). It can be achieved through any one function, although it is likely to be achieved through a unique and distinctive combination of functional activities. For each functional area of the business, such as production, marketing and human resources, the company will have a functional strategy. It is important that functional strategies are designed and managed in a co-ordinated way so that they interrelate with each other and at the same time collectively allow the competitive strategy to be implemented properly.

Successful competitive and functional strategies add value in ways which are perceived to be important by the company's stakeholders, especially its customers, and which help to distinguish the company from its competitors. Adding value is explained and discussed later in the chapter. Mathur and Kenyon (1997) reinforce these points and contend that competitive advantage is fundamentally about the positioning and fit of an organization in its industry or market, and that success is based on distinct differences and sound cost management.

Corporate strategy, essentially and simply, is deciding what businesses the organization should be in and how the overall group of activities should be structured and managed. It has been described by Porter as 'the overall plan for a diversified business', although it is perfectly acceptable for a business to elect to stay focused on only one product or service range. This does happen in many companies, especially small businesses. In this case the corporate and competitive strategies are synonymous. Corporate strategy for a multibusiness group is concerned with maintaining or improving overall growth and profit performance through acquisition, organic investment (internally funded growth), divestment and closure. The term strategic perspective is often used to describe the range and diversity of activities, in other words the corporate strategy. Each activity then has a competitive position or strategy. The management of corporate strategy concerns the creation and safeguarding of synergies from the portfolio of businesses and activities.

Studying strategy

Our study of strategy should embrace both its scope (the different levels we discussed in the previous section) and issues of choice and change, and this is emphasised by Figure 1.2, developed from ideas in Whittington (1999).

Taking each box in turn, the choice of corporate strategy will first relate to the debate about focus and diversification, which in turn is really a debate over sources of potential organization-level synergy. Global ambitions are also a key element here. Competitive strategy concerns activities, fit and positioning, as we have discussed. Competitive advantage is typically built around differentiation and cost management. Analysing the nature and logic of these choices, then, comprises a significant proportion of this book – but this type of analysis provides only a partial understanding of strategic management in organizations. We must also seek to understand how strategies are chosen and changed.

Some strategies are changed reactively when companies are surprised by their competitors or other events in their environment; in other instances we see evidence of proactive attempts to shape, mould and manage the business environment. We see later in this chapter how strategic change involves entrepreneurial leadership, planning and analysis and intrapreneurial change where

Figure 1.2   Studying strategy.

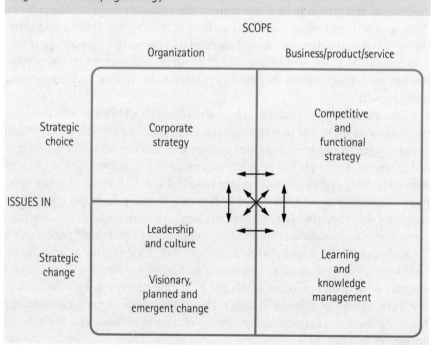

individual managers are empowered to act in a dynamic environment. The relative significance of each mode is dependent on the preference and style of the strategic leader and the culture of the organization, and it helps to determine the extent to which power and responsibility is centralized or decentralized. Consequently, and towards the end of the book, we study organizational structure and consider the link between structure and strategy implementation. As we stated earlier, strategy concerns people, and their influence on choice and change. While their willingness (or not) to accept empowerment in a devolved structure is critical, so too is the ability of the organization to share its knowledge and learn collectively if it is to enjoy the synergies we discussed above. Hence, we must also examine the way in which individual managers influence strategy, especially at the functional and competitive level.

Five perspectives on strategy

More than anyone else, Henry Mintzberg has been responsible for drawing our attention to alternative views and perspectives on strategy, all of them legitimate. Mintzberg *et al.* (1998) provides an excellent summary of his work on this topic.

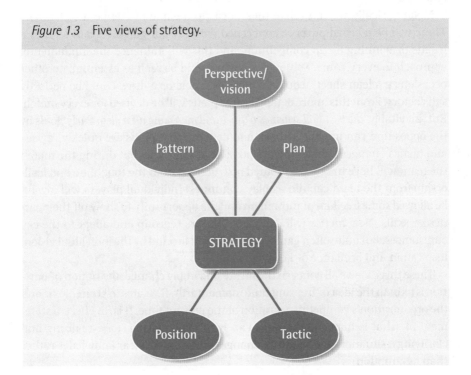

Figure 1.3 Five views of strategy.

The top oval in Figure 1.3 suggests that strategies can be seen in a visionary context. Here we imply that strategy can be considered as a clear strategic purpose, intent and direction for the organization, but without the detail worked out. In a dynamic environment, managers would then determine more detailed and specific strategies in *real time* rather than exclusively in advance. But they would always have a framework of direction to guide their decision making and help them to determine what is appropriate. In addition, some strategies come from a visionary input from an entrepreneurial manager – or strategic leader – who spots an opportunity and is minded to act on it.

This contrasts with some people's thinking that strategy and planning are synonymous. Certainly, as we shall see later in this chapter, strategic planning has a crucial role in strategy creation, but it does not fully explain how strategies are changed. Both the visionary and planning perspective are concerned with thinking ahead as far as it might be sensible to think and plan. While the tactical view is also about the future, it is really about the immediate future. The assumption being made here is that competitors in a dynamic market will constantly adopt new ploys in an attempt to steal a short-term gain or advantage. Their tactics may be easily copied, but there can be some temporary advantage when rivals are caught by surprise and need time to react.

Metaphorically we can relate these ideas to a game of competitive football. There will be a broad purpose concerned with finishing at a certain level in a league or winning a cup competition, and this will influence the fundamental approach to every game. Sometimes a win would be seen as essential; on other occasions a 'clean sheet' would be more desirable or a draw could be perfectly satisfactory. From this, more detailed game plans will be devised for every match. But, inevitably, *the best laid schemes o' mice and men gang aft a gley*. Early goals by the opposition can imply a setback and demand that plans are quickly revised and tactics changed. This is always possible at half-time, but during the match the team will have to rely on shouted instructions from the touchline and leadership from the team captain as play continues. Individual players will always be allowed some freedom of movement and the opportunity to show off their particular skills. New tactics will emerge as players regroup and adapt to the circumstances, but quite often games will be turned around by the individual vision, inspiration and brilliance of key players.

These three views all concern the future and imply change; the notion of position is akin to the idea of freezing time momentarily. It relates to strategic fit and the organization's competitive position at the present time. It is, in effect, a statement of what is happening; and it can be vital for *taking stock*, realizing and clarifying a situation so that future changes are based on clear knowledge rather than assumption.

Of course, organizations come to their present position as a result of decisions taken previously; plans have been implemented and tactics adjusted as events have unfolded. It is again crucial that we analyse and understand this evolving pattern, appreciating just what has happened, why and how. This can be a valuable foundation for future decisions, plans and actions, but, although history can be a guide to the future, rarely in strategy are events repeated without some amendment. The importance of clarifying the pattern from the various decisions and changes also explains why strategy has irreverently been described as a *series of, mindless, random events, rationalized in retrospect!*

In the next section of this chapter we build our understanding of these alternative perspectives as we look at how strategies are created and changed.

The Strategic Management Process

The strategic planning approach

Traditionally, courses in strategic management have been built around three important elements:

- strategic analysis
- strategy creation and choice
- strategy implementation.

Relevant frameworks for studying strategy, such as the one featured in the top half of Figure 1.4, tend to follow a pattern:

- appraisal of the current situation and current strategies – invariably using a SWOT (strengths, weaknesses, opportunities and threats) analysis
- determination of desirable changes to objectives and/or strategies
- a search for, and choice of, suitable courses of action
- implementation of the changes
- monitoring progress; ongoing appraisal.

Strategic management involves awareness of how successful and strong the organization and its strategies are, and of how circumstances are changing. At any time, previously sound products, services and strategies are likely to be in decline, or threatened by competition. As this happens, new 'windows of opportunity' are opening for the vigilant and proactive companies.

New strategies must be created which may be changes to the corporate portfolio or changes at the competitive level. Sometimes these strategic ideas will emerge from formal planning processes; at other times, and particularly in the

Figure 1.4   Strategic management: awareness and change.

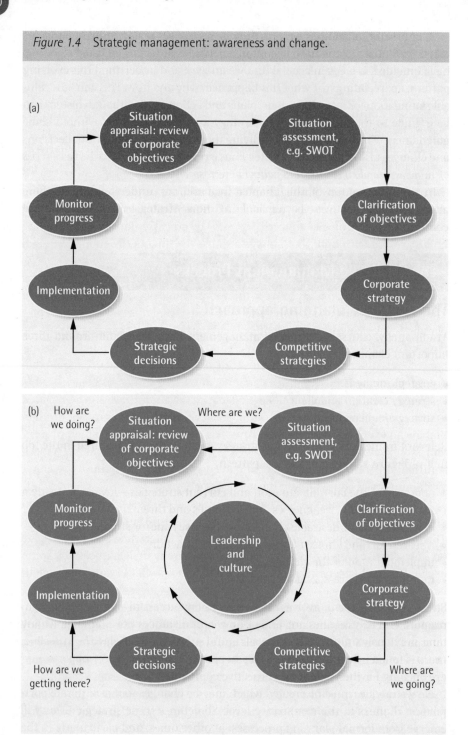

case of functional and competitive strategies, changes will emerge as managers throughout the organization try out new ideas.

The actual strategies being pursued at any time reflect the organization's strategy content, and the important issues are:

- the ability of the organization to add value in meaningful ways, which
- exploit organizational resources to achieve synergy and at the same time
- satisfy the needs of the organization's major stakeholders, particularly its shareholders and customers.

The selection of new strategies must take account of these criteria. Existing and new strategies must be implemented. Effective implementation and the creation of new strategies concern process. The processes involved in designing and carrying through any changes must be managed, monitored and controlled.

Figure 1.4(b) develops this basic process model by, first, adding a number of key questions which, realistically, organizations should be addressing all the time. These are not issues which only need to be considered once a year as part of a planning cycle; in dynamic environments circumstances are changing all the time and organizations must continuously search for new opportunities as well as appreciating the reactive changes to strategies and tactics that are required in order to remain effective. Strategic management is dynamic; strategies need to be reviewed and revised all the time. Leadership and culture have also been placed in the centre of the diagram, illustrating their critical impact on strategic decision making and strategic performance. Arguably we can never understand strategy and strategic change in organizations without some understanding of the contribution of the strategic leader and the way in which the culture acts either as stimulus or as constraint on the necessary changes.

The basic proposal here is that by a series of analyses and decisions an organization can determine the direction that its future strategy should follow. This approach provides an important underpinning framework, and it is adequate on a prescriptive basis for a study of strategic management. Realistically it cannot explain all that happens in practice and reality. Simply, while organizations might be described as goal-seeking machines, comprising managers who make and take decisions in pursuit of defined goals (or objectives), and using information to support their decision-making processes, people invariably disagree on how they interpret the meaning of both the goals and events in the environment. Moreover, there is frequently a conflict between the various goals or objectives, requiring prioritization, which demands more subjective value judgements. Nevertheless, there is always purposeful activity, ideally directed towards pursuit of the essential purpose of the organization. Strategies are, therefore, created in other ways than relatively formal planning, as we shall see later.

Figure 1.5 provides an alternative presentation of these ideas.

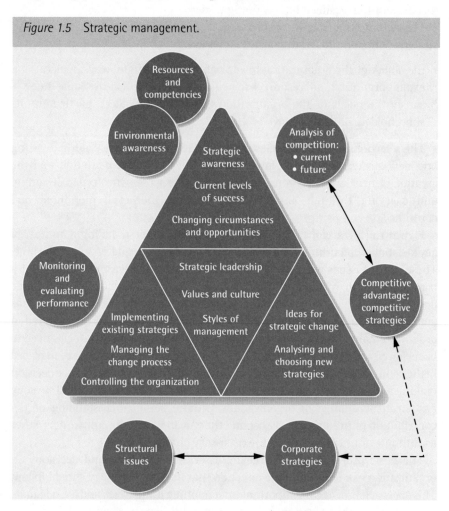

Figure 1.5   Strategic management.

The emergence of strategic management

In this section we refer to a number of approaches to strategic management, all of which are discussed in detail at different points in the book, where they are referenced more fully. The paper *The Emergence of Strategic Management* on the website elaborates our discussion.

From the 1960s, when we really began to study strategic management, the strategic planning framework has provided a valuable base for our understanding of the subject. Since then a number of other approaches have been added. They are all relevant and help to shed further light on this complex topic. If strategy were easy to understand and practice, then we might expect that more organizations would be successful and sustain this success over time. But, although it is based in many ways on some simple points and common sense, strategy remains enigmatic.

Figure 1.6 shows that when Porter (1980, 1985) drew our attention to the subject of competitive advantage, and the significance of strategic positioning, an important second layer was added to the planning foundation. The next important contribution was the clarification that many strategies emerge as decisions are taken all the time in dynamic circumstances, highlighting that while planning plays an important role, it is a partial one.

The general thrust of these approaches is market driven, based on the argument that organizations must react in a dynamic environment, seizing new opportunities and avoiding major potential threats. Responding to customers, suppliers and competitors will always be vital, but an alternative perspective is also relevant. This is a resource-based view which argues that organizations must discern their critical strategic strengths and look for ways of building and

Figure 1.6 Emerging views of strategic management.

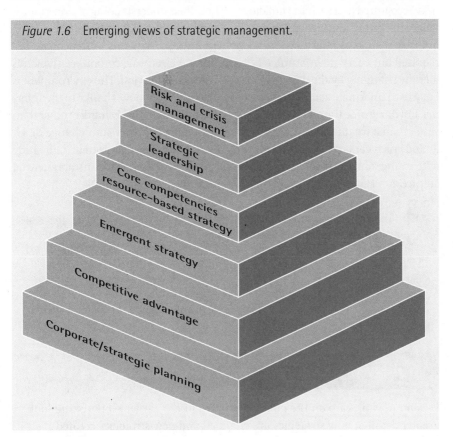

exploiting them in order to mould the competitive environment. In Chapter 2 we look at the relevant issues of core competency and strategic capability. Successful organizations will blend both the market and resource perspectives so that they do not overlook potentially good opportunities.

In recent years the subject of strategic leadership has received greater prominence, stimulated in part by the media. Business success stories have been popular items for newspapers and magazines, especially where there is a high-profile figure who can be identified with the organization and the story. In addition, the 'falls from grace' of some very high-profile businesspeople have proved newsworthy. The accompanying autobiographies of some of these people have added to our understanding. It should be pointed out, though, that academically rigorous research on the subject has also been carried out. When we incorporate the themes of leadership and entrepreneurship we are adding the dimension of aspiration to strategy creation, to accompany the analysis of the strategic planning model, as shown in Figure 1.6.

Most recently, risk and crisis management has joined the debate. Organizations have recognized that scenario building can help their understanding of uncertainty, where the future may depend in part on the past but will not replicate it. For some industries, such as pharmaceuticals (where huge investments in new drugs are required but carry no guarantee of success) and electronic commerce (which is literally changing by the day), serious risk assessment is vital. The environment is busy with information and triggers, never more so than now, thanks to the Internet, but discerning the real commercial opportunities is probably harder rather than easier than it was in the past. Organizational fortunes can, therefore, change rapidly, and crises can arise suddenly to catch out the unwary organization. Our study of learning, and the involvement of people in an empowered and intrapreneurial culture, is a key element of both this topic and emergent strategy.

The most important management technique is to understand the real situation in which you are operating.

Sir Paul Girolami, Chairman, Glaxo, 1987

The best way to predict the future is to invent it.

John Sculley, when Chairman, Apple Computers

Strategy Creation

We can now pick up on the points discussed in the earlier sections and look in greater detail at how strategies are changed and new strategies created.

Opportunities for change

It is essential that managers are strategically aware both of potentially threatening developments and of opportunities for profitable change, and that they seek to match and improve the fit between the environment and the organization's resources.

A wise man will make more opportunities than he finds.

Francis Bacon

There is, however, no single recommended approach for seeking out and pursuing new opportunities. There is a broad spectrum ranging from what might be termed entrepreneurial opportunism to what Quinn (1980) calls 'logical incrementalism'. These are analogous to the bird and squirrel approaches described in Box 1.3.

DISCUSSION – Box 1.3
Approaches to Strategic Management

The bird approach

Start with the entire world – scan it for opportunities to seize upon, trying to make the best of what you find.

You will resemble a bird, searching for a branch to land on in a large tree. You will see more opportunities than you can think of. You will have an almost unlimited choice.

But your decision, because you cannot stay up in the air for ever, is likely to be arbitrary, and because it is arbitrary, it will be risky.

The squirrel approach

Start with yourself and your company – where you are at with the skills and the experience you have – and what you can do best.

In this approach you will resemble a squirrel climbing that same large tree. But this time you are starting from the trunk, from familiar territory, working your way up cautiously, treefork by treefork, deciding on the branch that suits you best at each fork.

You will only have one or two alternatives to choose from at a time – but your decision, because it is made on a limited number of options, is likely to be more informed and less risky.

In contrast with the bird who makes single big decisions, the squirrel makes many small ones. The squirrel may never become aware of some of the opportunities the bird sees, but he is more likely to know where he is going.

Adapted from Cohen, P (1974) *The Gospel According to the Harvard Business School*, Penguin. Originally published by Doubleday, New York, 1973.

Strategic change can be relatively evolutionary or gradual, or much more dramatic or revolutionary. The nature of the opportunities (and threats) is directly related to both the general and the specific industry environments; and the approach that particular organizations take in seeking to match resources to the environment is dependent on the basic values of the organization and the style of the strategic leader. However, as will be seen, it does not follow that the strategic leader is the sole manager of strategic change.

Effectively managed change requires a vision of the future – where the organization is heading or wants to go – together with the means for creating and reaching this future. Planning a way forward from where the organization is now may not be enough to create the future vision; at the same time, when there is a vision, it is illogical to set off in pursuit without the appropriate 'equipment'. There must be a clear vision of a route, and this requires planning; on the way, managers should stay alert for dangers and opportunity (see Figure 1.7). Well-tracked routes (strategies which have proved successful in the past) and experience can both be beneficial, but in a dynamic environment, there will always be an element of the unknown.

Figure 1.7   Strategic change.

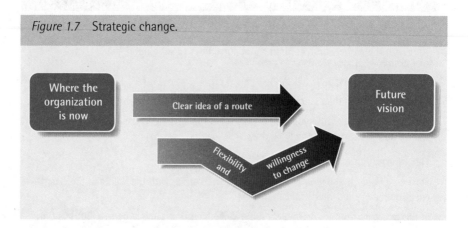

Planning and strategy creation

All managers plan. They plan how they might achieve objectives. Planning is essential to provide direction and to help ensure that the appropriate resources are available where and when they are needed for the pursuit of objectives. Sometimes the planning process is detailed and formal; on other occasions planning may be informal, unstructured and essentially 'in the mind'. In the context of strategy formulation a clear distinction needs to be made between the cerebral activity of informal planning and formalized planning systems.

Formal strategic planning systems are most useful in stable conditions. Environmental opportunities and threats are forecast, and then, as we saw earlier, strategies are planned and implemented. Strategies which are appropriate, feasible and desirable are most likely to help the organization to achieve its mission and objectives.

Where the environment is more turbulent and less predictable, strategic success requires flexibility, and the ability to learn about new opportunities and introduce appropriate changes continuously. Planning systems can still make a valuable contribution but the plans themselves must not be inflexible.

In addition it is important not to discount the contribution of visionary strategic leaders who become aware of opportunities – and on occasions, create new opportunities – and take risks based on their awareness and insight of markets and customers.

Formal strategic planning implies determined actions for achieving stated and desired objectives. For many organizations these objectives will focus on sales growth and profitability. A detailed analysis of the strategic situation will be used to create a number of strategic alternatives, and then certain options will be chosen and implemented.

Planning systems are useful, and arguably essential, for complex or diversified organizations with a large number of businesses which need integrating. There are, though, a number of possible approaches. Head office can delegate the detailed planning to each division, offering advice and making sure the plans can be co-ordinated into a sensible total package. Alternatively, the planning system can be controlled centrally in order to establish priorities for resource allocation.

While the discipline of planning and setting priorities is valuable, the plans must not be inflexible and incapable of being changed in a dynamic competitive environment. During implementation it is quite likely that some plans will be discarded and others modified.

Visionary leadership

Planning systems imply that strategies are selected carefully and systematically from an analytical process. In other instances major strategic changes will be decided on without lengthy formal analysis. Typically such changes will reflect strong, entrepreneurial leadership and be visionary and discontinuous: *I have seen the future and this is it!*

To an outsider it can often appear that the organization is pursuing growth with high-risk strategies, which are more reliant on luck than serious thought. This can underestimate the thinking that is involved, because quite often these entrepreneurs and visionary leaders have an instinctive feel for the products, services and markets involved, and enjoy a clear awareness and insight of the opportunities and risks.

This mode of strategy creation is most viable when the strategic leader has the full confidence of the organization, and he or she can persuade others to follow his or her ideas and implement the strategies successfully. Implementation requires more detailed planning and incremental changes with learning – initially it is the broad strategic idea that is formulated entrepreneurially.

Formal planning and/or visionary leadership will invariably determine important changes to corporate strategies; competitive and functional level changes are more likely to involve emergent strategy in the form of adaptive and incremental changes. The actual implementation of corporate-level decisions is also likely to be incremental.

> All newly-appointed chief executives should ask five key questions:
>
> - What are the basic goals of the company?
> - What is the strategy for achieving these goals?
> - What are the fundamental issues facing the company?
> - What is its culture?
> - And is the company organized in a way to support the goals, issues and culture?
>
> *Bob Bauman, ex-Chief Executive of SmithKline Beecham*

Adaptive strategic change

Some organizations will be characterized by extensive decentralization, empowerment and accountability. Here, managers throughout the organization are being encouraged to look for opportunities and threats and to innovate. The underlying argument is that managers 'at the coal face' are closest to the key changes in the organization's environment and should, therefore, be in a position where they can, on the one hand, react quickly, and, on the other hand, be proactive or intrapreneurial in attempting to change or manage the external environment. Managers will be encouraged and empowered to make changes in their areas of responsibility, and, ideally, rewarded for their initiatives. The implication is that functional changes will impact on competitive strategies in a positive way as the organization adapts to its changing environment. Conceptually this is similar to incremental change.

Proponents of chaos theory such as Ralph Stacey (1993) argue that intentional strategies are, per se, *too inflexible for unknown futures*. Relying on this approach is a *recipe for stagnation and failure because of the extent of the complexity*. Companies must seek to *achieve a state of creative tension on the edge of instability*. These theorists accept that organizational hierarchies and planning are needed to control day-to-day operations, but, long-term, strategies must be allowed to emerge from the *self-organizing activities of loose, informal, destabilizing networks.*

Incremental strategic change

In dynamic and turbulent competitive environments, detailed formal planning is problematical. The plans are only as good as any forecasts, which must be uncertain. It can make sense, therefore, not to rely on detailed plans, but instead to plan broad strategies within a clearly defined mission and purpose.

Having provided this direction the strategic leader will allow strategies to emerge in a decentralized organization structure. Managers will meet regularly, both formally and informally, to discuss progress and changing trends; they will plan new courses of action and then try them out – a form of 'real-time planning'.

> *When I was younger I always conceived of a room where all these [strategic] concepts were worked out for the whole company. Later I didn't find any such room. ... The strategy [of the company] may not even exist in the mind of one man. I certainly don't know where it is written down. It is simply transmitted in the series of decisions made.*
>
> James B Quinn (1980)

Quinn argues that organizations test out relatively small changes and develop with this approach rather than go for major changes. An example would be Marks and Spencer testing a proposed new line in a selected and limited number of stores before deciding to launch it nationally. Lex Group (see Box 1.2) followed an incremental approach when it diversified into hotels, building and buying properties one by one rather than acquiring a chain of hotels.

An organization can, of course, use more than one means of bringing about strategic changes at any one time. During the 1980s, for example, ASDA, the major food retailer, acquired, and later sold, the kitchen furniture group MFI. At the same time it was actively developing and pursuing growth strategies, involving opening new stores, redesigning and refurbishing existing stores, developing own-label goods, introducing more fresh foods and non-food items, using information technology and streamlining the distribution system.

Strategy, therefore, can result from a stream of decisions and information fed upwards from the lower management levels of the organization: Quinn contends that this is sensible, logical and positive.

> *The most effective strategies of major enterprises tend to emerge step by step from an iterative process in which the organization probes the future, experiments and learns from a series of partial (incremental) commitments rather than through global formulations of total strategies. Good managers are aware of this process and they consciously intervene in*

it. They use it to improve the information available for decisions and to build the psycho-logical identification essential to successful strategies. The process is both logical and incremental. Such logical incrementalism is not 'muddling' as most people understand that word. Properly managed it is a conscious, purposeful, proactive, executive practice.

Teamworking and learning are at the heart of the adaptive and incremental modes. Managers must learn about new opportunities and threats; they should also learn from the successes and mistakes of other managers. Managers must be willing to take measured risks; for this to happen understandable mistakes and errors of judgement should not be sanctioned harshly.

Change is gradual and comes from experimentation; new strategies involve an element of trial and error. Success is very dependent on communications. Managers must know of opportunities and threats facing them; the organization must be able to synthesize all the changes into a meaningful pattern, and spread learning and best practice.

Mintzberg (1989) argues that organizations should be structured and managed to ensure that formulators of strategies (managers whose decisions lead to strategic changes) have information, and that the implementers of strategies and changes have the appropriate degree of power to ensure that the desired changes are brought about.

It is quite normal to find all these modes in evidence simultaneously in an organization, although there is likely to be one dominant mode. Moreover different managers in the same organization will not necessarily agree on the relative significance of each mode; their perceptions of what is actually happening will vary.

The place of corporate planning today

During the past 40 years, a number of books have been written on the subject of corporate planning, where it is generally agreed that strategic change is the outcome of objective, systematic decision making which establishes objectives and then seeks and chooses ways of achieving them. As change is a planned activity, corporate planning is therefore prescriptive in its approach. It would be churlish to argue that formal planning has no role to play in strategic management but, quite simply, there is more to strategic management and strategic change than planning.

Planning activity will consider opportunities and threats (although this is not the only way they should be spotted); it will allow a thorough evaluation of strengths and weaknesses; it will allow an assessment of where competitive advantage is or is not and how it might be achieved; and future scenarios can be tested. Planning can be used to help to decide where the organization's scarce resources (for example, future investment capital) should be concentrated; and it can be used to establish tactics (actions) for carrying out strategies.

There are a number of useful planning techniques and these will be considered in Chapter 11. However, the overall role and relative importance of planning remains a controversial and disputed issue. As mentioned by Mintzberg (1982), *strategy need not always be a conscious and precise plan.*

Finally, it is quite plausible to argue that the outcome of planning need not be a plan. Rather than trying to produce a watertight document covering the next ten years, planning, as an exercise, should concentrate on identifying and evaluating alternative courses of action for the business, so that more opportunities are created. Planning therefore increases awareness.

In this section we have outlined the views of a number of contributors on strategy. It can usefully be summarized as follows. Strategic management is concerned with:

- deciding the future direction and scope of the business, in line with perceived opportunities and threats. This will clearly require awareness and planning. The planning, however, may be more cerebral and visionary than detailed, formal and quantitative
- ensuring that the required resources are, or will be, available in order that the chosen strategies can be implemented
- ensuring that there is innovation and change. These changes can be in relation to corporate, competitive or functional strategies. Equally, innovation can take place throughout the organization. If this is to happen then an appropriate organization structure and culture must be in place.

Figure 1.8 summarizes these ideas.

Figure 1.8 Strategy creation.

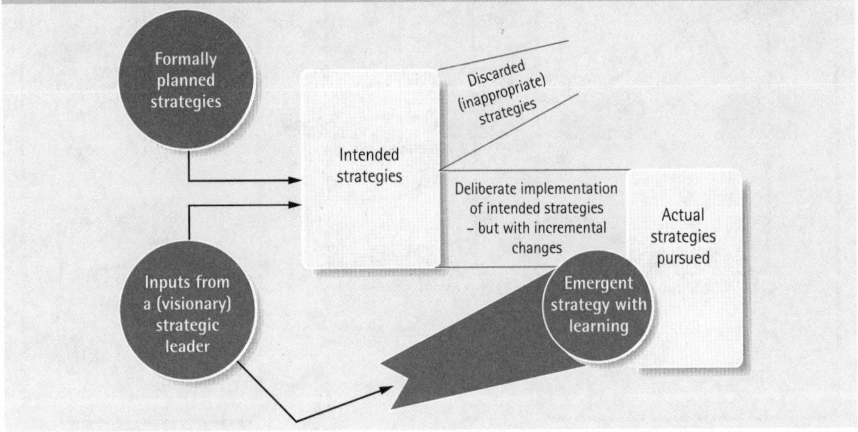

Figure 1.8 indicates that intended strategies can be the outcome of both a formal planning process and visionary leadership. On implementation some of these intended strategies will be discarded – they turn out to be based on misjudgements, or changing circumstances make them less viable. Meanwhile, in this changing environment, the organization does two other things as a result of learning. First, it incrementally changes the intended strategies as they are implemented. Second, it introduces new adaptive strategies when fresh opportunities are spotted. Consequently, the actual strategies pursued will relate to, but differ from, the intended strategies.

Mission, strategy, objectives and tactics

These four terms were all defined in Box 1.1 and they have either been introduced in brief or discussed in detail in this chapter. Figure 1.9 shows how they interrelate hierarchically, and looks at them in the context of intended and emergent strategy creation.

Strategies are means to ends, as we have said already. Where they are planned in some detail they will relate to specific objectives or targets. Both objectives and strategies set and pursued should help to achieve – or at least to pursue – the purpose or mission of the organization. Tactics and actions, carried out everywhere

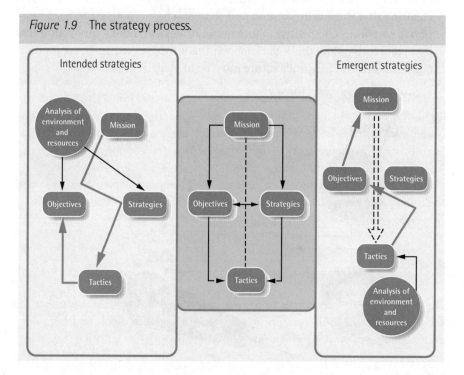

Figure 1.9 The strategy process.

in the organization by various managers and other staff, represent, on the one hand, the implementation of intended strategies, and, on the other hand, new strategic ideas being tried out by empowered managers.

The left-hand section of Figure 1.9 highlights how, with intended strategies, the mission is used to establish objectives, which in turn lead to strategies and tactics. With emergent strategy – the right-hand section of the diagram – managers are expected to appreciate and support the broad purpose and direction of the organization, and it is a key role of the strategic leader to ensure that they actually do this. Within this context they are then empowered to decide on, and try out, new strategic ideas. What they do determines the level of achievement and performance of the organization. In both cases environmental and resource considerations will guide decision making – but the information will be used by different people at different levels in the hierarchy.

With intended strategies, performance evaluation straightforwardly concerns the achievement (or not) of stated objectives with the strategies and tactics used. In the case of emergent strategy, performance evaluation is really an assessment of what has been achieved in the context of the mission.

Finally, it is important to recognize that specific issues and events will be perceived differently at different levels of the organizational hierarchy – partly because individual businesses in a diverse organization can – and often will – have their own mission statements. While they may differ, they should be complementary.

The subject of strategy has its origins in ancient warfare and a more recent military example provides a useful illustration of these points. In World War II the mission of the British government was, quite simply, to win the war. This required contributions from each of the armed services and from others. Winning the Battle of Britain was, consequently one objective, supported by various strategies concerned with, for example, training pilots and building aircraft. The recruitment of women to work in the aeroplane factories was one of many tactics. An individual front-line squadron would, however, define its mission differently. It might, for example, have been concerned with shooting down enemy planes and minimizing losses. To the government, with a higher level purpose, this would be seen as an objective.

Key Strategic Concerns

The purpose of this section is to introduce, outline and explain a number of key terms, themes and concepts which run through the book and help our understanding of strategy and strategic management. They will all be taken up and developed in greater detail at various points in the text.

Strategic leadership

It has been pointed out that a major aim of this book is to encourage readers to be more strategically aware. Long-term strategic success requires that the efforts of managers are co-ordinated. This is the task of the chief executive or managing director of the whole organization and in turn of general managers of subsidiaries or divisions in the case of large complex organizations. For simplicity in this book we shall use the term strategic leader to refer to this role.

The role is analogous to that of the captain of a ship. In a sailing race, for example, the captain must sail the ship possibly in uncertain or dangerous waters, with one or more clear goals in sight. The chosen strategy or strategies will be decided upon in the light of these goals, and the risks of any actions will be assessed. Nevertheless the captain's success will depend on the crew. It is essential that the crew act in a co-ordinated way, and therefore it is crucial that the strategies are communicated and understood.

Lee Iacocca, who became chairman of the Chrysler Corporation in the USA in the early 1980s and succeeded in turning it round, provides a useful example. Chrysler, faced with competition from General Motors, Ford and Japan, was nearly bankrupt and had lost its way. Iacocca changed some of his crew, but essentially his success lay in persuading his managers to think about how to succeed in the 1980s and to forget the strategies of the 1960s and 1970s. Cars were redesigned, marketing was improved, labour costs were lowered, productivity and quality were improved and government support was obtained. Chrysler recovered.

The strategic leader must build and lead a team of managers – and establish the goals or objectives. Styles will vary enormously, as will the scope of the objectives. Some leaders will be autocratic, others entrepreneurial. Some, arguably like Henry Ford of Ford Motor Company and Ray Kroc who started McDonald's, will be visionaries; others will set more modest goals. Others, such as Richard Branson, are not only idiosyncratic role models, they *are* their organization. The person and the business cannot be realistically separated.

The leader and his or her managers should be clear about where the organization is going, where they want to go and how they are going to get there. This requires an appreciation of the environment and an understanding of the organization's resources.

Culture and values

Schein (1985) defines culture as *the deeper level of basic assumptions and beliefs that are shared by members of an organization, that operate unconsciously, and that define in a basic 'taken for granted' fashion an organization's view of itself and its environment.*

Culture is *a pattern of basic assumptions that works well enough to be considered valid, and therefore is taught to new [organization] members as the correct way to perceive, think and feel in relation to problems of external adaptation and internal integration ... [it is] learned, evolves with new experiences, and can be changed if one understands the dynamics of the learning process.*

In the very simplest terms it is the way organizational members behave and the values that are important to them and it dictates the way decisions are made, the objectives of the organization, the type of competitive advantage sought, the organization structure and systems of management, functional strategies and policies, attitudes towards managing people, and information systems. Many of these are interrelated.

In the late 1980s, Woolworth's (the high-street retailer which is now part of the Kingfisher Group) identified that customer service, when compared with their main rivals, was a relative weakness and a major contributor to their disappointing performance. People, they concluded, are a major strategic resource, and they reflect the values of the organization. In common with many other service organizations, Woolworth's introduced a customer-care training programme entitled 'Excellence', and linked it to staff rewards. There have been two achievements. First, customer perception of staff helpfulness increased, and second, there were immediate financial gains.

Styles of corporate decision making and values are always important in strategy creation and implementation, and they are not easily changed without the appointment of a new chief executive.

Environmental fit and stakeholder satisfaction

Several authors have defined strategy in terms of the relationship between an organization and its environment. One such definition is:

> *The positioning and relating of the firm/organization to its environment in a way which will assure its continued success and make it secure from surprises.*

Ansoff (1984)

Figure 1.10 considers the organization in the context of its environment. Influenced by the strategic leader, and in the context of an ideally clear vision and direction, the organization draws its resources (employees, managers, plant, supplies, finance, etc.) from a competitive business environment. It has to compete with other firms for labour, supplies, loans, etc., and it operates in a network which includes its suppliers and financial backers, with whom one would expect it to have strong and robust relationships. With strategies and activities, it must then use these inputs in some organized way to produce products and services which can be marketed effectively and, where appropriate, profitably – thus generating

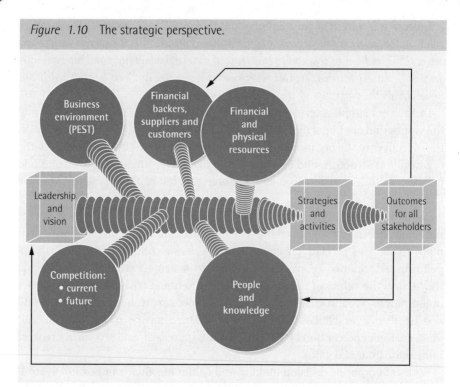

Figure 1.10 The strategic perspective.

outcomes which satisfy all key stakeholders. It must invariably succeed in a competitive marketplace. As well as appreciating market demand and the strengths, weaknesses and strategies of its competitors, it must also respond to fundamental changes in society and the economy. Over time people's tastes change, their discretionary purchasing power rises and falls, luxuries can become necessities and previously popular products can become unfashionable. The economy is not static, and it is strongly affected by government policy. While some companies influence government policy, many do not. We shall see later how a PEST (political, economic, social and technical) analysis can provide a straightforward and useful framework for analysing the external environment.

Therefore strategic management involves the following:

- a clear awareness of environmental forces and the ways in which they are changing
- an appreciation of potential and future threats and opportunities
- decisions on appropriate products and services for clearly defined markets
- the effective management of resources to develop and produce these products for the market – achieving the right quality for the right price at the right time

- appreciating how key strategic resources might be redeployed and exploited to create new market opportunities.

Strategic management, then, is effective when resources match stakeholder needs and expectations and change to maintain a fit in a turbulent environment. As we have seen, the external environment consists of suppliers, distributors and customers as well as bankers and other financial institutions and share-holders. It also includes competitors and sometimes the government. These stakeholders all expect something from a business in return for their support. If organizations are to be successful – and in many cases, profitable – they have to meet the needs and expectations of all their external stakeholders. It is also essential that the interests, needs and expectations of internal stakeholders, the employees, are not overlooked – after all, it is these employees who create the out-comes which satisfy external stakeholders. The relative demands of all the stake-holders determine what it is that a business must do well; and invariably their different requirements imply some difficult choices and trade-offs.

Innovation is an important element in maintaining fit as environmental forces and competitor strategies change. An innovative organization fosters learning which leads to continuous, managed change to products, services and process-es. In turn this demands an organization-wide commitment to improvement and change, together with the ability and willingness of managers to spot and seize change opportunities, factors again dependent upon leadership and cultural issues. Effective innovation is thus about people and the exploitation of the orga-nization's knowledge and intelligence.

Strategic positioning

A straightforward, popular and well-known technique, a SWOT analysis, implies that an organization's resources (which constitute its strengths and weakness-es) should match the demands and pressures from its external environment (man-ifest as a set of opportunities and threats) as effectively as possible, and, with change, stay matched in dynamic and turbulent times. The overlap of products and services (the outcome of the use of the organization's resources) with mar-ket needs are shown as strategic fit in Figure 1.11.

Here we can see illustrated two different, but complementary, approaches to strategy creation and strategic change. Market-driven strategy reflects the adop-tion of the marketing concept, and implies that strategies are designed – and resources developed and deployed – with customer and consumer needs in mind. Carefully and creatively defining the industry or industries in which an organi-zation competes can influence its perspective on the products and services it supplies. Marketing students will always remember that railway companies are in the transportation business! The approach is market-pull; and the value of a

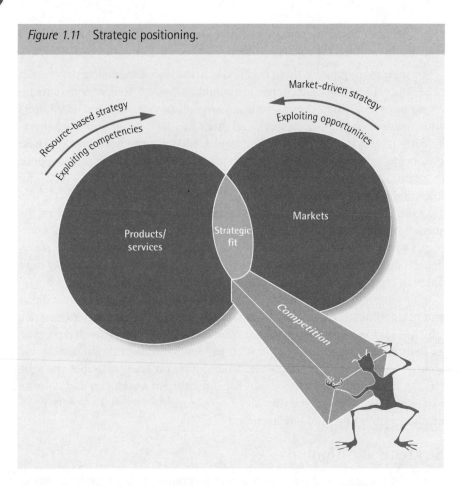

Figure 1.11   Strategic positioning.

distinct competitive advantage is clearly synonymous with this approach. It should, though, never be forgotten that different sectors of the same industry require different competencies, and that the demands of creating new competencies may be readily underestimated.

Although it is convenient to see resources as organizational strengths and weaknesses (which they very clearly are) and the environment as the source of opportunities and threats, this is too simplistic. Resources can also constitute both opportunities and strengths. Resource-based strategy, then, implies that the organization clarifies its core strategic competencies and capabilities and seeks to exploit these by finding new market opportunities where they can be used to create new values and competitive advantage. The assumption is that the organization can mould and develop its market with innovatory new ideas, sometimes changing the rules of competition in an industry. This can imply the creation of new customer preferences and perspectives in the process.

Resources which are central to an organization's success can be a threat if they could be lost. Particular people can be a major asset, and a key reason for organizational success, and people can be lost. Although rare, one reality is that they could die – more realistically they could leave and join a competitor. Obvious instances are professional sport and restaurant chefs. Some football clubs lose star players to rivals, sometimes for a transfer fee, sometimes when they are out of contract. Although this can affect the playing fortunes of the club, it is unlikely that fans will follow them. Loyalty goes too deep. The same cannot be said of chefs, however. Top-quality chefs can be the reason customers frequent a particular restaurant – and if they move, customers may well go with them.

All the time competitors will be attempting to accomplish the same ends. Hence, while a company is trying to create a stronger fit between itself and its customers, its competitors will be attempting to force them apart by offering something superior which draws customers away and destroys fit. Moreover, emerging opportunities can attract competitors with different backgrounds and motives. Developments in computer software and hardware (high-quality monitors, scanners and printers) have opened up an opportunity for digital cameras. Kodak were interested because of their dependency on the photography industry and the potential long-term threat to film-based photography. Canon and Hewlett-Packard were both interested as they could see a new opportunity for exploiting technological competencies which they already possessed. The challenge for each rival was quite different.

It is now appropriate to look further at market needs as key success factors for an organization, and at resources in the context of competency and capability. From that we can explore the concept of added value. It is this value which provides strategic fit and competitive advantage.

Key success factors

A company will have to produce to high and consistent quality levels and meet delivery promises to customers. Delivery times have been reducing gradually in very competitive industries. Suppliers and subcontractors expect regular orders and accurate forecasting when very quick deliveries are demanded from them. Without such support just-in-time production systems are impractical. Just-in-time systems rely on regular and reliable deliveries from suppliers in order to maintain constant production without the need for high parts inventories.

Companies will try to minimize their stockholding because this helps both cash flow and costs. Conglomerate subsidiaries will have to generate a positive cash flow in order to meet the financial expectations of the parent company which, in effect, acts as its banker. Costs have to be controlled so that companies remain price competitive, although low prices are not always a marketing weapon.

These stakeholder requirements represent key success factors, those things that an organization must do well if it is to be an effective competitor and thrive. In addition, many companies have to be innovative and improve both their product range and their customer service if they are to remain a leading competitor in a changing industry.

Some key success factors will be industry and sector specific. For example, successful consumer goods manufacturers will need skills in brand management. Charities need skills in fund raising and public relations. There is intense competition between charities for donations, and consequently they must be run as businesses. They can only spend what they can raise. It is also essential that they use their money appropriately, are seen to be doing so and are recognized for their efforts. The differing demands of fund raising and aid provision lead to complex cultures and organizations.

BUPA, a private medicine organization based in the UK, has a similar dilemma. Typical of such organizations around the world, the business comprises two parts: insurance, with a strong commercial culture and orientation, and hospitals, which are naturally more of a caring community.

Resources must be managed with stakeholder needs in mind. Consequently, it is important that everyone in the organization recognizes and is committed to meeting key success factors, and is additionally responsive to change pressures in a dynamic and competitive environment. Without this commitment companies will be unable to sustain a match with the environment as it changes.

Figure 1.12 illustrates that if organizations are to satisfy their stakeholders, especially their customers, while outperforming their rivals, their competitive offering should comprise:

- the ability to meet the recognized key success factors for the relevant industry or market
- distinctive competencies and capabilities which yield some form of competitive advantage, and
- the ability and willingness to deploy these competencies and capabilities to satisfy the special requirements of individual customers, for which a premium price can often be charged. Hall (1992) suggests using the term 'customerizing' instead of marketing to reflect the importance of customers as individuals rather than as a generic group who constitute a market.

Core competencies

In order to meet their key success factors organizations must develop core competencies (Prahalad and Hamel, 1990). These are distinctive skills which yield competitive advantage, and ideally they:

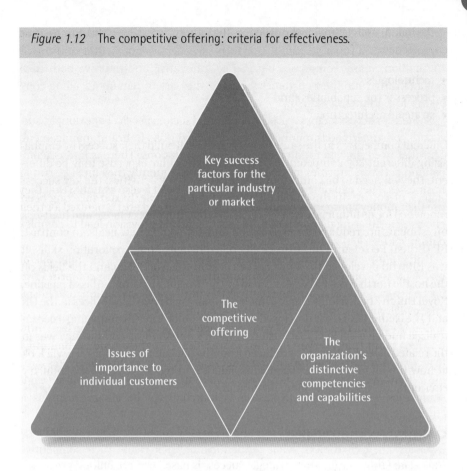

Figure 1.12 The competitive offering: criteria for effectiveness.

- provide access to important market areas or segments
- make a significant contribution to the perceived customer benefits of the product or service, and
- prove difficult for competitors to imitate.

Once developed they should be exploited, as, for example, Honda have exploited their skills at engine design and technology. Core competencies must, however, be flexible and responsive to changing customer demands and expectations. Canon have developed core competencies in precision mechanics, fibre optics and microelectronics, and these are spread across a range of products, including cameras, calculators, printers and photocopiers. There is constant product innovation.

Successful products and services, then, are the manifestation of important, underlying core competencies; and the true competition between organizations is at this competency level.

Prahalad and Hamel acknowledge that there are three strands to core competency:

- technologies
- processes (or capabilities) and
- strategic architecture.

Different competitors in the same industry may well build their success by emphasizing different key competencies. While the particular expertise may be different, they all need to be competent in a number of key activities, the key success factors, of course. In the global oil industry, for example, Exxon has long been renowned for its financial expertise, crucial when huge speculative and high-risk investments are required for exploration and developing new fields. In contrast, BP (British Petroleum) has historically relied heavily on its exploration skills. It was BP who developed the huge Forties field in the North Sea and the fields off the hostile north coast of Alaska, aided by the imaginative trans-Alaska pipeline. Royal Dutch Shell, a joint Anglo-Dutch company with two head offices in the UK and The Netherlands, has developed a valuable competency in managing a decentralized and diversified global business. Mobil's outstanding competency was in the related field of lubricants produced from the oil. Later in the book we will look at how the oil industry has been consolidating in recent years as the industry environment has become more demanding.

Strategic capabilities

Stalk *et al.* (1992) argue that strategic success is based on capabilities: processes which enable the company to be an effective competitor. Distribution networks which achieve both high service levels (effectiveness) and low costs (efficiency) would be an example. Typically these processes will cut across whole organizations, rather than be product specific, and they will rely heavily on information systems and technology.

In many respects Stalk's capabilities are the processes embedded in Hamel and Prahalad's core competencies. However, I personally think that a valuable distinction can be made between *competencies* largely rooted in technologies and process-based *capabilities*. While delivering similar outcomes, conceptually they are very different.

Retailers such as Boots in the UK (which has encompassed high-street department stores, specialist pharmacies, optical retailing, Halfords car products and service bays, Fads, Homestyle and Do-It-All DIY at various times) operate a number of different retail formats, capitalizing on their expertise in supply chain, information and service management.

Hamel and Prahalad (1993) developed these ideas further when they argued that understanding processes should generate intelligence which can be used to create added or greater value from resources, in order to strengthen or enhance competitiveness. They refer to this as stretching resources. The ability to stretch resources is very dependent on strategic architecture, which we discuss next.

Kay (1993) further stresses that, to be beneficial, both core competencies and strategic capabilities must be capable of exploitation and be *appropriable*. In other words, the firm must be able to realize the benefits of the competencies and capabilities for the company itself, rather than the main beneficiaries being its suppliers, customers or competitors.

Strategic architecture competencies

Strategic success requires:

- the organization to behave in a co-ordinated, synergy-creating manner, integrating functions and businesses
- the value adding network (links between manufacturers, retailers, suppliers and intermediate distributors) to be managed as an effective, integrated, system.

Kay (1993) refers to the ability to achieve these demands as strategic architecture. The ability to build and control a successful architecture is facilitated by strong technological competency and effective functional process competencies.

Honda, as we have seen, is renowned for its expertise in engine design and technology. However, its success as an international company has also been dependent on its ability to establish an effective distribution (dealer) network for all its products. This has been enhanced by sound, IT-supported, communications and control systems. As another example, Marks and Spencer's functional competencies and brand technology create both an image and a capability which enable it to trade in clothes, foods, cosmetics, household furnishings and credit. These competencies also bestow on the company the power to demand and obtain from its suppliers worldwide both a strict adherence to Marks' technological specifications and very keen prices.

The important themes in architecture are:

- 'systemic thinking', which leads to synergy from the fostering of inter-dependencies between people, functions and divisions in organizations and
- the establishment of linkages or even alliances between organizations at different stages of the added value chain.

Respectively, these refer to internal and external architecture.

Successful internal architecture requires that managers think 'organizationally' rather than put themselves first or promote their particular part of the organization to the detriment of other parts. Synergy from internal architecture also depends on the ability of the divisions or businesses in a conglomerate to support each other, transferring skills, competencies and capabilities and sometimes sharing common resources. This, in turn, is partially dependent on the ability of the organization to learn, and share learning. It is also affected by the actual portfolio of businesses managed by a corporation. Goold *et al.* (1994) use the term heartland to describe that range of businesses to which a corporate head office can add value, rather than see value destroyed through too much complexity and diversity.

Alliances enable companies to focus on their core skills and competencies. Nike, for example, a leading company in sporting and leisure footwear, focuses on product design, marketing and personality endorsements; it avoids manufacturing, which it subcontracts to specialists worldwide. Partners have to support each other, though, and understand each other's various needs and expectations. The main benefits will come from sharing information, which in turn should enable companies to respond more quickly to new opportunities and threats. Alliance partners can also be an excellent means of overcoming relative weaknesses.

Leveraging resources

Hamel and Prahalad (1993) also emphasize the need to manage the organization's strategic resources to achieve ambitious, stretching objectives. Productivity can be improved by gaining the same output from fewer resources – this is downsizing (sometimes called rightsizing) – and by leveraging, achieving more output from given resources.

Clearly internal and external architecture are both important for leveraging resources. In addition, organizations can benefit by ensuring that there is a clear and understood focus for the efforts. This could take the form of a properly communicated mission or purpose, which is acknowledged and understood. British Airways would claim that much of its success historically has been based around a commitment to the slogan *The World's Favourite Airline*. This example again emphasizes the significance of corporate image.

Adding value

A business must add value if it is to be successful. As supply potential has grown to exceed global demand in the majority of industries, adding value has become increasingly important. In simple terms the extent of the value added is the difference between the value of the outputs from an organization and the cost of the inputs or resources used. We are simply addressing two quite fundamental questions: what is the value created and what is the cost?

The traditional paradigm, based on the accountancy measure, is that prices reflect costs plus a profit margin. The lack of differentiation, for which a higher price can be charged, implies enormous downward pressures on costs. Performance measurement is then based upon *economy* (low input costs) and *efficiency* (minimizing the actual and attributed costs of the resources used for adding further value).

While it is important to use all resources efficiently and properly, it is also critical to ensure that the potential value of the outputs is maximized by ensuring that they fully meet the needs of the customers for whom they are intended. An organization achieves this when it sees its customers' objectives as its own objectives and *enables its customers to easily add more value or, in the case of final consumers, feel they are gaining true value for money*.

The new paradigm is as follows. The key is value for the customer; if resources are used to provide real value for customers, they will pay a price which reflects its worth to them.

John Kay (1993) researched the most successful European companies during the 1980s, measured by their average costs per unit of net output. He found that each company had developed an individual strategy for adding value and creating competitive success. Glaxo (number one in the ten) successfully exploited the international potential for its patented anti-ulcer drug Zantac. LVMH (Louis Vuitton, Moët Hennessy), sixth in the list, generated synergy from the global distribution of a diverse range of high-quality, premium-brand products. Benetton, second, enjoyed beneficially close links with its suppliers and distributors, again worldwide. Marks and Spencer (tenth, and this chapter's case study) was also expert at supply chain management and further benefited from its value-for-money image and reputation. In contrast, low-price food retailer Kwik Save, fifth in the list, was selling its products with a low margin but enjoying a relatively very high turnover to capital employed. BTR (number nine) had expertise in the management of a diversified conglomerate. Many of Kay's leading companies are featured in the case studies in this book, and it is important to emphasize that the relative fortunes of some of these organizations have declined. We mentioned earlier that Marks and Spencer has recently fallen from grace; the demise of both BTR and Kwik Save has been greater. Simply it cannot be assumed that what constitutes value for customers at some point in time will always constitute value. When needs and requirements change, companies must find new ways of creating high added value.

The important elements in adding value are:

- understanding and being close to customers, in particular understanding their perception of value
- a commitment to quality
- a high level of all-round service
- speedy reaction to competitive opportunities and threats
- innovation.

Organizations can seek to add value by, first, adding positive features, such as air conditioning, comfortable bucket seats and CD players in cars, and, second, by removing any features perceived as negatives or drawbacks. Anti-lock braking systems and four-wheel drive gearboxes reduce the concerns that some people have about driving in bad weather; extended warranty schemes remove the fear of unknown future repair costs. Each of these additions has a value for which some customers, not all, will pay a premium.

It is, of course, quite conceivable that organizations are pursuing strategies or policies which make life harder for their customers. Minimum order quantities, and, possibly, volume discounts, may force or encourage customers to buy more than they need or can afford to stock. Obsolescence can then become an issue. Organizations could evaluate the merit of discounts based on annual sales rather than only on individual orders. Simply, organizations should be looking to ensure that they follow the top loop of Figure 1.13 and not the bottom one.

Organizations which truly understand their customers can create competitive advantage and thereby benefit from higher prices and loyalty. High capacity utilization can then help to reduce costs.

As an example, the prices of airline seats are related to the value they have for customers, the benefits they offer, not simply the airline's cost for providing the seat and the associated service. The first-class cabin has traditionally offered space, comfortable seats which can be reclined almost to the horizontal, and high-quality food and service. Business class is based on similar principles but to a more limited degree. Now airlines are beginning to introduce sleeper seats (seats which can be converted into a horizontal bed) in these cabins for long-haul overnight flights. Both classes are quieter than the economy section, offering some opportunity for business travellers to work; and reservations can be changed. Economy seats at full fare allow for late bookings, open tickets allow for flexible return schedules, upstairs seats on Boeing 747s with some airlines and, clearly, more chance of an upgrade when a flight is not fully booked. Reduced apex fares can be very good value for money, but they are inflexible. Travellers must stay for a prescribed period, flights and tickets cannot be altered and sometimes payment must be made early and in full.

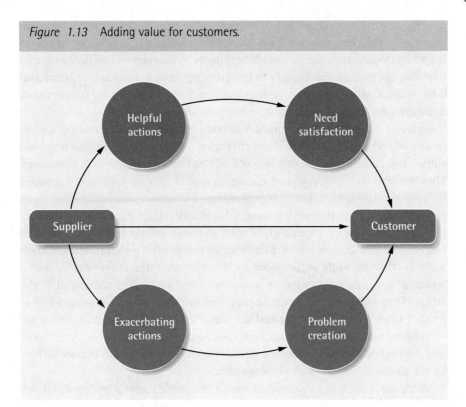

Figure 1.13   Adding value for customers.

One important key success factor for an airline is the ability to sell the right mix of tickets to maximize the revenue potential from every flight. Empty seats imply lost revenue; at the same time, if every ticket is sold at a discounted price, the flight is unlikely to be profitable. After flipping from profit to loss at the end of the 1990s, British Airways has switched its emphasis and increased the size of its premium-price business class cabins at the expense of low-margin economy seating.

Consequently the airline performance measures include: load factors; passenger kilometres (the numbers of passengers multiplied by the distance flown); and the revenue per passenger kilometre.

Opportunities for adding value which attracts customers must be sought and exploited. Numerous possible opportunities exist at corporate, competitive and functional strategy levels. Resources must be deployed to exploit these opportunities. Pümpin (1991), argues that multiplication – strategic consistency and performance improvement by concentrating on certain important strategies and learning how to implement them more effectively – promotes growth. The matching process is led and championed by the strategic leader, who is responsible for establishing the key values. While striving to improve performance with existing strategies the organization must constantly search for new windows of opportunity. McDonald's (see the case study in Chapter 8) provides an excellent example. Ray Kroc spotted an opportunity in the growing fast-food market and exploited it by concentrating on new product ideas and franchised outlets, supported by a culture which promoted *quality, service, cleanliness and value.*

Figures 1.14 and 1.15 now summarize our arguments about strategic competency and competitive success. We see in Figure 1.14 that organizations must add value – and continue to find new ways of adding fresh value – for their customers. They achieve this by developing, changing and exploiting core resource-based technological competencies. This exploitation involves organizational processes and capabilities, together with strong linkages with other companies in the supply chain (strategic architecture), in order to create differentiation and effective cost control and, thus, establish and superior competitive position. The situation is always fluid, though; organizations cannot assume that currently successful products, services and competitive strategies will be equally successful in the future. They must be changed at appropriate times. In turn, this requires competency in awareness, thinking and learning. Realizing which competencies are most important for long-term success, concentrating attention on them, developing them and measuring the desired improvements is a critically important task for the strategic leader, as we shall see later.

All the time, companies should carry out efficiently those activities which are essential for creating a distinctive or differentiated competitive position, and avoid

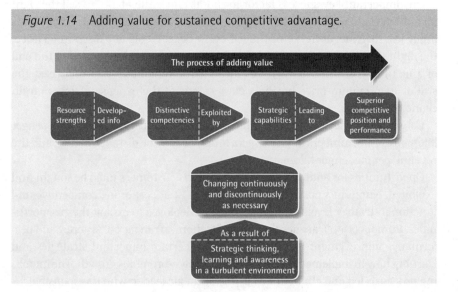

Figure 1.14   Adding value for sustained competitive advantage.

incurring unnecessary costs by providing non-essential values. This implies that they clearly understand their markets, their customers and the key success factors that they must meet – their defined competitive strategy. Moreover, they should constantly seek improvement by driving their operating efficiencies.

Figure 1.15 pulls together the market- and resource-based views of strategy with the analytical (planning) and aspirational (visionary and emergent) approaches to strategy creation introduced and explained earlier. The market-based approach can be manifest in either an analytical insight into the competitive environment or an endeavour to envision new opportunities for building value through an instinctive understanding of customers and their needs. The resource-based approach can build analytically on core competencies and capabilities. At the same time, real breakthroughs in processes or technologies can help to rewrite the rules of competition in an industry.

Figure 1.15 Changing strategies. Based on ideas in KPMG (1999) Change the Game, Change the Rules of the Game, ww.kpmg.co.uk/kpmg/uk/services/manage/ebook/change

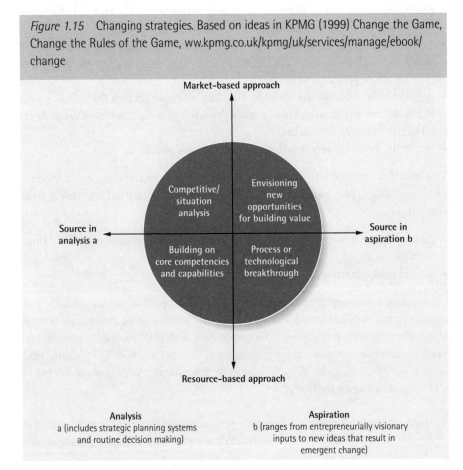

Market-based approach

Competitive/ situation analysis

Envisioning new opportunities for building value

Source in analysis a

Source in aspiration b

Building on core competencies and capabilities

Process or technological breakthrough

Resource-based approach

Analysis
a (includes strategic planning systems and routine decision making)

Aspiration
b (ranges from entrepreneurially visionary inputs to new ideas that result in emergent change)

Competitive advantage

Ohmae (1982) contends that business strategy is all about competitive advantage. He argues that without competitors there would be no need for strategy, for the sole purpose of strategic management is to enable the company to gain, as effectively as possible, a sustainable edge over its competitors – to alter a company's strength relative to that of its competitors in the most efficient way. Actions affecting the health of a business (value engineering or improved cash flow which improve profitability) widen the range of alternative strategies the company may choose to adopt *vis-à-vis* its competitors.

A good strategy is one by which a company can gain significant ground on its competitors at an acceptable cost to itself. There are basically four ways:

- Identify the key success factors in an industry and concentrate resources in a particular area where the company sees an opportunity to gain the most significant strategic advantage over its competitors.
- Exploit any area where a company enjoys relative superiority. This could include using technology or the sales network developed elsewhere in the organization for other products or services.
- Aggressively attempt to change the key success factors by challenging the accepted assumptions concerning the ways in which business is conducted in the industry or market.
- Innovate. Open up new markets or develop new products.

The principal concern is to avoid doing the same thing, on the same battleground, as competition. The aim is to attain a competitive situation in which your company can

- gain a relative advantage through measures that its competitors will find hard to follow and
- extend that advantage further.

Competitive advantage is more than the idea of a competitive strategy, which may or may not prove distinctive. Porter (1985), the author most commonly associated with this topic, has shown how companies can seek broad advantage within an industry or focus on one or a number of distinct segments. He argues that advantage can accrue from particular generic strategies which are available to all competitors in an industry:

(i) cost leadership, whereby a company prices around the average for the market (with a 'middle-of-the-road' product or service) and enjoys superior profits because its costs are lower than those of its rivals

(ii) differentiation, where value is added in areas of real significance for customers, who are then willing to pay a premium price for the distinctiveness.
A range of differentiated products (or services), each designed to appeal to
a different segment, is possible, as is focus on just one segment.

I believe that, in addition, speed (say quicker new product development) and fast
reaction to opportunities and threats can provide advantage, essentially by reducing costs and differentiating.

Real competitive advantage implies that companies are able to satisfy customer
needs more effectively than their competitors. Because few individual sources of
advantage are sustainable in the long run, the most successful companies innovate and continually seek new forms of advantage in order to open up a competitive gap and then maintain their lead. Successfully achieving this is a cultural
issue, as we have seen.

Ohmae (1982) offers an alternative, but clearly related, framework to that of
Michael Porter for studying competitive advantage. Ohmae focuses on three Cs:
customers, competitors and the corporation.

Customers will ultimately decide whether or not the business is successful by buying or not buying the product or service. But customers cannot be treated *en
masse*. Specific preferences should be sought and targeted. Products should be differentiated to appeal to defined market segments.

Competitors will similarly differentiate their products, goods and services, and
again incur costs in doing so. Competition can be based upon price, image, reputation, proven quality, particular performance characteristics, distribution or
after-sales service, for example.

Corporations are organized around particular functions (production, marketing,
etc.). The way in which they are structured and managed determines the cost of
the product or service.

There are opportunities to create competitive advantage in several areas of business, such as product design, packaging, delivery, service and customizing. Such
opportunities achieve differentiation, but they can increase costs. Costs must be
related to the price that customers are willing to pay for the particular product,
based to some extent on how they perceive its qualities – again in relation to
competitors.

Strategic success, in the end, requires a clear understanding of the needs of
the market, especially its segments, and the satisfaction of targeted customers
more effectively and more profitably than by competitors.

Achieving competitive advantage

Competitive advantage, then, does not come from simply being different. It is achieved if and when real value is added for customers. This often requires companies to stretch their resources to achieve higher returns (Hamel and Prahalad, 1993, and discussed earlier in this section). Improved productivity may be involved; ideally employees will come up with innovations, new and better ways of doing things for customers.

This innovation can result in lower costs, differentiation or a faster response to opportunities and threats, the bases of competitive advantage; and it is most likely to happen when the organization succeeds in harnessing and exploiting its core competencies and capabilities.

It also requires that employees are empowered. Authority, responsibility and accountability will be decentralized, *allowing employees to make decisions for themselves*. They should be able and willing to look for improvements. When this is managed well, a company may succeed in changing the rules of competition. Basically organizations should seek to encourage 'ordinary people to achieve extraordinary results'.

This will only happen if achievement is properly recognized, and initiative and success rewarded. Some people, though, are naturally reticent about taking risks. 3M, which developed Post-It Notes, Sony, Hewlett-Packard and Motorola are four organizations which are recognized as being highly creative and innovative. In each case employees are actively encouraged to look for, and try out, new ideas. In such businesses the majority of products in the corporate portfolio will have only existed for a few years. Effective empowerment can bring continual growth to successful companies and also provide ideas for turning around companies in decline.

Competitive advantage is also facilitated by good internal and external communications – achieving one of the potential benefits of linkages. Without this businesses cannot share and learn best practice. Moreover, information is a fundamental aspect of organizational control. Companies can learn from suppliers, from distributors, from customers, from other members of a large organization – and from competitors.

Companies should never overlook opportunities for communicating their achievements, strengths and successes. Image and reputation are vitally important; they help to retain business.

E-V-R congruence

If one wished to claim that an organization was being managed effectively from a strategic point of view, one would have to show, first, that its managers appreciated fully the dynamics, opportunities and threats present in their competitive environment, and that they were paying due regard to wider societal issues; and, second, that the organization's resources (inputs) were being managed strategically, taking into account its strengths and weaknesses, and that the organization was taking advantage of its opportunities. Key success factors and core competencies would be matched. This will not just happen, it needs to be managed. Moreover, potential new opportunities need to be sought and resources developed. It is also important, therefore, that the values of the organization match the needs of the environment and the key success factors. It is the values and culture which determine whether the environment and resources are currently matched, and whether they stay congruent in changing circumstances.

Values are traditionally subsumed as a resource in a SWOT (strengths, weaknesses, opportunities, threats) analysis, but I believe that they need to be separated out. The notion of E–V–R congruence then is an integration of these issues. Basically there is an overlap between the environment (key success factors) and resources (competencies and capabilities) and the organization is committed to sustaining this overlap with effective strategic change initiatives. This notion of E–V–R (environment–values–resources) congruence is illustrated in the top left diagram in Figure 1.16.

The value of E–V–R analysis is that it provides a straightforward framework for assessing the organization's existing strategies and strategic needs. It is crystal clear at a conceptual level what organizations have to achieve and sustain strategically; the challenge then is to use the logic to explore and create opportunities and ways for achieving and sustaining congruence by dealing with the various – but different – risks that organizations have to manage if they are to avoid crises in the face of constant uncertainty.

The other four illustrations in Figure 1.16 illustrate alternative instances of incongruence. E–V–R analysis can be applied at more than one level; and consequently different managers should be in positions where they can address which of the alternatives in Figure 1.16 best represents their organization and their individual business. Having selected the one that they feel best sums up the present situation, they can immediately see the direction and thrust of the changes that are needed to create or restore congruency.

Working downwards from the top left in the figure, we next see a 'lost organization'. Possibly there was congruency at some time, but now products, services and markets are out of alignment and the values inappropriate. Without major changes to strategy, structure and style, almost certainly involving a change of strategic leader, an organization in this situation has no future. This degree of incongruence would be relatively unusual, but the other three possibilities are not.

Figure 1.16   E–V–R congruence and incongruence.

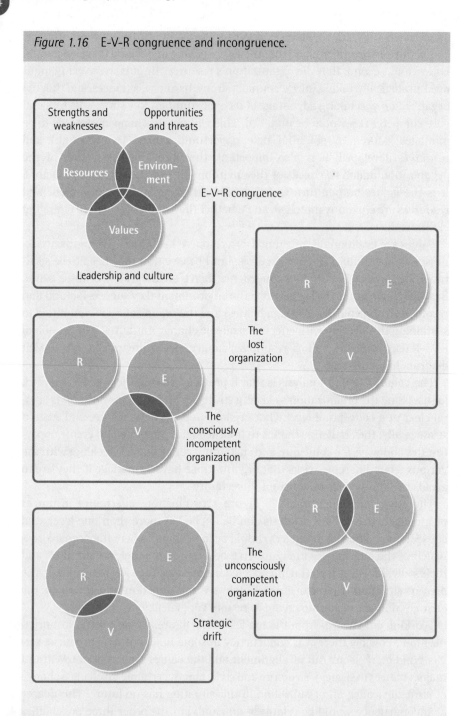

The 'consciously incompetent' organization is aware of the needs for success in its marketplace, and managers appreciate the importance of satisfying its customers – but it is simply not achieving the desired level of service and quality. Managers may well have some insight into what might be improved but not be in a position to achieve this improvement. Maybe there is a key resource shortage of some form or a lack of investment, or a person or people with key skills have left and not been replaced. Possibly too many managers are unwilling to grasp the changes that are needed and accept empowerment and responsibility. It is typical for a company in this situation to be constantly fighting crises and problems. Because of the customer orientation, there will be a commitment to resolving the problems and difficulties, and, for this reason, some customers may be somewhat tolerant. But the organization is likely to be highly reactive and, consequently, again the position cannot be sustained indefinitely. A more proactive and entrepreneurial approach will be required to strengthen the resource base and restore congruency with a fresh strategic position.

In contrast, the 'unconsciously competent' organization enjoys strategic positioning without any real commitment, especially to improvement and change. Things are working – at a surface level and possibly with some element of luck. Any success is taken for granted. The organization is unable to exploit its strengths and, if it fails to address this, then E and R will drift apart over time, possibly sooner rather than later, to create a lost organization. The required change in culture and values probably implies a change of leadership – certainly of leadership style – to increase decentralization and empowerment.

'Strategic drift' is commonplace. An organization which is internally cohesive simply loses touch with its environment. Demands may change; fresh competition may make the company's products and services less attractive than in the past. The challenge then concerns realignment in a dynamic environment, which certainly requires a change in management style and, possibly again, leadership. This organization desperately needs new ideas, which may already be available inside the organization, but not captured.

An article by Peter Drucker (1994) complements both this model and these arguments when he states that all organizations have implicit or explicit 'theories' for their business, incorporating:

- assumptions about the environment, specifically markets, customers and important technologies
- assumptions about its mission or purpose and
- assumptions about the core (content) competencies required to fulfil the mission.

These assumptions, at any time, must be realistic, congruent, communicated and understood; to achieve this they must be evaluated regularly and rigorously.

Pümpin (1987) uses the term strategic excellence positions (SEP's) to describe *capabilities which enable an organization to produce better-than-average results over the longer term compared with its competitors*. SEPs imply that·organizations appreciate the views of customers and develop the capabilities required to satisfy these needs. Moreover, they are perceived by their customers to be a superior competitor because of their skills and accomplishments.

It is important to deploy resources and to focus the drive for excellence (an aspect of the organization's culture) on issues which matter to customers. IBM, for example, has succeeded historically by concentrating on service, Rolls Royce (Motor Cars) on image and quality, and Procter and Gamble on advertising and branding.

Businesses should seek to develop competitive advantage and a strategic excellence position for each product and service. Overall E–V–R congruence then depends on these SEPs together with any corporate benefits from linkages and interrelationships.

The development of SEP's and E–V–R congruence takes time, and requires that all the functional areas of the business appreciate which factors are most significant to customers. Once achieved, though, it cannot be assumed that long-term success is guaranteed. Situations change, and new windows of opportunity open (Abell, 1978). The demand for guaranteed overnight parcel deliveries anywhere in the country, and immediate services within cities, opened up the opportunity for couriers; new technologies used in laptop computers, facsimile machines and the Internet have created demand and behaviour changes. Competitors may behave unexpectedly, and consequently there is a need for strategic awareness and for monitoring potential change situations.

Handy (1994) also stresses that timing plays a crucial role in the management of strategic change. He uses the sigmoid curve (Figure 1.17) to illustrate that organizations must change when they are successful, not when it is too late. His argument is that change should be initiated at point A, not point B. At point A there is time to be positive and embed change before a situation deteriorates, thus maintaining a positive momentum. If the change is delayed to point B, then there is a real chance that the organization will go into decline, albeit temporarily, and appear very reactive. The shaded area thus represents a period of uncertainty and turbulence.

Vigilance should help an organization to decide where it should be concentrating its resources at the moment, how it might usefully invest for the future, and where it needs to divest as existing windows of opportunity start to close.

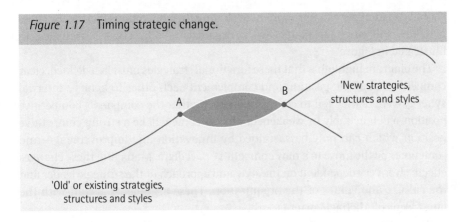

Figure 1.17   Timing strategic change.

New market needs may imply a change of values, and this again will take time and prove challenging. It is not easy, for instance, to change a strong cost culture into one which is more innovatory.

Bettis and Prahalad (1995) argue that business decisions are affected by a 'dominant logic', championed by the strategic leader and communicated through the organization. This could be an articulated vision or a culturally integrated paradigm concerning 'what the business is about and how things get done'. We shall see next how strategic regeneration implies this logic needs to be changed. IBM's growth and early industry dominance was built on a belief that mainframe computers were essential for organizations. Competitors such as Microsoft, which concentrated on software, highlighted that IBM's logic was outdated and it needed to be 'unlearned'. New products and new processes alone would prove inadequate. The new logic is one of decentralized personal computers in the hands of knowledgeable workers.

Organizations, therefore, should build on their past successes while always realizing that the past may not be the best guide to the future.

Synergy

Synergy (defined in Box 1.1) is a critical aspect of both corporate and competitive strategies. It is important that the functions and businesses within an organization work collectively and support each other to improve effectiveness and outcomes.

All the time, companies should carry out efficiently those activities which are essential for creating a distinctive or differentiated competitive position, and avoid incurring unnecessary costs by providing non-essential values. This implies that they clearly understand their markets, their customers and the key success factors that they must meet – their defined competitive strategy. Moreover, they should constantly seek improvement by driving their operating efficiencies. These activities will be encapsulated in the organization's functional strategies, as illustrated in Figure 1.18.

The diagram highlights that these functional strategies must fit a defined, clear competitive strategic position and complement each other to achieve internal synergy. Where they fail to complement each other the company's competitive position will inevitably be weakened. The outcome will be a strong competitive position which can only be sustained by innovation and improvement – and sometimes by the move to a new competitive paradigm. Managing these changes effectively is very dependent on the style and approach of the strategic leader and the culture and values of the organization. These arguments accord with the latest ideas of Michael Porter (1996).

People, however, are often naturally competitive and their competitive energy should be directed against external rivals rather than members of their own organization – although, carefully managed, internal competition for scarce resources can sharpen managerial skills.

Taking the logic a stage further: where the organization's various competitive strategies are also complementary, based around a fitting heartland of activities to which the corporation can add value, the organization will be able to maintain a strong corporate portfolio. Individual businesses should, therefore, benefit from being part of the organization; membership should reduce their costs or help to provide other competitive advantages. At the same time, the organiza-

Figure 1.18   Strategic success through complementary activities.

tion as a whole should derive benefit from the particular mix of businesses, which should, in some way, complement each other. There may be intergroup trading, for example, with one business unit supplying another; equally, skills could be transferred, factory units could be shared, or the businesses could join together to purchase common requirements with substantial discounts.

Major changes to the corporate perspective will invariably be board-level decisions and actively involve the organization's strategic leader. Changes at the corporate and functional levels are more likely to be delegated to other managers in the business. The nature and extent of such delegation will vary from organization to organization and should reflect a careful balance between, on the one hand, the need to maintain effective control and integrate the businesses to create synergy, and, on the other hand, the benefits which can be gained from empowering those managers who are most aware of environmental changes and new competitive opportunities.

Strategic regeneration

Organizations have to deal with dynamic and uncertain environments, as we have seen already. Some environments are more turbulent than others. Organizations should actively and continuously look for opportunities to exploit their competencies and strategic abilities, adapt and seek improvements in every area of the business – gradual change, building on an awareness and understanding of current strategies and successes. One difficulty is the fact that organizations are not always able to clarify exactly why they are successful. At the same time it is also valuable if they can think ahead discontinuously, trying to understand future demand, needs and expectations. By doing this they will be aiming to be the first competitor with solutions. Enormous benefits are available to the companies which succeed by, in effect, rewriting the rules of competition in an industry.

> *The future was predictable – though very few predicted it!*
> Allen Kay, when research fellow, Apple Computers

Hamel (1997) argues that a changing business (or external) environment opens up the possibility for finding new business and competitive opportunities all the time. There are opportunities for entrepreneurs and the entrepreneurially minded organization; for the others there are threats. He cites globalization, shorter product and service life cycles (linked to technology improvements and to consumer willingness to change more frequently than in the past) and faster, more sophisticated communication networks as typical sources of opportunity. He explains that there are known and visible areas of opportunity – such as gene-engineered drugs, non-branch banking and multimedia – but stresses that the secret lies in finding the 'right' strategic position to exploit the opportunity. As we have already said, because of the constant environmental turbulence any strategic position must be seen as temporary and sensitive to unexpected events; innovation is needed to reinforce and defend a position of strength.

Without constant improvement, renewal and intrapreneurship there are obvious dangers in this changing environment, but alone this may well prove inadequate. The most entrepreneurial companies will, at the same time, be searching for new ways of competing. Linked to this is the difficulty for many organizations that future competitive threats are as likely to come from unknown or unexpected organizations currently outside the industry as they are from existing, known rivals. In the early 1980s it is highly likely that British Airways was particularly concerned with the possible actions over routes and fares by its main American and European rivals; it seems much more improbable that they anticipated the threat that Richard Branson and Virgin Atlantic was going to pose. BA may well have recognized the potential for new competitors as deregulation changed the air travel environment, but predicting the source was another matter. The outsider Direct Line had the same impact on the insurance industry.

In a sense this process is an attempt to invent the future, and the resources of the organization, its people and technologies, will need to be applied creatively. Companies should *imagine new product opportunities* and strive to develop new products and services because they believe that customers will value them if they are available (Hamel and Prahalad, 1991). Sony, for example, developed a sketch pad for children, allowing them to project their drawings directly onto a TV screen as they drew them. Developments like this are based on ideas and 'dreams' rather than merely attempting to improve existing products. Asking customers is not enough – companies must be able to both to understand them and to think at least one jump ahead. There is a danger when companies 'follow their nose' but fail truly to understand their markets. In such cases, research and development may drive product development down an inappropriate track. In addition, caution is necessary when ideas are implemented because markets and customers are likely to resist changes which seem too radical.

To minimize the risk, 'expeditionary marketing' – low-risk incursions into the market to test out new features or new performances – can be useful. Here organizations are really attempting to create markets ahead of competitors and just slightly ahead of customers.

In summary, organizations are searching for:

- long-term product or service leadership, which is dictated by the environment
- long-term cost leadership, which is resource dependent

- product and service excellence, doing things more quickly than competitors without sacrificing quality-essential values.

Strategic regeneration refers to simultaneous changes to strategies and structures (organizational processes) in this search.

Strategies have to be reinvented. New products and services should be created by questioning how and why existing ones are popular and successful, and looking for new ways of adding extra value. Electronic publishing and CD-ROM technology, for example, have offered enormous potential for dramatically changing the ways people learn. Rewards have been available for those companies which have learnt how to exploit these *environmental opportunities*.

In thinking ahead, companies should consider both products (or services) and core competencies. Concentrating on products encourages a search for new competitive opportunities; thinking creatively about competencies (which transcend individual products and businesses) can generate radically new opportunities for adding value and establishing a different, future 'competitive high ground'.

Structural changes are designed to improve *resource efficiency and effectiveness*. Trends in the late 1990s have been:

- downsizing– splitting the organization into small, autonomous, decentralized units. Those organizations which have taken this too far have inadvertently lost key resources which were critical for their competitiveness. Consequently, the notion of 'right-sizing' is the important one
- delayering – using the power and potential of information technology for reducing the number of layers of managers, in order to speed up decision making,and
- process re-engineering – reviewing and redesigning processes in order that tasks can be performed better and more quickly.

Simply, changes are required to the structure of the organization, the nature and scope of jobs and the network of communications.

Empowerment and teamworking are also seen as essential for creating the values necessary to enable this degree of change.

On paper the idea of strategic regeneration can be justified as essential, exciting and rewarding, but, not unexpectedly, there are likely to be major barriers when applying the ideas. The most obvious hurdles are:

- the quality of leadership required to provide the necessary drive and direction
- an inability to create an internal culture of change – the most powerful inhibitors will be experienced, established managers who have become out of date
- uncertainty about changing needs and competitor activities.

Pascale (1992) uses the word *transformational* to describe organizations which succeed with simultaneous strategic and structural change. They become learning organizations which *encourage continuous learning and knowledge generation at all levels, have processes which can move knowledge around the organization easily to where it is needed, and can translate that knowledge quickly into changes in the way the organization acts, both internally and externally* (Senge, 1991).

Successful entrepreneurs and entrepreneurial organizations often find new products and new needs ahead of both their rivals and their customers. Market research can tap into issues that are important for customers, but it is unlikely to provide the answers. Creativity, insight and innovation stimulated within the organization is more likely to achieve this. Entrepreneurs and entrepreneurial organizations thus *create proprietary foresight from public knowledge* by synthesizing information and environmental signals and creating new patterns and opportunities.

This intellectual foresight has a number of possible sources according to Hamel and Prahalad (1994):

- It can be a personal restlessness with the existing status quo.
- It can be a natural curiosity – which the education system does not manage to stifle! – which leads to creativity. Sometimes the entrepreneurial people concerned have a childlike innocence in the questions they ask, and the process is stimulated by a wide network of contacts.
- It may be a willingness on the part of certain individuals to speculate and manage the risk of investigation. Invention has to precede learning.
- It is sometimes a desire to change things and 'leave footprints'.
- Often there is an empathy with the industry and market concerned, coupled with
- The ability to conceptualize what does not yet exist ... *you can't create a future you can't imagine.*

Strategic Management in Specific Contexts

Strategic ideas are relevant for every type of organization, and many of the key issues are the same, although they may differ in their relative significance. At the same time, there are some important differences, which we introduce in this section. Throughout the book we endeavour to use examples and cases which reflect a range of different types and size of organization, but, inevitably, large manufacturing and service businesses feature most prominently, largely because they are the organizations and brand names that most readers recognize and relate to easily.

Small businesses

Typically, small businesses will focus on a single product or service, or at least a restricted range of related products and services, targeted at a defined market niche. Competitive and functional strategies are important, but many of the corporate strategy issues we discuss will not be relevant until the organization grows larger, assuming it does do this. In addition, their customers may be concentrated in a single geographical area, but this will certainly not always be the case. In some large organizations, the structure is designed to encourage the individual businesses to behave as a typical small business with some of the things it does.

There is generally a great reliance on the owner–manager for all major strategic decisions. The advantage can be speed, as decisions need not get lost or slowed down in discussion or committee; the corresponding disadvantage can be an over-reliance on one person who may become overstretched as the business develops. Hence we see an emphasis on visionary strategy creation and on emergence, as new things are tried out. Sophisticated analysis and planning is less likely – and sometimes a lack of attention to detail can constitute another weakness.

The real challenge for small businesses is to develop and strengthen their resources once they start growing – if they fail they will lose their competitiveness. Some, of course, never possess any real competitive advantage in the first place and, while they may survive if they are run efficiently, they are unlikely to grow to any significant size.

Where a small business fails to grow it will always be dependent on the actions of others. Both its suppliers and customers could be larger and consequently more powerful, in which case it could find that it is paying cash for its supplies and giving extended credit to its customers, resulting in cashflow problems. It is also likely to be very reactive to competitor initiatives until it can become more prominent and proactive. The helpful publicity and visibility given to larger organizations may be withheld, even at a local level. High-quality managers and employees – who could fuel the growth – may not find a small, and perceptually inconsequential company, attractive to work for. Nevertheless, all companies start small, they are, after all, the seed bed for those successful entrepreneurs who do create growth businesses.

The success, or lack of it, then, will be hugely dependent on the strategic leader, and his or her culture and style. The future will be dictated by their ability and also by their ability to acquire resources, particularly in terms of finance. A lack of capital can often be a real restraint to growth. Banks often demand security and collateral; venture capitalists often only become interested once the business has reached a certain size and proved itself. This traditional logic concerning small businesses, however, is being turned on its head in the case of many new Internet or 'dot.com' companies who are raising millions of pounds on the strength of a barely proven idea which appears to offer a golden opportunity. Financiers are taking risks they have previously shunned because of the speed and growth of this sector and its inherent uncertainty.

Global companies

Here the emphasis is very much on corporate strategy – diversity, geographical scope and co-ordinating the countries where products are made with the countries where they are sold. Using low-cost labour factories in Eastern Europe and the Far East can prove controversial while still being an economic necessity. In addition we are often talking about very powerful companies whose annual turnover exceeds the GNP (gross national product) of many of the world's smaller countries. Nevertheless, issues of competitiveness and competitive advantage are as relevant as they are for a small business. One key complication can be currency fluctuations when component supplies and finished goods are moved around the world.

The major dilemma for many global companies concerns their need to achieve global scale economies from concentrating production in large plants while not sacrificing their local identity and relevance in the various markets. To accomplish this they must stay close to their customers and markets, whose specific tastes and preferences may differ markedly, even though they are buying essentially the same product.

The organizational structure can be, and often is, just as important as the strategy itself. This, in turn, raises a number of important people issues. People may be switched from business to business and from country to country as part of their personal progression. This movement also helps the whole organization to transfer skills and knowledge and to learn good practices from different parts of the business.

Global corporations also need to develop expertise in financial management. Attractive development grants and packages will be available in certain countries and influence strategic developments. Interest rates are not the same around the world and consequently loans can be relatively more attractive in certain countries and not in others. Moreover, tax rates vary and it can be very beneficial to be seen to be earning profits in low-tax countries instead of high-tax ones.

Not-for-profit organizations

Organizations such as churches and charities clearly fit into this sector very well, but certain other profit-generating businesses, such as museums, zoos and local theatres, are relatively closely aligned. In the case of the latter examples, the profit objective is often designed to create a 'war chest' for future investment rather than to reward an owner or group of investors. For this reason there are many common characteristics. Money may be perceived differently in not-for-profit organizations than in profit-seeking businesses, but there is still a need to create a positive cash flow. A charity, for example, can only spend on good causes if it can generate funds. For this reason, churches and charities can legitimately appear very commercial in their outlook, and this must be accepted alongside the cause they are targeting.

These not-for-profit organizations need social entrepreneurs or strategic leaders who, in many ways, will be similar to those found in the profit-seeking sector. They will possess similar entrepreneur and leader qualities, but they will be driven by a cause, and it is this which attracts them to the particular organization and sector. This, in turn, guides the mission, purpose and culture. In addition, there is likely to be a greater reliance on voluntary helpers and possibly managers and others who readily accept salaries and wages below those that they might earn in the profit sector.

We are likely to see variations on the modes of strategy creation discussed here. There is likely to be some committee structure, involving both salaried employees and unpaid volunteers, the latter often in senior roles. Decision making can be slow and political in nature, although clearly it does not have to be this way. However, strong and dominant leaders (either paid or unpaid) quite often emerge and are at the heart of strategy making. Because there is a need for accountability for the funds raised, planning systems are likely to be prominent.

Organizations in the public sector

In many countries around the world the composition of this sector has changed over recent years. Typically essential service industries, such as telecommunications, gas, electricity, water, and air, bus and rail transport, have been privatized, often resulting in the creation of a number of complementary or even competing businesses. The outcome in each industry has been one or more private company, some of which have since merged or been acquired, sometimes by overseas parents. In the case of the UK this privatization programme has also included individual companies such as British Airports Authority (BAA), which manages several airports but is largely a retail organization. Outside direct government control, BAA has expanded overseas and now manages a number of other airports around the world.

In every case there is some form of regulation and government influence, as distinct from the direct government control of the past. The trend towards privatization has gathered momentum for many reasons, one factor in Europe being the stronger stance on government subsidies to individual industries by the European Commission. The key appears to lie in the effectiveness of the regulation, which must attempt to balance the needs of all key stakeholders: customers, employees and investors.

As a result, we now tend to think of local authorities and public health and emergency services as the archetypal public sector organizations. Clearly we are talking about service businesses, and ones which will always have to choose and prioritize between different needs and stakeholders. Generally, they will always be able to achieve more outcomes if they can acquire more resources. However, they remain largely dependent on central government for their resources and are therefore influenced by the political agenda of the day. Increasingly some have greater involvement with the private sector than was the case in the past. The British National Health Service (NHS) works alongside the private health-care sector and, although their roles and remits differ, it is the same consultants who operate in both sectors. Many services in local communities were subjected to CCT (compulsory competitive tendering) and, as a result, have been outsourced to providers in the private, profit-seeking sector.

Decision making and style features some element of bureaucracy, in part because of the role of governing bodies, be they elected (local councillors) or appointed (e.g. NHS Trust Boards). As accountability has become increasingly public in recent years, analysis and planning will also be very prominent. Again, though, strong leaders can, and will, make an impact; and, as the public sector environment is no more stable than the one affecting commercial businesses, emergent strategy is also very important.

Summary

Strategies are means to ends – they are the means through which organizations seek to achieve objectives and fulfil their mission or purpose.

All managers can be strategy makers because of their influence in both strategy creation and strategy implementation.

Strategic management is a process which embraces the strategies themselves together with the themes of excellence in their implementation, creativity and innovation when they are changed and the effective and timely management of these changes.

There is evidence that strategic thinking – and hence strategic management – could be improved in many companies by:

- segmenting and targeting markets more crisply and definitively
- appreciating clearly what the key success factors are in the targeted markets and segments
- creating real competitive advantage
- out-thinking rivals.

There are three levels of strategy:

- corporate – the overall portfolio of businesses within an organization

- competitive – the search for, and maintenance of, competitive advantage in each and every business, product and/or service
- functional – the activities which deliver the competitive advantage.

These activities, products, services and businesses should be analysed not exclusively at an individual 'ring-fenced' level, but also in terms of the whole organization. Links should be forged wherever possible to generate synergies.

Strategies should not be thought of as having one single definition or perspective. Five have been discussed: visionary strategies, planned strategies and tactics, all of which address the future; present strategic positions; and patterns that have emerged with past decisions and strategies.

The strategic management process comprises three broad stages: analysis; creation and choice; and implementation. This three-stage approach can be linked to the popular and well-established concept of strategic planning.

Additional themes complement, but do not replace, strategic planning in our understanding of the realities of strategic management and strategic change – namely competitive advantage, emergent strategy creation, strategic competency, strategic leadership and risk and crisis management.

There are three ways in which strategies are created: with visionary leadership; from a planning process; and adaptively and incrementally as new decisions are taken in real time.

Strategic leadership, culture and values are at the heart of all strategic decision making. The role, style and contribution of the strategic leader affect both strategy creation and implementation. The culture can – and should – act as a spur to, and facilitator of, change ... however, in some organizations the culture will successfully frustrate important change initiatives.

Strategic management can be conceptualized as a process through which internal and external resources are brought together to produce products and services – and through these satisfactory (at least) outcomes for all the organization's stakeholders. Related to this there are two approaches to strategy – market driven and resource based – but these should not be seen as mutually exclusive. They are complementary.

The market-driven approach requires that organizations understand – and satisfy – key success factors. These relate to general industry requirements, organizational distinctiveness and specific efforts for individual customers.

The resource-based approach implies that organizations identify and exploit their core competencies and strategic capabilities.

Linked to both is the importance of strategic architecture – linkages and synergy between the activities, functions and businesses inside the organization, and also between the organization and other members of its supply chain, such as suppliers and distributors.

The common theme to all these approaches is the recognition that the organization must find suitable ways of creating and building value for its customers. This naturally impacts on the degree of competitive advantage (real differences) that it enjoys.

The E–V–R (environment–values–resources) model provides an ideal framework for pulling most of these ideas together. It is relevant at both the organization and individual business level.

On some occasions in turbulent environments, organizational renewal and regeneration will become essential, when strategies, structure and style will all need changing simultaneously. This level of change can be traumatic, especially if it is forced on the organization.

Strategy and strategic management in different sectors, such as small and global businesses, the public sector and not-for-profit organizations, have many similarities, but there are clear differences, especially of emphasis.

References

Abell, DF (1978) Strategic windows, *Journal of Marketing*, 42 (July).

Ansoff, HI (1984) *Implanting Strategic Management*, Prentice Hall.

Beck, P, quoted in Lorenz, C (1987) Crusading for a clear strategy, *Financial Times*, 25 February.

Bettis, R and Prahalad, CK (1995) The dominant logic: retrospective and extension, *Strategic Management Journal*, Volume 16, January.

Burns, T and Stalker, GM (1961) *The Management of Innovation*, Tavistock.

Caulkin, S (2000) How we manage to fail, *Management Today*, November.

Collins, J and Porras, J (1995) *Built to Last*, Century Business.

Drucker, PF (1994) The theory of business, *Harvard Business Review*, September–October.

Drucker, PF (1985) *Innovation and Entrepreneurship*, Heinemann.

Freeman, C (2000) Interview: *Management Today*, January.

Goold, M, Campbell, A and Alexander, M (1994) *Corporate Level Strategy*, John Wiley.

Hall, D (1992) *The Hallmarks for Successful Business*, Mercury Books.

Hamel, G (1997) Address to a Strategic Planning Society Conference, London.

Hamel, G and Prahalad, CK (1989) Strategic intent, *Harvard Business Review*, May–June.

Hamel, G and Prahalad, CK (1991) Corporate imagination and expeditionary marketing, *Harvard Business Review*, July–August.

Hamel, G and Prahalad, CK (1993) Strategy as stretch and leverage, *Harvard Business Review*, March–April.

Hamel, G and Prahalad, CK (1994) *Competing for the Future*, Harvard Business School Press.

Handy, C (1994) *The Empty Raincoat*, Hutchinson.

Kay, JA (1993) *Foundations of Corporate Success*, Oxford University Press.

Mathus, S S and Kenyon, A (1998) *Creating Value: Shaping Tomorrow's Business*, Butterworth-Heinemann.

Mintzberg, H (1989) *Mintzberg on Management*, Free Press.

Mintzberg, H, quoted in Lorenz, C (1982) Strategic doctrine under fire, *Financial Times*, 15 October. The themes are developed extensively in Quinn, JB, Mintzberg, H and James, RM (1987) *The Strategy Process*, Prentice-Hall.

Mintzberg, H, Ahlstrand, B and Lampel, J (1998) *Strategy Safari*, Prentice Hall.

Morrison, R and Lee, J (1979) From planning to clearer strategic thinking, *Financial Times*, 27 July.

Ohmae, K (1982) *The Mind of the Strategist*, McGraw-Hill.

Pascale, RT (1992) Paper presented at the *Strategic Renaissance Conference*, Strategic Planning Society, London, October.

Porter, ME (1980) *Competitive Strategy*, Free Press.

Porter, ME (1985) *Competitive Advantage*, Free Press.

Porter, ME (1996) What is Strategy? *Harvard Business Review*, November-December.

Prahalad, CK and Hamel, G (1990) The core competence of the corporation, *Harvard Business Review*, May/June.

Pümpin, C (1987) *The Essence of Corporate Strategy*, Gower.

Pümpin, C (1991) *Corporate Dynamism*, Gower.

Quinn, JB (1980) *Strategies for Change: Logical Incrementalism*, Irwin.

Schein, EH (1985) *Organization Culture and Leadership*, Jossey Bass.

Senge, P (1991) *The Fifth Discipline: The Art and Practise of the Learning Organization*, Doubleday.

Stacey, RD (1993) *Strategic Management and Organizational Dynamics*, Pitman.

Stalk, G, Evans, P and Shulman, LE (1992) Competing on capabilities: the new rules of corporate strategy, *Harvard Business Review*, March–April.

Whittington, R (1999) The 'how' is more important than the 'where', *Financial Times (Mastering Strategy supplement)*, 25 October.

Additional material on the website

Reference was made in the text to the paper 'The Emergence of Strategic Management'. In addition to this paper there is one additional case on Rubbermaid which, like the case study on Marks and Spencer, charts the progress of a successful business which, in part, lost its edge.

The Margaret Brooke case study on the website provides an annotated application of the strategic analysis-choice-implementation framework. In addition, there is a paper entitled *Effective Strategies for the 1990s* which expands on a number of the points discussed in this chapter.

Questions and Research Assignments

TEXT RELATED

1. What exactly is a strategy? What have you learned about different perspectives, levels and ways in which they are changed?

2. What are the key elements in the strategic management process?

3. From your background knowledge what might be the key success factors required for success in the airline business? How do you feel Virgin and EasyJet have embraced these? How important a factor is 'risk taking'?

4. What is 'added value'? In what ways might an organization add value for its customers?

5. What are key success factors and core competencies? How are they related?

6. Taking any organization with which you are familiar ... use the E–V–R framework to assess its current situation.

Internet and Library Projects

1. How has Marks and Spencer sought to attain and maintain competitive advantage? What do you think its objectives might have been?

2. Sainsbury's first became UK market leader for 'packaged groceries' in 1983, with some 16% market share. Tesco and the Co-op each had 14.5% and ASDA 8%.

   The company's shares continued to outperform the Financial Times Index of top shares throughout the 1980s, and an editorial in the *Financial Times* commented that Sainsbury's *'performance combines profitability, productivity and a sense of social purpose.'*

   However, there did not appear to be any 'grand strategy'.

   > *We did not sit down in the early 70s and work out any corporate plan, or say that by a particular time we intended to be in a particular business, or to be of a particular size.*
   >
   > Roy Griffiths, Managing Director

   Rather, Griffiths claimed, Sainsbury's had *'identified and obsessively pursued'* opportunities that fitted the company's corporate values, the *'basics of the business'*.

   These were:
   - selling quality products at competitive (though not necessarily the cheapest) prices
   - exacting quality-control standards
   - extensive research of competitors and customers
   - strict financial management
   - right control of suppliers
   - planned staff involvement.

   In recent years Tesco has overtaken Sainsbury to become UK market leader. Why?

   Try to identify the successful strategies pursued by Tesco and the comparative shortcomings in the Sainsbury strategy.

   Can you identify any influence from changes in strategic leadership?

3. The American engineering contractor Bechtel has acquired a reputation for its ability to rescue major public sector projects which have either been in difficulty, behind schedule or with cost over-runs. Specific examples of successful intervention by Bechtel as project managers include

Appointment date	Project	Cost
1990	Channel Tunnel	£10 billion
1993	Cardiff Bay Barrage	£200 million
1996	Channel Tunnel Rail Link	£5.8 billion
1998	Jubilee Line Extension	£3.5 billion

What are the competencies and capabilities possessed and exploited by Bechtel to create this record of success?

2

The Organizational Mission and Objectives

Strategies are means to ends; this chapter is about these ends. Organizations undertake purposeful activity; what they do is not without purpose. Ideally, that purpose will be understood, shared and supported by everyone in the organization such that there is a clear, if broad, direction for the activities and strategies. Establishing the purpose and direction is a key role of the strategic leader; and it will provide a basis for the more detailed objectives and performance targets for individual managers and employees. This does not imply that everyone always shares the more detailed objectives; indeed, there can often be internal conflicts over these. Moreover, what individual people actually do and achieve affects organizational performance. Hence, this chapter looks at the idea of purposeful activity by considering the organizational mission and objectives.

A number of economic and behavioural theories contributes to our understanding of this subject. Considered here are the potentially conflicting expectations of different stakeholders, the role of institutional shareholders, and whether the profit motive should be the key driving force. A separate section looks at inherent conflicts of interest in certain not-for-profit organizations and later at issues of social responsibility and business ethics which also affect behaviour, performance and outcomes in a variety of ways. The chapter begins with a case on Ben and Jerry's ice cream, a company which has always been proud of its commitment to social and environmental causes and which has recently been acquired by the Anglo-Dutch multinational corporation Unilever.

Case Study 2: Ben and Jerry's

This idiosyncratic business was founded and developed by two partners, both entrepreneurs but, at face value, unlikely businessmen. Ben Cohen was a college dropout who had become a potter. His friend from his schooldays was Jerry Greenfield, a laboratory assistant who had failed to make it into medical school. They had become 'seventies hippies with few real job prospects'. They decided they wanted to do something themselves and 'looked for something they might succeed at'. They 'liked food, so food it was!' They could not afford the machinery for making bagels, their first choice, but ice cream was affordable. In 1977 they opened an ice-cream parlour in Burlington, Vermont, where there were 'lots of students and no real competition'. They fostered a relaxed, hippy atmosphere and employed a blues pianist. Their ice cream was different, with large and unusual chunks.

They were instantly successful in their first summer, but sales fell off in the autumn and winter when the snow arrived. They realized they would have to find outlets outside Vermont if they were to survive. Ben went on the road. Always dressed casually, he would arrive somewhere around 4.00 am and then sleep in his car until a potential distributor opened. He was able to 'charm the distributors' and the business began to grow. Ben and Jerry's success provoked a response from the dominant market leader, Häagen Dazs, owned by Pillsbury. Their market share was 70% of the luxury ice-cream market. Häagen Dazs threatened to withdraw their product from any distributors who also handled Ben and Jerry's. The two partners employed a lawyer and threatened legal action, but their real weapon was a publicity campaign targeted at Pillsbury itself, and its famous 'dough boy' logo. 'What's the Dough Boy afraid of?' they asked. Their gimmicks generated massive publicity and they received an out-of-court settlement. More significantly, the publicity created new demand for luxury ice cream, and the company began to grow more rapidly than had ever been envisaged. A threat had been turned into a massive opportunity. Soon Ben and Jerry's had a segment market share of 39%, just 4% behind Häagen Dazs. The company has expanded internationally with mixed success. They have enjoyed only limited success in the UK 'because there was only limited marketing support'.

Perhaps not unexpectedly, given their background, Ben and Jerry have created a values-driven business; some of their ice creams have been linked to causes and interests they support and promote. Rainforest Crunch ice cream features nuts from Brazil; the key ingredients for

Chocolate Fudge Brownie are produced by an inner-city bakery in Yonkers, New York; and they favour Vermont's dairy-farming industry. When the business needed equity capital to support its growth, local Vermont residents were given priority treatment. Ben and Jerry argue that they are committed to their employees who 'bring their hearts and souls as well as their bodies and minds to work' but acknowledge that their internal opinion surveys show a degree of dissatisfaction with the amount of profits (7.5%) given away every year to good causes.

The two realists with an unusual but definite ego drive later dropped out of day-to-day management '. . . the company needed a greater breadth of management than we had . . .' and were content to be 'two casual, portly, middle-aged hippies'.

In early spring 2000 the business was acquired by Unilever, the multinational foods, detergents and cosmetics business. Unilever already owned the UK market leader, Walls ice cream. Unilever and Walls had recently been investigated by the UK competition authorities because of their strategy of insisting that retailers only stock Walls ice cream if Unilever provide them with a freezer cabinet on loan.

QUESTIONS: Do you think the objectives of Ben and Jerry's will have to change after this acquisition?
Do you think it will feel like 'a different place to work', with different priorities?

Ben and Jerry's   http://www.benjerry.com

If you don't know where you are going, any road will take you there.
Raymond G Viault,
when Chief Executive Officer,
Jacobs Suchard, Switzerland

A voyage of a thousand miles begins with a single step. It is important that that step is in the right direction.

Old Chinese saying, updated

How can we go forward when we don't know which way we are facing?
John Lennon, 1972

Life can only be understood backward, but it must be lived forward.
S Kierkegaard

Introduction

This chapter is about the idea of strategic direction and objectives – what is meant by the terminology used and the implications. Objectives (in some form or another) should be set and communicated so that people know where the strategic leader wants the organization to be at some time in the future. At the same time it is essential that the objectives currently being pursued are clearly understood. Because of incremental changes in strategies the actual or implicit objectives may have changed from those that were established and made explicit sometime in the past. Objectives, therefore, establish direction, and in some cases set specific end-points. They should have time-scales or end-dates attached to them. The attainment of them should be measurable in some way, and ideally they will encourage and motivate people.

It is important, straight away, to distinguish between the idea of a broad purpose and specific, measurable, milestones. The organization needs direction in terms of where the strategic leader wants it to go, and how he or she would wish it to develop. This is really related to the *mission* of the organization, and/or possibly a visionary statement concerning the future. This mission is likely to be stated broadly and generally, and it is unlikely that it can ever be achieved completely. Thus, the organization pursues the mission, looking for new opportunities and new ways of building value for customers, dealing with problems and seeking to progress continually in the chosen direction. Improvements in the overall situation towards the stated mission are the appropriate measure of performance. Managers at all levels are likely to be set specific objectives to achieve. These, logically, are quantifiable targets for sales, profit, productivity or output, and performance against them is measured and evaluated. Objectives then become measurable points which indicate how the organization is making definite progress towards its broad purpose or mission.

Intended strategies are developed from the mission and the desired objectives as they are the means of achieving them. Hence, a change in objectives is likely to result in changes in strategy. At the same time it is important to realize that incremental, adaptive and emergent changes in strategy, whether the result of internal or external pressure, affect the levels of performance of the organization, i.e. the growth, profit or market share, and these performance levels should be related to the objectives actually being pursued.

The central theme of the chapter is that it is essential that the most senior managers in an organization understand clearly where their company is going, and why. Ideally, all managers will appreciate the overall mission and how their own role contributes to its attainment. The strategies being followed may be different to those that were originally stated, and there may be good reasons for this. Thus, the situation should be reviewed constantly and the strategic leader should seek to remain informed and aware of what is happening.

Definitions, Terminology and Examples

Box 2.1 defines the terms *vision*, *mission* and *objectives* and provides a range of examples from the private and public sectors. Figure 2.1 shows the relationships between these terms, highlighting their key constituents. The examples in Box 2.1 were selected to illustrate the relevant points, not because they are superior or inferior to those of other organizations; they should be evaluated in this light.

> **STRATEGY IN ACTION – Box 2.1**
>
> Examples of Vision, Mission and Objectives Statements
>
> Vision statements
>
> A *vision statement* describes what the company is to become in the (long-term) future.
>
> **The Sony spirit** Sony is a trail blazer, always a seeker of the unknown. Sony will never follow old trails, yet to be trod. Through this progress Sony wants to serve mankind.
>
> *Sony* http://www.sony.com
>
> **WH Smith (1995)** There's nowhere quite like WH Smith. It's full of energy and colour and excitement.
>
> Just when you think you know them, they surprise you. Everywhere you look there are fresh, inspired ideas.
>
> Smith's is an essential part of life. It's a unique blend of information, inspiration and just plain fun.
>
> Everything is chosen with thought, designed with care and presented with imagination.
>
> Customer service is instinctive. It's the right help at the right time, by people who know what they're saying and love what they're doing.
>
> Smith's builds its reputation day by day, product by product and customer by customer.
>
> Always in Front.
>
> > We can see represented here: adding new values, innovation, products which match customer needs, effective presentation, service and constant improvement.
>
> *WH Smith*
> http://www.whsmith.co.uk

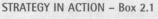

STRATEGY IN ACTION – Box 2.1
(Continued)

British Airways The world's favourite airline.

This vision focuses on employees and customers. The related mission emphasized BA's desire to be the world's first truly global airline, which in turn generated a corporate strategy of carefully selected alliances. To be feasible, however, it has always been essential that BA staff believe in the vision and act accordingly. In recent years staff trust and morale has declined as costs have been cut dramatically and the airline's profitability has declined.

British Airways   http://www.britishairways.com

Mission statements
The *mission* reflects the essential purpose of the organization, concerning particularly why it is in existence, the nature of the business(es) it is in, and the customers it seeks to serve and satisfy.

The Girl Guides Association To help a girl reach her highest potential.

These eight words cut straight to the heart of the movement; there is a clear and direct statement of purpose.

Girl Guides Association   http://www.wagggsworld.org

Financial Times Conferences The mission of the FTC is to organize conferences on subjects of interest to the international business community, using the highest calibre speakers and providing attending delegates with the finest service, thereby providing a low-cost and time efficient means of both obtaining impartial quality information and making senior-level industry contacts.

We can see a clear definition of the business, a formulation of objectives, delivery strategies, means of differentiating the service and stakeholder relevance.

Financial Times
http://www.news.ft.com

Virgin Atlantic Airways As the UK's second long-haul carrier, to build an intercontinental network concentrating on those routes with a substantial established market and clear indication of growth potential, by offering the highest possible service and lowest possible cost.

Not particularly elegant in style, but it does clarify both the target markets and the source of competitive advantage.

Virgin Atlantic
http://www.virgin-atlantic.com

Long-term objectives
Objectives are desired states or results linked to particular time-scales and concerning such things as size or type of organization, the nature and variety of the areas of interest and levels of success.

BAA – British Airports Authority: Open objectives BAA aims to enhance the value of the shareholders' investments by achieving steady and remunerative long-

STRATEGY IN ACTION – Box 2.1
(Continued)

term growth. Its strategy for developing and operating world-class international airports that are safe, secure, efficient and profitable is based on a commitment to continuously enhancing the quality of service to passengers and business partners alike. This process of constant improvement includes cost-effective investment in new airport facilities closely matched to customer demand.

These are in the context of a stated mission to 'make BAA the most successful airport company in the world'.

British Airports Authority   http://www.baa.co.uk

HP Bulmer Holdings: Multiple stakeholder objectives Our mission is to remain the world's most successful cider company. We will continue to measure our success in terms of market leadership, product quality, increasing shareholder value, and rewarding employment opportunities for our employees. This will be achieved by attaining the following objectives:

1. Lead and grow the UK and international cider markets through meeting consumer needs by superior marketing and sustained high levels of customer service.
2. Maintain lowest industry costs and ensure the most economical supply of essential and quality raw materials.
3. Be dedicated to fulfilling the requirements of all our customers through achieving excellence in our products, operations and service.
4. Adopt best practice across all of our activities through an innovative approach to product, process development and information technology.
5. Foster a culture of continuous improvement through self-motivation, team work and acceptance of change.
6. Provide competitive pay, employee share ownership and single status employment while achieving a link between performance, reward and shareholder interests.
7. Give all employees the opportunity to develop skills and potential through actively improving their own and the company's performance. Promote from within whenever appropriate.
8. Keep employees informed of policy, plans and performance. Invite comments and feedback and, through employee involvement, show how individual and team efforts contribute towards the company's success.
9. Provide a high quality working environment taking all appropriate steps to ensure the health and safety of our employees, customers and the community.
10. Preserve the quality of life and environment in our everyday work and to benefit our local communities whenever an affordable opportunity arises.

(Reproduced with permission.)

Multiple objectives, stated in this form, will demand priorities and trade-offs at different times, but their value is that they draw attention to the potentially conflicting needs of all the major stakeholders.

HP Bulmer Holdings   http://www.bulmer.co.uk

The expression *aims* is sometimes used as an alternative to mission. The term *goals* is seen as synonymous with objectives, and in this book the terms are used interchangeably. Specifically, where other works are being referred to and those authors have used the term goal as opposed to objective, their terminology is retained. It is also important to distinguish between long-term and short-term objectives or goals. Thompson and Strickland (1980) provide a useful distinction. They argue that objectives overall define the specific kinds of performance and results that the organization seeks to produce through its activities. The *long-term objectives* relate to the desired performance and results on an ongoing basis; *short-term objectives* are concerned with the near-term performance targets that the organization desires to reach in progressing towards its long-term objectives. Making use of such techniques as management by objectives, these performance targets can be agreed with individual managers, who are then given responsibility for their attainment and held accountable.

Measurement can be straightforward for an objective such as 'the achievement of a minimum return of 20% of net capital employed in the business, but with a target of 25%, in the next 12 months'. If the objective is less specific, for example, 'continued customer satisfaction, a competitive return on capital employed and real growth in earnings per share next year', measurement is still possible but requires a comparison of competitor returns and the monitoring of customer satisfaction through, say, the number of complaints received. Richards (1978) uses the terms 'open' and 'closed' to distinguish between objectives that are clearly measurable and typically finance based (closed) and those that are less specific and essentially continuing.

Vision statements

While mission statements have become increasingly popular for organizations, vision *statements* are less prevalent. The lack of a published statement, of course, is not necessarily an indication of a lack of vision. Where they exist they reflect the company's vision of some future state, which ideally the organization will achieve. Terminology and themes such as a world-class manufacturer, a quality organization, a provider of legendary service and a stimulating, rewarding place to work might well appear. The essential elements focus on those values to which the organization is committed and appropriate standards of behaviour for all employees. Possible improvement paths, employee development programmes and measures or indicators of progress should be established for each element of the vision.

Mission statements

The corporate mission is the overriding *raison d'être* for the business. Ackoff (1986), however, claimed that many corporate mission statements prove worth-

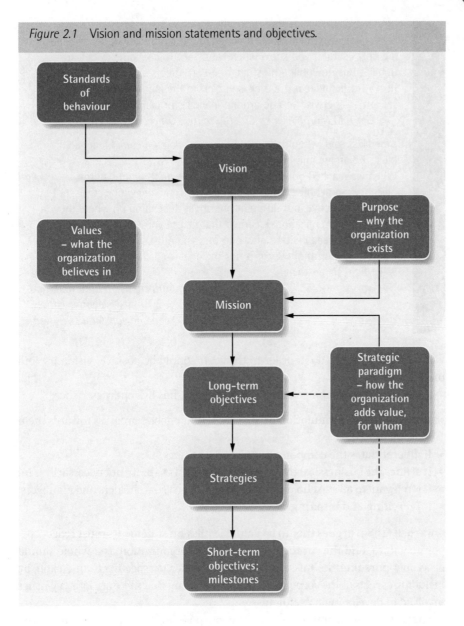

Figure 2.1   Vision and mission statements and objectives.

less, one reason being that they consist of loose expressions such as 'maximize growth potential' or 'provide products of the highest quality'. How, he queries, can a company determine whether it has attained its maximum growth potential or highest quality? His points are still valid today. Primarily, the mission statement should not address what an organization must do in order to survive, but

> Strategy development is like driving around a roundabout. The signposts are only useful if you know where you want to go. Some exits lead uphill, some downhill – most are one-way streets and some have very heavy traffic indeed. The trick is in picking the journey's end before you set out – otherwise you go around in circles or pick the wrong road.
>
> *Gerry M Murphy, when Chief Executive Officer, Greencore plc, Ireland*
>
> Arne Ness said, when he climbed Everest: I had a dream. I reached it. I lost the dream and I miss it.
> When we reached our dream we didn't have another long-term objective. So people started to produce their own new objectives, not a common objective, but different objectives depending on where they were in the organization. I learned that before you reach an objective you must be ready with a new one, and you must start to communicate it to the organization. But it is not the goal itself that is important . . . it is the fight to get there.
>
> *Jan Carlzon, when Chairman and*
> *Chief Executive Officer,*
> *Scandinavian Airlines System*

what it has chosen to do in order to thrive. It should be positive, visionary and motivating.

Ackoff suggests that a good mission statement has five characteristics.

- It will contain a formulation of objectives that enables progress towards them to be measured.
- It differentiates the company from its competitors.
- It defines the business(es) that the company wants to be in, not necessarily is in.
- It is relevant to all stakeholders in the firm, not just shareholders and managers.
- It is exciting and inspiring.

Campbell (1989) argues that to be valuable mission statements must reflect corporate values, and the strategic leader and the organization as a whole should be visibly pursuing the mission. He takes a wider perspective than Ackoff by including aspects of the corporate vision and arguing that there are four key issues involved in developing a useful mission.

First, it is important to clarify the purpose of the organization – why it exists.

Hanson plc, for example, which is referred to at various stages in this book, was led by Lord James Hanson for some 25 years and he stated:

> *It is the central tenet of my faith that the shareholder is king. My aim is to advance the shareholder's interest by increasing earnings per share.*

By contrast, and at the same time, Lex Service published an alternative view:

We will exercise responsibility in our dealings with all our stakeholders and, in the case of conflict, balance the interest of the employees and shareholders on an equal basis over time.

The implications of these contrasting perspectives are discussed in the next section of this chapter.

Secondly, the mission statement should describe the business and its activities, and the position that it wants to achieve in its field. Thirdly, the organization's values should be stated. How does the company intend to treat its employees, customers and suppliers, for example? Finally, it is important to ensure that the organization behaves in the way that it promises it will. This is important because it can inspire trust in employees and others who significantly influence the organization.

It is generally accepted that in successful companies middle and junior managers know where the strategic leaders are taking the company and why. In less successful organizations there is often confusion about this.

Mission statements, like vision statements, can all-too-easily just 'state the obvious' and as a result have little real value. The secret lies in clarifying what makes a company different and a more effective competitor, rather than simply restating those requirements that are essential for meeting key success factors. A mission (or vision) statement which could easily be used by another business, whether in the same industry or not – as many can be – is, simply, of no great value. Companies that succeed long term are those which create competitive advantages and sustain their strong positions with flexibility and improvement. The vision and mission should support this.

The principal purpose of these statements is communication, both externally and internally and, arguably, a major benefit for organizations is the thinking they are forced to do in order to establish sound statements. Nevertheless, many are still worded poorly. In addition, it is essential that the mission (or vision) is more than a plaque in a foyer; employees have to make the words mean something through their actions. For this to happen, employees must feel that the organization actually means what it is saying in the mission and vision statements. There must be an element of trust, for without it the desired outcomes will not be achieved.

The mission clearly corresponds closely to the basic philosophy or vision underlying the business, and if there is a sound philosophy, strategies that generate success will be derived from it. Sock Shop was founded in 1983, with a simple vision. One newspaper has summarized it as, 'shopping in big stores for basic items like stockings is a fag, but nipping into an attractive kiosk at an Underground station, British Rail concourse or busy high street is quick, convenient and can be fun'. From this have emerged six key marketing features or strategies, which have become the foundations of the company's success and rapid growth:

- shops located within areas of heavy pedestrian traffic
- easily accessible products
- friendly and efficient service
- a wide range of quality products designed to meet the needs of customers
- attractive presentations
- competitive selling prices.

In 1989, after a number of years of growth and success, Sock Shop began to lose money. The hot summer weather and the London Underground strikes were blamed for falling sales. Increasing interest rates caused additional financial problems. Moreover, Sock Shop expanded into the USA and this had proved costly. However, in February 1990 Sock Shop founder, Sophie Mirman, commented: 'We provide everyday necessities in a fashionable manner . . . our concept remains sound. Our merchandise continues to be not merely "lifestyle".' Sophie Mirman has since lost control of Sock Shop but her vision prevails.

Objectives: Issues and Perspectives

A full consideration of objectives incorporates three aspects:

- an appreciation of the objectives that the organization is actually pursuing and achieving – where it is going and why
- the objectives that it might pursue, and the freedom and opportunity it has to make changes
- specific objectives for the future.

This chapter looks at the issues that affect and determine the first two of these. Decisions about specific future objectives are considered later in the book (Chapter 9). We begin, though, by looking briefly at a number of theories of business organizations and considering the role and importance of stakeholders.

Market models

Basic microeconomic theory states that firms should seek to maximize profits and that this is achieved where marginal revenue is equal to marginal cost. A number of assumptions underpin this theory, including the assumptions that firms clearly understand the nature of the demand for their products, and why people buy, and that they are willing and able to control production and sales as the model demands. In reality, decision makers do not have perfect knowledge and production and sales are affected by suppliers and distributors.

However, this basic theory has resulted in the development of four market models (Table 2.1), and the characteristics of these in respect of barriers to entry into the industry and the marketing opportunities (differentiation potential; price and non-price competition) determine whether or not there is a real opportunity to achieve significant profits.

In markets which approach pure competition (pure competition as such is theoretical), firms will only make 'normal' profits, the amount required for them to stay in the industry. Products are 'commodities', not differentiated, and so premium prices for certain brands are not possible. There are no major barriers to entry into the industry and so new suppliers are attracted if there are profits to be made. Competition results, and if supply exceeds demand the ruling market price is forced down and only the efficient firms survive.

Table 2.1   Structural characteristics of four market models

Market model	Number of firms	Type of product	Control over price by supplier	Entry conditions	Non-price competition*	Examples†
Pure competition	Large	Standardized Identical or almost identical	None	Free	None	Agricultural products; some chemicals; printing; laundry services
Monopolistic competition	Large	Differentiated	Some	Relatively easy	Yes	Clothing; furniture; soft drinks; plumbers; restaurants
Oligopoly†	Few or a few dominant	Standardized or differentiated	Limited by mutual interdependence. Considerable if collusion takes place	Difficult	Yes	Standardized: cement; sugar; fertilizers. Differentiated: margarine; soaps; detergents
Pure monopoly	One	Unique	Considerable	Blocked	Yes	British Gas (domestic consumers); water companies in their regions; local bus companies in certain towns

*Non-price competition occurs in many ways, e.g. by attempts to increase the extent of product differentiation and buyer preference through advertising, brand names, trade marks, promotions, distribution outlets; by new product launch and innovation, etc.

†Useful further reading: Doyle, P and Gidengil, ZB (1977) An empirical study of market structures. *Journal of Management Studies*, 14(3), October, 316–28. Some of the examples are taken from this.

‡There are many oligopoly models of collusive and non-collusive type. They make varying behavioural and structural assumptions.

Journal of Management Studies   http://www.blackwellpublishers.co.uk/journals/JOMS

In monopolistic competition there are again several suppliers, some large, many small, but products are differentiated. However, as there are once more no major barriers to entry the above situation concerning profits applies. Newcomers increase supply and although those firms with distinctive products can charge some premium they will still have to move in line with market prices generally, and this will have a dampening effect on profits.

Only in oligopoly and monopoly markets, where a small number of large firms is dominant, is there real opportunity for 'supernormal' profits, in excess of what is required to stay in business. However, in oligopoly the small number of large firms tend to be wary of each other and prices are held back to some extent for fear of losing market share. Suppliers are interdependent and fear that a price decrease will be met by competitors (thus reducing profits) and price increases will not (hence market share will be threatened). There are two types of oligopoly, depending on whether opportunities exist for significant differentiation. In all of these models competition is a major determinant of profit potential and therefore objectives must be set with competitors in mind. In a monopoly (again somewhat theoretical in a pure sense) excess profits could be made if government did not act as a restraint. In the UK, although such public-sector organizations as British Gas and British Telecom have been privatized their actions in terms of supply and pricing are monitored and regulated.

Stakeholder theory

The influence of external stakeholders will be examined again in Chapter 5, which looks at the business environment, but it is important to introduce the topic at this stage. A further assumption of profit-maximizing theory is that shareholders in the business should be given first priority and be the major consideration in decision making, and this arose because early economic theorists saw owners and managers as being synonymous. This assumption no longer holds, however. A study of market models demonstrates the important role played by competitors and by government as a restraining force, and it was also suggested that organizations must pay some regard to their suppliers and distributors. In addition, managers and employees must be considered. The decisions taken by managers which create incremental change will be influenced by the objectives and values that they believe are important. Managers are paid employees, and whilst concerned about profits, they will also regard growth and security as important.

These are all *stakeholders*. Freeman (1984) defines stakeholders as any group or individual who can affect, or is affected by, the performance of the organization. Newbould and Luffman (1979) argue that current and future strategies are affected by

- external pressures from the marketplace, including competitors, buyers and suppliers; shareholders; pressure groups; and government
- internal pressures from existing commitments, managers, employees and their trade unions
- the personal ethical and moral perspectives of senior managers.

Figure 2.2 re-presents these ideas and also highlights the need for a solid base in the form of corporate values and priorities.

Stakeholder theory, then, postulates that the objectives of an organization will take account of the various needs of these different interested parties who will represent some type of informal coalition. Their relative power will be a key variable, and the organization will on occasions 'trade off' one against the other, establishing a hierarchy of relative importance. Stakeholders see different things as being important and receive benefits or rewards in a variety of ways, as featured in Table 2.2.

Stakeholder interests are not always consistent. For example, investment in new technology might improve product quality and as a result lead to increased profits. While customers who are shareholders might perceptively benefit, if the investment implies lost jobs then employees, possibly managers, and their trade unions

Table 2.2   Examples of stakeholder interests

Shareholders	Annual dividends; increasing the value of their investment in the company as the share price increases. Both are affected by growth and profits Institutional shareholders may balance high-risk investments and their anticipated high returns with more stable investments in their portfolio
Managers	Salaries and bonuses; perks; status from working for a well-known and successful organization; responsibility; challenge; security
Employees	Wages; holidays; conditions and job satisfaction; security – influenced by trade union involvement
Consumers	Desirable and quality products; competitive prices – very much in relation to competition; new products at appropriate times
Distributors	On-time and reliable deliveries
Suppliers	Consistent orders; payment on time
Financiers	Interest payments and loan repayments; like payment for supplies, affected by cash flow
Government	Payment of taxes and provision of employment; contribution to the nation's exports
Society in general	Socially responsible actions – sometimes reflected in pressure groups

NB. This is not intended to constitute a complete list.

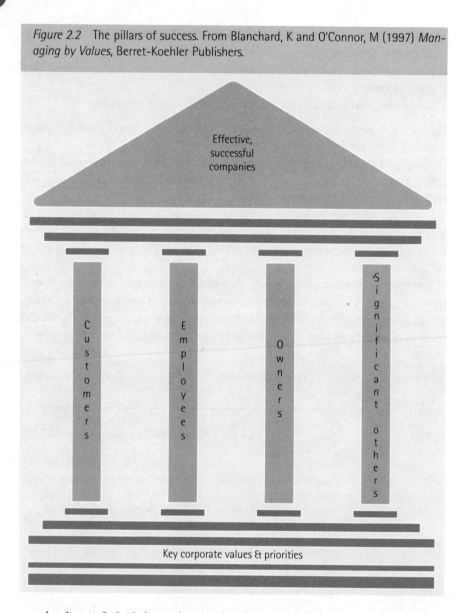

Figure 2.2   The pillars of success. From Blanchard, K and O'Connor, M (1997) *Managing by Values*, Berret-Koehler Publishers.

may be dissatisfied. If the scale of redundancy is large and results in militant resistance, the government may become involved.

The various stakeholders are not affected in the same way by every strategic decision and, consequently, their relative influence will vary from decision to decision. In 1995 Shell, one of Europe's most successful and respected companies, was forced to change an important strategic decision following a high-profile campaign by a leading pressure group. Shell wanted to sink its redundant Brent Spar oil platform in deep seas some 150 miles west of Scotland. It had reached an agreement with the UK government that, scientifically, this was the most appropriate means of disposal for the platform. Greenpeace objected and protesters boarded the platform, claiming that it still contained 5000 tonnes of oil which would eventually be released to pollute the sea. The ensuing and professionally orchestrated publicity fuelled public opinion, and there were protests in a number of European countries, including attacks on petrol stations in Germany. Shell backed down and agreed to investigate other possibilities for disposal. The UK government expressed both anger and disappointment with this decision. Independent inspectors later proved that Greenpeace's claims were gross exaggerations – the residual oil was much, much less than 5000 tonnes. The press concluded: 'Shell went wrong in spending too much time convincing government of the case for sea-bed dumping, but not attaching enough importance to consulting other stakeholder groups'.

Shell had been made to appear socially irresponsible, yet the ethics of the Greenpeace campaign are questionable; these issues are explored further at the end of this chapter.

Waterman (1994) contends that successful companies do not automatically make shareholders their first priority. Instead, they pay primary attention to employees and customers and, as a result, they perform more effectively than their rivals. The outcome is superior profits and wealth creation for the shareholders. Simon (1964) argues that one of the main reasons for an organization's collapse is a failure to incorporate the important motivational concerns of key stakeholders. Small businesses, for example, are generally weak in relation to their suppliers, especially if these are larger well-established concerns; and if they neglect managing their cash flow and fail to pay their accounts on time they will find their deliveries stopped. For any organization, if new products or services fail to provide consumers with what they are looking for, however well produced or low priced they might be, they will not sell.

A recent survey by Deloitte Consulting (1999) confirmed that 'customer-centric' manufacturing companies worldwide are 60% more profitable than those that are less committed to customers. In addition, they enjoy lower operating costs. Customer-centricity is seen as a 'systematic process which sets objectives for customer loyalty and retention and then tracks performance towards those goals'. It should facilitate the development of higher added value, premium-price products.

Figure 2.3 shows that shareholders, employees and customers are the three key stakeholders that the organization must satisfy, but invariably in a competitive environment: if they fail with any group long term they will place the organization in jeopardy through a spiral of decline. Figure 2.4 is an alternative presentation of the same points. On the left is a virtuous circle of growth and prosperity. Satisfied, perhaps even delighted, customers enable high financial returns, which can be used in part to reward employees. A perception of fairness here can be instrumental for motivating employees to keep customers satisfied and thus sustain the circle. The issues of measuring performance in relation to all of the stakeholders will be taken up in Chapter 3. The right-hand side clarifies that the needs of customers can sometimes conflict with the

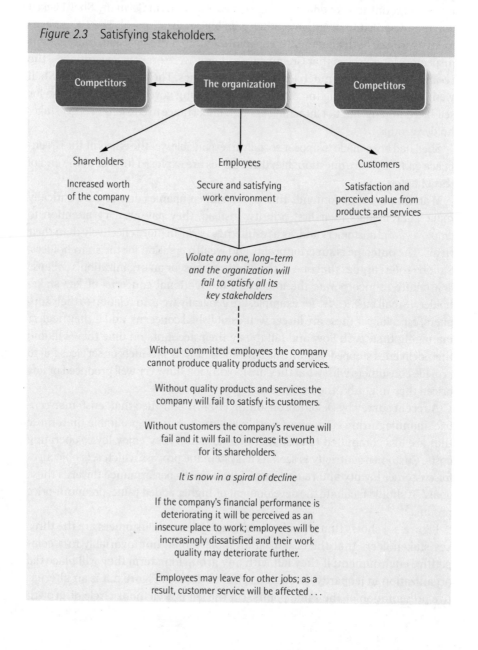

Figure 2.3   Satisfying stakeholders.

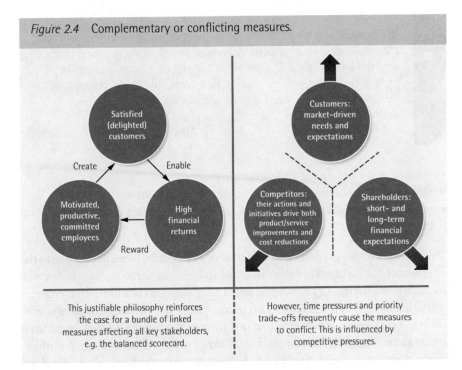

Figure 2.4   Complementary or conflicting measures.

demands of some shareholders, especially those who are willing to trade off long-term achievement for short-term financial returns. Competitors are always trying to persuade customers to switch allegiance and thus impact on an organization's success.

While these arguments are, in themselves, convincing, many organizations still fail to satisfy their stakeholders long term. The following theories provide some insight into this reality.

Cyert and March's behavioural theory

Stakeholder theory is closely related to the ideas in Cyert and March's *A Behavioural Theory of the Firm* (1963). Cyert and March argue that the goals of an organization are a *compromise* between members of a coalition comprising the parties affecting an organization. The word compromise is used as the actual choice is linked to relative power and there are inevitably conflicts of interest. Cyert and March argue that there are essentially five directional pulls to consider:

- production related, and encapsulating stable employment, ease of control and scheduling
- inventory related – customers and sales staff push for high stocks and wide choice, management accountants complain about the cost of too much stock

> The investor and the employee are in the same position, but sometimes the employee is more important, because he will be there a long time, whereas an investor will often get in and out on a whim in order to make a profit. The worker's mission is to contribute to the company's welfare, and his own, every day. All of his working life he is really needed.
>
> *Akio Morita, Joint Founder, Sony*

- sales related – obtaining and satisfying orders
- market share, which yields power relative to competitors
- profit, which concerns shareholders, senior management and the providers of loan capital.

This theory stresses the perceived importance of the short term, as opposed to the long term, because issues are more tangible and because decisions have to be taken as situations change. Organizations adapt over time and it is likely that changes will be limited unless it is necessary to change things more radically. In other words, once a compromise situation is reached there is a tendency to seek to retain it rather than change it, and the goals will change as the values and relative importance of coalition members change. As a result, 'organizational slack' develops. This is 'payments to members of the coalition in excess of what is required to keep them in the coalition'. It is difficult, for example, to determine the minimum acceptable reward for employees; assets are generally underexploited since it is difficult to know the maximum productivity of a person or machine; and uncertainties mean that less-than-optimal price, product and promotional policies will be pursued. The existence of slack does allow for extra effort in times of emergency.

This theory can be usefully considered alongside Herbert Simon's (1964) theory of satisficing. Here he contends that managers seek courses of action which are acceptable in the light of known objectives. These actions may not be optimal but they are chosen because of internal and external constraints such as time pressure, a lack of information and the vested interests of certain powerful stakeholders.

Objectives and constraints

Simon (1964) also makes an important distinction between objectives and constraints. Some of the ends that strategies are designed to achieve are not freely set objectives but constraints imposed on the organization by powerful stakeholders or agencies. Simply, organizational freedom – to set objectives – is constrained. For example, an animal food company might wish to offer low-priced feeds for livestock but be constrained by dietary requirements which, by determining ingredients, influence costs and hence prices.

In recent years, many of the world's leading drug companies have changed their strategies as a result of external constraints. Governments have been increasingly reluctant to fund expensive drugs and treatments. Some companies have closed plants, while others have relocated for lower costs. There has been an increased research focus on treatments that are most likely to receive funding, arguably at the expense of potential breakthroughs in other areas. Priorities and strategies in the UK National Health Service (NHS) are affected by the government's waiting-list targets. Although Railtrack (which manages and maintains the UK railway infrastructure) is a private-sector business, it has a regulator who imposes specific requirements and targets for safety which inevitably affect costs and profits.

Several other authors have offered theories in an attempt to explain the behaviour of organizations and the objectives they seek.

Baumol's theory of sales maximization

Baumol (1959) argues that firms seek to maximize sales rather than profits, but within the constraint of a minimum acceptable profit level. It can be demonstrated that profit maximizing is achieved at a level of output below that which would maximize sales revenue and that, as sales and revenue increase beyond profit maximizing, profits are sacrificed. Firms will increase sales and revenue as long as they are making profits in excess of what they regard as an acceptable minimum. Businessmen, Baumol argues, attach great importance to sales as salaries are often linked to the scale of operations. 'Whenever executives are asked "How's business?", the typical reply is that sales have been increasing or decreasing'.

Williamson's model of managerial discretion

Williamson (1964) argues that managers can set their own objectives, that these will be different from those of shareholders and that managerial satisfaction is the key. Satisfaction increases if a manager has a large staff reporting to him or her, if there are 'lavish perks' and if profits exceed the level required for the essential development of the business and the necessary replacement of equipment. This extra profit can be used for pet projects or the pursuit of non-profit objectives. The manner in which managers reward themselves for success is discretionary.

Marris's theory of managerial capitalism

Marris (1964) again postulates growth as a key concern, as managers derive utility from growth in the form of enhanced salaries, power and status. The constraint is one of security. If, as a result of growth strategies pursued by the firm, profits are held down, say because of interest charges, the market value of the firm's shares may fall relative to the book value of the assets. In such a case the firm may become increasingly vulnerable to take-over, and managers wish to avoid this situation.

Penrose's theory of growth

Penrose (1959) has offered another growth theory, arguing that an organization will seek to achieve the full potential from all its resources. Firms grow as long as there are unused resources, diversifying when they can no longer grow with existing products, services and markets. Growth continues until it is halted. A major limit, for example, could be production facilities either in terms of total output or because of a bottleneck in one part of the operation. Changes can free the limit, and growth continues until the next limiting factor appears. Another limit is the capacity of managers to plan and implement growth strategies. If managers are stretched, extra people can be employed, but the remedy is not immediate. New people have to be trained and integrated, and this takes up some of the time of existing managers. Penrose refers to this issue as the 'receding managerial limit' because again the limiting factor decreases over a period of time. In a climate of reasonably constant growth and change managers learn how to cope with the dynamics of change; and properly managed, given that overambition is constrained and that market opportunities exist, firms can enjoy steady and continuous growth.

Galbraith's views on technocracy

Finally, Galbraith (1969) highlighted the particular role of large corporations, whose pursuit of size requires very large investments associated with long-term commitments. Because of these financial commitments the corporations seek to control their environment as far as they possibly can, influencing both government and consumer, and they in turn are controlled by what Galbraith calls 'technocrats' – teams of powerful experts and specialists. Their purposes are, first, to protect as well as control the organization, and hence they seek financial security and profit, and, secondly, to 'affirm' the organization through growth, expansion and market share. As is typical of oligopolists, price competition is not seen to be in their interests, and hence aggressive marketing and non-price competition are stressed. In addition, such firms will seek to influence or even control (by acquisition) suppliers and distributors, and they may well see the world, rather than just the UK, as their market.

   Galbraith (1963) also identified the growth of 'countervailing power' to limit this technocracy. The growth of trade unions in the past is an example of this, but, as seen in recent years, the technocrats have fought back successfully. The increasing size and power of grocery retailers such as Sainsbury's and Tesco, and their success with own-label brands, has put pressure on all product manufacturers, especially those whose products are not the brand leader. As a consequence the owners of the strongest brands have invested heavily to promote their brands and ensure that they are selected, even though there may be cheaper alternatives. Moreover, there have been mergers within retailing in an attempt to strengthen power bases. Tesco has expanded from the UK into Europe, while Wal-Mart has acquired ASDA. Simply, over time there are swings in relative power and, as a result, the potential for consumer exploitation is checked and available profits are shared more widely.

Profit as an objective

Box 2.2 discusses whether profit is the ultimate objective of profit-seeking business organizations or whether it is merely a means to other ends, which themselves constitute the real objectives. Not-for-profit organizations are considered separately later in this chapter (p. 102).

Ackoff (1986) argues that both profit and growth are means to other ends rather than objectives in themselves. He argues that profit is necessary for the

---

DISCUSSION – Box 2.2
Profit

A business school is likely to teach that an organization must be good to people because then they will work harder; and if they work harder the business will make a profit.

They will also teach that a firm should strive to produce better products and services, because with better products the firm will make greater profits.

What if they told the story the other way round?

What if they taught managers: you have got to make a profit, because if you do not make a profit you cannot build offices that are pleasant to be in. Without profit you cannot pay decent wages. Without profit you cannot satisfy a lot of the needs of your employees. You have got to make a profit because without a profit you will never be able to develop a better product.

The profit would still be made. People would still get decent wages. Most employers would still make an effort to improve their products as they do now.

'But you would have a whole new ball game.'

Adapted from Cohen, P (1974) *The Gospel According to the Harvard Business School*, Penguin. Originally published by Doubleday, New York, 1973.

Harvard Business School   http://www.hbs.edu

survival of a business enterprise but is neither the reason for which the business is formed nor the reason why it stays in existence. Instead, Ackoff contends, 'those who manage organizations do so primarily to provide themselves with the quality of work life and standard of living they desire . . . their behaviour can be better understood by assuming this than by assuming that their objective is to maximize profit or growth'.

However, it is also important to consider the 'quality of life' of investors (shareholders), customers, suppliers and distributors, as well as other employees of the firm who are not involved in decision making. Developing earlier points, it can be argued that employees are the major stakeholders, because if the firm goes out of business they incur the greatest losses.

In many respects it does not matter whether profit is seen as an objective or as a means of providing service and satisfaction to stakeholders, as long as both are considered and not seen as mutually exclusive. However, the 'feel' and culture of an organization will be affected. In simple terms an organization will succeed if it survives and meets the expectations of its stakeholders. If its objectives relate to the stakeholders, it is successful if it attains its objectives.

The influence of shareholders

Some commentators hold the view that too many companies are still encouraged to seek short-term profits in order to please their major institutional shareholders, and that it is only by considering the long term and the interests of all stakeholders that companies will become more effective competitors in world markets. In the UK, for example, Constable (1980) stated: 'Britain's steady relative industrial decline over the past 30 years is related to an insistence on setting purely financial objectives which have been operated in relatively short time scales'. Institutions such as pension funds effectively control the UK's largest companies through the sizeable blocks of shares that they own; in contested take-

The purpose of industry is to serve the public by creating services to meet their needs. It is not to make profits for shareholders, nor to create salaries and wages for the industrial community. These are necessary conditions for success, but not its purpose.

Dr George Carey, Archbishop of Canterbury

The responsibility of business is not to create profits but to create live, vibrant, honourable organizations with a real commitment to the community.

Anita Roddick, The Body Shop

overs, for example, individual pension fund managers will be instrumental in determining the outcome. These managers have a remit to earn the best returns that they can obtain for their members. Since the mid-1990s there has been a drive to increase the 'transparency' of these large shareholder blocks, and companies have been required to publish more information.

The issue of short-termism is complex, however, and Box 2.3 investigates the debate. Companies, obviously, cannot disregard powerful institutional shareholders.What is crucial is to ensure that there is dialogue and mutual understanding and agreement concerning the best interests of the company, its shareholders and other stakeholders.

DISCUSSION – Box 2.3
Long- and Short-termism: The Debate

Laing (1987) has argued that where owners and managers are the same people, the goals and means of achieving them are not in conflict; but institutional fund managers, themselves under pressure to perform in the short term, have often put pressure on public companies to pursue strategies that may be incompatible with sound long-term management. It is, however, generally acknowledged that companies must pursue strategies that increase the long-term value of the business for its shareholders, or eventually they are likely to be under threat of acquisition. It is also often argued that many companies believe that they are likely to be under threat from powerful institutional shareholders if short-term performance is poor, i.e. if sales and profits fail to grow. The result can be a reluctance to undertake costly and risky investments, say, in research and development (R&D), if the payback is uncertain.

Thus, it would follow that if a manufacturing business were seeking to boost short-term profits and earnings per share for reasons of expedience, it might well reduce quality and service and fail to

invest adequately for the future. The price for this would be inevitable decline. This tendency could be worsened if the company were under threat of take-over and thus anxious to improve its immediate performance. For businesses in countries such as Germany and Japan, where historically 'the Damoclean sword of hostile take-overs was virtually unknown' (Laing, 1987), this has been less likely than in the UK.

Institutional shareholders must clearly want to be able to exercise some control or influence over large companies where they have substantial equity interests. One dilemma is that while they want to rein in powerful and risk-orientated strategic leaders, they do not want to forsake the potential benefits of strong, entrepreneurial leadership. They can exert influence by:

- pushing for the roles of chairman and chief executive to be separated, and arguing for a high proportion of carefully selected non-executive (external part-time) directors
- attempting to replace senior managers whose performance is poor or lacklustre, but this can be

difficult (it is often argued that shareholders are too passive about this option)
- selling their shares to predatory bidders.

While this final option is a perpetual threat, and the biggest fear of many strategic leaders, not all companies are prevented from investing in R&D. Logically, those which are well managed are in command of where they are going to invest. In addition, institutions argue that they are objective about their investments and turn down more offers for their shares than they accept.

In essence, 'managers should not be discouraged by their owners, their shareholders, from taking risks, from undertaking research and from investing in innovation' (Laing, 1987).

A more recent analysis by the *Financial Times* (Martinson, 1998) suggests that large institutional shareholders do take a long-term view but rarely make helpful comments on strategy. When they exercise their voting power it is generally clear and visible, rather than covert. Many fund managers were seen as professional but, at the same time, 'ill-informed fund managers are making increasing demands on executive time'.

Undoubtedly more communication between directors and their shareholders concerning results, plans and philosophies would be desirable in many cases. Would this resolve the difficulties, or is something more drastic still required?

Lipton (1990) has controversially suggested that Boards should be subject to quinquennial reviews of their performance (partially conducted by independent outsiders) and their plans for the next five years. Hostile bids could be considered at the same time, but not between reviews. Boards may or may not be re-elected, depending on their relative performance. The idea is to generate more stability and to 'unite directors and shareholders behind the goal of maximizing long-term profits'.

The late Lord White of Hanson plc (1990) stated his disagreement, arguing that if institutional shareholders are willing to sell their shares it is usually the result of poor management generally, and not merely a reluctance to invest in R&D. 'Under-performing companies are frequently typified by high top salaries, share options confined to a handful of apparatchiks and generous golden parachutes'. Such companies are often legitimate take-over targets, and inevitably the bids are likely to be perceived as hostile.

In summary, long-term success requires that companies and their strategic leaders are properly accountable for their performance and, for many businesses, this really has to be to their shareholders. At the same time, shareholders must be objective and take a long-term perspective, and they must be active, not passive, about replacing poor managers and about intervening when they feel that the corporate strategy is wrong.

The dilemmas relate to the implementation of these ideas and to the issue of whether institutions have advisers with enough detailed, industry-specific, knowledge to make an objective judgement.

DISCUSSION – Box 2.3
(Continued)

Sources
Laing, H (1987) quoted in *First*, **1** (2).
Lipton, M (1990) An end to hostile takeovers and short-termism, *Financial Times*, 27 June.
   Martinson, J (1998) Companies say big shareholders take long view, *Financial Times*, 27 April.

White, G (1990) Why management must be accountable, *Financial Times*, 12 July.

Financial Times
http://www.news.ft.com
Hanson plc
http://www.hansonplc.com

In his debate on the short- and long-term perspective, Constable (Table 2.3) contrasts two sets of objectives, ranked in order of priority. He contends that company B is likely to grow at the expense of company A, and that these objective sets, A and B, are essentially those adopted by large UK and Japanese companies, respectively, for much of the period since World War II. To suggest that Japanese success rests solely on a particular set of objectives is oversimplifying reality, but it has certainly contributed.

In Japan and Germany, however, shareholders do not exert pressure in the same way as they do in the UK. Cross shareholding between companies in Japan means that only 25% of shares in Japanese businesses are for trading and speculation, and this generates greater stability. In Germany the companies hold a higher proportion of their own shares, and banks act as proxy voters for private investors. Banks thereby control some 60% of the tradable shares, again generating stability.

Table 2.3 Contrasting company objectives

Company A	Company B
1. Return on net assets, 1–3 year time horizon	1. Maintenance and growth of market share
2. Cash flow	2. Maintenance and growth of employment
3. Maintenance and growth of market share	3. Cash flow
4. Maintenance and growth of employment	4. Return on net assets

Understanding Corporate Strategy

German companies also adopt a two-tier board structure. A supervisory board has overall control and reports to shareholders and employee unions; reporting to this board is a management board, elected for up to 5 years.

Table 2.4 pulls together a number of the points discussed here by showing how organizational strategic leaders and institutional investors do not share completely the same perspective on stakeholder priorities, although there are clear similarities with the most important stakeholders. Interestingly, suppliers, key partners in the supply chain, receive a higher priority from strategic leaders, while the institutions rate politicians more highly than do organizational leaders. It is both significant and realistic that small, individual shareholders are not particularly powerful, because they are generally too disparate to become organized. Individually, they may be able to embarrass an organization with difficult questions at its Annual General Meeting, but this is far from an expression of ongoing power.

The importance of the strategic leader

To conclude this section it is useful to emphasize the key role of the strategic leader, and his or her values, in establishing the main objectives and the direction in which they take the organization. Personal ambitions to build a large conglom-

Table 2.4 Perceptions of stakeholder importance

Stakeholder	Prioritization by industry strategic leaders	Prioritization by analysts with institutional investors
Existing customers	1	1
Existing employees	2	3
Potential customers	3	2
Institutional investors	4	4
Suppliers	5	7
Potential employees	6	6
City analysts	7	5
Private (individual) shareholders	8	10
Business media	9	9
General media	10	11
Local communities	11	12
Members of Parliament/Local Authorities	12	8

Source: Based on research by MORI (2000).

MORI   http://www.mori.com

erate or a multinational company may fuel growth; a determination to be socially responsible may restrain certain activities that other organizations would undertake; a commitment to high quality will influence the design, cost and marketing approach for products. A strong orientation towards employee welfare, as evidenced in such companies of Richer Sounds and ASDA, will again influence objectives quite markedly.

The objectives and values of the strategic leader are a particularly important consideration in the case of small firms. While it is possible for small firms to enjoy competitive advantage, say by providing products or services with values added to appeal to local customers in a limited geographical area, many are not distinctive in any marked way. Where this is the case, and where competition is strong, small firms will be price takers, and their profits and growth will be influenced substantially by external forces. Some small-firm owners will be entrepreneurial, willing to take risks and determined to build a bigger business, whereas others will be content to stay small. Some small businesses are started by people who essentially want to work for themselves rather than for a larger corporation, and their objectives could well be concerned with survival and the establishment of a sound business which can be passed on to the next generation of their family.

Each of the ideas and theories discussed in this section provides food for thought, but individually none of them explains fully what happens, or what should happen, in organizations. In the author's experience certain organizations are highly growth orientated, willing to diversify and take risks, while others, constrained by the difficulties of coping with rapid growth and implementing diversification strategies, are less ambitious in this respect. Each can be appropriate in certain circumstances and lead to high performance, but in different circumstances they may be the wrong strategy.

Stakeholder theory is extremely relevant conceptually, but organizations are affected by the stakeholders in a variety of ways. Priorities must be decided for companies on an individual basis. Moreover, the strategic leader, and in turn the organization, will seek to satisfy particular stakeholders rather than others because of their personal backgrounds and values. There is no right or wrong list of priorities. However, while priorities can and will be established, all stakeholders must be satisfied to some minimum level. In the final analysis the essential requirement is congruence among environment, values and resources.

So far this chapter has concentrated on profit-seeking organizations and considered just how important the profit motive might be. Not-for-profit organizations may be growth conscious, quality conscious or committed to employee welfare in the same way as profit seekers, but there are certain differences which require that they are considered separately.

Objectives of Public-sector and Not-for-profit Organizations

In order to understand the objectives of not-for-profit organizations and appreciate where they are aiming to go, several points need to be considered.

- Stakeholders are important, particularly those who are providers of financial support.
- There will be a number of potentially conflicting objectives, and quite typically the financial ones will not be seen as the most essential in terms of the mission.
- While there will be a mix of quantitative (financial) and qualitative objectives, the former will be easier to measure, although the latter relate more closely to the mission of the organization.
- For this reason the efficient use of resources becomes an important objective.

These points will now be examined in greater depth, making reference to a number of other examples, as public-sector and not-for-profit organizations are many and varied.

Historically, and at one extreme, certainly in terms of size, *nationalized industries* with essentially monopoly markets have been seen as both public sector and non-profit. Throughout their existence different governments have strived to establish acceptable and effective measures of performance for them. At various times both breakeven and return on capital employed have been stressed. There has always been an in-built objectives conflict between social needs (many of them provided essential services) and a requirement that the very substantial resources involved were managed commercially in order to avoid waste. The Conservative government of the 1980s followed a policy of privatizing certain nationalized industries partly on the grounds that in some cases more competition will be stimulating and create greater efficiency.

In Britain, the NHS can be viewed similarly. Fundamentally, its purpose relates to the health and well-being of the nation, and attention can be focused on both prevention and cure. The role of the police in terms of crime prevention and the solution of crimes that have taken place can be seen as synonymous. The health service can spend any money it is offered, as science continually improves what can be done for people. In a sense it is a chicken-and-egg situation. Resources improve treatments and open up new opportunities for prevention; and these in turn stimulate demand, particularly where they concern illnesses or diseases which historically have not been easily treated. However, these developments are often very expensive, and decisions have then to be made about where funds should be allocated. Quite simply, the decisions relate to priorities.

Customers of the health service are concerned with such things as the waiting time for admission to hospital and for operations, the quality of care as affected by staff attitudes and numbers, and arguably privacy in small wards, cleanliness and food. Doctors generally are concerned with the amount of resources and their ability to cope with demand; some consultants are anxious to work at the leading edge of their specialism; while administrators must ensure that resources are used efficiently.

The government funds the NHS, and as the major source of funds it is a key influence. It is very concerned with the political fallout from perceived weaknesses in the service, and inevitably its priorities are affected by this. It has been reported that the Labour government's emphasis on waiting lists, a key pledge in its 1997 election manifesto, has distorted clinical priorities, such that many minor ailments have been given priority for treatment over more major ones. Pfeffer (1981) has argued that the relative power of influencers is related to the funds that they provide. The less funding that is provided by customers, the weaker is their influence over decisions. Hence, a not-for-profit organization such as the NHS may be less customer orientated than a private competitive firm. Some would argue that the private medical sector is more marketing conscious. Without question, and in simple terms, the NHS is about patient care within imposed budgetary constraints. The issue really concerns whether patients perceive that it feels like a service driven by a culture of care or by a culture of resource management efficiency.

All organizations will seek to measure performance in some way. It was stated earlier in the chapter that performance against quantitative objectives can be measured directly, whereas performance against qualitative objectives is typically indirect and more difficult. If attention is focused on the aspects that are most easily measured there is a danger that these come to be perceived as the most important objectives. Hospital administrators can easily measure the number of admissions, the utilization of beds and theatres, the cost of laundry and food and so on. Fundamentally more important is who is being treated relative to the real needs of the community. Are the most urgent and needy cases receiving the priorities they deserve? How is this measured? Performance measures therefore tend to concentrate on the *efficient use of resources* rather than the effectiveness of the organization. Although profit may not be an important consideration, costs are. In addition, these measures may well be a source of conflict between medical and administrative staff and this is a reflection of the fact that there is likely to be disagreement and confusion about what the key objectives are.

Given this, the objectives that are perceived as important and are pursued at any time are very dependent on the relative power of the influencers and their ability to exercise power. Linked to this point is the relationship between hospitals and area and regional health authorities. Similarly, where not-for-profit organizations have advisory bodies, or boards of trustees, the relationship and relative power are important.

Tourist attractions such as London Zoo and leading museums (including the British Museum, the Natural History Museum and the Victoria and Albert, which is the National Museum of Art and Design) have a potential conflict of objectives concerning their inevitable educational and scientific orientations and the requirement that they address commercial issues. Museums can earn money from shops and cafeterias and they receive some private funding, but to a great extent they are reliant on government grants. In the 1980s these grants did not keep pace with their monetary demands and hence it has been necessary for them to seek additional revenue as well as manage resources and costs more efficiently. Admission charges to museums have become a controversial issue in the UK. In November 1985 the Victoria and Albert Museum introduced voluntary admission charges, and in April 1987 the Natural History Museum started charging for entry. Some potential visitors are lost as they refuse to pay, and this has implications for the educational objective. It has been reported that by 1987 admissions to the Victoria and Albert had fallen to one million a year from a peak of 1.75 million in 1983, but they began to increase again after 1988. However, the museum was criticized by some arts lovers for a poster campaign describing it as 'an ace caff with quite a nice museum attached', although museum staff claimed that this was a major reason for the increase in attendances. Some museums, including the British Museum, adamantly opposed charging. The new Tate Modern, opened in 2000, does not charge for admission.

At *The National Theatre* the issue addresses art and finance. Subsidized theatres, like The National, perceive their role to be different from that of commercial theatres and a number of them, including the Royal Shakespeare Company, English National Opera and the Royal Opera House, Covent Garden, competes for a percentage of Arts Council funding. When the Arts Council, as a major stakeholder and provider of funds, attempts to influence the strategies of the theatres they are often accused of meddling. Again there is a potential chicken-and-egg situation. If the theatres, under pressure from reduced subsidies (in real terms), raise more revenue and reduce their costs, they may find that this results in permanently reduced subsidies. Hence, as an alternative, they may choose to restrain their commercial orientation.

Cathedrals face a similar dilemma. The costs of repairs and maintenance are forcing some to charge visitors fixed amounts rather than rely on voluntary donations. Their mission is concerned with religion and charity but they are not immune from commercial realities.

Charities frequently have sets of interdependent commercial and non-commercial objectives. Oxfam's mission concerns the provision of relief and the provision of aid where it is most needed throughout the world. Additional objectives relate to teaching people how to look after themselves better through, say, irrigation and better farming techniques and to obtaining publicity to draw public attention to the plight of the needy. Their ability to pursue these objectives is constrained by resource availability. Consequently, Oxfam has fund-raising objectives and strategies (including retailing through Oxfam shops) to achieve them. It is difficult to say which receives most priority as they are so interdependent.

While the coverage of not-for-profit organizations in this section has been partial, as many other organizations, such as schools and universities, are fundamentally non-profitable, the points are representative of the sector.

The issue of the displacement of objectives has been discussed in some not-for-profit organizations. Attention is centred on quantitative measures as they are relatively easily carried out. The efficient use of resources replaces profit as the commercial objective, and while this may not be an essential aspect of the mission, it will be seen as important by certain stakeholders. In reality attention has switched from evaluating outputs and outcomes (the real objectives) to measuring inputs (resources) because it is easier to do. Where the stakeholders are major sponsors, and particularly in the case of government departments, there will be an insistence upon cost-effectiveness. Many of the organizations mentioned in this section are managed by people whose training and natural orientation is towards arts or science, and this can result in feelings of conflict with regard to objectives. Quite typically the organization will pursue certain objectives for a period of time, satisfying the most influential stakeholders in the coalition, and then change as the preferences of stakeholders, or their relative power and influence, change.

While profit-seeking and not-for-profit organizations have essentially different missions, the issue of profit making is complex. Some not-for-profit organizations rely on subsidies and these enable prices to be kept below what they would otherwise be. In nationalized industries the element of customer service has been seen to be important, with prices controlled or at least influenced by government. An independent regulator has been appointed when nationalized businesses have been privatized. However, unless the providers of grants and subsidies are willing to bear commercial trading losses and at the same time finance any necessary investment, there is a necessity for the organizations to generate revenue at least equal to the costs incurred. Where investment finance also needs to be generated a surplus of income over expenditure is important. This basically is profit. While profit may not therefore be an essential part of the mission it is still required.

The Impact of Personal Objectives

It has already been established that organizations are generally too large and complex to have only one objective. As a result, and influenced by stakeholders, there are typically several objectives with varying degrees of relative importance. It is now appropriate to consider why organizations cannot be treated separately from the people who work in them.

> The objectives pursued by organizations frequently differ from those proclaimed. Some years ago I assumed that the principal objective of universities was the education of students. Armed with this assumption I could make no sense of their behaviour. I learned that education, like profit, is a requirement not an objective and that the principal objective is to provide their faculties with the quality of work life and the standard of living they desire. That's why professors do so little teaching, give the same courses over and over again, arrange classes at their convenience, not that of their students, teach subjects they want to teach rather than students want to learn and skip classes to give lectures for a fee.
>
> *Russell Ackoff (1986)*

Objectives can be set (and changed) in any one of three ways.

- The strategic leader decides.
- Managers throughout the organization are either consulted or influence the objectives by their decisions and actions.
- All or some of the external stakeholders influence or constrain the organization in some way.

The second of these is addressed in this section. With emergent strategy the decisions made by managers determine the actual strategies pursued, and in turn revised, implicit, objectives replace those that were previously declared as intended objectives. The incidence or likelihood of this is affected by the culture of the organization, the relative power bases of managers, communication systems, and whether or not there are rigid policies and procedures or more informal management processes that allow managers considerable freedom. Box 2.4 defines policies and discusses their role in strategy implementation. The following brief example illustrates the impact of policies. Consider a multiple store that sells compact discs as one of its products and has nearby a small independent competitor that appeals to different customers. If the small store closed down there could be new opportunities for the manager of the multiple store if he changed his competitive strategy for CDs by changing his displays, improved his stock levels and supported these moves with window displays promoting the changes. Head-office merchandising policies concerning stocks and displays may or may not allow him this freedom.

In the case of intended strategy, the strategic leader determines and states the objectives, strategies and proposed changes for the organization. In arriving at decisions he or she may be influenced in a minor or major way by stakeholders outside the organization and the managers consulted. In order to ensure that the strategies are implemented (and the objectives achieved) the strategic leader will design and build an organization structure – which may restrict managers or

KEY CONCEPT – Box 2.4
Policies

You must provide a framework in which people can act. For example, we have said that our first priority is safety, second is punctuality, and third is other services. So if you risk flight safety by leaving on time, you have acted outside the framework of your authority. The same is true if you don't leave on time because you are missing two catering boxes of meat. That's what I mean by a framework. You give people a framework, and within the framework you let people act.

Jan Carlzon, when President and Chief Executive Officer, SAS
(Scandinavian Airlines System)

- *Policies* are guidelines relating to decisions and approaches which support organizational efforts to achieve *stated* and intended objectives.
- They are basically *guides to thoughts* (about how things might or should be done) *and actions*.
- They are therefore *guides to decision making*. For example, a policy which states that for supplies of a particular item three quotations should be sought and the cheapest selected, or a policy not to advertise in certain newspapers, or a policy not to trade with particular countries – all influence decisions. Policies are particularly useful for routine repetitive decisions.
- Policies can be at corporate, divisional [or strategic business unit (SBU)] or functional level, and they are normally stated in terms of management (of people), marketing, production, finance and research and development.
- If stated objectives are to be achieved, and the strategies designed to accomplish this implemented, the appropriate policies must be there in support. In other words, the behaviour of managers and the decisions that they make should be supportive of what the organization is seeking to achieve. Policies guide and constrain their actions.
- Policies can be mandatory (rules which allow little freedom for original thought or action) or advisory. The more rigid they are the less freedom managers have to change things with delegated authority, and this can be good or bad depending on change pressures from the environment.
- *It is vital to balance consistency and co-ordination* (between the various divisions, SBUs and departments in the organization) *with flexibility*.
- Policies need not be written down. They can be passed on verbally as part of the culture.
- Policies *must* be widely understood if they are to be useful.

allow them considerable freedom – and will determine policies which may be mandatory or advisory. This will tie in to the culture of the organization and will be influenced by the style and values of the strategic leader, both of which were introduced earlier.

However, the types of policy and the authority and freedom delegated to managers guide, influence and constrain decision making. The motives, values and relative power of individual managers, the relative importance of particular functions, divisions or strategic business units in the organization, and the system of communications are also influential. The stated or *official objectives* may or may not be achieved; there may be appropriate incremental decisions which reflect changes in the environment; or managers may be pursuing personal objectives, which Perrow (1961) has termed *operative goals*. This is happening when the behaviour taking place cannot be accounted for by official company objectives and policies. The aggregation of these various decisions determines the emergent strategic changes, the actual objectives followed and the results achieved.

Operative goals may complement official goals or they may conflict. A complementary situation would exist if the stated objective was in terms of a target return on capital employed, and if this was achieved through operative goals of managers and decisions taken by them regarding delivery times, quality and so on. If, however, a sales manager was favouring particular customers with discounts or priority deliveries on low-profit orders, or a production manager was setting unnecessarily high quality standards (as far as customers are concerned) which resulted in substantial rejections and high operating costs, profits would be threatened. In such cases operative goals would conflict with official goals.

In this context, a recent report from the Public Management Foundation (1999) highlights a dilemma. Arguing that the UK Government is feeling frustrated by the slow speed at which the public sector is embracing certain objectives and strategies from the profit-seeking private sector, the Foundation discovered a 'public-sector ethos' amongst its managers. They are driven to 'make a difference for the community'. Improving local services and increasing user satisfaction are their personal priorities. There are occasions when this conflicts with the prioritization, rather than the actual existence, of stated, intended objectives for cutting costs and improving efficiencies. There is also a perception among many public-sector managers that their funders prefer centralized management controls, while they would like more autonomy and delegated authority. The situation is confused further when changing political pressures and necessities impact upon objectives and priorities.

Social Responsibility and Business Ethics

Having looked at some of the theories which are relevant for a study of objectives, and at typical objectives that organizations pursue and why, it is appropriate to conclude this chapter with a consideration of wider societal aspects. Objectives that relate to social responsibility may be affected by stakeholders; in some cases they result from legislation, but often they are voluntary actions. The issue is one of how responsible a firm might choose to be, and why. Again, the particular values of the strategic leader will be very influential.

There are numerous ways in which a firm can behave responsibly in the interests of society, and examples are given below. It should not be thought, however, that social responsibility is a one-way process; organizations can benefit considerably from it. Social responsibility and profitability can be improved simultaneously (The Performance Group, 1999).

- Product safety: This can be the result of design or production and includes aspects of supply and supplier selection to obtain safe materials or components. Product safety will be influenced to an extent by legislation, but an organization can build in more safety features than the law requires. Some cars are an example of this, such as Volvo which is promoted and perceived as a relatively safe car. Product safety will have cost implications. Sometimes the safety is reflected in perceived higher quality, which adds value that the customer is willing to pay a premium for, but at other times it will be the result of the organization's choosing to sacrifice some potential profit.
- Working conditions: Linked to the previous point, these can include safety at work, which again is affected by legislation which sets minimum standards. Aspects of job design to improve working conditions and training to improve employees' prospects are further examples.
- Honesty, including not offering or accepting bribes.
- Avoiding pollution.
- Avoiding discrimination.

The above points are all subject to some legislation.

- Community action: This is a very broad category with numerous opportunities, ranging from charitable activities to concerted action to promote industry and jobs in areas which have suffered from economic recession. Many large organizations release executives on a temporary basis to help with specific community projects.
- Industry location: Organizations may locate new plants in areas of high unemployment for a variety of reasons. While aspects of social responsibility may be involved, the decision may well be more economic. Grants and rate concessions may be important.
- Other environmental concerns: These include recycling, waste disposal, protecting the ozone layer and energy efficiency. Box 2.5 illustrates a number of specific examples.

Porter (1995) contends that many companies mistakenly see environmental legislation as a threat, something to be resisted. Instead, he argues, they should see regulation as an indication the company is not using its resources efficiently. Toxic materials and discarded packaging are waste. The costs incurred in eliminating a number of environmental problems can be more than offset by other savings and improvements in product quality. Companies should be innovative and not reluctantly just complying with their legal requirements.

STRATEGY IN ACTION – Box 2.5
Examples of Environmental Strategies

1 **McDonald's** took an equity stake in a new venture for recycling the waste collected at their restaurants. Some plastic containers which cannot be recycled have been withdrawn; food scraps are used for making compost. **Sainsbury's** give a one-penny refund for every plastic carrier bag that customers reuse. This saves the retailer the cost of providing a new bag; it also reduces the amount of waste plastic.

2 **Electricity generating** has gradually switched to gas and cleaner coal (with a low sulphur content) because coal has been shown to cause acid rain.

3 **Packaging**. Smaller, lighter packages use fewer raw materials and they are cheaper to transport. Procter and Gamble and Unilever have both introduced more concentrated versions of their detergent brands which, ironically, many consumers have seen as poor value for money because they have been unconvinced by the instructions to use less of the product! Soft drinks manufacturers have switched to fully recyclable aluminium cans and plastic bottles.

4 **ICI** invested in the challenge to find a replacement for chlorofluorocarbons (CFCs), gases which are used extensively in aerosols and refrigeration equipment, and which are widely blamed for depleting the ozone layer.

5 **The Body Shop** produces a comprehensive, externally audited, environmental report, its *Green Book*. The emphasis on such factors as energy waste and product stewardship drives improvements. Among other initiatives, The Body Shop has sought to eliminate its use of polyvinylchloride (PVC) because of the environmental impact of such packaging.

6 **The motor vehicle industry**. Historically, car manufacturers exploited an opportunity very successfully: increased affluence and the desire for individual freedom had generated a demand for private cars. Their success in increasing levels of ownership created a number of threats: traffic density, pollution from exhaust emissions, material waste through obsolescence, the 'waste' of scarce resources in high-consumption, inefficient engines, and safety problems arising from the sheer volume of traffic, congestion and hurry.

   A response was needed, and this has involved both manufacturers and government:
   - Legislation has made catalytic converters compulsory on all new cars after January 1993.
   - New models invariably feature improvements in design and technology which reduce waste and increase fuel efficiency.
   - New concept vehicles are being developed, including electric cars and others which mix the traditionally contradictory high performance with environmental friendliness. These have a long-term time scale.
   - Links between different forms of transport (road, rail, air and water) are being strengthened. BMW, for example, has pioneered co-operative ventures in

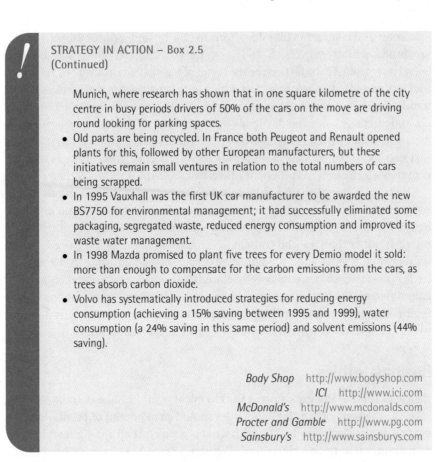

Munich, where research has shown that in one square kilometre of the city centre in busy periods drivers of 50% of the cars on the move are driving round looking for parking spaces.

- Old parts are being recycled. In France both Peugeot and Renault opened plants for this, followed by other European manufacturers, but these initiatives remain small ventures in relation to the total numbers of cars being scrapped.
- In 1995 Vauxhall was the first UK car manufacturer to be awarded the new BS7750 for environmental management; it had successfully eliminated some packaging, segregated waste, reduced energy consumption and improved its waste water management.
- In 1998 Mazda promised to plant five trees for every Demio model it sold: more than enough to compensate for the carbon emissions from the cars, as trees absorb carbon dioxide.
- Volvo has systematically introduced strategies for reducing energy consumption (achieving a 15% saving between 1995 and 1999), water consumption (a 24% saving in this same period) and solvent emissions (44% saving).

Body Shop   http://www.bodyshop.com
ICI   http://www.ici.com
McDonald's   http://www.mcdonalds.com
Procter and Gamble   http://www.pg.com
Sainsbury's   http://www.sainsburys.com

However, the European chemical industry has argued that bulk chemical manufacture has been largely driven out of EC countries by the costs of complying with environmental regulation. Standards in many Far Eastern countries are less restrictive.

- Attitude of food retailers: For example, accurate labelling (country of origin), free-range eggs, organic vegetables, biodegradable packaging, CFC-free aerosols and products containing certain dubious E-number additives. It is a moot point whether retailers or consumers should decide on these issues.

Objectives of this nature become part of the organization culture. Social responsibility is at the heart of activities and objectives because it is felt that the organization has an obligation both to the community and to society in general. However, it must not be assumed that the approach receives universal support. Milton Friedman (1979), the economist, argues that 'the business of business is business . . . the organization's only social responsibility is to increase its profit'.

Friedman also comments that donations to charity and sponsorship of the arts are 'fundamentally subversive' and not in the best interests of the shareholders. Social responsibility would then be the result of legislation. Drucker (1974) argues that businesses have a role in society which is 'to supply goods and services to customers and an economic surplus to society . . . rather than to supply jobs to workers and managers, or even dividends to shareholders'. The latter, he argues, are means not ends. Drucker contends that it is mismanagement to forget that a hospital exists for its patients and a university for its students. This contrasts with the comments by Russell Ackoff about university academics quoted earlier.

The topic is complex, and although the outcome of certain decisions can be seen to be bringing benefit to the community or employees the decision may have been influenced by legislation or perceived organizational benefit (enlightened self-interest) rather than a social conscience. One could argue that the organization will benefit if it looks after its employees; equally one could argue that it will suffer if it fails to consider employee welfare. The two approaches are philosophically different, but they may generate similar results. Some organizations feature their community role extensively in corporate advertising campaigns designed to bring them recognition and develop a caring, responsible image.

Business ethics

Disasters such as the explosion at the chemical plant in Bhopal, India, in 1984 raise the question of how far companies should go in pursuit of profits. Ethics is defined as 'the discipline dealing with what is good and bad and right and wrong or with moral duty and obligation' (Webster's Third New International Dictionary). Houlden (1988) suggests that business ethics encompasses the views of people throughout society concerning the morality of business, and not just the views of the particular business and the people who work in it.

Issues such as golden handshakes, insider dealing and very substantial salary increases for company chairmen and chief executives are topical and controversial.

The high-profile case of British Airways and Virgin Atlantic, where BA was accused of using privileged information to evaluate Virgin's route profitability and to persuade Virgin customers to switch airlines, suggested that BA acted unethically. In contrast, Hewlett-Packard, the US electronics multinational which is widely regarded as being highly ethical, operates an internal ban on the use of improper means for obtaining competitor information. The company also insists that any statements about its competitors must be fair, factual and complete.

Public attention is drawn to these issues, and people's perceptions of businesses generally and individually are affected. However, their responses differ markedly. Some people feel disgruntled but do nothing, whereas others take more positive actions. Managers, however, should not ignore the potential for resistance or opposition by their customers, who may refuse to buy their products or use their services.

Another ethical concern is individual managers or employees who adopt practices which senior managers or the strategic leader would consider unethical. These need to be identified and stopped. If they remain unchecked they are likely to spread, with the argument that 'everyone does it'. Sales staff using questionable methods of persuasion, even lying, would be an example. However, it does not follow that such practices would always be seen as unethical by senior managers – in some organizations they will be at least condoned, and possibly even encouraged.

The Co-operative Bank took an ethical stance in its customer strategy and advertising in the 1990s. This appealed to certain customers and thus gave the Co-operative Bank a competitive advantage.

Ethical dilemmas

One classic ethical dilemma concerns the employee who works for a competitor, is interviewed for a job, and who promises to bring confidential information if he is offered the post. Should the proposition be accepted or not? The issue featured at the beginning of this section, is how far companies should go in pursuit of profits. In such a case as this, long-term considerations are important as well as potential short-term benefits. If the competitor who loses the confidential information realizes what has happened it may seek to retaliate in some way. Arguably, the best interests of the industry as a whole should be considered. Box 2.6 presents three more ethical dilemmas.

Another example is the company with a plant that is surplus to requirements and which it would like to sell. The company knows the land beneath the plant contains radioactive waste. Legally it need not disclose this fact to prospective buyers, but is it ethical to keep quiet? Research commissioned by the Rowntree Foundation (see Taylor, 1997) concluded that housebuilders and estate agents generally do not warn buyers when new homes are built on previously contaminated industrial land. Petfood manufacturers, looking to expand their sales, would logically seek to differentiate their products by featuring particular benefits and satisfied, friendly pets, but they will also hope to persuade more people to become owners. Given the publicity on potentially dangerous breeds of dog, and the numbers of abandoned pets, particularly after Christmas, what would constitute an ethical approach to promotion? In 1991 a small number of ministers in the Church of England questioned whether the Church Commissioners, with £3 billion to invest to cover the future salaries and pensions of clergy, should be free to invest the

STRATEGY IN ACTION – Box 2.6
Three Ethical Dilemmas

A well-established European pharmaceutical company (X), in a country with a moderate but not large Catholic community, has developed and patented a new drug which safely induces abortion and has demonstrable health-care benefits for women seeking an abortion. For a variety of reasons, largely economic (health-care savings, benefit reductions and corporation tax revenues), its government is encouraging it to launch the drug in the home country and around the world at the earliest opportunity. Profits to the company would be good, but they would not have a dramatic impact on the company's overall profits. They would, however, ensure the future viability of a small production plant in an area of high unemployment. However, a sizeable block of the company's shares (but not a controlling interest) has recently been acquired by a foreign mini-conglomerate whose chief executive is a Catholic and opposed to the drug on religious grounds. As X's Managing Director you also know from your personal experience that if you launch the drug in America, one of your key export markets, you can expect protests from demonstrators opposed to abortion. What should you do?

A business manager for a well-known high-street bank is told by her manager that her function is shortly to be moved to a new regional centre some 25 miles away and that her own position is secure. She is personally delighted as her travel-to-work commute will be reduced, but she knows that there will be redundancies. Under instruction that for the moment the news is embargoed from other staff, she is concerned when her personal assistant approaches her a few days later. She has heard unsubstantiated rumours on the bank's grapevine and she would, for family reasons, be unable to move. She wants to know what she should do as she is about to pay a deposit on a new house. What should the business manager do? What is 'right by her employer' and what is 'right by her subordinate'?

A young consultant with a relatively new and small but fast-growing management consultancy is invited out-of-the-blue to be joint presenter (with the senior partner) of a bid to a potentially very large client. He is surprised; he has had no involvement in preparing the bid. Moreover, it is not in his area of expertise. Flattered with the wonderful opportunity, but at the same time concerned, he discusses the request with his mentor in the consultancy. He is informed that the contact person in the client organization is, like him, from an ethnic minority background. The senior partner felt that the client would like to see that the consultancy's only non-white consultant was a key member of the team. How should he react?

Developed from material in: Badaracco, JL Jr (1997) *Defining Moments – When Managers Must Choose Between Right and Right*, Harvard Business School Press.

money anywhere (in an attempt to maximize earnings) or whether they should be restricted to organizations which were known to be ethical in their business dealings. Interestingly, Martinson (1998) reported that the shares of companies widely perceived to be ethical in their strategies, policies and behaviour do not underperform when measured against the equity markets overall. In this context community involvement is seen as positive; any involvement with tobacco, alcohol or military equipment is negative.

Badaracco and Webb (1995) also highlight how internal decisions can be influenced by unethical practices. They quote instances of invented market-research findings, and altered investment returns which imply, erroneously, that the organization is meeting its published targets. They distinguish between 'expedient actions' and 'right actions'.

In contrast, a serious dilemma faces individuals in an organization who feel that their managers are pursuing unethical practices. There are several examples of individuals who have acted and suffered as a result of their actions. An accountant with an insurance company exposed a case of tax evasion by his bosses and jeopardized his career. Stanley Adams, an employee of Hoffman la Roche, the Swiss drug company, believed that his firm was making excessive profits and divulged commercially sensitive information to the European Commission. He also lost his career and suffered financially. There are similar examples of engineers who felt that design compromises were threatening consumer safety, complained, and lost their jobs.

Many of the ethical issues that affect strategic decisions are regulated directly by legislation. Equally, many companies do not operate in sensitive environments where serious ethical issues require thought and attention. However, some companies and their strategic leaders do need a clear policy regarding business ethics. Often they have to decide whether to increase costs in the short run, say to improve safety factors, on the assumption that this will bring longer-term benefits. Short-term profitability, important to shareholders, could be affected. Increased safety beyond minimum legal requirements, for example, would increase the construction costs of a new chemical plant. If safety were compromised to save money, nothing might actually go wrong and profits would be higher. However, an explosion or other disaster results in loss of life, personal injury, compensation and legal costs, lost production, adverse publicity and tension between the business and local community. The long-term losses can be substantial.

Reidenbach and Robin (1994) have produced a spectrum of five ethical/unethical responses.

- *Amoral companies* seek to 'win at all costs'; anything is seen as acceptable. The secret lies in not being found out.
- *Legalistic companies* obey the law and no more. There is no code of ethics; companies act only when it is essential.
- *Responsive companies* accept that being ethical can pay off.
- *Ethically engaged companies* actively want to 'do the right thing' and to be seen to be doing so. Ethical codes will exist, but ethical behaviour will not necessarily be a planned activity and fully integrated into the culture.

- *Ethical companies* such as The Body Shop have ethics as a core value, supported by appropriate strategies and actions which permeate the whole organization.

Because ethical standards and beliefs are aspects of the corporate culture, they are influenced markedly by the lead set by the strategic leader and his or her awareness of behaviour throughout the organization. If a proper lead is not provided, managers will be left to 'second guess' what would be seen as appropriate behaviour. Power, then, can be used ethically or unethically by individual managers.

Frederick (1988) contends that the corporate culture is the main source of any ethical problems. He argues that managers are encouraged to focus their professional energies on productivity, efficiency and leadership, and that their corporate values lead them to act in ways which place the company interests ahead of those of consumers or society

To guard against this it can be useful for a company to publish a corporate code of ethics, which all managers are expected to follow. Typically, large US companies have been more progressive with such codes than those in the UK. In the early 1990s, some 30% of large companies in the UK had published codes, but the number has since been growing all the time.

The typical issues covered in an ethics code include relationships with employees (the most prevalent factor in the UK codes of ethics), government (more important in the USA), the community and the environment.

Drawing on earlier points, attitudes towards bribery and inducement, and the use of privileged information, could also be incorporated in any code. Attention might also be paid to practices which are commonplace but arguably unethical. Examples would include a deliberate policy not to pay invoices on time, and creative accounting, presenting information in the most favourable light. The extent to which audited company accounts can be wholly relied upon is another interesting issue.

Business ethics is arguably important and worthy of serious attention. However, a consideration of ethical issues in strategic decisions typically requires that a long-term perspective is adopted. Objectives and strategies should be realistic and achievable rather than overambitious and very difficult to attain. In the latter case individual managers may be set high targets which encourage them to behave unethically, possibly making them feel uneasy. Results may be massaged, for instance, or deliberately presented with inaccuracies. Such practices spread quickly and dishonesty becomes acceptable. The longer-term perspective can reduce the need for immediate results and targets which managers feel have to be met at all costs. However, pressure from certain stakeholders, particularly institutional shareholders, may focus attention on the short term and on results which surpass those of the previous year. The longer-term perspective additionally allows for concern with processes and behaviour, and with how the results are obtained.

The drive for results is not allowed to override ethical and behavioural concerns.

Houlden (1988) concludes that strategic leaders should be objective about how society views their company and its products, and wherever possible should avoid actions that can damage its image. If an action or decision that certain stakeholders might view as unethical is unavoidable, such as the closure of a plant, it is important to use public relations to explain fully why the decision has been taken. The need for a good corporate image should not be underestimated.

Later chapters (particularly Chapter 6) include discussions on how organizations might achieve competitive advantage. Ethical considerations can make a significant contribution to this. A commitment to keeping promises about quality standards and delivery times, or not making promises which cannot be met, would be one example. If employees are honest and committed, and rewarded appropriately for this, then costs are likely to be contained and the overall level of customer service high, thereby improving profits.

To summarize briefly, this chapter has been about direction and about ends, the ends which help to determine the strategies that organizations select and pursue. A number of key terms have been defined and a number of important conflicts of interest explained. The next two chapters look first at how we might measure performance against these desired end-points and then at issues of organizational culture, which provide an important guide to why organizations pick particular strategies and follow certain routes.

Summary

The corporate *mission* represents the overriding purpose for the business, and ideally it should explain why the organization is different and set it apart from its main rivals. It should not be a statement that other organizations can readily adopt. Its main purpose is communication.

It is useful to separate the mission statement from a statement of corporate *vision* which concerns 'what the organization is to become'.

Both can provide a valuable starting point for more specific *objectives* and strategies. Shorter term objectives will normally have time-scales or end-dates attached to them and ideally they will be 'owned' by individual managers.

It is, therefore, feasible to argue that organizations (as a whole) have a purpose and individual managers have objectives.

Mission, vision and objectives all relate to the *direction* that the organization is taking – the ends from which strategies are derived.

It is not, however, feasible to assume that the organization will always be free to set these objectives for its managers: there may be constraints from key stakeholders. A number of theories and models, mainly from a study of economics, can help us to understand why organizations do the things they do.

In addition, individuals will have *personal objectives* that they wish (and intend) to pursue, which should not be allowed to work against the best interests of the organization.

External *stakeholders* also have expectations for the organization. These will not always be in accord with each other, and important trade-offs and priorities must be established. There is always the potential for conflicts of interest. As a result, the organization will be seen to have a multitude of objectives, but all contributory to a single purpose.

Profit is necessary for profit-seeking businesses; a positive cash flow is essential for not-for-profit organizations. Profit (or cash) can, however, be seen as either a means or an end, and this will impact upon the 'feel' or culture of the organization.

Regardless, there is a virtuous circle of financial returns, motivated employees and satisfied customers.

Issues of *social responsibility* and *business ethics* are important for all organizations. They will be seen by some organizations as a threat or constraint and encourage a strategy of compliance. Other organizations will perceive them as an opportunity to create a difference and in turn a positive image. They are becoming increasingly visible, issues which organizations should take seriously and not ignore.

References

Ackoff, RL (1986) *Management in Small Doses*, John Wiley.

Badaracco, JL and Webb, A (1995) Business ethics: a view from the trenches, *California Management Review*, 37.2, Winter.

Baumol, WJ (1959) *Business Behaviour, Value and Growth*, Macmillan.

Campbell, A (1989) Research findings discussed in Skapinker, M (1989) Mission accomplished or ignored? *Financial Times*, 11 January. See also: Campbell, A and Nash, L (1992) *A Sense of Mission: Defining Direction for the Large Corporation*, Addison-Wesley.

Constable, J (1980) The nature of company objectives. Unpublished paper, Cranfield School of Management.

Cyert, RM and March, JG (1963) *A Behavioural Theory of the Firm*, Prentice-Hall.

Deloitte (1999) *Making Customer Loyalty Real – A Global Manufacturing Study*, Deloitte Consulting and Deloitte & Touche, http://www.dc.com/research

Drucker, PF (1974) *Management: Tasks, Responsibilities, Practices*, Harper & Row.

Frederick, WC (1988) An ethics roundtable: the culprit is culture, *Management Review*, August.

Freeman, RE (1984) *Strategic Management: A Stakeholder Approach*, Pitman.

Friedman, M (1979) The social responsibility of business is to increase its profits. In *Business Policy and Strategy* (eds DJ McCarthy, RJ Minichiello and JR Curran), Irwin.

Galbraith, JK (1963) *American Capitalism. The Concept of Countervailing Power*, Penguin.

Galbraith, JK (1969) *The New Industrial State*, Penguin.

Houlden, B (1988) The corporate conscience, *Management Today*, August.

Marris, R (1964) *The Economic Theory of Managerial Capitalism*, Macmillan.

Martinson, J (1998) Ethical equities perform well, *Financial Times*, 21 July.

MORI (2000) See: Brown, K (2000) Survey exposes 'gulf' over the essentials for business success, *Financial Times*, 2 February.

Newbould, GD and Luffman, GA (1979) *Successful Business Policies*, Gower.

Penrose, E (1959) *The Theory of the Growth of the Firm*, Blackwell.

Performance Group, The (1999) *Sustainable Strategies for Value Creation*, Oslo, Norway.

Perrow, C (1961) The analysis of goals in complex organizations, *American Sociological Review*, 26, December.

Pfeffer, J (1981) *Power in Organizations*, Pitman.

Porter, ME (1995) Interviewed for the Green Management letter, *Euromanagement*, June.

Public Management Foundation (1999) *Wasted Values*, London.

Reidenbach, E and Robin, D (1995) Quoted in Drummond, J: Saints and sinners, *Financial Times*, 23 March.

Richards, MD (1978) *Organizational Goal Structures*, West.

Simon, HA (1964) On the concept of organizational goal, *Administrative Science Quarterly*, 9(1), June, 1–22.

Taylor, A (1997) Home buyers unaware of contamination, *Financial Times*, 24 October.

Thompson, AA and Strickland, AJ (1980) *Strategy Formulation and Implementation*, Irwin.

Waterman, R (1994) *The Frontiers of Excellence: Learning from Companies that Put People First*, Nicholas Brealey Publishing.

Williamson, OE (1964) *Economics of Discretionary Behaviour: Managerial Objectives in a Theory of the Firm*, Kershaw.

Test your knowledge of this chapter with our online quiz at:
http://www.thomsonlearning.co.uk

Explore The Organizational Mission and Objectives further at:
Administrative Science Quarterly   http://www.gsm.cornell.edu/ASQ/asq.html
California Management Review   http://www.haas.berkeley.edu/News/cmr/index.html
Sociological Review   http://www.blackwellpublishers.co.uk/journals/SOCREV/descript.htm
Rowntree Foundation   http://www.jrf.org.uk

Questions and Research Assignments

TEXT RELATED

1. Consider how the objectives of HP Bulmer Holdings, detailed in Box 2.1, might be ranked in order of priority. Is there a difference between an ideal ranking and the likely ranking in practice? Note: Members of the Bulmer family hold over 50% of the ordinary shares.

2. Thinking of any organization with which you have personal experience, do you believe that profit (or cash in the case of a non-profit organization) is seen as a means or an end by the key decision makers? Do they all agree on this?

3. What key issues do you believe should be incorporated in a company statement on ethics?

Internet and Library Projects

1. When Tottenham Hotspur became the first English Football League club with a stock-exchange listing (in 1983) the issue prospectus said: 'The Directors intend to ensure that the Club remains one of the leading football clubs in the country. They will seek to increase the Group's income by improving the return from existing assets and by establishing new sources of revenue in the leisure field'.

   (A) Research the strategies followed by Tottenham Hotspur plc since 1983. Do you believe that the interests of a plc and a professional football club are compatible or inevitably conflicting?

   (B) Which other clubs have followed Tottenham? Have they chosen similar or different strategies? How have they performed as businesses?

   (C) In view of the comments about social responsibility, how do you view the fact that football clubs generally invest far more money in players (wages and transfer fees) than they do in their grounds (amenities and safety)?

2. Have the objectives (in particular the order of priorities) of the Natural History Museum changed since the introduction of compulsory admission charges in April 1987?

3. In view of the findings after the *Herald of Free Enterprise* disaster at Zeebrugge in March 1987 and the *Estonia* disaster in 1994, how does a company such as P&O (the owners of the *Herald*) balance the extra costs involved in additional safety measures with the need to be competitive internationally, and the time added on to voyages by more rigorous safety procedures with customer irritation if they are delayed unnecessarily?

Natural History Museum http://www.nhm.ac.uk
P&O Group http://www.p-and-o.com
Tottenham Hotspur plc http://www.spurs.co.uk/corporatenew/index.html

Measuring Success

The performance of a company, the outcomes of the strategies that it is pursuing, is typically evaluated by financial ratios and other quantitative measures. In this chapter it is argued that while these are an essential element of the evaluation process, alone they are inadequate. To appreciate fully how well an organization is doing one needs to take a wider, more holistic, perspective, beginning with an assessment of the strategies themselves. We show how different measures and assessments can provide conflicting conclusions and finish the main body of the chapter with a comprehensive model based on E–V–R (environment–values–resources) congruence.

Financial ratio analysis is an important aspect of management case-study analysis and consequently a section explaining the main ratios is appended to this chapter.

Case Study 3: The New Internet Businesses

As we start the new millennium, cyberspace and e-commerce are providing another Klondike gold rush. Using the 'gold-rush' metaphor is interesting; it conjures up thoughts of huge fortunes and, without question, these fortunes are being made. There are 64 new millionaires every day in Silicon Valley alone, and Europe's first e-commerce millionaires have arrived. But we must not forget that only a small percentage of those prospectors attracted to Alaska really made their fortune. Most failed to find very much gold, and many perished in the harsh conditions. The Internet is a wonderful and attractive opportunity, but it will prove disappointing, even cruel, to many of those would-be entrepreneurs that it attracts. The commercial potential of new creative, innovative ideas is difficult to evaluate.

Brady (1999) argues that the success of any e-commerce business is dependent upon several factors. The idea must be innovatory, and while the business should be clearly focused it must be able to change and evolve speedily if it is to sustain growth. The people behind the business, their plans and their grasp of the issues, together with their ability to raise the necessary finance, are obviously critical issues. It is also essential that they develop a strong brand and, on the back of this, create and maintain very high levels of service. The site must be readily accessible, orders must be simple to place and then easily tracked while they are in the system, and deliveries should be on time.

How, then, might we evaluate these new businesses, remembering that at the moment only a minority is profitable? Partly concerned not to be left behind in this new gold rush, some financiers and venture capitalists seem willing to back some very high-risk proposals if they believe in the idea and the entrepreneur. Amazon.com, the most substantial and famous e-commerce company in the world, has secured enormous funding but has yet to declare a profit. The theoretical value of the company, a reflection of its current share price, varies dramatically – and many analysts have suggested that it is overvalued because of the relative uncertainty.

Management Today (see Gwyther, 1999) offers the following set of evaluation criteria.

Three factors which determine the extent and value of the opportunity

1. *The concept or idea*
   - How *value* is created and built
   - The potential for profit, based on costs and revenues
   - The size of the potential market
   - The potential to establish an advantage and reap the rewards, specifically the presence of effective barriers to entry by direct competitors.
2. *Innovation*
   - The initial difference and the potential to build new values and thus sustain any early advantage.
3. *Engagement and implementation*
   - The ability to set up the infrastructure and the business, which inevitably depends on the people behind the business.

Three further factors which reflect the project or business outcomes

4. *Traffic*
   Numbers of customers generated – linked to the extent of repeat business, which in turn is dependent on service levels achieved. Although web congestion can be a constraint, the fact that people recommend websites by word of mouth is a major opportunity.
5. *Financing*
   Financial resources secured, to fund continued expansion as well as start-up. Setting up a robust business and infrastructure on the web is expensive.
6. *Visibility*
   The critically important brand identity and image, remembering that a strong public profile and visibility can also act as a barrier to entry. This will often be in the form of media coverage for either an exciting new idea or the recognition of a new, successful entrepreneur or even web millionaire.

   The following two examples feature a company which disappeared almost as quickly as it appeared and one which is prospering as this book is being written. Things, however, change quickly in this sector.

Boo.com had a physical base in London's Carnaby Street, home of 1960s' fashion, and it was set up to sell sportswear. The idea was to widen the availability of the more exclusive designer-label items, which are typically only available in large cities. Two of its three founders (who were all in their twenties) had previously created Books.com, an early on-line bookseller; the third was an ex-model. It has been estimated that Boo.com was able to raise £100 million in venture capital, but this is still far less than the amount required to set up a physical retail infrastructure which could provide customers with these items on a wide scale. After a number of well-publicized false starts, the company went on-line in November 1999, offering deliveries in 18 countries from warehouses in Cologne and Kentucky. Boo.com did not own these warehouses but had a dedicated staff working there and an alliance with the owners. Goods were delivered to the warehouses by their manufacturers and then repackaged in distinctive Boo boxes before being posted on.

The website offered 40,000 items. Each had been photographed at least 24 times such that browsers could examine them from every angle. Clothes could be seen on their own and on particular mannequin figures. Product descriptions were available in eight languages and sales were in local currencies. In reality, this level of detail proved too complex for the memories of many computers that were used to browse the site. In addition, there was a sophisticated internal checking system to ensure that customers were never sold anything which was not immediately available from the relevant manufacturer.

The delayed start, revelations about inadequate computer memories and an early sale when orders appeared to be below initial targets, all combined to ensure that Boo.com began to receive hostile publicity, having previously been heralded as a 'company of the future'. By May 2000 there were reports that the company needed refinancing with an additional £30 million. Rumours that Boo.com might be acquired by a leading sportswear company were also beginning to circulate. In the event the business went into liquidation within a year of its launch. Most of the invested millions were lost.

Boo.com   http://www.boo.com

Lastminute.com deals in products and services with a finite shelf-life that are close to their sell-by date and are sometimes candidates for distress pricing. Seats for flights, sporting events, theatres and holidays would all qualify. Events in the UK, France and Germany are included. Lastminute.com brokers a deal and then takes a commission. Clearly this web company is not the only potential outlet for the products in question, and consequently its success will depend on the variety it can offer, the extent of the business it can generate through its site and its ability to bring buyer and seller together. The target market is cash-rich, time-constrained professionals who would like a bargain but who cannot invest the time and effort to find it personally. In mid-1999 Lastminute.com was declaring 300,000 registered subscribers with an average of almost 15 site visits per month. Revenues amounted to some £6 million, and no direct American equivalent had been identified.

The company was founded in November 1998 by two ex-consultants in their late twenties, Brent Hoberman and Martha Lane Fox. The basic idea was Hoberman's, who had become increasingly irritated with the process of price haggling with individual hotels and airlines when he was travelling. Mid-way through 1999 the two partners had raised over £6 million from, amongst others, Intel and Deutsche Telekom, and they were constantly seeking new backers to help to develop the scope and extent of the business. At this time it was being speculated that the company would be floated in 2000. A potential valuation of £400 million was featured in the reports. The two partners would be able to retain 45% of the equity.

Having expanded its activities into France, Germany and Sweden, the company was floated in early 2000. The valuation was now some 50% higher than the 1999 indication and the shares were oversubscribed. Investor allocations had to be rationed and the price soared immediately. The uncertainty of this sector ensured that they fell just as quickly and soon they were trading at just one-third of their post-flotation high. After all, for some, Lastminute.com is 'nothing more than an up-market bucket shop'.

When the company published its results for the 6 month period October 1999 to March 2000, revenues had grown to £11.4 million for the half-year. From these the company received £1.2 million income, but lost £17 million. Like Amazon.com, Lastminute.com has yet to make a profit. In fact, the company is not forecasting a profit until 2004 at the earliest. In Spring 2000, Martha Lane Fox was placed fifth in a *Management Today* listing of the most powerful women in Britain.

Brent Hoberman reacted to the adverse publicity that the company was beginning to attract and commented: 'People have chosen to focus on personalities and the share price, but the results should focus people's minds on the business and we have shown real growth'.

In August 2000 Lastminute.com acquired its French rival, Dégriftour, for £59 million in a mixture of cash and shares. The proclaimed benefits were economies of scale and the likelihood of reaching break-even point in a shorter period. The potential downside was the reality that it could prove a distraction for a rapidly expanding company.

Lastminute.com   http://www.lastminute.com

References

Brady, G (1999) The new rules for start-ups, *e-business*, December.
Gwyther, M (1999) Jewels in the web, *Management Today*, November.
Wheatcroft, P (2000) Britain's 50 most powerful women, *Management Today*, April.

QUESTIONS: Is Lastminute.com a successful company? If yes, on what criteria are you judging it? If not, why not? Do you know of any other companies which, like Boo.com, have failed?

Introduction

An organization is successful if it is meeting the needs and expectations of its stakeholders. This implies a mixture of common sense and competency. These two simple, bold statements explain how we should seek to measure the success of an organization. We certainly need to know how well the stakeholder expectations are being met; we also need to understand the 'why' and 'how' behind the 'how well', as otherwise we will not be in a strong position to remedy weaknesses or sustain success.

We may feel that we know instinctively whether an organization is doing relatively well or relatively poorly, but realistically we need to be more precise than this. For one thing, we could be deluding ourselves or misjudging a situation. We could be seduced into feeling complacent and ignoring environmental changes. Success, assuming the success is real and not imagined, can be transient.

Figure 3.1 therefore implies that it is essential that organizations and their managers know where, how and why a company is doing relatively well or relatively poorly and that they use this information to sustain success by improvement and change or remedy weaknesses by remedial action. Otherwise, if relative success is taken for granted, or if relative failure is not understood, the organization will experience decline, whether this is slowly or rapidly.

It is quite normal to look for explanations when results or outcomes are disappointing or below target. Attention is quickly focused on failure. This is not always the case with success. It is not unusual for a group of managers proverbially to pat themselves on the back and assume that the success is a result of

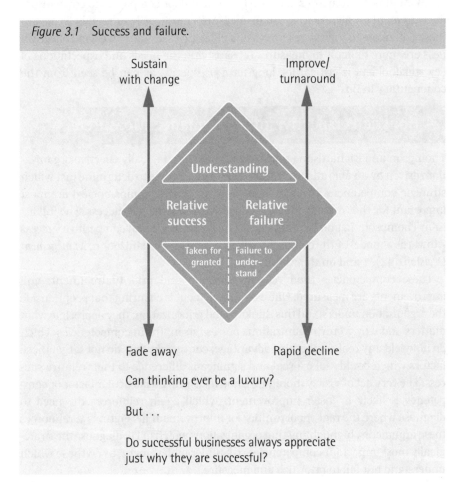

Figure 3.1 Success and failure.

Sustain with change

Improve/ turnaround

Understanding

Relative success

Relative failure

Taken for granted

Failure to under- stand

Fade away

Rapid decline

Can thinking ever be a luxury?

But . . .

Do successful businesses always appreciate just why they are successful?

their personal abilities and brilliance. The reality could be that the success lies more in good fortune and an absence of any strong, threatening competitors. Such advantages can prove very short lived. Success, when taken too much for granted, can quickly turn to failure.

It is also necessary to face up to the real issues and not attempt to 'spin' the figures to provide an attractive, but not entirely honest, explanation. Companies like to present and discuss their results in terms of absolute figures for revenue and profits, and the media seem happy to report these figures, frequently headlining any growth. Absolute growth in this form can – and can be used to – hide a deterioration in true performance. Profitability, for instance, is more important than profit per se for understanding how well a company is doing. Case Study 3 showed how growth alone could be a very dubious and misleading measure of success. Always remember – sales revenue is vanity; cash flow is clarity; profits are sanity.

Taking this point further, it is also not unusual for companies to concentrate measurement on factors that can be measured most easily or readily. Typically, these will relate to inputs, resources and efficiencies, as outcomes and effectiveness are more difficult to measure. Yet satisfying the needs and expectations of key stakeholders is critical for long-term prosperity, as can be seen from the commentary in Box 3.1.

A Holistic Perspective of Performance Measurement

Thompson and Richardson (1996) argue that a strategically effective organization, driven by an able and aware strategic leader, is able to determine just which strategic competencies (from a set of over 30 generic competencies) are most important for that organization's competitive and strategic success. The full list is in: Thompson, JL and Richardson, B (1996) Strategic and competitive success – towards a model of the comprehensively competent organization, *Management Decision*, (34), 1 and on the website.

These competencies then receive attention and priority treatment, and improvements are measured. One essential element is ensuring that people inside the organization understand this thinking and prioritization; they appreciate what matters and why. Many organizations possess strengths in competencies which do not yield any real competitive advantage; conversely, they do not target those factors which could make a real and significant difference to their relative success. The very act of visibly monitoring and measuring a particular factor or competency is likely to foster improvement, which again reinforces the need to diagnose where the real opportunities for improvement lie. Figure 3.2 reinforces these arguments, highlighting that organizations which fail to diagnose the strategically most important competencies risk underachievement, as do those which understand but fail to prioritize and measure.

STRATEGY IN ACTION – Box 3.1
Efficiency or Effectiveness?

There are three important measures of performance:

- Economy, which means 'doing things cost effectively'. Resources should be managed at the lowest possible cost consistent with achieving quantity and quality targets.
- Efficiency, which implies 'doing things right'. Resources should be deployed and utilized to maximize the returns from them.

    Economy and efficiency measures are essentially quantitative and objective.
- Effectiveness, or 'doing the right things'. Resources should be allocated to those activities which satisfy the needs, expectations and priorities of the various stakeholders in the business.

    Effectiveness relates to outcomes and need satisfaction, and consequently the measures are often qualitative and subjective.

Where economy, efficiency and effectiveness can be measured accurately and unambiguously it is appropriate to use the expression 'performance measures'. However, if, as is frequently the case with effectiveness, precise measures are not possible, it can be more useful to use the term 'performance indicators'.

As the following grid indicates, only efficient and effective organizations will grow and prosper. Effective but inefficient businesses will survive but underachieve because they are not using minimum resources; efficient but ineffective companies will decline as they cease to meet the expectations of their stakeholders – simply, the things they are doing are wrong, however well they might be doing them.

	Ineffective	Effective
Inefficient	Corporate collapse	Survival
Efficient	Gradual decline	Growth and prosperity

Possible performance measures for British Airways – an application

An airline is a people-dependent service business. Unquestionably, its revenue, profits, profitability, liquidity and market share (explained and discussed in the appendix to this chapter) are all important. But alone they are inadequate for assessing the overall performance.

The following list contains examples of appropriate measures that might also be used.

Economy measures

- Costs, e.g. the cost of fuel
- The cost of leasing aircraft
- Staff levels and costs – slimming these is acceptable as long as the appropriate quality of service is maintained. This could be measured as an overhead cost per passenger.

STRATEGY IN ACTION – Box 3.1
(Continued)

Efficiency measures

- Timekeeping/punctuality
- Revenue passenger kilometres (RPK), the number of passengers carried multiplied by the distances flown
- Available seat kilometres (ASK), the number of seats available for sale multiplied by the distances flown
- The overall load factor = RPK/ASK. (Similar measures for freight are also relevant.)

Solid performance with these measures is essential if the airline is to run at all profitably, but increasing them requires the airline to be more effective in persuading more customers to fly, utilizing marketing and consistently good service.

A related measure is:

- Passenger revenue per RPK. Improving this implies increasing the return from each flight, given that on any aircraft there are likely to be several pricing schemes in operation.
- Income (from all sources) related to the numbers of employees
- Reliability of the aircraft, i.e. continuous flying without breakdown (as a result of efficient maintenance, see below)
- The average age of the aircraft in the fleet.

Effectiveness

- Ability to meet all legislative requirements
- Image – which is based on several of the factors listed in this section
- Staff attitudes and contributions – both on the ground and on board the aircraft: care, courtesy, enthusiasm, friendliness, respect and efficiency
- The aeroplane – does it look and feel new and properly looked after?
- Other aspects of the on-board service, such as the cleanliness of the seating and toilet areas, food and entertainment
- Innovation – new standards of passenger comfort
- Safety record
- The number of routes offered, the timing of flights and the general availability of seats (this requires good links with travel agents)
- Recognition of, and rewards for, regular and loyal customers, reflected in the accumulation of air miles by passengers and the numbers of passengers who become 'gold-card' holders in regular flier schemes
- Having seats available for all people with tickets who check in. While airlines, like hotels, often overbook deliberately, they must ensure that they are not 'bumping' people onto the next available flight at a level which is causing ill-will and a poor reputation

- The compensation package when people are delayed
- Time taken at check-in
- Reliability of baggage service, particularly making sure that bags go on the right flight. This also involves the issue of bags being switched from one flight to another for transit passengers
- The time taken for baggage to be unloaded (this is partially in the hands of the airport management)
- The absence of any damage to luggage
- The systems for allocating particular seats in advance of the flight and at check-in
- The number of complaints; the number in relation to the number of passengers
- The way in which complaints are handled
- The ability to balance the cost of maintenance with the costs incurred if things go wrong. If there is inadequate maintenance there are likely to be incidents or accidents which are costly in lost revenue and goodwill. At the same time airlines could 'overmaintain' to a level where they are no longer able to compete because of too-high costs.

The additional factors below are not wholly the responsibility of airlines as they also involve the airport owners:

- Terminal provisions and comfort – seating, escalators, restaurants, duty-free shopping and toilets
- Security – evidence of security and the perception that it is being taken seriously
- Availability of trolleys.

Endnotes

It is also important to consider how all these factors might be measured and evaluated. Observation, passenger surveys, complaints and comparisons with other airlines are all possibilities.

The distinction between indicators (aspects of service which are actually difficult to measure), measures and performance targets (standards to measure against) needs to be recognized.

The following points are also worth noting:

- It is sensible not to be overambitious with both measures and targets.
- If something cannot be measured it is perhaps better to leave it out.
- The chosen measures must be relevant and easily understood; hopefully the very act of measurement will foster improvements.

Figure 3.2   Measuring strategic competencies.

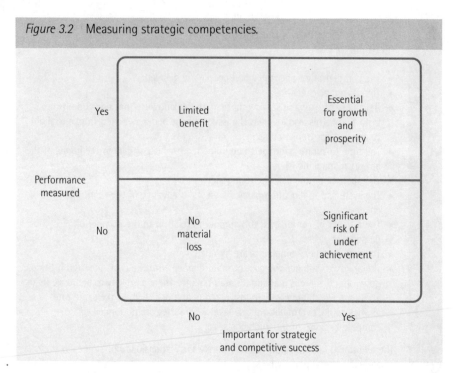

	No	Yes
Yes	Limited benefit	Essential for growth and prosperity
No	No material loss	Significant risk of under achievement

Performance measured

Important for strategic and competitive success

Simply and fundamentally, the act of measurement affects the behaviour of individual managers.

> What gets measured gets done. If you are looking for quick ways to change how an organization behaves, change the measurement system.
>
> *Mason Haire, University of California*
> *Institute of Industrial Relations*

Measurement and review not only clarify how well an organization is doing, the process informs and guides change, both continuous, improvemental, emergent change and discontinuous change to new competitive paradigms, as explained in Figure 3.3.

Thompson and Richardson (1996) have also shown how these generic strategic competencies can be categorized into three broad groups which influence the organization's efficiency and effectiveness and have a relevance for all of its stakeholders. *Content* competencies reflect the ways through which organizations add value, differentiate and manage their costs. They include functional and competitive strategies. *Process* competencies deal with the ways by which these content competencies are changed and improved in a dynamic and competitive

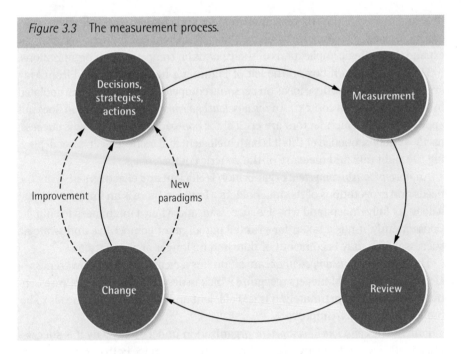

Figure 3.3 The measurement process.

environment, while *awareness and learning* competencies inform the change management process. Process competencies relate, for example, to strategy implementation and to quality and customer care; awareness and learning competencies include the ability to satisfy stakeholders, ethical and social issues, and the ability to avoid and manage crises.

Each organization has its own particular mix of critical competencies, and this mix changes in dynamic and competitive environments. Consequently, the measurement systems must be flexible and capable of dealing with both hard and soft issues. Some competencies will need to be evaluated by indicators which are inevitably subjective in nature rather than by formalized, hard measures. The fact that this may be more difficult is no excuse for concentrating on measuring those factors which are simply easy to measure, as they may not be the ones which make a real difference.

Improving competency

Where organizations need to become more successful and less crisis prone, it will be necessary for them to improve and/or reprioritize their competencies. It was suggested above that it is necessary, first, to evaluate which competencies are critical for strategic and competitive success and, secondly, to ensure that the organization possesses these competencies at an appropriate level. To facilitate this, and to ensure that there is improvement and change, it will clearly be necessary for organizations to measure their competencies. Figures 3.4 and 3.5 expand the strategic implications of these points on competency for organizations.

The four-quadrant box on the left of Figure 3.4 has been adapted from May and Kruger (1988), whose ideas on personal competency have been extrapolated to an organizational context. An *unconsciously incompetent* organization does not appreciate just which factors are critical for competitive and strategic success; partly as a consequence of this it is both inefficient and ineffective. It is not deploying the right mix and measure of the generic competencies.

An *unconsciously competent* organization is efficient and effective, satisfying the needs and expectations of its stakeholders. However, there is an implication that it does not fully understand why it is successful, and when it might need to change. Consequently, it has a taken-for-granted paradigm of competitive and strategic success which may become out of date and no longer appropriate.

The *consciously incompetent* organization has a clear and shared awareness of key success factors. Managers recognize which issues and competencies are essential for success. Unfortunately, it is less efficient and effective than it needs to be, but it is motivated to improve.

Finally, the *consciously competent* organization understands why it is successful. It is efficient and effective and it is motivated to manage both continuous and discontinuous change as necessary.

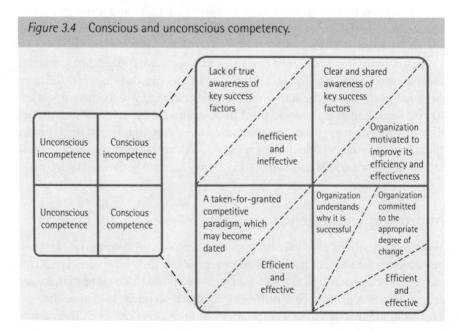

Figure 3.4 Conscious and unconscious competency.

Figure 3.5 illustrates the requirements for moving from one quadrant to another. An unconsciously incompetent organization becomes more competent (arrow 1) by efficiency and productivity drives, which may also improve effectiveness to some extent, but it may not become properly effective because it fails to clarify its key success factors. The same organization, alternatively, may become more conscious by attempting to clarify the key success factors (arrow 2). This, later, needs to be accompanied by a determined effort to improve efficiency and effectiveness (arrow 3) to generate competency.

Arrows 4 and 5, linking the bottom two quadrants, indicate an organization with E–V–R congruence. Once an organization has become consciously competent, these competencies and the associated competitive paradigm need to be fully accepted and absorbed into the organization's culture and values. Satisfying the key success factors happens almost automatically and unconsciously (arrow 4), and there is an ongoing commitment to continuous improvement. However, this state of affairs is only satisfactory while the underpinning competitive paradigm remains appropriate. Competitive pressures will at some

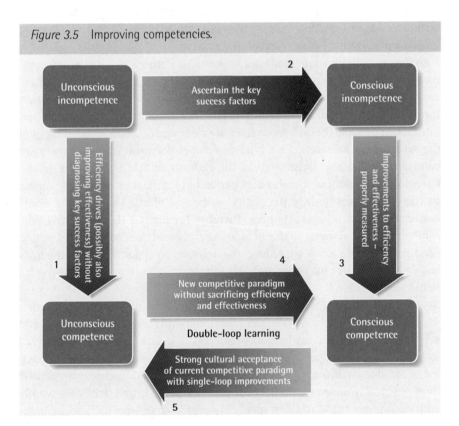

Figure 3.5 Improving competencies.

stage require most organizations to search for a new perspective of effective competition, and ideally reach the new 'competitive high ground' ahead of their rivals. This means that the competency package – and key success factors – should be evaluated constantly to ensure that they remain appropriate. When the competitive strategy is changed, efficiency and effectiveness must not be sacrificed (arrow 5).

What should we measure?

The three most important things you need to measure in business are customer satisfaction, employee satisfaction and cash flow.

Jack Welch, Chief Executive Officer,
General Electric (US)

The ultimate measure of success for any organization will invariably have a quantitative element. For profit-seeking businesses it will concern revenue growth, profits and profitability. For non-profits it will relate to an ability to raise sufficient funding to fulfil its purpose and objectives effectively. However, simply focusing on financial measures, important as they are, is woefully inadequate as they pay insufficient regard to issues of cause and outcome.

In the previous chapter, Figure 2.4 presented a virtuous circle whereby motivated, productive, committed employees create satisfied, maybe even 'delighted' customers, whose continued business enables high financial returns. To sustain the circle, this financial success must, in part, reward employees adequately and satisfactorily. While these dependencies are clear and obvious, measurement of the extent of the satisfaction is not always straightforward. Moreover, there are conflicting pulls, also illustrated on the right-hand side of Figure 2.3. The financial expectations of shareholders, particularly in the short term, may impose cost restraints which affect the ability of the organization to meet the needs and expectations of its customers, thereby threatening the virtuous circle. A further potential threat to the virtuous circle comes from competitors, whose actions and initiatives can reduce the relative perception of a company's ability to satisfy its customers and also put pressure on costs by forcing price reductions.

It is essential then, but only as a first step, to measure resource utilization efficiencies. But this, by nature, has a predominantly internal perspective, and a business cannot sustain long-term success if it fails to satisfy its external stakeholders. In a competitive environment, effectiveness measures, such as customer satisfaction linked to service, are equally critical, as many organizations have now realized. Selected aspects of this can be measured straightforwardly with various types of satisfaction survey, but other elements are more tricky. Innovation, supported by learning, underpins customer care and service. While this must by nature be difficult to measure objectively, attempts can be made to judge the level of activity and the extent to which it is growing.

Atkinson *et al.* (1997) support the contention that satisfied employees are productive, and productive employees are essential for financial success. They suggest that employee satisfaction depends on four key variables: compensation schemes and rewards; the culture of the organization; the prevailing style of management; and job design and responsibility.

Research by Industrial Relations Services, IRS (1997), confirms that an increasing number of UK organizations now accepts that they must measure customer satisfaction, 'employee well-being' and the contributions made by people at both the individual and team levels. This in part explains the increasing influence of measurement 'packages' such as Kaplan and Norton's *balanced scorecard* (1992), which is discussed later in this chapter (p. 147).

Organizations are now just as likely to have stated and measured objectives covering customer relations and people-related issues as they are profit and profitability improvement. While it is acknowledged that elements of this are difficult, there is increasing evidence – but certainly not universal practice – of surveys of employee morale, satisfaction and opinion. Leadership and team behaviour, for example, can be usefully evaluated with 360° appraisals, but attempts at this by various organizations have enjoyed mixed success.

Consequently, Ruddle and Feeny (1997) have concluded that, for some organizations '. . . in spite of all the rhetoric and new ideas, it is very difficult to get people away from the financial numbers.'

Furthermore, parallel research in the USA by Towers Perrin (1997) concludes that employees who have accepted and survived organizational restructuring and downsizing, together with the accompanying insecurity, do not feel that they are being rewarded justly now that the American economy is buoyant once again and corporate financial performances are generally improving. Productivity has increased and the satisfaction of employees with their individual jobs is relatively high and growing. People are accepting empowerment, responsibility and control of their jobs, but this is fuelling their expectations of higher rewards. However, there is only 'limited evidence of the partnerships employers have said they want to build with their workers'. The inherent danger is that the commitment level will plateau and turn down again, thus breaking the virtuous circle in Figure 2.4, instead of providing a platform for both corporate and personal growth now that the degree of job insecurity is reduced.

As a final qualification to this section, my own research suggests that even when softer issues are evaluated and measured, the results are not always communicated through the organization to an appropriate and desirable degree.

A holistic model

Accepting these reservations, it is next important to look at performance measures within a comprehensive cause and outcome framework. Manfred Kets de Vries (1996) argues that strategic leaders have two key roles to play. First a charismatic one, through which they ensure that the organization has an understood vision and direction, people are empowered and as a consequence they energize, stimulate and galvanize change. Secondly, an architectural role of establishing an appropriate structure and style for both control and reward. Effective leaders succeed when strategies are owned by those who must implement them, customers are satisfied, people enjoy their work and things happen in the organization – specifically, the necessary changes are quick and timely.

Extending the themes, Figure 3.6 reinforces earlier comments about how strategic leadership is crucial for establishing (and changing) both competency and the corporate 'strategic logic' of the organization. With the latter we are considering whether or not the organization's corporate portfolio and its competitive strategy or strategies 'make sense' and can be justified, or appear to be a recipe for poor or disappointing performance.

A strong and well-managed portfolio will be reflected in successful and effective competitive and functional strategies and in operating efficiency. Also important and relevant manifestations are the image, visibility and reputation of the organization, its strategic leader and its products and services, factors which can be managed and can have a bearing on many things, but which are tricky to evaluate and measure, particularly by the organization itself. Largely, they are the subjective opinion of external experts and stakeholders.

There are three distinctive broad approaches to measuring outcomes. These are:

- *Financial results* and other market-driven quantitative measures such as market share
- *Stakeholder satisfaction*, reflected in the balanced scorecard and similar packages
- *Admiration*, for example the annual reviews carried out by *Fortune* in the USA and *Management Today* in the UK.

This chapter now looks briefly at corporate logic, and then at admiration, image and reputation, financial measurement and stakeholder measures to explain the linkages in Figure 3.6.

Corporate strategic logic

Caulkin (1995) stresses that the average life expectancy of successful UK companies is some 40–50 years. He has shown how only nine of the 30 companies used to make up the first Financial Times share index in 1935 still existed in their

Figure 3.6   Strategic performance evaluation.

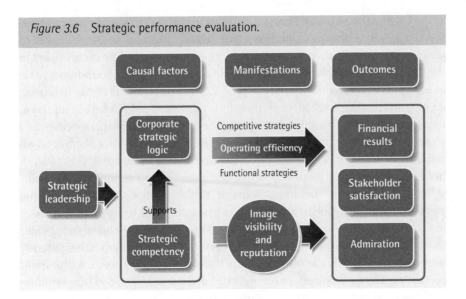

own right 60 years later. Several others were still in existence but under new ownership. Some had been liquidated; many had been acquired and absorbed by their new corporate parents. It is inevitable that every one of the companies will have seen major strategic and/or structural changes of some kind.

It has long been recognized that businesses which succeed in maintaining real growth over a number of years quickly abandon their early dependence on a single product or service. As they increase the range of activities in their portfolio, a key strategic issue is the extent of their diversity. Some will diversify only around related markets, processes and technologies; many others have historically chosen to move into completely unrelated areas. Although General Electric, a genuinely diversified conglomerate spanning manufacturing, television and financial services, enjoys the status of one of the world's largest and most successful companies – due in no small way to the style of its chief executive, Jack Welch – the attractiveness of real diversity has waned. Sadtler *et al.* (1997) defend the case for a clear focus, built around a defensible core of related activities, and in this they reflect current practice.

Admired companies

Sound profits and a strong balance sheet are very important, but alone they will not necessarily lead to a company being 'admired'. In the 1980s, and based on research in the USA by *Fortune*, the *Economist* began to investigate which companies are most admired by other business people, particularly those with whom they compete directly. More recently, *Management Today* has taken over the project in the UK and the *Financial Times* in association with Price Waterhouse later initiated a parallel European and then a global study. Business people are asked to allocate marks against certain criteria for their main rivals. The criteria used in the UK survey are as follows: quality of management; financial soundness; value as a long-term investment; quality of products and services; the ability to attract, develop and retain top talent; capacity to innovate; quality of marketing; and community and environmental responsibility. These reflect multiple perspectives and stakeholder interests; and consequently the *Economist* (1991) argues that admiration encourages customers to buy more and to stay loyal, employees to work harder, suppliers to be more supportive and shareholders also to remain loyal.

Table 3.1 features the most admired British companies for the period 1994–1999, tracking the relative progress in the charts of the top five businesses in both 1994 and 1999. The results for 2000 are listed at the end of the chapter (p. 155). Tesco stands out as the one business which has been ranked consistently over a period of years; the other winners have enjoyed more mixed fortunes. In particular, Marks and Spencer has declined dramatically in 1999 (the explanation can be found in Case Study 1 earlier). In general, British service businesses also score very highly in the European poll but, significantly, the manufacturing sections are normally dominated by German, Swedish and Swiss companies. In a second vote, business people have often been asked for their views on all companies, not just those in their own industry sector. Marks and Spencer was the clear winner here for several years in the mid-1990s, reinforcing the extent of its recent fall from grace.

Table 3.1 Britain's most admired companies, 1994–1999

Company	1994	1995	1996	1997	1998	1999
			Position			
Tesco	31	4	1	2	1	1
SmithKline Beecham	4	14	7	8	5	2
Glaxo (Wellcome)	2	13	11	4	6	3
Daily Mail	28	47	43	40	12	4
Cadbury Schweppes	7	1	5	16	2	5
Rentokil (Initial)	1	11	30	14	37	56
Marks and Spencer	3	7	4	3	11	> 125
Unilever	5	2	16	6	7	7

Covers the progress over 6 years of the top 5 in 1994 and top 5 in 1999.
Source: *Management Today* (every November issue).

The ten most admired American companies (*Fortune*, 2000) in 1999 were:

1. General Electric
2. Microsoft
3. Dell Computers
3. Cisco Systems
5. Wal-Mart
6. Southwest Airlines
7. Berkshire Hathaway
8. Intel
9. Home Depot
10. Lucent Technologies.

A number of observations can be made:

- In an era of strategic focus, an extensively diversified company is the most admired – and globally as well (see Table 3.2). The important contribution of General Electric's strategic leader, Jack Welch, in ensuring that there is a cohesive and synergistic link between strategy, structure and style will emerge throughout this book.
- Unlike the UK, the chart of winners is dominated by computing, networks and semiconductor companies, of which there are five in the top ten.

Table 3.2   The world's most respected companies, 1998–2000

		Year		
		1998	**1999**	**2000**
Position	1	General Electric	General Electric	General Electric
	2	Microsoft	Microsoft	Microsoft
	3	Coca-Cola	Coca-Cola	Sony
	4	IBM	IBM	Coca-Cola
	5	Toyota	Daimler-Chrysler	IBM

Position of best-placed UK companies

12	Royal Dutch Shell	20	Unilever	21	Vodaphone
27	Body Shop	21	Royal Dutch Shell	23 =	Royal Dutch Shell
35 =	British Airways	28	BP/Amoco	23 =	BP/Amoco
35 =	Marks and Spencer	32	British Airways	28 =	Virgin
35 =	Unilever	41	Lloyds/TSB	37	Unilever

Sources: The World's Most Respected Companies, *Financial Times* Survey, 7 December 1999; 15 December 2000.
http://surveys.ft.com (past surveys) – www.globalarchive.ft.com

- The extremely successful and remarkable Berkshire Hathaway is included. Run by entrepreneur Warren Buffett, Berkshire Hathaway is neither a manufacturing nor a service business; instead it is an investment vehicle for its shareholders' funds. Minority shareholdings in a range of companies, including Coca-Cola, are typically held for the long term. Notably, high-technology companies are avoided because of their perceived inherent uncertainty.

It is also interesting that McDonald's is perceived by American business people to be their most socially responsible company, a view clearly not held by many environmental protest groups around the world.

Table 3.2 shows the world's most respected companies for 1998–2000. Notably, General Electric also tops this poll, with Microsoft following up. The other American giants included here, Coca-Cola, IBM and Daimler-Chrysler are, interestingly, not in the US top ten listed above. It is also noticeable that the British companies which enjoy the most respect globally are quite different from those admired 'at home'.

Another survey in the UK by BMRB/Mintel (see Summers, 1995) asked a sample of consumers which companies they perceive offer good value for money, understand their market, are trustworthy and care about the environment. Boots won every category except for environmental concern, where it came second to The Body Shop. Inevitably, the winning companies in a poll such as this will be those with high visibility and presence, especially retailing organizations, reflecting the value of a good corporate image. Ironically, Marks and Spencer did not appear in the top ten in any category.

Yet another related survey is the British Quality of Management awards (see Houlder, 1997), where Marks and Spencer were again placed first for three consecutive years in the mid-1990s, this time followed by British Airways and Glaxo Wellcome. The polling here is conducted by MORI, who seek opinions on a selection of key issues from institutional investors, company chief executives and business journalists. One significant fact to emerge is that different categories of judges prioritize the significant issues in different ways. Journalists see innovation as vitally important, whereas it receives much lower priority from industrialists in the MORI poll. By contrast, Price Waterhouse concluded that both industrialists and analysts see innovation as the most important factor of all. Interestingly, strategic leadership is not recorded as a particularly high priority for fund managers by MORI, but the following comment was made about ABB's success in the European poll:

> *The biggest asset may well be the charismatic figure of its chairman [Percy Barnevik]*
> *. . . who is identified as an outstanding business leader.*

Asea Brown Boveri (ABB) is a Swedish–Swiss engineering conglomerate.

Financial success alone certainly does not guarantee admiration from competitors and popularity with all the stakeholders; at the same time, as evidenced by The Body Shop over a period of years, deteriorating financial returns will bother shareholders far more than customers! Fisher (1996) has argued that admiration placings in the USA can certainly affect the stock price both positively and negatively, yet the extent to which financial performance affects the admiration marks remains less clear.

While several tentative conclusions might be drawn from these polls, prolonged debate is outside the scope of this book. However, it is worth emphasizing three points: first, fortunes can change very quickly; secondly, admiration seems to be affected by short-term changes of fortune; and thirdly, the various polls on the same themes are themselves not always consistent, although some patterns can be traced.

Image, reputation and strategic panache

A well-recognized and positive image and reputation appear to improve the admiration rankings; and, correspondingly, linkage with a major corporate mistake or mishandled crisis has a negative effect, especially if social and ethical responsibilities are involved. The next issue to be addressed, therefore, concerns the relative value of a good reputation and high visibility. Could reputation, inevitably a subjective judgement, actually help to cover up a relatively poor financial performance, itself a more objective measurement? Fombrum (1996) contends that reputations create economic value, and that image, because it embodies the company's uniqueness, is a key competitive tool. He uses this as an argument in favour of benchmarking those companies perceived to be the leading performers, to ensure that no critical gaps are left open.

We have seen that General Electric, Microsoft and Coca-Cola are the world's most respected companies. It is significant that General Electric (Jack Welch) and Microsoft (Bill Gates) have highly respected strategic leaders and, if we accept Windows as a brand, two of the three have hugely popular and instantly recognizable *brands* that are systematically encircling the globe. Until his sudden, early death Coca-Cola's long-time strategic leader, Roberto Goizueta, was also highly respected.

> Virgin may be innovative and Body Shop may be ethical, but the main thing that distinguishes these companies from the pack is how hard they shout about their achievements.
>
> *Columnist Lucy Kellaway writing*
> *in the Financial Times,*
> *23 September 1996*

Brands can give a company visibility, sometimes international visibility. When a prominent brand becomes associated with trust and quality, its corporate owner should be in a position to command premium prices, although some of this is needed to cover the extra promotional costs required to sustain the brand's visibility. Companies are increasingly including their brands as balance-sheet assets and attempting to place a value on them. Usefully for consumers, sensible companies will invest in their brands in order to improve them and sustain their competitive leadership. We return to this issue in Chapter 7.

The relative value of a charismatic, high-profile and media-friendly – or even media-chasing – strategic leader is more difficult to quantify, although the reality of their impact is not in question.

The thinking behind Figure 3.7 recognizes that competency and reputation may or may not be aligned. Some companies enjoy a reputation which exceeds their true competency if it is evaluated objectively; as long as they are not actually incompetent this must surely be good for them, but only in the short run! This situation could be the product of history, trading on past success, which clearly can only last for some finite time; it could equally be that they are simply very good publicists. Meanwhile, others fail to exploit their real worth and competency.

Figure 3.7   Competency, recognition and success.

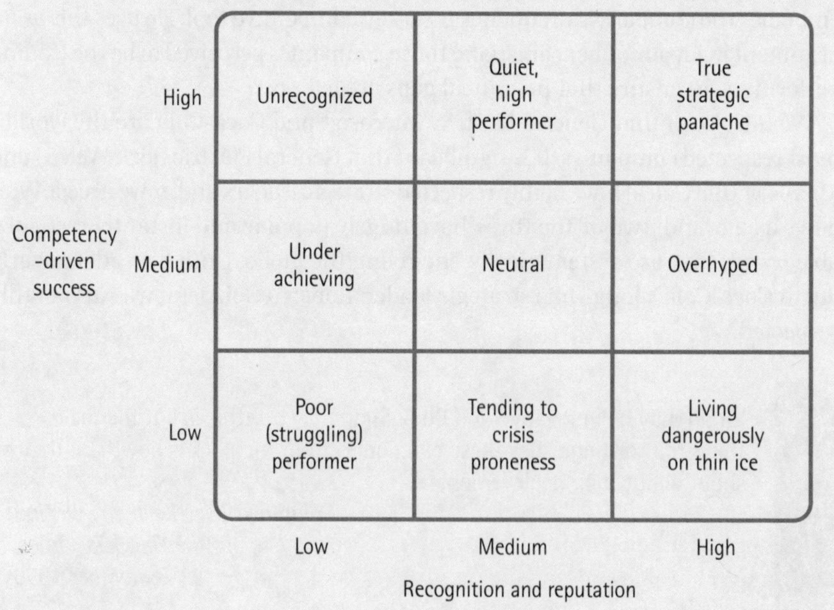

Competency-driven success		Recognition and reputation		
	High	Unrecognized	Quiet, high performer	True strategic panache
	Medium	Under achieving	Neutral	Overhyped
	Low	Poor (struggling) performer	Tending to crisis proneness	Living dangerously on thin ice
		Low	Medium	High

Figure 3.7 uses the phrase '*strategic panache companies*' to describe those organizations that are competent, successful, highly visible and widely recognized. Such companies are doing the right things (effectiveness), they know that they are doing them well (properly measured efficiency) and they are recognized for their achievements. Their challenge is to maintain both their competency and reputation, because otherwise their visibility could become their downfall. It is clearly a prized spot in the matrix, but it is not without a potential downside.

Quiet high performers are less visible and always really underachieving, but only to a limited degree. This is a lower-risk approach, but because the companies are less prominent, it could pay off in the long term. The secret lies in not becoming unrecognized.

Companies whose reputation exceeds their competency and success over a prolonged period must be in danger of becoming crisis prone as they increasingly fail to live up to the expectations of their stakeholders. Where success is drifting, but a company still enjoys a sound reputation, ideally this reputation should be used to 'buy time' and drive through competency improvements. Sadly, in a number of cases, it will not, and once-successful businesses will find themselves in need of major turnaround if they are to avoid liquidation. This frequently requires the creation of new strategic competencies, and is often associated with a change of leadership.

Admiration, image and reputation are not correlated closely with financial performance. While there are understandable reasons for this the implication has to be that no single 'measure' can be taken as a comprehensive assessment. This point is debated further in Thompson (1998).

Financial measures

A plethora of financial performance measures has long been used to help evaluate the relative success and progress of a business; there is no suggestion here that this should cease to be the case. These measures include ratios such as return on capital employed and return on shareholders' funds, earnings per share, the share price itself and the price to earnings ratio. Typically, a company's share price performance will be evaluated against the relevant industry average and against one of the *Financial Times* indices. While these are objective within the constraints of accounting practice and convention, there are two points to note. First, although analysts always seem to stress profitability, relating pre- or after-tax profits to either sales, capital employed or shareholders' funds, press headlines are more likely to focus on the specific growth or decline in revenues and actual profits made. Secondly, share prices are also affected by future expectation, and a plausible and convincing strategic leader can be persuasive about 'better times being on the way'.

An analysis of financial ratios is useful for a number of reasons.

- It enables a study of trends and progress over a number of years to be made.
- Comparisons with competitors and with general industry trends are possible.
- It can point the way towards possible or necessary improvements – necessary if the organization is performing less and less well than competitors, useful if new opportunities are spotted.
- It can reveal lost profit and growth potential.
- It can emphasize possible dangers – for example, if stock turnover is decreasing or ratios affecting cash flow are moving adversely.

Financial analysis concentrates on efficiency rather than effectiveness unless the objectives are essentially financial or economic ones. The real measure of success, as far as the strategic leader and the various stakeholders are concerned, is whether or not the objectives that they perceive as important are being achieved.

Outside analysts, such as students and interested readers, can gain some insight into the apparent objectives of an organization by reading annual reports, articles, press releases and so on, but only the people involved in decision making know the real objectives and whether they are being achieved. Financial analysis from the published (and easily obtained) results can be very informative and lead to conclusions about how well a company is performing, but certain aspects remain hidden. Decision makers inside an organization use financial analysis as part of the wider picture, but outsiders are more restricted. Financial analysis, then, is a very useful form of analysis, and it should be used, but the wider aspects should not be overlooked.

More recently, *economic value added* (EVA; see, for example, Lynn, 1995) has been adopted as another measure. EVA compares a company's after-tax operating profits with its cost of capital.

A more detailed treatment of financial measures is included as a Finance in Action supplement to this chapter.

Stakeholder measures

The important *Tomorrow's Company* report (RSA, 1995), written in an attempt to improve the competitiveness of UK industry in global markets, concluded that there is:

- complacency and ignorance about world-class standards
- an overreliance on financial measures which often focus attention on the short rather than the long term
- a national adversarial culture which fails to integrate stakeholders into a cohesive network of interdependent organizations.

The preferred solution lies in a more holistic approach which incorporates the interests of multiple stakeholders. Implicit here is a clear realization that both measurement and organizational learning must encompass both what is happening inside an organization and what is emerging in the outside environment. This accords with the ideas behind the '*balanced scorecard*' approach of Kaplan and Norton (1992, 1996).

Kaplan and Norton suggest that organizations should focus their efforts on a limited number of specific, critical performance measures which reflect stakeholders' key success factors. In this way managers can readily concentrate on those issues which are essential for corporate and competitive success.

Kaplan and Norton use the term 'balanced scorecard' to describe a framework of four groups of measures, and argue that organizations should select critical measures for each one of these areas. The four groups, and examples of possible measures, are:

- financial – return on capital employed; cash flow
- customers – perceived value for money; competitive prices
- internal processes – enquiry response time; enquiry to order conversion rate
- growth and improvement – number of new products/services; extent of employee empowerment.

These measures encapsulate both efficiency and effectiveness. Figure 3.8 illustrates the synergistic dependencies and linkages between the four groups of measures. These have a close relationship with the competency linkages mentioned in the Introduction to this chapter, and featured on the right-hand side of the figure.

Measuring effectiveness requires a recognition that quality does not mean the same things for every customer. Organizations must determine what will generate repeat business and seek to provide it. Supermarkets, for example, can offer service in the form of a wide range of products, brand choice for each product in the range, low prices, fast checkout and ample car parking. Stores can focus aggressively on one or more of these or seek a balanced profile. The major chains will have a basic competitive posture and then tailor each store to meet local conditions.

The Measurement of Success in Not-for-profit Organizations

It was suggested in Chapter 2 that the objectives of not-for-profit organizations are often stated in terms of resource efficiency because of the difficulty of quantifying their real purpose. As a result, the measures of their success that are used in practice may not be closely related to their real mission and purpose. Where

Figure 3.8   Stakeholder measurements.

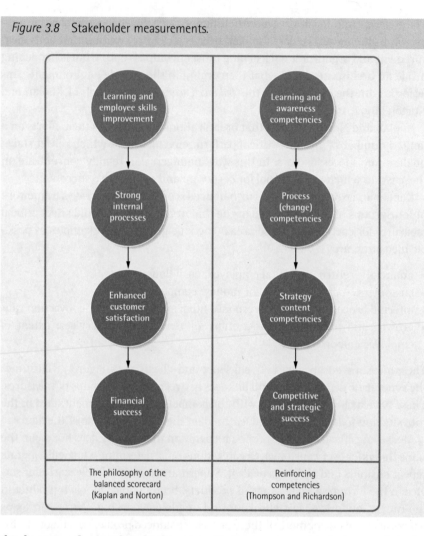

| The philosophy of the balanced scorecard (Kaplan and Norton) | Reinforcing competencies (Thompson and Richardson) |

this happens, financial and other quantitative measures are being used as the measures of performance, and efficiency not effectiveness is being evaluated. In other words, performance and success is being measured, but despite the usefulness of, and need for, the measures being used, they may not be assessing strategic performance directly in relation to the mission. These points are expanded below.

Drucker (1989) comments that many not-for-profit organizations are more money conscious than business enterprises are because the funding they need is hard to raise. Moreover, they could invariably use more money than they have available. Money, however, is less likely to be the key element of their mission and strategic thinking than are the provision of services and the satisfaction of client needs. Given this premise, the successful performance of a not-for-profit organization should be measured in terms of outcomes and need satisfaction. Money then becomes a major constraint upon what can be accomplished and the appropriate level of expectations.

The outcomes, in turn, must be analysed against the expectations of the important stakeholders. For many organizations in this sector this involves both beneficiaries of the service and volunteer helpers as well as financial supporters and paid employees. Typically their personal objectives and expectations will differ.

But what is the case in reality? How difficult is it to measure performance and success in this way? Fundamentally, the Boy Scout and Girl Guide organizations are concerned with helping youngsters to develop and grow into confident and capable young men and women. But do they evaluate their success in this respect or in terms of, say, membership and monetary income which, being essentially quantitative, are far easier to measure? Similarly, it would be inadequate to claim success because of a general feeling that good was being done and that young people must be benefiting from their membership. The real measures of success concern the changes that take place outside the organization as a result of the organization's efforts.

As another example, the success of local meals-on-wheels services is related to their impact on the health and life expectancy of the elderly rather than to the number of meals served or the cost per meal.

The performance and effectiveness of the education system relate to the impact on pupils after they leave the system, their parents, the taxpayers who fund education and future employers. Their perspectives will differ, and their individual aspirations and expectations will be difficult to quantify and measure. It is far easier to measure efficiency in the way that resources are utilized, for example by class sizes, staff/student or staff/pupil ratios, building occupancy and examination performance.

Similarly, local authorities exist to serve local residents, and their mission is concerned with making the area a better place in which to live. Would all the residents agree on what is implied by 'a better place in which to live', and could changes be objectively measured and evaluated? Because of the difficulties, value for money from the resources invested is more likely to be considered, and improvements in the efficiency of service provision sought.

If a charity seeks to save money by minimizing administration and promotion expenditures it is focusing on short-term efficiency. If it concentrates on long-term effectiveness it may well be able to justify investing in marketing and administration in order to raise even more money. A charity that spends some 60% of its current income on administration and marketing (and the rest on its directly charitable activities) could well, in the long run, be more effective than one that spends only 20% in this way. The aim is to establish the most appropriate structure, administration network and promotional expenditure to achieve the purpose, and then run it efficiently.

The not-for-profit sector is increasingly attempting to measure effectiveness in terms of impacts and outcomes rather than efficiency alone. The task is not straightforward.

Value for money looks at the relationship between the perceived value of the output (by the stakeholders involved) and the cost of inputs. Essentially it is used as a comparative measure. There are too many uncertainties for there to be any true agreement on the magnitude of 'very best value', and consequently one is seeking to ensure that good value is being provided, when measured against that of other similar, or competitive, providers.

If we consider both inputs and outcomes then we are considering the efficiency and effectiveness of the organization's transformation processes, its ability to add value. With certain non-profit organizations, such as the UK National Health Service (NHS), it is also tempting to make international comparisons. How much per head of the population is spent on health care? What percentage of gross domestic product does this represent? Again, these are input measures when it is outcomes that matter. The life expectancy of British people and the infant mortality rate are critically important outcomes but, while health care makes an important contribution, it is not the only causal factor.

Jackson and Palmer (1989) emphasize that if performance is to be measured more effectively in the public sector, then the implicit cultural and change issues must also be addressed, a point that was addressed in Chapter 2. The climate must be right, with managers committed to thinking clearly about what activities should be measured and what the objectives of these activities are. This may well involve different reward systems linked to revised expectations. This approach, they suggest, leads managers to move on from measuring the numbers of passengers on the railway network to analysing how many had seats and how punctual the trains were; and measuring and analysing the numbers of patients readmitted to hospital after treatment, rather than just the numbers of patients who are admitted and the rate of usage of hospital beds. Jackson and Palmer also emphasize the importance of asking users about how effective they perceive organizations to be.

A Holistic Framework of Measures

Figure 3.9 offers an outline framework for reflecting on the measurement demands facing an organization. It is based on the premise that a competitive and strategically successful organization will achieve and, with changes, sustain, a congruency among its environment (key success factors), resources (compe-

Figure 3.9   A holistic framework of measures.

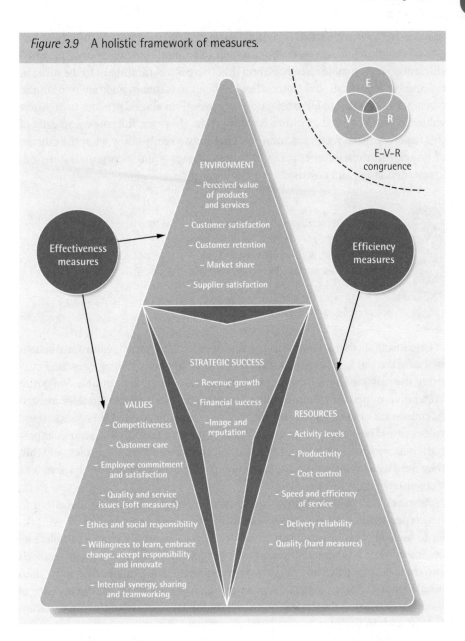

tencies and capabilities) and values (the ability to manage appropriate and timely continuous and discontinuous change). A small reminder of this E-V-R congruence model is provided in the top right corner.

While corporate strategic success is concerned with the mission and purpose of the organization, it will frequently be assessed by financial measures of some form, as highlighted earlier. Long-term strategic success requires that the interests of stakeholders are met, and are seen to be met, that this is accomplished efficiently with capable resources, and that there is a commitment to the mission reflected in organizational values. The implication is that in addition to resource efficiency and stakeholder satisfaction, organizations should attempt to measure values to ensure that the culture is appropriate. However, the true complexity of this task is realized when we question whether we really know what the culture of an organization in an era of continuous change – and incorporating periodic restructurings and downsizings – should be like.

> In a very turbulent, rapidly changing time what we need to give people is something they can depend on, something lasting. Every company needs to rethink what are the values and what are the operating principles that will be unchanging in time so that we can truly establish a new contract with all employees.
>
> *George Fisher, Chairman, Eastman Kodak*

Organizations that attempt this will first need to clarify which values and behaviours are critical for carrying out corporate and competitive strategies, and pursuing the mission, both now and in the future. In 1991, for example, Yorkshire Water determined that their key values were: trust, loyalty, pride, honesty, integrity, endeavour, quality, service/excellence and competitiveness. Adherence to these values would be manifested in a number of behaviour traits. It was seen as important that employees were committed to, and confident about, their roles, and that they were suitably empowered and rewarded. Effective communications networks were also thought to be vital.

Research can capture a snapshot of currently held values and the extent to which particular behaviours are being manifested. Some organizations will prefer to use volunteers from among the workforce rather than select a sample. The findings should be evaluated against a set of expectancies, and follow-up research can track both positive and negative developments. The organization must then decide what action to take if there is any deterioration or the initial absence of a critical value or behaviour pattern. Changing the culture of the organization is dealt with in Chapter 4.

It will, therefore, be realized that the Figure 3.9 framework implies a series of both hard and soft measures and indicators. Some will be straightforward, others far more difficult and subjective. Arguably the real key to success lies in those issues that are most difficult to assess. This is no excuse for not attempting a robust assessment of some form, even though it is sometimes easy to argue a case based on unsubstantiated opinion which, when rigorously probed, turns out to be a delusion. It is all too easy for senior managers to argue for what they would like to believe is a reality: that their company is competitive, that it is committed to quality and service, and that their employees are committed and supportive. They need to check these things out!

Summary

At a most basic level of argument, an organization is successful if it is meeting the needs and expectations of its stakeholders, such that their support and commitment are maintained.

Strategically, this will imply a clear direction, from which are derived corporate, competitive and functional strategies, the implementation of which brings about the desired results. This needs both common sense and strategic competency.

Measurement matters. Apparent success cannot, and must not, be taken for granted. Nor must weaknesses be overlooked. We must measure those issues which really matter. The act of measurement focuses attention and endeavour on that which is being measured: being brilliant at things that do not really matter to stakeholders will not add and build value.

Some key elements will, through their very nature, be difficult to measure. They are essentially subjective and qualitative issues rather than objective and quantifiable. This is no excuse to avoid tackling them; instead we have to rely on indicators rather than measures of performance.

In some cases attention is focused on *efficiency* measures, which largely concern the utilization of resources. We are evaluating whether or not we are 'doing things right'. Measures and indicators of *effectiveness* look more at outcomes (for stakeholders) and provide a check on whether we are 'doing the right things'.

Most organizations use a raft of quantitative *measures*, embracing sales and production. Analysts external to the organization, such as students – and lecturers, come to that – will not normally have access to this information to draw conclusions from. However, financial data have to be published and can be used to calculate a number of valuable ratios which provide some insight into organizational performance. In the Finance in Action supplement to this chapter investment, performance, solvency and liquidity ratios are explained.

The '*balanced scorecard*' approach provides a more comprehensive set of measures which cover stakeholders. The four categories for measurement are: finance; customers; internal processes; and growth and improvement.

It is also relevant to look at issues of *admiration, image* and *reputation*. These evaluations are normally by people inside the relevant industries and therefore provide an insight into how organizations are rated by their competitors and peers. There is, however, a short-term focus in this approach. Companies that are highly regarded will not necessarily be those with the strongest financial results. Although there is some link between the most admired American and the most respected global companies, those British companies that enjoy the greatest international admiration are not those held in the highest regard 'at home'.

The term '*strategic panache*' has been adopted to cover those companies that are not only successful but also seen to be successful and thus are highly regarded. Charismatic strategic leadership and strong brands are often major contributors to strategic pananche.

In isolation, therefore, any single measure or type of measure must be treated cautiously.

Consequently, the chapter concluded with a holistic framework of measures derived from the E–V–R congruence model.

References

Atkinson, AA *et al.* (1997) A stakeholder approach to strategic performance measurement, *Sloan Management Review*, Spring.

Caulkin, S (1995) The pursuit of immortality, *Management Today*, May.

Drucker, PF (1989) What businesses can learn from nonprofits, *Harvard Business Review*, July–August.

Economist (1991) Britain's Most Admired Companies, 26 January.

Fisher, AB (1996) Corporate reputations, *Fortune*, 4 March.

Fombrum, CJ (1996) *Reputation – Realising the Value from the Corporate Image*, Harvard Business School Press.

Houlder, V (1997) What makes a winner? *Financial Times*, 19 March.

IRS (1997) IRS Management Review No. 5, *Measuring Performance*, April.

Jackson, P and Palmer, R (1989) *First Steps in Measuring Performance in the Public Sector*, Public Finance Foundation, London.

Kaplan, RS and Norton DP (1996) *The Balanced Scorecard*, Harvard Business School Press. See also: The balanced scorecard – measures that drive performance, *Harvard Business Review*, January–February 1992.

Kets de Vries, M (1996) Leaders who make a difference, *European Management Journal*, 14, 5, October.

Lynn, M (1995) Creating wealth: the best and the worst, *Sunday Times*, 10 December.

May, GD and Kruger, MJ (1988) The manager within, *Personnel Journal*, 67, 2.

Reid, W and Myddelton, DR (1974) *The Meaning of Company Accounts*, 2nd edn, Gower. The quotation in the Finance in Action supplement was taken from this second edition, but there are later editions.

RSA (1995) *Tomorrow's Company: The Role of Business in a Changing World*.

Ruddle, K and Feeny, D (1997) Transforming the Organization: New Approaches to Management, Measurement and Leadership, Research Report, Templeton College, Oxford.

Sadtler, D, Campbell, A and Koch, R (1997) *Break-up. When Large Companies are Worth More Dead Than Alive*, Capstone.

Summers, D (1995) Boots comes top in corporate image poll, *Financial Times*, 23 October.

Thompson, JL (1998) Competency and measured performance outcomes, *Journal of Workplace Learning – Employee Counselling Today*, 10, 5. This paper can be found in full on the website accompanying this book.

Thompson, JL and Richardson, B (1996) Strategic and competitive success – towards a model of the comprehensively competent organization, *Management Decision*, 34, 2.

Towers Perrin (1997) Workplace index. Summarized in Bolger, A (1997) Workers feel their just reward, *Financial Times*, 26 September.

Notes

Britain's most admired companies 2000 – see *Management Today*, December (2000).

1 Glaxo/SmithKline (recently merged)
2 BP/Amoco
3 Shell Transport
4 Cadbury Schweppes
5 Tesco

Test your knowledge of this chapter with our online quiz at:
http://www.thomsonlearning.co.uk

Explore Measuring Success further at:

Economist   http://www.economist.com
Fortune   http://www.fortune.com/fortune
IRS Management Review   http://www.irseclipse.co.uk/publications/irsmr.html
Journal of Workplace Learning   http://www.mcb.co.uk/jurl.htm
Management Decision   http://www.mcb.co.uk/md.htm
RSA Journal   http://www.rsa.org.uk/publications/journal.html
Sloan Management Review   http://www.mitsloan.mit.edu/smr/main.html
Sunday Times   http://www.sunday-times.co.uk

Questions and Research Assignments

TEXT RELATED

1. The purpose of the Metropolitan Police Service is to: 'uphold the law fairly and firmly; to prevent crime; to pursue and bring to justice those who break the law; to keep the Queen's peace; to protect, help and reassure people in London; and to be seen to do all this with integrity, common sense and sound judgement'. How might they measure their success?

2. The Royal Charter for the Royal National Institute for the Blind (RNIB), granted originally in 1949, states that the RNIB exists in order to:
   - 'promote the better education, training, employment and welfare of the blind
   - protect the interests of the blind; and
   - prevent blindness.'
   How might they assess how well they are doing?

Internet and Library Projects

1. In early 2000 Microsoft was judged by the American courts to have been operating as a monopoly and stifling competition. How have its reputation, respect and admiration been affected by this judgement and also by subsequent moves by both the company and the competition authorities?

   Microsoft   http://www.microsoft.com

2. Select a number of organizations from Tables 3.1 and/or 3.2 (or the *Fortune* list), picking out ones that interest you personally. Obtain their financial results for at least two years which correspond with the admiration rankings. To what extent are financial performance and admiration linked? By also checking the movements in the company's share prices over the same period, does the company's market valuation more closely reflect financial performance or a wider perception of its relative performance?

3. The National Health Service
   British Prime Minister John Major announced a new Citizen's Charter in July 1991. This implied a change of attitude for the NHS: patients should be seen as customers with rights, rather than people who should be grateful for treatment, however long the wait. From April 1992 hospitals would have to set standards for maximum waiting times.

This followed on from the 1989 NHS White Paper, *Working for Patients*, which was designed to achieve:

- raising the performance of all hospitals and general practitioners (GPs) to the level of the best (significant differences existed in measured performances)
- patients receiving better health care and a greater choice of services through improved efficiencies and effectiveness in the use of NHS resources
- greater satisfaction and rewards for NHS staff.

In subsequent years, how has this impacted on NHS strategies, and how have these also been affected by a change of government? How have performance measures and indicators been brought into line?

Citizen's Charter   http://www.cabinet-office.gov.uk/servicefirst

NHS   http://www.nhs50,nhs.uk

Finance in Action

Financial Analysis

The published financial accounts of a company, as long as they are interpreted carefully, can tell a good deal about the company's activities and about how well it is doing. This section concentrates on three main aspects, examining the financial measures and what they can tell us, and considers the strategic implications. The three aspects are as follows.

- *Investment*: How do the results relate to shareholders and the funds they have provided, and to the company's share price?
- *Performance*: How successfully is the business being run as a trading concern? Here we are concerned not so much with profit as with profitability. How well is the company using the capital it employs to generate sales and in turn profits?
- *Financial status*: Is the company solvent and liquid? Is it financially sound?

The ratios calculated in each of these categories have relevance for different stakeholders. Shareholders, and potential investors, are particularly concerned with the investment ratios. Performance ratios tell the strategic leader how well the company is doing as a business. Bankers and other providers of loan capital will want to know that the business is solvent and liquid in addition to how well it is performing.

This form of analysis is most relevant for profit-seeking businesses, although some of the measures can prove quite enlightening when applied to not-for-profit organizations.

Ratios are calculated from the published accounts of organizations, but an analysis of just one set of results will only be partly helpful. Trends are particularly important, and therefore the changes in results over a number of years should be evaluated. Care should be taken to ensure that the results are not considered in isolation of external trends in the economy or industry. For example, the company's sales may be growing quickly, but how do they compare with those of their competitors and the industry as a whole? Similarly, slow growth may be explained by industry contraction, although in turn this might indicate the need for diversification.

Hence, industry averages and competitor performance should be used for comparisons. One problem here is that different companies may present their accounts in different ways and the figures will have to be interpreted before any meaningful comparisons can be made. Furthermore, the industry may be composed of companies of varying sizes and various degrees of conglomeration and diversification. For this reason certain companies may be expected to behave differently from their competitors.

In addition, it can be useful to compare the actual results with forecasts, although these will not normally be available to people outside the organization. The usefulness is dependent on how well the forecasts and budgets were prepared.

Financial Statements

The two most important statements used for calculating ratios are the profit and loss account and the balance sheet, simplified versions of which are illustrated in Tables 3.3 and 3.4. The full accounts may be required in order to make certain adjustments.

From the profit and loss account (Table 3.3) we wish to extract a number of figures. Gross profit is the trading profit before overheads are allocated. It is the difference between the value of sales (or turnover) and the direct costs involved

Table 3.3 Simplified profit and loss account

			£
	Sales/turnover		
less:	Costs of goods sold		
		equals	Gross profit
less:	Depreciation Selling costs Administration costs		
		equals	Profit before interest and tax*
less:	Interest on loans		
		equals	Profit before tax
less:	Tax		
		equals	Profit after tax
less:	Dividends		
		equals	Retained earnings (transferred to balance sheet)

*In published accounts this figure will not always be shown. It is required, however, for the calculation of certain ratios.

in producing the product(s) or service(s), which is known as the contribution. In the case of multiproduct or multiservice organizations, where it may be difficult to attribute overheads to different products and services accurately, comparison should be made between the contributions from different divisions or strategic business units.

When depreciation and selling and administrative overheads are subtracted from gross profit the remainder is profit before interest and before tax. This is the net profit that the organization has achieved from its trading activities; no account has yet been taken of the cost of funding. This figure is not normally shown in published accounts; it has to be calculated by adding interest back onto profit before tax.

Table 3.4 Simplified balance sheet

Information required for ratio calculations			Conventional presentation of figures in published accounts
	Fixed assets	(Land; property buildings; plant and equipment)	**Fixed assets**
plus	**Current assets**	(Stock; debtors; cash and investments)	plus **Current assets**
less	**Current liabilities**	(Creditors: amounts falling due within one year; specifically trade creditors, overdraft, taxation not yet paid)	less **Current liabilities**
equals	**Net assets**		equals **Total assets** less **Current liabilities**
	Long-term loans	Generally termed creditors: amounts falling due after more than one year)	plus **long-term loans**
			equals **Total net assets**
plus	**Shareholders' funds**	(Called-up share capital: share premium account; revaluation reserve; profit and loss account)	**Shareholders' funds**
equals	**Total capital employed**		
Net assets equals		**Total capital employed**	**Total net assets** = **Shareholders' funds**

Profit before tax is the figure resulting when interest charges have been removed. Tax is levied on this profit figure, and when this is deducted profit after tax remains. This represents the profits left for shareholders, and a proportion will be paid over to them immediately in the form of dividends; the remainder will be reinvested in the future growth of the company. It will be transferred to the balance sheet as retained earnings (or profit and loss) and shown as a reserve attributable to shareholders.

This simplified outline excludes the need to, and value of, clearly separating the revenue and profits from ongoing businesses or continuing activities, recent acquisitions and discontinued activities.

Balance sheets are now normally laid out in the format illustrated on the right in Table 3.4. Assets are shown at the top and the capital employed to finance the assets below.

Fixed assets comprise all the land, property, plant and equipment owned by the business. These will be depreciated annually at varying rates. Balance sheets generally reflect historical costs (the preferred accounting convention), but occasionally assets may be revalued to account for inflation (land and property values can increase significantly over a number of years) and any ratios calculated from an asset figure will be affected by this issue of up-to-date valuations.

Current assets, assets which are passing through the business rather than more permanent features and which comprise stocks (raw materials, work-in-progress and finished goods), debtors (customers who are allowed to buy on credit rather than for cash), investments and cash, are added on. Current liabilities, short-term financial commitments, are deducted. These include the overdraft, tax payments due and trade creditors (suppliers who have yet to be paid for goods and services supplied).

The left-hand column of Table 3.4 shows the resultant figure as net assets, which is equal to the total capital employed in the business, or the sum of long-term loans and shareholders' funds. The right-hand column differs slightly and presents net assets as total assets minus the sum of current liabilities and long-term loans – and therefore equal to shareholders' funds. This is the normal way in which a company will present its accounts, leaving us to calculate a figure for total capital employed.

Long-term loans are typically called 'creditors: amounts falling due after more than one year'. Shareholders' funds are made up of the called-up share capital (the face value of the shares issued), the share premium account (money accrued as shareholders have bought shares for more than their face value, dependent on stock market prices at the time of sale), any revaluation reserve (resulting from revaluation of assets) and retained earnings (past profits reinvested in the business).

Balance sheets balance. Net assets are equal to the capital employed to finance them.

Investment Ratios

The five key investment ratios are explained in Table 3.5, and the linkages between four of them are illustrated in Figure 3.10.

The return on shareholders' funds deals with the profit available for ordinary shareholders after all other commitments (including preference share dividends) have been met; and it is divided by all the funds provided both directly and

Table 3.5 Investment ratios

Ratio	Calculation	Comments
Return on shareholders' funds (%)	$\dfrac{\text{Profit after tax}}{\text{Total shareholders' funds}}$	Measures the return on investment by shareholders in the company
Earning per share (pence)	$\dfrac{\text{Profit after tax}}{\text{Number of ordinary shares issued}}$	Profit after tax represents earnings for the shareholders. It can be returned to them immediately as dividends or reinvested as additional shareholders' funds (retained earnings)
Price-to-earnings ratio *P/E*	$\dfrac{\text{Current market price of ordinary shares}}{\text{Earnings per share}}$	Indicates the multiple of earnings that investors are willing to pay for shares in the stock market The higher the ratio, the more favourably the company is perceived
Dividend yield	$\dfrac{\text{Dividend per share}}{\text{Market price per share}}$	Equivalent to rate of interest per cent paid on the investment Shareholders will not expect it to equal say building society rates – reinvested profits should generate longer-term increases in the share price
Dividend cover (number of times)	$\dfrac{\text{Earnings per share}}{\text{Dividend per share}}$	The number of times the dividends *could* have been paid from the earnings: the higher the better

indirectly by ordinary shareholders. 'The return on shareholders' funds is probably the most important single measure of all. It takes into account the return on net assets, the company's tax position, and the extent to which capital employed has been supplied other than by the ordinary shareholders (for example by loans)' (Reid and Myddelton, 1974).

Earnings per share indicates how much money the company has earned in relation to the number of ordinary shares. Taken in isolation this measure is useful if considered over a number of years. Companies can be compared with each other if the ratio is linked to the current market price of shares. This calculation provides the price-to-earnings ratio *P/E*.

The *P/E* ratio indicates the amount (how many times the current earnings figure) that potential shareholders are willing to pay in order to buy shares in the company at a particular time. It is affected by previous success and profits, but really it is an indication of expectations. The more confidence the market has in

Figure 3.10   Linkages between four investment ratios: the squares represent the investment ratios; the circles the figures required for calculating ratios. (Note: the two figures required to calculate each ratio are shown leading into the box.)

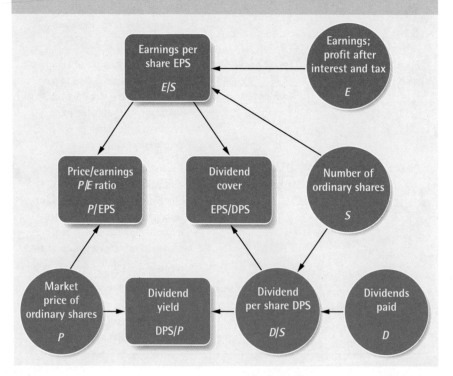

a company, generally the higher will be its *P/E*. It can also indicate relatively how expensive borrowing is for the company. If the company opts to raise money from existing shareholders by offering new shares in a rights issue (the shareholders are invited to buy new shares in fixed proportion to those they already hold) the higher the *P/E* is, the cheaper is the capital. A high *P/E* implies that shareholders will pay many times current earnings to obtain shares.

The *P/E* ratio is also very important in acquisition situations. Consider two companies as an example. Company A has issued 500,000 ordinary shares with a face value of 25p and their current market price is 600p. Current earnings per share are 20p (£100,000 in total). Hence, the *P/E* is 600/20 = 30. Company A looks attractive to the shareholders of company B when it makes a bid for their shares. B also has 500,000 shares issued, again with a face value of 25p, but they are trading at only 150p as company B has been relatively sleepy of late and growth has been below the average for the industry. With earnings per share of 10p (£50,000 in total) the *P/E* is 15. A offers one new share in company A for every three shares in B (perhaps more generous than it need be), and the shareholders in B accept. A–B now has 666,667 shares issued; at the moment the combined earnings are £150,000. If the stock market, and the shareholders, are confident that A can turn B round and increase earnings significantly the current *P/E* of 30 could remain. If so, the new price of shares in the combined A–B is 675p. Earnings per share are 22.5p (£150,000/666,667 shares).

A's share price has in effect risen, possibly making it appear an even more successful company. Any company wishing to acquire A will now have to pay more. Equally, A's ability to acquire further companies on the above lines has been enhanced.

The price-to-earnings ratio and earnings per share are measures which are most applicable to companies whose shares are traded on the stock market.

Two dividend ratios

The dividend yield provides the rate of interest that shareholders are receiving in relation to the current market price for shares. It must be used cautiously as it takes no account of the price that people actually paid (historically) to buy their shares; and in any case shareholders are often more interested in long-term capital growth.

The dividend cover indicates the proportion of earnings paid out in dividends and the proportion reinvested. Company dividend policies will vary between companies and, for example, a decision to maintain or reduce dividends in the face of reduced earnings will be influenced by the predicted effect on share prices and in turn the valuation of the company, which as we saw above can be an issue in acquisitions.

Quoted companies can also be analysed by considering the movement of their share price against the Financial Times 100 Shares Index or the All Shares Index, and against the index of shares for their particular industry. Under- and over-performance of the shares are further reflections of investors' confidence and expectations.

Performance Ratios

Tables 3.6 and 3.7 explain the various performance ratios.

Profitability

The return on net assets or the return on capital employed uses profit before interest and before tax and compares it with the assets, or capital employed, used in the business to create the profit. Actual profit is important as it determines the

Table 3.6   Performance ratios

Ratio	Calculation	Comments
Return on net assets Return on capital employed (%)	$\dfrac{\text{Profit before interest and before tax}}{\text{Total capital employed in the business}}$	Measures the relative success of the business as a trading concern Trading profit less overheads is divided by shareholders' funds and other long-term loans Useful for measuring and comparing the relative performance of different divisions/strategic business units
Profit margin (%)	$\dfrac{\text{Profit before interest and before tax}}{\text{Sales (turnover)}}$	Shows trading profit less overheads as a percentage of turnover Again useful for comparing divisions, products, markets
Net asset turnover (number of times)	$\dfrac{\text{Sales}}{\text{Total net assets or capital employed in the business}}$	Measures the number of times the capital is 'turned over' in a year Or: the number of pounds of sales generated for every pound invested in the company

Table 3.7 Other useful performance ratios

Ratio	Calculation	Comments
Stock turnover (number of times)	$\dfrac{\text{Turnover}}{\text{Stock}}$	Shows how quickly stocks move through the business Logically the quicker the better – as long as it does not result in stock shortages Most accurate measurement from *average* stock level over the year rather than the balance-sheet figure
Debtor turnover (number of times; or days of credit given)	$\dfrac{\text{Turnover}}{\text{Debtors}}$ $\dfrac{\text{Debtors}}{\text{Turnover} \times 365}$	Shows how quickly credit customers pay. Again, use *average* debtors. Retail organizations, such as Marks & Spencer, sell mostly for cash, or charge interest for credit through their credit cards A similar measure, credit purchases/ average creditors, shows how much credit time is received by the company
Gross profit margin (%)	$\dfrac{\text{Gross profit}}{\text{Turnover (sales)}}$	Indicates percentage profit before overheads
and		
Selling and administration costs to sales (%)	$\dfrac{\text{Selling and administration costs}}{\text{Turnover (sales)}}$	Shows overheads (indirect costs) in relation to turnover

amount of money that a company has available for paying dividends (once interest and tax are deducted) and for reinvestment. But it is also important to examine how well the money invested in the business is being used – this is profitability. This particular ratio ignores how the business is actually funded, making it a measure of how well the business is performing as a trading concern. It was mentioned earlier that contributions from different products or strategic business units should be compared in the case of multiproduct organizations. The return on net assets should also be used to compare the profitabilities of products and strategic business units. In this way the ratio can be used for evaluating particular competitive strategies and the relative importance to the business of different products. However, this measure should not be used in isolation from an assessment of the relative importance of different products in terms of turnover. High-volume products or divisions may be less profitable than smaller volume ones for a variety of reasons, which are examined in the section on portfolio analysis.

This ratio is particularly useful when it is examined in the light of the two ratios that comprise it. The return on net assets is equal to the profit margin times the net asset turnover. The profit margin is the proportion of sales revenue represented by profits (before interest and tax); the net asset turnover illustrates how well the company is utilizing its assets in order to generate sales.

Certain companies will adopt strategies that are designed to yield good profit margins on every item sold, and as a result probably add value into the product or service in such a way that their assets are not producing the same amount of sales per pound sterling as is the case for a company which uses assets more aggressively, adds less value and makes a lower profit margin. Particular industries and businesses may offer little choice in this respect; others offer considerable choice.

If a decision is reached that for the business as a whole, or some part of it, the return on net assets (profitability) must be improved, there are two approaches. Either profits must be increased, or assets reduced, or both. Figure 3.11 illustrates the alternatives available to the organization, and at the bottom the functional responsibilities. Hence, a corporate or competitive strategy change will result in changes to functional strategies.

Other useful performance ratios

Table 3.7 explains stock turnover and debtor turnover, which both indicate how well the company is managing two of its current assets. The stock turnover will depend on how the company is managing its operations – different strategies will lead to higher or lower stocks. Low stocks (high stock turnover) save costs, but they can make the business vulnerable if they are reduced to too low a level in order to save money and result in production delays. Debtor turnover, for certain types of business, looked at over a period can show whether the company is successful at persuading credit customers to pay quickly. This can affect the marketing strategy if decisions have to be taken not to supply certain customers who are slow payers.

The gross profit margin and the selling and administration costs to sales ratio are useful for indicating the percentage of turnover attributable to overheads. If a company has a high gross profit margin but is relatively unprofitable after accounting for overheads it is a sign of poor management. The product or service is able to command a price comfortably in excess of direct costs (direct labour and materials) but this contribution is being swallowed by overheads which are pos-

Figure 3.11 Improving profitability.

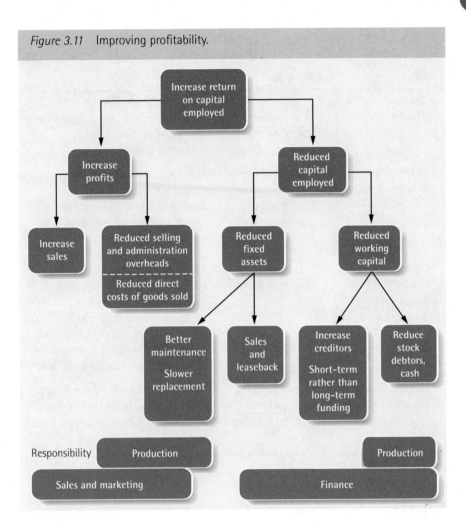

sibly too high and in need of reduction. Such a company is appropriate for restructuring and perhaps acquisition. Again, these ratios should be examined over a period of years to ensure that the overhead burden is not creeping up without just cause. In terms of increasing profits (to improve profitability; Figure 3.11) it may be easier to reduce overheads than to reduce direct costs.

Measures of Financial Status

Measures of financial status can be divided into two groups: solvency and liquidity. The ratios are explained in Table 3.8.

Table 3.8 Measures of financial status

Ratio	Calculation	Comments
Solvency		
Debt ratio (%)	$\dfrac{\text{Long-term loans}}{\text{Total capital employed}}$	The lower the debt ratio the more the company is cushioned against fluctuation in trading profits
Interest cover (number of times)	$\dfrac{\text{Profit before interest and before tax}}{\text{Interest on long-term loans}}$	Indicates how many times the interest is covered by earnings Sometimes argued that banks expect a figure of at least three times
Liquidity		
Current ratio (ratio *x*:1) (also known as working capital ratio)	$\dfrac{\text{Current assets}}{\text{Current liabilities}}$	Shows the extent to which short-term assets are able to meet short-term liabilities 1.5:1 and 2:1 both suggested as indicative targets. Also suggested that working capital (current assets minus current liabilities) should exceed stock
Liquidity or acid test ratio (ratio *x*:1)	$\dfrac{\text{Liquid assets (i.e. current assets less stock)}}{\text{Current liabilities}}$	This shows how liquid the company is relative to short-term liabilities. Stock is excluded as it can take months to turn into cash

Solvency

The major ratios are the debt ratio and interest cover. The debt ratio relates to the company's gearing – how much it is funded by equity capital (shareholders' funds) and how much by long-term loans. Loans generally carry fixed interest payments, and these must be met regardless of any profit fluctuations; a company can elect not to pay dividends to shareholders if profits collapse, which gives it more flexibility.

Managers and investors will both be wary of the debt ratio creeping up, as it does when companies borrow money from the banking system to finance investment or acquisitions. In fact, acquisitive companies must relate their acquisition strategies to their ability to finance them. Sometimes money can be raised from shareholders, but the company must be confident that shareholders will subscribe to rights issues. If not, and the shares have to be sold to the banks who underwrite the issue (who then sell them when the price is appropriate), blocks of shares can be bought up by other acquisitive companies and this can pose a threat. The alternative is long-term loans, and the higher the proportion these constitute, the more stable profits need to be. This is taken up later in the book (a Finance in Action supplement to Chapter 12).

Interest cover shows by how much the interest payments are covered by profits.

Liquidity

The two main liquidity ratios, the current ratio and the acid test (liquidity) ratio, relate to working capital. Has the company sufficient money available to meet its short-term commitments? They are determined by the flow of cash in and out of the business. A shortage of cash, and commitments to meet, will push the company towards increased borrowings (say a larger overdraft), and this will increase interest commitments.

While targets of 1.5:1 and 2.0:1 are sometimes quoted for the current ratio, these should be treated with some caution. Companies who trade mainly in cash, rather than allow credit, are likely to have a ratio much nearer 1:1 and still be perfectly liquid. Retailers and breweries are cases in point.

A company will experience liquidity problems if it invests in stock and then fails to win orders or if it fails to control its debtors. Conversely, a successful company can have cash problems. Success at winning orders may require investment in machinery or stocks and labour, and these may have to be paid for before and during production and before the goods are delivered and paid for by customers. This can lead to temporary illiquidity, and is known as overtrading.

Managing Cash

Cash flow, therefore, can be just as important as profitability. Where demand is seasonal for certain products production may take place when sales are low, in advance of peak demand. This puts pressure on cash flow in the way outlined above. A perfect example of this is Standard Fireworks, a largely focused business, whose sales are concentrated in the weeks before bonfire night (5 November), but who produce all through the year.

Cash reserves built up in good years can be run down to finance a company during lean years or a recession.

Cash-flow issues affect corporate strategy in terms of the range of products, services and businesses selected, competitive strategies in terms of the way they are marketed (to avoid the worst implications of seasonal fluctuations) and functional production, marketing and financial strategies.

Table 3.9 A typical cash-flow statement

Cash generated by operating activities (including operating profits, changes in stocks, debtors, and creditors and depreciation charged in the accounts)

Add:	Interest from investments
	Proceeds from any share issues
	Receipts from any asset sales
	New loans taken out
Deduct:	Interest paid on loans
	Loans repaid
	Tax paid
	Dividend paid
	Fixed assets purchased
Leaving:	Money available for further investment

It is not unusual for companies to be slow in paying their bills when their performance is poor. This impacts upon their customers, and highlights the importance of cash flow, particularly in a recession. Table 3.9 shows how cash is generated and spent.

Cash flow can be improved in a number of ways, for example, by

- increased turnover – but only if linked to
- effective management of debtors and creditors
- higher operating profit margins
- reduced tax payments
- reduced investment in working capital and/or fixed assets
- improved gearing to reduce interest payments.

Simply, a company must be able to produce cash in order to finance future investments and acquisitions, meet outstanding payments on earlier acquisitions and cover any unexpected events requiring extraordinary charges.

Accounting for Inflation

It is an accounting convention to use historical costs, and within the accountancy profession there is ongoing debate and disagreement about how best to treat inflation. This topic is outside the scope of this book. However, it is important to take some account of inflation when looking at growth rates for actual data such as turnover and profits as otherwise companies appear to be doing far better than in reality they are.

Other Quantitative Performance Indicators

In addition to all of these financial ratios, businesses will typically collect and evaluate information concerning the performance of all the activities being undertaken. For each functional area there will be a number of measures, such as the value of orders acquired by every salesperson, machine utilization, turnover at every retail outlet, output per shift, productivity per employee and absenteeism. Performance will be evaluated against targets or objectives agreed with individual managers who should be held accountable. These are measures of resource efficiency. They are important control measures which evaluate the efficiency of each functional area of the business.

Similarly, individual sectors will favour particular measures. Retailers will typically consider sales per square foot of trading space, sales per employee, average shopping spend per trip and the number of new store openings or refits.

Improvements can strengthen the company's competitive capability. In isolation, however, these measures do not indicate how successful the company is strategically. This particular issue is very significant for not-for-profit organizations which cannot use the traditional profitability ratios sensibly and at the same time cannot readily measure their effectiveness in relation to their fundamental purpose. Consequently, they often rely more on quantitative measures of efficiency.

These measures are not developed in the same detail as the financial ones in this chapter as they will not be available to students tackling management case studies, whereas key financial data are normally obtainable.

Service Businesses

In addition to the above measures, the ability to retain customers is a key requirement for service businesses. Retention implies customer satisfaction and probably word-of-mouth recommendation. It is likely to result in higher profits because of the high costs incurred in attracting new business. Moreover, customers are likely to increase their level of spending over time. For insurance companies the cost of processing renewals is far cheaper than the cost of finding new clients; and many people will take out additional policies with a company on which they feel they can rely.

Key performance measures for solicitors are their ability to achieve results for their clients, and the service they offer, measurable by, for instance, the speed with which they respond to letters and telephone calls.

Applying the Ratios – A Library/Internet Project

Table 3.10 provides selected financial data for British Airways in 1994–95, and Table 3.11 a worked analysis of the following ratios:

Investment ratios:
Return on shareholders' funds
Earnings per share
Price/earnings ratio
Dividend yield
Dividend cover

Performance ratios:
Return on net assets
Profit margin
Net asset turnover
Stock turnover
Debtor turnover
Gross profit margin

Solvency ratios:
Debt ratio
Interest cover

Liquidity ratios:
Current ratio
Liquidity ratio

Check how these ratios have been calculated. Then update the figures for subsequent years and calculate the relevant ratios. Consider the trends with what you know (or can find out) about BA's strategy and general fortunes since 1995.

Table 3.10 British Airways: extracts from profit and loss account and balance sheet, 31 March 1995

	£million		£million	£million
Turnover	7177	Fixed assets	6163	
		Investments	471	
Cost of sales	6436			6634
Gross profit	741	Current assets		
		Stock	70	
Overheads/administration	123	Debtors	1182	
		Short-term loans	1099	
Operating profit	618	Cash	64	
Other income/provisions	(76)			2415
Interest	215	Current liabilities	2320	
Tax	77	Working capital	95	
Profit after interest and tax	250	Total net assets		6729
Dividend paid	119	Long-term loans	4582	
Retained profit	131	Provisions for charges	57	
		Shareholders' funds	2090	
Number of ordinary shares	954,605,000			
Year-end share price	402 pence	Total capital employed		6729

Table 3.11 British Airways: worked ratio analysis for 1994–95

Investment ratios

Return on shareholders' funds	=	$\dfrac{250}{2090}$	=	11.96%
Earnings per share	=	$\dfrac{250}{954.605}$	=	26.2 pence
Price/earnings ratio	=	$\dfrac{402}{26.2}$	=	15.34
Dividend yield	=	$\dfrac{12.46}{402}$	=	3.1%
Dividend cover	=	$\dfrac{26.2}{12.46}$	=	2.1 times

Performance ratios

Return on net assets	=	$\dfrac{618}{6279}$	=	9.2%
Profit margin	=	$\dfrac{618}{7177}$	=	8.6%
Net asset turnover	=	$\dfrac{7177}{6729}$	=	1.07 times
Stock turnover	=	$\dfrac{7177}{70}$	=	102 times
Debtor turnover	=	$\dfrac{7177}{1182}$	=	6.1 times (or 60 days)
Gross profit margin	=	$\dfrac{741}{7177}$	=	10.3%

Solvency ratios

Debt ratio	=	$\dfrac{4582}{6729}$	=	68%
Interest cover	=	$\dfrac{542}{215}$	=	2.5 times

Liquidity ratios

Current ratio	=	2415:2320	=	1.04:1
Liquidity ratio	=	2345:2320	=	1.01:1

Culture and Values

4

Culture affects every element of strategy and strategic management and consequently this topic is studied early in the book.

The key decision elements of strategic management concern strategic choice (deciding what to do), and strategy implementation and change (making things happen). Chapter 1 showed briefly how strategic leadership and values are at the heart of the decision-making processes. Simply, they influence the choices that are made and the feasibility of change. Can ideas for change be implemented smoothly? Will there be major barriers and resistance? If we do not understand the culture of an organization, and the impact of the strategic leader who underpins the culture, we cannot understand strategic management in that organization. The culture varies between organizations, although some elements will be common and transferable. It also varies between countries, influencing the relative competitiveness of industries and organizations in different countries. This chapter looks into these implications and into the determinants of culture and cultural differences.

Case Study 4: IKEA

IKEA was started in Sweden by Ingvar Kamprad, who pioneered the idea of self-assembly furniture in handy packs. His vision of 'a better, more beautiful, everyday life for the many' led to 'a wide range of home furnishings, of good function and style, at low prices, for mass consumer markets'. Kamprad began with a mail-order business in 1943; the first IKEA store was opened in 1958.

Growth has been carefully regulated. IKEA waited for seven years before opening a second branch; the first branch outside Sweden was in the early 1970s; the first US store opened in 1985, with typically one new store being added every year. This approach allows IKEA to establish local supply networks and ensures that it does not become stretched financially. The expansion programme has always been funded from cash generated by the retail activities. IKEA does not have a large market share in any single country; instead, it has a global brand and an intriguing reputation which draws customers from substantial distances away. On busy weekends in the UK, long queues at the checkouts and to get into and out of the car parks are legendary.

By the late 1990s, IKEA had some 150 shops in 30 countries. IKEA's strategy has always involved high-quality merchandise at prices which undercut the competition. In the mid-1990s IKEA's annual turnover passed the $5 billion mark; after-tax profits were estimated to be 8% of revenue. Reputedly worth at least $12.5 billion, IKEA has always been reticent about the financial data it releases.

IKEA stores focus on sales of self-assembly packs which customers take away themselves. IKEA will, however, deliver fully assembled pieces for a premium price. The stores have a wide range of facilities, typically including restaurants and games and video rooms for children; these are normally on the top floor, which is where customers come in. People are then routed carefully through a series of display areas to the downstairs purchase points which resemble a typical discount warehouse.

The furniture packs are commissioned from over 2300 suppliers in some 70 countries, many of them low labour cost countries in the Far East and Eastern Europe. IKEA has an equity stake in several of its suppliers and insists on tight stock control programmes to reduce costs through the whole supply chain. IKEA designs all its own products and aims to lead customer taste. There is just one range of products for the global market, but not every country and store stocks the full range. IKEA chooses not to have mini-ranges for specific countries and prides itself on an ability to respond to local fashion and opportunities by quickly adjusting the range in any one store. Sales per square foot invariably exceed industry averages.

Manifestations of IKEA's distinctive culture

The *artefacts* clearly include the stores, the products and the prices. There are (like Marks and Spencer) no brands other than IKEA's own. There are no annual or seasonal sales; prices stay valid for a whole year. There is a plethora of in-store information and communications, but there are no commissioned sales people.

Values – IKEA use the word 'prosumers' to imply that value is added by both IKEA and their customers in partnership. Employees are empowered to be innovative and helpful and challenged to 'dare to be different'. IKEA recognizes that always offering prices substantially below those of its competitors places considerable pressure on its staff.

Underlying assumptions can be summarized in the following quotes:

> We do not need to do things in traditional ways (window manufacturers have been approached to make table frames; shirt manufacturers for seat cushions).

> Break your chains and you are free; cut your roots and you die. IKEA should look for constant renewal. Experiments matter; mistakes (within reason) will be tolerated.

Behaviours – Every IKEA manager flies economy class and uses taxis only if there is no suitable alternative. In The Netherlands, managers have been encouraged to stay with typical IKEA customer families to learn more about their needs.

People

A variety of *stories* permeates the IKEA culture. Initially customers in the US stores were simply not buying any beds – there had been no market research into US tastes; it was IKEA's global product. Eventually, it was realized that Americans sleep in bigger beds than Swedes. Similarly, kitchen units had to be adjusted to handle extra-large pizza plates.

Leadership and management style – Kamprad rarely shows his face to the public. At one stage there was some adverse publicity concerning alleged wartime allegiances, but no lasting damage. The lack of published financial information reinforces this hidden aspect of IKEA.

The *organization* is structured as an inverted pyramid – employees are there to serve customers – and based on managers and co-workers. There are no directors, no formal titles and no dining rooms or reserved parking spaces for executives. Managers are quite likely to switch between functions and countries. The organization is fundamentally informal with 'few instructions'. Every year there is an 'anti-bureaucracy' week when everyone dresses casually.

Communications – Both customers and employees are encouraged to provide ideas and suggestions, which may be translated into new products. Information enters the system from several points.

Ownership and structural issues

IKEA remains a private company which owns all of its sites. It pays for new sites in cash. 'We don't like to be in the hands of the banks'. There are no plans to become a limited company either; Kamprad has criticized the short-term interests of many investors.

The company operates as three distinct activities. The core retailing business is now a Dutch-registered charitable foundation. The profits of the operations are subjected to a top-slice of 3% to fund a separate business which has responsibility for managing the brand and IKEA's franchisees. The third arm is a banking and finance business; IKEA, for example, owns a majority shareholding in Habitat in the UK.

QUESTION: IKEA believes that fashionable and modern furniture and furnishings can be affordable for most families. It need not be prohibitively expensive. How does it achieve this?

IKEA   http://www.ikea.com

Introduction

When any group of people live and work together for any length of time, they form and share certain beliefs about what is right and proper. They establish behaviour patterns based on their beliefs, and their actions often become matters of habit which they follow routinely. These beliefs and ways of behaving constitute the organization's *culture*.

Culture is reflected in the way in which people in an organization perform tasks, set objectives and administer resources to achieve them. It affects the way that they make decisions, think, feel and act in response to opportunities and threats. Culture also influences the selection of people for particular jobs, which in turn affects the way in which tasks are carried out and decisions are made. Culture is so fundamental that it affects behaviour unconsciously. Managers do things in particular ways because it is expected behaviour.

The culture of an organization is therefore related to the people, their behaviour and the operation of the structure. It is encapsulated in beliefs, customs and values, and manifested in a number of symbolic ways.

The formation of, and any changes to, the culture of an organization is dependent on the leadership and example of particular individuals, and their ability to control or influence situations. This is itself dependent on a person's ability to obtain and use power.

The Body Shop provides an ideal example how the values of the founder, in this case Anita Roddick, can inspire employees and attract customers. Its distinctive culture enabled The Body Shop to grow and prosper, but it was not totally appropriate for the large, international business that The Body Shop became. As a consequence, Anita Roddick has relinquished day-to-day control and a number of changes has been made to the strategies.

Culture and power, then, affect the choice, incidence and application of the modes of strategy creation, which will also reflect the values and preferences of the strategic leader. The preferred mode must, however, be appropriate for the organization's strategic needs, which are affected by competition. Moreover, culture and power are such strong forces that, if the prevailing culture is overlooked, implementation may not happen. Strong cultures can obstruct strategic change, particularly if companies are in decline and people feel vulnerable.

Quite simply, culture is at the heart of all strategy creation and implementation. Organizations are seeking to respond to perceived strategic issues. Resources must be deployed and committed, but successful change also requires the 'right' attitude, approach and commitment from people. This mindset, which might, for example, reflect a strong customer and service focus, could imply further empowerment and consequently cultural change.

In the early 1980s, Berry (1983) claimed that after some 20 years of emphasis on analytical techniques in strategic management, the concentration switched to the softer aspect of culture. The emphasis was no longer on the marketplace, but on what managers could do to resolve internal problems; by using culture, companies could become more strategically effective. The perspective of this book is that both the hard and soft aspects of strategy have important roles to play in strategic management.

Strong cultures, then, are an important strategic asset. Internalized beliefs can motivate people to exceptional levels of performance. An effective strategic leader will understand and mould the culture in order that a vision can be pursued and intended strategies implemented. Most successful companies develop strong cultures; the major doubt concerns an organization's ability to change the culture.

Moreover, large organizations formed by a series of acquisitions will frequently exhibit different cultures in the various divisions or businesses; in many international businesses this is inevitable. The challenge for corporate headquarters is to ensure that certain critically important values are reflected in all branches of the corporation and cultural differences do not inhibit internal architecture and synergy.

At the same time, cross-border mergers and alliances promise to fuse together the best features of different cultures, but this may prove more idealistic than realistic. For example, the acquisition of Rover by BMW appeared to offer an opportunity to bring together the longer-term German perspective on investment, training and employee consultation and the UK's flexibility in working practices and lower manufacturing costs. In the event the marketing aspects were ineffective and well-reviewed Rover cars did not sell in the showrooms. In spring 2000 Rover was resold by BMW to the specially formed Phoenix Group.

Aspects of Culture

The points discussed in this section are summarized in Figure 4.1.

Manifestations of culture

Edgar Schein (1985) contends that it is important to consider culture as having a number of levels, some of which are essentially manifestations of underlying beliefs.

The first and most visible level Schein terms *'artefacts'*. These include the physical and social environment and the outputs of the organization. Written communications, advertisements and the reception that visitors receive are all included.

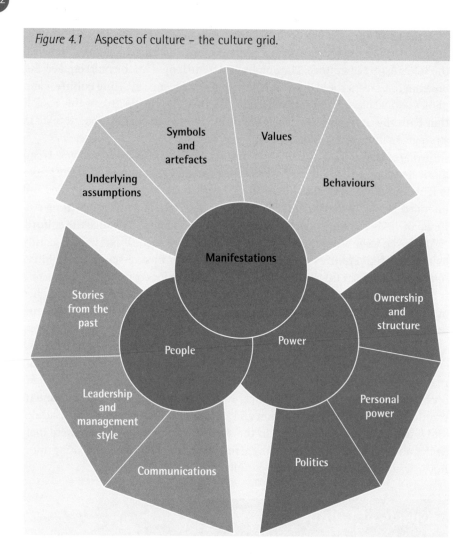

Figure 4.1   Aspects of culture – the culture grid.

Values are the second level, and they represent a sense of 'what ought to be' based on convictions held by certain key people. For example, if an organization has a problem such as low sales or a high level of rejections in production, decisions might be made to advertise more aggressively or to use high-quality but more expensive raw materials. These are seen initially as the decision maker's values, which can be debated or questioned. Many of the strategies followed by organizations start in this way, and many will reflect values held by the strategic leader.

If the alternative is successful it may well be tried again and again until it becomes common practice. In this way the value becomes a belief and ultimately an assumption about behaviour practised by the organization. These basic *under-*

lying assumptions are Schein's third level, and they represent the taken-for-granted ways of doing things or solutions to problems.

One belief accepted by employees within a bank might be that all lending must be secure. A football team could be committed to always playing attractive, open football. A university might be expected to have clear beliefs about the relative importance of research and teaching, but this is likely to be an issue where employees 'agree to disagree', leading to a fragmented culture. Examples of *behaviours* are speedy new product development, long working hours, formal management meetings and regular informal meetings or contacts with colleagues, suppliers and customers.

It is also important to appreciate that certain organizations may state that they have particular values but in reality these will be little more than verbal or written statements or aspirations for the future.

Schein argues that cultural paradigms are formed which determine how 'organization members perceive, think about, feel about, and judge situations and relationships' and these are based on a number of underlying assumptions.

People and culture

For Schwartz and Davis (1981) culture is 'a pattern of beliefs and expectations shared by the organization's members, and which produce norms that powerfully shape the behaviour of individuals and groups in the organization'. They argue that the beliefs held by the company are seen as major aspects of corporate policy as they evolve from interactions with, and in turn form policy towards, the marketplace. As a result, rules or norms for internal and external behaviour are developed and eventually both performance and reward systems will be affected. These aspects of the culture are often transmitted through *stories* of past events, glories and heroes.

Success is measured by, and culture therefore becomes based on, past activities. Current decisions by managers reflect the values, beliefs and norms that have proved beneficial in the past and in the development and growth of the organization. Moreover, they reinforce the corporate culture and expected behaviour throughout the organization.

The culture affects suppliers and customers, and their reactions are important. They will feed back impressions about the organization, and their views should be sought. Successful organizations will ensure that there is congruence between these environmental influences and the organization culture. In this way key success factors can be met if resources are administered, controlled and developed appropriately.

Organizations need a cohesive blend of the philosophies introduced earlier. A cohesive culture would exhibit strong leadership, whereby the strategic leader is sensitive to the degrees of decentralization and informality necessary for satisfying customer needs efficiently, and managing change pressures, in order to keep the business strong and profitable. At the same time a centralized information network will ensure that communications are effective and that managers are both kept aware and rewarded properly for their contributions. A fragmented culture, in contrast, would suggest that the needs of certain stakeholders were perhaps not being satisfied adequately, or that strategies and changes were not being co-ordinated, or that managers or business units were in conflict and working against each other, or that the most deserving people were not being rewarded.

Linked to this is *communication*, an essential aspect of culture. The organization might be seen as open or closed, formal or informal. Ideally, employees from different parts of the business, and at different levels in the hierarchy, will feel willing and able to talk openly with each other, sharing problems, ideas and learning. 'Doors should be left open'. Employees should also be trusted and empowered to the appropriate degree. Good communications can 'stop nasty surprises'. It is helpful if employees know how well competitors are performing, where they are particularly strong, so they can commit themselves to high levels of achievement in order to outperform their rivals.

Communication is clearly essential for creating effective internal and external architecture.

Hampden-Turner (1990) argues that culture is based on communication and learning. The strategic leader's vision for the organization must be communicated and understood; events and changes affecting the organization also need to be communicated widely. Managers should be encouraged to seek out new opportunities by learning about new technology and customer expectations, and to innovate. The organization should help them to share their experiences and their learning.

Power and culture

Power is reflected in the *ownership* of the business. It may be a family company with strong, concentrated power. A small group of institutional shareholders could control the business, in which case it is conceivable that short-term financial targets will dictate strategies. *Structural issues* include the extent to which the organization is centralized or decentralized, the role and contribution of corporate headquarters, and control and reward systems. *Personal power* is discussed later in this chapter; *politics* refers to the ways in which managers use power and influence to affect decisions and actions.

Case Study 4 analyses IKEA against this model. IKEA focuses on being a low-cost competitor and achieves this while maintaining a complex supply-chain network. IKEA also has an ability to be flexible in response to local opportunities, which could easily add costs as well as value. The company is product and production driven, but able to capture and use ideas from customers and employees.

Determinants of Culture

Deal and Kennedy (1982) have conducted research into US companies in an attempt to ascertain what factors lead to consistently outstanding (above average for the industry) performance. They found that over the long term the companies that are the most successful are those that believe in something and those where the belief or beliefs have permeated through the whole organization, i.e. they are communicated and understood. Examples quoted are progress via innovation and technology and 'excellence' in something that customers value, say service or delivery on time.

Deal and Kennedy argue that employees must be rewarded for compliance with the essential cultural aspects if these values are to be developed and retained over time; and they conclude that people who build, develop and run successful companies invariably work hard to create strong cultures within their organizations.

From their research Deal and Kennedy isolated five key elements or determinants of culture.

- The environment and key success factors: what the organization must do well if it is to be an effective competitor. Innovation and fast delivery are examples quoted.
- The values that the strategic leader considers important and wishes to see adopted and followed in the organization. These should relate to the key success factors, and to employee reward systems.
- Heroes: the visionaries who create the culture. They can come from any background and could be, for example, product or service innovators, engineers who build the appropriate quality into the product, or creative marketing people who provide the slogans which make the product or brand name a household word.
- Rites and rituals: the behaviour patterns in which the culture is manifest. Again there are any number of ways in which this can happen, including employees helping each other out when there are difficulties, the way in which sales people deal with customers, and the care and attention that go into production.
- The cultural network: the communications system around which the culture revolves and which determines just how aware employees are about the essential issues.

When the culture is strong, people know what is expected of them and they understand how to act and decide in particular circumstances. They appreciate the issues that are important. When it is weak, time can be wasted in trying to decide what should be done and how. Moreover, it is argued that employees feel better about their companies if they are recognized, known about and regarded as successful, and these aspects will be reflected in the culture.

There can be a number of separate strands to the culture in any organization, which should complement each other. For example, there can be aspects relating to the strategic leader, the environment and the employees. There could be a strong power culture related to an influential strategic leader who is firmly in charge of the organization and whose values are widely understood and followed. This could be linked to a culture of market orientation, which ensures that customer needs are considered and satisfied, and to a work culture if employees feel committed to the organization and wish to help in achieving success.

Implications of Culture

Pümpin (1987) suggests that seven aspects comprise the culture of an organization, and that the relative significance of each of these will vary from industry to industry. The seven aspects are:

1. The extent to which the organization is marketing orientated, giving customers high priority.
2. The relationships between management and staff, manifested through communication and participation systems, for example.
3. The extent to which people are target orientated and committed to achieving agreed levels of performance.
4. Attitudes towards innovation. It is particularly important that the risks associated with failure are perceived as acceptable by all levels of management if innovation and entrepreneurship are to be fostered.
5. Attitudes towards costs and cost reduction.
6. The commitment and loyalty to the organization felt, and shown, by staff.
7. The impact of, and reaction to, technology and technological change and development. One major issue concerns whether or not the opportunities offered by information technology are being harnessed by the firm.

Many of these aspects are developed further in later chapters of the book.

Hampden-Turner (1990) believes that the culture is a manifestation of how the organization has chosen to deal with specific dilemmas and conflicts. Each of these can be viewed as a continuum, and the organization needs a clear position on each one. One dilemma might be the conflict between, on the one hand, the need to develop new products and services quickly and ahead of competitors and, on the other hand, the need for thorough development and planning to ensure adequate quality and safety. Another dilemma is the need for managers to be adaptive and responsive in a changing environment, but not at the expense of organization-wide communication and awareness. Such change orientation may also conflict with a desire for continuity and consistency of strategy and policy.

Tables 4.1 and 4.2 take this idea further. Table 4.1 highlights how every apparent virtue also has a 'flip side', and consequently something which is positive at one point may suddenly prove disadvantageous. Table 4.2 looks at the advantages and drawbacks of three business paradigms: a market-orientated business, an organization focused on resource efficiency, and a growth-driven business. Taken together, these confirm that there can never be one best or ideal culture. The culture needs to be flexible and adaptive as circumstances change. The cultural factors that bring initial success may need to be changed if success is to be sustained. Similarly, it is not enough simply to look at what other successful organizations are doing and copy them. Benchmarking and teasing out good practices are both important and beneficial, but these practices again need customizing and adapting to the unique circumstances facing an individual organization.

Culture and Strategy Creation

We have already seen that the essential cultural characteristics will dictate the preferred mode of strategy creation in an organization; all the modes are likely to be present to some degree.

Table 4.1   Every coin, every virtue, has a flip side!

Team players	May be indecisive and avoid risks
Customer focus	Can lead to reactivity and lack of innovation
Action orientation	Can become reckless and dictatorial
Analytical thinking	Can result in paralysis
Innovation	Which is impractical, unrealistic, ill thought through, wastes time and money
A global vision	May mean valuable local opportunities are missed
Being a good 'people manager'	May allow someone to become soft and walk away from tough decisions

Developed from ideas in McCall, MW (1998) *High Flyers*, Harvard Business School Press.

Table 4.2 The imperfect world of organizations

A market-driven business is likely to be:	An efficient operations-driven business is likely to be:	A growth-orientated business is likely to be:
Resourceful	Efficient	Competitive
Entrepreneurial	Strong on teamworking	Strong on targets and achieving results
Risk orientated	Good at executing plans	Full of hard-working people
Pragmatic in terms of getting things done	Sophisticated with its systems and procedures	Flexible
		Changing quickly
But it may not be:	**But it may not be:**	**But it may not be:**
Consistent	Responsive to customers	Taking a long-term perspective
Disciplined in what it does	Good at managing change	
Adhering to systems and procedures	Able to see 'the big picture'	Offering a balanced lifestyle for its employees
Strong on teamworking		Sensitive to people's needs

Developed from ideas in McCall, MW (1998) *High-flyers*, Harvard Business School Press.

The culture will influence the ability of a strategic visionary to 'sell' his or her ideas to other members of the organization and gain their support and commitment to change. The planning mode is most suitable in a reasonably stable and predictable environment, but a reliance on it in a more unstable situation can lead to missed opportunities. It is an ideal mode for a conservative, risk-averse, slow-to-change organization.

Where environmental opportunities and threats arise continuously in a situation of competitive chaos an organization must be able to deal with them if it is to survive. It is the culture, with its amalgam of attitudes, values, perceptions and experiences, which determines the outcomes and relative success. The structure must facilitate awareness, sharing and learning, and people must be willing and able to act. People 'learn by doing' and they must be able to learn from mistakes. Peters (1988) states that 'managers have to learn how to make mistakes faster'. The reward system is critical here. Managers and employees should be praised and rewarded for exercising initiative and taking risks which prove successful; failures should not be sanctioned too harshly, as long as they are not repeated!

Berry (1983) argues that if a strategic leader really understands the company culture he or she must, by definition, be better equipped to make wise decisions.

He or she might conclude that 'cultural change will be so difficult we had better be sure to select a business or strategy that our kind of company can handle well'. This is just as valid as, and perhaps more useful than, believing that one can accomplish cultural change in order to shift the firm towards a new strategy.

Moreover, if business strategies and culture are intertwined, the ability to analyse and construct strategies and the ability to manage and inspire people are also intertwined. Hence, a good strategy acknowledges, 'where we are, what we have got, and what therefore managerially helps us to get where we want to be' and this is substantially different from selecting business options exclusively on their product/market dynamics. In other words, developing and implementing strategy is a human and political process that starts as much with the visions, hopes and aspirations of a company's leaders as it does with market or business analysis. Ideas drive organizations.

With ever-shortening product lifecycles, intense global competition and unstable economies and currencies the future is going to require organizations that are ready to commit themselves to change. Strategy is going to be about intertwining analysis and adaptation. The challenge is to develop more effective organizations.

Miles and Snow (1978), whose research has been used to develop Table 4.3, have suggested a typology of organizations which can be looked at in relation to culture and strategy formation. The typology distinguishes organizations in terms of their values and objectives, and different types will typically prefer particular approaches to strategy creation. Defenders, prospectors and analysers are all regarded by Miles and Snow as positive organizations; reactors must ultimately adopt one of the other three approaches or suffer long-term decline. Suggested examples of each type are as follows. GEC, despite being in high-technology industries, has been relatively conservative and a defender. The risk-orientated innovative Amstrad has always been a prospector. The respective strategic leaders of these organizations, Lord Weinstock (until his retirement in 1996) and entrepreneur Sir Alan Sugar, have adopted different styles of management and exhibited different corporate values. Historically, many public-sector bureaucracies have been stable analysers, while Marks and Spencer has long been a changing analyser. Prior to its decline and acquisition by BTR, Dunlop, in the 1970s, exhibited many of the characteristics of a reactor organization, and failed to change sufficiently in line with environmental changes.

Miles and Snow argue that, as well as being a classification, their typology can be used to predict behaviour. For example, a defender organization, in a search for greater operating efficiency, might consider investing in the latest technology, but reject the strategy if it has high risk attached.

Table 4.3   Organizational values and strategies

Type	Characteristics	Strategy formation
Defenders	Conservative beliefs	Emphasis on planning
	Low-risk strategies	
	Secure markets	
	Concentration on narrow segments	
	Considerable expertise in narrow areas of specialism	
	Preference for well-tried resolutions to problems	
	Little search for anything really 'new'	
	Attention given to improving efficiency of present operations	
Prospectors	Innovative	Visionary mode
	Looking to break new ground	
	High-risk strategies	
	Search for new opportunities	
	Can create change and uncertainty, forcing a response from competitors	
	More attention given to market changes than to improving internal efficiency	
Analysers	Two aspects: stable and changing	
	Stable: formal structures and search for efficiencies	Planning mode
	Changing: competitors monitored and strategies amended as promising ideas seen (followers)	Adaptive/Incremental mode
Reactors	Characterized by an inability to respond effectively to change pressures	Adaptive mode
	Adjustments are therefore forced on the firm in order to avert crises	

The power of 'corporate culture' should not be underestimated, both for a company's success and, if it is inappropriate, in frustrating change. Values, strategies, systems, organization and accountabilities – the components of culture – are a very strong mix which can either make a company successful or, alternatively, lead to its decline. The task of corporate leadership is to apply energy and judgement to the corporate culture to ensure its relevance.

Sir Allen Sheppard, when Chairman, Grand Metropolitan plc

Culture, Structure and Styles of Management

Charles Handy (1976), building on earlier work by Harrison (1972), has developed an alternative classification of organizations based on cultural differences, and this is illustrated in Figure 4.2.

Figure 4.2   Handy's four cultures. Adapted from Handy, CB (1976) *Understanding Organizations*, Penguin.

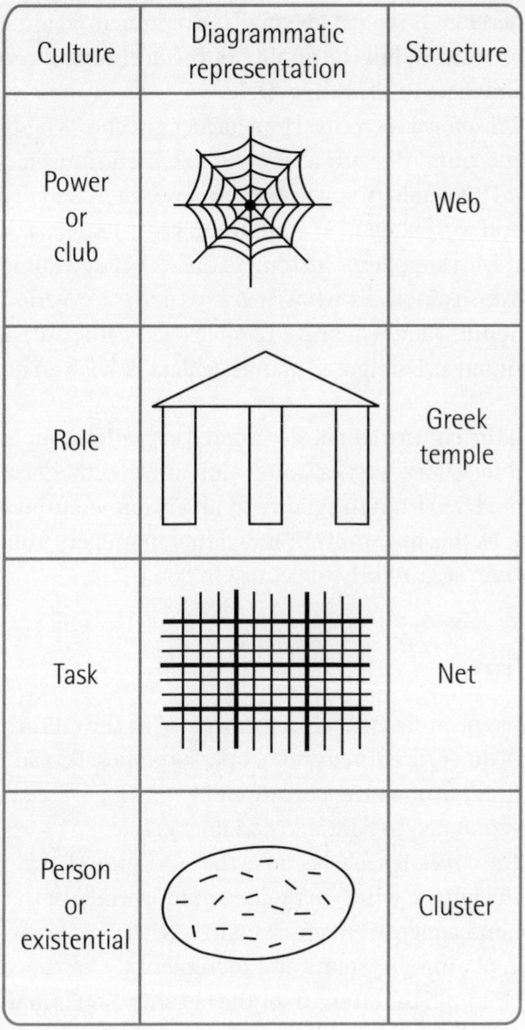

Culture	Diagrammatic representation	Structure
Power or club		Web
Role		Greek temple
Task		Net
Person or existential		Cluster

The club culture or power culture

In the club culture type of organization, work is divided by function or product and a diagram of the organization structure would be quite traditional. There would be departments for sales, production, finance and so on, and possibly product-based divisions or strategic business units if the organization was larger. However, this structure is mostly found in smaller firms.

These functions or departments are represented in Handy's figure by the lines radiating out from the centre; but the essential point is that there are also concentric lines representing communications and power. The further away from the centre, the weaker is the power and influence. This structure is dominated from the centre and therefore is typical for small entrepreneurial organizations. Decisions can be taken quickly, but the quality of the decisions is very dependent on the abilities of managers in the inner circle.

In its heyday Hanson was described by a former director as a 'solar system, with everyone circling around the sun in the middle, Lord Hanson' (see Leadbeater and Rudd, 1991). This analogy suggests both movement and dependency.

Decisions depend a great deal on empathy, affinity and trust, both within the organization and with suppliers, customers and other key influences.

People learn to do instinctively what their boss and the organization expect and require. Consequently, they will prove reliable even if they are allowed to exercise a degree of initiative. Foreign-exchange dealers provide an illustration of this point.

For this reason the culture can be designated either 'club' or 'power'. Employees are rewarded for effort, success and compliance with essential values; and change is very much led from the centre in an entrepreneurial style.

A culture such as this may prevent individual managers from speaking their minds, but decisions are unlikely to get lost in committees.

The role culture

The role culture is the more typical 'organization' as the culture is built around defined jobs, rules and procedures and not personalities. People fit into jobs, and are recruited for this purpose. Hence, rationality and logic are at the heart of the culture, which is designed to be stable and predictable.

The design is the Greek temple because the strengths of the organization are deemed to lie in the pillars, which are joined managerially at the top. One essential role of top management is to co-ordinate activity, and consequently it will be seen that both planning systems and incremental changes can be a feature of this culture. Although the strength of the organization is in the pillars, power lies at the top.

As well as being designed for stability the structure is designed to allow for continuity and changes of personnel, and for this reason dramatic changes are less likely than more gradual ones.

High efficiency is possible in stable environments, but the structure can be slow to change and is therefore less suitable for dynamic situations.

Aspects of this culture can prove beneficial for transport businesses such as railways and airlines, where reliability and timekeeping are essential. Unfortunately, it is not by nature a flexible, service-orientated culture. Intrapreneurship or elements of the task culture are also required for effectiveness.

The task culture

Management in the task culture is concerned with the continuous and successful solution of problems, and performance is judged by the success of the outcomes.

The challenge is more important than the routine.

The culture is shown as a net, because for particular problem situations people and other resources can be drawn from various parts of the organization on a temporary basis. Once the problem is dealt with people will move on to other tasks, and consequently discontinuity is a key element. Expertise is the major source of individual power and it will determine a person's relative power in a given situation. Power basically lies in the interstices of the net, because of the reliance on task forces.

The culture is ideal for consultancies, advertising agencies, and research and development departments. It can also be useful within the role culture for tackling particularly difficult or unusual problem situations.

In dynamic environments a major challenge for large organizations is the design of a structure and systems which allow for proper management and integration without losing the spirit and excitement typical of small, entrepreneurial businesses. Elements of the task culture superimposed over formal roles can help by widening communications and engendering greater commitment within the organization. One feature is cost. This culture is expensive as there is a reliance on talking and discussion, experimentation and learning by trial. Although Handy uses the expression problem solving, there can be problem resolutions or moves towards a solution along more incremental lines, as well as decisions concerning major changes. If successful changes are implemented the expense can often be justified.

The person culture or existential culture

The person culture is completely different from the other three, for here the organization exists to help the individual rather than the other way round. Groups of professional people, such as doctors, architects, dentists and solicitors, provide excellent examples. The organization, with secretarial help, printing and telephone facilities and so on, provides a service for individual specialists and reduces the need for costly duplication. If a member of the circle leaves or retires, he or she is replaced by another who may have to buy in.

Some professional groups exhibit interdependencies and collaboration, allocating work among the members, although management of such an organization is difficult because of individual expertise and because the rewards and sanctions are different from those found in most other situations.

However, in an environment where government is attempting to increase competition between professional organizations, and in some cases to reduce barriers to entering the profession, it is arguable that effective management, particularly at the strategic level, will become increasingly necessary. Efforts will need co-ordinating and harnessing if organizations are to become strong competitors.

Management philosophies

Press (1990) suggests that the culture of an organization is based upon one or more philosophies. His ideas are developed in Figure 4.3. The specific philosophies

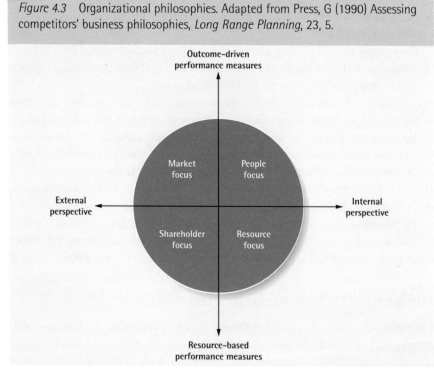

Figure 4.3   Organizational philosophies. Adapted from Press, G (1990) Assessing competitors' business philosophies, *Long Range Planning*, 23, 5.

are related to the various stakeholders in the business, and are determined by two intersecting axes. One relates to whether the business is focused more internally or externally; the other is based on performance measures. Do they concentrate more on resource management and efficiency, or outcomes and effectiveness? This creates four discrete philosophies:

- the resource focus, which concentrates on internal efficiencies and cost management
- the shareholder focus, which sees the business as a portfolio of activities which should be managed to maximize the value of the business for its shareholders
- the people focus, which emphasizes the skills and contribution of employees, and their needs and expectations
- the market focus, which stresses the importance of satisfying customers by adding value and differentiating products and services.

All of these are important; none of them can be ignored. The culture can be analysed in terms of how these four philosophies are perceived and prioritized. As pointed out earlier, the philosophy may have to change if success is to be sustained.

A company which relies heavily upon formal strategic planning, for example, is likely to concentrate more upon shareholders and resources. It may be argued that, at a corporate level Hanson was similarly inclined; the individual subsidiary businesses typically had a resource focus supported by people and market philosophies. (Hanson was ultimately split into five separate businesses.) General Electric (GE) of the USA is another diversified conglomerate but with a different policy and style from Hanson on empowerment and decentralization. GE places most emphasis upon people and its style and culture have proved more enduring. Japanese companies, discussed later in this chapter, exhibit a particular blend of people, markets and resources.

Styles of management

The style adopted by the strategic leader can have a strong influence on the culture of the organization. Individual leaders can, for example, be relatively autocratic or democratic, visionary or essentially champions of the past, orientated more towards markets or more towards financial controls.

Styles which differ from the 'normal and traditional' can prove to be very effective in particular circumstances. The John Lewis Partnership, Britain's third largest department store chain after Debenhams and House of Fraser, practises worker participation and democracy. John Lewis is also diversified into supermarkets with its Waitrose chain. The company has a chairman, a board of directors and a management structure, as do most companies, but parallel to this commercial structure stands a second structure which represents the interests of the ordinary worker who is also a partner in John Lewis. While a partner working in a department in a store cannot directly influence management decisions, as a result of the partnership and its constitution the ordinary workers are again in ultimate control of the company for which they work. This is supplemented by a profit-sharing scheme. Decision making and communications within the organization must be affected by high levels of participation. John Lewis's motto of 'never knowingly undersold' is based on value for money which is helped by employee involvement. Through its workforce the company can relate well to its customers.

> Everyone in the business feels (and is) involved. Everyone also feels (and is) accountable, especially those at the top. Top management are given lots of freedom to determine and change strategy, but they can be questioned on anything by the rank-and-file partners . . . this . . . makes people think ahead and consider the consequences of their actions.
>
> *Stuart Hampson, Chairman, John Lewis Partnership, since 1993.*
> *Hampson is only the fourth Chairman since*
> *the Partnership was formed in 1929*

Culture and Power

In Charles Handy's classification of organizations in terms of their culture, power is an important element which needs further consideration.

Power is related to the potential or ability to do something. Consequently, strategic change will be strongly influenced by the bases of power within an organization and by the power of the organization in relation to is environment.

Internal power

Change is brought about if the necessary resources can be harnessed and if people can be persuaded to behave in a particular way. Both of these require power. Power results in part from the structure of the organization, and it needs exercising in different ways in different cultures if it is to be used effectively. At the same time power can be a feature of an individual manager's personality, and managers who are personally powerful will be in a position to influence change.

The ways in which managers apply power are known as 'power levers'; Box 4.1 describes seven major sources of power. The classifications of power bases produced by a number of authors differ only slightly. Box 4.1 has been developed from a classification by Andrew Kakabadse (1982), who has built on the earlier work of French and Raven (1959).

KEY CONCEPT – Box 4.1
Power Levers

- **Reward power** is the ability to influence the rewards given to others. These can be tangible (money) or intangible (status). Owner managers enjoy considerable reward power, managers in larger public-sector organizations very little. For reward power to be useful, the rewards being offered must be important to the potential recipients.

- **Coercive power** is power based on the threat of punishment for non-compliance, and the ability to impose the punishment. The source can be the person's role or position in the organization, or physical attributes and personality.

- **Legitimate power** is synonymous with authority, and relates to an individual manager's position within the structure of the organization. It is an entitlement from the role a person occupies. The effective use of legitimate power is dependent on three things: access to relevant information; access to other people and communication networks inside the organization; and approaches to setting priorities – this determines what is asked of others.

- **Personal power** depends on individual characteristics (personality) and physical characteristics. Charm, charisma and flair are terms used to describe people with personality-based power. Physical attributes such as height, size, weight and strength also affect personal power.

- **Expert power** is held by a person with specialist knowledge or skills in a particular field. It is particularly useful for tackling complex problem areas. It is possible for people to be attributed expert power through reputation rather than proven ability.

- **Information power** is the ability to access and use information to defend a stance or viewpoint – or to question an alternative view held by someone else – and is important as it can affect strategic choices.

- **Connection power** results from personal and professional access to key people inside and outside the organization, who themselves can influence what happens. This relates particularly to information power.

In order to understand the reality of change in an organization and to examine how change might be managed, it is important to consider where power lies, which managers are powerful, and where their sources of power are. While a visible, powerful and influential strategic leader is often a feature of an entrepreneurial organization, the nature and direction of incremental change will be influenced significantly by which managers are powerful and how they choose to exercise their power.

A power culture has strong central leadership as a key feature and power lies with the individual or small group at the centre who controls most of the activity in the organization. In contrast, role cultures are based on the legitimacy of rules and procedures and individual managers are expected to work within these. Task cultures are dependent on the expertise of individuals, and their success, in some part, depends on the ability of the individuals to share their power and work as a team. Managers are expected to apply power levers in ways that are acceptable to the predominant culture of the organization, and at the same time the manner in which power levers are actually used affects what happens in the organization. Power is required for change; change results from the application of power. Hence the implementation of desired changes to strategies requires the effective use of power bases; but other strategic changes will result from the exercise of power by individual managers. It is important for the organization to monitor such activity and ensure that such emergent changes and strategies are desirable or acceptable.

The relative power of the organization

The ability of an organization to effect change within its environment will similarly depend on the exercise of power. A strong competitor with, say, a very distinctive product or service, or with substantial market share, may be more powerful than its rivals. A manufacturer who is able to influence distributors or suppliers will be similarly powerful. The issue is the relative power in relation to those other individuals, organizations and institutions – its stakeholders – on whom it relies, with whom it trades, or which influence it in some way.

The Search for Excellence

Research into US companies

McKinsey and Company, well-known US management consultants, initiated an investigation in the 1970s into why certain companies were more successful than their rivals. The findings were published in 1980 in a *Business Week* article and they eventually became the basis for the book *In Search of Excellence* (Peters and Waterman, 1982). The research emphasizes the important contribution of culture and values to organizational success.

At successful companies, strong cultures are clearly a strategic asset as internalized beliefs motivate people to unusual performance levels. We must, however, be cautious. While much may be known about the culture of a successful organization, we may not learn 'how to get it'. *In Search of Excellence* (in common with similar books) is descriptive, not prescriptive.

Table 4.4 In search of excellence: characteristics of the most successful organizations

A bias for action	Greater emphasis on trying things rather than talking about them and seeking 'solutions' rather than 'resolutions' Avoidance of long, complicated business plans Use of task forces to tackle special problems (Handy's task culture)
Close to the customer	Companies are 'customer-driven, not technology-driven, not product-driven, not strategy-driven' They 'know what the customer wants, and provide it – better than competitors'
Autonomy and entrepreneurship	Managers are authorized to act entrepreneurially rather than be tied too rigidly by rules and systems
Productivity through people	Productivity improvements by motivating and stimulating employees, using involvement and communications 'Corny merit awards, like badges and stars work' if they are properly managed and not just used as a gimmick
Hands on, value driven	Values are established with good communications People must 'believe' The power and personality of the strategic leader is crucial
Stick to the knitting	Successful companies know what they do well and concentrate on doing it well
Simple form, lean staff	Simple structures
Simultaneous loose–tight properties	An effective combination of central direction and individual autonomy Certain control variables, such as a particular financial return measure or the number of employees, are managed tightly; for other things managers are encouraged to be flexible

Summarized from Peters, TJ and Waterman, RH Jr (1982) In *Search of Excellence*, Harper and Row.

Some 40 companies were surveyed in a cross-section of industries and included IBM, Texas Instruments, Hewlett-Packard, 3M, Procter and Gamble, Johnson and Johnson, and McDonald's. The companies were selected for being well-run and successful organizations. Most of the companies were well established and large. In the selection process 20 years of financial data were analysed and the companies under consideration were evaluated relative to competitors in their industry. In addition, a subjective assessment of their innovation records was used as a final screen. The research concluded that the most successful companies exhibited eight common attributes, which are featured in Table 4.4, and that their success was based primarily on good management practice. Managers had invested time, energy and thought into doing certain important things well, and those activities and values were understood by employees and appreciated by customers. In other words they had become part of the culture of the organization.

In most companies the role of one or more strategic leaders had proved to be very influential in establishing and developing the values, and in many cases the values had been established early in the company's history. In other words growth had been assisted by the culture. Peters and Waterman conclude that 'the real role of the chief executive is to manage the values of the organization'.

Peters and Waterman argued that 'excellent' companies are successful in their management of the basic fundamentals with respect to their environment: customer service; low-cost manufacturing; productivity improvement; innovation; and risk taking. In order to ensure that the key values are understood and practised throughout the organization there is an emphasis on simplicity: simple organization structures; simple strategies; simple goals; and simple communications systems.

The attributes featured in Table 4.4 are essentially basic rather than startling, and they are very much related to the contribution made by people. 'The excellent companies live their commitment to people'. Not all the attributes were visible in each of the companies studied, nor were they given the same priority in different organizations, but in every case there was a preponderance of the attributes and they were both visible and distinctive. In less successful companies, argue Peters and Waterman, 'far too many managers have lost sight of the basics: quick action, service to customers, practical innovation, and the fact that you can't get any of these without virtually everyone's commitment'.

Since the book was published some of the 'excellent' companies, most notably People Express and Caterpillar Tractor, have been less successful and so the findings of *In Search of Excellence* should be treated carefully. Basically, the research found a number of common attributes to be present in the organizations studied rather than providing a set of recommendations concerning how unsuccessful companies could be transformed. It provided food for thought rather than answers.

In a more recent book Robert Waterman (1988), writing independently, argued that in order to become and remain successful organizations must master the management of change. However, there is often a fear of change and hostility towards it. These must be overcome, claims Waterman, because competition changes too quickly to allow companies to fall into what he calls the 'habit trap'. He further argues that strategies should be based on 'informed opportunism', developing from effective information systems which ensure that customers, suppliers and other key influences are consulted. Waterman emphasizes that for an information system to be effective it should not be allowed to become too rigid or bureaucratic.

Peters (1988) also asserts that there are no long-term excellent companies. 'The pace of change has become far too rapid to make any enterprise secure. Tomorrow's winners will have to view chaos, external and internal, not as a problem, but as a prime source of competitive advantage'. Peters quoted Ford of Europe as an example of a company which was dealing successfully with the challenge of change by stressing a new set of basic values: world-class quality and service; greater flexibility and responsiveness; continuous and rapid product and service innovation. Arguably, however, the change had been forced on Ford by strong Japanese competition and it has not prevented Ford having to reduce production capacity in Europe in recent years. Simply, we need companies that are flexible and innovative, companies that can learn from the past and find new opportunities and new ways of competing as markets and industries change.

After the success of *In Search of Excellence* it was inevitable that there would be a parallel study in the UK. This was reported originally by Goldsmith and Clutterbuck in *The Winning Streak* (1984), with the work updated in 1997. In this more recent book Goldsmith and Clutterbuck conclude that success lies not with specific strategies, structures and styles but with the dexterity with which organizations deal with the pressures they face. Their ability to do this, of course, is culture related and culture dependent.

Goldsmith and Clutterbuck identify a number of cultural dilemmas facing organizations. These include:

- Pride and humility – realizing that internal self-belief and pride in what the organization is doing and achieving are crucial, but that they must not become arrogance and a belief the organization is untouchable.
- Values and rules – finding the appropriate degree of effective empowerment.

- Customer care versus customer count – finding new customers will always be important, but this should not be at the expense of looking after existing ones properly.
- Challenging and nurturing people at the same time – setting stretching targets, but providing support.

There will never be straightforward answers to these issues and dilemmas, but the current style and approach of an organization will affect its relative fortunes.

The limits to excellence

To summarize, some firms do appear to obtain superior financial performance from their cultures, but it does not follow that firms who succeed in copying these cultural attributes will necessarily also achieve superior financial results. Organizations which pursue the excellence factors must surely improve their chances of success, but clearly there can be no guarantees. Ignoring these issues will, however, increase the chances of failure.

However, the need to maintain E–V–R congruence in a dynamic, competitive environment must never be forgotten.

During the early 1980s Jan Carlzon turned around the struggling SAS (Scandinavian Airlines System) by focusing on improvements in service and communications. Profits were restored with improved revenues, but costs later increased as well. As a driving philosophy, the service culture had to give way to a focus strategy and rationalization.

> *Everything that does not further the competitiveness of our airline activities must be removed, sold or turned into separate entities.*
>
> Jan Carlzon

Carlzon was successful for a period, but 'fell from grace' when SAS profits later declined again. BA, which followed SAS with a service culture, was, for a number of years, more successful in simultaneously controlling costs, and it became one of the world's most successful and admired airlines. Again fortunes have changed, illustrating how the trust that is required to underpin a service culture can easily be lost when difficult strategies have to be implemented and are not handled well.

In my opinion effective strategic management requires:

- a sound strategy, which implies an effective match between the resources and the environment
- a well-managed execution and implementation of the strategy
- appropriate strategic change. While it can be important to 'stick to the knitting', firms must watch for signs indicating that strategies need to be improved or changed.

Culture and competitive advantage

Barney (1986) has examined further the relationship between culture and 'superior financial performance'. He has used microeconomics for his definition of superior financial performance, arguing that firms record either below-normal returns (insufficient for long-term survival in the industry), normal returns (enough for survival, but no more) or superior results, which are more than those required for long-term survival. Superior results, which result from some form of competitive advantage, attract competitors who seek to copy whatever is thought to be the source of competitive advantage and generating the success. This in turn affects supply and margins and can reduce profitability to only normal returns and, in some cases, below normal. Therefore, sustained superior financial performance requires sustained competitive advantage. Barney concluded that culture can, and does, generate sustained competitive advantage, and hence long-term superior financial performance, when three conditions are met.

- The culture is valuable. The culture must enable things to happen which themselves result in high sales, low costs or high margins.
- The culture is rare.
- The culture is imperfectly imitable, i.e. it cannot be copied easily by competitors.

Hence, if the cultural factors identified by Peters and Waterman are in fact transferable easily to other organizations, can they be the source of superior financial performance? Barney contends that valuable and rare cultures may be difficult, if not impossible, to imitate. For one thing, it is very difficult to define culture clearly, particularly in respect of how it adds value to the product or service. For another, culture is often tied to historical aspects of company development and to the beliefs, personality and charisma of a particular strategic leader.

Club Méditerranée and The Body Shop provide examples of companies which have gained success and renown with a culture-based competitive advantage. While maintaining the underlying principles and values, both companies have had to rethink their strategies to remain competitive.

Changing Culture

The culture of an organization may appear to be in need of change for any one of a number of reasons. It could be that the culture does not fit well with the needs of the environment or with the organization's resources, or that the company is not performing well and needs major strategic changes, or even that the company is growing rapidly in a changing environment and needs to adapt.

Ideally, the culture and strategies being pursued will complement each other and, again ideally, the organization will be flexible and adaptable to change when it is appropriate. But these ideals will not always be achieved.

The culture of an organization can be changed, but it may not be easy. Strong leadership and vision is always required to champion the change process. If an organization is in real difficulty, and the threat to its survival is clearly recognized, behaviour can be changed through fear and necessity. However, people may not feel comfortable and committed to the changes they accept or are coerced into accepting. Behaviour may change, but not attitudes and beliefs. When an organization is basically successful the process of change again needs careful management – changing attitudes and beliefs does not itself guarantee a change in behaviour. It is not unusual for a team of senior managers to spend time, frequently at a location away from the organization itself, discussing these issues and becoming excited about a set of new values that they proclaim are the way forward. After the workshop any commitment to the new values and to change can be easily lost once managers return to the 'daily grind' and they become caught up again in immediate problems and difficulties. Their behaviour does not change and so the culture remains largely untouched.

The potential for changing the culture is affected by:

- the strength and history of the existing culture
- how well the culture is understood
- the personality and beliefs of the strategic leader and
- the extent of the strategic need.

Lewin (1947) contends that there are three important stages in the process of change: unfreezing existing behaviour, changing attitudes and behaviour, and refreezing the new behaviour as accepted common practice.

The first steps in changing culture are recognizing and diagnosing the existing culture, highlighting any weaknesses and stressing the magnitude of the need to change.

One way of changing behaviour would be the establishment of internal groups to study and benchmark competitors and set new performance standards. This would lead to wider discussion throughout the organization, supported by skills training – possibly including communication, motivation and financial awareness skills. People must become committed to the changes, which requires persistence by those who are championing the change and an emphasis on the significance and the desired outcomes.

Unless the changes become established and part of the culture, there will be a steady drift back to the previous pattern. While critical aspects of the culture should remain rock solid and generate strategic consistency, this must not mean that the organization becomes resistant to change without some major upheaval. Competitive pressures require organizations to be vigilant, aware and constantly change orientated, not change resistant.

Resistance to change should always be expected. People may simply be afraid because they do not understand the reasons behind the proposed changes; they may mistrust colleagues or management because of previous experiences; communications may be poor; motivation and commitment may be missing; internal architecture may be weak, causing internal conflict and hostility; and the organization may simply not be good at sharing best practice and learning.

Culture – An International Dimension

There are cultural differences between nations and ethnic groups. What constitutes acceptable behaviour in one country (for example, bribes) would be totally unacceptable in others. Ways of conducting discussions and deals vary – Indians always like and expect to negotiate, for instance. Some countries, such as France, have a high respect for tradition and the past, while others, such as the USA, are more interested in future prospects. This influences the extent to which both individuals and organizations are judged on their track record and on their promise. These differences are important because business is conducted across frontiers and because many organizations have bases in several countries. Organizations, therefore, have to adjust their style for different customers and markets and accept that there will be cultural differences between the various parts of the organization. This reality affects the ability of the strategic leader to synthesize the various parts of the organization and achieve the potential synergies.

Related to these issues, research by Kanter (1991) drew out different perspectives on competitive success between the leading nations, where she argued that these stemmed from national cultures and cultural differences. Her findings indicated the following priorities:

- Japan –   Product development
                Management
                Product quality
- USA –   Customer service
                Product quality
                Technology
- Germany –   Workforce skills
                Problem solving
                Management.

These conclusions may be summarized by arguing that Japan is driven by a commitment to innovation, America by customers and Germany by engineering.

Interestingly, the report highlighted how UK competitiveness had been enhanced by its drive to privatize public services and other state-owned organizations, the opening up of its capital markets and its encouragement of inward investment. At the same time it is arguably inhibited by an education system which discourages rather than encourages creativity, individualism and entrepreneurship, by a general lack of language skills and, for many, a preference for leisure over work. While a case can be made that these issues are being addressed in various ways, they remain relative weaknesses.

Differences in international cultures have been examined by various authors, including Hofstede (1991), Kluckhohn and Strodtbeck (1961) and Trompenaars and Hampden-Turner (1997). The following points have been distilled from their findings. From these points general conclusions may be drawn about cultural differences between nations; but it must also be recognized that certain organizations in the same country do not automatically fit the national picture in every respect. In some respects, for example, Sony is typically Japanese. In other respects it behaves more like an American company, such that research has confirmed that many US citizens think that Sony is American!

- Some countries and cultures prefer a watertight contractual approach while others are more comfortable with trust and 'a handshake'. The appropriate way of conducting business therefore varies accordingly.
- In some countries managers operate with individual freedom and responsibility, and negotiations are on a one-to-one basis. In others there will invariably be a team of people involved. Where there are multiple decision makers like this, there will sometimes be a clear hierarchy and recognition of the relative power of various individuals. On other occasions such demarcations will be less obvious or visible.
- In addition, individual managers can be relatively selfish in their outlook, or far more corporate. This can have a particular bearing on where managers' natural competitive energy is channelled. Is it directed at outside competitors, as realistically it should be, or at perceived internal rivals? Simply, would a culture of internal rivalry inside an organization be typical or rare?
- There is also an issue of women managers. In some countries they will not be found, either at all, or at least in positions of real authority.
- Leisure activities can play a relatively minor or more prominent role in business. The image of the British bank manager who enjoys long lunches and regular golf matches with clients has been largely confined to history, but negotiations and networking away from the place of business can still be important. Corporate hospitality at major sporting events would be one example, but it is not practised universally.

- Senses of humour also vary, which begs the question: is creativity more likely to be found in some countries than others? Creativity implies elements of fun and irreverence, challenging existing ways and looking for new and different alternatives. Certainly humour, together with other issues, such as the symbolism of certain objects and colours, affects advertising and promotion. The same campaigns cannot necessarily be used on a global scale.
- This leads on to a final point: do managers in different countries have similar or different perspectives on uncertainty? Some countries, organizations and managers are relatively risk orientated and view environmental turbulence as a source of opportunity. They look to be proactive. Others seek to be more reactive and adaptive, attempting to find positions of stability amongst the perceived chaos.

Since the end of World War II Japan has risen to become a major economic force around the world, with some Japanese companies extremely prominent in certain industries. The Japanese style of management is very different in some respects from that found in most Western countries and, while it cannot simply be copied – largely because of cultural differences – it offers a number of important and valuable lessons. Consequently, this chapter finishes with a section on Japanese culture and management style.

The Japanese Culture and Style of Management

Without question, Japanese companies have become formidable competitors in several industries. For many years they have been the principal challengers of Western firms serious about world markets. More recently domestic recession, a high yen and intensifying competition from other Pacific Rim countries (many with lower wages) have restrained Japan's global expansion. However, a study of the philosophies, strategies and tactics adopted by Japanese companies will yield a number of valuable insights into competitive strategy, even though it is impractical to suggest that Western businesses could simply learn to copy their Japanese rivals. This section looks at some of the reasons for Japan's economic rise and success; it has to be acknowledged that in the 1990s some of the practices have changed. 'In the long-run the only feasible response is to do better what the Japanese are doing well already – developing management systems that motivate employees from top to bottom to pursue growth-oriented, innovation-focused competitive strategies' (Pucik and Hatvany, 1983).

Deal and Kennedy (1982) have argued that 'Japan Inc.' is a culture, with considerable co-operation between industry, the banking systems and government. For this reason certain aspects of the Japanese culture are difficult to imitate. For example, banks in the UK are public companies with their own shareholders and they borrow and lend money in order to make profit; this is their basic 'mission'.

Another key structural feature historically has been the keiretsu, or corporate families, whereby a unique mix of ownerships and alliances makes hostile take-overs very unlikely. At its height, for example, the powerful Mitsubishi keiretsu represented 216,000 employees in 29 organizations as diverse as banking, brewing, shipping, shipbuilding, property, oil, aerospace and textiles. The companies held, on average, 38% of each other's shares; directors were exchanged; and the fact that 15 of the companies were located together in one district of Tokyo facilitated linkages of various forms, including intertrading wherever this was practical. The keiretsu influence is fading as Japanese companies are locating more and more production overseas in their search for lower manufacturing costs. Mitsubishi's shipping company, for instance, has begun to buy vessels manufactured in Korean yards; Japanese shipbuilders are no longer an automatic low-price competitor.

Culture plays a significant role at the heart of the Japanese strategy process.

In Japan the historic focus has been on human resources (Pucik and Hatvany, 1983) and this became the basis for three key strategic thrusts which are expressed as a number of management techniques. These have acted as key determinants of the actual strategies pursued (Figure 4.4). The three strategic thrusts are the notion of an internal labour market within the organization, a unique company philosophy, and intensive socialization throughout the working life.

The internal labour market is based on the tradition of lifetime employment whereby young men (not women) who joined large companies after school or university were expected to remain with them for life and in return were offered job security. Commitment and loyalty to the employer result. With recession in recent years this practice has been less widespread.

The articulated and enacted unique philosophy is again designed to generate commitment and loyalty with the argument that familiarity with the goals of a company helps to establish values and provides direction for effort and behaviour. YKK's 'Cycle of Goodness' (Box 4.2) is an excellent example.

The potential benefits of a company philosophy will only be gained if the philosophy is communicated to employees and demonstrated by managers. Hence this is a key aspect of company socialization in Japan, which starts with initial training and continues with further training throughout the working life.

These three strategic thrusts are closely linked to six management techniques used extensively in Japanese firms.

Open communication and sharing information across departmental boundaries aims to develop a climate of trust and a team spirit within the organization. This is enhanced by close integration between managers and employees. Job rotation and the internal training programmes supplement this communication system because through them employees become more aware of what happens throughout the organization. Because of relatively low labour turnover, promotion oppor-

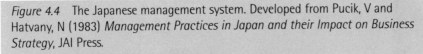

Figure 4.4 The Japanese management system. Developed from Pucik, V and Hatvany, N (1983) *Management Practices in Japan and their Impact on Business Strategy*, JAI Press.

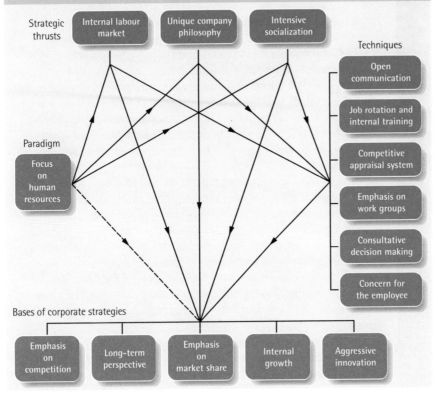

tunities are very limited and advancement is slow and often based on seniority. However, performance is essential, and employees are carefully and regularly appraised in their abilities to get things done and to co-operate with others.

This is particularly important as Japanese companies revolve around groups rather than individuals, with work being assigned to teams of employees. This, together with the use of quality circles (whereby groups of employees are encouraged to discuss issues and problems and suggest improvements), is seen as a key motivator. There is considerable emphasis on consultative decision making, involving these working groups, and a desire for consensus decisions. This generates greater loyalty to the decisions and to implementation. Finally, managers are encouraged to spend time with employees discussing both performance and personal problems. Companies have also frequently provided housing and various other services for employees.

!

STRATEGY IN ACTION – Box 4.1
The Cycle of Goodness
Attributed to Tadeo Yoshida, President, YKK

YKK is the world's leading manufacturer of zip fasteners. YKK produces and markets zips throughout the world, and is vertically integrated, designing and manufacturing much of its own machinery.

I firmly believe in the spirit of social service.

Wages alone are not sufficient to assure our employees of a stable life and a rising standard of living. For this reason we return to them a large share of the fruits of their labour, so that they may also participate in capital accumulation and share in the profits of the firm. Each employee, depending on his means, deposits with the company at least ten per cent of his wages and monthly allowances, and 50 per cent of his bonus; the company, in turn, pays interest on these savings. Moreover, as this increases capital, the employees benefit further as stockholders of the firm. It is said that the accumulation of savings distinguishes man from animals. Yet, if the receipts of a day are spent within that day, there can be no such cycle of saving.

The savings of all YKK employees are used to improve production facilities, and contribute directly to the prosperity of the firm. Superior production facilities improve the quality of the goods produced. Lower prices increase demand. And both factors contribute to the prosperity of other industries that use our products.

As society prospers, the need for raw materials and machinery of all sorts increases, and the benefits of this cycle spread out not just to this firm, but to all related industries. Thus the savings of our employees, by enhancing the prosperity of the firm, are returned to them as dividends that enrich their lives. This results in increased savings which further advance the firm. Higher incomes mean higher tax payments, and higher tax payments enrich the lives of every citizen. In this manner, business income directly affects the prosperity of society; for businesses are not mere seekers after profit, but vital instruments for the improvement of society.

This cycle enriches our free society and contributes to the happiness of those who work within it. The perpetual working of this cycle produces perpetual prosperity for all. This is the cycle of goodness.

YKK http://www.ykk.com

Several Japanese companies have invested in manufacturing plants in the USA and Europe in recent years. In a number of cases they have selected industries where the country had already ceased to manufacture products because of an inability to compete (e.g. television sets and video recorders) or where the competitive edge had declined. Motor vehicles is an example of the latter. The British car industry fell behind the Japanese and German producers in terms of quality and productivity and has struggled to catch up. The first Japanese car plant in the UK was built by Nissan near Sunderland and, using a Japanese approach – rather than adopting all the techniques described in this section – it has become the most productive car plant in the UK, and one of Nissan's most efficient anywhere in the world.

Hill (1990) explains that the key human resources aspects of the Nissan UK strategy are as follows.

- There is a single union agreement, with the AEU.
- All employees (including managers) have the same conditions of employment, and wear similar blue overalls at work.
- There are no (inflexible) written job descriptions.
- There is no clocking on and no privileged parking.
- Absenteeism has remained very low.
- There are daily communications meetings – searching for continuous improvement.
- Employees often go to Japan for training – skilled workers learn both operational and maintenance skills.
- The training budget, equivalent to 14% of sales revenue, is exceptionally high for a British company. A typical employee will receive 9 days on-the-job and 12 days off-the-job training each year.
- Supervisors are empowered managers. They recruit and select their own staff (individually they are responsible for about 20 employees), and they control the layout and operation of their own part of the production line.

The core of management is the art of mobilizing every ounce of intelligence in the organization and pulling together the intellectual resources of all employees in the service of the firm. We know that the intelligence of a handful of technocrats, however brilliant and smart they may be, is no longer enough. Only by drawing on the combined brain power of all its employees can a firm face up to the turbulence and constraints of today's environment.

Mr Konosuke Matsushita, Matsushita Electrical Industrial Company Ltd

Quality and competition

Although there are close supporting links between companies, government and the banking system, there is intense and aggressive competition between the individual firms in an industry, fostered by growth objectives and the loyalty of employees to their firm.

Prahalad and Hamel (1985) have suggested that the Japanese 'rewrite the rules of the game to take their competitors by surprise'. Through technology, design, production costs, distribution and selling arrangements, pricing and service they seek to build 'layers of competitive advantage' rather than concentrate on just one aspect. Many competitors in the West think more narrowly. Prahalad and Hamel suggest that Japanese companies are successful in part because they have a clear mission and statement of strategic intent, and a culture which provides both opportunity and encouragement to change things incrementally. Getting things right first time and every time – total quality management – is endemic in the culture.

Internationally, Japanese companies may not be consistent with their strategies; instead they will seek the best competitive opportunities in different places and they will change continually as new opportunities arise and are created.

Japanese companies benchmark against the best in the world and willingly customize their products to meet local market demand.

Long-term perspective

It was shown in Chapter 2 that while many Western companies concentrate on short-term strategies, influenced often by financial pressures, the Japanese take a long-term perspective.

Emphasis on market share

Japanese companies are competitive, growth orientated and anxious to build and sustain high market shares in world markets. This will enable them to provide the job security that is a fundamental aspect of the culture. They often use their experience curve (which is examined in detail in the Finance in Action supplement to Chapter 5) to develop strategies aimed at market dominance with a long-term view of costs and prices.

Internal growth

Mergers, acquisitions and divestitures are relatively uncommon in Japan – the Japanese favour the internal production system and innovation.

In a book on Japanese manufacturing techniques, Schonberger (1984) argued that a major reason for Japan's success has been its ability to use its resources well, better than many Western competitors. In many factories, he contends, the equipment is no better than that used elsewhere in the world, but wherever they can Japanese companies invest in the best equipment available. Managerial skills are used in improvement drives, a search for simple solutions and, in particular, a meticulous attention to detail. Simplicity is important since management and shopfloor can relate better to each other; and flexible techniques and workforces result in low stock production systems, efficiency and lower costs.

The ability to trust and establish close links with other companies in the supply chain allows focused specialization and just-in-time manufacturing with low inventories. However, this type of dependency can act as a hindrance to global expansion until comparative supplier links can be established.

Innovation

Research and development is deemed important and funded appropriately. As a result much of Japan's technology has advanced quickly, and firms who fail to innovate go out of business. Ohmae (1985) has described Japan as a 'very unforgiving economy', with thousands of corporations destroyed every year through bankruptcy. He points out that Japan is selective about the industries in which research and development will be concentrated. Japan has, for example, spent a relatively high proportion of its research and development money in ceramics and steel, and as a result has become a world leader in fibre optics, ceramics and mass-produced large-scale integrated circuits. For similar reasons the USA is world leader in biotechnology and specialized semiconductors, and Europe in chemicals and pharmaceuticals.

Product innovation in Japan is fast and competitive. For example, Sony launched the first miniaturized camcorder (hand-held video camera and recorder) in June 1989. Weighing less than 700 g (1.5 lb) it was one-quarter of the size of existing camcorders. Within six months Matsushita and JVC had introduced lighter models. Within a further six months there was additional competition from Canon, Sanyo, Ricoh and Hitachi. Sony introduced two new models in Summer 1990. One was the lightest then available; the other had superior technical features. More recent models feature larger viewfinders and allow the user to hold the camcorder at arm's length instead of up-to-the-eye.

This faster model replacement is linked to an ability to break even financially with fewer sales of each model. Japan has achieved this with efficient and flexible manufacturing systems and a greater willingness to use common, rather than model-specific, components.

Individual Western companies have proved that it is possible, with determination and distinctive products, to penetrate Japanese markets successfully, but contenders can expect fierce resistance and defensive competition.

Summary

Culture is the way in which an organization performs its tasks, the way its people think, feel and act in response to opportunities and threats, the ways in which objectives and strategies are set and decisions made. It reflects emotional issues and it is not easily analysed, quantified or changed. Nevertheless, it is a key influence on strategic choice, strategy implementation and strategic change – until we understand the culture of an organization we cannot understand strategic management in that organization.

A large organization is unlikely to be just one single, definable culture. It is more likely to be a loose or tight amalgam of different cultures.

It is quite normal for the culture to be influenced by a strong strategic leader and his or her beliefs and values.

In a very broad sense we can think of culture as a mixture of *behaviours* (manifestations) and underlying *attitudes and values*. It is easier to change one of these rather than both simultaneously.

There is no 'ideal culture' as such. Key elements typically have a 'flip side' and, therefore, a style and approach that is appropriate at a particular time can quickly become out of date and in need of change.

An useful grid for analysing the culture of any organization would comprise:

Manifestations – artefacts; values; underlying assumptions; behaviours
People   – stories; leadership; communications
Power   – ownership and structure; personal power; organizational politics.

Charles Handy proposes *four cultural types* which help to explain the culture, style and approach of different organizations. These are the power culture (typical of small, entrepreneurial organizations), the role culture (larger and more formal organizations), the task culture (the complex organization seeking to achieve internal synergies through effective linkages) and the person culture (built around the individual managers' needs).

In an alternative and equally significant contribution Miles and Snow differentiate among *defenders* (conservative and low-risk organizations), *prospectors* (innovative and entrepreneurial), *analysers* (limited change with measured steps) and *reactors* (followers). These can be readily linked to styles of strategy creation.

We can only understand culture when we understand power inside an organization. Who has power, how do they acquire it and how do they use it?

A number of books on the general theme of 'organizational excellence' has highlighted how it is culture that is at the heart of success. Although general themes and lessons can be teased out, an organization cannot simply replicate the culture of another successful organization and become successful itself.

There are important cultural differences between nations. This has implications for businesses which operate or trade globally.

References

Barney, JB (1986) Organization culture: can it be a source of sustained competitive advantage? *Academy of Management Review*, 11 (3).

Berry, D (1983) The perils of trying to change corporate culture, *Financial Times*, 14 December.

Deal, T and Kennedy, A (1982) *Corporate Cultures. The Rites and Rituals of Corporate Life*, Addison-Wesley.

French, JRP and Raven, B (1959) The bases of social power. In *Studies in Social Power* (ed. D Cartwright), University of Michigan Press.

Goldsmith, W and Clutterbuck, D (1997) *The Winning Streak Mark II*, Orion Business. The first edition, *The Winning Streak*, was originally published in 1984 by Weidenfeld and Nicolson.

Hampden-Turner, C (1990) Corporate culture – from vicious to virtuous circles, *Economist*.

Handy, CB (1976) *Understanding Organizations*, Penguin. The ideas are elaborated in Handy, CB (1978) *Gods of Management*, Souvenir Press.

Harrison, R (1972) Understanding your organization's character, *Harvard Business Review*, May/June.

Hill, R (1990) Nissan and the art of people management, *Director*, March.

Hofstede, G (1991) *Cultures and Organization: Software of the Mind*, McGraw Hill.

Kakabadse, A (1982) *Culture of the Social Services*, Gower.

Kanter, RM (1991) Transcending business boundaries: 12000 world managers view change, *Harvard Business Review*, May–June.

Kluckhohn, C and Strodtbeck, F (1961) *Variations in Value Orientations*, Peterson.

Leadbeater, C and Rudd, R (1991) What drives the lords of the deal? *Financial Times*, 20 July.

Lewin, K (1947) Frontiers in group dynamics: concept, method and reality in social science, *Human Relations*, 1.

Miles, RE and Snow, CC (1978) *Organization Strategy, Structure and Process*, McGraw-Hill.

Ohmae, K (1985) *Triad Power*, Free Press.

Peters, TJ (1988) *Thriving on Chaos*, Knopf.

Peters, TJ and Waterman, RH Jr (1982) *In Search of Excellence: Lessons from America's Best Run Companies*, Harper and Row. Original article: Peters, TJ (1980) Putting excellence into management, *Business Week*, 21 July.

Prahalad, CK and Hamel, G (1985) Address to the Annual Conference of the Strategic Management Society, Barcelona, October.

Press, G (1990) Assessing competitors' business philosophies, *Long Range Planning*, 23, 5.

Pucik, V and Hatvany, N (1983) Management practices in Japan and their impact on business strategy, *Advances in Strategic Management*, Vol. 1, JAI Press.

Pümpin, C (1987) *The Essence of Corporate Strategy*, Gower.

Schein, EH (1985) *Organizational Culture and Leadership*, Jossey Bass.

Schonberger, RJ (1984) *Japanese Manufacturing Techniques*, Free Press.

Schwartz, H and Davis, SM (1981) Matching corporate culture and business strategy, *Organizational Dynamics*, Summer.

Trompenaars, F and Hampden-Turner, C (1997) *Riding the Waves of Culture: Understanding Cultural Diversity in Business*, Nicholas Brealey Publishing.

Waterman, RH Jr (1988) *The Renewal Factor*, Bantam.

Test your knowledge of this chapter with our online quiz at:
http://www.thomsonlearning.co.uk

Explore Culture and Values further at:

Academy of Management Review   http://www.aom.pace.edu/amr

Business Week   http://www.businessweek.com

Long Range Planning   http://www.lrp.ac

Strategic Management Journal   http://www.smsweb.org/about/SMJ/SMJ.html

Questions and Research Assignments

TEXT RELATED

1. Use the text in Case Study 4.2 (IKEA) to complete a culture grid (Figure 4.1) for IKEA.

2. Take an organization with which you are familiar and evaluate it in terms of Handy's and Miles and Snow's typologies.

3. List other organizations that you know which would fit into the categories not covered in your answer to Question 2.

For both Questions 2 and 3 you should comment on whether or not you feel your categorization is appropriate.

4. Considering the organization that you used for Question 2, assess the power levers of the strategic leader and other identifiable managers.

5. Thinking of the identified cultural priorities for Japan, Germany and the USA, listed in the text, what do you think the cultural priorities of UK businesses are?

Internet and Library Projects

1. From the 1980s to the mid-1990s Rover had a strategic alliance with Honda. When its then owner, British Aerospace, sold Rover to BMW this alliance was wound down and then terminated. A Japanese influence was replaced by a German one. Rover developed a number of new models but by early 2000 its trading losses were so significant that BMW decided to 'sell or close'. The Phoenix group was pulled together by a

previous Rover manager, John Towers, and he acquired the business for a mere £10. Rover became British once more. How has the culture and style changed with these various changes of ownership?

Rover Group http://www.rovergroup.com

Honda http://www.honda.com

British Aerospace http://www.bae.co.uk

BMW http://www.bmw.com

2. Research how profitable John Lewis and Waitrose have been in comparison with their major competitors in the 1990s. What conclusions can you draw?

John Lewis Partnership http://www.johnlewis.co.uk

Waitrose http://www.waitrose.com

3. Find out where your nearest John Lewis or Waitrose store is and if possible visit it. Can you detect any differences in attitude between the John Lewis staff and those who work in similar stores?

John Lewis Partnership http://www.johnlewis.co.uk

Waitrose http://www.waitrose.com

4. Our Price, once part of WH Smith, is a leading specialist retailer of music and video products, including computer games – markets where the majority of competing products are identical. At the end of the 1980s, following years of growth, this market had flattened out. Our Price was acknowledged to be a company which provided excellent service but its stores were seen as 'dull, drab, boring and intimidating'.

WH Smith was determined to 'reposition the brand' to revitalize it while ensuring that it was easily distinguishable from its major competitors, especially the informal Virgin Megastores and the mainstream WH Smith stores, which are more formal and traditional. It was thought necessary to change the ways in which products are displayed and sold, media and in-store promotions, aspects of the service and, especially, staff attitudes and behaviour.

A new vision and values was defined 'to build an attitude and way of behaving in all that we do in the business that will support . . . the re-positioning of the brand'.

The Our Price vision
- The first place everybody thinks of for music
- The place its customers keep coming back to
- The place where the involvement and fulfilment of its people creates commercial success.

The required values

To pursue the vision effectively Our Price would need:

- To 'delight' its customers, who need to feel satisfied even if they leave the store without purchasing
- To empower its people
- To drive itself forward and embrace change . . . while recognizing the need to be commercially successful.

Visit your nearest Our Price store and evaluate whether this vision and values are still relevant. Compare and contrast Our Price with competing HMV stores (or Virgin Megastores) and sounds departments within WH Smith high-street stores. Do they seem and feel to be different? What are the implications of any differences?

WH Smith   http://www.whsmith.co.uk

Virgin Megastores   http://www.virginmega.com

HMV   http://www.hmv.co.uk

Environmental Analysis, Synergy and Strategic Positioning

The notion of strategic positioning helps us to understand the fit between an organization and its external environment. Positions are related to the organization's ability to create and add value and consequently added value can be analysed in relation to a SWOT (strengths, weaknesses, opportunities and threats) analysis.

In simple terms, an organization should be asking and addressing two questions simultaneously:

- *What distinctive competencies and relative strengths does the organization possess – and where are there opportunities to exploit this further and more effectively? This is the resource-based approach.*

- *What new opportunities can be spotted and identified for which the organization has, or can, obtain the strengths and competencies which would be needed to exploit them? This is the opportunity-driven approach.*

It is important to hold these two approaches in mind when reading Chapter 5, 6 and 7. In essence, this chapter and much of Chapter 6 (on competitive dynamics) concentrate on the opportunity-driven approach. The resource-based approach is touched on in Chapter 6 when activity mapping is introduced and then it is developed in greater detail in Chapter 7. However, successful organizations do not adopt one approach rather than the other: they address both issues simultaneously and blend them together.

However, we begin this chapter by explaining strategic thinking and synergy, two key strategic issues which impact on both the opportunity-driven and resource-based approaches to strategy.

We continue by examining the nature of the business environment, followed by a consideration of the impact of competition regulations on industry and company strategies to which the opening case study refers. Positions also have to be changed, as seen in the discussion of E–V–R congruence. Sometimes the change is continuous and incremental; sometimes is is more dramatic or discontinuous. To help with the understanding of the latter the chapter concludes with a discussion of scenario building.

Case study 5: Regulation and the Brewing Industry

When governments interfere in industries, there will be forced changes which often open up new opportunities. After all, detailed reports from the UK Competition Commission often contain significant information which becomes freely available to competitors and industry outsiders.

An investigation by the Monopolies and Mergers Commission (the predecessor to the Competition Commission) into brewing resulted in the 1991 Beer Orders. The investigation was prompted by four brewers controlling 60% of brewing and 80% of the UK's 60,000 public houses. The Beer Orders required that brewers with over 2000 pubs had to divest half their estate. In addition, all pubs they retained had to offer 'guest beers', ones not produced by the owner–brewer. The intention was to break the tied link whereby particular beers could be forced on to tenants by the powerful brewers.

In response, the leading brewers set up independent companies to buy out their own pubs, typically with links back to the brewers who were loaning the money. Naturally, the brewers retained the most lucrative pubs in their estates. In reality, the tied link was never truly broken. At the same time, the brewers began to diversify into hotels and restaurants because they were unable to open any new pubs. Bass acquired Holiday Inn, for example. Bass also owns Harvester restaurants and Britvic soft drinks.Whitbread similarly built a portfolio which included Travel Inn, Marriott Hotels (in the UK), Beefeater, Brewers Fayre, the Bella Pasta, TGI Fridays (UK franchise) and Pizza Hut (another UK franchise) restaurants, and the wine and spirits retailers Wine Rack, Threshers and Victoria Wine.

The Beer Orders provided new opportunities for entrepreneurial outsiders. The guest beer requirement, for example, led to the growth of microbreweries, which produce only very limited quantities of generally very strong ales. Some pubs brew their own beer on-site. One manager with the Japanese bank, Nomura, came up with an idea to buy 2000 pubs from Bass for £2 billion. The bank had no interest in running pubs, but it was interested in property which could earn it some £300 million per year in rent. The bank raised the money for the deal by issuing bonds with a 10% annual interest. Simply, the bank raised £2 billion for an annual interest payment of £200 million and earned £300 million in rents – a £100 million annual profit. Simple, really, if you have the idea and the resources to back the deal!

By 1999 the situation was:

	Percentage of UK beer sales	
	On-trade	Take home
Scottish and Newcastle	27	22
Bass	23	17
Whitbread	14	20
Carlsberg–Tetley	13	9
Other companies	23	32

The activity profile (percentages of total turnover) of the four leading brewers was as follows:

	Bass	Whitbread	Scottish and Newcastle	Carlsberg–Tetley
Brewing	33	22	61	77
Retail	30	30	27	0
Soft drinks	11	10	0	8
Other leisure activities	26	38	12	15

Shortly afterwards, both Bass and Whitbread announced that they were to withdraw from brewing in favour of other leisure activities. The Belgian brewer of Stella Artois, Interbrew, expressed interest in acquiring breweries from both companies, thus becoming the UK market leader. However, after Interbrew acquired Bass' Breweries the UK government acted on a competition commission report and demanded the breweries should be re-sold. Meanwhile, Scottish and Newcastle (S&N) acquired Kronenbourg to become Europe's second largest brewer, second only to Heineken. S&N also owns Lodge Inns, Chef and Brewer restaurants, and the Center Parcs and Pontin's holiday resorts. In 2000 S&N was looking to divest its least profitable pubs and Center Parcs.

QUESTION: Overall, have the Beer Orders really affected power and industry concentration in favour of the consumer?

Bass   http://www.bass-brewers.com
Carlsberg-Tetley   http://www.carlsberg.com
Heineken   http://www.heineken.com
Interbrew   http://www.interbrew.com
Scottish and Newcastle   http://www.scottish-newcastle.com
Whitbread   http://www.whitbread.co.uk

Introduction

Good ideas for the future can either start inside the organization or be obtained from external contacts, and they require that organization strengths are matched with external, environmental opportunities. The ability to create and sustain an effective match is a reflection of the organization's *strategic thinking* capabilities.

At one level, matching, exploiting and changing the linkages between resource competency and environmental opportunity is an expression of organizational competitiveness, and the presence (or absence) of competitive advantage. It was shown earlier (Chapter 1) how it is essential for organizations to seek competitive advantage for every product, service and business in their portfolios. Competitiveness comes from functions and activities, and the effectiveness of the links between them. This is one aspect of *synergy*. The second aspect of synergy is the relatedness and interdependency of the different products, services and businesses and their ability to support each other in some way.

Figure 5.1 illustrates the organization in the context of its external environment. Its suppliers and customers, upon whom it depends, and its competitors – both existing and new-in-the-future – are shown as having an immediate impact. Wider environmental forces bear on all the 'players' in the industry, and these are shown in the outer circle as political, economic, social and technological (PEST) forces.

The forces and influences have been deliberately shown in concentric circles. It is quite typical for us to think of the organization as a group of activities (and/or functions) and then to place everything and everyone else, including suppliers and customers, in a so-called external business environment. Increasingly, it

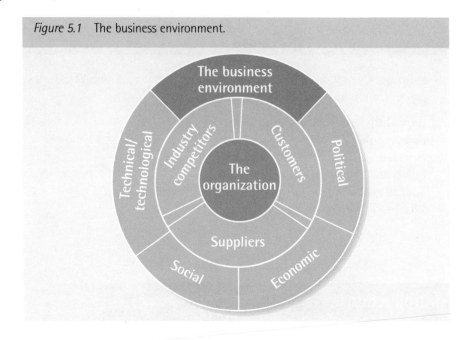

Figure 5.1 The business environment.

makes considerable sense for the organization to see itself working in partnership with its suppliers, distributors and customers. When this perspective is adopted, then only competitors from the middle ring would be placed in the external environment, together with the general forces which impact upon the whole industry.

Figure 5.2 extends this point, and shows the various concepts and techniques discussed in Chapters 5, 6 and 7 in diagrammatic form.

Strategic Thinking

Strategic thinking embraces the past, present and future. Understanding patterns and lessons from the past will certainly inform the future – but given the dynamic, turbulent and uncertain business environments that affect many industries and organizations, it would be dangerous to assume that the future will reflect the past and be a continuation of either past or existing trends.

Figure 5.3 shows (bottom right triangle) how strategies which link competencies with a strategic vision for the future embrace learning from the past, an awareness of existing competencies and some insight into likely future trends. The main part of the figure highlights that *organizational learning* is required to build the future and that it encompasses:

Figure 5.2   Competitive strategy: a summary of techniques.

Figure 5.3   Organizational learning.

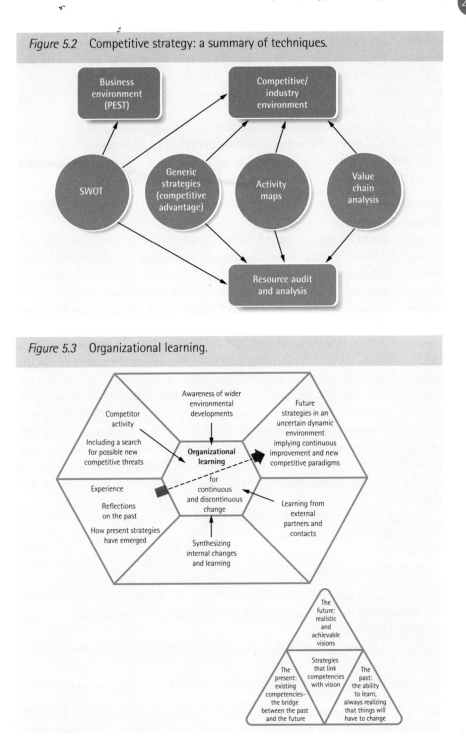

- a reflection on how present strategies have emerged over time
- an understanding of current competencies and the strategic value of particular resources and the linkages between them
- knowledge of existing competitors and what they are doing at the moment – and preparing to do in the future
- an appreciation of possible new sources of competition
- an awareness of wider environmental opportunities and threats
- an ability to share information with, and thus learn from, external partners and contacts, including suppliers, distributors and customers.

The effective organization will synthesize this learning into insightful strategies for dealing with future uncertainties.

Campbell and Alexander (1997) offer a different, but clearly related, approach to strategic thinking. They delineate three elements. First, insight into operating issues: with benchmarking other organizations (searching for good practices), process re-engineering and total quality management organizations should look for opportunities to improve continuously the way they do things. Secondly, future gazing: exponents of chaos theory warn of the need always to be ready for the unexpected and unpredictable; and so here the emphasis is on discontinuous change, and the idea of reinventing and thus controlling developments in the industry. Put another way, establishing new rules of competition and seizing the 'high ground' ahead of any rivals. Scenario building (which is discussed later) plays an important role. The third element is behaviour and culture. Without a clear and communicated vision and direction, and with an absence of employees who are willing to engage the future and look for change opportunities, strategic thinking will be very limited and unimaginative. Simply, the organization must become more entrepreneurial in a dynamic environment, as discussed later in Chapter 10.

Courtney *et al.* (1997) distinguish four alternative future patterns and three broad approaches, which have different degrees of relevance for different situations.

The four futures are:

- a clear and definable future, which implies a continuation of present trends
- a limited and definable number of discrete alternatives which can be evaluated and judged
- a known range of possibilities, which can be defined only in more general terms
- real uncertainty, and with the possibility of major disruption and change.

The three broad approaches, which should not be seen as mutually exclusive, for utilizing organizational learning to deal with the relevant future pattern are:

Figure 5.4 Strategic thinking: purposes and elements.

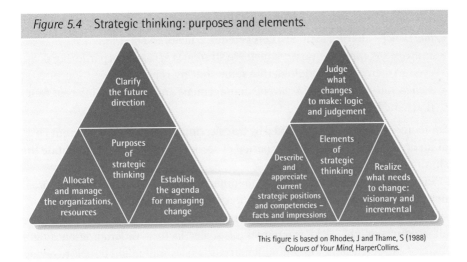

This figure is based on Rhodes, J and Thame, S (1988)
Colours of Your Mind, HarperCollins.

- being relatively clear, or confident, about the direction, attempting to play an important influence and shape events
- accepting that there will be some uncertainty, staying vigilant and in close touch with events and happenings, and adapting to retain a strong position
- monitoring events and waiting for an appropriate opportunity to intervene in some way.

Figure 5.4 completes this section and summarizes the purposes and broad elements of strategic thinking.

Throughout this section on strategic thinking, the emphasis has been on the ability to take a holistic view and synthesize information. We need to synthesize information from the past and present and combine it with a view of the future. This embraces information which originates inside the organization and information that can be obtained from external partners and contacts. Synergy, which is discussed next, explains the importance of linkages and synthesis.

Synergy

Synergy is either a path to sustained growth or a 'bridge too far' for organizations. It is concerned with the returns that are obtained from resources. Ansoff (1987) argues that resources should be combined and managed in such a way that the benefits which accrue exceed those which would result if the parts were kept separate, describing synergy as the 2 + 2 = 5 effect. Simply, the combination of the parts produces results of greater magnitude than would be the case if the parts operated independently.

There are three basic synergy opportunities:

- *functional* – sharing facilities, competencies, ideas and best practice
- *strategic* – complementary competitive strategies across a corporate portfolio: even in a diversified conglomerate some sharing is possible
- *managerial* – compatible styles of management and values in different functions and businesses.

Sometimes the synergy is obtained by transferring people between different parts of an organization, possibly for a period of secondment, in order to facilitate the sharing.

In simple terms, if an organization manufactures and markets six different products, the organization should be structured to yield the benefits that might be possible from combining these different interests. For example, central purchasing for all products might yield economies of scale; factory rationalization might increase productivity or lower production costs; sales staff might be able to obtain more or larger orders if they are selling more than one product; each product might gain from name association with the others; and distributors might be more satisfied than if the company offered only a very limited range or a single product. Some of the benefits are clearly measurable, whereas others are more subjective; and the search for synergy clearly embraces structural as well as strategic decisions.

Similarly, if functions, products or business units were not co-ordinated, then efforts may well be duplicated, or delays might be built into the organization system because of a lack of understanding.

Table 5.1 explains how corporate strategy decisions, such as acquisitions, alliances or divestments, should be made in the light of the overall synergistic

Table 5.1 Synergy

Corporate strategy	Acquisitions – Horizontal
	– Vertical
	Alliances/joint ventures
	Divestment for greater focus
Impacting on	
Competitive strategy	Lower costs
	Shared resources
	'Know-how' – transferable skills and learning
	Negotiating, bargaining power
	Foundations for a new spinoff business

implications of the change. Some – strategically sound – changes imply increased synergy opportunities, while others imply complexity, fragmentation and lost synergy. The synergy impact is seen in the competitive strategies and competitive success for each relevant activity. Simply, where an organization is considering increasing its range of products and services, or merging with or acquiring another company, synergy is an important consideration. In the case of an acquisition the combination of the companies should produce greater returns than the two on their own. Adding new products or services should not affect existing products or services in any adverse way, unless they are intended to be replacements. When such strategic changes take place the deployment of resources should be re-evaluated to ensure that they are being utilized both efficiently and effectively.

Obtaining synergy may well imply the sharing of knowledge and other resources between divisions or business units, possibly attempting to disseminate best practice. This is only feasible if resource efficiencies are measured and compared in order to identify which practices are best. Internal rivalries may prevent the attainment of the potential benefits from sharing. Synergy is more likely to occur if all the relevant activities are linked in such a way that the organization as a whole is managed effectively, which Drucker (1973) has defined as 'doing the right things'. Individual business units and functions must themselves be managed efficiently or, as Drucker would say, they must be 'doing things right'. As seen in Chapter 3, resource efficiency considers how well resources are being utilized and the returns being obtained from them. Effectiveness incorporates an evaluation of whether the resources are being deployed in the most beneficial manner.

There are four key elements which must come together if potential synergy is to be achieved:

- *effective leadership* – which emphasizes the importance of co-operation, sharing, transfer and learning throughout the organization
- *facilitative structure* – which allows co-operation and inhibits internal conflict
- *supportive systems* – which encourage sharing and transfer. Examples include cross-functional and cross-business project teams and the provision of opportunities for managers to spend time in other parts of an organization
- *appropriate rewards* – such that parts of an organization can benefit from helping others.

Figure 5.5 pulls these themes together and shows how synergy potential must be examined inside a framework of strategic resources, strategic thinking and the relevant business environment. Potential exists from effectively combining the various functions and activities in each business, from sharing and learning between businesses and from the overall corporate strategic logic.

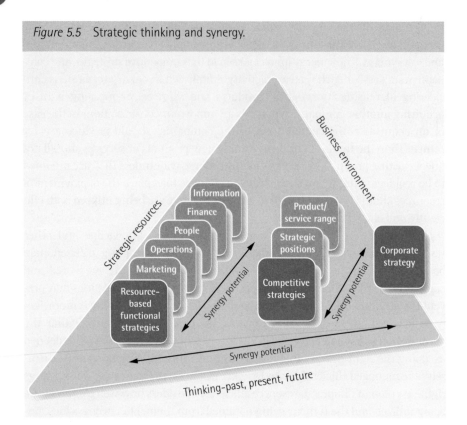

Figure 5.5   Strategic thinking and synergy.

At the same time, though, it must be realized that the anticipated synergy from strategic changes is easily overestimated and quite frequently it does not accrue. Potential benefits from adding new activities may be misjudged. After all, there is always an element of subjective anticipation and promise – the synergy is justified with strategic logic but delivered through people and their behaviour – and this should not be an excuse for delusion. Admitting to strategic misjudgements rarely comes easy to strategic leaders and managers and, as a result, the appropriate exit or withdrawal when synergy is not obtained may not happen when it should. Internal politics and conflicts, because businesses and divisions see themselves as rivals rather than partners, all too often inhibit synergy.

Box 1.2 mentioned one diversification by the Lex Service Group in the 1970s. Lex were successful and profitable essentially with car distribution and felt that their resources and skills would be ideally suitable for transfer into hotel management. They anticipated synergy because of their management skills. Their level of success from the change, however, was below their expectations and they withdrew from this industry.

Searching for synergy – two examples

Sony

A number of Japanese electronics companies (specifically manufacturers of 'hardware' – televisions, videos and hi-fi equipment) has sought links with the US makers of music and films, the related 'software', arguing that there is potential synergy from merging the two. An array of new products continues to become technologically feasible and the manufacturers want to secure their commercial exploitation. Such developments have included high-definition and digital televisions, flat-screen TVs (both large and small for mounting on walls, like a picture, and carrying around), personal video disc players the same size as personal cassette players, miniaturized compact discs (CDs) and CD players and digital versatile discs (DVDs). Films can also be the basis for computer games. The large film companies have huge film libraries for video and games exploitation, both growth markets. The strategy is similar to that of the manufacturers of razors who have derived benefits and synergy from also manufacturing razor blades.

Not every product was a success, of course. Record companies were always reluctant to release music in the new high-technology digital audio tape (DAT) format when it was introduced. While Sony pioneered the hardware, its subsidiary CBS chose not to break industry ranks. DAT has never really taken off.

Sony acquired CBS Records in 1987 and Columbia Pictures from Coca-Cola in 1989. Previously, Coca-Cola had anticipated synergy from linking soft drinks and entertainment, but it had not accrued. Matsushita acquired MCA (Universal Pictures, record labels and part-ownership of a network TV station) in 1990. Toshiba negotiated a joint venture with Time Warner. Earlier, Rupert Murdoch had bought Twentieth Century Fox to exploit the film library on his cable and satellite TV networks worldwide.

The strategy has been defended with logical arguments. It has been suggested that if Sony had owned Columbia in the 1970s their Betamax video format would have proved more successful because more prerecorded videos would have been available in this format rather than the successful VHS – developed by Matsushita who were more resourceful in striking agreements with video makers. Similarly, CBS would prove a useful vehicle for forcing the pace of the switch from records to CDs.

Sceptics always argued that the synergy would not accrue, contending that the typical Japanese company and Hollywood film makers have dramatically different cultures which would not prove compatible. Moreover, Japan is not noted for creativity in entertainment.

In 1995 Matsushita divested MCA, selling it to Seagram. At this time, Sony was still not in a position to claim that it had effectively integrated its entertainments subsidiaries to deliver the anticipated benefits, profits and synergies. However, it has persevered and financial and other benefits have since accrued from the integration.

LVMH (Louis Vuitton, Moët Hennessy)

LVMH, which describes itself as the world's leading luxury products group, 'brings together a unique collection of crafts and brands well known in prestige circles: champagne, cognac, luggage, watches, jewellery, perfumes and haute couture'. LVMH brands include: Moët and Chandon, Veuve Clicquot, Hennessy, Hine, Tag Heuer, Zenith, Christian Dior, Givenchy and Christian Lacroix, as well as the Louis Vuitton leather products. In 1993 LVMH sold its Roc Skincare subsidiary to Johnson and Johnson, as its products did not fit properly since they sell exclusively through pharmacies. More recently LVMH expanded into selective retailing with chains such as Le Bon Marché and Sephora.

These are all products with a global appeal, albeit to relatively limited market niches. For such products, the marketing/selling network has to be extensive or it cannot support the global distribution; consequently, there can be major benefits from linking together an appropriate range of products and brands. LVMH's synergistic benefits are:

- name association, particularly with fashion and perfumes
- advertising – savings by advertising several brands in the same magazines
- distribution – although there are specialist outlets for different products, large department stores sell many LVMH brands. Because the LVMH range as a whole is vital for these stores, LVMH can command premium positions and displays
- sales – a worldwide sales force and network yields savings.

In November 1999 LVMH appeared to depart from its traditional pattern of acquisitions and bought Phillips, the world's third largest fine art auction house. Could it see hidden synergy potential?

> One thing is clear. Even if you're on the right track, you'll get run over if you just sit there!
>
> *Sir Allen Sheppard, when Chairman,*
> *Grand Metropolitan plc (now Diageo)*

Analysing the Business Environment

Managing in an increasingly turbulent world

This chapter now examines in detail the environment in which the organization operates and considers how the forces present in the environment pose both opportunities and threats. The topic of stakeholders is developed further as several of the environmental forces which affect the organization clearly have a stake in the business. Simply, stakeholders should be categorized in terms of their power and their interest – a simple four-quadrant grid can easily be used for this, as shown in Figure 5.6. Those with power must be satisfied, especially if they are also interested in the activities of the organization. Those with relatively low power but high interest should certainly be kept informed. Competitors inevitably constitute a major influence on corporate, competitive and functional strategies and they are the subject of Chapter 6.

If a firm is to control its growth, change and development it must seek to control the forces that provide the opportunities for growth and change, and those that pose threats and demand responses. Not only must managers be aware of environmental forces and environmental change, they must manage the organization's resources to take advantage of opportunities and counter threats. In turn, the strategic leader should ensure that this happens and that the values and

Figure 5.6   Stakeholder significance grid. Developed from ideas in Mendelow, A (1991) *Proceedings of 2nd International Conference on Information Systems*, Cambridge, MA.

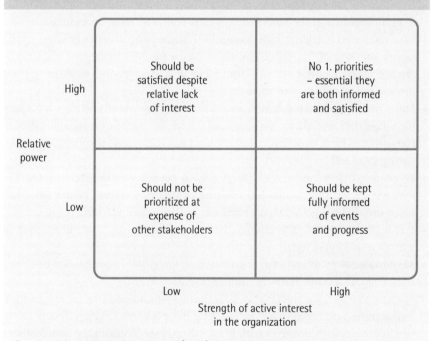

Developed from ideas in Mendelow, A (1991) *Proceedings of 2nd International Conference on Information Systems*, Cambridge, MA.

culture of the organization are appropriate for satisfying the key success factors. Quite simply, the environment delivers shocks to an organization, and the way in which resources are deployed and managed determines the ability to handle these shocks. This relates to E-V-R (environment–values– resources) congruence.

Over time, paradigms concerning 'what will work' to bring about success in a particular industry or competitive environment will be created and maintained. However, as environmental and competitive forces change, the current reality (at any time) of what is required for competitive success may be drifting away from the organization's paradigm; consequently, a new paradigm will be essential. In an age of discontinuity, paradigms will need changing more frequently and more dramatically; expediting these changes is a key managerial task.

Put another way, in a turbulent environment, the organization must change its strategies and possibly its beliefs if it is to maintain E–V–R congruence. For example, farmers now look at their farms as potentially diversified businesses.

A number of key themes underpins the issues discussed in this chapter:

- Traditional industries such as manufacturing and mining have given way to new, more technological – and frequently electronics-based – industries which demand new labour skills, and where 'knowledge workers' are of prime importance.
- New technologies can generate opportunities for substitutability, different forms of competition and the emergence of new competitors in an industry.
- In addition to changing skills demands, there have been other changes in the labour markets of developed countries. Many families have joint wage earners and more women are working. More and more people work from their homes, at least for part of their time.
- Many managers and employees are more time constrained and have less spare time than they would like. Not only does this imply less time for shopping (hence the potential for e-commerce), but demand has increased for convenient, time-saving products.
- People are living longer and, coupled with periods of lower birth rates, the average age of the population and the number of retired people are both increasing. These groups have more leisure time than working people.
- The Internet continues to change the way in which we access information in a quite remarkable way.
- Multinational businesses have grown in strength and significance and they have become the norm for manufacturing industries.
- Manufacturers from the UK, USA, Germany, Japan and other nations with a longstanding tradition in manufacturing have been willing to relocate factories in developing countries with lower wage costs. Technology which allows increasing levels of output from the same-size factory has facilitated these changes.

- Consequently, the competitive arena has been changing with, recently, the highest economic growth being enjoyed by the USA, although during the early and mid-1990s it was the Pacific Rim countries. In many industries, global supply potential exceeds demand, placing downward pressures on real prices.
- Product and service markets, supply chains, capital markets and communication systems have become global in nature.
- The speed of change in most industries and markets has increased and product lifecycles have shortened. For some companies, success can be very transient.
- Governments have masterminded increasing degrees of deregulation. Other countries have followed the UK's lead and privatized public-sector utilities; air travel and telecommunications markets have been opened up to more competition.
- Consumers are more aware and more knowledgeable; environmental groups have begun to wield increasing influence.
- Changes in politics and regimes in different parts of the world, such as Eastern Europe and the Far East, have introduced an element of chaos and greater unpredictability. Opportunities open up but carry a significant downside risk.

Simply, environments are more turbulent; managing them and managing *in* them demand more flexibility and more discontinuity than in the past.

> There is no doubt that the world is becoming one marketplace. Capital markets, products and services, management and manufacturing techniques have all become global in nature. As a result, companies increasingly find that they must compete all over the world – in the global marketplace.
> *Maurice Saatchi, when Chairman, Saatchi and Saatchi Company plc*
>
> In my experience, corporate life-threatening problems in large manufacturing companies have developed over a long period. These problems should never have been permitted to grow so large, but they were allowed to do so by top management who were lethargic and self-satisfied, who engaged in self-delusion and congratulated themselves on their exalted status. In short, the managements were the problem.
> *Eugene Anderson,*
> *ex-Chairman and Chief Executive, Ferranti International plc*
>
> How can we expect to succeed when we are playing cricket and the rest of the world is practising karate?
> *Sir Edwin Nixon, when Chairman, Amersham International*

Figure 5.7 emphasizes that as industries and markets become increasingly global, quality is more important than origin. People in Britain might like to claim 'British is best' – as might other people in other countries – but a statement such as this is meaningless unless it can be demonstrate that British (or other) products and services really are world class. To achieve world-class quality and reputation, companies must use knowledge and ideas to be innovative, operate at the level of the best in the world and form international networks and partnerships to access the best resources from around the world.

In this dynamic environment, the USA has become the most competitive nation because it has taken a lead in technically advanced industries and transformed itself into a service economy. It has found ways of generating the private-sector finances required for investment in new and relatively high-risk sectors, and it has ensured that regulations do not inhibit labour-force flexibility. Europe is generally more restrictive, although practices do vary between countries, even within the European Union.

Figure 5.7   World-class strategic performance. Developed by John Thompson from ideas in Kanter, RM (1996) *World Class – Thriving Locally in the Global Economy*, Simon and Schuster.

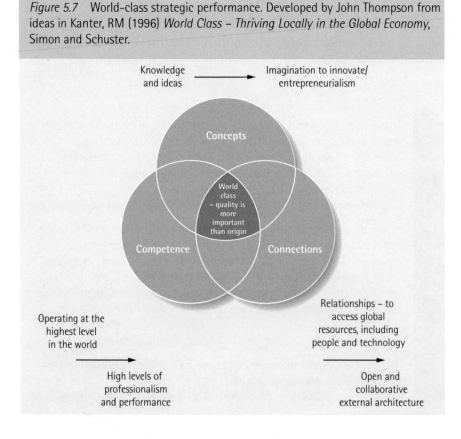

Although the following examples are British in origin and used to illustrate an important theme, similar stories can readily be told of other parts of the world. When the former British Prime Minister, Margaret Thatcher, came to power in 1979 she quickly identified a wide productivity gap between many British companies and those perceived to be the best in the world. She set about reducing the gap for both large and small companies – and she was successful, although in many industries a gap remains, albeit smaller than it otherwise would have been. In some industries Britain does have 'best in the world' companies, but relatively few industry-wide centres of excellence. In motor cars, really only two truly British companies remain. These, Morgan and TVR, are very small niche players. Rover is manufacturing again, having recently been divested by BMW, but it is financially weak with vehicles dependent upon competitors' technology. Ford now owns Jaguar and Land Rover; Vauxhall is a subsidiary of General Motors. Peugeot, Honda, Nissan and Toyota all assemble vehicles in UK factories. Nissan's Sunderland factory is their most productive plant. Yet, British companies are dominant in the high-profile, advanced technology, segment of Formula One racing. UK-based McLaren and Williams have only one serious rival, Ferrari. Television assembly is similar in principle, with British plants owned and operated by French and Japanese manufacturers.

Where there are individual world-class companies in an industry, there is also often a long tail of low performers. Most significantly, though, average productivity in Britain remains below the average for many of its leading competitors. Simply, while British companies have improved, so too have most others! Britain may have reduced the productivity gap, and may seem able and committed to it not widening again, but the gap has not been closed, and rivals have certainly not been overtaken.

The competitive future for the UK, however, does not lie in reducing wages to compete with the Far East and Eastern Europe, and thus creating a downward spiral of expectation; rather it lies in finding new ways of innovating, adding value, differentiating and *leading* consumers. Notwithstanding this, some cutting back to create and maintain trim and efficient organizations will always be essential.

These points are explored further in Box 5.1.

There are several frameworks for studying the environment of an organization. In addition to considering the company's *stakeholders* in terms of their relative power, influence, needs and expectations, a PEST analysis can prove useful. This is an objective and straightforward consideration of changing Political, Economic, Social and Technological influences. This review should help to clarify changing opportunities and threats.

The nature of the stakeholders and the environmental forces is a useful indicator of the most appropriate strategic approach for the organization to take.

KEY CONCEPT – Box 5.1
Competitive Advantage and Strategy in the Late 1990s

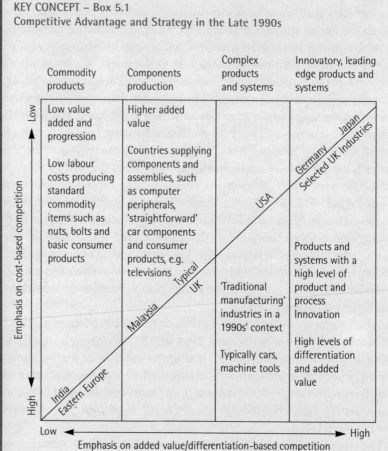

Commodity products	Components production	Complex products and systems	Innovatory, leading edge products and systems
Low value added and progression Low labour costs producing standard commodity items such as nuts, bolts and basic consumer products	Higher added value Countries supplying components and assemblies, such as computer peripherals, 'straightforward' car components and consumer products, e.g. televisions	'Traditional manufacturing' industries in a 1990s' context Typically cars, machine tools	Products and systems with a high level of product and process Innovation High levels of differentiation and added value

Emphasis on cost-based competition (Low ↑ / High ↓)

Diagonal labels (low to high): India, Eastern Europe, Malaysia, Typical UK, USA, Germany, Selected UK Industries, Japan

Emphasis on added value/differentiation-based competition (Low ← → High)

- Countries progress up and down the diagonal over time.
- Within each country different industries will be in different sectors. The position shown here on the diagonal is that with which the country is typically associated.
- The UK has drifted down to 'components' by offering incentives and relatively low labour costs to attract inward investments. However, with aerospace and pharmaceuticals, for example, the UK is clearly in the 'innovatory' sector.
- Arguably, the UK should focus more intently on innovation to reverse the trend, otherwise it will increasingly become a mere supplier to the industry leaders and drivers. However, innovation requires managerial and workforce strengths and skills that the UK may not have.

KEY CONCEPT – Box 5.1
(Continued)

- Innovation relates to products and services (radical improvements in value; reconceiving form and function) and market boundaries (attracting new customers; providing new values by satisfying individual needs more effectively).

Thompson, J (1997) based on ideas in Kruse, G and Berry, C (1997) A nation of shopkeepers, *Management Today*, April.

Where the environment is complex, turbulent and uncertain it will be necessary for the organization to be vigilant and speedily reactive. A carefully planned approach is ideal in stable and predictable circumstances; and a positive and proactive approach should be adopted where the environment can be changed or influenced.

Understanding the environment

Although the constituent forces of the environment can be listed and assessed for opportunities and threats, and the forecasting of possible changes can be attempted, of most importance for managers is ongoing insight and awareness. The important issues might well be listed as part of a SWOT (strengths, weaknesses, opportunities and threats) analysis: they constitute an essential part of the planning process and can be used for developing and evaluating possible strategic changes. Managers, however, should always be attentive to changes and their decisions and actions should be both reactive and proactive as appropriate. In other words, their awareness should result from constant vigilance and attentiveness rather than from any isolated clinical analysis. This will in turn be dependent on the information system within the organization, sources of external information and the uses made of it, and the ability of individual managers to evaluate the importance and potential significance of events of which they become aware. While environmental forces and influences clearly exist and change, what matters is the perception that managers place on their observations and experiences, i.e. the meaning that they attribute to information. Manager capabilities are dependent on experience and basic understanding of the overall strategic process. It is particularly useful if managers are able to take a strategic perspective rather than a functional one because then they may perceive opportunities and threats in areas outside their own particular specialisms.

Uncertainty, complexity and dynamism

Duncan (1972) argued that the environment is more uncertain the more complex it is or the more dynamic it is. An example of an organization facing a generally stable, non-dynamic and hence fairly certain environment is a small rural village post office. While most organizations face far more uncertainty, their managers also enjoy more challenges. In recent years the position of small village post offices has become more uncertain and many have closed. At the same time, however, The Post Office is looking at the possibility of offering a new range of banking services. The Post Office has realized that there is a window of opportunity as high-street banks consolidate and shut small branches. Moreover, they already have branches in every town and city that possess both spare capacity and a secure environment for handling cash. This development is not feasible without support and co-operation from the main clearing banks who, on the one hand, could benefit from the beneficial publicity, but, on the other hand, might see it constituting a new form of competition for some of their services. So far the banks have only co-operated reluctantly. The government has also announced plans for new computers which will allow post offices to become Internet centres with access to information of a variety of government services. If trials are successful this could enable more and more rural post offices to stay open.

While windows of opportunity are opening all the time, windows also close. In Spring 2000 the Dutch retail chain C & A announced that it was to close all its branches in the UK. The stores and their ranges had become unfashionable for many customers at a time when retail spending was pretty static, electronic commerce was increasing and new, more focused rivals, together with supermarkets such as ASDA, were selling fashionable designs at low prices.

The dynamic environment

Dynamism can be increased by a number of factors. Rapid technological change involving either products, processes or uses will mean that changes are likely to occur quickly and that organizations must stay aware of the activities of their suppliers and potential suppliers, customers and competitors. Where competition is on a global scale the pace of change may vary in different markets, and competition may be harder to monitor. In such cases the future is likely to be uncertain. Risk taking and creative entrepreneurial leadership may well be required as strategies pursued in the past, or modifications of them, may no longer be appropriate.

The complex environment

An environment is complex where the forces and the changes involving them are difficult to understand. Quite often complexity and dynamism occur together.

Technology-based industries and Internet-based businesses are excellent examples of this. The structure of the organization, the degree of decentralization and the responsibility and authority delegated to managers throughout the organization, and information systems can render complexity more manageable. Managers will need to be open and responsive to the need for change and flexible in their approach if they are to handle complexity successfully.

Managerial awareness and the approach to the management of change are therefore key issues in uncertain environments. If managers are strategically aware, and flexible and responsive concerning change, then they will perceive the complex and dynamic conditions as manageable. Other less aware managers may find the conditions so uncertain that they are always responding to pressures placed on the organization rather than appearing to be in control and managing the environment. Hence a crucial aspect of strategic management is understanding and negotiating with the environment in order to influence and ideally to control events.

Environmental influences

Figure 5.1 showed how the organization is typically one of a number of competitors in an industry; and to a greater or lesser degree these competitors will be affected by the decisions, competitive strategies and innovation of the others. These interdependencies are crucial and consequently strategic decisions should always involve some assessment of their impact on other companies, and their likely reaction. Equally, a company should seek to be fully aware of what competitors are doing at any time.

Furthermore, this industry will be linked to, and dependent on, other industries: industries from which it buys supplies, and industries to which it markets products and services. Essentially this relates to Porter's model of the forces that determine industry profitability, which will be considered in Chapter 6. The relationships between a firm and its buyers and suppliers are again crucial for a number of reasons. Suppliers might be performing badly and as a result future supplies might be threatened; equally they might be working on innovations that will impact on organizations to which they supply. Buyers might be under pressure from competitors to switch suppliers. It is important to be strategically aware, and to seek to exert influence over organizations where there are dependencies.

These industries and the firms that comprise them are additionally part of a wider environment. This environment is composed of forces that influence the organizations, and which in turn can be influenced by them. Particular forces will be more or less important for individual organizations and in certain circumstances. It is important that managers appreciate the existence of these forces, how they might influence the organization, and how they might be influenced.

Mintzberg (1987) has used the term 'crafting strategy' to explain how managers learn by experience and by doing and adapting strategies to environmental needs. He sees the process as being analogous to a potter moulding clay and creating a finished object. If an organization embarks upon a determined change of strategy certain aspects of implementation will be changed as it becomes increasingly clear with experience how best to manage the environmental forces. Equally, managers adapt existing competitive and functional strategies as they see opportunities and threats and gradually change things. In each case the aim is to ensure that the organization's resources and values are matched with the changing environment.

External forces: a PEST analysis

A PEST analysis is merely a framework that categorizes environmental influences as political, economic, social and technological forces. Sometimes two additional factors, environmental and legal, will be added to make a PESTEL analysis, but these themes can easily be subsumed in the others.

Economic conditions affect how easy or how difficult it is to be successful and profitable at any time because they affect both capital availability and cost, and demand. If demand is buoyant, for example, and the cost of capital is low, it will be attractive for firms to invest and grow with expectations of being profitable. In opposite circumstances firms might find that profitability throughout the industry is low. The timing and relative success of particular strategies can be influenced by economic conditions. When the economy as a whole or certain sectors of the economy are growing, demand may exist for a product or service which would not be in demand in more depressed circumstances. Similarly, the opportunity to exploit a particular strategy successfully may depend on demand which exists in growth conditions and does not in recession. Although a depressed economy will generally be a threat which results in a number of organizations going out of business, it can provide opportunities for some.

Economic conditions are influenced by *politics and government policy*; equally, they are a major influence affecting government decisions. The issue of whether European countries join, or remain outside, the single European currency is a case in point. At any one time either exported or imported goods can seem expensive or inexpensive, dependent upon currency exchange rates. There are many other ways, however, in which government decisions will affect organizations both directly and indirectly as they provide both opportunities and threats.

While economic conditions and government policy are closely related, they both influence a number of other environmental forces that can affect organizations. Capital markets determine the conditions for alternative types of funding for organizations; they can be subject to government controls, and they will be guided by the prevailing economic conditions. The rate of interest charged for loans will be affected by inflation and by international economics and, although the determining rate may be fixed by a central bank (as, for example, it is by the Bank of England) it will always be influenced by stated government priorities. Government spending can increase the money supply and make capital markets more buoyant. The expectations of shareholders with regard to company performance, their willingness to provide more equity funding or their willingness to sell their shares will also be affected.

The labour market reflects the availability of particular skills at national and regional levels; this is affected by training, which is influenced by government and other regional agencies. Labour costs will be influenced by inflation and by general trends in other industries, and by the role and power of trade unions.

The *sociocultural environment* encapsulates demand and tastes, which vary with fashion and disposable income, and general changes can again provide both opportunities and threats for particular firms. Over time most products change from being a novelty to a situation of market saturation, and as this happens pricing and promotion strategies have to change. Similarly, some products and services will sell around the world with little variation, but these are relatively unusual. Figure 5.8 shows how washing-machine designs are different for different European countries to reflect consumer preferences. Organizations should be aware of demographic changes as the structure of the population by age, affluence, regions, numbers working and so on can have an important

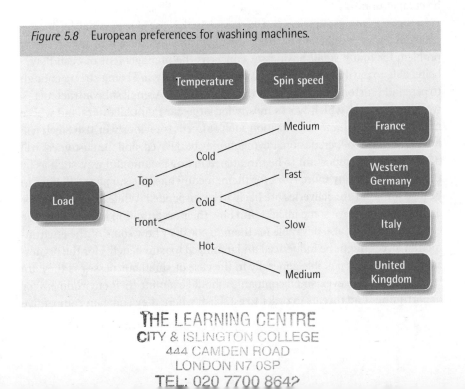

Figure 5.8   European preferences for washing machines.

bearing on demand as a whole and on demand for particular products and services. Threats to existing products might be increasing; opportunities for differentiation and market segmentation might be emerging.

Technology in one respect is part of the organization and the industry part of the model as it is used for the creation of competitive advantage. However, technology external to the industry can also be captured and used, and this again can be influenced by government support and encouragement. Technological breakthroughs can create new industries which might prove a threat to existing organizations whose products or services might be rendered redundant, and those firms which might be affected in this way should be alert to the possibility. Equally, new technology could provide a useful input, perhaps in both manufacturing and service industries, but in turn its purchase will require funding and possibly employee training before it can be used.

The examples referred to here are only a sample of many, and individual managers need to appreciate how these general forces affect their organization in particular ways. Table 5.2 provides a general list of environmental influences and forces. To provide a specific example, Box 5.2 includes a short and very selective PEST analysis of environmental forces affecting the credit-card industry and picks out a number of key influences. It will be realized how such an analysis can be useful for helping to identify emerging opportunities and threats.

For any organization certain environmental influences will constitute powerful forces which affect decision making significantly. For some manufacturing and service businesses the most powerful force will be customers; for others it may be competition.

In some situations suppliers can be crucial. In the case of some small businesses external forces can dictate whether the business stays solvent or not. A major problem for many small businesses concerns the management of cash flow – being able to pay bills when they are due for payment and being strong enough to persuade customers to pay their invoices on time. A small subcontract metal-working business which works mostly for large car manufacturers and whose main supplier is a large organization such as Corus (previously British Steel) will have little power of persuasion. Payments may be delayed, and the customers will be too large and important to be threatened in any meaningful way, such as by the refusal to do any more work for them; meanwhile, the supplies will have to be paid for or future deliveries are likely to be suspended. While it is essential for all managers to have some insight into how their organization is affected by the environment, it is also desirable for them to consider how some of the environmental forces might be influenced and managed to gain benefits for the organization. This is less possible generally in the case of small businesses as they are less powerful. However, small companies should examine their environment for opportunities and threats in order to establish where they can gain competitive

Table 5.2 Environmental influences

Influence	Examples of threats and opportunities
The economy	The strength of the economy influences the availability of credit and the willingness of people to borrow. This affects the level of demand. Interest rates and currency fluctuations affect both the cost and demand of imports and exports
Capital markets	This includes shareholders, and their satisfaction with company success. Are they willing to buy more shares if offered them to increase equity funding? Would they willingly sell if someone bid for the organization? Also included are the banking system, and the cost and availability of loan capital
Labour market	Changes in structure with an ageing population and more women seeking work Availability of skills, possibly in particular regions Influence of trade unions Contribution of government training schemes
Technology	Robotics in manufacturing in such industries as car assembly Computers for design and manufacturing Information technology such as electronic point of sale in retailing
Sociocultural environment	Pressure groups affecting demand or industry location Changing population – by age groups Changing tastes and values Regional movements
Government	Regional aid policies Special industry initiatives, e.g. where high technology is involved The legal environment is part of this, including the regulation of competition Restraints on car exhaust emissions (pollution control) and labelling requirements would be other examples
Suppliers	Availability and cost of supplies, possibly involving vertical integration and decisions concerning whether to make or buy in essential components
Customers	Changes in preferences and purchasing power Changes in the distribution system
Competitors	Changes in competitive strategies Innovation
The media	Effects of good and bad publicity, drawing attention to companies, products and services

STRATEGY IN ACTION – Box 5.2
A PEST Analysis of the Credit-card Industry

Political	Legislation allowing young people to own credit cards
	The threat of restrictions on Internet trading
Economic	The future presence – or not – of the UK, Denmark and Sweden in the Euro-Zone and the European single currency, and the impact of the single currency on interest rates generally
	Future economic trends which will affect demand for consumption and credit
	Freedom for, or restrictions on, new entrants to the industry
Social	The willingness or reluctance to buy on credit – while credit is readily available for many people, there can be a rebellion against high interest charges
	The increasing acceptance of Internet shopping, which depends on credit-card transactions – possibly affected by the age profile of the population
Technical	Internet and e-business possibilities – and security.

advantage and where their resources might most usefully be concentrated. For many not-for-profit organizations, such as subsidized theatres and major museums, the government constitutes a major environmental force because each of these organizations is dependent in different ways on government grants. In the UK, the National Health Service (NHS) is similarly very dependent upon government policies which affect all decision areas. Consultants' salaries, nurses' pay, new hospitals and wards, and new equipment are substantially determined by government decisions, which they will seek to influence.

Ansoff's model

Ansoff (1987) contends that 'to survive and succeed in an industry, the firm must match the aggressiveness of its operating and strategic behaviours to the changeability of demands and opportunities in the market-place'. The extent to which the environment is changeable or turbulent depends on six factors:

- changeability of the market environment
- speed of change
- intensity of competition
- fertility of technology
- discrimination by customers
- pressures from governments and influence groups.

Ansoff suggests that the more turbulent the environment is, the more aggressive the firm must be in terms of competitive strategies and entrepreneurialism or change orientation if it is to succeed. The firms in an industry will be distributed such that a small number is insufficiently aggressive for the requirements of the industry, and as a result they are unprofitable or go out of business. Another small number will be above average in terms of success because they are best able to match the demands of the environment. Many will achieve results above average; and some others may also fail because they are too aggressive and try to change things too quickly through lack of awareness.

Where an organization is multiproduct or multinational the various parts of the business are likely to experience some common environmental influences and some which are distinctive, which reinforces the need for managers who are closest to the market and to competitors to be able to change things.

Ansoff suggests that the environment should be analysed in terms of competition and entrepreneurship or change. By attributing scores to various factors the degree of competitive and entrepreneurial turbulence can be calculated. The competitive environment is affected by market structure and profitability, the intensity of competitive rivalry and the degree of differentiation, market growth, the stage in the life of the products or services in question and the frequency of new product launches, capital intensity and economies of scale. Certain of these factors, namely market growth, the stage in the life of the product and profitability, also help to determine the extent to which the environment is entrepreneurial. Changes in structure and technology, social pressures and innovation are also influential.

The culture of the organization and managerial competencies should then be examined to see whether they match and be changed as appropriate if they do not. Again, scores are attributed to various factors. Culture encompasses factors such as values, reaction and response to change, and risk orientation. Problem-solving approaches, information systems, environmental forecasting and surveillance, and management systems are included in the competencies. Ansoff is really arguing that the resources of the organization and the values must be congruent with the needs of the environment.

Competition and the Structure and Regulation of Industry

The four economic models of pure or perfect competition, monopolistic competition, oligopoly and monopoly, were introduced in Chapter 2, when it was pointed out that the opportunity for substantial profits was most likely to be found in oligopoly and monopoly structures. Competition in the other models, resulting mainly from lower barriers to entry, has the effect of reducing profit margins. It is now useful to consider which models are dominant in the UK, and most other developed nations, as this influences the ways in which firms compete. Specifically, it affects the opportunities for differentiation and for the achievement of cost advantages which, as will be seen in Chapter 6, are major determinants of competitive advantage.

Monopoly power

It is important to point out here that as far as the regulatory authorities are concerned a 25% market share offers opportunities for a company to exploit monopoly power, Hence, although the model of pure monopoly assumes only one producer with absolute power in the marketplace, a large producer with a substantial share will be regarded as having monopoly power. It does not follow that such power will be used against the consumer; on the contrary, it can be to the consumer's advantage. Large companies with market shares in excess of their rivals may be able to produce at lower cost (and sell at lower prices) for any one of several reasons, including the ability to invest in high-output, low unit cost technology; the ability to buy supplies in bulk and receive discounts; the ability to achieve distribution savings; and the opportunity to improve productivity as more and more units are produced. In fact, savings are possible in every area of the business. Economists call these savings economies of scale, and they are related to the notion of the experience or learning curve which is explained in a Finance in Action supplement to this chapter.

A cost advantage, then, can be a major source of competitive advantage, and this point will be developed in greater detail later. The producer who is able to produce at a lower cost than his or her rivals may choose to price very competitively with a view to driving competitors out of the market and thereby increasing market share. Equally he or she may not; and by charging a higher price can make a greater profit per unit and thereby seek profit in preference to market share. In the first case the consumer benefits from lower prices and therefore monopoly power is not being used against the consumer. However, once a firm has built up a truly dominant market share it might seek to change its strategy and exploit its power more. This is when governments need to intervene in some way.

Concentration

Concentration is the measure of control exercised by organizations. There are two types.

Aggregate concentration, which will be mentioned only briefly, considers the power of the largest privately owned manufacturing firms in the economy as a whole.

Sectoral or market concentration traditionally considers the percentage of net output or employment (assets, sales or profits can also be measured) controlled by the largest firms in a particular industry, be it manufacturing or service. High concentration figures tend to encourage monopoly or oligopoly behaviour, most probably the latter, which implies substantial emphasis on differentiation and non-price competition, with rivals seeing themselves as interdependent.

Many industries worldwide are essentially oligopolistic in structure, with a limited number of major competitors and barriers to entry in individual countries. In general, competition will be non-price rather than price, but price competition will be seen in situations where supply exceeds demand and there is aggressive competition for market share.

There may well be marketing and distribution advantages for companies which belong to conglomerates and this could increase their relative market power. Similarly, products which dominate particular market segments will yield advantages. Consequently, there is still opportunity for smaller companies to compete successfully in certain oligopoly markets, especially if they can differentiate their product so that it has appeal for particular segments of the market.

In the chocolate industry Thornton's has been successful with a limited range of high-quality products distributed through the company's own specialist outlets. In contrast, certain industries exhibit very low concentration. Ladies' dresses are one example, and they are very much affected by fashion and the nature of the businesses which involve large numbers of part-time workers; leather goods are another, and here the barriers to entry are very low.

The UK exhibits higher concentration overall than is found in rival countries such as the USA and Germany, which have generally larger economies. However, UK companies, like many others around the world, have to compete in global markets, and therefore size is an important issue. After all, few British companies are dominant producers when considered in world terms.

The dilemma for government is to encourage firms to grow in size and become powerful competitive forces in world markets but at the same time to ensure that such size and power are not used to exploit consumers in the UK.

The regulation of monopoly power

It is generally accepted in many countries that it is the state's role to monitor the forces of competition, to minimize any waste of resources due to economic inefficiency, to guard against any exploitation of relatively weak buyers or suppliers, and to ensure that powerful companies do not seek to eliminate their competitors purely to gain monopoly power.

Regulations are passed and implemented to police these issues. This section uses the situation in the UK to illustrate the point, but the principles and general approach are not unique to the UK. A new UK Competition Bill, passed in 1997 and operational in 1999, put the following structure in place.

In overall charge is the Department (or Minister) for Trade and Industry (DTI). Reporting to the DTI are two bodies. First, the Office of Fair Trading (OFT), headed by a Director-General, which has powers to carry out preliminary investigations of all proposed mergers or take-overs involving market shares of 25% or more, or combined assets in excess of £75 million. If the OFT believes that major competition concerns are present, then it can refer the proposal to a second body, the Competition Commission, for further investigation.

Each case is considered on merit, and the presumption is not automatically that monopoly power is against the public interest. High profitability is considered acceptable if it reflects efficiency, but not if it is sustained by artificial barriers to entry.

The delay involved in an investigation can be important strategically. The process is likely to take at least six months and in that time a company which opposes the take-over bid against it will work hard to improve its performance and prospects. If this results in a substantial increase in the share price the acquisitive company may withdraw on the grounds that the cost has become too high. Companies may seek to prevent a reference by undertaking to sell off part of the businesses involved in an acquisition if competition concerns are raised.

The DTI retains secondary powers to refer any bid directly to the Competition Commission.

In line with other countries in Europe, the OFT also polices a ban on anti-competitive agreements (such as price fixing or market share cartels) and anti-competitive behaviour such as predatory pricing by a dominant company. Offending firms can be fined up to 10% of their global turnover. Firms found guilty by the OFT have a right of appeal to the Competition Commission.

Since September 1990 the European Commission has also been able to influence the growing number of corporate mergers and acquisitions in the European Union (EU). Mergers are exempted, though, if each company has more than two-thirds of its EU-wide turnover in any one EU country.

Examples of intervention

In February 2000 the Competition Commission in the UK ruled that Unilever should be banned from distributing its own Wall's ice cream direct to retailers. Wall's ice-cream products hold the largest market share in the UK, in excess of 50%. The argument was that a newly formed subsidiary, Wall's Direct, was undermining independent wholesalers and, as a consequence, competitors such as Nestlé and Mars were being squeezed out of the supply chain. The DTI chose to water down the ban and recommended a capping of the scope and extent of the distribution operation. Unilever, however, concluded that a cap was not feasible and it began to wind down its distribution.

In parallel with this investigation the Competition Commission had also looked at Unilever's practice of providing retailers with free freezer cabinets but insisting that they were used only for Wall's products. Small retailers, with room for just one freezer cabinet, were effectively prevented from stocking other brands. The Commission recommended that retailers should be allowed to fill up to half of the cabinet with rival products.

In 1998 BSkyB, part of the media group controlled by Rupert Murdoch, sought to buy a major shareholding in Manchester United, acknowledged to be the most valuable football club in the world. While the two activities may not appear to compete, the contractual arrangement between Sky Television and football's Premier League meant that there was a very clear relationship. It was felt that Manchester United and Sky could both benefit at the expense of rival football clubs and media companies, and consequently the OFT began an investigation. The concern was that Sky could be placed in a position where it could drive down the price that it paid for televising Premier League matches, particularly as Manchester United's matches are very popular with viewers as well as fans. The situation was compounded by the growing incidence of pay-per-view football. In the event the merger was not allowed to proceed. Instead, BSkyB, other media groups including Carlton and Granada, and the cable television company ntl, have all bought minority stakes in the most successful Premier League clubs.

Highlighting the global nature of competition regulation, Microsoft, dominant in personal computer operating systems, has been judged by an American court to be exploiting its monopoly power. In early 2000 it was ruled that the basic operating systems (based on Windows) and the applications (Microsoft Office and Internet Explorer) should be separated into two separate businesses, and that Microsoft should also be required to give away to its competitors some of its operating systems code. Inevitably the company has appealed against the ruling. The *Financial Times* commented: 'Surely, most seriously of all, is that at a time Microsoft should be focusing all its talent on keeping up with technological innovation, it is hamstrung by this case'.

Case Study 5 described the impact of regulation on the structure of the UK brewing industry over a period of years. Sometimes regulation produces unexpected and unpredicted outcomes; it is a grey world.

Strategic Positioning and Adding Value

Strategic positioning and added value were defined and explained in Chapter 1, and this section builds on that introduction.

Strategic positioning

Figure 5.9 emphasizes that effective strategic positions ensure that corporate strategic resources meet and satisfy key (or critical) success factors for customers and markets. Strategically valuable resources translate into core competencies and strategic capabilities (as explained in Chapter 1), which are then manifest in a whole range of activities that the organization undertakes. The idea of activity mapping is developed in Chapter 6.

Competencies and capabilities can be separated by thinking of core competencies being built around technologies and technological skills, and strategic capabilities referring to processes and ways of doing things. Capabilities thus exploit the competencies; technology must, however, be developed to a particular level for a company to be influential in an industry or market. Hence, while the real competitive strength of an organization can be built around either competencies or capabilities, both must be present for relative success. Over time, both competency and capability must be improved with innovation. In Chapter 10 it is shown that people, learning and information are critical elements of this innovation. In addition, companies can benefit markedly from exploiting the linkages and relationships that they have with their suppliers and distributors.

It will be appreciated that an emphasis on key success factors – with a search for efficient, effective and imaginatively different ways of satisfying them – represents the market- or opportunity-driven approach to strategy, while exploiting competencies and capabilities is the resource-based approach. The market-driven approach places customers first, clarifying their needs and looking for new and

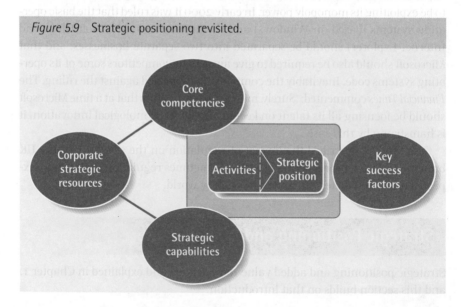

Figure 5.9   Strategic positioning revisited.

> In a fast-changing world where businesses are buffeted by external forces, managers need to be nimble to respond capably, to keep the company on track and to meet its objectives. They must be outwardly focused, aware of important trends that will impact on business or industry. They need to be opportunity-aware, without losing the more usual inward-looking focus on doing things better and responding to threats.
>
> *Neville Bain, when Group Chief Executive, Coats Viyella*

different ways of satisfying them. The emphasis is on finding opportunities that competitors have yet to realize, and which ideally they will not be able to copy quickly. The resource-based approach is a search for better ways of utilizing and exploiting the strategic resources possessed by the organization.

It should be understood that strategic positioning, per se, is not a source of competitive advantage. Any relative advantage enjoyed by the organization comes from the resources and activities which establish and support the position. This can be tangible or intangible in nature. It could come from specific technological skills, from the reputation that an organization enjoys or from the way that its people deliver service. Simply, these are the ways through which it creates and adds value.

Added value

Added value was introduced and explained in Chapter 1. In essence, an organization uses its various resources, tangible and intangible, to create value. In Chapter 7 it is shown how a value chain can be built which links the various internal activities and blends them with other key members of the whole supply chain. This value is then manifest in either differentiated products or services, or a cost advantage which can be partially passed on to customers in the form of lower prices. Figure 5.10 delineates two value-adding cycles, both of which can establish superior profits and allow for ongoing investment and innovation. They are not mutually exclusive, because whatever the competitive strategy, strong cost management is essential.

To be successful, products and services must fit into markets (Marketing and operations strategies are critical elements of competitive strategy but it is assumed that most readers will have already studied these topics elsewhere. However, a number of key points are included on the website to act as a reminder and reinforcement of the most significant aspects). These could be global or local markets, mass or niche markets. The products could be essentially commodities or substantially customized. The market (or the relevant niche) could be growing, static or declining. Every one can be profitable, but in different ways, with different strategies. Companies which target new markets, segments or niches may find that they are hard

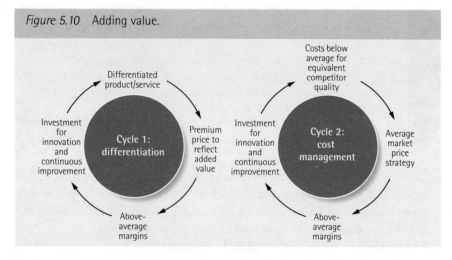

Figure 5.10 Adding value.

to penetrate, unless they have developed something radically new and different which is seen as a valuable alternative by customers. After all, most successful companies have realized that it is more expensive to win new business than it is to retain existing customers and, as a result, look after their customers. While patents can provide a barrier to new entrants and new rivals, so too can loyal customers!

However, some markets may equally be difficult to defend. This would be the case where the wider business environment is dynamic and turbulent, where the organization enjoys only a relatively weak strategic fit and where the service being provided is below the level expected. Hence, positioning and fit can be improved with customer care, product and service innovation and improvement, and by developing new products. All of this requires that companies take their competitors seriously, defend against any initiatives that they start and, on occasion, attack them. This can imply any or all of the following:

- finding and opening new windows of opportunity
- product and service development, improvement and enhancement
- direct attacks, such as price wars, either 'all-out' and sustained or short-term and guerrilla. Special discount promotions would be an example of the latter
- attempting to change the 'rules of engagement or competition' either openly (with genuinely new ideas) or more deviously (lobbying government for new regulations or buying out a key supplier or competitor)
- a 'war of words', seeking publicity for your activities and carefully disparaging your competitors. Sir Richard Branson was able to strengthen the image and position of Virgin Atlantic when he drew attention to British Airways' so-called 'dirty tricks' campaign to win over Virgin customers
- networking and collaboration with key partners in the supply chain.

To summarize this section, Markides (1999) provides a list of six factors for competitive and strategic success. These are:

1. Choose a potentially winning position. This requires understanding *who* your customers are, *what* they require and expect and *how* they can be reached. This corresponds with Porter's (1996) view that it is essential to focus on certain activities and ignore others, not attempting to be 'all things to all people'.
2. Make this choice by a proper exploration of options, which implies:
3. An active search for opportunities to be different in a meaningful way, not just adopting a strategy because it seems to work.
4. Ensure all the support activities work together effectively and synergistically.
5. Create a real strategic fit and position which links the organization with its customers.
6. Ensure there is flexibility in both the activities and the fit so that innovation and change can sustain competitiveness.

Appropriability

Kay (1993) uses the term 'appropriability' to make the point that organizations must seek to ensure that they see the benefits of the value which they create and add. After all, few things cannot be copied and some positions of advantage will be transient without improvement.

Value can be provided for customers in a whole variety of ways, but unless they are willing to pay a premium price which at least offsets the cost of adding the value, then it is the customer and not the organization that benefits. Even if a premium price can be charged, if this is then used to reward suppliers and employees, additional profits may not accrue. Sometimes higher profits are used primarily to reward shareholders, or owner–managers in the case of small organizations. All of these possibilities imply that the organization is not creating and sustaining a position where it makes superior profits and uses these (at least in part) to reinvest and help to build new values through improvement and innovation. Quite simply, the ideal scenario is a virtuous one, where every stakeholder benefits.

Regulation of railways in the UK provides an excellent example of the inherent tensions. The network and infrastructure provider (Railtrack, which essentially maintains the lines, signalling and stations) and the train operating companies (such as Virgin Rail, GNER and the French company Connex and who provide the actual train services) are independent businesses with their own employees and shareholders. Sometimes customers travel on services provided by just one train operator, but many journeys mean that customers are shared. Standards of reliability and service do vary. The government wants more people to use the railways (and other forms of public transport) to reduce traffic on the roads. This will only happen if services are good and prices acceptable. But attractive wages, required to recruit and retain a high calibre of employee, impact on costs and prices. So too do requirements for investment in new infrastructure (to improve services) and safety, particularly after a series of high-profile crashes. If investment demands, together with restraints on prices and profits imposed by the rail regulator, result in reduced profits and dividends, the individual train companies will find it increasingly difficult to generate and raise the funds they need for ongoing investment and improvement. Without the improvement, of course, they are likely to be fined by the regulator, making the profit situation even more precarious. There could very easily be a vicious rather than a virtuous circle.

SWOT (Strengths, Weaknesses, Opportunities and Threats) Analysis

Environmental opportunities are only potential opportunities unless the organization can utilize resources to take advantage of them and until the strategic leader decides that it is appropriate to pursue the opportunity. It is therefore important to evaluate environmental opportunities in relation to the strengths and weaknesses of the organization's resources, and in relation to the organizational culture. Real opportunities exist when there is a close fit between environment, values and resources. Similarly, the resources and culture will determine the extent to which any potential threat becomes a real threat. This is E–V–R congruence, which was explained in Chapter 1.

All of the resources at the disposal of the organization can be deployed strategically, including strategic leadership. It is therefore useful to consider the resources in terms of where they are strong and where they are weak as this will provide an indication of their strategic value. However, this should not be seen as a list of absolute strengths and weaknesses seen from an internal perspective; rather, the evaluation should consider the strengths and weaknesses in relation to the needs of the environment and in relation to competition. The views of external stakeholders may differ from those of internal managers (who in turn may disagree among themselves) when evaluating the relative strength of a particular product, resource or skill. Resources should be evaluated for their relative strengths and weaknesses in the light of key success factors.

Even though an organization may be strong or weak in a particular function, the corresponding position of its major competitors must also be taken into account. For example, it might have sophisticated computer-controlled machine tools in its factory, but if its competitors have the same or even better equipment, the plant should not be seen as a relative strength. This issue refers to distinctive competencies – relative strengths which can be used to create competitive advantage. As any resource can be deployed strategically, competitive advantage can be gained from any area of the total business.

An evaluation of an organization's strengths and weaknesses in relation to environmental opportunities and threats is generally referred to as a SWOT analysis.

As mentioned above, a mere list of absolute factors is of little use. The opportunities which matter are those that can be capitalized on because they fit the organization's values and resources; the threats which matter are those that the organization must deal with and which it is not well equipped to deal with; the key strengths are those where the organization enjoys a relatively strong competitive position and which relate to key success factors; the key weaknesses are those which prevent the organization from attaining competitive advantage.

Again, to be useful the lists of factors should be limited to those which matter the most, so that attention can be concentrated on them. In arriving at such a summary SWOT statement it can therefore be useful to start by drawing up a large grid and using it for assessing relative importances.

The example in Box 5.3 (developed from Benoit, 1999) considers Saga, founded originally in 1951, which now provides a wide range of holidays and other services (including insurance and home shopping) for people over 50 years old, a clearly identified and targeted segment.

STRATEGY IN ACTION – Box 5.3
A SWOT Analysis of Saga

Strengths	Strong and visible brand and reputation
	Increasingly wide range of products and services
	Valuable database for cross-selling
Weaknesses	Ill-judged move into the USA which reduced profits
	Late entrant into e-commerce – many over-50s do use the Internet!
Opportunities	E-commerce, especially for deeper penetration into the USA. The issue for Saga is thus one of reach not further diversification
	Europe, where so far there has been only limited marketing effort to date
Threats	Developing e-commerce may now prove to be too late, as others have targeted Saga's market – the power of the brand may, however, overcome the issue of the delay.

Saga http://www.sagaholidays.com

Figure 5.11 illustrates a popular and useful framework for a SWOT analysis applied to ASDA earlier in the 1990s, before the introduction of new strategies focusing on the product ranges, in-store layouts and a clear distinction between large ASDA superstores and smaller units with a limited range and discounted prices (called Dales), and finally its acquisition by Wal-Mart. The chart highlights

Figure 5.11   ASDA: SWOT analysis, early 1990s.

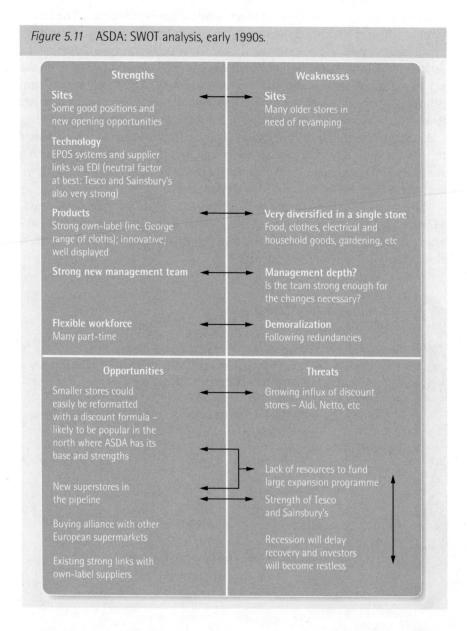

how certain issues can be considered as either a strength or a weakness, an opportunity or a threat, depending on how they are managed in the future.

Once all of the important strategic issues have been teased out from a long list of strengths, weaknesses, opportunities and threats, the following questions should be asked.

- How can we either neutralize critical weaknesses or convert them into strengths?
- Similarly, can we neutralize critical threats or even build them into new opportunities?
- How can we best exploit our strengths in relation to our opportunities?
- What new markets and market segments might be suitable for our existing strengths and capabilities?
- Given the (changing) demands of our existing markets, what changes do we need to make to our products, processes and services?

Finally, alongside a general SWOT analysis, it is essential to evaluate the relative strengths and weaknesses of the company's leading competitors.

Forecasting the Environment

A complex and dynamic modern environment is inevitably difficult to forecast; the inherent uncertainties can make it highly unpredictable and potentially chaotic. External events and competitor activities can trigger a chain reaction of responses and new scenarios; but Handy (1989) contends that 'those who know why changes come waste less effort in protecting themselves or in fighting the inevitable'. Consequently, however difficult it may be to forecast environmental change, organizations must attempt to stay strategically aware. They should reflect upon their experiences and look for emerging patterns or trends in the industry and business environment. They should be vigilant in tracking technological and other developments which may affect, possibly radically, their industries and markets. They should look for, and maybe even borrow or 'steal', appropriate ideas. New management literature can help; so too can reports of good practice in a whole variety of different organizations.

In analysing the environment managers should seek to do the following.

- Identify which forces are most important, and why they are critical. This will reflect opportunities and threats.
- Forecast how these forces might change in the future, using whatever methods are appropriate.

- Incorporate these expectations and predictions into decision making and management thinking. Fahey and King (1983) have emphasized the usefulness of including line managers from the whole organization in any teams which are specifically charged with environmental analysis, as this can lead to more effective dissemination of information to enable it to be used in decision making. Managers will be individually aware of many changes in the environment. Where strategic change takes place incrementally through managers with delegated authority, this information can be easily incorporated in decisions. However, where major strategic change is being considered centrally by the strategic leader it is important to gather the relevant data together.
- Be honest and realistic when evaluating strengths and weaknesses relative to competitors, and when considering the organization's ability to respond to opportunities and threats. The environment should be managed wherever possible, and managers should seek to ensure that their resources are compatible with the organization's environment and the factors and forces that will influence and determine success.

This last factor implies that forecasts should be as realistic as possible; they should be used in decision making and for the determination of future strategy; and the implications of changes in the environment should be acted upon and not ignored.

Individual managers will develop their environmental and strategic awareness through experience and perception, and by thinking about their observations and experiences. It is particularly important to assess the significance of what happens and what can be observed to be happening. However, in considering future strategic changes there will be an additional need to forecast the changes that might take place in the environment concerning supplies, customers, competitors, demand, technology, government legislation and so on. Some of the future changes may be forecast through straightforward extrapolation of past events; many will not. Some of the environmental forces can be better quantified than others, and consequently some subjectivity will be involved. Hogarth and Makridakis (1981) have argued that the overall performance of organizations in predicting future changes is poor, and that the most sophisticated methods of forecasting are not necessarily the best. However, despite the difficulties, forecasting is important. Managers who are encouraged to think about future changes, to ask questions and to query assumptions will increase their insight and awareness and this should help decision making.

What, then, do managers need to forecast, and how might the forecasting be carried out?

The economy and the possible impact of economic changes can be assessed in a number of ways. Economic growth, inflation, government spending, interest rates, exchange rates, the money supply, investment and taxation may all be influential. The Treasury provides forecasts periodically, based on its own econometric model. Some universities and business schools also publish predictions based on their econometric models. Sometimes they are in agreement, but often they are not. Analysts from City institutions are regularly quoted on television and radio news programmes, and again there is often disagreement. The problem lies in the number of interrelationships and interdependencies amongst the economic variables and in imperfect understanding of the cause and effect relationships. In addition, economic forces and changes around the world, such as changes in the exchange value of key currencies, inflation rates in major markets such as the USA and balances of payments in different countries, can all affect the UK and organizations based in the UK, especially those with overseas interests. Although not all changes can be forecast with great accuracy, managers should be aware of what is happening at the moment and the implications of any trends that can be observed.

Demographic influences include some that can be forecast reasonably well and some that are more unpredictable. Changes in population structure can be readily forecast; changes in tastes and values are more difficult. Again, it is essential to be able to appreciate the significance of observed events and changes. The government provides statistics on social trends, which give some insight, but organizations need to be continually aware rather than rely on statistics which are a little dated when published.

At one level this issue is relatively clear: there is a general breakdown of two-parent families, a growth in the number of older and retired people, and a decline in those aged 15–24. But what are the implications? Categorizing people into socioeconomic or house-type groupings has often been used to try and understand demand patterns, but the situation remains complex. Individual firms must conduct attitude and behavioural research. Why, for example, does a friend of the author drive a £30,000 car but wear a £20 wristwatch? Why does his wife buy premium-price luxury ice cream and the cheapest own-label toilet paper?

Political influences relate to changes in governments and their priorities and legislation programmes. Opinion polls help in forecasting the former, and indications of the latter are readily available. However, planned legislation is not always passed, for various reasons.

Developing from this is the need to forecast how certain laws and regulations might be implemented. Organizations considering mergers or acquisitions must try to predict whether a referral to the Competition Commission is likely before mounting their bid. Contacts within the so-called corridors of power can be of great benefit.

Demographic and political forecasting often relies on expert opinion, which can be obtained through personal contacts, commissioned research or published information in journals and newspapers. Outside opinions may well be biased or prejudiced because of strong views on certain issues or because of political perspectives, and this must be taken into account. Wilson (1977) has shown how probability-diffusion matrices can be useful here. Where opinions concerning the likelihood or probability of certain events are being gathered it is useful to plot both the strength of feeling (high or low probability of occurrence) and the diffusion of opinion (consistency or dispersion) among the sources or experts.

Technological forecasting covers changes in technology generally, and the possible impact of innovations which result from research and development by an organization, by its competitors and by other firms with which it is involved in some way. Expert opinion through scenario planning and from technical journals can be useful. Technological changes can have an impact throughout an organization and consequently it is useful for managers in various functions to consider the possible effects on them.

This issue has been manifested in the need for organizations to come to terms with the threats and opportunities posed by the Internet, both for information movement and for e-commerce. The Internet has expanded more rapidly than many people thought credible just a few years ago and many organizations are a long way from exploiting its potential. However, there are inbuilt dilemmas. For example, only one in seven German and Italian adults possesses a credit card, essential for buying on-line. Buying on-line for home delivery has varying degrees of relevance in different countries. Many Europeans live relatively close to the shops concerned and can easily fetch the goods themselves. In addition, relatively few Europeans have the larger, American-style, outside postboxes which can accept small parcel deliveries when people are out.

Scenario Planning

Scenarios are often used in strategic management to explore future possibilities. Possible happenings and events are considered by looking at potential outcomes from particular causes and seeking to explain why things might occur. The value is in increased awareness by exploring possibilities and asking and attempting to answer 'what if' questions. Although scenario planning can be predictive and can be used to plan strategic changes, it can also help decision making by providing managers with insight so that they can react better when things happen or change. It can also be helpful for conceptualizing possible new competitive paradigms.

Environments for many organizations have become – and continue to become – increasingly dynamic, turbulent and uncertain. They feature an ele-

> Don't try to eliminate uncertainty ... embrace it. Despite overwhelming evidence to the contrary many of us still view the future as an extension of the past.
> *Clem Sunter, Anglo American Corporation of South Africa (the world's largest mining group)*
>
> The world's changing. People in the US and Europe aren't going to live the way they do 100 years from now unless they do a lot of things differently. Who says that because we have 240 million people on this big piece of land [USA] we should have two cars and second homes, while 800 million people in India and 1 billion in China should live the way they live? We've only been wealthy in this country for 70 years. Who said we ought to have all this? Is it ordained?
> *John F Welch, Chairman and CEO, General Electric*

ment of competitive chaos, where companies continually thrust and parry with new ploys and stratagems in an attempt to, at the very least, stay 'in the game' and, ideally, get ahead of their rivals. Scenarios and scenario planning concern the medium- or long-term future and they embrace the possibility of real and dramatic change. Anticipation and creativity can be invaluable in dealing with the turbulence and uncertainty. By considering and evaluating future possibilities, organizations can put themselves in positions where they might be better placed to deal with the unpredictable challenges of the future. Put another way: simply engaging in the process of acknowledging and anticipating change enables managers to be less shocked by whatever change does occur.

Three central themes underpin effective scenario planning:

- It is important to clarify just what a business can and cannot change. Small farmers, for example, cannot enjoy the scale economies of large farms, nor can they affect the climate. They can, within reason, improve their soil and they can change their crops.
- What seems trivial or a pipe-dream today could be crucial in the future. In 1874, Western Union in America turned down Alexander Graham Bell's prototype telephone!
- Multiple scenarios need to be explored and then *held* as real possibilities. Shell, which pioneered scenario planning, is arguably ready to respond quickly to shocks which affect supply or prevailing prices.

The scenarios considered may involve modified versions of current competitive paradigms (the future is not the past, but at least the two are related) or radically new paradigms (everything changes in the end). The implications of the scenarios will tend towards one of two themes: first, there will be environmental changes but organizations can learn to cope with, and influence or manage events, and thereby enjoy some degree of relative stability; secondly, the environmental turbulence will be so great that the competitive situation will become ever more chaotic in nature.

Readers might like to consider a number of emerging issues in the UK, evaluate their significance and implications and, where appropriate, consider how they might apply in their own countries.

- People are living longer; there is an ageing population. But will the more recent trend of people retiring earlier, many on good pensions, continue? As people are healthier, is it not logical for them to work longer, as long as employers do not discriminate on age grounds? Of course, for some jobs skills can become outdated and people do become less useful. There is also the key dilemma of pensions. If people retire relatively early and live longer, there are two implications: one is that they will have to accept lower pensions; the other is that those people still in employment will have to pay far higher contributions to build up and sustain the pension funds.
- According to most published statistics, unemployment is coming down, yet, at the same time, there are growing skills shortages. Developing the point above, raising the retirement age could help here, but only for some jobs. In a knowledge-based society, does the need for skill retraining and updating become more critical through a person's working life?
- The NHS is stretched and private medicine is expensive. This could become more problematical as people live longer and especially if pensions are reduced. Hence, economically, people might need to work longer.
- However, if the relative balance between salaried and 'permanent' career posts and self-employed people who contract themselves to various organizations continues to change, this issue of the length of working lives could be exacerbated.
- In addition, it is becoming increasingly difficult for many families to prepare for retirement because of the increasing costs of educating their children. In turn, this increases the number of two-income families and creates a larger number of child-care positions.

Developing useful scenarios

Organizations should really be looking to develop a number of scenarios that can be used to provoke debate among managers and possibly generate new creative ideas in the process – ideas that can be used as a basis for new strategies and action plans.

The first step is to clarify the *key strategic issues*, mainly external, which will impact on the future that the company will face. Internally, many managers will already have formed views, which may not always accord, and which may be partial rather than comprehensive, but these preliminary views will have caused the development of current working assumptions about future trends. It is invariably invaluable also to consult outside experts.

There are three types of issue to consider:

- *predetermined elements* – for example, *social* changes to the size and structure of the population, lifestyles and values
- *key uncertainties* – *political* changes and the inevitable *economic* changes which accompany them; the entry of new competitors; possible changes of corporate ownership
- *driving forces* – developments in *technology* and education.

The link to a PEST analysis will be clearly seen.

The next step is to examine a number of *plausible outcomes* from the various key issues. It is particularly important to debate issues of positive and negative synergy, specifically the impact of interconnectedness. The discussions should generate some consensus, or possibly, and more realistically, accommodation on priorities, in the form of *viable scenarios* to test further.

These will often be presented as *stories*, illustrated creatively to generate interest and enthusiasm.

The *tests* against which they will be ultimately evaluated are:

- What has been left out? – in effect, the extent of the comprehensiveness and the absence of key omissions – and
- Do they lead to clearer understanding which informs future decisions and actions, while winning the commitment of everyone involved?

Box 5.4 provides a number of examples.

The dream society

Jensen (1999) contends that we shall soon be living in a 'dream society' where the stories attributed to products and services – their image and reputation – will be an increasingly significant aspect of competitive advantage. Examples might relate to free-range eggs, organic vegetables and celebrity-endorsed training shoes. Simply, the story adds value.

Jensen provides a number of themes for those organizations interested in creating 'dreams':

British Airways (BA)

BA believes that annual planning meetings (which are valuable and have a role to play) 'do not help people think about what might happen a decade from now'. Moreover, 'people have difficulty envisaging dramatic change'.

Consequently, in the mid-1990s, BA created two scenarios for the period to 2005, which it used in management meetings to provoke discussion about the implications of possible changes. These are known as *Wild Gardens* and *New Structures*.

Wild Gardens postulates a world where market forces are unleashed. Asian markets in particular grow rapidly and, early in the twenty-first century, after a period of strong growth, the USA falls into a long recession. The 1996/97 general election in the UK is won for a fifth consecutive time by the Conservatives; the country remains divided over Europe. The EU is enlarged to bring in more Eastern countries, but there is no single currency. The European Commission takes over negotiation of airline agreements from member governments, and concludes an Atlantic open-skies agreement which gives free access to transatlantic routes to carriers from both Europe and the USA. Access to domestic airports in Europe and the USA is widened.

The *New Structures* scenario is more stable, and gives greater control to individual governments. Asia's rise proves to be slower than initially anticipated, and Asian investment is reduced. Labour comes to power in the UK and joins France and Germany in promoting stronger European integration. A single currency (the Euromarque) is agreed, together with integrated air-traffic control and a European high-speed rail network. There is increased commitment to the environment. In the USA, President Clinton remains in power and reaches agreement with the Republicans to work together to increase investment and productivity. Taxes are increased; defence expenditure is reduced. North Korea provokes a security crisis in Asia and China suffers unrest after the death of Deng Xiaoping.

In discussions, BA managers believed that *New Structures* implied greater emphasis on ethical issues and customers who demand increased personal attention. *Wild Gardens* could mean that English ceases to be the international language and that fluency in Asian languages would inevitably be more important. As outcomes:

- BA decided to trial interactive television screens in airport lounges, allowing travellers to raise issues with an employee whose face they can see
- BA began investigating a single database covering its customers around the world

- there were discussions with partner airlines Qantas and US Air, concerning the implications of *Wild Gardens*. Even if Asia developed more slowly, the language implications would not disappear.

British Airways   http://www.britishairways.com

Motor vehicles

Historically, most car makers have seen engine and other technologies as key core competencies – and they have invested in research and development to enhance their competency. Many would argue that they have placed less emphasis on marketing issues. This might well reflect a harder, male image of cars and, as a possible scenario, a softer and so-called female style might be envisioned. While technology improvements tend to be incremental, this might imply more radical changes of design.

Areas for debate might then include the following.

- Why not see the driver's side and the passenger side as quite separate instead of basically replicating the layout of one in the other? Do the seats need to be designed the same? Would passengers enjoy more working or reading space?
- Should optional and child-orientated rear seating areas be considered? Could these be flexible and easily changed when the car changes hands?
- Could doors which are ideal for older and more infirm people be another option?

The debate could be extended to consider cars as something more than a means of transport. For some, they are almost a mobile office in any case. Certain customized – and premium-price – cars already provide telecommunications links.

Can lessons be applied to less expensive cars? This could, of course, be tied in with the whole issue of how motorists might receive more accurate and timely information about road and weather conditions on both the route they are following and the alternative rerouting options open to them. As motorists, we often feel frustrated about the lack of hard information while realizing we are in an information age!

References

Barnett, S (1996) Style and strategy: new metaphors, new insights, *European Management Journal*, **14**, 4, August.

Moyer, K (1996) Scenario planning at British Airways – a case study, *Long Range Planning*, **29**, 2.

- ADVENTURE   Involvement in the 'great outdoors' or leisure activities. Manchester United branded clothing appears to combine both

- NETWORKS   BT (British Telecom) capitalized on this with its 'family and friends' name for its discounted call scheme as well as the television advertisements which feature ET and which, for example, link an absent father with his son for a game of chess

- SELF-DISCOVERY Linked to products which allow people to say something about themselves. This theme has been exploited by VW (Volkswagen) with advertisements for the Golf which claim the only statement it needs to make is 'gone shopping'

- PEACE OF MIND   Security, often linked to the perceived safety of the known past. Perhaps this explains why VW has been able to relaunch the Beetle model and BMW a new Mini (a model that it acquired when it owned Rover)

- CARING   Businesses can exploit their community links and programmes

- CONVICTIONS   Ethical and environmental concerns are prominent. The Body Shop built a successful business around this.

Summary

Organizations operate with external environments that spring surprises on them from time to time. Indeed, many industries and markets are characterized by a form of 'competitive chaos' which arises from the natural dynamism, turbulence and uncertainty of both the industry and the environment.

It can make sense for the organization to see its boundary with the environment as relatively fluid. While suppliers, distributors and customers can be seen as outside the organizational boundary, they can also be identified as partners in a collaborative network which, more holistically, bounds with a number of external influences and forces.

Organizations must be able to react to the change pressures imposed by their environment (potential threats) and, at the same time, take advantage of opportunities which seem worthwhile. But this is arguably not enough. Leading organizations will create and sustain positions of strength by seeking to influence – and maybe even manage – their external environment.

A *PEST* (political, economic, social and technological forces) analysis provides a valuable framework for analysing relevant environmental forces.

Over time, strong competitors create and seek to hold positions of power in markets and industries. For this reason governments everywhere will seek to exercise some degree of control. In the UK the relevant bodies are the Office of Fair

Trading and the Competition Commission. However, in certain instances, UK companies will also be subject to regulation by the European Union.

Regulation is rarely clear-cut or 'black and white' and sometimes the outcomes are not quite the ones desired.

To manage, and manage in, its environment an organization will need strong strategic positions. This implies finding and exploiting opportunities for adding value, in ways that consumers value and for which they will reward the organization with prices that imply superior margins.

Here we are talking about finding an effective blend between the opportunity-driven approach to strategy creation and the resource-based approach.

As organizations seek to exploit their *core competencies* and *strategic capabilities* to add value in this way, it is important that the value is appropriable. In other words, the benefits should not all go to shareholders (through high dividends), consumers (in, say, the form of relatively low prices) or employees (generous remuneration) such that the organization has inadequate resources for investment to build new ways of adding value for the future.

A *SWOT* (strengths, weaknesses, opportunities and threats) analysis is a second valuable framework for evaluating the position of an organization in relation to its environment. It is, however, important that the SWOT analysis is used to create ideas and is not just seen as a static statement of position.

Taking this further, it is important that organizations attempt to forecast their environment, however difficult this may prove. Scenario planning can make a very valuable contribution here.

References

Ansoff, HI (1987) *Corporate Strategy*, Penguin. Revised from the original 1965 edition.

Benoit, B (1999) Nearing 50, hale and hearty on home ground – a corporate profile of SAGA, *Financial Times*, 23 November.

Campbell, A and Alexander, M (1997) What's wrong with strategy? *Harvard Business Review*, November– December.

Courtney, H, Kirkland, J and Viguerie, P (1997) Strategy under uncertainty, *Harvard Business Review*, November–December.

Drucker, PF (1973) *Management*, Harper and Row.

Duncan, R (1972) Characteristics of organizational environments and perceived environmental uncertainty, *Administrative Science Quarterly*, 313–27.

Fahey, L and King, R (1983) Environmental scanning for corporate planning. In *Business Policy and Strategy: Concepts and Readings*, 3rd edn (eds DJ McCarthy *et al.*), Irwin.

Handy, C (1989) *The Age Of Unreason*, Hutchinson.

Hogarth, RM and Makridakis, S (1981) Forecasting and planning: an evaluation, *Management Science*, 27, 115–38.

Jensen, R (1999) *The Dream Society*, McGraw Hill.

Kay, JA (1993) *Foundations of Corporate Success*, Oxford University Press.

Markides, C (1999) Six principles of breakthrough strategy, *Business Strategy Review*, 10, 2, Summer.

Mintzberg, H (1987) Crafting strategy, *Harvard Business Review*, July–August.

Porter, ME (1996) What is strategy? *Harvard Business Review*, November–December.

Wilson, IH (1977) Forecasting social and political trends. In *Corporate Strategy and Planning* (eds B Taylor and J Sparkes), Heinemann.

Test your knowledge of this chapter with our online quiz at:
http://www.thomsonlearning.co.uk

Explore Environmental Analysis, Synergy and Strategic Positioning further at:
Business Strategy Review   http://www.blackwellpublishers.co.uk/journals/BSR

Questions and Research Assignments

TEXT RELATED

1. Draw a diagram incorporating the environmental influences and stakeholders for any pub, discotheque or nightclub with which you are familiar.

2. Evaluate the threats and opportunities faced by any organization with which you are familiar.

3. From this evaluation, develop a SWOT analysis and consider the strategic implications.

4. Possibly in a group discussion, build a scenario relevant for the motor vehicle industry in ten years' time. How will people be using their cars? What will they expect in terms of size, performance, and external and interior design?

Internet and Library Projects

1. How have changes in competition from around the world affected the UK footwear industry? What are the strategies of the leading, remaining manufacturers?
   You may wish to use a leading retailer such as C&J Clark as a key reference point. You should also look at a specialist such as Grenson or Church's. You might also investigate the source of your personal wardrobe of shoes, boots and trainers.

   C&J Clark   http://www.clarks.com
   Church's   http://www.churchsshoes.com
   Grenson   http://www.grenson.co.uk

2. How has Steve Pateman, owner of a family boot and shoe business in Northamptonshire, dealt with the pressures for change in this industry? How has the company diversified, and what do you think the implications are?

3. From your own experience, and from newspaper and other articles you have read or seen, list examples of where monopoly power and restrictive practices have been investigated, and where proposed mergers have been considered by the Competition Commission (or its predecessor, the Monopolies and Mergers Commission). Evaluate the recommendations and outcomes. If you wish to follow up any of these investigations, all of the reports are published by HMSO.

Monopolies and Mergers Commission UK
http://www.coi.gov.uk/coi/depts/GMM/GMM.html
HMSO UK   http://www.hmso.gov.uk

Finance in Action

The Experience Curve

A large size, relative to competitors, can bring benefits. In particular, if a company has a market share substantially greater than its competitors it has opportunities to achieve greater profitability. Lower costs can be achieved if the company is managed well and takes advantage of the opportunities offered by being larger. These lower costs can be passed on to the consumer in the form of lower prices, which in turn puts pressure on competitors' profit margins and strengthens the position of the market leader.

Lower costs are achieved through economies of scale and the experience or learning effect. In the 1960s the Boston Consulting Group in the USA estimated that the cost of production decreases by between 10% and 30% each time that a company's experience in producing the product or service doubles, as long as the company is managed well. In other words, as cumulative production increases over time there is a potential cost reduction at a predictable rate. The company learns how to do things better. The savings are spread across all value-added costs: manufacturing, administration, sales, marketing and distribution. In addition, the cost of supplies decreases as suppliers experience the same learning benefits.

The experience effect has been observed in high- and low-technology industries, in new and mature industries, in both manufacturing and service businesses, and in relation to consumer and industrial markets. Specific examples are cars, semiconductors, petrochemicals, long-distance telephone calls, synthetic fibres, airline transportation, crushed limestone and the cost of administering life insurance.

The experience curve is illustrated by plotting on a graph the cumulative number of units produced over time (the horizontal axis) and the cost per unit (the vertical axis), as shown in Exhibit 1. This particular curve is called an '85% experience curve' as every time output is doubled the cost per unit falls to 85% of what it was. In reality, the plot will be of a least-squares line but the trend will

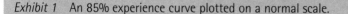

Exhibit 1   An 85% experience curve plotted on a normal scale.

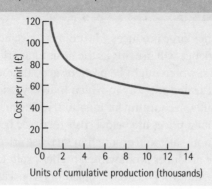

Units of cumulative production (thousands)

be clear. However, it is more common to plot the data on logarithmic scales on both axes, and this shows the straight-line effect illustrated in Exhibit 2.

Sources of the experience effect include:

- increased labour efficiency through learning and consequent skills improvement
- the opportunity for greater specialization in production methods
- innovations in the production process
- greater productivity from equipment as people learn how to use it more efficiently
- improved resource mix as products are redesigned with cost savings in mind.

This is not an exhaustive list and the savings will not occur naturally. They result from good management.

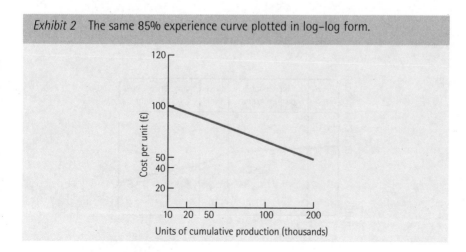

Exhibit 2   The same 85% experience curve plotted in log–log form.

Units of cumulative production (thousands)

Pricing Decisions and the Experience Effect

A market leader or other large producer who enjoys a cost advantage as a result of accumulated experience will use this as the basis for a pricing strategy linked to his or her objectives, which might be profit or growth and market share orientated. Exhibit 3 illustrates one way in which industry prices might be forced down (in real terms, after accounting for inflation) as the market leader benefits from lower costs. Initially, prices are below costs incurred because of the cost of development. As demand, sales and production increase prices fall, but at a slower rate than costs; the producer is enjoying a higher profit margin. This will be attractive to any competitors or potential competitors who feel that they can compete at this price even if their costs are higher. If competition becomes intensive and the major producer(s) wish to assert authority over the market they will decrease prices quickly and force out manufacturers whose costs are substantially above theirs. Stability might then be restored.

Companies with large market shares can therefore dictate what happens in a market, but there is a need for caution. If a company ruthlessly chases a cost advantage via the experience effect the implication could be ever-increasing efficiency as a result of less flexibility. The whole operating system is geared towards efficiency and cost savings. If demand changes or competitors innovate unexpectedly the strategy will have run out of time, as we have already seen. Companies should ensure that they are flexible enough to respond.

This material has mainly been summarized from Abell, DF and Hammond, JS (1979) *Strategic Market Planning: Problems, and Analytical Approaches*, Prentice-Hall.

Exhibit 3 is adapted from The Boston Consulting Group (1972) *Perspectives on Experience*.

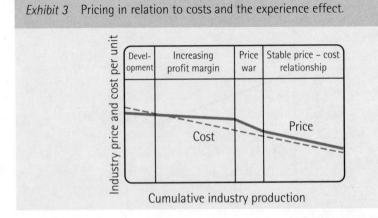

Exhibit 3   Pricing in relation to costs and the experience effect.

The Dynamics of Competition

Few companies enjoy the luxury of having no serious competitors or little likelihood of any need to change their competitive strategy. It is essential for companies to look for opportunities to create – and sustain – a competitive edge over their rivals and build customer loyalty that provides something of a comfort zone. Logically this should lead to superior profits.

However, competitive advantage, as a term, is easily misunderstood. Some organizations clearly believe, and thus delude themselves, that a clear competitive strategy constitutes advantage. It does not. Advantage comes from being better or different in some meaningful way.

Even the strongest companies cannot afford to stand still, as shown in Case Study 6.1. A cynic would argue that a company must change more rapidly than its rivals can steal its ideas!

This chapter begins by looking at the nature of competition in general, before discussing models and frameworks which help us to understand industries, competitive strategy, competitive advantage and competitive dynamics.

Case Study 6: Coca-Cola

Although it is typically priced higher than many competing products, Coca-Cola (Coke) remains the world's best-selling soft drink and the world's best-known brand name. Coca-Cola is reputed to see its only serious competitor as water! Ideally an adult requires a daily liquid intake of 64 ounces, and overall Coke provides just two of these. The Coca-Cola company was founded over 100 years ago, and today it remains largely focused; Columbia Pictures was acquired some years ago, but later sold to Sony. Seventy per cent of Coke's sales and 80% of its operating profits are now earned outside the USA. The company has a 50% share of the world market for carbonated drinks, including 44% of the US market. A typical American adult who drinks Coke will consume 400 eight-ounce servings in a year, just over one a day. Because Americans own very large refrigerators which can store the largest bottles available, this can work out relatively inexpensive. By contrast, a regular British Coke drinker consumes 120 eight-ounce servings in a year, from smaller and more expensive bottles and cans. The UK is still perceived to be a developing market for the product. Other 'established' territories, which include Switzerland, Chile and Mexico, have a consumption of 300 eight-ounce servings per year.

Over the years critics have predicted that something would happen to stem the continual and successful growth of the business, possibly changing tastes, stronger competition or market saturation. This really has not happened; Coca-Cola has continued to increase worldwide sales through clever marketing and occasional new products. In 1996 Coca-Cola was America's most admired company in the *Fortune* rankings but, as seen in Chapter 3, it had not sustained this position in the late 1990s, although it continues to enjoy high global admiration. In terms of increases in shareholder wealth, Coca-Cola was unrivalled in the USA throughout the leadership of its charismatic chief executive, Roberto Goizueta. Goizueta was the strategic leader from 1981 until his death in post in 1997. Nevertheless, Coca-Cola still made a number of strategic misjudgements.

Competitive strategies

Coke had successfully established Fanta (the fizzy orange drink launched in 1960) and Tab (sugar-free Coca-Cola, 1963) when Goizueta took over.

In 1982 Diet Coke was launched. Diet products are particularly important for the American market, but generally less significant elsewhere. However, in 1985, New Coke was launched to replace the original blending, but subsequently withdrawn after a consumer outcry. The Fresca range has also been launched. Sprite is another famous Coca-Cola brand, as are Minute Maid fruit juices. In 1998, an agreement to buy the Schweppes soft drinks businesses outside the USA from Cadbury's was thwarted by the European regulatory authorities. Coca-Cola has also been affected by economic crises and recessions in countries where it is particularly popular, especially Russia and Asia. In 1999 it was forced to withdraw the product in Belgium after a health scare resulting from minor contamination. Arguably, the company's public relations could have been better.

Coke really became popular overseas when it was shipped out to GIs during World War II, and systematically it has been introduced to more and more countries. For many years its stated goal was to 'always have Coca-Cola within an arm's reach of desire' and preferably in chilled storage, whether this was on retail shelves or through vending machines. It has benefited from being associated with the image and persona of America. When GIs drank it during World War II – and subsequent wars in Korea and Vietnam – it was seen as a reminder of exactly what they were fighting for. Early in 1999 Coca-Cola's name was linked to a line of fashion and sports clothing, the first significant extension of the brand.

Coca-Cola controls production of the concentrated syrup from Atlanta; mixing, bottling/canning and distribution are franchised to independent businesses worldwide. In truth, the issue of the 'secret formula' is more mystique than necessity, but it provides another valuable story to reinforce the brand and its image. Goizueta inherited a distribution network which was underperforming and he set about strengthening it with proper joint venture agreements and tight controls. Effective supply management is absolutely vital for the business.

Goizueta chose to acquire its smaller, underperforming bottlers, invested in them and, when they were turned around, sold them to stronger anchor bottlers – specifically those with the financial resources to invest in developing the business. 'Coca-Cola's distribution machine is [now] the most powerful and pervasive on the planet.'

Coca-Cola has always advertised heavily and prominently; and Goizueta has also negotiated a number of important promotional agreements. Coca-Cola has special aisles in Wal-Mart stores; Coke's Hi-C orange juice is supplied to McDonald's, for example. In recent years there has been increased emphasis on branding and packaging at the expense of pure advertising. 'We had really lost focus on who our customer was. We felt our customer was the bottler, as opposed to the McDonald's and the Wal-Marts' (Goizueta).

Faced with increased competition from retail own-label brands sold mainly through supermarket chains, Coca-Cola has carefully defended and strengthened its other distribution outlets such as convenience stores, fast-food restaurants and vending machines.

Competition

Coca-Cola's main rival is Pepsi Cola, which has a 30% share of the US market and 20% of the world market. Its share has been growing since the 1993 introduction of Pepsi Max, a sugar-free product with the taste of the original Pepsi. Pepsi diversified into snack foods (Frito-Lay in the USA, Walkers and Smiths crisps in the UK) and restaurants (Pizza Hut, Taco Bell and Kentucky Fried in the USA); just one-third of global profits came from soft drinks in the mid-1990s. Pepsi also owns much of its bottling network. In 1996 the Pepsi brand was relaunched with a massive international promotional campaign. The new Pepsi colours, predominantly blue, were chosen to appeal to the younger buyer. In 1997 PepsiCo divested its restaurants into a separate business, and followed this up with the acquisition of the French company Orangina – after the European competition regulators had prevented Coca-Cola from buying the business. A year later Pepsi acquired Tropicana, the world's largest marketer of branded juices, which it bought from the Canadian company Seagram. With this purchase, Pepsi controlled 40% of the US chilled orange juice market, twice the share of Coca-Cola.

Another significant competitor is Cott of Canada, which produces discounted colas with acceptable alternative tastes. Cott produces concentrate for Wal-Mart in the USA and for Sainsbury's and Virgin in the UK.

QUESTIONS: Why is Coca-Cola 'number one' in its industry?
Where is its competitive advantage?
If it avoids *serious* mistakes, does it need to do anything radically different to retain its position?
Can you think of anything its leading rivals might do to 'upset the applecart'?

Coca Cola   http://www.coca-cola.com

One advantage when you're No. 1 or 2 in an industry is that you can really have a hell of a lot of say in what the future's going to be like by what you do. I'm not a believer in always forecasting the future. But if you take actions that can create that future, at least shape it, then you can benefit from it.

They say: 'Do you sleep well at night with all the competition?' I say: 'I sleep like a baby'. They say: 'That's wonderful'. I say: 'No, no. I wake up every two hours and cry!' Because it's true, you know. You have to feel that restlessness.

Roberto Goizueta,
late Chief Executive,
Coca-Cola Corporation

Competition: An Introduction

Causes generate effects. Actions lead to outcomes. On occasions companies may attempt to seize the competitive initiative and introduce an innovatory change. An action by one competitor which affects the relative success of rivals provokes responses. One action can therefore provoke several reactions, depending on the extent of the impact and the general nature of competition. Each reaction in turn further affects the other rival competitors in the industry. New responses will again follow. What we have in many markets and industries is a form of *competitive chaos*. Figure 6.1 shows a competitive business environment which is permanently fluid and unpredictable. For example, the Post Office continues to experience new forms of competition from cheaper telephone calls, courier services and fax machines; it must adapt and respond to defend its place in the market.

In spring 2000, a proposed acquisition of US Air by market leader, United, was expected to provoke a hostile reaction by United's leading rivals, American and Delta Airlines. Quite the contrary – American and Delta both realized that if the United/US Air merger was allowed to proceed it would open up opportunities for further consolidation and rationalization. American was interested in linking with NorthWestern and Delta with Continental. This would, simply, create three larger and stronger companies from the current top six.

It is important to differentiate between two sets of similar, but nevertheless different, decisions. First, some actions are innovatory and represent one competitor acting upon a perceived opportunity ahead of its rivals; other actions constitute reactions to these competitive initiatives. Secondly, some decisions imply incremental strategic change to existing, intended strategies; on different occasions companies are adapting their strategies (adaptive strategic change) as they

Figure 6.1   Dynamic competition.

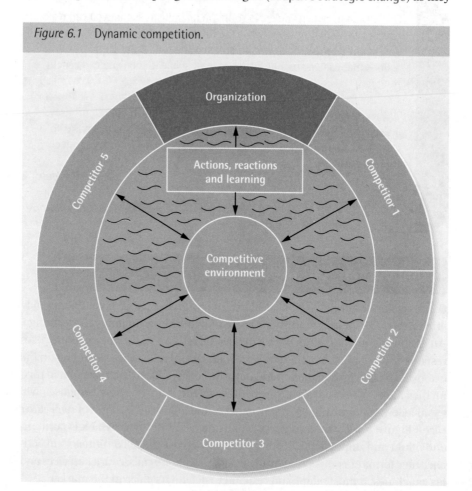

see new opportunities which they can seize early, or possible future threats which they are seeking to avoid. The process is about *learning and flexibility*. Often, as shown in Chapter 10, they involve an *intrapreneur*, an internal entrepreneur.

The skills required by organizations are:

- the ability to discern patterns in this dynamic environment and competitive chaos, and spot opportunities ahead of their rivals
- the ability to anticipate competitor actions and reactions
- the ability to use this intelligence and insight to lead customer opinion and outperform competitors.

3M (the Minnesota Mining and Manufacturing Company) is based in St. Paul, Minnesota, USA, and has developed a leading reputation for being innovative and creative. The story of 3M's Post-It Notes is really 'the stuff of legends'. Post-It Notes are one instance where a manufacturer 'knew' that there was a demand before consumers realized it themselves, awareness and insight which clearly requires more than simple market research. The intrapreneur in this case was an employee called Arthur Fry, who had become annoyed that pieces of paper he placed inside his Church hymn book as markers kept falling out when he was singing. Fry was a 3M chemical engineer who knew about an invention by a scientist colleague called Spencer Silver. Silver had developed a new glue which possessed only a very low sticking power, and for this reason was being perceived as a failure! Fry saw the new glue as the answer to his problem – when he applied it to his paper markers, they stayed put but they were easily removed. Realizing that many others also shared the same problem, Fry sought approval to commercialize his idea, but initially he met with scepticism. The idea took hold when he passed samples around to secretaries within 3M and other organizations. The rest, as they say, is history! Over the years the company has developed over 60,000 new products, including everything that bears the Scotch brand name, for example Sellotape and video cassettes.

Ocean Spray has been cited by Rosabeth Moss Kanter (1990) as another US company which spotted a potentially lucrative competitive opportunity missed by its rivals. Small 'paper bottles' for soft drinks were being used in Europe, but the leading US manufacturers did not see them taking off in America and were not enthusiastic. Ocean Spray, which manufactures a range of products, including drinks, from cranberries (sometimes mixed with other fruits) had empowered a middle manager from engineering to look for new ideas for the company – an aspect of their planned strategy – and he saw the potential. The result was an 18-month exclusive rights agreement. The packaging concept proved attractive and the final outcome was a substantial increase in the popularity of cranberry juice drinks. Simply, children liked the package and came to love the drink. Ocean Spray products are now much more evident around the world.

The Ocean Spray example illustrates how competition can come from unexpected sources. It is dangerous for any organization to assume that future competitive threats will only come from rivals, products and services that they already know and understand; in reality, it can be the unrecognized, unexpected newcomers which pose the real threat because, in an attempt to break into an established market, they may introduce some new way of adding value and 'rewrite the rules of competition'.

Bill Gates' 'view of the future', based on personal computers on every desk, was radically different from that of long-time industry leader, IBM, and it enabled Microsoft to enter and dominate the computer industry. British Airways was surprised by the entry and success of Virgin Atlantic Airways on profitable trans-Atlantic routes, as it perceived its main competition to come from the leading US carriers. Virgin was adding new values, offering high and differentiated levels of service at very competitive prices. The success of Direct Line, with telephone insurance services at very competitive prices, has provoked a response from existing companies; telephone banking is having a similar effect. In both cases the nature of the service has been changed dramatically, and improved for many customers.

Figure 6.2 shows how organizational resources need to be used to drive the competitive cycle. Constant, or ideally growing, sales and market share can lead to economies of scale and learning and, in turn, cost reductions and improved profits. The profits could, in a particularly competitive situation, be passed back to customers in the form of lower prices, but more normally they will be reinvested in the organization. This can generate productivity improvements, sometimes with new capacity and, then, lower prices and/or further cost reductions. The investment can also bring about new sources of added value and differentiation, possibly allowing higher prices and further profit growth. The improved competitiveness should also increase sales and market share and drive the cycle round again. These changes might take the form of gradual, continuous improvements or radical changes to establish new rules of competition.

To drive the cycle continuously, organizations will need a mix of steady-state managers to maintain efficiencies and more creative change agents to develop new initiatives.

Competitive themes and frameworks

According to Michael Porter (1980) effective strategic management is the positioning of an organization, relative to its competitors, in such a way that it outperforms them. Marketing, operations and personnel, in fact all aspects of the business, are capable of providing a competitive edge – an advantage which leads to superior performance and superior profits for profit-orientated firms.

Figure 6.2   The competitive cycle.

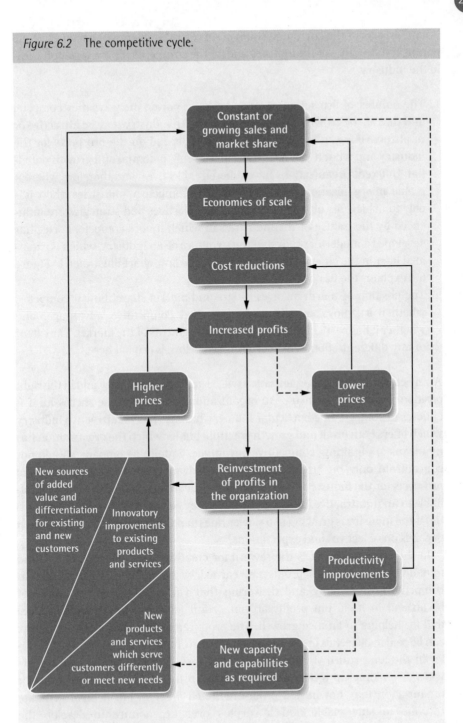

Two aspects of the current position of an organization are important: (1) the nature and structure of the industry and (2) the position of the organization within the industry.

1. The number of firms, their sizes and relative power, the ways they compete, and the rate of growth must be considered. An industry may be attractive or unattractive for an organization. This will depend on the prospects for the industry and what it can offer in terms of profit potential and growth potential. Different organizations have different objectives, and therefore where it is able an organization should be looking to compete in industries where it is able to achieve its objectives. In turn, its objectives and strategies are influenced by the nature of the industries in which it does compete. Porter has developed a model for analysing the structure of an industry, which is examined later in the chapter. For the moment, the flow chart illustrated in Figure 6.3 explains the basic principles.

2. The position of a firm involves its size and market share, how it competes, whether it enjoys specific and recognized competitive advantage, and whether it has particular appeal to selected segments of the market. The extent of any differentiation, which is discussed below, is crucial here.

An effective and superior organization will be in the right industry and in the right position within that industry. An organization is unlikely to be successful if it chooses to compete in a particular industry because it is an attractive industry which offers both profit and growth potential but for which the organization has no means of obtaining competitive advantage. Equally, a company should not concentrate only on creating competitive advantage without assessing the prospects for the industry. With competitive advantage a company can be profitable in an unattractive industry, but there may be very few growth opportunities if the industry is growing at a slower rate than the economy generally. Much depends on objectives and expectations.

In the economy profit is the reward for creating value for consumers; and in individual businesses profits are earned by being more successful than competitors in creating and delivering that value. Profit may or may not be an end in itself, but profits are important for achieving other objectives and for helping to finance growth. The profit remaining after interest and tax can be paid in dividends or reinvested in the firm (Chapter 3). A firm will be healthier in the long run if it can invest as it wishes and finance the investments without building up too substantial a debt. In the same way, a not-for-profit organization may not have a profit-orientated mission, but it must generate revenue to stay viable and a surplus over expenditure to develop the organization.

Figure 6.3   Industry growth prospects.

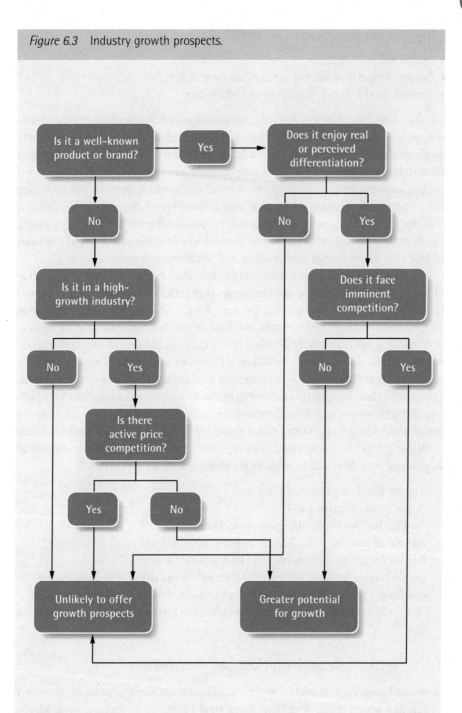

The most successful competitors will:

- create value
- create competitive advantage in delivering that value and
- operate the business effectively and efficiently.

For above-average performance all three are required. It is possible to run a business well – efficiently – but never create competitive advantage. Certain products and services may have competitive advantage and yet be produced by organizations that are not run well. In both, potential is not fully exploited. Moreover, competitive advantage must be sustained. A good new product, for example, may offer the consumer something new, something different, and thus add value; but if it is easily imitated by competitors there is no sustainable competitive advantage. For example, Freddie Laker pioneered cheap trans-Atlantic air travel but went out of business in the face of competition and management weaknesses.

In the author's experience sustaining competitive advantage, rather than creating it initially, presents the real challenge. Competitive advantage cannot be sustained for ever and probably not for very long without changes in products, services and strategies which take account of market demand, market saturation and competitor activity. People's tastes change, the size of markets is limited not infinite, and competitors will seek to imitate successful products, services and strategies. Competitive advantage can be sustained by constant innovation. Companies that are change orientated and seek to stay ahead of their competitors through innovatory ideas develop new forms of advantage. Case Study 6 earlier considers how Coca-Cola retains global leadership of the soft drinks market.

Heller (1998) has suggested that organizations which sustain competitive advantage over time will be addressing seven questions effectively:

1. Are we supplying the 'right' things?
2. In the most effective way?
3. And at the lowest possible economic cost?
4. Are we as good as – and ideally better than – our strongest competitor?
5. Are we targeting and serving the widest possible market?
6. Do we have a 'unique selling proposition' – something which will persuade customers to buy from us rather than anyone else?
7. Are we innovating to make sure the answer to all these questions will remain 'yes'?

Differentiation and market segmentation

A product or service is said to be differentiated if consumers perceive it to have properties which make it distinct from rival products or services, and ideally unique in some particular way. Differentiation is most beneficial when consumers value the cause of the difference and will pay a premium price to obtain it, and where competitors are unable to emulate it.

Differentiation recognizes that customers are too numerous and widely scattered, and with heterogeneous needs and adequate spending power, for them all to prefer exactly the same product or service. Hence competitors will distinguish their brand, product or service in some way, perhaps size, quality or style, to give it greater appeal for certain customers. Those customers who value the difference will be willing to pay a premium price for it and ideally buy it consistently in preference to the alternatives.

Consequently, effective organizations will be both customer-driven (responsive) and customer-driving (innovative).

Sources of differentiation

- *Speed* – high-street opticians and photo developers compete on their speed of service; courier businesses are successful because of the speed at which they can move items.
- *Reliability* – consistent quality and the ability to keep promises: providing what customers want, where, when and how. One example is McDonald's.
- *Service* – adding extra values to augment the service and thereby satisfy customers. Staff in certain hotels illustrate this point; some years ago Xerox provided a new level of service by incorporating a self-diagnostic computer chip in its copying machines.
- *Design* – both in the product itself (Bang & Olufsen hi-fi equipment, for instance) and in its reparability. This also relates to:
- *Features* – such as cordless irons, kettles and drills. The balance, though, is critical; some video cassette recorders now have too many features for most customers.
- *Technology* – which, say, led to the development of laser printers.
- *Corporate personality* – there is a value in certain corporate names and images, such as The Body Shop.
- *Relationships with customers* – through effective supply-chain management.

The differentiation need not be clearly tangible as long as customers believe that it exists.

Where specific groups of customers with broadly similar needs can be identified and targeted they are known as market segments, and often products and services are differentiated to appeal to specific segments. The segmentation might be based on ages, socioeconomic groups, lifestyle, income, benefits sought or usage rate for consumer markets, and size of buyer and reasons for buying in the case of industrial markets. To be viable the segment must be clearly identifiable, separated from other segments, easily reached with advertising and large enough to be profitable. Given these factors and a differentiated product, prices, distribution and advertising can all be targeted specifically at the segment.

Successful differentiation and segmentation require that products and services are clearly positioned. Toyota, for example, wanted to appeal to the lucrative executive market with a car that offered the 'ultimate in quality' and succeeded against BMW, Mercedes and Volvo. The car needed to be differentiated from the main Toyota brand and consequently it was named Lexus.

Both differentiation and market segmentation are key aspects of marketing strategy, a more detailed treatment of which can be found on the accompanying website.

The importance of timing

Products and services have finite lives, and broadly speaking they follow a lifecycle pattern. Strategies also have lifecycles. Strategies which deliver value and competitive advantage will bring benefits to the organization in terms of success, growth and profits. However, if consumer preferences change, and the factors creating the advantage are no longer perceived as valuable, the advantage is lost. A change of competitive strategy is required. Similarly, if the advantage is cost based and the factors generating the cost advantage change, such that the advantage is lost, a new strategy is required. Again, any advantage is potentially vulnerable to copying or improvements in some way by competitors, particularly if it is seen to be generating success.

Referring back to E–V–R (environment–values–resources) congruence, at times particular strategies reflect a congruence between resources and the environment. However, demand can change, or investment resources to strengthen competitive advantage may not be available. The congruence may disappear and withdrawal or divestment may well be appropriate.

Towards the end of 1992 it was being claimed that Porsche sports cars had become 'an extravagance which increasingly few people are able to afford'. Sales were around half those of the mid-1980s. Production costs had to be slashed and the company rationalized. Fortunately, Porsche was a family company with no debt and a strong cash base; it was therefore able to survive on its reserves until a new range of sports models was ready (in 1996). Referring back to the sigmoid curve (Figure 1.17), Porsche's timing was flawed; it was not ready to change at the most appropriate time.

In this context it is important to remember that all strengths are potential weaknesses. Tizer and Lesney (Matchbox toys) are companies which failed to appreciate when the effective life of a particular strategy was coming to an end, as much as anything because it had proved so successful in the past. As a result, the strategy became a weakness. As a consequence, both have been acquired by other companies.

Analysing an Industry

Porter (1980) argues that five forces determine the profitability of an industry. They are featured in Figure 6.4. At the heart of the industry are rivals and their competitive strategies linked to, say, pricing or advertising; but, he contends, it is important to look beyond one's immediate competitors as there are other determinants of profitability. Specifically, there might be competition from substitute products or services. These alternatives may be perceived as substitutes by buyers even though they are part of a different industry. An example would be plastic bottles, cans and glass bottles for packaging soft drinks. There may also be a potential threat of new entrants, although some competitors will see this as an opportunity to strengthen their position in the market by ensuring, as far as they can, customer loyalty. Finally, it is important to appreciate that companies purchase from suppliers and sell to buyers. If they are powerful they are in a position to bargain profits away through reduced margins, by forcing either cost increases or price decreases. This relates to the strategic option of vertical integration, which will be considered in detail later in the book (Chapter 11). Vertical integration occurs where a company acquires, or merges with, a supplier or

Figure 6.4   Determining industry profitability: the five forces. Adapted from Porter, ME (1980) *Competitive Strategy: Techniques for Analysing Industries and Competitors*, Free Press.

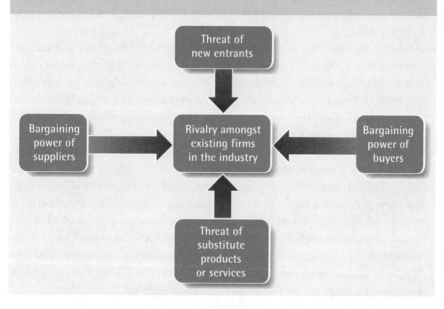

customer and thereby gains greater control over the chain of activities which leads from basic materials through to final consumption.

Any company must seek to understand the nature of its competitive environment if it is to be successful in achieving its objectives and in establishing appropriate strategies. If a company fully understands the nature of the five forces, and particularly appreciates which one is the most important, it will be in a stronger position to defend itself against any threats and to influence the forces with its strategy. The situation, of course, is fluid, and the nature and relative power of the forces will change. Consequently, the need to monitor and stay aware is continuous.

The threat of new entrants: barriers to entry

Where barriers to entry are high new entrants are likely to be deterred, and if they do attempt entry they are likely to provoke a quick reaction from existing competitors. Low barriers generally mean that responses will be slower, offering more opportunities. A number of factors can create barriers:

- *Economies of scale* – Some of the possible ways of achieving economies of scale have been considered earlier. In addition, the experience curve (see the Finance in Action supplement to Chapter 5) can be important. If there is a need for substantial investment to allow a new entrant to achieve cost parity with existing firms this may well be a deterrent. In such a case if a newcomer enters the market with only limited investment and is not able to achieve comparable economies of scale, he or she will be at a cost disadvantage from the start, in which case substantial differentiation will be required, but this introduces another issue.
- *Product differentiation* – If consumers perceive rival products or services to be clearly differentiated then newcomers must also seek to establish a distinct identity. Newcomers will therefore have to invest in advertising and promotion to establish their new brand, and this may be expensive. The major brewers and chocolate manufacturers, for example, spend millions of pounds each year promoting specific products and brands.
- *Capital requirements* – Any requirement for substantial investment capital in order to enter a market is a barrier to entry. The investment may be on capital equipment, research and development, or advertising to establish a market presence, and it may deter many aspiring competitors. However, large multiproduct companies who wish to break into a market may finance the necessary investment with profits from other areas of the business. Drugs is one industry where huge investments are required to develop and test possible new products over several years. While *patent protection* allows the costs to be recouped through prices, the investment is all 'up front'.

- *Switching costs* – These are costs incurred not by the company wishing to enter the market but by the existing customers. If a buyer were to change his supplier from an established manufacturer to a newcomer costs may be incurred in a number of ways. New handling equipment and employee training are examples. Buyers may not be willing to change their suppliers because of these costs, thereby making it very difficult for any newcomer to poach existing business.
- *Access to distribution channels* – Existing relationships and agreements between manufacturers and the key distributors in a market may also create barriers to entry. Some manufacturers may be vertically integrated and own or control their distributors. Other distributors may have established and successful working relationships with particular manufacturers and have little incentive to change. Companies aspiring to enter a market may look for unique distribution opportunities to provide both access and immediate differentiation.
- *Cost advantages independent of scale* – This represents factors which are valuable to existing companies in an industry and which newcomers may not be able to replicate. Essential technology may be protected by patent; the supply of necessary raw materials may be controlled; or favourable locations near to supplies or markets may not be accessible. Government restrictions on competition may apply in certain circumstances.

Potential entrants, attracted by high margins in an industry and not detracted by any of the above barriers, must try to gauge any likely retaliation by existing manufacturers; and Porter argues that this can be assessed by examining:

- past behaviour when newcomers have entered or tried to enter the market
- the resource capabilities of existing companies which will affect their ability to retaliate
- the investment and commitment of existing companies which may make retaliation inevitable if they are to protect their investment and position
- the rate of growth of the industry – the faster it is the more possibilities for a newcomer to be absorbed.

Existing firms may be prepared to reduce prices to deter entry and protect their market shares, especially if supply already exceeds demand. As a result, even in an oligopoly, profitability can be contained.

The bargaining power of suppliers

The behaviour of suppliers, and their relative power, can squeeze industry profits. Equally, the ability of a firm to control its supplies by vertical integration (acquiring its suppliers) or long-term supply arrangements can be very beneficial. The relative power is affected by five major factors.

- Concentration among suppliers *vis-à-vis* the industry they sell to – if the supply industry is very concentrated then buyers have little opportunity for bargaining on prices and deliveries as suppliers recognize that their opportunities for switching suppliers are limited.
- The degree of substitutability between the products of various suppliers and the amount of product differentiation – a buyer could be tied to a particular supplier if his or her requirements cannot be met by other suppliers.
- The amount of, and potential for, vertical integration which might be initiated by either the supplier or the buyer – again, government regulation on competition may prevent this.
- The extent to which the buyer is important to the supplier – if a buyer is regarded as a key customer he or she may well receive preferential treatment.
- Any switching costs that might be incurred by buyers will strengthen the position of suppliers.

The bargaining power of buyers

Any competitive action by buyers will act to depress industry profits, but specific arrangements with distributors or customers can be mutually beneficial. Vertical integration is again a possibility. The major supermarket grocery stores with their multiple outlets nationwide are in a very strong bargaining position with most of their suppliers.

This power has been strengthened by the success of private- label brands, whose prices can be up to 60% below those for the recognized major brands. Private labels have grown to over one-third of UK retail food sales. They have proved most successful with chilled meals, frozen vegetables, fruit juices and cheese; and least successful with pet foods, sugar, coffee and, for a long time, breakfast cereals. Barriers against private-label products are provided by innovation and aggressive marketing and promotion.

As the market for overseas travel grew in the UK, the power of the leading travel agency groups also grew *vis-à-vis* the tour operators – it is, after all, the travel agency that actually sells the holiday and has direct contact with customers, whom they are able to influence. As a consequence the leading tour operators (Thomson and Airtours) sought to acquire their own agencies and exercise greater control over the supply chain. At the same time, industry rationalization has meant that a small number of tour operators (all of whom also own their own airline) dominates the market.

The bargaining power of buyers is determined by:

- the concentration and size of buyer

- the importance to the buyer of the purchase in terms of both cost and quality (the more important it is the more he or she must ensure good relations with the supplier)
- the degree of product standardization, which affects substitutability
- the costs, practicability and opportunity for buyers to switch supplier
- the possibility of vertical integration, initiated by either the supplier or the buyer.

The threat of product substitutes

The existence or non-existence of close substitutes helps to determine the elasticity of demand for a product or service. In simple terms this is price sensitivity. If there are close substitutes, demand for a particular brand will increase or decrease as its price moves downwards or upwards relative to competitors. Price changes can be initiated by any firm, but other competitors will be affected and forced to react. If products are not seen as close substitutes then they will be less price sensitive to competitor price changes.

For this reason firms will seek to establish clear product or service differentiation in order to create customer preference and loyalty and thereby make their product or service less price sensitive. Where this is accomplished industry profits are likely to rise, which may be attractive to prospective newcomers who will seek to create further differentiation in order to encourage customers to switch to them and enable them to establish a presence in the market.

Products and services can be substituted for something completely different, reflecting the ever-present possibility that new competitors can change the 'rules of competition' in a market or industry.

Rivalry among existing competitors

Porter terms rivalry amongst existing competitors 'jockeying for position'. Competition may take the form of price competition, advertising and promotion, innovation, or service during and after sale. Where competitive firms are mutually interdependent retaliation is a key issue. Before deciding upon aggressive competitive actions firms must attempt to predict how their competitors will react; when other firms are proactive an organization must at least be defensive in order to protect market share and profitability. The intensity of competition is affected by the market structure and depends on the following:

- the number of competitors and the degree of concentration
- the rate of growth of the industry – slow growth increases the pressure upon competitors to fight for market share

- the degree of differentiation – the less there is the more likely is price competition
- cost structures – where fixed costs are high relative to variable costs companies are very sensitive around the break-even point. Profits are very dependent upon volume.

  As passenger aircraft become larger and more technologically sophisticated, the cost of buying (or leasing) and insuring them grows. The operating cost per seat mile – and break-even loadings – increases steadily, but with international overcapacity and competition, the revenue per seat mile has been falling. Some airlines have closed or been acquired; others have had to reduce salaries and numbers of employees.

- The implications of changing size or supply capability through investment – although demand may be increasing at a relatively gradual and consistent rate, supply provision may increase in sizeable blocks as a result of the necessary investment. If a firm wishes to increase output and it has exhausted the possibilities from increased usage of existing plant it will have to invest in new plant. When this is commissioned it may increase supply potential substantially and affect competitors as the company seeks orders to utilize its new capacity. Consider as examples a small charter airline which has three freight aeroplanes. If it buys a fourth it increases its capacity by 25% overnight. Similarly, if there are two three-star hotels in a medium-sized town and a third is opened, the competitive situation changes markedly.
- The extent to which competitors are aware of the strategies of their rivals – one issue in this is the relative importance of the product or service to the various competitors. If a product is a byproduct of another more important operation, for example, then the company concerned may compete very aggressively for sales and be far more concerned with volume than profits.
- The objectives of the competing firms – what matters to them. Are they more interested in profit, turnover or percentage market share? The objectives determine the strategies.
- Exit barriers, and the costs of leaving the industry – if these are high for any reason firms may be willing to accept low margins and limited profit opportunities in order to remain in the industry. The types of factor that determine exit costs are dedicated assets which have no profitable alternative use; the costs of redundancy; interrelationships within a conglomerate, whereby a product may be either a byproduct or an essential component for another division; emotional ties related to the history of the product and its association with the business; and pressure from government not to close down.

An example of dedicated assets which have no obvious alternative use is multiplex cinema complexes. As the number of these has grown, cinema audiences have also grown, and an industry in decline has been given a new lease of life. In addition, it is quite normal for several fast-food and retail outlets to open alongside the cinemas, helping to boost their traffic. But what would happen to the cinema buildings if audiences declined again?

Manufacturers of consumer electronics products have to invest continually to maintain the technology required for the necessary product improvements. To generate revenues to fund further investment they need volume sales; to create these they price with low, competitive margins. Profits are very slim, but the sunk costs are such that the cycle continues; it is too costly to come out of the industry. The cycle is reinforced by consumer purchasing behaviour. Consumers know which brands they are happy to consider, their short-list depending upon the quality and differentiation they are seeking. They then buy on price, seeing certain brands as interchangeable. Inevitably, the retailers also earn only low margins.

Table 6.1 provides a summary checklist of factors for industry analysis, and Box 6.1 analyses the supermarket industry against Porter's model of five forces.

The rivalry factors discussed above, and the rivalry strategies, are both affected by any slowing down in the rate of industry growth, by acquisitions, and by changes in the marketing strategy of any one competitor resulting from the perception of new opportunities for differentiation or segmentation.

Table 6.1 Checklist for industry analysis

1. How many firms are in the industry, and what size are they?
2. How concentrated is the industry?
3. To what degree are products substitutes?
4. Is the industry growing or contracting?
5. What are the relative powers of suppliers, buyers and competitors?
6. What are the prevailing competitive strategies?
7. What entry barriers exist?
8. What economies of scale are present?
9. What experience/learning curve effects are important?
10. What exit barriers exist (if any)?
11. What important external factors affect competition?

STRATEGY IN ACTION – Box 6.1
Industry Analysis – Supermarkets

Threat of new entrants

Barriers to entry are very high, because of the necessary supply network and distribution infrastructure. The continual investment in EPOS (electronic point-of-sale) and EDI (electronic data interchange) systems creates further barriers. In addition, it is very difficult and very expensive to acquire new sites in prime positions. It is possible, given financial reserves, to build a position in selected market niches. Of course, powerful companies, able to command huge financial resources, can break in with an acquisition, as was seen when Wal-Mart bought ASDA.

Relative strength of suppliers

Supply agreements with major retail chains, using EDI, make the leading suppliers and supermarkets more and more interdependent. Ownership of a leading brand yields power, but secondary and tertiary brands must be more vulnerable. There is further interdependency with own-label supply agreements.

Relative strength of buyers

Most buyers will have more than one supermarket that they can access, especially if they are car owners. The power of the Internet to promote home deliveries also opens up choice. There will be some loyalty, but only if prices and service are competitive.

Threat of substitutes

Small independent stores have a niche and a role, but the supermarkets are dominant. However, they are vulnerable on price for those products/brands offered by smaller, discount stores, especially where customers are willing to multishop. Home shopping via IT continues to be a sector of the market that supermarkets must develop rather than relinquish.

Existing rivalries

The industry is very competitive, with four or five chains competing for the family shopping budget. Sainsbury's, Tesco, ASDA (Wal-Mart) and Safeway have different competitive strategies (product ranges, pricing strategies, etc.) and have differing appeals, but they remain largely interchangeable. These companies must all invest to try and create differences as well as pricing competitively. The relative speedy demise of the Co-op to a predominantly niche role illustrates how intense the rivalry is.

STRATEGY IN ACTION – Box 6.1
(Continued)

Summary:
Barriers to entry – high
Power of suppliers – medium
Power of buyers – medium/high
Threat of substitutes – medium
Existing rivalries – intense

To be an effective competitor, a company must:

- appreciate which of the five forces is the most significant (it can be different for different industries) and concentrate strategic attention in this area
- position itself for the best possible defence against any threats from rivals
- influence the forces detailed above through its own corporate and competitive strategies
- anticipate changes or shifts in the forces – the factors that are generating success in the short term may not succeed long term.

Much will depend upon the strategic leader, the quality of management in the organization and the prevailing culture.

The role of government

Rather than incorporation as a separate sixth factor, Porter maintains that the importance of government lies in an ability to affect the other five forces through changes in policy and new legislation. The examples below are not exhaustive.

1. The introduction of competition and an internal market in the UK National Health Service, a Conservative policy abandoned by the Blair Labour government.
2. A series of privatizations during the 1980s and 1990s, including British Aerospace, Rolls Royce, British Airways, British Telecom (BT), British Rail and British Steel, along with the critically important gas, water and electricity utility industries.

To prevent the businesses becoming national or local monopolies in private ownership, with enormous potential to exploit their customers, industry regulators have been appointed in a number of cases. The regulators and the newly privatized businesses have at times disagreed over important strategic issues. Individual regulators are given freedom to establish specific guidelines within clear broad principles, and some would argue that this makes conflict between them and the regulated businesses inevitable. One of the reasons for the diversification strategies by privatized companies is that they create business activities which are outside the direct control of the regulator. Given a general trend away from diversification to a concentration on core businesses and competencies, this has sometimes proved to be risky. Maybe the impact of the regulators also needs regulating.

Regulation has also allowed, and even encouraged, acquisitions and the entry of new competitors into a market. A number of the regional water companies has been acquired by French rivals; some electricity suppliers are now owned by American energy businesses. With the emergence of mobile and cable telephony, BT has been subject to several new competitors, some with overseas financial backing. Customers can now buy their gas and electricity from several suppliers. Electricity companies can supply domestic gas, and vice versa. For example, someone living in Yorkshire can buy their electricity from Lancashire-based Norweb.

3. Deregulation of particular industries, such as air transport.

The lessening of restrictions and regulations unleashes new competitive forces and changes the nature of the industry. Some competitors will benefit, while others will suffer.

In the UK the changes in air transport created an interesting dilemma. British Airports Authority (BAA), which runs most of the major airports in the UK (the exception is Manchester), was privatized in 1987. Airport charges are regulated by the Civil Aviation Authority (CAA) which, for example, insisted on a new five-year formula covering the period April 1992 to March 1997. In years 1 and 2 charges would change by a figure 8% below retail price index (RPI), in year 3 by RPI less 4%, and in years 4 and 5 by RPI less 1%. These implied a need for major cost savings, together with greater efficiency and productivity. At the same time the need continues to grow for both a fifth runway in the London area (to add to two at Heathrow and one each at Gatwick and Stansted) and a fifth terminal at Heathrow. If either or both finally goes ahead, BAA will be the developers, assuming that their finances are sufficiently robust – because they have recently been further affected by the abolition of duty-free prices for travel inside the European Union.

The forces described above determine the profitability of an industry, and hence the attractiveness of the industry for companies already competing in it and for companies who might wish to enter it. As well as understanding the nature and structure of the industry it is important for organizations to decide how best to compete. In other words, firms must appreciate the opportunities for creating and sustaining competitive advantage.

Competitive Strategy

As far as customers are concerned, the link between price and perceived quality must make sense. Products and services should be neither overpriced (resulting in a loss of goodwill and often lost business) nor underpriced. In this latter case, potential profits must be lost and, perversely, orders may be lost as well – people may become suspicious of the unexpectedly low price and begin to question their perception of the relative quality. Companies must, therefore, also be realistic about customer perception of the relative quality of their products and services and neither overestimate nor underestimate the situation. Companies may think, or wish to believe, that they are 'the best'; customers may disagree.

Figure 6.5 offers a simple matrix of competitive strategies developed from this reasoning.

Porter (1985) developed his work on industry analysis to examine how a company might compete in the industry in order to create and sustain a position of strength. In simple terms, he argued, there are two basic parameters:

- Parameter 1. A company can seek to compete:
  - by achieving lower costs than its rivals and, by charging comparable prices for its products or services, creating a superior position through superior profitability,

  or

  - through differentiation, adding value in an area that the customer regards as important, charging a premium price, and again creating a superior position through superior profitability.
- Parameter 2. The arena in which the company seeks to compete can be a broad range of segments or a narrow range, perhaps just one.

This line of argument led Porter to develop his valuable model of generic strategies, which is discussed below. It also focused attention on the relevance of differentiation, adding value and cost management for helping to create – and sustain – competitive advantage. It is important, first, to appreciate that the generic strategy framework is a reflection of current (or targeted) positioning, and that competitive advantage is by nature a relative (to other competitors) and dynamic notion. Secondly, as mentioned briefly before, it is essential to realize that competitive strategy and competitive advantage, although clearly linked, are not one and the same. Competitive strategy concerns the way in which organizations choose to compete and position themselves – competitive advantage may or may not be an outcome of this. To achieve true advantage an organization must find opportunities to be different in ways which are meaningful for customers. The activities which create the position are the key to advantage.

Figure 6.5   Simple competitive strategy matrix. Based on an idea found on the Abram Hawkes plc website.

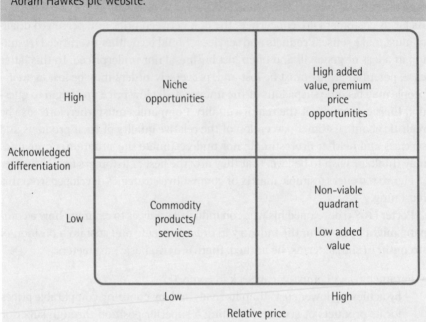

Generic competitive strategies

Porter's two parameters lead to the three generic strategies illustrated in Figure 6.6(a). Cost leadership is where the company achieves lower costs than its rivals and competes across a broad range of segments. Differentiation occurs when the company has a range of clearly differentiated products which appeal to different segments of the market. Focus strategies are where a company chooses to concentrate on only one segment or a limited range of segments. With this approach it can again seek either lower costs or differentiation.

Before considering these generic strategies in greater detail it is useful to apply them to particular industries. Porter argues that in the motor vehicle industry (Figure 6.6(b)) Toyota became the overall cost leader. The company is successful in a number of segments with a full range of cars, and its mission is to be a low-cost producer. Box 6.2 outlines Toyota's competitive strategy. In contrast, General Motors (GM) also competes in most segments of the market but seeks to differentiate each of its products with superior styling and features. GM also offers a wider choice of models for each car in its range.

Hyundai became successful around the world with a restricted range of small and medium size cars which it produced at relatively low cost and priced

Figure 6.6   (a) Porter's model of generic strategies. Adapted with permission of the Free Press, a division of Macmillan Inc., from Porter, ME (1985) *Competitive Advantage: Creating and Sustaining Superior Performance.* ©Michael E Porter, 1985.
(b) Porter's model of generic strategies applied to the world motor industry. Source: Porter, ME (1985) *Competitive Advantage: Creating and Sustaining Superior Performance,* Free Press.

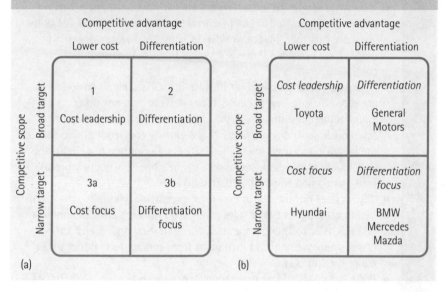

(a)   (b)

competitively. It should be noted that neither Toyota nor Hyundai markets the *cheapest* cars available. BMW and Mercedes have both succeeded by producing a narrow line of more exclusive cars for the price-insensitive, quality-conscious customer. There are several cars available from both companies but they are clearly targeted at people who are willing to pay premium prices for perceived higher quality. Mazda was similarly successful with a narrow and sporty range.

It is never going to be easy to identify who the true cost leader is in any industry or segment. To ascertain this we need accurate information on gross margins and profitability together with an acceptance of the relevant segment boundaries. We can, nevertheless, make educated guesses.

Applying the same ideas to credit cards, it is quickly and readily appreciated that Barclaycard, by offering both Visa and Mastercard credit cards, together with platinum, gold and special business versions, is differentiated and covers most segments of the market. American Express, and the increasingly popular 'affinity cards', such as those linked to football clubs, are focused differentiators because they concentrate on identifiable interest groups. Some would argue that MBNA, because of its international coverage and strategy of persuading other

cardholders to transfer, has become the overall cost leader. Egg, linked to Pru-dential's competitive but niched banking activity, is following a strategy of focused cost leadership.

In Chapter 5 the position of Unilever and its Wall's ice cream was discussed. This would appear to be the cost leader. Mars and Nestlé pursue differentiation strategies successfully; premium ice creams such as Ben and Jerry's and Häagen-Dazs are focused differentiators. Small, local retailers with low overheads will be following a cost focus strategy.

Using these ideas in a slightly different way, we can see that retailers seek to compete on either image or cost. Image-based retailers add value to either or both the product and the service provided to customers. Success in differentiating generates customer loyalty and premium prices. Cost-based retailers operate with competitive margins, searching for strategies that balance high turnover with low costs resulting from operating efficiencies.

Porter argues that a company cannot achieve superior profitability if it is 'stuck in the middle' with no clear strategy for competitive advantage and no clearly delineated position, a point that is debated later. Moreover, competitors seeking cost advantages should not lose sight of the need to maintain distinctiveness; and competitive differentiators should be vigilant in managing their costs. Otherwise, the potential for superior profits is lost.

The cost leadership strategy

To achieve substantial rewards from this strategy Porter argues that the organization must be *the* cost leader, and unchallenged in this position. There is room for only one; and if there is competition for market leadership based on this strategy there will be price competition.

Cost leadership as a generic strategy does not imply that the company will market the lowest price product or service in the industry. Quite often the lowest price products are perceived as inferior, and as such appeal to only a proportion of the market. Consequently, low price related to lower quality is a differentiation strategy. Low cost therefore does not necessarily mean 'cheap' and low-cost companies can have upmarket rather than downmarket appeal. Equally, low cost does not imply lower rewards for employees or other stakeholders as successful cost leaders can be very profitable. Their aim is to secure a cost advantage over their rivals, price competitively and relative to how their product is perceived by customers, and achieve a high profit margin. Where this applies across a broad range of segments turnover and market share should also be high for the industry. They are seeking above-average profits with industry-average prices.

Cost focus strategies can be based on finding a distinct group of customers whose needs are slightly below average. Costs are saved by meeting their needs specifically and avoiding unnecessary additional costs.

Figure 6.7 illustrates the above points and relates the generic strategies to efficiency and effectiveness.

There is little advantage in being only one of a number of low-cost producers. The advantage is gained by superior management, concentrating on

Figure 6.7 Competitive strategies.

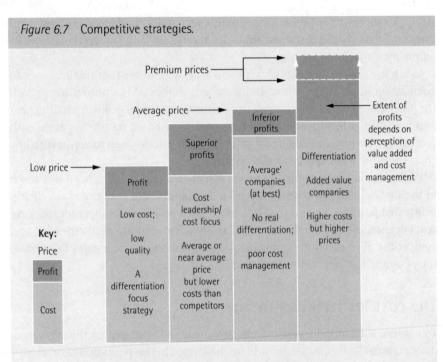

Efficiency, effectiveness and competitive strategies

	Cost leadership	Differentiation
Efficiency via	Driving costs downwards	Doing things well
Effectiveness via	Knowing what is important and unimportant to customers – saving on latter	Finding and sustaining unique or different ways of competing

cost-saving opportunities, minimizing waste, and not adding values which customers regard as unimportant to the product or service. Many products do have values added which are not regarded as necessary by the market. Cost savings can generally be achieved in any and every area of the business, and quite often they begin with the strategic leader. Senior executives who enjoy substantial perks are unlikely to pursue a cost leadership strategy. Porter suggests that it is a mistake to believe that cost savings are only possible in the manufacturing function and that this strategy is only applicable to the largest producers in an industry. However, where cost leadership generates market share and volume production opportunities, economies of scale in manufacturing do apply.

The differentiation strategy

Cost leadership is usually traded off against differentiation, with the two regarded as pulling in opposite directions. Differentiation adds costs in order to add value for which customers are willing to pay premium prices. For a differentiation focus strategy to be successful the market must be capable of clear segmentation, and the requirements for this were highlighted earlier.

With differentiation superior performance is achieved by serving customer needs differently, ideally uniquely. The more unique the difference, the more sustainable is any advantage which accrues. Differentiation must inevitably add costs, which can only be recouped if the market is willing to pay the necessary premium prices. It is crucial that costs are only added in areas that customers perceive as important, and again this can relate to any area of the operation. A solicitors' practice, for example, might find competitive advantage in the manner and promptness with which customer queries are dealt, both over the telephone and in person. A fuller list might include the following possibilities:

- quality of materials used (related to purchasing)
- superior performance (design)
- high quality (production; inspection)
- superior packaging (distribution)
- delivery (sales; production)
- prompt answer of queries (customer relations; sales)
- efficient paperwork (administration).

Furthermore, it is insufficient merely to add value; customers must recognize and appreciate the difference. If it cannot be seen easily it should be communicated, perhaps through advertising. Communication between manufacturer and customer is vital, for it is only by understanding customer needs that the most appropriate value can be added. Take as an example the supplier of a component to an assembly company. At face value the supplier will seek to help the assembler to lower his or her costs, or enhance the quality of his or her product, the choice depending upon the competitive strategy of the assembler. But this level of thinking alone might overlook further worthwhile opportunities. How does the assembler handle and store the components? And so on. If a supplier understands fully his or her customers' operations he might find new ways of adding value.

The differentiation strategy can be easily misjudged, however, for a number of reasons, including:

- by choosing something that buyers fail to recognize, appreciate or value
- by over-fulfilling needs and as a consequence failing to achieve cost-effectiveness
- by selecting something that competitors can either improve on or undercut
- by attempting to overcharge for the differentiation
- by thinking too narrowly, missing opportunities and being outflanked by competitors.

Box 6.3 illustrates three differentiation strategies.

A critique of Porter's generic strategies

Care must be taken not to misunderstand the implications of delineation. Porter has stated that successful organizations will select and concentrate their efforts on effectively implementing one of the generic strategies that he identified; they will avoid being 'stuck in the middle'. However, it does appear that while cost leadership and differentiation may be seen as mutually exclusive, successful strategies can be based on a mix of the two. YKK, the Japanese zip manufacturer and world market leader, achieves both cost leadership and significant differentiation, for example.

At the same time, Sainsbury's has argued that its strategy has been based on providing good food at low cost for the broad middle ground in the market. They do not offer the cheapest food; equally they do not offer the choice or range of a specialist delicatessen. Really what Sainsbury's was arguing was that it sought to ensure that it has relatively low costs but is seen as differentiated. However, Sainsbury's has lower margins than its main rivals – it is not enjoying the benefits of relatively low costs. Sainsbury's has lost market leadership to Tesco.

Hendry (1990) has suggested that as there can be only one cost leader, cost leadership is not so much a strategy as a position that one company – which is almost certainly differentiated – enjoys. Toyota may be overall cost leader, but it still differentiates all of its cars. There are different models for different market segments, as well as the associated Lexus range. Because it is a position, and because competitors are always likely to be following cost reduction strategies, it can be a very risky and precarious position if other opportunities for adding value are ignored. Simply, cost leadership is based on efficiencies and sound cost management, but being different still matters.

Similarly, differentiation may be concerned with adding value, and therefore costs, but costs must still be managed. We must understand the cost drivers for any business, a topic taken up in the next chapter. It is important to incur and add costs only where they can be recouped in the form of premium prices. Yet, where a company is particularly concerned with issues of size and market share

STRATEGY IN ACTION – Box 6.3
Three Differentiation Strategies: BMW, Bang & Olufsen and James Purdey

BMW

BMW follows a number of strategies designed to protect its market niche, especially from Japanese competition. Notably, these cover both the cars and the overall service package provided by BMW for its customers.

- Cars can be tailored and customized substantially. Customers can choose any colour they want, a benefit normally restricted to Rolls Royce and Aston Martin; and there is a wide range of interior options and 'performance extras'.
- Safety, environment, economy and comfort are featured and stressed in every model.
- National BMW sales companies are wholly owned, together with strategically located parts warehouses. The independent distributors place their orders directly into BMW's central computer.
- There are fleets of specially equipped cars to assist BMW motorists who break down.
- In 1994 BMW became the first European car manufacturer to produce in the USA.
- Historically, BMW chose to ignore sports cars and hatchbacks, which it saw as downmarket from luxury saloon cars. However, market trends and preferences brought a change of heart. The 1994 BMW Compact was launched as a hatchback version of the successful 3-series; a BMW sports model was used for the James Bond film Goldeneye.

The acquisition of Rover gave BMW a range of successful, smaller hatchbacks, along with Land Rover recreational and multipurpose vehicles. But the two companies, with their very different histories and cultures, were not easily integrated. In 2000 Rover was bought back by a financial consortium and Land Rover was sold to Ford.

BMW   http://www.bmw.com

Bang & Olufsen

Now 75 years old, Bang & Olufsen is a Danish manufacturer of hi-fi equipment and televisions, which enjoys an elite reputation and status worldwide for the quality of its products. Its customers tend to be very loyal.

The company has adopted sleek, tasteful designs, clever technologies and high standards of manufacture for many years. During the 1980s its performance deteriorated because it was seen as too much of a niche

STRATEGY IN ACTION – Box 6.3
(Continued)

competitor. As a response, ranges of slightly less expensive – but still exceptionally high-quality – products were launched. From this a new philosophy has emerged – that the products are about lifestyle and technical excellence is more of a 'given'.

Company advertising uses the slogan 'a life less ordinary' to suggest that 'distinctiveness is a value in itself'. Clearly, this fits with the paradigm of the 'dream society' discussed in Chapter 5.

Bang & Olufsen never asks its customers about future designs and products. Instead, its 'free thinking designers plant their ideas in the marketplace'. The company sees itself as a fashion leader. In addition, the company is very concerned to maintain control over who retails its products and how they are displayed in stores.

The company's niche must be potentially under threat if its rivals are able to improve the quality and reliability of their designs and exploit the manufacturing competencies of lower-cost labour countries.

Bang & Olufsen   http://www.bang-olufsen.com

James Purdey

Purdey firearms would be classified as a super-luxury product; they retail at 'prices more normally associated with small houses'. The company manufactures something in the order of 60 guns per year, 90% of which are sold abroad.

There is close attention to detail, and quality control is incredibly tight. Every order is perceived as a special; nothing is seen as standard. The stocks are oil polished rather than varnished in a lengthy, labour-intensive process; and buyers can choose almost any special, idiosyncratic feature as long as they are happy to pay the appropriate premium. Typically, orders are placed two years in advance of delivery.

Because they appeal to a very limited market segment, and because they literally last a lifetime (and sometimes longer), growth potential for James Purdey, without diversification, is clearly limited.

James Purdey   http://www.purdey.com

it may deliberately choose to charge relatively low prices and not attempt to recover the extra costs it has added in its search to be different. It sacrifices superior profits, at least in the short term while it builds a power base.

Hendry also questions the value of broad and narrow focus, arguing that internal industry boundaries are always changing, enhanced by the speed of technological change. New niches are emerging all the time, such that what appears to be a solid niche can quickly become a tomb.

To summarize, while the ideas of Michael Porter can be questioned and debated, they nevertheless provide an extremely useful framework for analysing industries and competitive strategy. It is important not to take them simply at face value and assume that the idea of generic strategies is the key which unlocks the secret of competitive advantage. They are not prescriptive.

Competitive Advantage and Competitive Success

So far it has been argued that competitive strategies are *built around* differentiation and cost leadership. Competitive advantage is *reflected in* and accrues from perceived differences and real cost advantages, both of these relative to competitors. Hence, competitive advantage is *dependent upon* strategic positioning, but the two are not the same. Competitive advantage will normally, at least in the long term, result in superior margins. Table 6.2 shows that any individual functional area, or a combination of several functions, can be the actual source of the advantage.

Porter (1996) later reinforced these points, and attempted to answer some of the criticisms of his generic strategy approach, when he restated that competitive success is based on one of two alternatives. First, an organization can aim to be better than its rivals and focus on operating efficiencies to achieve this. Secondly, it can seek either to do different things, or to do things differently. This concerns effectiveness, and it relates to strategic positioning. He identified three broad approaches to positioning:

- An organization can focus on a particular product or service – or an identifiable and limited range – and sell it to every customer who is interested. This is the approach favoured by BMW and EasyJet.
- It can, alternatively, target a segment group and provide a wider range of products which can serve a variety of their needs. This is the IKEA approach.
- Thirdly, it can identify and focus on an carefully defined niche with a single product or service. James Purdey (Box 6.3) provides an ideal example.

Porter pointed out that it is activities – what the organization actually does both directly and indirectly for its customers, its functional strategies – that create and build value and, in turn, advantage. Together these activities determine the strategic position that an organization enjoys, and competitive advantage comes from the strength of the position. While being able to do something better or differently is essential, the way in which the activities are combined to generate synergy is also critical. Most individual activities can be copied, but it is much more difficult to replicate what might be a unique combination of activities.

Table 6.2 Functional strategies and competitive advantage

	Competitive strategy	
Functional strategy	**Low cost**	**Differentiation**
Marketing	Large companies can obtain media discounts	Image – reinforced by well-known strategic leader
Operations	Efficient plant management and utilization (productivity)	Low defect rate and high quality
	Re-engineered processes which reduce costs	Re-engineered processes which add extra value
Human resources	Training to achieve low rejections and high-quality policies which keep turnover low	Incentives to encourage innovation
Research and development	Reformulated processes which reduce costs	New, patented breakthroughs
Finance	Low-cost loans (improve profit after interest and before tax)	Ability to finance corporate strategic change, investments and acquisitions
Information technology	Faster decision making in flatter organization structure	Creative use of information to understand customer needs, meet them and outperform competitors
Distribution logistics	Lower stock-holding costs	Alliances with suppliers and/or distributors which are long-term mutually supportive

This list of examples is indicative only, and not an exhaustive set of possibilities.

Consequently, organizations must choose what to do and what not to do, which activities to undertake and which to ignore, and how they might be fused into a powerful mix. Activities that affect the value proposition must not be neglected, but those that have little impact should not consume resources. Critical trade-offs must be made in an attempt to find a 'unique' position. It can be expensive, even self-destructive, to try and do too much and not focus on what does make a difference.

IKEA (Case Study 4) has chosen to trade off in a number of ways, for example. It sacrifices being able to offer a wide range of bought-in products by designing and manufacturing its own. By choosing to hold stock in all of its stores and warehouses IKEA sacrifices the low inventory costs some of its competitors enjoy by only delivering against orders. It sacrifices the use of the highest quality materials in favour of function and affordable prices. IKEA also sacrifices sales assistance in favour of self-service; and it opts for only out-of-town locations.

Activity mapping

Ideally, all of the selected activities will fit together and complement the corporate and competitive strategies in order to yield uniqueness and synergy. Porter uses the metaphor of a comparison of two people to make his point. They each have hands, feet, eyes, ears and so on which, by-and-large, perform similar functions. While there will be differences between two people's hands or feet, the real difference is in the way all the parts combine into a whole. Individual differences in parts, such as colour blindness or arthritis in a hand, do not in themselves explain different behaviours and outcomes. To understand this we need to understand more about the workings of the brain. In a similar way, if we are to understand organizations and organizational differences, we must understand how different organizations acquire and use knowledge, which is frequently related to the synergy created by the interactions of the functions and activities.

Figure 6.8 is an example of Porter's activity mapping idea. The organization selected is Lilliput Lane, manufacturer of plaster cottages and other collectable items. Using innovatory moulding technology, much of it invented by founder, David Tate, the company casts intricate figures and models out of plaster, a cheap and readily obtainable commodity. Individual painters then transform a relatively bland model into a unique finished article. Simply, the five larger circles represent what I believe are the key activities in terms of difference and competitive strength; the smaller circles are important support activities. It will be realized that the key activities are all linked and complementary and that the other activities often support more than one key activity.

Over time, activities will be abandoned, added or changed to affect the competitive position. To a large extent the way in which activities are carried out by people is crucially important and, consequently, the culture and style of management in the organization is a major determinant of the organization's ability to change and find new opportunities for creating different values for customers.

Figure 6.8   Lilliput Lane activity system.

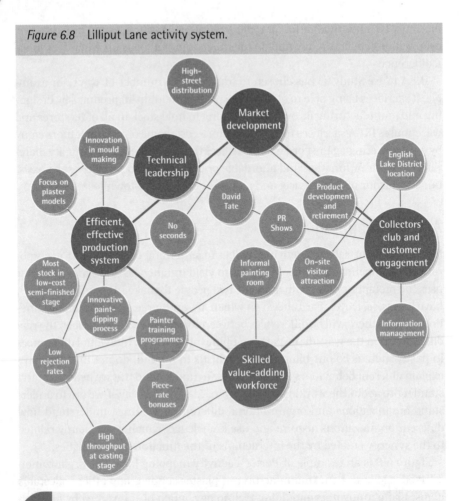

Many companies spend a lot of time and money researching customers' views, but most spend nothing like enough on observing competitors. The main reason for change is to keep ahead of competitors or to catch up on the complacent market leaders. Companies must invest in development – it's a case of 'duck or no dinner'.

Sir Simon Hornby,
ex-Chairman, WH Smith plc

When I'm on a plane, I prowl around and talk to passengers and ask the staff about everything. I normally come back with a hundred notes in my pocket scribbled on little pieces of paper. Direct feedback is far better than market research.

Sir Richard Branson, Chairman,
Virgin Group, quoted in Ferry (1989)

The strategy of Virgin Atlantic Airways is built around quality service and differentiation. Virgin's 'Upper Class' aims to offer a first-class-equivalent service at business-class prices and has provided for a number of years, for example, electrostatic headphones that customers can keep afterwards, a large selection of films to watch on personal mini video-cassette players, and chauffeur-driven rides to and from airports.

Activity mapping is clearly related to the value chain which is explained in Chapter 7.

Sustaining competitive advantage

Few positions are defensible long term against rivals. Competitors will copy good ideas and maybe even improve on them. Change is the key. Competitors, having created a competitive advantage, will stay ahead if they innovate and look for improvements on a continuous basis and, at the same time, look for discontinuous opportunities to effect change on industries and markets.

Figure 6.9 combines a number of the points made here, emphasizing that successful companies create advantage and success by being committed to their customers through careful positioning and managed change. The differences and cost advantages which create a position must be supported by high levels of service in strategy implementation and ideally by a strong reputation and brand, as discussed further in Chapter 7.

Figure 6.10 shows that competitive advantage can be rooted in technology, organization and people, but that it is people and people-driven processes that are the real source of *sustained* advantage, because it is these that are most difficult for rivals to copy. People must be convinced that they are important, and that their contribution is valued – logically through an appropriate reward system – as otherwise they may not deliver and improve the all-important service. This will always prove difficult in a culture where cost management and resource savings have become dominant.

There are many examples where once-powerful and prominent companies have lost their edge and failed to sustain their competitive advantage:

- Case Study 1.1 showed how Marks and Spencer 'took its eye off the ball' and allowed some of its ranges, particularly clothing, to become tired. Large retailers such as M&S normally control buying, product and range selection for every

Figure 6.9 Competitive advantage through customer commitment. Developed by John Thompson from material in de Kare-Silver, M (1997) *Strategy in Crisis*, Macmillan.

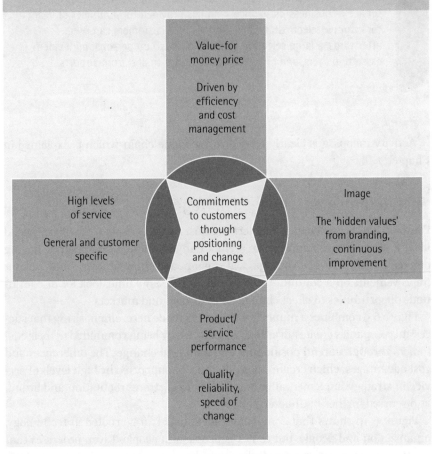

store centrally, because this can save costs. In an attempt to re-establish its position, M&S is allowing individual store managers to have more of an input than in the past. After all, they are closest to local customers.

- With Next, George Davies opened a niche for stylish clothing for slightly older age groups. However, once such a niche has been opened it is relatively easy for rivals to copy the broad strategy, and they did. When Next failed to defend its position by improvements, and instead committed resources to the acquisition of other retail brands and formats, its early advantage was lost. Davies was a corporate casualty, and Next has been turned around under different leadership.

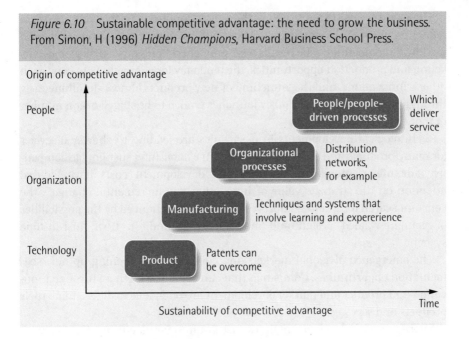

Figure 6.10 Sustainable competitive advantage: the need to grow the business. From Simon, H (1996) *Hidden Champions*, Harvard Business School Press.

- Toys R Us are the American toy superstores who grew at the expense of independent retailers. More recently, Toys R Us has suffered at the hands of Wal-Mart, which has used its purchasing power to compete on price and gain a significant market share. Wal-Mart simply focuses on the best-selling toys which it offers at rock-bottom prices. Toys R Us has a wider choice but that clearly is not what every customer wants. According to Tomkins (1998), 'the company's big mistake was complacency ... they stopped renewing and refreshing their stores', and thus provided a way in for Wal-Mart. Toys R Us became 'stuck in the middle'. The remaining high-street independents are often more convenient and the discounters are cheaper. Their demise was exacerbated by a reputation for relatively poor in-store service.

Speed and competitive advantage

Companies, then, however successful they might be, are likely to be knocked over by innovative competitors if they stand still and ignore a changing environment. They must adapt and improve if they are to retain their position. To sustain any competitive advantage and grow they must innovate more quickly than their rivals. Consequently, speed is becoming an increasingly important factor in the search for competitive advantage.

The world recession at the end of the 1980s, coupled with the continued economic progress of developing countries such as Taiwan and Korea, increased worldwide competition. The results were greater cost pressures, new global marketing and production opportunities, the tendency for competitors to copy each other's innovations, and the launching of new products almost simultaneously throughout the world – previously launches tended to be staged over a number of months or even years.

Technological developments in electronics are leading to shorter lifecycles for many products and growing difficulties in establishing sustainable competitive advantage. Increasing research and development costs have focused attention on the strategic value of innovation and incremental change – the constant search for gradual improvements. This is enhanced by the possibilities of computer-aided design and manufacturing and, in turn, just-in-time systems.

The emergence of global markets and competition is opening up new segmentation opportunities. Companies that can capitalize on these through innovation and product and market development are often able to differentiate their products and services.

Shorter product development times, just-in-time manufacturing, together with the benefits of learning and incremental improvements, can all lead to lower costs. Hence cost leadership and differentiation remain key sources of competitive advantage, and speed can enhance their potential.

Speed can, therefore, be manifested in a number of ways. Product development times can be reduced; deliveries from suppliers can be speeded up through just-in-time; and, by utilizing information technology, distributor and retail stocks can be replenished more quickly. Speed can relate to the whole of the value chain. However, obtaining the competitive benefits of speed is likely to involve more than improved efficiencies through cutting the time taken to do things. A change of attitude towards providing faster, better and customized service is also required. All activities need reviewing in an attempt to improve effectiveness.

Competitive advantage through speed will only be feasible if the organization structure facilitates the changes implied, rather than constrains them. Ideas and information must be able to permeate quickly through the organization; and managers at the operational level must be empowered to make decisions. This implies decentralization and possibly fewer levels of management in the hierarchy.

Successful organizations will become fast learners, ideally finding out about changing customer preferences and expectations ahead of their competitors. They will also need to be able to respond quickly to changes in competitor strategies. This again emphasizes the importance of decentralization.

When speed was less important it was normal for products to be developed and tested in advance of any investment in the new plant which would eventually be required to produce them in volume. These must now be seen as parallel, not sequential, activities. This necessitates close co-operation between the various functional areas of the business, perhaps using special project teams. Such changes can prove difficult to implement.

Finally, the notion of speed must be considered very carefully in certain industries. The design and development of new drugs and new aeroplanes, for example, should not be hurried if safety and reliability could be compromised.

The Dynamics of Competition

Competitor benchmarking

Recapping key points from earlier in the chapter, a true cost leader will also enjoy some form of differentiation, and successful differentiators will be effective cost managers. Differentiation and cost control are compatible. All companies should continually search for innovatory differentiation opportunities and for ways of improving their cost efficiencies. As seen in earlier chapters, leveraging resources and setting stretching targets for employees can help to bring about innovation and savings; benchmarking good or best practice in other organizations (a process of measurement and comparison) can also provide new ideas and suggestions for reducing costs and improving efficiency. Organizations from different sectors and industries can be a useful source of ideas if they have developed a high level of expertise. It should be stressed that this process is a search for ideas that can be customized for a different organization rather than an exercise in simply copying. Managers should be open-minded and inquisitive and look 'everywhere' for ideas.

At the same time, it is vital for an organization to understand clearly its position relative to its competitors. Table 6.3 provides a general framework for considering competitive strategies and Figure 6.11 shows how we might benchmark competitors for comparison with an organization and with customer preferences. The key order criteria – key success factors – are listed down the left-hand side and ranked in order of their importance to customers. Their relative significance is plotted against the horizontal axis. The ability of different competitors to meet these key success factors is illustrated by the dotted lines. Competitor A is clearly relying on its quality and technical back-up, for which it has a good reputation, but is it truly satisfying customer needs? Competitor B seems to offer an all-round better service, and in a number of areas is providing a service beyond that demanded. Given the areas, this may be good as it will indicate a reliable supplier.

How would our customers rank our products/services in relation to those of our competitors?

Not as good as. We must improve!

No worse than. This implies a general dissatisfaction, so there must be real opportunities to benefit from improvement and differentiation.

As good as the others, no better, no worse. Again opportunity to benefit if new values can be added and real differentiation perceived.

Better than. We must still work hard to retain our lead.

I subscribe absolutely to the concept of stealing shamelessly! Wherever you come across a good idea, if it's likely to work, pinch it. There's nothing wrong with that. There is a quite respectable word – benchmarking – which is the same thing if you think about it.

Bill Cockburn, British Telecom,
when Group Chief Executive, WH Smith plc

Changing competitive positions

A successful competitive position implies a match between customers' perceptions of the relative quality or value of a product or service – in comparison to rival offerings – and its price, again in relation to the prices of competing products or services. The relevant area of analysis is the segment or segments in which an organization chooses to compete; and, in addition, the 'total price' should be used for comparison purposes. Customers, for example, may willingly pay a premium purchase price initially for a particular brand of, say, an electrical good or car if they believe that over its life it will incur lower maintenance and service costs than competing brands. Products offered at initially lower prices may be perceived to be more expensive overall.

Figure 6.12 (which develops Figure 6.5) features a competitive positioning grid. Three basic positions are shown by sectors 1, 2 and 3. Sector 6, high perceived prices but only average (at best) quality, is an untenable position in the long run. Sector 4 illustrates a company competing on price, which can be a successful strategy, but it can provoke competitive responses; in which case, it may only serve in driving down all prices and making all competitors less profitable. Do-it-yourself chains, such as B&Q, have come to believe that the key to survival in a crowded market is to offer permanently competitive prices as well as developing a unique identity. Sporadic high discounts are being replaced by 'everyday low prices'; success is more dependent on volume sales than the actual margins on individual products.

Table 6.3 A framework for evaluating competitive strategies

Scope	Global; industry-wide; niche
	Single or multiproduct/service
	Focused or diversified
	Vertical linkages with suppliers/distributors
Objectives	Ambitious for market or segment leadership
	Market presence just to support other (more important) activities
Success	Market share
	Image and reputation
	Profitability
Commitment	Aggressive – willing to acquire to grow
	Passive survivor
	Willing to divest if opportunity arises
Approach	Offensive – attacking other competitors
	Defending a strong position [note: the same strategy (new products, price cuts) can be used both offensively and defensively]
	Risk taking or risk averse
	Teasing out new segments or niches
Strategy	High quality – perhaps with technological support
	High service
	Low price
Position	Cost advantage or even cost leadership enjoyed
	Clearly differentiated
Competitive resources	High technology base; modern plant
	Location relative to markets
	Quality of people (ability to add value)
	Reputation

The examples provided for each of the eight criteria are not offered as an exhaustive list.

Effective differentiators, commanding premium prices and earning superior profits with high margins, are shown as sector 5. Their success is partially dependent upon sound cost management.

Figure 6.13 illustrates a number of possible competitive strategy changes for companies in selected positions in the matrix.

Figure 6.11   Competitor gap analysis.

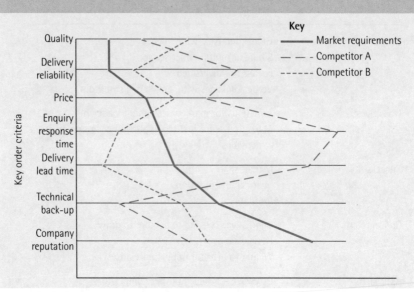

Figure 6.12   A competitive position matrix.

		Low	Average	High
Perception of relative quality and added value	High	**Low price/discount strategies** • can be attractive for new customers and those willing to switch brands **but** • price cuts can be followed readily • customers may become suspicious of quality if prices seem 'too low'	**Differentiation and product improvement** – coupled with greater efficiencies	**High price/high quality position**
	Average		**Market average position**	**Uncompetitive positions:**
	Low	**Low price/quality position**	• Prices not justified through lower quality perceptions • Possibly a company has failed to innovate and slipped back in comparison to competitors • Possibly it is relatively inefficient with a high cost base	

Perception of relative price

	5	3
4		1
2		6

1, 2, 3 acceptable strategies and positions
4   competition on price – successful if not copied and costs controlled
5   effective differentiation
6   uncompetitive, unsustainable positions

Figure 6.13   Possible competitive strategy changes.

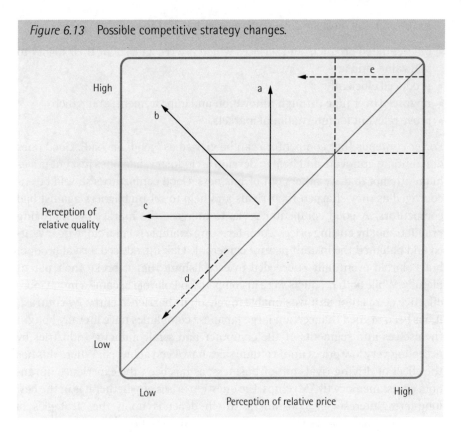

Concluding Comments

This chapter has concentrated on how an organization can gain a deeper under-standing of its competitive environment with a view to becoming a stronger, more effective competitor through creating and sustaining competitive advantage. The closer a business is to its customers, the more it will understand the market and the industry. Competitive strategy, essential for every product and service that the organization makes and markets, involves a vision about how best to com-pete. There is a number of ways to generate competitive advantage, and the process is both logical and creative. The choice will also be influenced by the strate-gic leader and by the organization's culture. However, every employee contributes in some way to both lower costs and uniqueness, and therefore it is important that the competitive strategy is communicated and understood throughout the organization.

In the end, the most successful companies will be those with:

- differentiated products and services which are recognized for their ability to add value, and are
- produced efficiently
- upgraded over time through innovation and improvement, and which
- prove relevant for international markets.

Porter contends that competitors can be viewed as 'good' or 'bad'. Good ones differentiate, innovate and help to develop an industry; bad ones just cut prices in an attempt to drive others out of business. Good competitors should be encouraged as they sharpen their rivals and help to set up barriers against bad competitors. A good competitor seeks to increase the market by improving products, not by cutting prices. An interesting example is Polaroid, who invented and patented the instant picture camera. Kodak introduced a rival product but Polaroid eventually succeeded in establishing that it broke their patent illegally. While both products were in competition Polaroid became a much more effective competitor as it was unable to rely on its barrier to entry. By contrast, it has been argued that certain large Japanese companies have literally bought themselves into segments of the computer and semiconductor industries by accepting very low prices until volume sales have been achieved. Where this has the effect of driving rivals out of business, as has been the experience in random access memory (RAM) chips, the question arises of whether it is in the best long-term interests of consumers. Much depends upon the strategies of companies when they reach a stage of market domination.

New windows of competitive opportunity are always opening:

- Products and services can be improved to open up new markets and segments, as was the case with organizers which competed for the market pioneered by Filofax.
- New technologies change behaviour and demand, e.g. personal computers, personal cassette players such as the Sony Walkman, and hole-in-the-wall cash dispensers.
- Changes in attitude – concern for the environment created the opportunity for unleaded petrol; acceptance of fast foods led to the growth of McDonald's and Pizza Hut.

Summary

Many industries and markets are characterized by competitive 'chaos' – they are dynamic and uncertain. All the time rivals may be trying out new initiatives which cannot be ignored. To succeed long term, organizations must be able to manage both continuous and discontinuous change pressures. This is achieved with a mix of incremental and more dramatic changes to competitive and corporate strategies.

In an endeavour to manage in, and manage, their competitive environment, organizations must understand the nature and attractiveness of their industry, and their relative position in it.

Industry attractiveness affects profit potential, and it can be assessed by considering five forces: barriers to entry; the relative power of suppliers; the relative power of buyers; the potential for substitutability; and interfirm rivalry. Governments affect all five.

Positioning can be examined against a framework of generic strategies, which are based on differentiation and cost leadership. The issue of a broad or narrow market focus is another important consideration.

Michael Porter has provided two useful frameworks to help with these assessments.

However, competitive positions, per se, do not yield competitive advantage. Advantage is a reflection of a strong position, but it is the result of the activities which create the position and, in particular, the synergistic links between them. Successful organizations achieve a unique mix which is hard to replicate, although the individual activities, at a basic level, can be copied.

While competitive advantage comes from technologies, organization and people, it is the people-driven processes that enable advantage to be sustained and extended.

All the time the pace of change and competition is speeding up in many markets and industries. To deal with this it is essential for organizations to benchmark both their competitors and other high-performing organizations in a search for good ideas and best practice. Specifically, they are looking for new opportunities to add or build value in ways that are meaningful for customers.

References

Ferry, I (1989) Branson's misunderstood Midas touch, *Business*, November.

Heller, R (1998) *Goldfinger – How Entrepreneurs Grow Rich by Starting Small*, HarperCollins.

Hendry, J (1990) The problem with Porter's generic strategies, *European Management Journal*, December.

Kanter, RM (1990) Strategic alliances and new ventures, Harvard Business School Video Series.

Porter, ME (1980) *Competitive Strategy: Techniques for Analysing Industries and Competitors*, Free Press.

Porter, ME (1985) *Competitive Advantage: Creating and Sustaining Superior Performance*, Free Press.

Porter, ME (1996) What is strategy? *Harvard Business Review*, November–December.

Tomkins, R (1998) Trouble in toyland pushes Toys R Us on the defensive, *Financial Times*, 29 May.

Additional material on the website

The website contains extra material for readers who want reinforcement of key issues in:

- marketing strategy
- operations strategy
- management and strategy issues in service businesses.

There is also a summary and critique of Michael Porter's work on how we might analyse the relative competitive strengths of nations.

Test your knowledge of this chapter with our online quiz at:
http://www.thomsonlearning.co.uk

Questions and Research Assignments

TEXT RELATED

1. Study Figure 6.6(b) and consider where you would place other major car manufacturers and why. Where should Rover be categorized? Which companies appear to be 'stuck in the middle' without a clear strategy for competitive advantage?

2. Apply the Competitor Grid (Figure 6.11) to this industry.

Internet and Library Projects

1. Take an industry of your choice, perhaps the one in which you work, and assess it in terms of:
   (a) concentration
   (b) Porter's model of five forces.

From this, analyse one or more of the major competitors in terms of their chosen competitive strategies.

As well as the Internet the following library sources might prove useful sources of information:

- Business Monitors (PA and PQ series)
- Annual Report of the Director General of Fair Trading (as a source of ideas)
- Monopolies and Mergers Commission reports, and Competition Commission reports, which usually feature a comprehensive industry analysis

- McCarthy's (or similar) Index (press-cutting service for firms and industries).

2. How successful has Porsche been since the introduction of its new models? Do you believe that the size of its niche is viable, or might the company have to extend its range?

Porsche http://www.porsche.com

3. Laura Ashley was started in the 1950s by the late Laura Ashley and her husband, Bernard. The company was very successful, with an instinctive approach to designs for fashions and fabrics. Laura Ashley designed, manufactured and retailed mostly clothes and furnishings. The company later diversified with a chain of perfume stores, leather goods stores and a knitwear business in Scotland. The company fared badly in the recession, and by 1991 was losing money.

The company's success has always depended upon the strength of the Laura Ashley name and brand, but the company has struggled after the death of Laura Ashley. In 1995 American Ann Iverson became the fourth chief executive of the decade. She inherited a company which was still clearly differentiated and popular with customers but where costs had escalated, resulting in margins of just 2%.

Ann Iverson declared she would tackle the cost base while 'preserving the mood and emotion, the countryside feeling' of the brand.

Her strategies have involved:

- selected store closures around the world, particularly in the USA
- a consolidation of the design, buying and merchandising functions
- a slimming of the product range.

The need for the company to manufacture, rather than focus on its core strengths of design and retailing, has been questioned.

Ann Iverson is no longer with the company; she too has been replaced.

What is the current position with Laura Ashley? Has the company been turned around or is it still struggling to find a strong competitive position?

Laura Ashley http://www.laura-ashley.com

7

Strategic Resources

Auditing Strategic Resources

Strategic Architecture

The Organization's Value Chain

The Value Chain and Competitive Advantage

Reputation and Branding

Summary

The resource-based view of strategy gradually emerged during the 1980s and 1990s with a series of important contributions, in particular work on core competency from Prahalad and Hamel (1990) and on added value by Kay (1993). This view helps to explain why some organizations succeed in creating competitive advantage and earning superior profits, while others do not. Consequently, it looks at strategies which can be identified with an individual company as distinct from those that are available to all competitors through an understanding of industries and markets. In other words, market opportunities have to be identified and then satisfied in an individual and distinctive way.

Supporters of the resource-based view put forward a number of arguments. As long as there are opportunities which can be identified, it will normally be easier and less risky for organizations to exploit their existing resources in new ways than to seek to acquire and learn new skills and competencies. Innovation matters and new ways of exploiting resources must be found to sustain any competitive advantage. Relative differences which separate a company from its rivals are critical. Just having a resource is not enough. For this reason, it can be useful if particular strengths are not easily learned and imitated by rivals. The opening case on Dyson shows how innovation and new ways of creating and adding value through design can markedly change an industry. In this particular case, innovation allowed a newcomer to establish a position of market dominance and force a reaction from established manufacturers.

This chapter looks firstly and briefly at the idea of a resource audit before considering resource linkages and synergy through architecture and the notion of the value chain. The idea of the activity maps, explained in Chapter 6, is developed here. The chapter concludes with a section on reputation and branding, key intangible assets.

Before reading this chapter you might usefully re-read the sections on core competencies and leveraging resources in Chapter 1.

Case Study 7: James Dyson

James Dyson is an entrepreneur who challenged the industry giants, in his case with a revolutionary vacuum cleaner. His dual cyclone cleaner now has a UK market share in excess of 50% and international sales are booming. A Hoover spokesman has said on the *BBC Money Programme*: 'I regret Hoover as a company did not take the product technology of Dyson ... it would have been lain on a shelf and not been used'. Dyson has been compared by Professor Christopher Frayling, Rector of the Royal College of Art, with 'the great Victorian ironmasters ... a one-man attempt to revive British manufacturing industry through design'. Dyson is creative, innovative, totally focused on customers and driven by a desire to improve everyday products. His dedication and ego drive is reflected in the following comment: 'the only way to make a genuine breakthrough is to pursue a vision with a single-minded determination in the face of criticism ...' and this is exactly what he has done. Clearly a risk taker, he invested all of his resources in his venture. In the end his rise to fame and fortune came quickly, but the preceding years had been painful and protracted, and characterized by courage and persistence. They reflect the adage that 'instant success takes time.'

James Dyson's schoolmaster father died when he was just nine years old. The public school to which he was then sent 'made him a fighter'. At school he excelled in running, practising by running cross-countries on his own; and it was on these runs that he began to appreciate the magnificence of the railway bridges constructed by Brunel in the nineteenth century, an experience which helped to form his personal vision. An early leap in the dark came when he volunteered to play bassoon in the school orchestra, without ever having seen a bassoon! Naturally artistic, he won a painting competition sponsored by the *Eagle* comic when he was ten years old. Art became a passion and he later went on to complete a degree in interior design. Dyson may be an inventor, but he has no formal engineering background.

Dyson's first successful product and business was a flat-bottomed boat, the Sea Truck. At this time he learnt how a spherical plastic ball could be moulded, an idea that he turned to good use in the wild garden of his new home. His wheelbarrow was inadequate as the wheels sank into the ground, so he substituted the wheel with a light plastic ball and thus invented the Ballbarrow. Backed by his brother-in-law on a 50:50 basis,

Dyson invested in his new idea. Made of colourful, light plastic the barrow was offered to garden centres and the building trade, both of whom were less than enthusiastic. With a switch to direct mail via newspaper advertisements, the business took off. A new sales manager was appointed but his renewed attempt to sell the barrow through more traditional retail channels was again a failure. The financial penalty was the need for external investors, who later persuaded Dyson's brother-in-law to sell the business. A second painful experience came when the sales manager took the idea and design to the USA, where Dyson later failed with a legal action against him.

Dyson's idea for a dual cyclone household cleaner came in 1979, when he was 31 years old. Again, it was a case of a need creating an opportunity. He was converting his old house and becoming frustrated that his vacuum cleaner would not clear all of the dust that he was creating. Particles were clogging the pores of the dust bags and reducing the suction capability of the cleaner. Needing something to collect paint particles from his plastic spraying operation for the ballbarrows, Dyson had developed a smaller version of the large industrial cyclone machines, which separate particles from air by using centrifugal forces in spinning cylinders. He believed that this technology could be adapted for home vacuum cleaners, removing the need for bags, but his partners in the Ballbarrow business failed to share his enthusiasm. Out of work when the business was sold, his previous employer, Jeremy Fry (for whom he had developed the Sea Truck), loaned him £25,000. Dyson matched this by selling his vegetable garden for £18,000 and taking out an additional £7000 overdraft on his house. Working from home, risking everything and drawing just £10,000 a year to keep himself, his wife and three children, he pursued his idea. Over the years he produced 5000 different prototypes.

When he ultimately approached the established manufacturers his idea was, perhaps predictably, rejected. Replacement dust bags are an important source of additional revenue. A series of discussions with potential partners who might license his idea brought mixed results. Fresh legal actions in the USA for patent infringement – 'with hindsight I didn't patent enough features' – were only partially offset by a deal with Apex of Japan. Dyson designed the G-Force upright cleaner which Apex manufactured and sold to a niche in the Japanese market for the equivalent of £1200 per machine, from which Dyson received just £20. At least there was now an income stream, but this had taken seven years to achieve. Finally, in 1991 Lloyds Bank provided finance for the design and manufacture of a machine in the UK. Several venture capitalists and the Welsh Development Agency had turned him down. Dyson was determined to give his latest version the looks of NASA technology, but further setbacks were still to occur. Dyson was let down by the plastic moulder and assembler with whom he contracted, and was eventually forced to set up his own plant. Early sales through mail-order catalogues were followed by deals with John Lewis and eventually (in 1995) with Comet and Curry's. In this year a cylinder version joined the upright. Dyson continues to improve the designs to extend his patent protection. By 1999 his personal wealth was estimated to be £500 million.

Dyson has always seen himself as more of an inventor than a businessman. He runs two separate businesses, both in Malmesbury, Wiltshire, and he keeps Dyson Manufacturing and Dyson Research (design and patenting) apart. The dress code for employees is perpetually informal and communications are predominantly face-to-face. Memos are banned and even e-mails discouraged. Every employee is encouraged to be creative and contribute ideas. Most new employees are young – 'not contaminated by other employers' – and they all begin by assembling their own vacuum cleaner, which they can then buy for £20. There are over 60 designers, who work on improvements to the dual cyclone cleaners as well as new product ideas. In early 2000 Dyson launched a robot version of the dual cyclone cleaner, which is battery-powered, self-propelled and able to manoeuvre itself around furniture. It retails at some £2500, which may limit it to a select segment of the market. Later in 2000 Dyson launched a revolutionary super-fast washing machine with short wash cycles and an ability to spin clothes almost dry, presenting a challenge to the manufacturers of both washing machines and tumble dryers. This time, however, Dyson had his own resources to launch the product. Moreover, Dyson controls 100% of the shares in the business. He has learnt some painful lessons but is now enjoying the rewards of his dogged determination.

QUESTIONS: Thinking about the issues of core competency and strategic capability, what is the 'secret' of James Dyson's competitive advantage? Has he been able to appropriate the rewards of the value he has added?

Dyson   http://www.dyson.com

> People feel the best about their work when they do a high-quality job! Getting a job done quickly is satisfying. Getting a job done at low cost is rewarding. But getting a job done quickly, at low cost and with high quality is exciting!
>
> *Robert C Stempel, when Chairman, General Motors Corporation*

Auditing Strategic Resources

Chapters 5 and 6 looked at organizations in the context of their environments, somewhat artificially separating their general and competitive environments. Environments spring surprises on organizations from time to time. Sometimes the surprises constitute opportunities; at other times, threats. The most vigilant and aware organizations will be better placed to respond. Success lies in seeing opportunities 'ahead of the game' and responding in some individual way, ideally one that is genuinely different, appreciated by customers and not easily copied by rivals. The ability to do this comes down to individual, specific to the organization, competencies and capabilities, which in turn emanate from the organization's resources. Resources, therefore, make the difference. In this chapter this argument is explored in greater depth and frameworks are provided which can help us to audit and evaluate strategic resources.

The relationship between environmental forces and internal resources is at the heart of Figure 7.1, which has been adapted from the Harvard Business School approach to strategy (Kelly and Kelly, 1987). Here, selected products, services and markets are seen as environment driven and the competitive environment and stakeholders are shown with resources and values as four key strategic elements linked to corporate objectives. These elements can be changed, but in many cases not readily and not quickly, and consequently at any point in time they are reasonably fixed.

Six operating elements are also incorporated. *Marketing* relates to how the various products and services are positioned in relation to competitors, and how they are priced, advertised and distributed. *Manufacturing* involves the types of production process, location issues and technology utilization. *Finance* incorporates both performance targets and sources of funding. *Research and development* considers how much to spend on research and development and whether the perspective is short or long term. *Human resources* relates to the types of people utilized and how they are rewarded. The *organization structure* encompasses how these functions are co-ordinated and controlled.

These operating elements determine whether or not the corporate objectives are achieved. The different functions in the organization are affected to varying

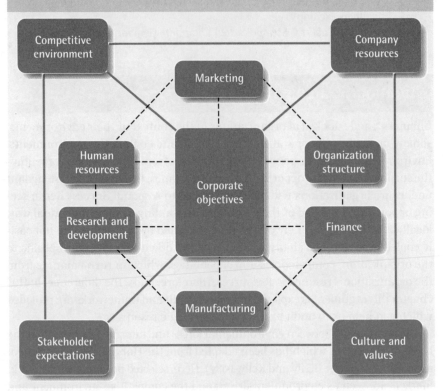

Figure 7.1   Matching the organization and the environment. Adapted from Kelly, FJ and Kelly, HM (1987) *What They Really Teach You at the Harvard Business School*, Piatkus.

degrees by different stakeholders, and certain stakeholders who have a significant impact on certain functions may have little direct importance for others. Equally, the specific stakeholders may influence individual functions in quite different ways. Their impact upon the whole organization is therefore affected by the organization structure and relative power and influence within the firm. The figure also highlights the strategic value of functional managers taking a more holistic view of the organization and their role and contribution.

How, then, might we audit and evaluate these operating elements or strategic resources?

An internal analysis should be a three-stage process:

1. an evaluation of the profile of the principal skills and resources of an organization
2. a comparison of this resource base with the requirements for competitive success in the industry

3. a comparison with competitors to determine the relative strengths and weaknesses and any significant comparative advantage.

Where internal managers carry out this analysis, it is inevitable that there will be some subjective judgement and it will be affected by their position in the organization.

In a SWOT (strengths, weaknesses, opportunities and threats) analysis, then, the strengths and weaknesses of resources must be considered in relative and not absolute terms. It is important to consider whether they are being managed effectively as well as efficiently. Resources, therefore, are not strong or weak purely because they exist or do not exist. Rather, their value depends on how they are being managed, controlled and used.

In auditing resources we consider the functional areas of the business, as this is where the human, financial and physical resources are deployed. These areas might include finance, production, marketing, research and development, procurement, personnel and administration. However, it is also important to consider how they are related together in the organization's structure and control systems. A brilliant and successful marketing manager, for example, might seem to represent a strength; however, if there is no adequate cover for him and he leaves or falls ill, it is arguable that the firm has a marketing weakness.

Control systems, such as production and financial control, and the ways in which managers co-operate within the organization influence how well resources are managed for efficiency and effectiveness. Table 7.1, which is not meant to be fully comprehensive, provides a sample of key resource considerations. In completing such an audit the various resources should be evaluated: their existence, the ways in which they are deployed and utilized, and the control systems that are used to manage them.

Efficiency measures of the salesforce might include sales per person or sales per region, but the effectiveness of the salesforce relates to their ability to sell the most profitable products or those products or services that the organization is keen to promote at a particular time, perhaps to reduce a high level of stocks. The efficiency of individual distribution outlets can be measured by sales revenue in a similar way. However, the effectiveness of the distribution activity relates to exactly which products are being sold and to whom, whether they are available where customers expect them, and how much investment in stock is required to maintain the outlets. The efficiency of plant and equipment is linked to percentage utilization. The effectiveness involves an assessment of which products are being manufactured in relation to orders and delivery requirements, to what quality and with what rejection levels.

It is also important to assess the relative strengths and weaknesses in relation to competition.

Table 7.1 Aspects of the resource audit

Resource/function	Key considerations
Marketing	Products and services: range, brand names and stage in lifecycle
	Patents
	Strength of salesforce
	Distribution channels
	Market information
Operations	Location and plant
	Capital equipment
	Capacity
	Processes
	Planning and manufacturing systems
	Quality control
	Supplies
Research and development	Annual budget
	Technology support
	Quality of researchers
	Record of success and reputation
	Spending in relation to industry norm
Information	Organizational knowledge and extent of sharing
	Information systems
	Problem-solving capabilities and procedures
Finance	Capital structure
	Working capital
	Cash flow
	Costing systems and variances
	Nature of shareholders
	Relations with bankers
Human resources	Numbers and qualifications
	Skills and experience
	Age profile
	Labour turnover and absenteeism
	Flexibility
	Development and training record and policies
	Motivation and culture
	Managerial competencies and capacity

Managers must be aware of and must address strategic issues if the resources are to be used for creating and sustaining competitive advantage. *Marketing* can be looked at from the point of view of managing the activities which comprise the marketing function. Product design and pricing, advertising, selling and distribution would be included here. However, if an organization is marketing orientated there is an implication that employees throughout the organization are aware of consumers and customers, their needs, and how they might be satisfied effectively while enabling the organization to achieve its objectives. Consumer concern becomes part of the culture and values. Consumers and customers are mentioned separately because for many organizations, particularly the manufacturers of products for consumer markets, their customers are distributors and their ultimate consumers are customers of the retailers that they supply.

Innovation and quality can be seen as aspects of production or *operations management*. Again, it is helpful if these factors become part of the culture. An innovatory organization is ready for change, and looking to make positive changes, in order to get ahead and stay ahead of competition. A concern for quality in all activities will affect both costs and consumer satisfaction.

In *human resources management* values are communicated and spread throughout the organization.

Financial management includes the control of costs so that profit is achieved and value is added to products and services primarily in areas that matter to consumers. This should provide differentiation and competitive advantage.

Lower costs and differentiation are important themes in competitive strategy. They relate to both an awareness of consumer needs and the management of resources to satisfy these needs effectively and, where relevant, profitably. Marketing orientation and the effective management of production and operations, people and finance are all essential aspects of the creation and maintenance of competitive strength and advantage.

Functional and competitive strategies are important for an understanding of strategic management in all types of organization, and they are especially important for a large proportion of small businesses and many not-for-profit organizations. Corporate strategic changes such as major diversification and acquisition, divestment of business units which are underperforming or international expansion may not be relevant for small firms with a limited range of products or services and a primarily local market, or for not-for-profit organizations with very specific missions. However, these organizations must compete effectively, operate efficiently and provide their customers and clients with products and services that satisfy their needs. Competitive and functional strategies are therefore the relevant issue.

As the Internet becomes more pervasive in our lives some organizations and industries are being presented with wonderful opportunities and, at the same time, real threats. Book retailing has changed with the growth of Amazon.com and the opening of on-line bookshops by the leading book retailers. Similarly, domestic banking has been changed with the growth of ATMs (automated teller machines or 'holes in the wall'), telephone call centres and Internet accounts. Competitors have had to develop new skills, competencies and capabilities in order to survive, let alone thrive. The challenge, though, did not stop here. It has also been necessary to clarify the key success factors for those customers who opted to avoid the Internet and stick with a personal service. What exactly are their needs and preferences? How can they be satisfied 'wonderfully well'? How can costs be trimmed in the process?

Success, then, depends upon understanding and linking with customers, and these points are explored further through the remainder of this chapter.

Strategic Architecture

Kay (1993) adopted the word 'architecture' to emphasize the importance of corporate networks and relationships. He argued that companies depend upon their people for their competitiveness and success, but strong and capable individuals, while important, are not enough. They must work together well and synergistically. Football clubs, and their need for skilled individuals to be moulded into a strong, winning team, provide a valuable metaphor. In addition, people's natural energies should be focused not on internal rivalries but on managing external demands. Success here can be enhanced through effective links between an organization, its suppliers, its distributors and its ultimate customers.

In summary, we should consider:

- The way in which managers and other employees co-operate within the organization. Communications and co-operation should work both horizontally and vertically. Transfer pricing arrangements and poorly crafted internal performance measures can all too easily set division against division and department against department, and create real internal competition for resources. Where managers find delight when another manager, department or division finds itself in trouble, something is wrong. But it still happens. Similarly, in some organizations, there is a reliance on top–down communications for issuing instructions coupled with an ability for managers lower down the organization to feed only good news upwards and suppress bad news. The valuable ideas that some junior and middle managers have are, consequently, neither sought nor listened to by their superiors. Kay calls this 'internal architecture'.
- Suppliers, organizations, distributors and final customers and consumers working together supportively in a 'seamless' chain which builds and provides value for all the participants, or 'external architecture'. Members of this value chain

can make life either relatively easy or problematical for the other members, depending on their philosophy. The ideal outcome is one where everyone feels that they are gaining some benefit rather than they are being exploited by someone who is ruthless or selfish. It is a feeling of 'win–win' rather than 'I win, you lose' or 'you win at my expense', which happens in many negotiations and deals. Sometimes the members of such a value chain will establish formalized partnerships or alliances to seal the relationship more firmly.

The outcome should be shared knowledge, co-operation and the development of trust and trusted routines, as illustrated in Figure 7.2. All parties should feel that they can rely on each other. Benetton provides an example of a successful international business which has built a strong network of dedicated suppliers.

> The driving force in all the world's markets is competition. And the most aggressive drivers are the Japanese. Their competitive strength and ambitions are apparent around the world. Ultimately the only way to succeed is to be fully competitive in the marketplace. Fundamentally this means offering products with utility, style and value that the buyers want, making them with world-class productivity and quality, and serving the customers better than anyone else.
>
> *John F Smith Jr, Vice Chairman (International Operations),*
> *General Motors Corporation*

A number of useful examples highlight the benefit of strong strategic architecture:

- For many years Japanese organizations have benefited from membership of corporate families or 'keiretsu'. Businesses, typically those clustered together in a geographical area, will all own shares in each other. Their directors will hold part-time directorships in other organizations in the keiretsu. The whole philosophy will be one of helping each other with either preferred supplier arrangements or the provision of help and advice. It will be realized how a base like this can foster benchmarking and the exchange of ideas and good practice, and the ability to exploit just-in-time supply arrangement. Here, manufacturers can avoid inventory costs by relying on their suppliers to deliver the quantities they need exactly when they are required for production.
- For many years Marks and Spencer was credited with having a valuable portfolio of key suppliers, many of them British, who were committed to it. Typically, M&S would take a substantial proportion of a supplier's annual output and would work with it on designs and quality. M&S knew that it was buying reliable, quality products; the suppliers knew that they were working with one of the UK's strongest retailers. Customers were equally satisfied. M&S

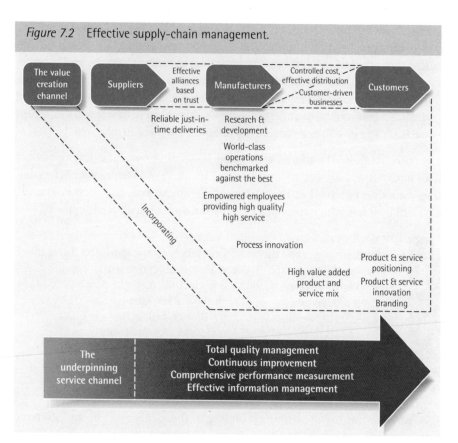

Figure 7.2   Effective supply-chain management.

standards and expectations were exacting, but the mutual rewards were high and shared. Towards the end of the 1990s, as M&S was accused of having 'tired' ranges and manufacturing costs in Britain for many clothing and food products seemed relatively expensive, some of these arrangements broke down. One clothing supplier, William Baird, sued M&S for alleged breach of contract.

- The legendary Silicon Valley, heart of the American, and arguably the global, computer and semiconductor industries, has long benefited from networks and alliances. Companies spinoff from each other, sometimes as rivals, but more often to develop new products or to supply each other. In the early days of the industry young entrepreneurs readily shared their ideas and knowledge. As a result, Silicon Valley as a whole became an opportunity which attracted people with ideas and ambition.

Sometimes the value and constituency of these networks and partnerships can be hard to quantify or even explain. They owe a lot to people and to their history. They are relationships which emerge and strengthen over many years. They are dependent upon personal relations and interactions. This often serves to make them even more powerful as they are automatically difficult to replicate. Consequently, architecture can be a vital element of competitive advantage.

As more and more organizations opt to focus on core strengths, activities and competencies, and divest those that are peripheral, the significance of architecture is reinforced and increased. When companies outsource important services such as information technology (IT) or payroll management, or choose to buy in key components they once made for themselves, they need to be able to rely upon, and trust, their new suppliers. Managing relationships, therefore, becomes an important new capability.

Buckingham and Coffman (1999) also draw attention to the importance of architecture in their delineation of four levels of customer service. Level 1 is accuracy and level 2, availability. These, they argue, have to be seen as the relatively easy levels, and are generally taken for granted. In other words, without them, a company cannot hope to win repeated business. Levels 3 and 4 are working partnerships and the provision of advice and support. These relate to strategic architecture.

Porter also made a contribution to strategic architecture by providing a value chain framework for helping to identify valuable differences and manage cost drivers. This is looked at in the next section.

Supply-chain partnerships

Developing his earlier work on industry structure (Porter, 1980), where he highlights the significance of the relative power of buyers and suppliers, Porter (1985) argues that in the search for competitive advantage a firm must be considered as part of a wider system:

suppliers → firm → distributors → consumers.

As well as seeking improvements in its own activities, a firm should assess the opportunities and potential benefits from improving its links with other organizations. A firm is linked to the marketing and selling activities of its suppliers, and to the purchasing and materials handling activities of its distributors or customers.

The supply chain, then, is a process, and managing it is a key *strategic capability*. Cost savings and service differentiation can be achieved.

Organizations can create synergy, and enjoy the appropriate benefits, if they can successfully link their value chain with those of their suppliers and distributors. Just-in-time (JIT) deliveries integrate a supplier's outbound logistics with the organization's inbound logistics. Stock and costs can be reduced for the manufacturer, whose delivery lead time and reliability should also be improved. Set up properly, a JIT system can enable suppliers to plan their work more effectively and reduce their uncertainty. This requires an open exchange of reliable, up-to-date information and medium- to long-term supply arrangements. When Nissan was developing the supply chain for its UK manufacturing plant in Sunderland, it deliberately forged links with its suppliers' suppliers in its search to control costs without sacrificing quality and service. A retail bookseller, taking orders for non-stock items, needs to be sure of the delivery lead time from his publishers or wholesaler before quoting a date to the customer. This again demands accurate information, supported by reliable supply.

Carphone Warehouse, a leading retailer of mobile phones, retails telephones at prices ranging from 50p to over £300. Where the phone is sold as part of a package which involves a monthly line rental, the phone will typically have been provided free to the Carphone Warehouse by one of the major networks, such as BT Cellnet or Vodafone, who in turn will have a supply arrangement with a manufacturer, perhaps Nokia or Motorola. The retailer will later receive a share of the future call revenues, normally between 3 and 5%. The ultimate value to Carphone Warehouse of the sale will average £300, regardless of the apparent selling price. In the case of phones used for prepaid calls without any monthly line rental, a typical sale will yield £200.

Organizations looking to launch a new product need to ensure that their supply and distribution networks are properly in place; given this, all interested parties can benefit. Retailers will need to be convinced of a new product's viability and potential before they agree to stock it, normally at the expense of taking something else off their shelves. Manufacturers must be sure that stocks are available where customers expect to find them before they proceed with launch advertising.

The key lies in an integrated network, where all members of the supply chain see themselves as mutual beneficiaries from an effective total system; however, this does not always happen.

Supply-chain management issues become increasingly important where organizations seek to reduce the number of their suppliers, buying as many items as possible from each selected supplier. It is quite feasible that these major suppliers will have to buy in products that they do not make themselves in order to create the 'basket' of items demanded by their customer. This strategy has been adopted by the leading oil companies and car manufacturers. In 1994 Ford in the USA included components from 700 US suppliers in its Tempo model; in 1995 the company's equivalent Mercury Mystique was using 227 suppliers worldwide. One supplier, for example, was now required to provide a fully assembled dashboard, ready for immediate installation; it is likely that the electronic instrumentation will be bought in by the relevant supplier. In 1999 Ford of Brazil went further. For the first time a supplier was given responsibility for part of the production line in a Ford assembly plant. Simply, the workers are employed by the supplier but work inside a plant owned by Ford.

Preece *et al.* (1995) use the value chain to explain how Levi Strauss, producer of the internationally successful Levi's jeans, has created value and used its value-creating activities carefully to establish a distinctive corporate reputation, which is a form of competitive advantage. Key aspects include:

- established links with suppliers from around the world
- team manufacturing (underpinned by training and empowerment) and linked to high-technology equipment and sophisticated information support
- global advertising and branding
- alliances with retailers who concentrate on Levi's jeans and do not stock competitor products
- a programme of 'marketing revitalization' designed to reduce lead times and improve the availability of the products.

Strengthening the processes involved in managing the supply chain relates to the level of service that companies are able to offer their customers and to total quality management, topics which are discussed in the supplementary pages on the website.

Corporate restructuring to improve international competitiveness is a vital priority for British and European businesses in the 1990s. However, such restructuring must be a continual process of change and revitalization if we are to consistently satisfy the consumer's need for the highest quality products and services at the most competitive cost. The leadership of this process is the primary role of management in the modern company.

Ian G McAllister, when Chairman and Managing Director, Ford Motor Company Limited, UK

ICI Explosives Division, who manufacture a range of explosive products, have also developed expertise in detonating explosions; quarry managers, who buy the products, really want stones and rocks on a quarry floor rather than the explosives. As a consequence ICI offered to produce a three-dimensional map of a quarry for their customers, indicating where the charges need to be placed, and then, when suitable holes have been drilled in the quarry face (by the quarry owners), carry out controlled explosions. In this way they add value for their customers and link the two value chains.

The Organization's Value Chain

While strategic success depends upon the way in which the organization as a whole behaves, and the ways in which managers and functions are integrated, competitive advantage stems from the individual and discrete activities that a firm performs. A cost advantage can arise from low-cost distribution, efficient production or an excellent salesforce that succeeds in winning the most appropriate orders. Differentiation can be the result of having an excellent design team or being able to source high-quality materials or high-quality production. Value-chain analysis is a systematic way of studying the direct and support activities undertaken by a firm. From this analysis should arise greater awareness concerning costs and the potential for lower costs and for differentiation. Quite simply, argues Porter (1985), competitive advantage is created and sustained when a firm performs the most critical functions either more cheaply or better than its competitors. But what are the most critical factors? Why? How and where might costs be reduced? How and where might differentiation be created?

In this section we are extending the ideas behind activity mapping which we introduced in Chapter 6.

Activities in the value chain

The value chain developed by Michael Porter is illustrated in Figure 7.3. There are five primary activities, namely inbound logistics, operations, outbound logistics, marketing and sales, and service. In the diagram they are illustrated as a chain

Figure 7.3 The value chain. Source: Porter, ME (1985) *Competitive Advantage: Creating and Sustaining Superior Performance*, Free Press. © Michael E Porter, 1985. Adapted with permission of the Free Press.

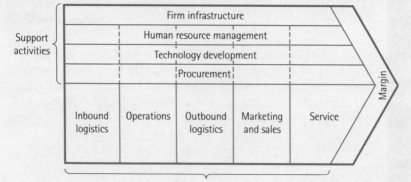

moving from left to right, and they represent activities of physically creating the product or service and transferring it to the buyer, together with any necessary after-sale service. They are linked to four support activities: procurement, technology development, human resource management, and the firm's infrastructure. The support activities are drawn laterally as they can affect any one or more of the primary activities, although the firm's infrastructure generally supports the whole value chain. Every one of the primary and support activities incurs costs and should add value to the product or service in excess of these costs. It is important always to look for ways of reducing costs sensibly; cost reductions should not be at the expense of lost quality in areas that matter to customers and consumers. Equally, costs can be added justifiably if they add qualities that the customer values and is willing to pay for. The difference between the total costs and the selling price is the margin. The margin is increased by widening the gap between costs and price. The activities are described in greater depth below.

Primary activities

- *Inbound logistics* are activities relating to receiving, storing and distributing internally the inputs to the product or service. They include warehousing, stock control and internal transportation systems.
- *Operations* are activities relating to the transformation of inputs into finished products and services. Operations includes machining, assembly and packaging.
- *Outbound logistics* are activities relating to the distribution of finished goods and services to customers.
- *Marketing and sales* includes such activities as advertising and promotion, pricing and salesforce activity.
- *Service* relates to the provision of any necessary service with a product, such as installation, repair, extended warranty or training in how to use the product.

Each of these might be crucial for competitive advantage. The nature of the industry will determine which factors are the most significant.

Support activities

- *Procurement* refers to the function or process of purchasing any inputs used in the value chain, as distinct from issues of their application. Procurement may take place within defined policies or procedures, and it might be evidenced within a number of functional areas. Production managers and engineers, for example, are very important in many purchasing decisions to ensure that the specification and quality are appropriate.
- *Technology development*: technology is defined here in its broadest sense to include know-how, research and development, product design and process improvement and information technology.

- *Human resource management* involves all activities relating to recruiting, training, developing and rewarding people throughout the organization.
- *The firm's infrastructure* includes the structure of the organization, planning, financial controls and quality management designed to support the whole of the value chain.

Again, each of these support activities can be very important in creating and sustaining competitive advantage.

Subactivities

Porter argues that it can often be valuable to subdivide the primary and support activities into their component parts when analysing costs and opportunities for differentiation. For example, it is less meaningful to argue that an organization provides good service than to explain it in terms of installation, repair or training. The competitive advantage is likely to result from a specific subactivity. Similarly, the marketing mix comprises a set of linked activities which should be managed to complement each other. However, competitive advantage can arise from just one activity in the mix, possibly the product design, its price or advertising, technical support literature, or from the skills and activities of the salesforce.

Linkages within the value chain

Although competitive advantage arises from one or more subactivities within the primary and support activities comprising the value chain, it is important not to think of the chain merely as a set of independent activities. Rather, it is a system of interdependent activities. Linkages in the value chain, which are relationships between the activities, are very important. Behaviour in one part of the organization can affect the costs and performance of other business units and functions, and this quite frequently involves trade-off decisions. For example, more expensive materials and more stringent inspection will increase costs in the inbound logistics and operations activities, but the savings in service costs resulting from these strategies may be greater. The choice of functional strategies and where to concentrate efforts will relate to the organization's competitive and corporate strategies concerning competitive advantage.

Similarly, several activities and subactivities depend on each other. The extent to which operations, outbound logistics and installation are co-ordinated can be a source of competitive advantage through lower costs (reduced stockholding) or differentiation (high-quality, customer-orientated service). This last example uses linkages between primary activities, but there are also clear linkages between primary and support activities. Product design affects manufacturing costs, purchasing policies affect operations and production costs, and so on.

Having introduced and discussed the concept of the value chain, it is now important to consider how it might be applied in the evaluation of costs and differentiation opportunities.

The Value Chain and Competitive Advantage

Cost leadership and differentiation strategies

Cost leadership
Chapter 6 discussed the argument of Porter (1985) that the lowest cost producer in either a broad or narrow competitive scope:

- delivers acceptable quality but produces the product or service with lower costs than competitors
- sustains this cost gap
- achieves above-average profits from industry-average prices.

This cost advantage will be achieved by the effective management of the key determinants of costs.

The differentiation strategy
Similarly, Porter argues that the successful application of a differentiation strategy involves:

- the selection of one or more key characteristics which are widely valued by buyers (there are any number of opportunities relating to different needs and market segments)
- adding costs selectively in the areas perceived to be important to buyers, and charging a premium price in excess of the added costs.

The success of this strategy lies in finding opportunities for differentiation which cannot be matched easily by competitors, and being clear about the costs involved and the price potential. Costs in areas not perceived to be significant to buyers must be controlled, and in line with competitor costs, for otherwise above-average profits will not be achieved.

The successful implementation of both of these strategies therefore requires an understanding of where costs are incurred throughout the organization. Understanding costs and the search for appropriate cost reductions involves an appreciation of how costs should be attributed to the various discrete activities which comprise the value chain. Table 7.2 compares a possible cost breakdown for a manufacturing firm with that for a firm of professional accountants. If an analysis of the value chain is to be meaningful, it is important that the costs are

Table 7.2 Indicative cost breakdown of a manufacturing and a service business

	Manufacturing firm (% of total)	Professional firm of accountants (% of total)	
Primary activities			
Inbound logistics	4	8	(data collection for audits)
Operations	64	26	(actual auditing)
Outbound logistics	1	5	(report writing and presentations)
Marketing and sales	7	21	(getting new business)
Service	1	3	(general client liaison)
	77	63	
Support activities			
Procurement	1	1	
Technology development	10	8	(IT development)
Human resources management	2	16	
Firm's infrastructure	10	12	
	100	100	

These figures are only indicative, and should not be seen as targets for any particular firm.

genuinely attributed to the activities that generate them, and not simply apportioned in some convenient way, however difficult this might prove in practice. Given the figures in Table 7.2 one might question whether the manufacturing firm is spending enough on human resources management and marketing, and the accountancy practice too much.

Cost drivers

It is important to appreciate which cost drivers are the most significant. The following cost drivers can all influence the value chain.

- Economies of scale and potential experience and learning curve benefits.
- Capacity utilization, linked to production control and the existence of bottlenecks.
- Linkages – Time spent liaising with other departments can incur costs, but at the same time create savings and differentiation through interrelationships and shared activities.

- Interrelationships and shared activities – Shared activities, possibly a shared sales force, shared advertising or shared plant, can generate savings. Close links between activities or departments can increase quality and ensure that the needs of customers are matched more effectively.
- Integration – This incorporates the extent to which the organization is vertically integrated, say manufacturing its own component parts instead of assembling bought-in components, or even designing and manufacturing its own machinery. This again can influence costs and differentiation, and is an important element of the strategy of YKK, which is featured as an example later in this chapter.
- Timing – Buying and selling at the appropriate time. It is important to invest in stocks to ensure deliveries when customers want them, but at the same time stockholding costs must be monitored and controlled.
- Policies – Policy standards for procurement or production may be wrong. If they are set too low, quality may be lost and prove detrimental. If they are too high in relation to the actual needs of the market, costs are incurred unnecessarily.
- Location issues – This includes wage costs, which can vary between different regions, and the costs of supporting a particular organization structure.
- Institutional factors – Specific regulations concerning materials content or usage would be an example.

Porter argues that sustained competitive advantage requires effective control of the cost drivers, and that scale economies, learning, linkages, interrelationships and timing provide the key opportunities for creating advantage. In the case of a cost leadership strategy, the cost advantage is relative to the costs of competitors, and over time these could change if competitors concentrate on their cost drivers. Consequently, it is useful to attempt to monitor and predict how competitor costs might change in the future linked to any changes in their competitive and functional strategies.

Box 7.1 provides details of some cost drivers in the car industry.

STRATEGY IN ACTION – Box 7.1
Cost Drivers – An Application

A key challenge for motor car manufacturers is one of reducing new product development times and costs while increasing the number of models that they offer their customers. To succeed, a car must look and feel different from its rivals, but the manufacturers have found that they can save both time and cost if they share components which are hidden from view. Examples would include floor pans (or platforms), engines and

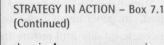

STRATEGY IN ACTION – Box 7.1
(Continued)

chassis. As a consequence, in recent years, there has been a tendency for new partnerships to emerge, as well as a number of important mergers.

Fiat, for example, owns the Alfa Romeo and Lancia marques and uses the same platforms for similar-sized models with the Fiat, Alfa Romeo and Lancia names.

Similarly, Volkswagen has acquired Audi, Seat and Skoda and adopts similar strategies. The platforms account for one-third of the costs incurred in designing a new car.

Manufacturers trade engines. Ford, for example, sells engines to other companies, as well as sharing components across the businesses it owns, which now include Jaguar, Land Rover and Volvo. In the same way, Peugeot diesel engines are common to Citroën and Peugeot cars.

Common problems in cost control through the value chain

It was mentioned above that it can prove difficult to assign costs to activities properly, and this is one of the difficulties likely to be encountered in using value-chain analysis as a basis for more effective cost management. Porter contends that there are several common pitfalls in managing costs for competitive advantage:

- misunderstanding of actual costs and misperceptions of the key cost drivers
- concentrating on manufacturing when cost savings are required. Often it is not the area to cut if quality is to be maintained, especially once a certain level of manufacturing efficiency has been achieved
- failing to take advantage of the potential gains from linkages
- ignoring competitor behaviour
- relying on small incremental cost savings when needs arise rather than introducing a long-term, permanently installed cost-management programme.

Differentiation opportunities

It has been mentioned on a number of occasions that competitive advantage through differentiation can arise from any and every area of the business. In relation to the component parts of the value chain, the following are examples of where differentiation might originate.

Primary activities

- *Inbound logistics* – careful and thoughtful handling to ensure that incoming materials are not damaged and are easily accessed when necessary, and the linking of purchases to production requirements, especially important in the case of JIT manufacturing systems.

- *Operations* – high quality; high output levels and few rejections; and delivery on time.
- *Outbound logistics* – rapid delivery when and where customers need the product or service.
- *Marketing and sales* – advertising closely tied to defined market segments; a well-trained, knowledgeable and motivated salesforce; and good technical literature, especially for industrial products.
- *Service* – rapid installation; speedy after-sales service and repair; and immediate availability of spare parts.

Support activities

- *Procurement* – purchasing high-quality materials (to assist operations); regional warehousing of finished products (to enable speedy delivery to customers).
- *Technology development* – the development of unique features, and new products and services; the use of IT to manage inbound and outbound logistics most effectively; and sophisticated market analyses to enable segmentation, targeting and positioning for differentiation.
- *Human resources management* – high-quality training and development; recruitment of the right people; and appropriate reward systems which help to motivate people.
- *Firm's infrastructure* – support from senior executives in customer relations; investment in suitable physical facilities to improve working conditions; and investment in carefully designed IT systems.

In searching for the most appropriate means of differentiating for competitive advantage it is important to look at which activities are the most essential as far as consumers and customers are concerned, and to isolate the key success factors. It is a search for opportunities to be different from competitors in ways which matter, and through this the creation of a superior competitive position. The Japanese zip manufacturer YKK, the world market leader, grew to enjoy a superior competitive position, and the company's strategy is analysed against the value chain in the next section. The underlying philosophy of YKK, the 'cycle of goodness', was illustrated in Chapter 4, Box 4.2.

An application of the value chain

YKK has arguably succeeded in creating both cost leadership and substantial differentiation with its corporate, competitive and functional strategies, and these

Figure 7.4

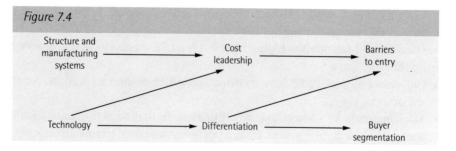

have resulted in effective barriers to entry into the industry and close relationships with customers. The idea is illustrated in Figure 7.4.

The essential components of the strategy, summarized below, are illustrated in Figure 7.5, which places them in the context of the value chain and highlights the linkages.

YKK is structured as a multiplant multinational company with both wholly owned subsidiary companies and joint ventures throughout the world. The latter organizations are primarily the result of local politics, particularly in low

Figure 7.5   YKK's competitive advantage and the value chain. Developed from Channon, DF and Mayeda, K (1979) *Yoshida Kogyo KK'A' and 'B' Case Studies.* Available from the European Case Clearing House and Ireland. The dashed lines illustrate the linkages.

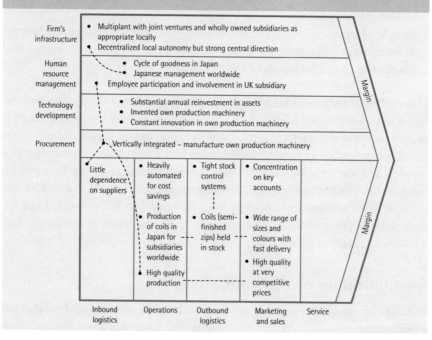

labour cost countries in the Far East. While the subsidiaries are decentralized and enjoy some local autonomy, they are invariably managed at the top by Japanese executives on a period of secondment. Consequently, there is substantial influence from the Japanese parent.

YKK invests a significant percentage of after-tax profits back in the business, and as a result is heavily automated and able to enjoy the benefits of the experience/learning curve. Moreover, YKK prices its finished products very competitively both to generate customer satisfaction and to create barriers to entry. The company is vertically integrated, designing and manufacturing its own production machinery, and this gives it a unique competitive edge. It is also particularly innovative as far as both machinery and finished products are concerned.

Coils of semifinished zips are produced in the Far East, particularly Japan, and exported to such countries as the UK, where they are cut to size and finished in response to customer orders. This results in both cost advantages and speedy deliveries from semifinished stocks. A wide range of colours and sizes is kept ready for finishing. In the UK the key garment manufacturers and the retail outlets that they serve are targeted by YKK and are given special service.

The 'cycle of goodness' philosophy has not been exported in its complete form, but employee relations are an important aspect of the human resources strategy. Participation and involvement are essential features, and total quality management is a key feature.

Conceptually, the value chain is a useful way of analysing resources and functions within the organization in the context of how they might individually contribute to competitive advantage. At the same time the linkages between them should be assessed, because it is from these interrelationships and linkages that synergy in the form of additional cost savings or differentiation is created.

To apply the value chain properly it is important also to allocate costs to activities and to evaluate whether costs could be saved in various areas or whether additional spending on certain activities might yield additional benefits by adding value in ways which are important to consumers. In practice it can be difficult to assign costs accurately. In this respect the actual application, rather than the concept, of the value chain is more applicable for managers than for students of this subject. In the author's experience, applications of the value chain pose difficulties for managers, primarily because the management accounting systems in many organizations do not readily provide the data in the form required. Developing this theme, Johnson and Kaplan (1987) contend that certain costs are extremely difficult to allocate to certain individual products, but they are the costs of activities which are very significant in relation to total quality and in turn competitive advantage. Machine failures are one example, and they affect a number of products and can mean that deliveries are late and possibly priorities are changed. But how should the costs be allocated? As production systems become increasingly sophisticated, overheads, as a proportion of total costs, increase relative to the direct costs of labour and materials. Genuinely allocating these production overheads is difficult.

Nevertheless, the value chain can provide an extremely useful framework for considering the activities involved in producing products and services and considering their significance for customers.

> We are students of Japan here in General Electric. We think they're marvellous, marvellous industrialists. We like their new product development, we like their speed, we like their quality focus. I put them at the pinnacle, and we're working every day to learn everything we can from them.
>
> *John F Welch, Chairman and CEO, General Electric*

Reputation and Branding

Reputation and branding are clearly linked but they are not one and the same. In a sense, a brand is a label that is attached to an organization's reputation. Kay (1993) contends that reputation is a key element of differentiation and that both reputation and branding are key intangible resources. What matters with differentiation is the customers' perception of the difference and what it means or conveys. It is, therefore, a qualitative indicator of quality; where quantitative measurement is difficult it can be a significant variable in decision making and choice.

The reputation of Sir Richard Branson's Virgin brand has allowed him to diversify into a wide range of activities – customer confidence in the brand provides reassurance and allows him entry into areas where he has little if any previous experience or expertise. It is critically important, therefore, never to disappoint customers in ways which tarnish a reputation; somewhat paradoxically, this means that there can be a huge downside risk for companies with the strongest reputations if they make strategic errors of judgement.

In similar vein, a strong reputation provides a 'safe choice' for customers who are new entrants to a market. A strong reputation therefore can help to sustain and build a strong position in a market. Moreover, it can sometimes be used to justify a premium price.

Famous-name endorsements provide an ideal opportunity for enhancing a company's reputation. Ownership of an endorsed product 'makes a statement' about a person. People hold certain personalities in very high regard and would find it hard to imagine that they would endorse anything that was not good, even the best in the market. Whether such people actually use the products and services that they endorse is an entirely different matter!

Branding

Many differentiated products, and some services, are identified by brand names. These brand names, and/or the identity of the companies that own them, convey an image to customers. Simply, brands reflect reputations; and advertising is often used to create and reinforce this image and reputation. As competition intensifies, more and more products are perceived as commodities, sold essentially on price. When this happens, differentiation and branding become increasingly significant. The product needs a clear brand identity; a supportive corporate image, a company brand, is also valuable.

Brands add value, possibly the promise of some particular satisfaction or experience, a 'guarantee' of a specific level of quality, or reliability. Consequently, a brand can be seen as an actual product or service augmented by some additional added value. Branding is important and valuable; the drive to establish and maintain a recognized brand image can bring about differentiation and innovation. Nescafé, for example, has had several variants and improvements over the years. However, the value added must be real, as informed customers today will quickly see through any marketing hype. Moreover, the distinctiveness will not be achieved without investment, in both research and development and advertising, an issue which is taken up later.

Ideally, successful branding will generate customer loyalty and repeat purchases, enable higher prices and margins, and provide a springboard for additional products and services. Customers expect to find the leading brand names widely available in distribution outlets but, in the case of, say, grocery products, the supermarkets will typically only offer the number one and number two brands alongside their own-label competitor. In the case of groceries, strong branding has been essential for enabling the leading manufacturers to contain the growing power of the leading supermarket chains. Nevertheless, branding has not exempted them from tight pricing strategies. Edwin Artzt, until the mid-1990s a powerful and renowned Chief Executive of Procter and Gamble, has stated that 'winning companies offer lower prices, better quality, continuous improvement and/or high profits to retailers'.

The quality of own-label products has increased, and consequently the magnitude of the premium that customers will pay for the leading manufacturer brand has declined in recent years. Procter and Gamble, which is not alone in this strategy, has adopted perpetual 'everyday low prices' for all of its products. Marlboro cigarettes, the world's leading cigarette brand, were reduced in price dramatically in the mid-1990s. In the competitive food sector, product innovation, quality, specific features and, to a lesser extent, packaging are seen as the most effective means of distinguishing brands from own-label alternatives.

Examples of leading brands

- *Persil* and *Pampers*: brand names not used in conjunction with the manufacturer's name – they are produced by Unilever and Procter and Gamble, respectively.
- *Coca-Cola*: manufacturer's name attributed to a product.
- *Cadbury's Dairy Milk* and *Barclaycard Visa*: the first is a combination of a company and a product name, the second a combination of an organization (Barclays) and a service provided by a separate business.
- *St Michael*: the personalized brand name used historically on all products sold by Marks and Spencer.
- *Hoover*: a company name which historically became irrevocably associated with a particular product, although it is just one of a range of products produced by Hoover.

Several large organizations have, through strategic acquisitions and investments in brands, established themselves as global corporations. Examples include:

- *Unilever*: now owns a variety of food (Bird's Eye, Batchelors, Walls, John West, Boursin, Blue Band, Flora), household goods (Shield soap, Persil, Lux and Surf detergents) and cosmetics (Brut, Fabergé and Calvin Klein) brands.
- *Philip Morris*: US tobacco company which has acquired General Foods (US; Maxwell House coffee) and Jacobs Suchard (Switzerland; confectionery and coffee).
- *Nestlé*: including Chambourcy (France), Rowntree (UK) and Buitoni (Italy).
- *LVMH*: discussed earlier, in Chapter 5.

These companies can afford substantial investments in research and development to innovate and:

- strengthen the brand, say by extending the range of products carrying the name
- develop new opportunities, for example, Mars Bars Ice Cream, which was launched simultaneously in 15 European countries and priced at a premium over normal ice-cream bars
- transform competition in the market. Pampers disposable nappies have been developed into a very successful range of segmented products selling throughout the USA and Europe.

Brand names are clearly an asset for an organization. The value of the brand, the so-called brand equity, relates to the totality of all the stored beliefs, likes/dislikes and behaviours associated with it. Customer attitudes are critical; so too are those of distributors. The fact that a brand can command a certain amount of shelf space in all leading stores carries a value. However, creating and maintaining the image is expensive. It has been estimated that manufacturers spend on average 7% of sales revenue to support the top ten leading brands, covering all product groups; this percentage increases as the brand recognition factor decreases. Because of this, manufacturers need to control the number of brands that they market at any time; Procter and Gamble withdrew over 25% of their brands in the 1990s. Similarly, new product launches need to be managed effectively.

There is a so-far unresolved debate concerning how these assets might be properly valued in a company balance sheet. In the mid-1990s the US magazine *Financial Week* postulated that the world's most valuable brand name was Marlboro (owned by Philip Morris) and that it was then worth in excess of $30 million. In terms of monetary value, Coca-Cola was perceived to be second, although it is generally accepted that it is better known. The most valuable European brand is Nestlé's Nescafé; the three leading British brands (worldwide) are Johnnie Walker Red Label whisky (owned by Guinness), Guinness itself and Smirnoff Vodka (Diageo). Where the most recognized brand names are tied to high market shares and above-average margins, they are typically valued at over twice their annual revenues.

Relationship marketing

Branding helps to establish, build and cement relationships among manufacturers, their customers and their distributors. The term 'relationship marketing' is used to reinforce the argument that marketing should be perceived as the management of a network of relationships between the brand and its various customers. Marketing, therefore, aims to enhance brand equity and thus ensure continued satisfaction for customers and increased profits for the brand owner. Implicit in this is the realization that new customers are harder, and more expensive, to find than existing ones are to retain. This potent mix of brand identity and customer care is clearly related to the whole service package offered by manufacturers to their customers, and to total quality management.

We always travel with our teddy bears. When we got back to our room at the hotel we saw that the maid had arranged our bears very comfortably in a chair. The bears were holding hands.

I needed a few more minutes to decide on dinner. The waitress said: 'If you would read the menu and not the road map, you would know what you want to order'.

Binter et al. (1990)

Summary

The *opportunity-driven* approach to strategy starts with the environment, and the relevant markets, and looks into emerging trends, possible new opportunities and potential threats. All competitors in an industry can, should and invariably will carry out an analysis along these lines. Some will see opportunities where others, provided with the same data or information, will miss them. Critically, some will be in a better position than their rivals to deal with opportunities and threats.

Acquiring, deploying and exploiting key resources in an individual and effective way is the source of important differences and, in turn, competitive advantage. The resource-based view of strategy looks at how organizations *individually* respond, and at how their core competencies and strategic capabilities determine their success as a competitor.

A simple *resource audit* is an attempt to assess the strengths and weaknesses of an organization; typically it will be carried in conjunction with an assessment of opportunities and threats. However, any evaluation should be relative. The assessment should be in the context of, first, the key success factors for the markets and industries in question and, secondly, the comparable strengths and weaknesses of competitors for the same customers.

Strategic architecture refers to the linkages inside the organization (between different divisions, departments and managers) and the relationships, possibly partnerships, that an organization has with other members of the relevant value chain, such as suppliers and distributors. Synergy, mutual dependency and trust are key issues in the relationships.

Michael Porter has provided a useful value-chain framework for helping to understand where differences are created, where costs are incurred and how synergy might be generated through linkages. His value chain comprises:

five primary activities – inbound logistics;
                                      operations;
                                      outbound logistics;
                                      marketing and sales
                                      service; and

four support activities – procurement;
                                      technology development;
                                      human resource management;
                                      the firm's infrastructure.

Organizations must understand and manage their cost drivers. They should not attempt to 'cut corners' with things that really matter for customers; at the same time, they should not incur unnecessary costs with things that do not add value in ways that customers believe are important.

The value of a strong reputation must not be underestimated. A sound corporate reputation reassures customers. It generates sales and, very significantly, repeat sales. It can enable price premiums. It is a crucially important intangible resource. It is frequently manifested in a strong, visible and readily identified brand name.

References

Binter, MJ, Booms, B and Tetreault, MS (1990) The service encounter: diagnosing favourable and unfavourable incidents, *Journal of Marketing*, 54, January.

Buckingham, M and Coffman, C (1999) *First, Break all the Rules*, Simon and Schuster.

Johnson, HT and Kaplan, RS (1987) *Relevance Lost: The Rise and Fall of Management Accounting*, Harvard Business School Press.

Kay, JA (1993) *Foundations of Corporate Success*, Oxford University Press.

Kelly, FJ and Kelly, HM (1987) *What they Really Teach you at the Harvard Business School*, Piatkus.

Porter, ME (1980) *Competitive Strategy: Techniques for Analysing Industries and Competitors*, Free Press.

Porter, ME (1985) *Competitive Advantage: Creating and Sustaining Superior Performance*, Free Press.

Prahalad, CK and Hamel, G (1990) The core competency of the corporation, *Harvard Business Review*, May/June.

Preece, S, Fleisher, C and Toccacelli, J (1995) Building a reputation along the value chain at Levi Strauss, *Long Range Planning*, 28, 6.

Test your knowledge of this chapter with our online quiz at: http://www.thomsonlearning.co.uk

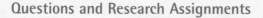

Questions and Research Assignments

TEXT RELATED

1. What are the opportunity-driven and resource-based views of strategy? Where and why are they different? Why is it important for organizations to embrace both views simultaneously?

2. Think about your own buying habits and choices. Where do you specifically choose high-profile branded items, and where are you less concerned? Why? What do you think this behaviour is saying about you?

Internet and Library Projects

1. Using the Internet to look at the current status of Dyson and the other main manufacturers of vacuum cleaners, to what extent has James Dyson transformed an industry? How has he now extended the product range for his dual cyclone cleaners? In what ways are his washing machines different?

   Dyson   http://www.dyson.com

2. Selecting an organization of your choice, and ideally one with which you are familiar, carry out a resource audit. Make sure that you take account of industry key success factors and competitors' relative strengths in your evaluation.

3. Using the same organization, apply Porter's value chain. As far as you are able, and accepting that there may be elements of subjectivity, allocate the costs and consider whether your breakdown matches your initial expectations. Where are the all-important linkages?

An Introduction to Strategy Creation and Strategic Change

Introduction

Strategy Creation

Entrepreneurs and Entrepreneurship

Visionary Leadership

Changing Strategies

Summary

This chapter recaps on themes introduced in Chapter 1. Figure 1.8 summarized the situation, by showing the linkages between the ideas of intended strategy (through strategic planning and entrepreneurial leadership) and emergent strategies when intended strategies are changed incrementally as they are implemented and new strategies are created as managers adapt in a changing environment.

Chapters 9 and 10 examine strategic planning and emergent strategy in greater detail and so this chapter includes a discussion of entrepreneurial and visionary strategic leadership. We conclude with a brief consideration of why strategies and the prevailing mode of strategy creation need to change at certain critical times.

The opening case illustrates how the three broad modes of strategy creation can be seen working together in one organization, McDonald's.

Case Study 8: McDonald's

McDonald's, built by a visionary, the late Ray Kroc, has become a very successful international company, with outlets in nearly 120 countries. Its products are popular with large numbers of customers, and certainly not just children. In 1996, according to Interbrand consultants, McDonald's ousted Coca-Cola as the world's best-known brand.

Ray Kroc has been described by *Time Magazine* as 'one of the most influential builders of the twentieth century'. Few children refuse a McDonald's burger – and its golden arches logo symbolizes American enterprise. Kroc was a truly opportunistic and focused entrepreneur who built an organizational network of dedicated franchisees. Yet his entrepreneurial contribution began late in life and the McDonald's chain of hamburger restaurants was certainly not his own invention. Instead he saw – really he stumbled on – an opportunity where others missed the true potential for an idea. Once he had seen the opportunity he rigorously applied business acumen and techniques to focus on providing value for his customers. By standardizing his product and restaurants he was able to guarantee high and consistent quality at relatively low cost. Kroc was also wise enough to use the expertise that his franchisees were developing.

In 1955, at the age of 52, Ray Kroc completed 30 years as a salesman, mainly selling milkshake machines to various types of restaurant across America, including hamburger joints. His customers included the McDonald brothers who, having moved from New Hampshire to Hollywood but failing to make any headway in the movie business, had opened a small drive-through restaurant in San Bernadino, California. They offered a limited menu, paper plates and plastic cups, and guaranteed the food in 60 seconds. When their success drove them to buy eight milkshake machines, instead of the two their small size would logically suggest, Ray Kroc's interest was alerted and he set off to see the restaurant. Kroc's vision was for a national chain which could benefit from organization and business techniques. He bought out the McDonald brothers and set about building a global empire. After he officially retired from running the business, and until his death in 1984, Ray Kroc stayed on as President and visited two or three different restaurants every week. He saw himself as the 'company's conscience', checking standards against his QSCV vision – quality food, fast and friendly service, clean restaurants and value for money.

By the late 1990s McDonald's had well over 20,000 restaurants worldwide; approximately 60% are in America. Up to 3000 new ones have been opened in a single year. The basic formula works as well in Moscow and Beijing as it does in the USA. Although the products available are broadly similar in the USA and Europe, menus are seen as flexible in other parts of the world. Japanese stores, for example, feature Teriyaki Burgers, sausage patties with teriyaki sauce. Half the stores are franchises; the rest are mainly joint ventures but some 2500 are company owned.

The growth and success in an industry where 'fast food is a by-word for low wages and an unskilled temporary workforce' is not accidental. It has been very carefully planned and managed, although McDonald's relies a lot on the people at the sharp end. Employees are often young; they work a closely prescribed system, operating internationally established rules and procedures for preparing, storing and selling food. Various incentive schemes are practised. Labour turnover is high, however, and consequently McDonald's has its critics as well as its supporters. Nevertheless, it is obvious that some competitors seek to emulate McDonald's in a number of ways: products, systems and employee attitudes.

Our competitors can copy many of our secrets, but they cannot duplicate our pride, our enthusiasm and our dedication for this business.

McDonald's is profitable because it is efficient and productive; and it stays ahead of its competitors by being innovative and looking for new opportunities.

A lot of the developments are planned and imaginative. McDonald's does not move into new countries without thorough investigation of the potential; the same is true for new locations. There are now McDonald's branches in American hospitals, military bases and zoos; worldwide they can be found in airport terminals, motorway service stations, supermarkets (Tesco), and on board cruise ships and Swiss trains.

McDonald's relies heavily on its suppliers for fresh food; again, arrangements are carefully planned, monitored and controlled. The in-store systems for cooking and running branches are very tight, to ensure that products and service standards are the same worldwide. New product development has utilized all of the group's resources. The Big Mac, which was introduced nationally in the USA in 1968, was the idea of a Pittsburgh franchisee who had seen a similar product elsewhere. The aim was to broaden the customer base and make McDonald's more adult orientated. The company allowed the franchisee to try the product in his restaurant in 1967, although there was some initial resistance amongst executives who wished to retain a narrow product line, and it proved highly successful.

Egg McMuffins in the early 1970s were a response to a perceived opportunity – a breakfast menu and earlier opening times. Previously the restaurants opened at 11.00 am. Although the opportunity was appreciated the development of the product took place over 4 years, and the final launch version was created by a Santa Barbara franchisee who had to invent a new cooking utensil.

When Chicken McNuggets were launched in 1982 it was the first time that small boneless pieces of chicken had been mass produced. The difficult development of the product was carried out in conjunction with a supplier and there was immediate competitive advantage. The product was not readily copied. From being essentially a hamburger chain McDonald's quickly became number 2 to Kentucky Fried Chicken for fast-food chicken meals.

McDonald's continually tries out new menus, such as pizzas, in order to extend its share of the overall fast-food market, but for many years it avoided any diversification, nor did it offer any different 'food concept'. To enhance its image of good value, and to compete in a very dynamic industry, McDonald's offers 'extra-value meals', special combinations at low prices. There is innovation and the ability to create and adapt strategies to capitalize on opportunities.

In addition, McDonald's is a 'penny profit' business. It takes hard work and attention to detail to be financially successful. Store managers must do two things well: control costs and increase sales. Increased sales come from the products, certainly, but also from service. Cost control is vital, but it must not be achieved by compromising product quality, customer service or restaurant appearance. Instead, it requires a focus on productivity and attention to detail. Success with these strategies has been achieved partly through serious attempts to share learning and best practice throughout the global network.

The company is an industry leader and contends that there are six main reasons behind this:

- Visibility: to this end substantial resources are devoted to marketing. The golden arches symbol is instantly recognizable.
- Ownership or control of real-estate sites: McDonald's argues that this factor differentiates it from its competitors who lease more.
- Its commitment to franchising and supplier partnerships.
- It is worldwide, with restaurants in some 118 countries, and uses local managers and employees.
- The structure is very decentralized but lines of responsibility and accountability are clear.
- It is a growth company.

By the mid-1990s, the company held 40% of the US market for its products, and yet its burgers were not coming out as superior to Wendy's and Burger King in taste tests. In addition, a special promotion in America, based around burgers for 55 cents each, had not proved successful because of the conditions attached to the offer. A new spicier – and premium price – burger for adults, the Arch Deluxe, had not taken off. New restaurants in the USA were beginning to take sales away from existing ones, rather than generating new business. Established franchisees were hardly delighted! A leading franchisee pressure group expressed the view that the entrepreneurial drive of founder Ray Kroc (who died in 1984) had been lost and replaced by a non-entrepreneurial bureaucracy. This change of culture was one reason why McDonald's recently pursued a libel action in the UK against two environmentalists: a case where McDonald's won the legal argument but lost the accompanying public-relations battle.

After a period of criticism and disappointing results McDonald's has, however, fought back courageously. With franchisees paying half the costs, new computerized kitchen equipment has been systematically installed in its 25,000 restaurants, allowing fast cooking to order. Ready-to-serve meals no longer have to stand for a few minutes on heated trays. In addition, McDonald's has begun to experiment with new low-risk opportunities for its competencies in supply-chain management, franchising, promotion and merchandising by acquiring new restaurant chains. Included are a group of 18 Mexican restaurants in Colorado, 143 pizza outlets in Ohio, a chain of 23 Aroma coffee shops in London and the Boston Market chain of chicken restaurants. The US operations have been split into five independent geographical regions.

Ray Kroc has been dead for over 15 years but his legacy lives on in a brand name that is recognized and revered around the world.

QUESTIONS: How does McDonald's create value for its customers? What are its important competencies and capabilities? To what extent do you think issues of strategic leadership and culture have influenced its growth and prosperity? Where can we see evidence of strategic planning and emergent strategy?

McDonald's   http://www.mcdonalds.com

We're not necessarily great overall strategists [at Virgin] ... we often do things and then work out afterwards what the overall strategy was.
Sir Richard Branson, Chairman, Virgin Group

If you're in the penalty area and aren't quite sure what to do with the ball, just stick it in the net and we'll discuss your options afterwards.
Bill Shankly (1914–1981), once Manager, Liverpool Football Club

Introduction

Football, or really any professional sport, provides a useful metaphor for understanding strategy creation. Teams – or, in the case of sports such as tennis, individuals – will begin all important matches with a game plan. They will have studied their opponents, assessed their relative strengths and weaknesses, thought about their natural game and about how they might approach this particular match, and worked out how they might be beaten. Led by the manager, coaches will have helped the players with the analysis and the tactics. Normally, the objective will be about winning. In some instances it can be about not losing (a subtle difference) or winning might be qualified by adding a 'means' objective related to approach and style. These game plans will undoubtedly *inform* the players, but it may be impossible to carry them out to the letter. Unexpected tactics from their opponents will ensure that this is the case.

Once the game is underway, the intended plans and strategies will be adjusted – there will be incremental changes. Broadly, however, they may well be implemented, certainly as long as the game is being won and not lost. At the same time, new, unexpected opportunities will be presented during the game, and good teams will be able to adapt.

Of course, 'the best laid plans o' mice and men gang aft a gley'. The opponents may prove stronger and more disciplined than predicted. They may take the lead and seize control of the game. In this case, there will be a need to adapt to the threats and change the tactics. When this happens, the ability to remain cohesive and disciplined as a team is essential.

At any time there is always the opportunity for individuals to show initiative and to shine. A strong, experienced and maybe visionary team manager (the strategic leader in this example) can act as a master tactician and an inspiration both beforehand and from the sidelines during the game. Talented players, with individual goals, spectacular saves or important tackles at key moments, will often make important contributions and, by doing so, encourage their colleagues also to make the extra effort that 'tips the balance'. As they always say, a game is not lost until the final whistle: teams often do go one or two goals down before recovering to win. Tennis players do not have to win the first set to win a match.

Strategy Creation

Chapter 1 explained how strategy creation involves three strands:

- *planning*, both systematic and formal strategic planning systems and informal, cerebral planning
- *vision* and visionary leadership, and
- *emergent strategies* – incremental changes to predetermined, intended strategies and adaptive additions with learning and responsiveness to opportunities and threats.

Figure 8.1 reiterates that strategy and strategic management embrace the corporate portfolio of businesses and the search for competitiveness and competitive advantage with each business, product and service, and that this competitiveness arises from the functional activities that an organization undertakes. Visionary ideas pull the organization forward. Where these result in significant changes, they will often be associated with the strategic leader. Planning pushes everything forward. Emergent changes, improvements and adjustments – intrapreneurial changes initiated and implemented by individual managers throughout the organization – support and complete the process.

Figure 8.1 Strategy creation.

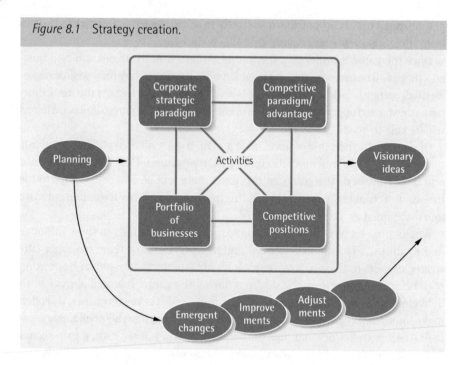

If all strategies were planned formally, then organizations would be able to look back and review the decisions that they had made over a period of time. At some stage in the past there would have been a clear recorded statement of intent which matched these events closely. In reality, stated plans and actual events are unlikely to match closely. In addition to strategies that have emerged and been introduced entrepreneurially, there are likely to have been expectations and planned possible strategies that have not proved to be viable. However, broad directions can be established and planned and then detailed strategies allowed to emerge as part of an ongoing learning experience within the organization.

Idenburg (1993) presents these ideas in a slightly modified way, distinguishing between the following strategies.

- Formal planning systems, through which clear objectives should lead to intended strategies.
- Learning or real-time planning, which represents a formal approach to adaptive strategy creation. Managers meet regularly, both formally and informally, and debate how key strategic issues are changing and emerging. Objectives and strategies will be changed in a turbulent environment.
- Incremental change and logical incrementalism. The organization will have a clear mission and directional objectives, and it will be recognized that pursu-

ing these requires flexibility. Managers will be encouraged to experiment with new ideas and strategies, learning and adapting all the time. Internal politics and systems will play an important role in this mode.

- Emergent strategies. Specific objectives will not be set; instead, organizations will be seen as fully flexible, 'muddling through' environmental turbulence. Opportunism, being ready and able to 'seize the main chance', is critical.

Mintzberg and Waters (1985) and Bailey and Johnson (1992) have also shown how the simple three-mode categorization might be extended, but the underlying implications remain unchanged. A number of points should be noted:

- Although it is not made explicit, some strategies, especially those formulated by a visionary entrepreneur, attempt to shape and change the environment, rather than react to changing circumstances.
- The organization structure and the actual planning process will affect the nature of planned objectives and strategies. Wherever a group of managers is involved in planning, their personal values and relative power will be reflected. See Cyert and March's behavioural theory in Chapter 3.
- Adaptive changes will also reflect the values, power and influence of managers.

It is important to appreciate that the three modes described above are not mutually exclusive, and that one mode frequently leads on from another. The implementation of visionary ideas and strategies typically requires careful planning, for example, and this will invariably bring about incremental changes. In Chapter 1 it was confirmed that all three modes will be found in an organization simultaneously, but the mix and prioritization will be particular to an individual company. This key point is illustrated in Figure 8.2. It was also emphasized that individual managers, depending largely on their position within the organization, will not necessarily agree on the relative significance of each mode. It is essential that managers understand and support the processes.

The mixed approach is both sensible and justifiable. In some manufacturing industries the time taken from starting to plan a substantive innovatory change to peak profit performance can be ten years. This needs planning, although the concept may be visionary. Throughout the implementation there has to be adaptive and incremental learning and change. Where strategies are being changed in a dynamic environment it is also useful, on occasions, to evaluate the current situation and assess the implications. This could well be part of an annual planning cycle.

Case Study 8 looks at how the three modes can be seen in practice in McDonald's. McDonald's has a clear and understood vision which also embraces its thousands of franchisees worldwide. In the late 1990s its annual rate of global expansion grew to over 3000 new restaurants; this requires

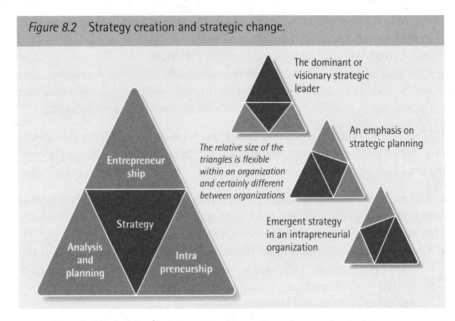

Figure 8.2   Strategy creation and strategic change.

Table 8.1   Levels of strategy and modes of strategy creation

| | | Levels of strategy |
Modes of strategy creation	Corporate strategy	Competitive and functional strategies
Planning	Formal planning systems	Planning the detail for implementing corporate strategies
Visionary	Seizing opportunities – limited planning only	Innovation throughout the organization
Adaptive/Incremental	Reacting to environmental opportunities and threats, e.g. businesses for sale; divestment opportunity	Reacting to competitor threats and new environmental opportunities
		Learning and adjustment as planned and visionary strategies are implemented

careful planning. This planning, together with arrangements with building contractors and suppliers, has also allowed McDonald's to cut 30% off the cost of opening every new restaurant, through the use of more efficient building systems, standardized equipment and global sourcing. As a consequence, it can now afford to open restaurants in locations which, in the past, had been seen as uneconomical. Given the intense competition in the fast-food industry, it is also essential for McDonald's to remain flexible and responsive, internationally, nationally and locally.

Table 8.1 further relates these themes to the three levels of strategy: corporate, competitive and functional. In large organizations much of the responsibility for corporate strategic change will be centralized at the head office, although the businesses and divisions can be involved or consulted. Competitive and functional change decisions are more likely to be decentralized, but again, not exclusively. Corporate policies can require or constrain changes at these levels.

Planning and strategy creation

Mintzberg (1989) contends that the strategic leader should be the chief architect, in conjunction with planners, of corporate plans; the process should be explicit, conscious and controlled; and issues of implementation should be incorporated. Essentially, analysis leads to choice, which leads on to implementation. The process is sequential:

$$Analysis \rightarrow Choice \rightarrow Implementation$$

Certain organizations might claim that detailed long-term planning is essential for them. An airline, for example, must plan capacity several years ahead because of the long delivery lead times for new aeroplanes and the related need to manage cash flow and funding. In addition, resources must be co-ordinated on an international scale. While planes are utilized on most days and fly as many hours in the day as possible, crews work only limited hours, and typically finish a flight or series of flights in a location which is different from their starting point.

However, Mintzberg argues that this is planning the implications and consequences of the strategic perspective, not necessarily the perspective itself. Detailed planning of this type should not inhibit creativity concerning the perspective.

Planning of some form will always be required in large organizations. It forces thinking and enables and supports resource allocation and budgeting. However, the extent and nature of the overall planning contribution will relate to the industry and the environment and be affected by both leadership and culture.

The visionary mode

A visionary strategic leader who formulates strategic change in his or her mind may only be semiconscious of the process involved. He or she will clearly understand the current and desired strategic perspective, and ideally the culture of the organization will be one in which other managers are receptive of the changes in perspective. The personality and charisma of the leader, and the ability to sell his or her ideas, will be crucial issues, and as speed of action, timing and commitment are typical features the strategy can prove highly successful.

The visionary or entrepreneurial approach suggests that the strategic leader is very aware of the strengths, weaknesses and capabilities of the organization; the current matching with the environment; a wide range of possibly diverse opportunities for change; and the likely reaction of managers to certain changes. Similar to the 'bird approach' described in Chapter 1, Box 1.3, the selection is made somewhat arbitrarily without careful and detailed planning, and therefore an element of risk is involved. This informality in the process is important to allow for creativity and flair. The strategic leader then sells the idea to other managers, and the strategy is implemented and changed incrementally as experience is gained and learning takes place. In other words, the vision acts as an umbrella and within it specific decisions can be taken which lead to the emergence of more detailed strategies.

With this mode it is difficult to separate analysis and choice, so that

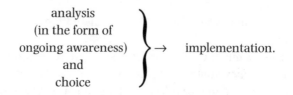

$$
\left.\begin{array}{c}
\text{analysis} \\
\text{(in the form of} \\
\text{ongoing awareness)} \\
\text{and} \\
\text{choice}
\end{array}\right\} \rightarrow \quad \text{implementation.}
$$

Dangers

The success of this mode in the long term depends on the continued strategic awareness and insight of the strategic leader, particularly if the organization revolves around a visionary leader and becomes heavily dependent upon him or her. People may be visionary for only a certain length of time, and then they become blinkered by the success of current strategies and adopt tunnel vision, or they somehow lose the ability to spot good new opportunities. It might also be argued that, if luck is involved, their luck runs out. The problems occur if the strategic leader has failed to develop a strong organization with other visionaries who can take over.

On a current basis the strategy requires management as well as leadership. In other words, managers within the organization must be able to capitalize on the new opportunities and develop successful competitive positions within the revised strategic perspective. This might involve an element of planning; equally it might rely more on the adaptive approach described below. We explore these issues in greater detail later in the chapter.

The adaptive and incremental modes

Under the adaptive and incremental modes strategies are formed and evolve as managers throughout the organization learn from their experiences and adapt to changing circumstances. They perceive how tasks might be performed, and products and services managed, more effectively, and they make changes. They also respond to pressures and new strategic issues. There will again be elements of semiconsciousness and informality in the process. Some changes will be gradual, others spontaneous, and they will act collectively to alter and improve competitive positions. As individual decisions will often involve only limited change, little risk and possibly the opportunity to change back, this is essentially the 'squirrel approach' described in Chapter 1, Box 1.3. Managers learn whether their choice is successful or unsuccessful through implementation.

Hence this mode implies limited analysis preceding choice and implementation, which are intertwined and difficult to separate. A proper analysis follows in the form of an evaluation of the relative success:

$$\text{Analysis} \rightarrow \text{Choice and}$$
$$\text{(limited)} \quad \text{implementation} \rightarrow \text{Analysis.}$$

Adaptive strategic change requires decentralization and clear support from the strategic leader, who also seeks to stay aware of progress and link the changes into an integrated pattern. It is often based on setting challenges for managers: challenging them to hit targets, improve competitiveness and stretch or exploit internal systems and policies to obtain the best possible returns. The greater the challenge, the more care needs to go into establishing a suitable reward system. When the structure enables effective adaptive change, then intrapreneurship can be fostered throughout the organization and individual managers can be allowed the necessary freedom. However, if adaptive changes are taking place in a highly centralized organization, and despite rigid policies, there is a problem which should be investigated. The major potential drawbacks concern the ability of the organization and the strategic leader to synthesize all the changes into a coherent pattern, and the willingness and ability of individual managers to take an organization-wide perspective. This latter point is examined later in Chapter 10.

Information technology provides opportunities for collecting and co-ordinating information and should be harnessed to support decentralization. In

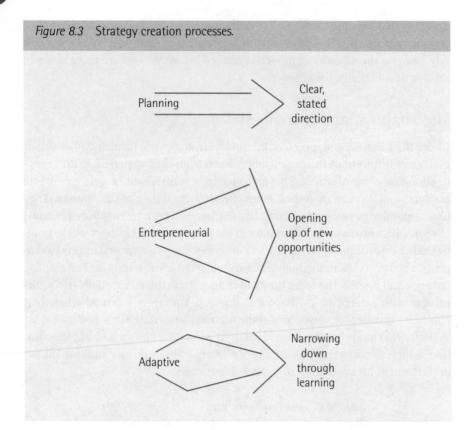

Figure 8.3   Strategy creation processes.

addition, team briefing can prove useful. Here, a strategic leader would regularly brief his or her senior executives, discussing progress and any proposed changes to the corporate strategy and policies. On a cascading basis managers would quickly and systematically communicate this information downwards and throughout the organization by meeting teams of people responsible to them. The secret lies in using team briefing meetings also to communicate information upwards by reporting on new strategic issues and how they are being handled.

Figure 8.3 provides a short summary of the processes. Planning is shown at the top as a 'closed funnel' activity. The entrepreneurial, visionary style is more one of diverging and opening things up, widening the scope of the ideas considered. Adaptive strategy (responding to new opportunities) is, conversely, illustrated as a convergent process. Here, learning and synthesis are required to form cohesive patterns which bind the emerging strategies. In the entrepreneurial mode, planning is required during implementation; and in the adaptive mode, individual managers are doing their own planning, sometimes informally, sometimes more formally.

Entrepreneurs and Entrepreneurship

Bolton and Thompson (2000) define an entrepreneur as a person who 'habitually creates and innovates to build something of recognized value around perceived opportunities'. Entrepreneurs can be found starting organizations, running organizations and working in organizations as employees. In the latter case they are typically called intrapreneurs, i.e. internal entrepreneurs. Two issues now need to be examined:

- the strategic leader as an entrepreneur
- whether the strategic leader has built an organization which fosters intrapreneurship.

Strategic management is concerned with environmental fit and it is important to achieve congruence between environment, values and resources for both existing and potential future products and services. Figure 8.4 revisits the model of E–V–R congruence and presents it in a marginally different way, one which implies action rather than being an expression of a state. The environment is presented as a number of windows of opportunity, and resources are represented by organizational competencies and capabilities. The argument is that entrepreneurship in the organization, both at the level of the leader and throughout the whole organization, is required to ensure that resources are developed and changed and used to exploit the windows of opportunity ahead of rival organizations.

The management of existing businesses should ensure that attention is focused on costs and prices (as they determine profits) and on ways of reducing costs by improving productivity. Technology changes, and new operating systems, may

Figure 8.4   E–V–R congruence and entrepreneurship.

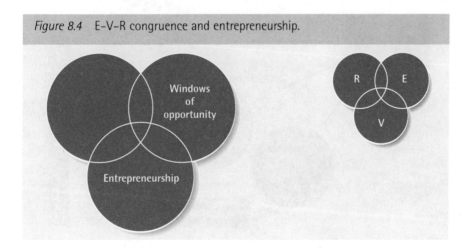

reduce costs; equally they may improve product quality for which premium prices might be charged.

Future developments might concern new products (or services) or new markets or both, and they might involve diversification. For different alternatives the magnitude of the change implied and the risk involved will vary.

For both areas the changes that take place can be gradual or incremental, or they can be more dynamic or individually significant. Real innovation can be costly in terms of investment required, and consequently can involve a high level of risk, but sometimes it is necessary.

Figure 8.5 shows alternative development paths for a business. We normally think of entrepreneurs as the people who develop new ideas and new businesses, but there are different views on the implications of an entrepreneurial start-up. Schumpeter (1949), for example, argues that entrepreneurs bring innovative ideas into a situation of some stability and create disequilibrium. The 'Austrian School' of economists (see Kirzner, 1973) suggests that entrepreneurs create equi-

Figure 8.5   Business development paths.

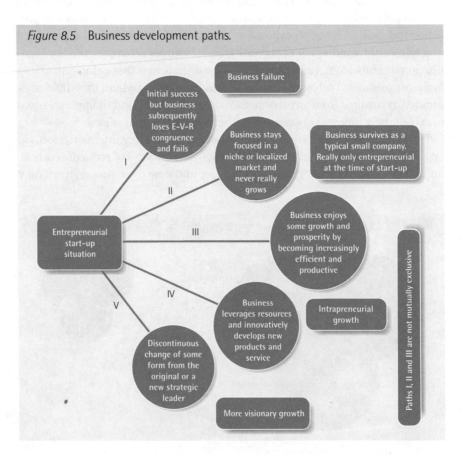

librium (in the form of E–V–R congruence) by matching demand and supply in a creative way. However, it is the path of future progress that really matters.

From its initial position the business could at first be successful but then fade away without further innovation and renewal (path I). The original window of opportunity closes and the business fails to find or capitalize on a new one.

Some businesses never really improve and grow (path II), sometimes by deliberate choice, sometimes through lack of insight and awareness; however, they survive as long as they can satisfy a particular niche or localized market. If one window of opportunity closes they find a new one, but in this respect they are more likely to be reactive rather than proactive. It is quite feasible for path II businesses to *expand*, as distinct from true growth based on improvement and excellence. In reality, many businesses fall into this category. They are the archetypal small business – and they are not run by 'real' entrepreneurs as they fail the 'habitual' requirement included in the definition. They can legitimately be called 'lifestyle businesses' and their founders are sometimes described as lifestyle entrepreneurs.

Paths III and IV feature more proactive entrepreneurial businesses which *grow* via productivity improvements and/or by leveraging their resources to develop new products and service opportunities. Sometimes, but certainly not always, such businesses will be decentralized, empowered and *intrapreneurial*.

Path V implies discontinuous change and requires visionary leadership, from either the original founding entrepreneur or a new strategic leader, which Mintzberg (1973) summarizes as follows:

- Strategy making is dominated by the active search for new opportunities.
- Power is centralized in the hands of the chief executive – certainly as far as corporate strategy changes are concerned.
- Strategic change is characterized by dramatic leaps forward in the face of uncertainty.
- Growth is the dominant goal of the organization.

Implicit is an attempt to be proactive and manage the environment. Paths III, IV and V are clearly not mutually exclusive; they can all be present simultaneously in an organization.

Sustained entrepreneurial behaviour is required for a successful economy; organizations must innovate and search for opportunities to rewrite the rules of competition. In this way home industries can succeed against foreign competitors (whose products and services may be differentiated successfully or priced very competitively because of cost advantages such as low wages) and find overseas markets. Paths I and II are not entrepreneurial businesses; in a different way, nor is an organization which grows via acquisitions but then fails to add new values and drive improvements along either path III or IV. Ironically, the nature of the strategic changes and the increases in size and revenue can suggest that these organizations are visionary and on path V. However, where an organization that has been following path II, III or IV merges with, or is taken over by, another organization, there is likely to be a change of strategy, culture and possibly leadership. The acquired business may therefore experience a path V change.

As well as sustained entrepreneurial behaviour, new entrepreneurs are required to start new businesses to replace the jobs which are lost when other companies collapse and certain industries decline, as have coal mining, steel making and shipbuilding, for example. Typically, a different type of business, with dissimilar labour requirements, will emerge. In general, the issue is not so much in stimulating business start-ups, but in encouraging them to grow. However, growth demands changes in structure and style and requires the owner–manager to relinquish some power and control. Growing too quickly often implies problems with cash flow and co-ordination.

Intrapreneurship

Entrepreneurial activity, innovation and growth are affected greatly by the ambition and style of the strategic leader, his or her values, and the culture that he or she creates, but arguably they should be spread throughout the organization. Intrapreneurship is the term given to the establishment and fostering of entrepreneurial activity within large organizations. Many new ideas for innovation, for product or service developments, can come from managers within organizations if the structure and climate encourage and allow them to contribute. There is a number of ways. Special task forces and development groups are one alternative. Allowing individual managers the opportunity, freedom and, if necessary, the capital to try new ideas is another. Success requires that change is perceived more as an opportunity than a threat, that the company is aware of market opportunities and is customer orientated, and that the financial implications are thought through.

The subject of intrapreneurship is explored in greater depth in Chapter 10.

Visionary Leadership

Visionary leadership is often associated with an organization that might be described as entrepreneurial, and many visionary leaders are legitimately entrepreneurs, but not always. Moreover, it is not a requirement that, to be effective, a strategic leader has to be personally visionary.

Mintzberg *et al.* (1998) contend that for a visionary strategic leader, strategy is a mental representation of the successful position or competitive paradigm inside his or her head. It could be thought through quite carefully or it could be largely intuitive. This representation or insight then serves as an inspirational driving force for the organization. The vision or idea alone is inadequate; the leader must persuade others – customers, partners, employees and suppliers – to see it, share it and support it. Flexibility will always be an inherent factor, and detail emerges through experience and learning.

For Mintzberg *et al.* (1998), visionary entrepreneurs often, but not always, conceptualize the winning strategic position as a result of immersion in the industry. They may simply have a genuine interest; equally they may have worked in the industry for some length of time. Their secret is an ability to learn and understand, making sense of their experiences and the signals they see. While some people would never be able to make sense of a pattern of strategic signals pertinent to an industry, others learn very quickly.

> *There are two types of people in the world – reasonable and unreasonable. A reasonable man adapts himself to the world; the unreasonable man persists in trying to adapt the world to himself.*

> George Bernard Shaw

This quotation from Shaw appears to reinforce the relative merits of two schools of thought concerning what entrepreneurs are actually doing: Schumpeter's (1949) belief that entrepreneurs disturb the existing market equilibrium and stability with innovation, contrasted with the Austrian contention that entrepreneurs actually create equilibrium and market stability by finding new, clear, positive strategic positions in a business environment characterized by chaos and turbulence. The Austrian perspective is that of the reasonable man who observes chaos and uncertainty and looks for an opportunity gap that others have missed. Schumpeter's innovators are unreasonable; they are trying to disturb the status quo, turn things upside down, find new strategic positions and make life hard for any existing competitors. Blanchard and Waghorn (1997) claim that Ted Turner (with CNN 24 hour network news) and Steve Jobs (Apple, a case discussed in Chapter 13) are unreasonable men who, like entrepreneurs in the mobile phones business, have been instrumental in changing the world we know.

Successful visionary, aspirational leaders and entrepreneurs are clearly not all 'from the same mould'. This author believes that there is a hypothetical 'well of talent' and as individuals we possess the potential most suitable for us to become either a leader, an entrepreneur, an intrapreneurial manager, an inventor, a 'follower' or whatever. We remain in the well until we are released. We can, of course, propel ourselves out with sheer determination; equally, if we are fortunate, we can be spotted, nurtured and encouraged. It is not inconceivable that our true talents will lie buried for many years. The point is that when people with entrepreneurial talents emerge from the so-called well, they follow different paths. In Figure 8.6, hard entrepreneurship represents the paradigm of the independent,

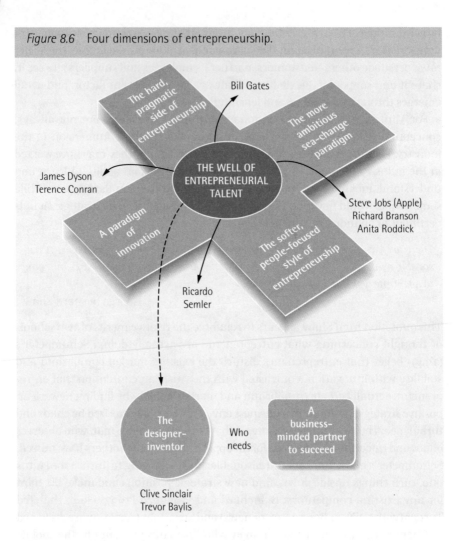

Figure 8.6   Four dimensions of entrepreneurship.

pragmatic, opportunistic and competitive entrepreneur. These achievement-orientated people are the typical managed risk takers and natural networkers in search of a deal. Not every entrepreneur fits this pattern. Some present a softer image. They operate in a more informal manner; they are strong on communication and they sell their vision to engage and motivate others. The hard and soft approaches lead to quite different cultures.

Some visionary, adventurous entrepreneurs set out to change the world. These are people with a real ability to galvanize others; they work hard, play hard and operate at the leading edge. They have to have enormous energy and generally they would be described as 'having a presence'. Again, this approach is not, and need not, be ubiquitous. The fourth arm, innovation, still requires imagination, creativity, passion and a commitment to bring about change (see Lessem, 1986, 1998).

It may be suggested that Bill Gates is a typical hard adventurer – Microsoft has literally changed the world of computing – while James Dyson is a hard innovator. Steve Jobs (Apple), Richard Branson and Anita Roddick are certainly visionaries, whose products have again had a major impact on our lives, but they have all adopted a softer style and approach. Brazilian Ricardo Semler is a visionary as far as management style is concerned, but Semco's (his family company) engineering products, including pumps and industrial dishwashers, are hardly revolutionary. Semler, who transformed Semco's fortunes by releasing the abilities and energies of its people, appears to typify the soft innovator.

There is, however, one final category: the designer–inventor who lacks the necessary business acumen or interest to build the business on his or her own, but who can, with help, be part of a successful and entrepreneurial business. Sir Clive Sinclair is a designer–inventor who has come up with a number of truly innovative ideas and products, but he has never found the right partner and built a winning business. Trevor Baylis also fits here. Baylis did find the right partner and his Bay-Gen clockwork radio has provided the foundation for a successful business.

Visionary leadership and strategy creation

Visionary leadership, then, implies a strategic leader with a personal vision for the future of the organization and at least a broad idea of the strategies for pursuing the vision. Such leadership often appears to be based on intuition and possibly experience rather than detailed analysis, but truly visionary leaders possess strategic awareness and insight and do not require extensive analyses to understand key success factors and how the organization can use its abilities and competencies to satisfy needs and expectations. There is a 'feel' for which strategies will be appropriate and feasible and for the potential of the opportunity.

When a visionary leader pursues new opportunities and introduces changes the detailed plans for implementing the new strategies are unlikely to be in place; instead, there will be a reliance on incremental learning, flexibility and adaptation. For the approach to succeed, the leader must be able to inspire others and persuade them of the logic and merits of the new strategies. This is true for all important strategic changes, but when new proposals have emerged from a more formal strategic planning system there will be substantive detail and analysis to justify the case instead of a strong reliance on vision and intuition.

Where major changes to the corporate strategy are being considered it may be necessary for the strategic leader to convince other members of the board of directors and, if new funding is needed, the institutional shareholders and bankers.

The strategy cannot be successful until it has been implemented and has brought the desired results and rewards. Such outcomes require the support and commitment of other managers, and consequently effective visionaries are often articulate, communicative and persuasive leaders.

In simple terms, then, visionary strategic leadership implies three steps: step one is the vision, step two is selling it to other stakeholders and managers, and step three is making sure it happens – aspects of vision, communication and pragmatism.

Richardson (1994) suggests that the following factors are typical of visionary leadership:

- 'covert' planning – planning is often cerebral rather than formal and systematic, such that planning *systems* are not a major aspect of strategy creation
- a passion about what they are doing and their business
- they are instrumental in creating and fostering a particular culture
- they are highly persuasive when encouraging others to implement their ideas and strategies
- they rely on charisma and personal power.

Although visionary leaders are sometimes entrepreneurs, and some entrepreneurs are visionary leaders, the two terms are not synonymous. In this book a visionary strategic leader is seen, typically, as someone who is a persuasive and charismatic agent of change, either starting a new, differentiated business which takes off, or changing the direction and corporate strategy of a business in order to maintain or improve its rate of growth. Major, discontinuous change is implied. The growth can be fuelled by astute acquisition. While entrepreneurship again implies growth, the growth need not always be visionary or discontinuous. Equally, many entrepreneurs are not, and need not be, charismatic figures. The key element of visionary strategic leadership is a visionary impact on strategy creation.

Remember, however, that a strategic leader who succeeds in turning around a company in crisis and *restores growth* – a process sometimes called corporate entrepreneurship – can be a visionary. At the same time, it does not follow that visionary leadership is necessary for either new ventures or successful turnaround situations. When a company is in trouble, a good, analytical 'company doctor' who can restructure, rationalize and refocus the business can be very effective.

Individual managers, responsible for competitive and functional strategies, can act as internal entrepreneurs (intrapreneurs) and lead incremental or adaptive changes on a relatively small scale. Again, they are agents of change in a decentralized organization. They drive innovation, they make a difference, but they are not visionary leaders.

Changing Strategies

Two important strategic pressures can leave the unprepared organization weakened: competitive and other environmental pressures, and focusing too much on controls at the expense of flexibility.

Hurst (1995) has shown how management and control become increasingly necessary as organizations grow and become more complex, but that this development contains the seeds of potential failure. Figure 8.7 shows that organizations often start life with an entrepreneurial vision but that the significance of this vision soon gives way to learning and emergence as the entrepreneur and the organization learn to cope with the pressures of a dynamic and competitive environment. This flexibility maintains the momentum and the organization grows and prospers. To ensure that the organization is managed efficiently, planning and control systems run by specialist professional managers become increasingly prominent, but this often reduces the flexibility which has proved so valuable. If the flexibility is lost, if the organization fails to address what it is doing wrong while it is still succeeding, some of the momentum for innovation is lost.

Figure 8.7   Strategic change.

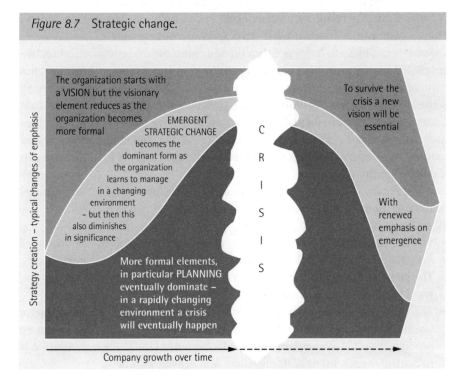

Unless the entrepreneur and the organization foresee the impending problem and find a major new initiative, a crisis is likely to happen. If the organization is to survive the crisis it will need a substantial new opportunity, together with a renewed reliance on innovation and learning.

Businesses hit these crisis points when they run short of money, usually because they have failed to remain competitive and to attract sufficient resource contributions from customers and other important resource suppliers. Sometimes turnaround is possible, frequently accompanied by a change of strategic leader to input the new vision and inspiration. On other occasions the intervention is too late, and the organization either collapses or is taken over as a means of providing the necessary new leadership and resourcing.

Businesses in trouble, then, may be realistically irrecoverable, recoverable but only to a level of survival, or capable of genuine renewal. The immediate need is to stop any financial haemorrhaging before new opportunities are sought and pursued. The first step does not need someone with entrepreneurial talent and temperament – it is largely based on technique, backed by a willingness to take tough decisions – but the second stage does.

Hurst further argues that on occasions it can be valuable to engineer an internal crisis and upset in order to drive through major changes in an organization that has lost its dynamism and become too resistant to change. A controlled crisis is better than one resulting from external events as it can be used for positive change rather than constitute a more desperate reaction.

Stasis is less likely to happen if the company employs and encourages creative people who drive innovation and intrapreneurship. But if momentum is lost, the company may need more than creative people: it may need a 'maverick', perhaps someone who is normally ill-at-ease in a typical organization or a new strategic leader who will come in for just a short period. The maverick manager is unorthodox, individualistic and outspoken, someone who will challenge mediocrity and existing ways of doing things and someone who is not afraid to upset others in the drive for change.

Another way of presenting these arguments is the following four-stage model of organizational progression and development.

- The first step is a *creative* one, when new ideas are put forward.
- *Reflection and nurturing* follow as the idea is crafted into a winning opportunity. The person who has the original idea may not be the person who takes it forward in the most opportune way.
- The third stage is an *action* stage as the organization grows by developing a business from the opportunity. As the business takes off, and more and more products are sold, some element of order becomes vital if the organization is to control events, manage its cash flow and deliver on time.

- The fourth stage then becomes one of *management* and administration with clear policies and procedures which deliver smooth running and efficiencies. This can become a dangerous stage if stasis sets in and new, creative ideas are not forthcoming.

Clearly, each stage has a downside. A constant stream of new ideas may not constitute entrepreneurial opportunities. Too much deliberation may inhibit action. An overemphasis on 'doing' and competitiveness may mean that inadequate attention is given to structural necessities. Finally, too much bureaucracy can mean missed opportunities. The organization begins to need a fresh input of creative ideas. Individually, we are all different and our affinity and fit with each of these stages vary; some of us are not able to switch styles. While the most successful and habitual entrepreneurs will ensure that there is a constant flow of activity between these stages and the potential downsides do not materialize, other strategic leaders will need to recognize their relative strengths and weaknesses and recruit other people carefully to ensure that there is a balance of skills and constant progression. Moreover, the positive organization implied here will be in a better position to exploit and retain its most talented intrapreneurial managers.

Summary

There are three key elements in how organizations might, and in reality do, generate new ideas for future strategies:

- Planning – which in turn is dependent upon the quality of the available information.
- Leadership – to provide both ideas and a clear framework in which other decision makers can operate effectively.
- Innovation – intrapreneurship within the organization to ensure that new opportunities are found and threats are avoided, such that the organization stays strong, competitive, effective and successful in a dynamic environment. This is again dependent upon communications and information.

These elements are reflected in three modes of strategic creation:

1. Strategic planning
2. Visionary leadership } both leading to intended strategies

3. Emergent strategy creation as intended strategies are changed incrementally when they are implemented in a dynamic environment and in the form of new adaptive strategies as the organization responds to new strategic opportunities.

All three modes involve the key strategic themes of analysis, choice and implementation, but these themes are manifested in different ways in each case.

Visionary strategic leaders typically provide a strategic vision and rely on formal planning systems to only a limited extent. They are often persuasive and charismatic, operating through the organization structure.

Entrepreneurs are similar in many respects, but they are different. Entrepreneurs build value around opportunities. Internal entrepreneurs (intrapreneurs) will be provided with opportunity and encouragement in some organizations where they will then drive emergent change.

As an organization grows the relative significance of the three modes changes. In its early days an organization is likely to be influenced markedly by its founding strategic leader, but if it is successful and grows, the emergent and planning approaches will become increasingly important. If planning becomes dominant and causes the organization to be relatively inflexible in the dynamic environment a crisis is likely to occur, demanding a new visionary input and possibly a new strategic leader.

Sometimes it is necessary to engineer an internal crisis to bring about this level of change rather than wait for an externally driven crisis, maybe in the form of a new competitor or new competitive paradigm.

References

Bailey, A and Johnson, G (1992) How strategies develop in organizations. In *The Challenge of Strategic Management* (eds G Johnson and D Faulkner), Kogan Page.

Bolton, WK and Thompson, JL (2000) *Entrepreneurs: Talent, Temperament, Technique*, Butterworth-Heinemann.

Hurst, DK (1995) *Crisis and Renewal – Meeting the Challenge of Organizational Change*, Harvard Business School Press.

Idenburg, PJ (1993) Four styles of strategy development, *Long Range Planning*, 26, 6.

Kirzner, IM (1973) *Competition and Entrepreneurship*, Cambridge University Press.

Lessem, R (1986) *Enterprising Development*, Gower.

Lessem, R (1998) *Managing Development Through Cultural Diversity*, Routledge.

Mintzberg, H (1973) Strategy making in three modes, *California Management Review*, 16(2), Winter.

Mintzberg, H (1989) Presentation to the Strategic Planning Society, London, 2 February. Further details can be found in Mintzberg, H (1973).

Mintzberg, H and Waters, JA (1985) Of strategy deliberate and emergent, *Strategic Management Journal*, 6(3).

Mintzberg, H, Ahlstrand, B and Lampel, J (1998) *Strategy Safari*, Prentice-Hall.

Richardson, B (1994) Towards a profile of the visionary leader, *Small Business Enterprise and Development*, 1, 1, Spring.

Schumpeter, J (1949) *The Theory of Economic Development*, Harvard University Press; original German edition, 1911.

Questions and Research Assignments

TEXT RELATED

1. Explain the following terms and provide examples of each one from your own experiences or reading:
   - Strategic planning systems
   - Visionary leadership
   - Incremental change
   - New, adaptive strategies.

2. Where do the entrepreneur and the visionary leader overlap, and where are they different?

Internet and Library Projects

1. Take one or more – and possibly all – of the entrepreneurs/strategic leaders included in Figure 8.6 and who are not discussed in the case studies in this book, namely:
   - Bill Gates (Microsoft)
   - Sir Richard Branson (Virgin)
   - Anita Roddick (The Body Shop)
   - Sir Terence Conran (Conran Design)
   - Ricardo Semler (Semco)
   - Sir Clive Sinclair
   - Trevor Baylis

   and establish their impact upon strategy creation in the organizations they founded. How has their style of leadership changed as the organization they founded has grown?

   Microsoft http://www.microsoft.com
   Virgin http://www.virgin.com
   Body Shop http://www.bodyshop.com

2. The following facts relate to Sir Alan Sugar, founder of Amstrad, and one of Britain's richest businessmen.
   - 1947   Born Hackney, East London
   - 1963   Left school
   - 1966   Began selling car aerials from a van
   - 1968   Founded Amstrad to sell plastic covers for record players. Involvement in televisions, video receivers and CB radio led to
   - 1985   Launch of a low-cost word-processor and compact disc player
   - 1986   Acquisition of the intellectual property rights of Sinclair computers from Clive Sinclair and launch of an IBM-compatible microcomputer

1988   Entered satellite dish market

1991   Entered laptop computer market.

Research the growth and success of Amstrad in the consumer electronics and microcomputers markets and assess what has happened to Alan Sugar in the past 10 years.

What can you conclude about his style of leadership? Is he an entrepreneur?

Amstrad   http://www.amstrad.com

Strategic Planning

Planning the future – thinking about the most appropriate strategies, and changes in strategic direction – is essential for organizations, particularly those experiencing turbulent environments. Rigid systematic planning – based on techniques and formalized procedures is, however, no longer as fashionable as it was, nor is it the only way in which strategic change decisions are made. There are dangers if organizations become reliant upon professional planners and where the only outcome of planning is a plan. This may not allow for effective strategic thinking, and may not result in a clear direction for the future.

There are dangers, then, in thinking that all strategic changes can be planned systematically and procedurally. Whether it is the result of formal and systematic planning, or much more informal and ad hoc leadership and management – which, paradoxically, still implies an element of planning – an organization will have strategies and processes whereby these strategies are changed. The processes need to be understood, and in many cases improved. It is important to assess where and how the organization should change and develop in the light of market opportunities and competitive threats, but there are lessons to be learnt about their appropriateness to certain strategic opportunities. Managers should know clearly where the organization is, and where it might sensibly go, and start making appropriate changes. They should then monitor progress and be aware of changes in the environment; in this way they can be flexible and responsive. After all, all managers are strategy makers.

In this context, this chapter considers what is meant by the term planning, and what is involved in the systematic planning cycle approach to the management of strategic change. The contribution of a number of planning techniques will be evaluated, and possible pitfalls and human issues in planning will be pinpointed.

Case Study 9: Strategic issues and high-street Banking

During the 1990s, and following the worldwide economic recession and the ensuing bad debts, the UK high-street clearing banks changed their strategies as a response to a number of key challenges and issues.

Strategic issues

- They faced a need to switch from a position of high overheads with an extensive branch infrastructure and the associated high-risk lending (required to cover the overheads) to one where their (lower) cost base is in equilibrium with the type and volume of lower risk business that can be more readily justified.
- Information technology, exploited effectively, offered opportunities for providing new and more efficient services without sacrificing either quality or reliability. In addition, the Internet was forecast to attract up to 10 million personal accounts by 2003.

Both of these issues implied restructuring and job losses, although there was always the possibility that once the banks had re-established strong controls and truly efficient systems they would reconsider taking higher risks again.

- The entry of new competitors, particularly linked to Internet banking (Prudential's Egg) and savings accounts (the leading supermarkets).
- A prediction that many personal customers would switch emphasis from borrowing to saving as the economy strengthened. The high-street banks were not perceived to be good for savers, offering relatively low rates of interest in comparison to the building societies and PEP-linked (subsequently ISA-linked) unit trusts.
- A possibility that customers would be more willing to switch bank accounts than has generally been the case historically. The reasoning was that the Internet was making everything, including comparable interest rates, much more visible.
- Changes in capital markets were taking away some of the bank's leading corporate customers.

New strategies

- High-street banks now typically offer a wider range of financial services, which they promote aggressively, often using their extensive databases for direct-mail campaigns.
- Attempts by certain banks to charge customers from other banks who use their 'hole-in-the-wall' automated teller machines (ATMs) – this strategy provoked considerable controversy.
- Efforts to reinforce brand names and strengthen reputations – difficult for some who faced customer resistance to branch closures.
- Stronger credit controls for more effective loan management – implying both improved information and tracking and a reduction in the number of loans.
- Computerized credit and loan assessments to link charges with risks more closely than in the past. This has changed the role of individual bank managers and, for some businesses, made borrowing more difficult. Many business managers now offer counselling and advice rather than negotiate and track loans.
- A tighter focus on specific market segments, looking for positions of strength, rather than 'being involved in everything'. In particular, UK banks have reviewed their overseas exposure.
- A search for more attractive savings products in an increasingly competitive environment.
- New forms of service. Following the pioneering work of First Direct (a subsidiary of the old Midland, now owned by HSBC) other clearing banks have introduced telephone banking services. This would not have been possible without information technology. Some, such as the Co-op Bank with 'Smile', have started Internet bank accounts.
- Mergers between banks, building societies and insurance companies to create a more comprehensive financial services corporation. The systematic amalgamation of Lloyds, TSB, Cheltenham & Gloucester and Scottish Widows is an excellent example of this.

QUESTION: From your own experiences, what changes have you noticed in the service and the range of services offered by your bank?

> The planning era, if one may call it that, occurred some time ago, and has been discredited as we have moved on to the greater belief in the development of common values in the organization, and are rediscovering again today the necessity to be close to the market.
>
> *Sir John Harvey-Jones, Past Chairman, ICI, 1987*

> Planning is one of the most complex and difficult intellectual activities in which man can engage. Not to do it well is not a sin; but to settle for doing it less than well is.
>
> *Russell Ackoff, 1970*

Strategic Thinking and Strategic Planning

Robinson (1986) argues that the role of the planner should be not to plan but to enable good managers to plan. It is not the task of the planner to state the objectives; rather he or she should elicit and clarify them. Planning should concentrate on understanding the future, which is uncertain and unpredictable, and helping managers to make decisions about strategic changes. Thus, the aim of planning should be to force people to think and examine, not to produce a rigid plan.

It is worth reinforcing here that the real value of planning is not the plan which emerges, and which might be produced as a summary document which is worth little more than the paper it is printed on! Rather, the value lies in the thinking that the act and process of planning forces people to do.

Undoubtedly, planning techniques, used carefully, can provide a valuable description and analysis of the current situation. But the future is not necessarily the past extrapolated forwards, and while we can learn from past decisions, actions and events, companies must develop new competitive and corporate paradigms for managing the future and its inherent uncertainties. Vision and flexibility will be essential, alongside a clear direction and purpose. New thinking is essential for reaching the new competitive high ground first.

Strategic planning systems, popular and dominant in the 1960s and 1970s, became less fashionable in the 1980s and 1990s, but they still have an important contribution to make. In most companies planning had not contributed to strategic thinking and, because strategic thinking is essential, a new role has had to be found for strategic planning.

Strategic planning became fashionable for two basic reasons. First, it provided a means for allocating resources and managing budgets in complex multiproduct organizations and, second, it helped to pull together the disparate activities and businesses in organizations. These needs remain.

The outcome for many organizations was formal planning systems, heavily reliant on financial data, and supported by thick planning manuals. This was the downside.

On the positive side, planning can encourage managers to think about the need and opportunities for change, and to communicate strategy to those who must implement it. This was particularly important in the 1960s and early 1970s when there was an abundance of investment opportunities and a dearth of capital and key priorities needed to be established. In complex multiactivity organizations, decisions have to be made concerning where to concentrate investment capital in relation to future earnings potential, and this has generated a number of port-folio analysis techniques, some of which are studied later in the chapter. Rather than use these techniques for gaining greater awareness and insight, for which they are well suited, managers sought to use them prescriptively to determine future plans.

Formal strategic planning had become unfashionable by the 1980s for a number of reasons:

- Planning was often carried out by planners, rather than the managers who would be affected by the resultant plans.
- As a result, the outcome of planning was often a plan which in reality had little impact on actual management decisions, and therefore was not implemented.
- The planning techniques used were criticized primarily because of the way in which they were used.
- The important elements of culture and total quality management were usually left out.

However, many industries continue to experience turbulent environments caused by such factors as slower economic growth, globalization and technological change, and consequently strategic thinking is extremely important. The following questions must be addressed:

- What is the future direction of competition?
- What are the future needs of customers?
- How are competitors likely to behave?
- How might competitive advantage be gained and sustained?

Organizations must ensure that these questions are constantly addressed rather than addressed occasionally as part of an annual cycle. Line managers who implement plans must be involved throughout the process. 'Every executive needs to understand how to think strategically'. Rigorous frameworks and planning manuals are not necessary as long as the proper thinking takes place.

There should be a strategic plan for each business unit in a complex organization, i.e. clear competitive strategies built around an understanding of the nature of the industry in which the business competes, and sources of competitive advantage. Chosen strategies must have action plans for implementing them, including an assessment of the needs for finance and for staff training and development. This is generally less difficult than formulating a corporate strategy for the whole organization.

Planning and Planning Systems

What do we mean by planning?

All managers plan. They plan how they might achieve objectives. However, a clear distinction needs to be made between the cerebral activity of informal planning and formalized planning systems.

A visionary strategic leader, aware of strategic opportunities and convinced that they can be capitalized upon, may decide independently where the organization should go and how the strategies are to be implemented. Very little needs to be recorded formally. Conversations between managers may result in plans which again exist only in individual managers' heads or in the form of scribbled notes. Equally, time, money and other resources may be invested by the organization in the production of elaborate and formally documented plans.

In all cases planning is part of an ongoing continuous activity which addresses where the organization as a whole, or individual parts of it, should be going. At one level a plan may simply describe the activities and tasks that must be carried out in the next day or week in order to meet specific targets. At a much higher level the plan may seek to define the mission and objectives, and establish guidelines, strategies and policies that will enable the organization to adapt to, and to shape and exploit, its environment over a period of years. In both cases, if events turn out to be different from those which were forecast, the plans will need to be changed.

The value of strategic planning

When managers and organizations plan strategies they are seeking to:

- be clearer about the business(es) that the organization is in, and should be in
- increase awareness about strengths and weaknesses
- be able to recognize and capitalize on opportunities, and to defend against threats
- be more effective in the allocation and use of resources.

Irrespective of the quality or format of the actual plans, engaging in the planning process can be valuable. It helps individual managers to establish priorities and address problems; it can bring managers together so that they can share their problems and perspectives. Ideally, the result will be improved communication, co-ordination and commitment. Hence there can be real benefit from planning or thinking about the future. What form should the thinking and planning take? Should it be part of a formalized system making use of strategic planning techniques?

Corporate and functional plans

Corporate and strategic plans concern the number and variety of product markets and service markets in which the organization will compete, together with the development of the necessary resources (people, capacity, finance, research and so on) required to support the competitive strategies. Strategic plans, therefore, relate to the whole organization, cover several years and are generally not highly detailed. They are concerned with future needs and how to obtain and develop the desired businesses, products, services and resources. The actual timescale involved will be affected by the nature of the industry and the number of years ahead that investments must be planned if growth and change are to be brought about.

Functional plans are derived from corporate strategy and strategic plans, and they relate to the implementation of functional strategies. They cover specific areas of the business; there can be plans relating to product development, production control and cash budgeting, for example. Functional plans will usually have shorter time horizons than is the case for strategic plans, and invariably they will incorporate greater detail. However, they will be reviewed and updated, and they may very well become ongoing rolling plans. While strategic plans are used to direct the whole organization, functional plans are used for the short-term management of parts of the organization.

Competitive strategies and functional strategies and plans are essential if products and services are to be managed effectively, but they should be flexible and capable of being changed if managers responsible for their implementation feel it necessary.

Ohmae (1982) emphasizes that individual products must be seen as part of wider systems or product groups/business units, and that although short-term plans must be drawn up for the effective management of individual products, it is important to ensure that thinking about the future is done at the appropriate level. As an example, a particular brand or type of shampoo targeted at a specific market segment would constitute a product market. The company's range of shampoos should be produced and marketed in a co-ordinated way, and consequently they might constitute a strategic planning unit. The relevant strategic business unit might incorporate all of the company's cosmetics products and there should be a competitive strategy to ensure that the various products are co-ordinated and support each other. In terms of strategic thinking Ohmae suggests that it is more important to consider listening devices as a whole than radios specifically, and that this type of thinking resulted in the Sony Walkman and similar products. In the same way, the Japanese realized a new opportunity for black and white television receivers in the form of small portable sets, when other manufacturers had switched all of their attention to the development of colour sets. If the level of thinking is appropriate, resources are likely to be allocated more effectively.

Alternative approaches to planning

Taylor and Hussey (1982) feature seven different approaches to planning which are detailed briefly below.

- *Informal planning* takes place in someone's head, and the decisions reached may not be written down in any extensive form. It is often practised by managers with real entrepreneurial flair, and it can be highly successful. It is less likely to be effective if used by managers who lack flair and creativity.
- *Extended budgeting* is rarely used as it is only feasible if the environment is stable and predictable. Extended budgeting is primarily financial planning based on the extrapolation of past trends.
- *Top–down planning* relates to decisions taken at the top of the organization and passed down to other managers for implementation. These managers will have had little or no input into the planning process. Major change decisions reached informally may be incorporated here, and then a great deal depends upon the strength and personality of the strategic leader in persuading other managers to accept the changes. At the other extreme, top–down plans may emanate from professional planners using planning techniques extensively and reporting directly to the strategic leader. These are the type of plans that may not be implemented.
- *Strategic analysis/policy options* again uses planning techniques, and involves the creation and analytical evaluation of alternative options. Where future possible scenarios are explored for their implications, and possible courses of action are tested for sensitivity, this form of planning can be valuable for strategic thinking. It is an appropriate use of planning techniques, but it is important to consider the potential impact on people.
- *Bottom–up planning* involves managers throughout the organization, and therefore ensures that people who will be involved in implementing plans are consulted. Specifically, functional and business unit managers are charged with

evaluating the future potential for their areas of responsibility and are invited to make a case for future resources. All of the detail is analysed and the future allocation of resources is decided. In an extreme form thick planning manuals will be involved, and the process may be slow and rigid. Necessary changes may be inhibited if managerial freedom to act outside the plan is constrained. A formal system of this nature is likely to involve an annual planning cycle, which is discussed later in the chapter.

- *Behavioural approaches* can take several forms, but essentially the behavioural approach requires that managers spend time discussing the future opportunities and threats and areas in which the organization might develop. The idea is that if managers are encouraged to discuss their problems and objectives for the business freely, and if they are able to reach agreement concerning future priorities and developments, then they will be committed to implementing the changes. However, it is quite likely that not all of the conflicts concerning resource allocation and priorities will be resolved. Clearly, scenario planning can be very useful here.

- The *strategic review* was developed to take the best features of the other six approaches and blend them together into a systematic and comprehensive planning system. A typical system is discussed in detail in the next section.

All of these approaches have individual advantages and disadvantages, and they are not mutually exclusive. The approach adopted will depend on the style and preferences of the strategic leader, who must:

- clarify the mission and corporate objectives and establish the extent and nature of changes to the corporate perspective
- approve competitive and functional strategies and plans for each part of the business, however they might be created, and
- establish appropriate control mechanisms, which may or may not involve substantial decentralization.

It has been established that planning may be either informal or formal. Informal planning, as such, cannot be taught; but formal planning systems can. These are the subject of the next sections.

The planning gap

A number of essentially similar models of systematic planning has been developed by such authors as Argenti (1980), Hussey (1976), Cohen and Cyert (1973) and Glueck and Jauch (1984). All of these models use the concept of gap analysis, which is extremely useful for strategic thinking purposes and which is explained in Box 9.1.

DISCUSSION – Box 9.1
The Planning Gap

The planning gap should be seen as an idea which can be adapted to suit particular circumstances, although gap analysis could be regarded as a planning technique.

An example of the planning gap is illustrated in Figure 9.1. The horizontal axis represents the planning time horizon, stretching forward from the present day; either sales volume or revenue, or profits, could be used on the vertical axis as a measure of anticipated performance. The lowest solid line on the graph indicates expected sales or profits if the organization continues with present corporate, competitive and functional strategies; it does not have to slope downwards. The top dashed line represents ideal objectives, which imply growth and which may or may not ultimately be realized. The difference between these two lines is the gap. The gap is the difference between the results that the organization can expect to achieve from present strategies continued forward and the results that the strategic leader would like to attain.

The example illustrated in Figure 9.1 shows the gap filled in by a series of alternative courses of strategic action ordered in an ascending hierarchy of risk. Risk is constituted by the extent to which future products and markets are related to existing ones; and this idea of increased risk and strategic alternatives is developed further in Figures 9.2 and 9.3.

The lowest risk alternative is to seek to manage present products and services more effectively, aiming to sell more of them and to reduce their costs in order to generate increased sales and profits. This is termed market penetration in the simple growth vector developed by H Igor Ansoff and illustrated in Figure 9.2. It can be extended to strategies of market and product development, which imply, respectively:

- new customers or even new market segments for existing products, which might be modified in some way to provide increased differentiation; and
- new products, ideally using related technology and skills, for sale to existing markets.

(In this context 'new' implies new to the firm rather than something that is necessarily completely new and innovative, although it could well be this.) Figure 9.1 distinguishes between market and product development strategies that are already under way and those that have yet to be started.

The highest risk alternative is diversification because this involves both new products and new markets. Figure 9.3 develops these simple themes further and distinguishes between the following:

DISCUSSION – Box 9.1
(Continued)

- replacement products and product line extensions based on existing technologies and skills, which represent improved products for existing customers
- new products based on new or unrelated technologies and skills, which constitute concentric diversification (these may be sold to either existing or new customers)
- completely new and unrelated products for sale to new customers. This is known as conglomerate diversification and is regarded as a high-risk strategic alternative.

Using the planning gap

Thinking about the extent of the initial gap between present strategies and ideal objectives enables managers to consider how much change and how much risk would be involved in closing the gap and achieving the target objectives. Some of the strategies considered might be neither feasible nor desirable, and consequently the gap might be too wide to close. Similarly, the degree of risk, especially if a number of changes is involved, might be greater than the strategic leader is willing to accept. In these cases it will be necessary to revise the desired objectives downwards so that they finally represent realistic targets which should be achieved by strategic changes that are acceptable and achievable.

This type of thinking is related to specific objectives concerning growth and profitability. It does not follow, as was discussed in Chapter 2, that either growth or profitability maximization will be the major priority of the organization, or that the personal objectives of individual managers will not be an issue.

The concept of the planning gap relates very closely to issues which were raised in Chapter 2 on objectives. It addresses the following questions:

- Where do we want to go?
- Where can we go realistically?

When considering where and how an organization might develop in the future, both the desired and realistic objectives are essential considerations. Desired objectives relate to where the strategic leader and other decision makers would like to take the organization if it is possible to do so. Realistic objectives incorporate the influence of the various stakeholders in the business, and their expectations; the existence of suitable opportunities; and the availability of the necessary

Figure 9.1   An example of the planning gap.

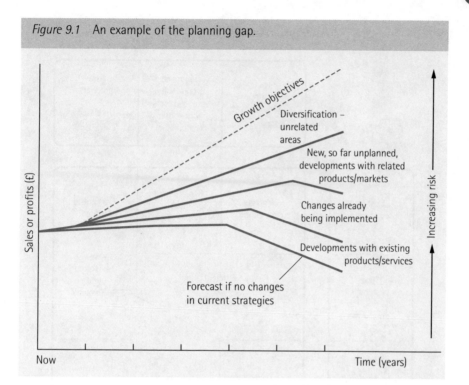

Figure 9.2   Ansoff's growth vector. Source: Ansoff, HI (1987) *Corporate Strategy*, revised edn, Penguin.

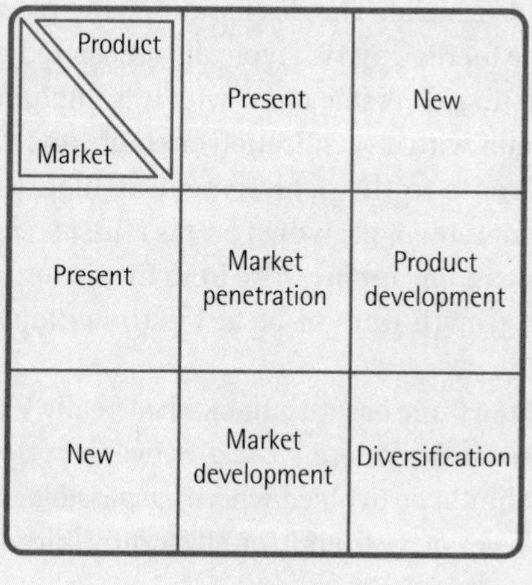

Figure 9.3   An extended growth vector.

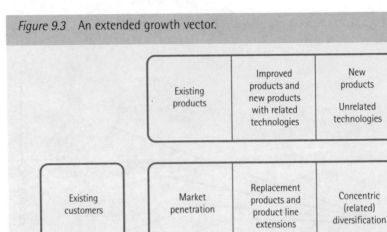

	Existing products	Improved products and new products with related technologies	New products / Unrelated technologies
Existing customers	Market penetration	Replacement products and product line extensions	Concentric (related) diversification
New customers in existing markets	Product differentiation and market segmentation		– based on marketing and technology
New markets	Market development		Unrelated (conglomerate) diversification

resources. The issue of the risk involved in the alternative courses of action that might be considered is crucial. The discussion of the planning gap in Box 9.1 draws attention to the increasing risk typically associated with certain strategic alternatives, in particular diversification, which is often implemented through acquisition. Failure rates with diversification are high, and yet diversification may be the only feasible route to the achievement of high growth targets or the maintenance of present rates of growth in profits and sales revenues. The strategic leader, perhaps under significant pressure from City investors, shareholders and analysts who expect growth rates to be at least maintained, may be forced to pursue high-risk strategies.

Table 9.1 looks at how three organizations, specifically Virgin, McDonald's and Sony, have pursued several different strategies over a period of years.

While undue risk should be avoided wherever possible, it is always important to accept a certain level of risk and set stretching targets for managers and businesses.

Table 9.1 Applications of the simple growth vector

	Virgin	McDonald's	Sony
Market penetration	Publicity, self-publicity and exploitation of Virgin name, e.g. Branson's balloon challenges	Sponsorship of major sporting activities Opening restaurants in different types of location: supermarkets, hospitals, military bases Special value meals	
Market development	Before divesting the businesses: opening Virgin Megastores around the world and a music business in the USA	Opening new restaurants all round the world The Big Mac, a hamburger for adults not children	The Sony Walkman and associated derivatives: – effectively existing products repackaged
Product development	Music retailing led to music production and publishing and later music videos	Chicken McNuggets, McChicken Sandwiches, Egg McMuffins, etc.	Tape recorders to videos Televisions Compact discs (some limited diversification involved)
Related diversification	Films, computer games		Computers, Sony Playstation (related technologies)
Unrelated diversification	Virgin Atlantic Airways, Virgin Holidays, Virgin Cola, Virgin Financial Services		CBS Records, Columbia Pictures

A contemporary approach to strategic planning

In order to ensure that planning does not become an end in itself, and that planners facilitate management thinking, many large companies have evolved personalized contemporary planning systems along the lines of the one illustrated in Figure 9.4.

The organization's culture and the expectations of the strategic leader and the key stakeholders influence the whole process of analysis and decision making. The thinking starts with an assessment of the current position of the organization, its skills and resources, and an evaluation of whether there is a clear understanding of the 'mission', the broad objectives and directions for the future.

Figure 9.4   A contemporary approach to strategic planning.

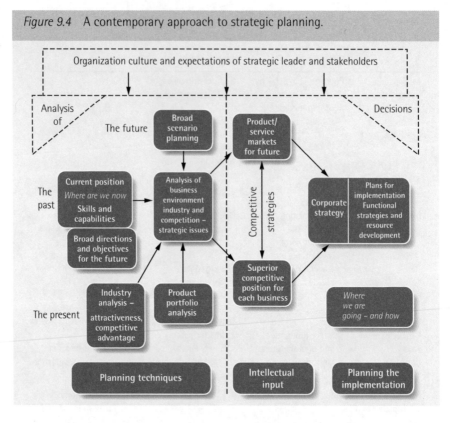

Then the business environment is analysed thoroughly, concentrating on the industries in which the organization currently competes and those in which it might apply its skills and resources. Feeding into this analysis are three other analyses:

- broad scenario planning – conceptualizing a range of different futures with which the organization might have to deal, to ensure that the less likely possibilities, threats and opportunities are not overlooked, and to encourage a high level of flair and creativity in strategic thinking (see Chapter 5)
- product portfolio analyses, which are discussed in greater detail in the next section; contingency and possible crisis planning considerations can be incorporated in this
- industry analyses, following the Porter criteria for judging attractiveness and opportunities for competitive advantage.

This environmental analysis should focus on any *strategic issues* – current or forthcoming developments, inside or outside the organization, which will impact upon the ability of the organization to pursue its mission and meet its objectives. Ideally, these would be opportunities related to organizational strengths. Wherever possible any unwelcome, but significant, potential threats should be turned into competitive opportunities.

Case Study 9 looks at the strategic issues facing high-street banks in the 1990s and how they have affected strategic developments.

From these analyses competitive strategy decisions must be reached concerning:

- the reinforcement or establishment of a superior competitive position, or competitive advantage, for each business within the existing portfolio of products and services
- product markets and service markets for future development, and the appropriate functional strategies for establishing a superior competitive position.

Amalgamated, these functional and competitive strategies constitute the corporate strategy for the future, which in turn needs to be broken down into resource development plans and any decisions relating to changes in the structure of the organization, i.e. decisions that reflect where the organization is going and how the inherent changes are to be managed. The band across the bottom of Figure 9.4 shows how this contemporary approach blends planning techniques with an intellectual input and later action plans for implementing strategic choices.

Simply, planning techniques and analyses are used to clarify the key strategic issues. Discerning the issues and deciding what should be done to address them require creativity (the search for something different) and hence a more intellectual input. Once broad strategic directions are clarified, detailed implementation planning will follow. Like the strategies, these detailed implementation plans should not be seen as inflexible.

It is important that new strategic issues are spotted and dealt with continuously, and the organization structure must enable this to happen, either by decentralization and empowerment or by effective communications.

An example of a systematic corporate planning system for a large organization

A corporate planning team for a large corporation, based at its head office, will typically comprise both planners and analysts. The analysts are responsible for monitoring the external environment, searching for new opportunities and threats. They also model the implications of possible future events and scenarios for the group. The planners consolidate the individual plans for every business in the group to create the overall corporate plan. Group progress against the plan is continuously monitored and evaluated by the planners.

Table 9.2   A typical corporate planning timetable for a diversified organization

	Head-office corporate planning team	Individual businesses
March	Review of progress and corporate objectives	
April	Strategic review for the group	
	⟶	
May		Strategic review for each business
		and
June		Presentation to divisional boards
	⟵	
	Divisional strategies and bids presented	
July/August	Search for new strategies – growth and divestment	
September	Final corporate plan agreed	
	⟶	
		Action plans and target milestones
October⟶March	Ongoing search for further strategic opportunities; monitoring, control and change	

A timetable for a typical planning system is included in Table 9.2. Say the company's financial year end is 31 March: around this time, when the relative success of the group for the year is becoming clear, the planners will produce a final review of progress towards corporate objectives. They evaluate where the group is doing well and where it is less successful, and the extent to which it is satisfying its major stakeholders. To this is added a rigorous internal (corporate resources) and external (environmental developments) assessment of the group, provided by the analysts. They specifically highlight the important *strategic issues* facing the group – appropriate and feasible opportunities and critical threats – together with details about current and (if known) planned competitor strategies.

During April the group chief executive (the strategic leader) convenes his corporate strategy committee, which comprises senior board members and the head of the corporate planning group. The divisional managing directors are not members, although on occasions they will be asked to attend. They are excluded on the grounds that when bids from the divisions for additional investment capital are being considered later in the year, they would all support each other's projects. Any opposition by one divisional head would provoke counter-hostility from the others.

The outcome of the April meeting is a preliminary statement of corporate objectives for the year ahead; these will normally reaffirm the company's mission statement, although it may be reviewed and amended. Typically, the objectives will summarize:

- growth and profit aspirations
- the company's strategy for exploiting core competencies and capabilities and its willingness to diversify (possible acquisition targets and divestments may be discussed but not announced)
- international/geographical objectives
- the commitment to, and standards for, quality, service and customer care
- the resources available to support expansion.

This is broadly equivalent to the top line of the planning gap illustrated in Box 9.1.

During May and early June each business unit finalizes its own strategic review, which is presented to the relevant divisional board of directors. Each company is likely to carry out comprehensive SWOT (strengths, weaknesses, opportunities and threats) competitor and portfolio analyses (portfolio analysis is explained on p. 414) and indicates:

(i)   the anticipated revenue and profit targets if there are no *major* changes to competitive and functional strategies
(ii) the requirements for the company to achieve or maintain competitive advantage
(iii) strategic changes that it would like to make, the anticipated returns and the resource implications.

Each business may be asked to submit proposals based on a range of financial assumptions, ranging from limitless resources to very tight funding. All significant investments will need to be justified in detail; the assistance of head-office planners could be enlisted in formulating proposals.

Items (i) and (ii) will be used immediately for updating the company's action plans and budgets, recognizing that these may have to be adjusted later.

The role of the divisional board is to question and challenge before reaching a set of recommendations for the chief executive. The strategy committee then meets for a second time at the end of June to discuss these recommendations, which may be accepted (and the necessary resources provided) or rejected. Portfolio analysis is again used to consider the current and emerging state of the group; and strategic opportunities for interdivisional support and internally generated synergies are sought.

At the same time the committee compares the promised returns from all the businesses with their own initial growth objectives. If a gap remains, and further resources are available or can be found, the corporate analysts will be asked for costed options and recommendations. The strategic leader may have ideas of his or her own to input. In addition, the analysts will be asked for recommendations concerning how the group might rationalize and achieve further cost savings, beyond those being offered by the divisions. Divisional boards may suggest the divestment of particular businesses, but this is unusual; such decisions are more likely to start with the strategic leader or the analysts.

This evaluation takes place throughout the summer, and the strategy committee meets for a third time in September to agree the corporate strategy. Final targets are issued to the divisions and business units, enabling them to review, and if necessary change, their current plans and budgets. It is these final plans which are co-ordinated by the head-office planners into the corporate plan and used for committing and managing the group's strategic resources.

Different reactions will be provoked by these strategic decisions. Business units that are allocated resources and given support for their proposed strategies tend to be euphoric, whereas those which see themselves as 'losers' are frequently demotivated, an inevitable drawback of this approach.

The divisions and individual businesses are not precluded from changing functional and competitive strategies at any time in response to competitive threats and opportunities, but if they require additional resources, outside their budgeted allocation, they have to apply to the chief executive.

A planning system along the lines of this example is basically a process which forces managers to address key questions and issues. Head office is likely to find that the detailed plan can be a useful document for explaining their basic intentions to the major institutional shareholders. The value of the finished plan to the individual subsidiaries, as distinct from the *process* of planning its content, is more questionable. They should see the document as a *summary of thinking* and a statement of intent, rather than a rigid plan that must be executed.

The corporate strategy may also be changed by the strategic leader at any time during the year if new windows of opportunity become available; such changes may imply either a visionary approach to major strategy additions or more emergent, opportunistic responses to events.

In addition, the planning exercise can be essential for providing a framework against which the strategic leader can monitor the commitment of resources and the emergent outcomes.

Commentary

This approach to corporate planning may well succeed in the essential task of co-ordinating the plans for all the divisions and businesses, enabling the strategic leader to exercise control over a conglomerate. In addition, the system should not prohibit vision and learning within the corporation, which is important as these are the two modes of strategy creation most likely to take the organization forward in a competitive and uncertain environment. Unfortunately, the vision and learning may be concentrated within each division. Ideally, it will permeate the whole organization.

Typically, strategic planning systems used to be very formal. All ideas from the individual businesses had to be supported by comprehensive, documented analyses. Now it is frequently accepted that many proposals cannot be fully justified quantitatively; instead, the assumptions and justifications will be probed and challenged by divisional boards. Care must also be taken to ensure that the evaluation and resource allocation processes do not create too high a level of internal competition. Divisions and businesses should have to justify their intentions and proposals, and it is inevitable they will be competing for scarce resources. Nevertheless, the 'real enemy' is external competitors, not other parts of the organization, and this must never be forgotten.

In addition, some organizations still tend to use the performance targets as the primary means of control, which sometimes results in short-term thinking. Once a business drops below its target it is put under considerable pressure to reduce costs, and this may restrict its ability to be creative and innovative. Many strategic planning systems could be improved if the head-office corporate planners had more contact and involvement with the businesses; they sometimes tend to be remote and detached.

In summary, formalized planning systems may be imperfect, but a system of some form remains essential for control and co-ordination. Alone it cannot enable the company to deal with competitive uncertainties and pressures. Vision and learning are essential, but planning must not be abandoned.

This section has considered the important role and contribution of strategic planning in large, and possibly diverse, organizations. The next section considers strategic planning in small businesses. Box 9.2 examines a number of relevant planning issues in local government.

Strategic planning and small businesses

Many small companies stay focused and do not diversify or acquire another business. Their corporate perspective stays the same, but they still need to create some form of competitive advantage and develop and integrate functional plans. In this respect, small business planning is similar to that for an individual

STRATEGY IN ACTION – Box 9.2
Strategy and Local Government

A typical UK local authority is likely to perceive the aim of the activities it carries out as the provision of more, and ideally better, services for the local community. These services fall into three broad categories: front-line (housing, education and leisure), regulatory (environmental health, planning and building control), and promotional (economic development and tourism).

How does local government 'work' strategically? Strategic decisions at the top policy level demand an input from two groups of people: the elected councillors who exert a controlling influence, and the salaried managers. The councillors may be politically very experienced and, working on behalf of their constituents, they should be in a position to reflect local needs. The specialist expertise is more likely to come from the salaried staff. There are, therefore, two strategic leaders – the Leader of the Council and the Chief Executive – who ideally will be able to work together harmoniously and synergistically. On occasions there will be clear evidence of visionary leadership. Some leaders, either individually or in partnership, will transform the character and infrastructure of a town or city. At the other extreme, other leaders really do little more than manage budgets and carry through central government initiatives.

There is an obvious role for strategic planning as local authorities have to work within guidelines and budget restraints set by central government. They have to decide upon how, at least, to maintain local services, improve efficiencies and implement any central government requirements.

Councillors will form into policy-making groups, and the salaried employees will operate with some degree of delegated authority in discrete service areas. Each service will have policy guidelines, output targets and a budget. Normally they will be free to develop and adapt strategies as long as they operate within their budget and achieve their outputs.

Many councils will want to increase spending wherever possible, as more or better services are popular with the electorate. In simple terms, spending minus income (including grants from central government) equals the sum to be raised from householders and businesses, and generally more spending is likely to lead to higher local taxes. The freedom to increase these is constrained by central government. Borrowing is used primarily to fund new capital programmes and for managing the cash flow on a temporary basis. It is, for example, being suggested that in the future local councils will borrow money to build new roads or improve existing ones and repay the money with congestion charges on motorists.

STRATEGY IN ACTION – Box 9.2
(Continued)

Some councils establish partnerships with specific developers. An independent company might, for example, develop a new shopping centre in partnership with a local authority. Together they will put up or raise substantial sums of development capital which will be repaid later through rents and business rates.

It is very difficult to measure quantitatively the benefits that accrue from certain services, such as parks and gardens for public recreation. Information from the Audit Commission enables one authority to compare its costs and spending in total, and per head of the population, for individual services with those incurred by similar authorities in the UK. Where this is utilized it is basically a measure of efficiency, rather than an assessment of the overall effectiveness of the service provision.

Until the 1980s it was usual for a local authority to carry out most of its activities in-house. External contractors were used for some building and engineering work, and in other instances where very specialized skills were required. However, the first Thatcher government required that councils put out to tender all major new build projects, together with significant projects in housing and highways maintenance. Later in the 1980s school catering, refuse collection, street cleaning and most white-collar services were also subject to compulsory competitive tendering (CCT). Where services were put out for tender an authority continued to determine the specific level of service to be provided, and then sought quotations for this provision. Tendering organizations neither suggested nor influenced the actual level of service. This power remained firmly with the local authority. As more and more services were compulsorily put out to tender local authorities essentially became purchasers of services on behalf of the local community.

The Blair Labour government, elected in 1997, was determined to abolish CCT and replace it with 'Best Value'. CCT was abandoned in 2000. Best Value requires a local authority to review each of its services over five-year periods, assessing whether it should be provided in-house, via the voluntary sector or by private-sector contractors. There are four key themes:

- challenge
- consult (stakeholders)
- compare (by benchmarking external and other local authority providers)
- compete (with the best providers that can be identified).

Audit Commission UK http://www.audit-commission.gov.uk

business inside a conglomerate. Aram and Cowen (1990) believe that small businesses can improve their performance by limited investment in strategic planning and development, and returns well in excess of costs can be generated. Unfortunately, many small owner–managers misguidedly believe that:

- strategic planning is too expensive and only belongs in large organizations
- formalized processes, requiring expert planners, are essential
- the benefits are too long term and there are no immediate payoffs.

As a result they adopt a more seat-of-the-pants reactive approach. Both vision and flexibility are important features of most successful small businesses, but these can be built on to provide greater strength and stability. Simply, and reinforcing points made earlier in the chapter, small companies can benefit in the same way as large ones from discerning the important *strategic issues* and from involving managers from the various functions in deciding how they might best be tackled.

Aram and Cowen recommend that small companies should involve all relevant managers in discussions about priorities, opportunities, problems and preferences. They should look ahead and not just consider immediate problems and crises. Objective information and analyses (albeit limited in scope) are required to underpin the process, which must be actively and visibly supported by the owner–manager or strategic leader, who, in turn, must be willing to accept ideas from other managers. Adequate time must also be found, and sound financial systems should be in place to support the implementation of new strategies and plans.

Strategic Planning Issues

Who should plan?

Among the various authors on corporate planning who have been referred to earlier in this chapter, there is a consensus of opinion that strategic planning should not be undertaken by the chief executive alone, planning specialists divorced from operating managers, marketing executives or finance departments. An individual or specialist department may be biased and fail to produce a balanced plan. Instead, it is important to involve, in some way, all managers who will be affected by the plan, and who will be charged with implementing it. However, all of these managers together cannot constitute an effective working team, and therefore a small team representing the whole organization should be constituted, and other managers consulted. This will require a schedule for the planning activities and a formalized system for carrying out the tasks. As discussed above, it is important that planning systems do not inhibit ongoing strategic thinking by managers throughout the organization. Threats must still be spotted early and potential opportunities must not be lost.

Planning traps

Ringbakk (1971) and Steiner (1972) have documented several reasons why formal planning might fail and have discussed the potential traps to avoid. Among their conclusions are the following.

- Planning should not be left exclusively to planners who might see their job as being the production of a plan and who might also concentrate on procedures and detail at the expense of wide strategic thinking.
- Planning should be seen as a support activity in strategic decision making and not a once-a-year ritual.
- There must be a commitment and an allocation of time from the strategic leader. Without this managers lower down the organization might not feel that planning matters within the firm.
- Planning is not likely to prove effective unless the broad directional objectives for the firm are agreed and communicated widely.
- Implementers must be involved, both in drawing up the plan (or essential information might be missed) and afterwards. The plan should be communicated throughout the organization, and efforts should be made to ensure that managers appreciate what is expected of them.
- Targets, once established, should be used as a measure of performance and variances should be analysed properly. However, there can be a danger in over-concentrating on targets and financial data at the expense of more creative strategic thinking.
- The organizational climate must be appropriate for the planning system adopted, and consequently structural and cultural issues have an important role to play.
- Inflexibility in drawing up and using the plan can be a trap. Inflexibility in drawing up the plan might be reflected in tunnel vision, a lack of flair and creativity, and in assuming that past trends can be extrapolated forwards.
- If planning is seen as an exercise rather than a support to strategy creation, it is quite possible that the plan will be ignored and not implemented.

The impact of planning on managers

Unless the above traps are avoided and the human aspects of planning are considered, the planning activity is unlikely to prove effective. Abell and Hammond (1979) and Mills (1985) highlight the following important people considerations.

- Ensure the support of senior executives.
- Ensure that every manager who is involved understands what is expected of him or her and that any required training in planning techniques is provided.
- Use specialist planners carefully.
- Keep planning simple, and ensure that techniques never become a doctrine.
- Particularly where detailed planning is involved, ensure that the time horizon is appropriate. It is harder to forecast and plan detail the further into the future one looks.
- Never plan for the sake of planning.
- Link managerial rewards and sanctions to any targets for achievement which are established.
- Allow managers of business units and functions some freedom to develop their own planning systems rather than impose rigid ones, especially if they produce the desired results.

In summary, planning activities can take a number of forms, and organizations should seek to develop systems that provide the results they want. Ideally, these should encapsulate both strategic thinking and the establishment of realistic objectives and expectations and the strategies to achieve them. Planning techniques can be used supportively, and their potential contribution is evaluated in the next section. Systematic corporate planning, though, should not be seen as the only way in which strategic changes are formulated.

The role of planning and planners

In the light of the comments above on strategy formulation, this section concludes by considering further the role of planning and planners. Planning and strategy creation are different in the sense that planners may or may not be strategists but strategists might be found anywhere in the organization. Mintzberg (1989) suggests that planning activities are likely to involve a series of different and very useful analyses, but it does not follow that these must be synthesized into a systematic planning system. Planners can make a valuable contribution to the organization and to strategic thinking by:

- programming strategies into finite detail to enable effective implementation (this will involve budgeting and ensuring that strategies are communicated properly, plus the establishment of monitoring and control processes)
- formalizing ongoing strategic awareness – carrying out SWOT analyses and establishing what strategic changes are emerging at any time
- using scenarios and planning techniques to stimulate and encourage thinking
- searching for new competitive opportunities and strategic alternatives, and scrutinizing and evaluating them.

In other words, all of the activities incorporated in the planning systems discussed earlier in the chapter are seen to be making an important contribution, but they need not be component parts of a systematic model. Rather, they are contributors towards strategic thinking, awareness and insight.

Johnson (1992) further points out that on occasions plans are documented in detail only because particular stakeholders, say institutional shareholders or bankers, expect to see them as justification for proposals. There is never any real intention that they should be implemented in full.

Figure 9.5 draws together a number of these themes and illustrates the various contributions that planning and planners can make. In conjunction with this, the next section considers the relative value and contribution of selected planning techniques.

> The key macro and micro variables of our business are so dynamic that poker becomes more predictable than planning and reactivity more profitable than rumination.
> *Dr John White, ex-Managing Director, BBA, whose customers were involved in the motor vehicle industry*
>
> I have a saying: 'Every plan is an opportunity lost' . . . because I feel that if you try to plan the way your business will go, down to the last detail, you are no longer able to seize any opportunity that may arise unexpectedly.
> *Debbie Moore, Founder Chairman, Pineapple (dance studios) Ltd*

Strategic Planning Techniques

It has already been explained that different strategists and authors of strategy texts adopt different stances on the significance of vision, culture and strategic planning techniques in effective strategic planning. In this book the view is held that the role of the strategic leader, styles of corporate decision making and organization culture are key driving forces in strategy creation and implementation. However, strategic planning techniques, which rely heavily on the collection and analysis of quantitative data, do have an important contribution to make. They help to increase awareness, and thereby reduce the risk involved in certain decisions. They can indicate the incidence of potential threats and limitations which might reduce the future value and contribution of individual products and services. They can help in establishing priorities in large complex multiproduct multinational organizations. They can provide appropriate frameworks for evaluating the relative importance of very different businesses in a portfolio.

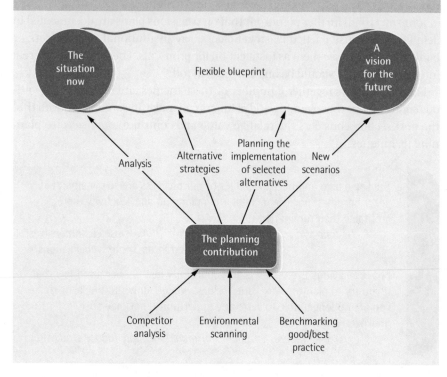

Figure 9.5 The planning contribution. Systematic planning (in isolation) will not create a vision – but you can plan your own way towards a vision. Ideas generated through planning may well change the vision.

However, their value is dependent on the validity and reliability of the information fed into them. Where comparisons with competitors are involved, the data for other companies may well involve 'guesstimation'.

Judgement is required for assessing the significance of events and competitor strategies; vision is essential in discontinuous change management.

In the author's opinion strategic planning techniques should be used to help and facilitate decision makers. They should not be used to make decisions without any necessary qualifications to the data and assumptions.

Portfolio analysis

The Boston Consulting Group growth-share matrix (Box 9.3) can be very useful for positioning products in relation to their stage in the product lifecycle as long as one is both careful and honest in the use of data. It can provide insight into the likely cash needs and the potential for earnings generation. However, while

KEY CONCEPT – Box 9.3
The Boston Consulting Group (BCG) Growth-share Matrix

Basic premises

Bruce Henderson (1970) of BCG has suggested firstly that the margins earned by a product, and the cash generated by it, are a function of market share. The higher the market share, relative to competitors, the greater the earnings potential; high margins and market share are correlated. A second premise is that sales and revenue growth requires investment. Sales of a product will only increase if there is appropriate expenditure on advertising, distribution and development; and the rate of market growth determines the required investment. Third, high market share must be earned or bought, which requires additional investment. Finally, no business can grow indefinitely. As a result, products will at times not be profitable because the amount of money being spent to develop them exceeds their earnings potential; at other times, and particularly where the company has a high relative market share, earnings exceed expenditure and products are profitable.

Profitability is therefore affected by market growth, market share, and the stage in the product lifecycle. A company with a number of products might expect to have some that are profitable and some that are not. In general, mature products, where growth has slowed down and the required investment has decreased, are the most profitable, and the profits they earn should not be reinvested in them but used instead to finance growth products that offer future earnings potential.

The matrix

The matrix is illustrated in Figure 9.6. Chart (a) shows the composition of the axes and the names given to products or business units which fall in each of the four quadrants; chart (b) features 15 products or business units in a hypothetical company portfolio. The sterling-volume size of each product or business is proportional to the areas of the circles, and the positioning of each one is determined by its market growth rate and relative market share.

The *market growth rate* on the vertical axis is the annual growth rate of the market in which the company competes, and really any range starting with zero could be used. The problem is where to draw the horizontal dividing line which separates high-growth from low-growth markets.

The *relative market share* on the horizontal axis indicates market share in relation to the largest competitor in the market. A relative market share

KEY CONCEPT – Box 9.3
(Continued)

of 0.25 would indicate a market share one-quarter of that of the market leader; a figure of 2.5 would represent a market leader with a market share that is 2.5 times as big as that of the nearest rival. The vertical dividing line is normally 1.0, so that market leadership is found to the left-hand side of the divider. It is important to consider market segmentation when deciding upon the market share figure to use, rather than using the share of the total market.

The growth-share matrix is thus divided into four cells or quadrants, each representing a particular type of business.

- *Question marks* are products or businesses which compete in high growth markets but where market share is relatively low. A new product launched into a high growth market and with an existing market leader would normally constitute a question mark. High expenditure is required to develop and launch the product, and consequently it is unlikely to be profitable and may instead require subsidy from more profitable products. Once the product is established, further investment will be required if the company attempts to claim market leadership.

- Successful question marks become *stars*, market leaders in growth markets. However, investment is still required to maintain the rate of growth and to defend the leadership position. Stars are marginally profitable only, but as they reach a more mature market position as growth slows down they will become increasingly profitable.

- *Cash cows* are therefore mature products which are well-established market leaders. As market growth slows down there is less need for high investment, and hence they are the most profitable products in the portfolio. This is boosted by any economies of scale resulting from the position of market leadership. Cash cows are used to fund the businesses in the other three quadrants.

- *Dogs* describe businesses that have low market shares in slower growth markets. They may well be previous cash cows, which still enjoy some loyal market support although they have been replaced as market leader by a newer rival. They should be marginally profitable, and should be withdrawn when they become loss makers, if not before. The opportunity cost of the resources that they tie up is an important issue in this decision.

Boston Consulting Group http://www.bcg.com

a particular matrix position indicates potential needs and prospects it should not be seen as prescriptive for future strategy. In certain respects, all competitive positions are unique, and it is very important to consider the actual industry involved and the nature and behaviour of competitors. Business unit and product managers are likely to be able to do this with greater insight than specialist planners as they are in a better position to appreciate the peculiarities of the market.

The product portfolio suggests the following strategies for products or business units falling into certain categories:

- cash cow – milk and redeploy the cash flow
- dog – liquidate or divest and redeploy the freed resources or proceeds
- star – strengthen competitive position in growth industry
- question – invest as appropriate to secure and improve competitive position.

Given that a dog represents a product or service in a relatively low-growth industry sector, and one which does not enjoy market segment leadership, it follows that many companies will have a number of dogs in their portfolios. Liquidation or divestment will not always be justified. Products which have a strong market position, even though they are not the market leader, and which have a distinctive competitive advantage can have a healthy cash flow and profitability. Such products are sometimes referred to as cash dogs. Divestment is most appropriate when the market position is weak and when there is no real opportunity to create sustainable competitive advantage, as long as a buyer can be found. Turnaround

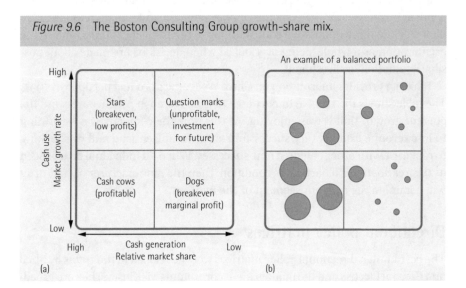

Figure 9.6   The Boston Consulting Group growth-share mix.

strategies for products which are performing very poorly are examined further in Chapter II.

According to Hamermesch (1986) many businesses that are classified as cash cows should be managed for innovation and growth, especially if the industry is dynamic or volatile, or can be made so. In other words, strategies that succeed in extending the product lifecycle can move it from a state of maturity into further growth. One example quoted is coffee. This market experienced renewed growth when the success of automatic coffee makers increased demand for new varieties of fresh ground coffee. The success of Starbucks (coffee) illustrates shows how a single organization which spots and seizes an opportunity can change an industry and provide an impetus for growth.

At one time in the ballpoint pen market Bic was the clear market leader and a cash cow when the market reached a stage of maturity. However, the introduction of rollerball pens and erasable ballpoint pens generated new growth and marketing opportunities for other competitors. Bic, meanwhile, has ensured its continued success by producing pens as 'give-away' corporate products for clients such as the main hotel chains, who mainly place them in hotel rooms and expect that guests will remove them.

When 'milking' products care also has to be taken not to reduce capacity if there is a chance that demand and growth opportunities might return as a result of scarcities or changes in taste. When restrictions on the import of Scotch whisky into Japan were eased in the late 1980s, the product enjoyed star status even though it was seen as a cash cow in the UK.

Strategic decisions based on portfolio positions may also ignore crucial issues of interdependence and synergy. Business units may be treated as separate independent businesses for the purposes of planning, and this can increase the likelihood of the more qualitative contributions to other business units, and to the organization as a whole, being overlooked when decisions are made about possible liquidation or divestment.

Table 9.3 provides information on Glaxo Wellcome's product portfolio in 1997. The table shows the relative importance to Glaxo of each product area and the current growth that it was enjoying. At this time the company was beginning to lose revenue from its very successful Zantac antiulcer drug and was looking to replace it with other patented new successes. When an individual drug is seen as *the* treatment for a particular condition, then the manufacturer of that drug will dominate the relevant segment of the industry.

Directional policy matrices

The best-known directional policy matrices were developed in the 1970s by Shell and General Electric and the management consultants McKinsey. They are broad-

Table 9.3   Glaxo Wellcome (1997)

Area of treatment	Revenue contribution (%)	Current rate of growth/decline (%)
Gastrointestinal, including Zantac	23	−13
Respiratory	21	+11
Viral infections	16	+28
Bacterial infections	11	+2
Migraine-type drugs	9	+47
Oncology	6	−3
Others	14	+8

At this time (and prior to its merger with SmithKline Beecham), Glaxo Wellcome was focusing its research efforts on viral infections (two separate AIDS drugs), asthma, influenza and hepatitis B.

Glaxo Wellcome   http://www.glaxowellcome.co.uk

ly similar and aim to assist large complex multiactivity enterprises with decisions concerning investment and divestment priorities. A version of the Shell matrix is illustrated in Figure 9.7; a fuller explanation can be found in Robinson *et al.* (1978).

In using such a matrix there is an assumption that resources are scarce, and that there never will be, or should be, enough financial and other resources for the implementation of all the project ideas and opportunities which can be conceived in a successful, creative and innovative organization. Choices will always have to be made about investment priorities. The development of an effective corporate strategy therefore involves an evaluation of the potential for existing businesses together with new possibilities in order to determine the priorities.

The matrix is constructed within two axes: the horizontal axis represents industry attractiveness, or the prospects for profitable operation in the sector concerned; the vertical axis indicates the company's existing competitive position in relation to other companies in the industry. New possibilities can be evaluated initially along the vertical axis by considering their likely prospects for establishing competitive advantage. It will be appreciated that Michael Porter's work links closely to this.

In placing individual products in the matrix the factors shown in Table 9.4 are typical of those that might be used.

Each factor would be given a weighting relative to its perceived importance, and each product being evaluated would be given a score for every factor. The aggregate weighted scores for both axes determine the final position in the matrix.

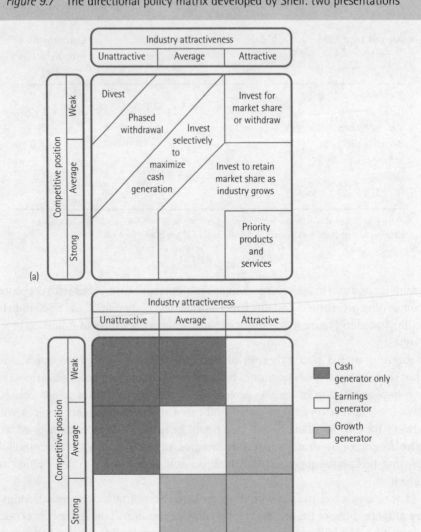

Figure 9.7 The directional policy matrix developed by Shell: two presentations

Using the matrix

Figure 9.7(a) illustrates that the overall attractiveness of products diminishes as one moves diagonally from the bottom right-hand corner of the matrix to the top left. Priority products, in the bottom right-hand corner, are those which score highly on both axes. As a result they should receive priority for development, and the resources necessary for this should be allocated to them.

Table 9.4	Factors in the directional policy matrix

Industry attractiveness	Market growth
	Market quality, or the ability for new products to achieve higher or more stable profitability than other sectors
	Supplier pressure
	Customer pressure
	Substitute products
	Government action
	Entry barriers
	Competitive pressure
Competitive position and relative strength	Competition
	Relative market shares
	Competitive postures and opportunities
	Production capability
	Research and development record and strengths
	Success rate to date, measured in terms of market share and financial success (earnings in excess of the cost of capital)

Products bordering on the priority box should receive the appropriate level of investment to ensure that at the very least market share is retained as the industry grows.

Products currently with a weak competitive position in an attractive industry are placed in the top right-hand corner of the matrix. They should be evaluated in respect of the potential to establish and sustain real competitive advantage. If the prospects seem good, then carefully targeted investment should be considered seriously. If the prospects are poor it is appropriate to withdraw from the market. A weak position in an attractive industry might be remedied by the acquisition of an appropriate competitor.

Products across the middle diagonal should receive custodial treatment. It is argued that a good proportion of products is likely to fall into this strategic category, which implies attempting to maximize cash generation with only a limited commitment of additional resources.

Currently profitable products with little future potential should be withdrawn gradually, but retained as long as they are profitable and while the resources committed to them cannot be allocated more effectively elsewhere.

Products for divestment are likely already to be losing money if all of their costs are properly assigned.

Figure 9.7(b) provides an alternative presentation and flags that products should been seen as either cash generators at best, earnings generators or true growth generators, dependent upon their relative positioning.

The directional policy matrix, like other matrices, is only a technique which assists in determining the industry and product sectors that are most worthy of additional investment capital. Issues of synergy and overall strategic fit require further managerial judgement before final decisions are reached.

SPACE (strategic position and action evaluation)

Rowe *et al.* (1989) have developed a model based on four important variables:

- the relative stability/turbulence of the environment
- industry attractiveness
- the extent of any competitive advantage
- the company's financial strengths – incorporating profitability, liquidity and current exposure to risk.

Scores are awarded for each factor, and then put into a diagram (see Box 9.4). This particular illustration features a financially strong company (or division or product) enjoying competitive advantage in an attractive industry with a relatively stable environment. The appropriate strategy is an aggressive one. The table shows the appropriate strategies for four clearly delineated positions, and judgement has to be applied when the situation is less clear cut.

This technique usefully incorporates finance, which will affect the feasibility of particular strategic alternatives and the ability of a company to implement them. It has similar limitations to directional policy matrices.

PIMS (profit impact of market strategy)

According to Buzzell and Gale (1987) the profit impact of market strategy (PIMS) approach is similar to portfolio analysis in that industry characteristics and strategic position are seen as important determinants of strategy and strategic success. However, PIMS was designed to explore the impact of a wide variety of strategic and environmental issues on business performance, and to provide principles that will help managers to understand how market conditions and particular strategic choices might affect business performance.

PIMS was invented by General Electric in the 1960s as an internal analysis technique to identify which strategic factors most influence cash flow and investment needs and success. Its scope was extended by the Harvard Business School and eventually in 1975 the Strategic Planning Institute (SPI) was established to develop PIMS for a variety of clients.

PIMS is a very sophisticated computer model and its database is information submitted by clients. They provide about 100 pieces of information about the

KEY CONCEPT – Box 9.4
SPACE; Strategic position and Action Evaluation

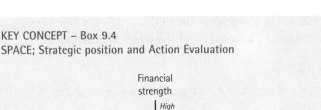

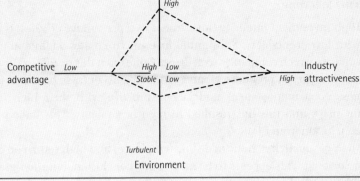

Strategic thrust	Aggressive	Competitive	Conservative	Defensive
Features:				
Environment	Stable	Unstable	Stable	Unstable
Industry	Attractive	Attractive	Unattractive	Unattractive
Competitiveness	Strong	Strong	Weak	Weak
Financial strength	High	Weak	High	Weak
Appropriate strategies	Growth, possibly by acquisition	Cost reduction, productivity improvement, raising more capital to follow opportunities and strengthen competitiveness	Cost reduction and product/service rationalization	Rationalization
	Capitalize on opportunities		Invest in search for new products, services and competitive opportunities	Divestment as appropriate
	Innovate to sustain competitive advantage			
		Possibly merge with a less competitive but cash-rich company		

Source: Rowe, AJ, Mason, RO, Dickel, KE and Snyder, NH (1989) *Strategic Management: A Methodological Approach*, 3rd edn, Addison-Wesley.

business environment and the competitive position of each product, production processes, research and development, sales and marketing activities and financial performance. From an analysis of the data those elements that are most significant to the performance for each business are identified and the information is relayed to the client.

PIMS can be used for:

- evaluating business performance relative to competitors, and
- establishing targets for return on investment and cash flow.

The SPI claims that variables in the PIMS models are able to explain some 80% of the variations in performance of the businesses included.

Major findings

Among the most significant findings that have emerged from the PIMS models are the following.

- High investment intensity (investment as a percentage of sales) is associated with low profitability. Substantial investment creates additional production capacity which companies seek to use. Quite often this results in low prices and low margins for products. Japanese industry, in contrast, has been able to harness good management and labour practice with their high investment intensity, and this has resulted in high profitability. This links to the next conclusion from PIMS.
- High productivity (value added per employee) and high return on capital are associated. This appears to be an obvious conclusion, but the significance of the point is that, while the previous finding indicates that high investment in capital and the corresponding reduction in labour intensity do not create profits, improvements in working practices have a more positive impact on profitability.
- Additional investment in products and industries that are currently performing well is not guaranteed to bring increased profits.
- High relative market share has a strong influence on profitability but is not the only factor.
- High industry growth rates absorb cash, and can have a harmful effect on cash flow – this is made worse by high capital intensity.
- High relative product quality is related to high return on investment. An element of managerial judgement is involved in the data substantiating this.
- High relative quality is said to exist when managers in the organization believe that they have a superior competitive position.
- Product innovation and differentiation lead to profitability, especially in mature markets, but relative market share also has a considerable influence on this factor.
- Vertical integration is more likely to prove successful in stable industries than in unstable ones. Vertical integration tends to increase fixed costs, making the firm more vulnerable if there is intense competition or technological change.
- The conclusion of the experience curve is sound in that unit cost reductions over time prove profitable for companies with high market share.

Limitations of PIMS

It is important to appreciate that there are certain drawbacks which Constable (1980), among others, has listed. These include the following.

- PIMS assumes that short-term profitability is the prime objective of the organization.
- The analysis is based on historical data and the model does not take account of future changes in the company's external environment.
- The model cannot take account of interdependencies and potential synergy within organizations. Each business unit is analysed in isolation.

Planning techniques, then, can be extremely useful, particularly as they force managers and organizations to ask themselves many relevant and searching questions and compile and analyse important information. But the techniques do not, and cannot, provide answers; they merely generate the questions. The danger is that some managers may perceive the output of a technique such as PIMS or a matrix analysis as an answer to strategic issues.

Summary

Strategic planning – using techniques and formalized procedures – is just one of the ways in which strategies are created. Strategies can also be provided by the strategic leader and be decided by managers 'in real time'. Intended strategies, say those selected by the leader or a formal planning system, have to be implemented, and during this implementation they may well be changed incrementally. After all, intended strategies imply forecasting, and, to some extent, all forecasts are wrong. In addition, flexible organizations will adapt all the time by responding to new opportunities and threats.

In the 1960s and 1970s the predominant view with academics and organizations was that formalized strategic planning was at the heart of strategy creation, and should be used to manage future direction. It became clear, however, that a planning approach that relies on quantitative data, forecasts and manuals, can restrict creativity, thinking, flexibility and, critically, the support and engagement of the managers who must implement strategy. Many organizations fell into the trap of believing the key outcome of planning is the plan!

Nevertheless, it is important to realize that all managers plan, all the time. Evaluating the current situation, and discussing possible changes and improvements with colleagues, implies planning. Simply, this is informal planning rather than the formalized systems implied by the term strategic planning.

There are at least seven approaches to planning, which should not necessarily be seen as mutually exclusive. Formal planning is separate from informal planning. The process can be largely top–down or bottom–up. It can take the form of extended budgeting and be numbers driven, or be more behavioural in approach, possibly using scenarios.

The '*planning gap*' is a very flexible concept and technique which can be used in a variety of ways. Broadly, it is used to clarify the extent of the revenue or profits gap that might emerge if current strategies are left largely unchanged. The more ambitious the objectives set by the company, the greater the risk that is likely to be involved in the strategies required to close the gap.

Our contemporary approach to strategic planning is based on a mixture of planning techniques, intellectual input and action plans for implementing strategies; and central to the whole process are current strategic issues.

With any form of strategic planning it is important to decide upon who should be involved and what they should contribute. Professional or specialist planners have an important role to play, but others must be involved as well. Where there is an overreliance on planners, or where there is inadequate flexibility with the plan itself, the organization is likely to fall into one of the obvious planning traps.

Planning has a number of important contributions to make and individual organizations will not all adopt the same approach.

There is a number of useful planning techniques, specifically:

- the Boston Consulting Group (BCG) 2 × 2 matrix
- directional policy matrices
- SPACE
- PIMS.

In various ways all of these techniques can be valuable. They will always be dangerous if they are used too rigidly and allowed to drive decisions without reference to, or qualification by, managerial judgement.

References

Abell, DF and Hammond, JS (1979) *Strategic Market Planning*, Prentice-Hall.

Ackoff, RL (1970) *A Concept of Corporate Planning*, John Wiley.

Ansoff, HI (1987) *Corporate Strategy*, revised edn, Penguin.

Aram, JD and Cowen, SS (1990) Strategic planning for increased profit in the small business, *Long Range Planning*, 23, 6.

Argenti, J (1980) *Practical Corporate Planning*, George Allen & Unwin.

Buzzell, RD and Gale, BT (1987) *The PIMS Principles – Linking Strategy to Performance*, Free Press.

Cohen, KJ and Cyert, RM (1973) Strategy formulation, implementation and monitoring, *Journal of Business*, 46(3), 349–67.

Constable, J (1980) Business strategy. Unpublished paper, Cranfield School of Management.

Glueck, WF and Jauch, LR (1984) *Business Policy and Strategic Management*, 4th edn, McGraw-Hill.

Hamermesch, R (1986) Making planning strategic, *Harvard Business Review*, July–August.

Harvey-Jones, JH (1987) In an introduction to Ansoff, HI, *Corporate Strategy*, Penguin.

Henderson, B (1970) *The Product Portfolio*, Boston Consulting Group.

Hussey, D (1976) *Corporate Planning – Theory and Practice*, Pergamon.

Johnson, G (1992) Strategic direction and strategic decisions, presented at 'Managing Strategically: Gateways and Barriers', Strategic Planning Society Conference, 12 February.

Mills, DQ (1985) Planning with people in mind, *Harvard Business Review*, July–August.

Mintzberg, H (1989) Presentation to the Strategic Planning Society, London, 2 February.

Further detail can be found in Mintzberg, H (1973).

Ohmae, K (1982) *The Mind of the Strategist*, McGraw-Hill.

Ringbakk, KA (1971) Why planning fails, *European Business*, Spring.

Robinson, J (1986) Paradoxes in planning, *Long Range Planning*, 19(6).

Robinson, SJQ, Hitchens, RE and Wade, DP (1978) The directional policy matrix – tool for strategic planning, *Long Range Planning*, 21, June.

Rowe, AJ, Mason, RO, Dickel, KE and Snyder, NH (1989) *Strategic Management: A Methodological Approach*, 3rd edn, Addison-Wesley.

Steiner, G (1972) *Pitfalls in Comprehensive Long Range Planning*, Planning Executives Institute.

Taylor, B and Hussey, DE (1982) *The Realities of Planning*, Pergamon.

Test your knowledge of this chapter with our online quiz at:
http://www.thomsonlearning.co.uk

Explore Strategic Planning further at:

Journal of Business   http://www.journals.uchicago.edu/JB

Questions and Research Assignments

TEXT RELATED

1. Mintzberg has distinguished between 'grass-roots' strategies (which can take root anywhere in the organization but eventually proliferate once they become more widely adopted) and 'hothouse' strategies which are deliberately grown and cultured. What do you think he means?

2. Who should plan? What should they plan, how and when?

3. A manufacturer of industrial products is structured around five separate strategic business units (SBUs). Use the data below to construct a Boston matrix and assess how balanced the portfolio seems. Where are the strengths? Where are the weaknesses?

SBU	Sales £ million	Number of competitors	Sales of top three companies £ million	Market growth rate %
A	0.4	6	0.8, 0.7, 0.4	16
B	1.8	20	1.8, 1.8, 1.2	18
C	1.7	16	1.7, 1.3, 0.9	8
D	3.5	3	3.5, 1.0, 0.8	5
E	0.6	8	2.8, 2.0, 1.5	2

4. In the context of the Boston matrix, is the Big Mac a cash cow? What do you feel McDonald's competitive strategy for the Big Mac should be?

Internet and Library Projects

1. For an organization of your choice, ideally one with which you are familiar:

   (a) Ascertain how the planning, entrepreneurial and emergent modes might apply currently to strategic change in the organization. Which mode is predominant? Why do you think it is the preferred mode? How successful is it?

   (b) What would be the opportunities and concerns from greater utilization of the other modes?

   (c) As far as you are able, draw up a directional policy matrix for the products and services of the organization. (Use your own judgement in assigning weights to the various factors for assessing industry attractiveness and competitive position.)

2. Update Table 9.3 on Glaxo's 1997 portfolio of products. How strong and how balanced is the portfolio? To what extent has the merger with SmithKline Beecham strengthened the portfolio?

   Glaxo Wellcome   http://www.glaxowellcome.co.uk

3. In 1975 the Boston Consulting Group wrote a report for the British government concerning the penetration of Honda motorcycles in the USA. They concluded that the success was the result of meticulous staff work and planning.

Pascale (1984) disagrees and argues that the success was entirely due to learning and persistence, and that it was Honda's learning experience concerning operating in the USA that eventually led to a more rationally planned approach.

Both arguments are documented in Pascale, R (1984) Perspectives on strategy – the real story behind Honda's success, *California Management Review*, 26 (3). Read this article and assess the points that Pascale makes.

Boston Consulting Group   http://www.bcg.com
Honda   http://www.honda.com
California Management Review
http://www.has.berkeley.edu/News/cmr/index_.html

Emergent Strategy and Intrapreneurship: The Contribution of People and Information

Emergent strategy takes two forms: incremental changes as intended strategies are implemented, and new strategies as the organization adapts to opportunities and threats in a dynamic environment. The idea is that the organization stays flexible in order that it might get ahead and stay ahead of its rivals, and to accomplish this it needs to be innovative and intrapreneurial. Emergent strategy is clearly dependent upon decision-making processes in the organization: who makes the decisions, how, their quality, and their outcomes. In turn, this comes down to people and information.

Companies comprise physical, technical and human resources, and it is these resources that create new value. Arguably, people are the most precious resource. There is evidence that 'ordinary people can be inspired to produce extraordinary results' in particular circumstances. Where this happens in successful organizations, power has been handed over to people by the strategic leader, and they have been offered the appropriate support and encouragement. We can see where this has happened, but that does not mean that it is easily replicated by other organizations, and for this reason it is often the key to sustained competitive advantage. Communications, information and organizational knowledge provide the lubrication for the processes.

Simply, we cannot understand emergent strategy in an organization if we do not examine the relevant people and information strategies and achievements. Together with an examination of intrapreneurship and innovation, these themes provide the content of this chapter, which concludes with a short assessment of the impact of the Internet.

Case Study 10: Richer Sounds

Electrical goods retailers are not new. The dominant names in the UK are Comet and Curry's, but Richer Sounds is different, and very successful. Richer is more focused than its main rivals, specialising in hi-fi, especially separate units. According to the *Guinness Book of Records*, Richer achieves the highest sales per square foot of any retailer in the world. Sales per employee are also high. Stock is piled high to the ceilings in relatively small stores in typically low-rent locations. All the main brands can be found; the latest models feature alongside discontinued ones, these at very competitive prices. 'We just aren't that ambitious [to justify diversifying] . . . we feel that by staying with what we know best we can concentrate our effort and resources in one field and hopefully do it well'.

Julian Richer was born in 1959; his parents both worked for Marks and Spencer. He was just 19 when he opened his first shop at London Bridge: 'seventy thousand commuters passed the shop every day'. He now owns 39 stores in the UK and Eire and two more in The Netherlands. Apart from Christmas, Richer will not open on Sundays. His employees are known as colleagues and they are empowered to work 'The Richer Way'. He claims that his suggestion scheme has generated the highest number of suggestions per employee of any scheme anywhere in the world, and the best ideas are rewarded with trips on the Orient Express. The most successful employees (in terms of sales) can win free use of a holiday home; the most successful shops earn the free use of a Bentley or Jaguar for a month. Every employee is allowed £5 per month 'to go to the pub and brainstorm'. Julian Richer has advised ASDA on suggestion schemes, and ex-ASDA Chairman, Archie Norman, has said: 'Julian has gone to great lengths to create a system that works without him, but, to a great extent, his business is his personality'.

Richer has established a parallel consulting arm, with eight consultants who offer 'The Richer Way as a philosophy for delighting customers'. Consultancy is provided free to charities and good causes. Richer has also established a foundation to help selected good causes, and he owns a number of other small businesses. These include a retail recruitment agency, a property portfolio, and an award-winning tapas bar in Fulham. He has, however, 'one business and a number of hobbies'.

QUESTIONS: Is 'The Richer Way' a key to sustained competitive advantage? Why do you think it has been successful?

Richer Sounds http://www.richer-sounds.co.uk

The executives and employees who go to make up a total work force are the most important assets of the company. They always have been and always will be. The real issue is how to maximize the value from those assets and that is why all senior executives irrespective of function have an obligation to contribute to people development at every level.

Unattributed quotation from a manufacturing company director.
Taken from Coulson-Thomas and Brown (1989)

In times of discontinuity and accelerated change, survival depends on flexibility, on our ability to learn to adapt. Organizations which learn fast will survive. Management must take the lead. We must mobilize our greatest asset, our people, invest in their training and orchestrate their talents, skills and expertise. Their commitment, dedication, quality and care will build the competitive advantage of a winning team. Only they can provide our customers with the best product and service in the industry. The management of change takes tenacity, time, talent and training.

JFA de Soet, President, KLM Royal Dutch Airlines

Intrapreneurship

Building the organization

Effective leaders possess a number of characteristics, they set direction and they inspire others. However, their strong leadership should not throttle flexibility and learning by a resistance to trusting other managers and involving them in key decisions. The most successful strategic leaders realize that they cannot do everything on their own and build a team to whom they can delegate important decisions and contributions. While some of these people will, by necessity, be specialists, professionals and technocrats, Horovitz (1997) stresses the importance of also recruiting or developing entrepreneurial managers to ensure the flow of innovation and change and prevent entropy. He argues that one of the reasons for the once very successful Club Méditerranée losing momentum in the 1990s was the result of a failure to accomplish this back-filling effectively. Quinn (1980) also emphasizes the importance of innovation and ongoing learning by this team because not all of the issues and difficulties that will have to be faced can be foreseen.

> *The aim in a global business is to get the best ideas from everywhere.* [In General Electric] *each team puts up its best ideas and processes – constantly. That raises the bar. Our culture is designed around making a hero out of those who translate ideas from one place to another, who get help from somebody else. They get an award, they get praised and promoted.*
>
> (Jack Welch, Chief Executive,
> General Electric)

Horovitz (1997) contends that organizations should look for the problems before they even arise, by questioning what the (possibly very successful) organization is doing wrong. At times it is important to abandon products, services and strategies which have served the organization well in the past, as they are not the future. de Geus (1997) contends that businesses need to become 'living organizations' if they are to enjoy long and sustained success. This requires that the company:

- knows 'what it is about'
- understands where 'it fits in the world'
- values new ideas, new people, and fresh views and opinions
- manages its resources (especially financial resources) in a way which places it in a position to govern its own future; in other words, it is prudent and does not spend beyond a level it can earn.

These requirements are manifest in:

- clear direction and purpose (awareness of its identity)
- strategic positioning (its sensitivity to its environment)
- the management of change (its tolerance of new ideas) and
- the efficient use of its capital investment.

People, then, must been seen as key assets and managed accordingly; controls must have some element of looseness and flexibility; and constant learning must be possible.

Rosabeth Moss Kanter (1989) clearly supports this view when she argues that the whole organization holds the key to competitive advantage. She suggests that five criteria are found in successful, entrepreneurial organizations:

- *focused* on essential core competencies and long-term values
- *flexible* – searching for new opportunities and new internal and external synergies with the belief that ever-increasing returns and results can be obtained from the same resources if they are developed properly and innovative
- *friendly* – recognizing the power of alliances in the search for new competencies
- *fast* and able to act at the right time to get ahead and stay ahead of competitors
- *fun* – creative and with a culture which features some irreverence in the search for ways to be different; people feel free to express themselves.

This argument is revisited in Chapter 13.

In her earlier work, Kanter (1983) warned about the potential for stifling innovation by:

- blocking ideas from lower down the organization, on the grounds that only senior or very experienced managers are in a position to spot new opportunities. On the contrary, she argues, younger people with fresh minds are in an excellent position to question and challenge the status quo
- building too many levels in the hierarchy so that decision making is slowed almost to a point of non-existence
- withholding praise from people who do offer good, innovative ideas, and instilling a culture of insecurity so that people feel too terrified even to question authority, policies or procedures
- being unwilling to innovate until someone else has tried out the idea – a fear of leading change.

Case Study 10, Richer Sounds, illustrates an organization that has benefited substantially from involving employees widely in new strategy creation.

While robust questioning and assumption-testing of new ideas is crucial, it is particularly important to remember that many people fear change, partly because of uncertainty about its impact on them personally. As a result, some people will seek to resist valuable change initiatives, and may even attempt to mount an active and orchestrated opposition. They are, in fact, enterprising and entrepreneurial, but they channel their energy in an unhelpful way. Their tactics may be aimed at preventing an idea ever taking off; equally, they may wait until it has taken root and is gaining some support and momentum. Managing change effectively, therefore, requires continuous effort and sometimes patience, reinforcing the significant contribution made by the project champion.

The process of intrapreneurship

Bridge *et al.* (1998) highlight the importance of recruiting, spotting and using people with entrepreneurial talent who are motivated to use their abilities and initiative and do something on their own, but who may not want to start their own business. These internal entrepreneurs have been called *intrapreneurs* by Pinchot (1985). Intrapreneurship, then, is the term given to the establishment and fostering of entrepreneurial activity in large organizations which results in incremental improvements to existing products and services and occasionally to brand-new products.

Figure 10.1 shows that both entrepreneurship (creating outcomes which imply a real difference) and intrapreneurship (less ambitious changes which are more likely to be based around improvements than major changes of direction) are broadly similar. They both begin when someone has a personal vision from which an idea and a related opportunity emerge. The opportunity must then be engaged and resources acquired as prerequisites to action and implementation. Intrapreneurship happens as individual managers promote and sell their ideas inside the organization and build a team of supporters. They drive change.

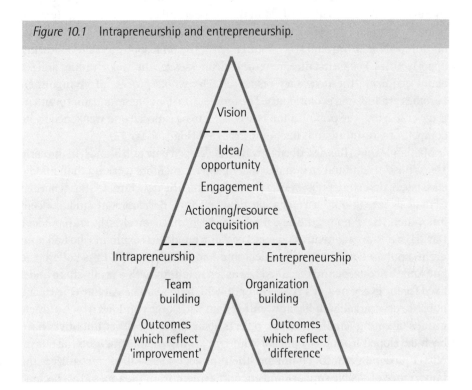

Figure 10.1 Intrapreneurship and entrepreneurship.

This was illustrated in Chapter 6 (p. 281) with the example of 3M and Post-It Notes, but realistically this is an extreme case. The innovation is more likely to be a minor, but significant improvement to a product or service or process: anything that makes a valuable difference.

Intrapreneurs, typically, are strategically aware, ideas-driven, creative, flexible, innovative, good networkers, individualistic but also able to work well in a team, persistent and courageous. If frustrated by a lack of freedom they will underachieve or possibly leave. But they are volunteers; intrapreneurship is not right for everyone.

According to Pinchot (1985), the key lies in engaging people's efforts and energy for championing, capturing and exploiting new ideas and strategic changes. This must stretch beyond the most senior managers in the organization, who do not have a monopoly on good ideas. On the contrary, the potentially most valuable and lucrative ideas are likely to come from those people who are closest to the latest developments in technology or to customers. Suggestion schemes are linked in, but on their own do not constitute intrapreneurship. The ideas need to be taken forward, and they can only be developed if the potential intrapreneurs are able to obtain the necessary internal resources and, moreover, they are willing to do something. This in turn requires encouragement and appropriate rewards for success. People must feel involved in the process and comfortable that they are being supported. Intrapreneurship cannot work where people feel 'frozen out' or 'dumped on'. Churchill (1997) summarizes the philosophy as skills following opportunities. People in entrepreneurial businesses see the opportunities and set about acquiring the necessary resources. The whole process of change then becomes gradual and evolutionary. The momentum for change and improvement is never lost and the organization is less likely to be exposed and weakened by its competitors, resulting in it having to cross a 'bridge too far'.

Maitland (1999) has described how Bass developed new pub brands. In the early 1990s Bass' traditional customers (older people, and more working than middle class) were deserting pubs; young people became the new target. '[Bass] needed a radical "break-out" strategy of new product development and concept innovation'. Bass spotted the new It's A Scream format, conceived by entrepreneur David Lee and popular with students. Lee was a builder in Farnham who had been given a pub in lieu of an unpaid debt and had transformed it. Bass bought the pub and the concept and recruited Lee as a consultant with a profit-share and a fixed fee for every new It's A Scream pub which opens. The All Bar One theme pubs, an up-market, well-lit, city-centre chain with large windows which attracts groups of young female drinkers, reflects a similar story. Other initiatives have been developed from ideas put forward by existing managers, who have been offered secondment to champion their project ideas. Bass recognized the importance of visible support and encouragement from the top, so this became an engineered and not a random process. Bass ensured that adequate financial resources were available and also utilized sophisticated computer mapping systems to help with location issues. The two parallel questions are: Where are the ideal places for siting a particular format? What would be the best format for a site they already own? The key variables are age, affluence and car ownership, linked to how far people are willing to travel to eat or drink out. In other words, Bass brought together ideas, talented intrapreneurs and the resources that they needed.

To summarize these points, Hurst (1995) likens entrepreneurial strategic leaders to gardeners. They prune. They clear out. They plant, by recruiting other entrepreneurial managers. They feed, by encouraging and rewarding managers for being creative and innovative. Simply, they nurture and manage the organization as they would a garden. Paradoxically, many good ideas begin in the same way that weeds emerge in a garden, i.e. randomly. They then need spotting and looking after – the equivalent of transfer to a hothouse?

The intrapreneurial organization

Fradette and Michaud (1998) describe four main elements to an organization which succeeds with intrapreneurship. First, the strategic and structural environment is 'right'. The purpose and direction implies a realistic vision and it is widely understood and shared. Formal systems and controls do not stifle innovation and people are free to make limited changes. Inhibitive internal 'chimneys' are pulled down so that people can collaborate and share ideas readily. Secondly, an appropriate workforce has been built. Enterprising people have been recruited. They have been trained in key skills and there is an appropriate reward system. The organization's main heroes are the entrepreneurial ones. Thirdly, the workforce is backed by the necessary support systems. Teamworking is commonplace, people collaborate and network naturally, information is shared and learning is fostered. After all, several people in the organization may be thinking along the same lines at the same time concerning future possibilities. Fourthly, successes are visibly rewarded and mistakes are not sanctioned so harshly that people are dissuaded from further initiatives. These points are discussed further later in this chapter.

An intrapreneurial organization will often feature a relatively flat structure with few layers in the hierarchy; too many layers tend to slow decision making down. The culture and atmosphere will be one of collaboration and trust. The style of management will be more coaching than instructional, and mentoring will be in evidence. Ideally it will be an exciting place to work. The entrepreneur's enthusiasm will have spread to others. In other words, it will be decentralized.

The centralization–decentralization issue is central to this. Centralization of decision-making power with the strategic leadership allows for more straight-forward controls: intended information flows are clear and it is not essential that information is shared widely through the organization. However, decision making can be relatively slow and potentially valuable information that individual managers have may well not be available. Intrapreneurship and individual innovation are restrained. While decentralization can overcome these drawbacks, it demands a different form of control system, based on information *sharing* rather than instructions, if the organization is to stay cohesive and synergistic. To many strategic leaders decentralization will appear to imply a greater risk because centralization seems easier to operate.

Terazano (1999) also reminds us that effective intrapreneurship is not that easily achieved, and that many organizations set off down the road but fail to reap the anticipated rewards. Balancing control (to ensure that current activi-ties and strategies are implemented efficiently) with flexibility (to foster and embrace changes to the same strategies) can imply different cultures, which are difficult to achieve without tension and conflict. Another difficulty frequently lies with finding the appropriate reward and remuneration systems to ensure fairness. It is a brave organization which only awards bonuses to the visibly entrepreneurial people. Managers in established companies often find it difficult to handle setbacks and disappointments when initiatives fail. But there always has to be the risk of failure, albeit temporary, when experimenting with new and unproven ideas. While intrapreneurs often have the security of large company employment, such that the penalty for failure is to some extent reduced, the rewards for real success are unlikely to equal those of the true entrepreneur. Nevertheless, 'increased competition in global markets and the pressure for innovation is forcing Britain's large companies to look for methods to stimulate ideas for new products'.

Innovation

Innovation takes place when an organization makes a technical change, e.g. pro-duces a product or service that is new to it, or uses a method or input that is new and original. If a direct competitor has already introduced the product or method then it is imitation, not innovation. However, introducing a practice from a different country or industry rather than a direct competitor would constitute innovation.

Innovation implies change and the introduction of something new. Creating the idea, or inventing something, is not innovation but a part of the total process. While at one level it can relate to new or novel products, it may also be related to production processes, approaches to marketing a product or service, or the way in which jobs are carried out within the organization. The aim is to add value for the consumer or customer by reducing costs or differentiating the product or total service in some sustainable way. In other words, innovation relates to the creation of competitive advantage; and, to summarize, there are four main forms of innovation:

- new products, which are either radically new or which extend the product lifecycle
- process innovation leading to reduced production costs, and affected partially by the learning and experience effect
- innovations within the umbrella of marketing, which increase differentiation
- organizational changes, which reduce costs or improve total quality.

Where the innovation reflects continuous improvement, product or service *enhancement*, and only minor changes in established patterns of consumer behaviour, the likelihood of success is greater than for those changes that demand new patterns of usage and consumption. Examples of the latter include personal computers and compact disc players. Discontinuous innovations such as these are more risky for manufacturers, but if they are successful the financial payoffs can be huge. By contrast, continuous improvements – which, realistically, are essential in a dynamic, competitive environment – have much lower revenue potential.

Innovation can come about in a variety of ways:

- Ideas can come out research and development departments, where people are employed to come up with new ideas or inventions. Some would argue that there is a risk that departments such as this are not in direct touch with customers; however, while customers may sense that a product or service has drawbacks, they may have no idea how it might be improved. This requires a technical expert.
- People from various parts of an organization working on special projects.
- Employees being given freedom and encouragement to work on ideas of their own, e.g. the 3M approach mentioned earlier.
- Everyday events as people interact and discuss problems and issues.

There is a mix of routine, structured events and unstructured activities.

Changes in the service provided to customers and the development of new products and services imply changes in operating systems and in the work of employees, and some of the proposed changes may well be the result of ideas generated internally. However, many of the ideas for innovations come from outside the organization, from changes in the environment. This emphasizes the crucial importance of linking together marketing and operations and harnessing the contribution of people. For example, Ford in the USA realized some years ago that a number of its engineers had a tendency to 'over-engineer' solutions to relatively simple problems. As a result, its costs were higher than those of its rivals, particularly Japanese and Korean companies, and its new product development times were considerably longer. Instead, the company needed 'creative engineers' with a fresh perspective and greater realization of customer expectations.

Creativity, innovation and entrepreneurship

'There is a great myth about innovation – that it is all about an idea. But the idea is almost incidental – innovation is about making it work as a business'. There is a clear link between entrepreneurship and innovation; indeed, Drucker (1985) argues that innovation is the tool of entrepreneurs. In addition, both innovation and entrepreneurship demand creativity. The link between these terms is therefore in need of clarification.

Creativity implies conceptualizing, visualizing or bringing into being something that does not yet exist. It is about curiosity and observation. Creativity often seems to come 'out of the blue' triggered by a problem to be solved or an idea to be expressed. Its roots and origins are mysterious and unknown but its existence cannot be denied.

Entrepreneurs (and intrapreneurs) are familiar with ideas that suddenly come to mind and are not too concerned with their origins. This is the starting point of the entrepreneurial process. Creativity is seen as a talent, an innate ability, although we recognize that it can be developed and that there are techniques that promote creativity and problem solving. Creativity is also a function of how people feel. Some are more creative under pressure while others need complete relaxation. Some use divergent thinking in their creativity while others prefer convergent thinking.

One thing that seems common to all forms of creativity is joy. Einstein comments that the idea that 'the gravitational field has only a relative existence was the happiest thought of my life' (Pais, 1982). His creative genius had come up with the idea of relativity and it made him happy. There is an intense personal satisfaction in having come up with something new and novel.

This is one reason why many entrepreneurial people see their activities and contributions as fun. There is the joy of creativity all around them. For the entrepreneur creativity is both the starting point and the reason for continued success. It is the secret formula by which he or she overcomes obstacles and outsmarts the competition.

Arguably every one of us has the ability to be creative, but do we all use and exploit this ability? Many of us simply do not act creatively much of the time. Possibly we are not motivated and encouraged; maybe we do not believe in ourselves and the contribution and difference that we could make. There is certainly a skills and technique element to creativity; in a business context, for example, we can be taught creative thinking and behaviour in the context of decision making, but this is clearly only part of the explanation.

Innovation builds on creativity when something new, tangible and value-creating is developed from the ideas. Innovation is about seeing the creative new idea through to completion, to final application, but, of course, this will not necessarily be a business. It is the *entrepreneur* who builds a business around the idea and the innovation. Both can be difficult roads and require courage and perseverance as well as creativity and imagination. These are attributes that the entrepreneur brings and his or her role in innovation is crucial.

There are three basic approaches with innovation, which are not mutually exclusive. First, it is possible to have a problem and to be seeking a solution, or at least a resolution. Edwin Land invented the Polaroid camera because his young daughter could not understand why she had to wait for the pictures to be printed when he took her photograph. Secondly, we might have an idea – in effect a solution – and be searching for a problem to which it can be applied. 3M's Post-It Notes happened when a 3M employee created a glue with only loose sticking properties, and a colleague applied it to a need he had for marking pages in a manuscript. Thirdly, we might identify a need and design something which fits. James Dyson's innovatory dual cyclone cleaner came about because of his frustration with his existing machine, which was proving inadequate for cleaning up the dirt and dust generated when he converted an old property.

Generating opportunities from ideas requires us to attribute meaning to the ideas. Ideas form in our minds and at this stage they mean something to us, personally. Typically, they become a real opportunity when we expose the ideas and share them with other people, who may well have different perceptions, attribute different meanings and see something that we miss initially. This process of exploration is fundamental for determining where the opportunities for building new values are. In other words, innovation comes from the way in which we use our ideas. Crucially, the person with the initial idea may not be the one who realizes where the real opportunity lies. An inventor is not always an opportunity spotter, and often not a natural project champion who masterminds the implementation. Picasso claimed that 'great people steal ideas and create opportunities where others cannot see the potential'.

The *Sony Walkman* provides an excellent illustration of these points. The idea came to Sony co-founder Akio Morita when he was questioning why he was finding it difficult to listen to music when he was in public places or walking round a golf course. The idea became an innovative new product, and a valuable opportunity, when Morita shared his idea with other colleagues in Sony, and existing technologies and competencies were used to develop the compact personal radio with adequate playing time from its batteries and individual headphones. The project was championed, resourced and implemented. The original radio has systematically been joined by personal cassette and CD players. It was simply a great idea which rejuvenated Sony at the time it was conceived, and it has brought value and affected the lives of millions of people around the world.

Disruptive technology

Christensen (1998) uses the term 'disruptive technology' to explain partially why it is often outsiders that succeed in changing the rules of competition in an industry. His arguments are illustrated in the case of James Dyson (Case Study 7).

When a new idea is very much at the embryo stage, and not particularly thought through, the conclusion could be that there 'might be something in it' but it is by no means certain. Whether the idea starts with their own people, or is offered to them by an outside inventor, large, established organizations may at this stage disregard the idea because it has no clear and outstanding advantages. A smaller, entrepreneurial company, in contrast, as long as it can somehow find the necessary resources, is much more likely to accept the risk associated with the idea and pursue it. Eventually the idea might well turn out to have real value – it is truly different and may offer a cost advantage as well. By the time the large company is in a position to respond it could well have lost market share.

Why does this happen? Paradoxically, according to Christensen, because large companies become very customer focused and avoid disruptive ideas or technologies that might put existing relationships and loyalties at risk. Of course, large companies can set up and resource smaller subsidiaries, and charge them with developing this form of disruption.

Human Resource Strategies

The 'people contribution'

Successful organizations meet the needs and expectations of their customers more effectively than their competitors; at the same time, they generate acceptable financial returns. Achieving these outcomes requires competent and committed people. People, then, are critically important strategic resources. Successful companies will be able to attract, motivate, develop, reward and keep skilled and competent managers and other employees. They will be able to create and implement strategic changes in a supportive culture. People need to be used and stretched to get the best out of them but, correspondingly, they need to be looked after and rewarded. However, even successful companies have lean periods, and when these occur, they will again be able to retain their most important people. There is no 'one best way' of achieving this.

Everything that an organization does, in the end, depends on people. Although technology and information technology (IT) can make a major strategic impact, it is people who exploit their potential. Managers and employees are needed to implement strategies and to this end they must understand and share the values of the organization. They must be committed to the organization and they must work together well. At the same time, where an organization is decentralized and operating in a turbulent environment, the strategic leader will rely on people to spot opportunities and threats, to adapt and create new strategies.

Consequently, it is people who ultimately determine whether or not competitive advantage is created and sustained. Adding new values with innovation, they can be an opportunity and a source of competitive advantage; equally, unenthusiastic, uncommitted, untrained employees can act as a constraint. People's capabilities are infinite and resourceful in the appropriate organizational climate. The basic test of their value concerns how much they – and their contribution – would be missed if they left or, possibly worse, left and joined a competitor. They could take customers with them and not be easily replaced.

Achieving the highest level of outcomes that people are capable of producing will therefore depend upon the human resource practices adopted by the organization. While the issues are clear and straightforward – they involve selection, training, rewards and work organization – there is no single 'best approach' to the challenge. A relatively formal, 'hard' approach can prove very successful in certain circumstances; other organizations will derive significant benefits from a 'softer', more empowered style. One issue here is whether the business is being driven by a small number of identifiable, key decision makers or by the employees collectively.

To bring out the best in people, they have to be managed well, and this requires leadership. A useful metaphor is that of an orchestra. Every member (manager/employee) is a specialist, with some making a unique contribution which, on occasions, can take the form of a solo performance. Nevertheless, all the contributions must be synthesized to create harmony (synergy), which is the role of the conductor (strategic leader). A single musician (weak link) can destroy a performance; a chain is only as strong as its weakest link.

A successful organization, therefore, needs people with appropriate skills and competencies who can work together effectively. People must be:

- committed (commitment can be improved)
- competent (competencies can be developed, and can bring improved product quality and productivity)
- cost-effective (ideally costs should be low and performance high, although this does not imply low rewards for success)
- in sympathy with the aims of the organization (are the values and expectations of all parties in agreement?)

Where people grow, profits grow.
Dr Alex Krauer, when Chairman and Managing Director, Ciba-Geigy

Involving and empowering people

There are two recognized approaches to human resource management: the 'hard' approach and the 'soft' approach. The key tension or dilemma that is being addressed is the balance between centralization for control and decentralization for greater empowerment. The two approaches imply contrasting styles, but they can both be appropriate in certain circumstances. Moreover, companies can be hard on certain aspects and soft on others. In addition, the style may alter with the strategic demands placed on an organization. When times are difficult and a company must rationalize and downsize, a hard approach may prove to be appropriate for driving through the changes quickly. However, a softer, more empowered style may be required to rejuvenate the company and bring new sources of competitive advantage.

Hard human resource management assumes that:

- people are viewed as a resource and, like all resources, companies gain competitive advantage by using them efficiently and effectively
- the deployment and development of employees – who are essentially there to implement corporate and competitive strategies – is delegated to line managers who are responsible for groups of people
- scientific management principles and systems can be useful but should be used cautiously.

Soft human resource management assumes that:

- workers are most productive if they are committed to the company, informed about its mission, strategies and current levels of success, and
- involved in teams which collectively decide how things are to be done
- employees have to be trusted to take the right decisions rather than controlled at every stage by managers above them.

Soft human resource management argues that people are different from other resources (and often more costly) but they can create added value and sustainable competitive advantage from the other resources. Therefore, soft human resource management places greater emphasis on control through review and evaluation of outcomes, such that employees are led rather than managed.

Empowerment is explored more fully in Box 10.1, which also describes the Wal-Mart approach. United Airlines in the USA provides another but quite different example. In 1994, the employees of United Airlines, the largest airline in the world,

KEY CONCEPT – Box 10.1
Empowerment

Empowerment means freeing employees from instructions and controls and allowing them to take decisions themselves. Total quality management implies constant improvement; to achieve this employees should be contributing to the best of their ability. Proponents argue that rules stifle innovation and that future success relies not on past results but on the continuing ability to manage change pressures. Managers must be free to make appropriate changes in a decentralized structure.

There are three main objectives of empowerment:

- to make organizations more responsive to external pressures
- to 'delayer' organizations in order to make them more cost effective. British Airways, for example, now has five layers of management between the chief executive and the front line who interface with customers. It used to be nine.
  Managers become responsible for more employees, who they are expected to coach and support rather than direct
- to create employee networks featuring teamworking, collaboration and horizontal communications. This implies changes in the ways in which decisions are made.

The important questions are why, how and when. The leading retailers, for example, benefited from increasing centralization throughout the 1980s. Information technology enabled cost savings and efficiencies from centrally controlled buying, store and shelf layouts, stocking policies and reordering. In the 1990s there was little support for changing this in any marked way and delegating these decisions to store level. In its early years, Waterstone's delegated book-buying responsibility to individual store managers, and this was regarded as exceptional. Once the company was acquired by WH Smith this decentralization was systematically removed. At the same time individual stores are judged in part on the quality of service provided to their customers; and it is in this area that there has always been considerable scope for empowering managers. However, in 2000, in an attempt to win back market share, Marks and Spencer has begun to decentralize purchasing and stock decisions and give store managers more opportunity to ensure that they stock ranges which best match local needs.

Since C&A announced it was closing all its stores it has allowed individual store managers the freedom to stock and sell what they think is appropriate locally. Both sales and profits have improved!

As empowerment is increased it is important that employees are adequately informed and knowledgeable, that they are motivated to exercise power, and that they are rewarded for successful outcomes. In

KEY CONCEPT – Box 10.1
(Continued)

flatter organization structures there are fewer opportunities for promotion.

There are, then, three basic empowerment options:

- Employees can be encouraged to contribute ideas. As seen in Case Study 8, several new product ideas for McDonald's have come from individual franchisees. In reality, however, this may represent only token empowerment.
- Employees work in teams which share and manage their own work, but within clearly defined policies and limits. This should increase both efficiency and job satisfaction.
- More extensive decentralization means that individuals are much freer to change certain parameters and strategies. Evaluating outcomes is seen as the important control mechanism rather than rules and guidelines. An important distinction here is between making people accountable for their individual actions and making them accountable for the overall result. Constructive accountability gives people freedom to make decisions and demands that they accept responsibility for the consequences. This requires strong leadership, a clear mission and effective communications, rewards and sanctions. Information must flow openly upwards and sideways as well as downwards. In many organizations there is a tendency for 'bad news' to be selectively hidden, with perhaps two-thirds not flowing up to the next layer. Many potential threats are thereby not shared within the company. This would be unacceptable in an empowered organization.

For many organizations empowerment implies that the core organization strategies are decided centrally, with individual managers delegated a discretionary layer around the core (as shown in Chart A).

It is crucial first to find the right balance between the core and discretionary elements, and secondly to ensure that managers support and own the core strategy.

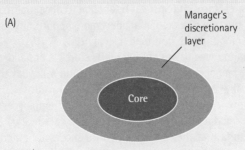

(A)

Manager's discretionary layer

Core

KEY CONCEPT – Box 10.1
(Continued)

The deciding factors are:

- The competitive strategies and the relative importance of close linkages with customers in order to differentiate and provide high levels of service. When this becomes essential empowerment may imply an inverted pyramid structure. The structure exists to support frontline managers, as shown in Chart B.

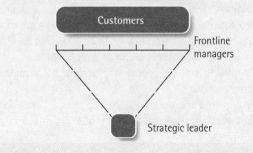

- Successful empowerment means putting the 'right' people in place and ensuring that they are able to do their job, which they understand and own. In this way they feel important.
- The extent to which the environment is turbulent and decisions are varied rather than routine.
- The expectations and preferences of managers and employees, and their ability and willingness to accept responsibility. Not everyone wants accountability and high visibility. If empowerment is mishandled it is possible that work will be simply pushed down a shorter hierarchy as managers seek to avoid responsibility.

Successful empowerment requires appropriate skills, which in turn frequently implies training. The appropriate style of management is coaching. Moreover, it is important to link in monitoring systems together with rewards and sanctions. Finally, empowerment must be taken seriously and not simply limited to non-essential decisions. Empowerment implies risk taking, and any mistakes, while not overlooked, must be handled carefully.

Empowerment is a powerful motivator as long as it does not suddenly stop when the really important and interesting decisions have to be taken.

Jeremy Soper, ex Retail Sales Director, WH Smith

KEY CONCEPT – Box 10.1
(Continued)

Wal-Mart's strategies for empowering people:

- Every project has a clear end-date.
- Everybody must experience success. Success can be built on success and people must never become complacent. People are therefore moved from clearly successful to less successful activities, so they can experience elements of both success and relative failure. In this way, 'winners' help others improve their standards and confidence; and people who are experiencing disappointment are moved into positions where morale is much higher. Linked to this,
- There is a 'no-blame' culture and no 'victims'.
- By moving around, people also become more multi-skilled and thereby grow personally.
- People are encouraged to become involved in several, small, improvemental projects – many of them driven by ideas from customers
- New ideas are tried out locally before being rolled-out more extensively.
- People are required to 'think, react and break-down barriers'.
- There is a philosophy that: *Track record + Empathy = Credibility.* Empathy develops as people 'get out', network and meet people so they can better understand their needs. It is credibility that 'gets things done'.
- To get ahead and stay ahead, speed is 'everything'.

Source for Wal-Mart material: Turner, K (1999) *The Wal-Mart Experience*, Presentation to a Retail Solutions International Conference, May.

agreed to accept paycuts in exchange for majority control of the company, which was experiencing financial difficulties. As an outcome, decision making was decentralized more. One example was the bringing together of 350 pilots, flight attendants, mechanics and other employees to plan the development of a new, low-cost, short-haul shuttle service on the West Coast. United had to achieve very high service levels and low prices to compete with SouthWest Airlines. The new venture was established reportedly 'without a single flaw'.

In an instance such as this, people who normally deal with problems and 'fire-fight', with a tactical perspective, are being encouraged to think more operationally and strategically: designing a service and the necessary systems whereby, ideally, many of the problems with which they are familiar are eliminated at the design stage.

Many organizations, however, still prefer more rigid controls from the centre, even though they may have reduced the number of layers in the organizational hierarchy and widened managers' spans of control. This, they believe, is the way to achieve efficiency and managed costs. Tighter systems inevitably constrain innovation and employee development; but, they assume, new ideas and people can be bought in or recruited.

Manager competency

Simply, some companies will seek to develop their employees and managers, invariably promoting from within. A strong culture and vision should foster both commitment and continuous, emergent change. Necessary new competencies are *learned*. In such organizations, teamworking and networking are likely to be prominent. Other organizations prefer to search for the best people who might be available; they willingly recruit outsiders. They are seeking to *buy in* the new competencies that they require. People may feel less committed to such organizations in the long term, and consequently there will be a greater reliance on individualism and individual contributions.

The challenge for companies growing from within is that they need to become and stay very aware strategically if they are to remain ahead of their rivals; they will actively benchmark and look for new ideas that might be helpful. Companies securing new skills and competencies from outside face a different dilemma. If the competencies are available, and can be bought by any competitor, how can they ensure that they find the best ideas and people, and how can they generate some unique competency and competitive advantage?

Some companies will look to do both, finding, in the process, an appropriate balance. An analogy would be a leading football club which buys expensive, talented players in the transfer market while, at the same time, nurturing young players. There are many instances where highly skilled, experienced players do not fit in at a new club, certainly not at first; and when several arrive at once, it can be very disruptive until they are moulded into an effective team.

Capelli and Crocker-Hefter (1995) further distinguish between companies that seek to compete by moving quickly, perhaps by necessity, responding speedily to new opportunities, and those that have developed a more sustainable advantage in a longstanding market. They conclude that organizations competing on flexibility will typically find it more appropriate to recruit from outside. A reliance on developing new competencies internally may mean that they are too slow to gain early advantage from new opportunities. By contrast, organizations competing in established markets with longstanding relationships are more likely to rely on internally developed, organization-specific skills and strong internal and external architecture.

There are, inevitably, implications. In general, industries and markets are becoming more dynamic and turbulent, demanding that companies develop new product and market niche opportunities. This appears to imply an increasing reliance on recruiting strong, competent people from outside. In turn, this means that internal relationships and the culture may be under constant pressure to change. Companies are recruiting and rewarding individual experts; at the same time, synergistic opportunities demand strong internal architecture and co-operation. This is another organizational dilemma. Companies that succeed in establishing a strong, cohesive and motivating culture while developing new competencies flexibly and quickly are likely to be the future high performers.

Reinforcing points from earlier chapters, this demands effective strategic leadership and a shared, understood vision for the organization. The extent to which an organization can become a 'learning organization', discussed later in this chapter, is of great significance.

Figure 10.2 repackages the notion of manager competency in the form of five distinct mindsets. Managers, in different degrees, will and must possess all of these abilities. The issues concern the balance and the opportunity. Some managers will be extremely competent in certain areas, but their profile, approach and style may not be appropriate for the demands placed on them. In addition, and given the way in which managers work with constant interruptions, and performing a series of short, pragmatic tasks, it can be difficult for them to find time to think, reflect and challenge. Short-termism and 'more-of-the-same' can all too readily be the result.

Many books have been written, and continue to be written, describing the behaviour patterns and practices of successful organizations. While there is inevitably some element of idiosyncrasy and uniqueness, this approach is interesting and valuable. It can be a rich source of ideas. However, it is not the same as identifying those competencies which have been shown empirically to be associated with the creation of superior performance.

> A *real manager* has to be a good leader in the sense that he has to embody an open-minded attitude of leadership in himself, in his fellow managers and even in the heads of each employee of his organization. *Leadership*, therefore, means to enable and help people to act as individual entrepreneurs within the frame of a commonly born vision of the business. A *bad manager*, on the other hand, is more an administrator who follows severe rules and customs within a stiff bureaucratical hierarchy.
>
> *Dr Hugo M Sekyra, CEO and Chairman, Austrian Industries*

It is because these questions are complex that some organizations will adopt and build human resource practices that help to create and sustain

Figure 10.2   Five managerial mindsets.

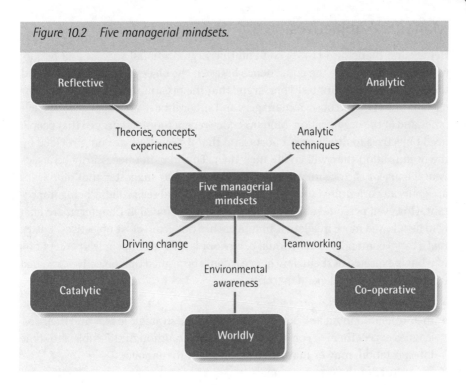

competitive advantage. They are peculiar to that organization's environmental matching challenge. Such organizations enjoy strong E–V–R (environment–values–resources) congruence. The competitive value of their competencies lies in the fact that while the general approach may be transferable, the specifics are not.

Managing Human Resources

We need the 'right' people if we are to foster effective emergent strategy. Appropriate people with the required and desired competencies, and/or the potential for growth and development, need to be recruited. They require clear objectives to give them both direction and performance yardsticks, backed by training and development opportunities. Outcomes should be measured, and performance reviewed and rewarded as appropriate. Underperformance or failure should be sanctioned in some way. This section looks briefly at a number of these issues, and also considers the importance of motivating employees, team building and succession planning.

Managers' objectives

Hersey and Blanchard (1982) contend that organizational success and performance are affected by the congruence between the objectives of managers and those of their subordinates. They argue that the organization can only accomplish its objectives if those of managers and subordinates are supportive of each other and of the organization. Moreover, McGregor (1960) has argued that people need objectives to direct their efforts, and that if objectives are not provided by the organization they will create their own. This may not necessarily be disadvantageous for the organization as Schein (1983) has suggested that managers are generally orientated towards economic goals and see profit as being important. However, personal objectives, which were discussed in Chapter 2, are likely to be allowed more freedom if managers are not given clear objectives. Porter *et al.* (1975) contend that individual behaviour is affected by people's perceptions of what is expected of them; and hence it could be argued that objectives pursued by managers will be dependent on:

- personal motives
- their understanding and perception of what the strategic leader and their colleagues expect them to contribute (expectations, although still subject to some interpretation, may or may not be made clear to managers)
- the culture of the organization.

Various systems and policies for setting and agreeing managers' objectives are available, but they are outside the scope of this book. Ideally, the resultant objectives will be 'SMART': specific, measurable, achievable, realistic and with a timescale.

While objective setting is important for dealing with tasks and priorities, it should never be forgotten that managing people effectively also involves communicating and interacting, and making sure there is always time and opportunity available for dealing with unexpected events.

Rewards

Rewards are an important motivator, but it is important to appreciate that an individual may feel rewarded by things other than money or promotion (see Figure 10.3). The demands and responsibilities of a job, and the freedom that people are given to decide how to do things, can be rewarding. In addition, working with a particular group of people, especially if they are seen to be successful, can be rewarding. If people feel that their efforts are being rewarded and that future efforts will also be rewarded, their quality of work is likely to improve. In this way, total quality can be improved. Moreover, where incremental strategic change is dependent on individual managers seeing, and acting upon, opportunities and threats, the reward system must be appropriate and motivating.

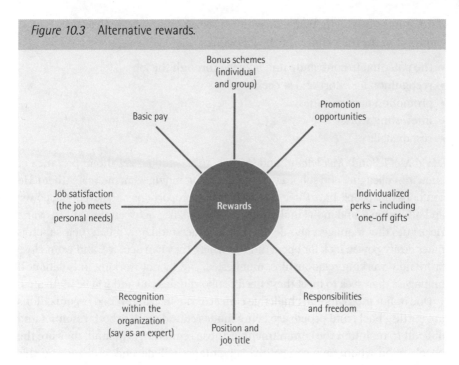

Figure 10.3 Alternative rewards.

A number of organizations, including BP, WH Smith and Federal Express, have experimented with formalized upward feedback as well as manager/subordinate appraisal. Although difficult to implement successfully, such systems can be very useful for increasing managers' awareness concerning their style and effectiveness. It is crucial that any performance evaluation systems which influence or determine rewards are open and fair, and perceived as such.

Rewards depend upon the success of the organization as a whole as well as individual contributions. Hence, individual motivation and the issues involved in building successful management teams are looked at next.

Involving and motivating people

If people are to be committed to the organization, and to the achievement of key objectives, they must be involved. Employees at the so-called grass-roots level are likely to know the details of the business and what really happens better than their superiors and managers. If they are involved and encouraged to contribute their ideas for improvements, the result can be innovation or quality improvement.

Moreover, if managers and other employees are to make effective strategic contributions it is important that they feel motivated. While money and position in the organization can motivate, there are other essential factors. Hertzberg (1968) emphasized the importance of the following:

- the potential to contribute and achieve through the job
- recognition for effort and success
- promotion opportunities
- interesting work
- responsibility.

David McClelland (McClelland and Winter, 1971) emphasizes the importance of knowing colleagues and subordinates and understanding what motivates them. He contends that people have three needs in varying proportions – achievement, power and affiliation – and individual profiles of the balance between these needs vary. He argues that managers should attempt to understand how much their subordinates desire power, look for opportunities where they can achieve, and want close or friendly working relationships, manifested, say, by not working in isolation. If managers then seek to meet these needs, subordinates can and will be motivated.

One major motivational challenge concerns downsizing. When organizations are cutting back, and people are being made redundant, it is both essential and difficult to maintain the commitment of those remaining. After all, they are the people upon whom new competitive advantages will depend, and without this the company cannot successfully rejuvenate.

Research by Roffey Park Management Centre (1995) established that while there is considerable enthusiasm among authors, consultants and senior managers for teamworking, empowerment and flexibility, many employees remain 'cynical, overworked, insecure and despondent' about the impact of flatter organization structures and the consequent reduction in promotion prospects. Employees frequently perceive delayering to be a cost-cutting exercise which actually reduces morale. When such rationalization is essential, and often it is, the real challenge comes afterwards, in encouraging the remaining managers to look for innovative new ways of adding value and to take risks, albeit limited and measured risks. This reinforces the critical importance of finding the most appropriate reward systems, together with mechanisms for involving, managing and leading people to achieve superior levels of performance.

Succession issues

Succession problems can concern both strategic leadership and managerial positions throughout the organization. Small firms whose growth and success have been dependent upon one person, most probably the founder, often experience problems when he or she retires, especially where there has been a failure to develop a successor in readiness. Some very large organizations also experience problems when particularly charismatic and influential strategic leaders resign or retire. Although they may be replaced by other strong leaders there may be changes to either or both the strategy or culture which do not prove successful.

However, succession problems can be seen with key people in any specialism and at any level of the organization. Firms need management in depth in order to cope with growth and with people leaving or being promoted. This implies that people are being developed constantly in line with, and in readiness for, strategic change; and this relates back to appraisal and reward systems. Many global companies deliberately move managers between countries and product groups as part of their management planning. This, they claim, opens the company up to 'different ideas and outside perceptions'.

Team building

Both formal and informal teams exist within organizations. Formal teams comprise sections or departments of people who work directly together on a continuous basis and in pursuit of particular specified objectives, and teams of senior managers who meet on a regular basis with an agreed agenda. Informal teams can relate to managers from different departments, or even divisions, who agree informally to meet to discuss and deal with a particular issue, or who are charged with forming a temporary group to handle an organization-wide problem. In both cases relationships determine effectiveness. Ideally, all members will contribute and support each other, and synergy will result from their interactions. Simply putting a group of people together in a meeting, however, does not ensure that they will necessarily work well together and form an effective and successful team.

A successful team needs:

- shared and agreed objectives
- a working language, or effective communications
- the ability to manage both the tasks and the relationships.

Cummings (1981) contends that individual contributions to the overall team effort are determined by personal growth needs (for achievement and personal development) and social needs – perceived benefits from working with others to complete tasks, rather than working alone.

Within any team, therefore, there will be a variety of skills, abilities and commitments. Some people will be natural hard workers who need little supervision or external motivation; others, who may be diligent and committed, may need all aspects of their task spelt out clearly; the major contribution of particular members might be in terms of their creativity and ideas. Meredith Belbin (1981) argues that a good team of people will have compensating strengths and weaknesses, and that as a group they will be able to perform a series of necessary and related tasks. Belbin has identified a number of characteristics or contributions that individuals make to teams. They relate to the provision of ideas, leadership, the resolution of conflict, the gathering and analysing of data and information, carrying out certain detailed work which might be regarded as boring by certain members, organizing people to make their most useful contributions, and developing relationships within the group. Individuals will contribute in a number of areas, not just one or two, but they will often be particularly strong in some and weak in others. A balance is required if the team is to work well together and complete the task satisfactorily.

Whoever is responsible for leading the team – it might be the strategic leader and his or her team of senior managers, or department managers – should consider the various strengths and weaknesses of people and seek to develop them into an effective and cohesive team. If any essential areas of contribution are missing this should be dealt with, and any potential conflicts of strong personalities should be determined early.

The 'learning organization'

When we think of building strong, cohesive and integrated teams, we generally, and quite rightly, think of small groups of employees. However, the same themes can be extended to the scale of the whole organization. Where all the parts can be integrated effectively, share with each other and learn from each other we have what Senge (1991) has called a 'learning organization' – which is explained in Box 10.2. Simply, as shown in Figure 10.4, the whole organization is able to think strategically and create synergy by sharing its knowledge and ideas and generating actions which contribute to the interests of the whole. The process is self-reinforcing as managers objectively review their progress.

Figure 10.4 The learning organization – leadership and vision. Based on ideas of Charles Handy (1989).

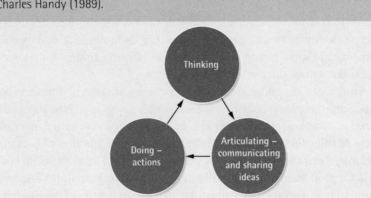

KEY CONCEPT – Box 10.2
The Learning Organization

The basic arguments are as follows:

- When quality, technology and product/service variety are all becoming widely available at relatively low cost, speed of change is essential for sustained competitive advantage.
- If an organization, therefore, fails to keep up with, or ahead of, the rate of change in its environment it will either be destroyed by stronger competitors, or lapse into sudden death or slow decline. The ideal is to be marginally ahead of competitors – opening up too wide a gap might unsettle customers.
- An organization can only adapt if it is first able to learn, and this learning must be cross-functional as well as specialist.

  Hence a learning organization encourages continuous learning and knowledge generation at all levels, has processes which can move knowledge around the organization easily to where it is needed, and can translate that knowledge quickly into changes in the way the organization acts, both internally and externally.

  Senge (1991)

Strategically important information, together with lessons and best practice, will thus be spread around; and ideally this learning will also be protected from competitors.

Essential requirements

- Systemic thinking, such that decision makers will be able to use the perspective of the whole organization; and there will be significant environmental awareness and internal co-operation. For many organizations the systemic perspective will be widened to incorporate collaboration and strategic alliances with other organizations in the added value chain.
- Management development and personal growth – to enable effective empowerment and leadership throughout the organization, and in turn allow managers to respond to perceived environmental changes and opportunities.
- A shared vision and clarity about both core competencies and key success factors. Changes should be consistent through strategic and operational levels.
- Appropriate values and corporate culture – to exploit fully core competencies and satisfy key success factors.

KEY CONCEPT – Box 10.2
(Continued)

- A commitment to customer service, quality and continuous improvement.
- Kotter and Heskett (1992) argue that the appropriate culture is one which is capable of constant adaptation as the needs of customers, shareholders and employees change.
- Team learning within the organization through problem sharing and discussion.

These points have been used to develop the following matrix which draws together a number of points discussed in this chapter and relates them to key issues of change management.

	Effectiveness orientated	The learning organization
Employment and development	Focus on problem-solving approach	Innovative intrapreneurial risk taking
	Change accepted	
Culture and values		Change initiated
Orientation towards efficiency and results	Concentration on resource efficiency	Supportive organization
	Consistent and systematic	Cross-functional co-operation
	Change resisted	Response to change pressures
	Individuals and tasks	Teams and integration
	Structural focus	

Information and Information Technology

The strategic value of information

Information is the fuel used in decision making; it can also be an important source of competitive advantage in certain circumstances. It must be stressed that IT, per se, is rarely a source of advantage, but information management can be. So, what exactly do we mean by 'information' and how might it be exploited?

Information has been defined as 'some tangible or intangible entity that reduces uncertainty about a state or event' (Lucas, 1976), which is a way of saying that information increases knowledge in a particular situation. When information is received, some degree of order can be imposed on a previously less well-ordered situation.

Information is needed for, and used in, decision making. Information, information systems and information technology are all aids to decision making. The more information managers and other employees have about what is happening in the organization, and in its environment, the more strategically aware they are likely to be. Information about other functional areas and business units can be particularly helpful in this respect.

Ackoff (1967), however, suggested that management information systems can easily be based on three erroneous assumptions:

- Managers are short of information. In many cases managers have too much irrelevant information.
- Managers know the information they require for a decision. However, when asked what information they might need, managers play safe and ask for everything which might be relevant, and thereby contribute to the overabundance of irrelevant information.
- If a manager is provided with the information required for a decision he or she will have no further problem in using it effectively. How information is used depends on perceptions of the issues involved. Moreover, if any additional quantitative analysis or interpretation is required, many managers are weak in these skills.

Nevertheless, decisions and decision making do involve both facts and people. While the right information available at the right time can be extremely useful, the real value of information relates to how it is used by decision makers, particularly for generating and evaluating alternative possible courses of action. In designing and introducing IT and management information systems into organizations it is necessary to consider the likely reaction of people as well as the potential benefits that can accrue from having more up-to-date and accurate information available. Information gathering should never become an end in itself, for the expertise and experience in people's heads can be more useful than facts on paper.

Moreover, it is important to evaluate who actually needs the information, rather than who might find it useful for increasing awareness, and to ensure that those people receive it. Although information technology and information systems can be expensive to introduce, those organizations that receive information, analyse and distribute it to the appropriate decision makers more quickly than their competitors can achieve a competitive edge, particularly in a turbulent environment.

Hence, the structure and culture of the organization should ensure that managers who need information receive it, and at the right time. However, while information can lead to more effective decision making, it remains a manifestation of power within the organization, and this aspect needs monitoring. If information that could prove useful is withheld from decision makers, negligently or deliberately by political managers pursuing personal objectives, the effectiveness of decision making is reduced.

Information is used through a filter of experience and judgement in decision making, and its relative value varies between one decision maker and another. In certain instances the available information will be accurate, reliable and up to date. In other circumstances the information provided may already be biased because it is the result of the interpretation of a situation by someone who may have introduced subjectivity. Some managers, perhaps those who are less experienced, will rely more heavily on specific information than others, for whom experience, general awareness and insight into the situation are more important.

To complicate matters further, Day (1996) argues that organizations do not know what they know. In other words, they are awash with data that do not get translated into valuable information and hence real organizational knowledge. Linked to this, it is clear that quite frequently they also fail to realize the value of some of the information that some people in the organization possess. This can be taken even further. If organizations do not know what they know, it must follow that they do not know what they do not know. They remain unaware of certain opportunities that others will seize and that they would have found valuable if they knew of their existence. Correspondingly, they do not find out about certain threats until it is too late to act.

Decision making and the interpretation of information

Spear (1980) argues that when information systems and the provision of information for managers are being considered it is important to bear in mind how people make decisions, interpret data and information, and give meaning to them. In decision making managers sometimes behave in a stereotyped way and follow past courses of action; sometimes they are relatively unconcerned with the particular decision and may behave inconsistently. In each case they may ignore information which is available and which if used objectively would lead to a different conclusion and decision. At other times information is used selectively and ignored if it conflicts with strongly held beliefs or views about certain things. In other words, information may be either misused or not used effectively.

Moreover, when considering a problem situation managers have to interpret the events that they are able to observe and draw certain conclusions about what they believe is happening. The question is: do managers perceive reality? Is there even such a thing as reality, or are there simply the meanings that we give to events? The following example will explain the point. Worker directors, popular in some other European countries, have always been a controversial issue among managers and trade union officials in the UK, with some of them supportive and others, in reality a majority, strongly opposed to their introduction. Managers who oppose them argue that they will reduce managerial power to run an organization; union opponents argue they would increase managerial power because the directors would be carefully selected or co-opted to include mainly those who were antagonistic to many of the aims of the union. These views represent meaning systems. The idea of worker directors, and what they are, is definite and agreed; their meaning and the implications of using them are subjective and interpretative.

A parallel situation would concern the interpretation of economic data. If, say, interest rates are rising, share prices are falling or the value of the pound is strengthening, do economic analysts agree or disagree on their meaning?

Counterintuitive behaviour

A failure to think through the implications of certain decisions on other managers, departments or business units can have effects that are unwelcome. The same can happen if there is an inability to appreciate the consequences because of a lack of information, or if there is a misunderstanding resulting from the wrong interpretation of information. Such an event is known as counterintuitive behaviour, and it often creates a new set of problems that may be more serious than those that existed originally.

Jay Forrester, in his book *Urban Dynamics* (1969), discusses how a strategy of building low-cost housing by the US equivalent of a local authority in order to improve living conditions for low-income earners in inner city areas has done more harm than good. The new houses draw in more low-income people who need jobs, but at the same time they make the area less attractive for those employers who might create employment. General social conditions decline. The area becomes even more destitute, creating again more pressure for low-cost housing. 'The consequence is a downward spiral that draws in the low-income population, depresses their condition, prevents escape and reduces hope. All of this done with the best of intentions.'

A more recent and real example concerns horse racing. It has always been the case that flat racing is cheaper and easier to stage than National Hunt racing over hurdles. Generally, but not exclusively, and dictated by ground conditions, flat racing is focused on the summer with National Hunt in the winter months. Weather conditions are more likely to be adverse in the winter, and so artificial turf all-weather surfaces were put on trial to see test their value in overcoming the problem for horses of hard, frozen ground. The intention was to make National Hunt economically more attractive. Paradoxically, the all-weather surfaces proved too tough for chasers and hurdlers when they landed from jumping, but they proved ideal for flat racing. The outcome is that the flat racing season can be extended, giving it even more of a relative advantage over National Hunt.

Related problems occur with misinterpretation of information. Consider the example of a small independent retailer who finds that he is selling more of a particular item than normal and more than he expected to sell. Deliveries from his wholesaler or other suppliers require a waiting period. Does he simply replace his stock, or increase his stockholding levels? How does he forecast or interpret future demand? When he starts ordering and buying more, or buying more frequently, how do his suppliers, and ultimately the manufacturer, respond? On what do they base their stockholding and production decisions, given that there will be penalties for misunderstanding the situation? Such problems are made worse by time-lags or delays. The use of IT by major retail organizations has proved that the impact of this dilemma can be reduced.

Summarizing, the fact that information is available does not necessarily mean that more effective decisions will result.

Information technology is a solution looking for a problem.

Donald Jones, CEO, ETSI
(Consultants in call centre technology)

Information systems and information technology: a cautionary comment

IT can be regarded as 'the application of hardware (machinery) and software (systems and techniques) to methods of processing and presenting data into a meaningful form which helps reduce uncertainty and is of real perceived value in current or future decisions'.

A management information system collects, processes and distributes the information required for managers to make decisions. It should be designed to be cost-effective, in that the additional revenue or profits generated by more effective decisions exceed the cost of designing, introducing and running the system, or that the value of management time saved is greater than the cost of the system. In addition, the information provided should be valid, reliable and up to date for the decisions concerned.

It should be realized that while computers and IT might be an essential feature of a management information system, the basic ideas behind an information system have little concern with computers. The terms are not synonymous.

Earl and Hopwood (1980) expressed a concern that there would be a tendency for the potential of IT to lead to an increasingly technological perspective on the way in which information is processed by managers. This would lead to increasingly formal systems and bureaucratic procedures which 'neither fit nor suit the realities of organizational activity'. On many occasions, informally exchanged information between managers who trust and respect each other is extremely important, and in some organizations political activity and power is important in certain decisions. In addition, organizations can become over-loaded with information that they cannot utilize effectively.

In the mid-1990s Tesco introduced its customer loyalty card, Clubcard, and was later followed by Safeway (ABC card) and Sainsbury's (Reward Card). Every time shoppers pass through a till their card is swiped to record their purchases. Customers build up points which can be used as a discount on future purchases either with the supermarket in question or with partner organizations. At the same time the computer records every item the customer has bought. The idea was that this could be used to profile people's habits and preferences so that special promotions could be targeted, instead of the more traditional 'blanket coverage' approach. Safeway invested £50 million a year for five years to run its system and then abandoned it. Customers had used the cards, but many possess more than one supermarket card in any case, reducing the value of the loyalty element. Safeway also admitted that it had underestimated the scope of the systems needed to handle, analyse and exploit the data it was collecting. In the end, Safeway concluded the £50 million per year would be better spent on reducing prices. ASDA, incidentally, had not gone down this route. A company survey of 5500 shoppers in 1999 was used to justify this decision: only five wanted a loyalty card, they said!

With the complexities discussed above as a backcloth, it is now important to examine the strategic information challenge facing organizations.

The strategic information challenge

Why do some organizations, which are currently enjoying success and high profits, fail to realize when products, services or strategies are about to lose customer support? Why do they fail to anticipate competitor initiatives? Why are others able to be more proactive?

Being close to customers, and in touch with new developments in a dynamic and possibly chaotic marketplace, requires information, intelligence and learning. Successful organizations monitor the activities of their customers, suppliers and competitors; they ask questions and test out new ideas. They express a willingness to learn and to change both their perspective on competition – their mindset concerning which factors determine competitive success – and the things they actually do. Sophisticated analyses and models of past and current results and behaviour patterns make an important contribution but, as Day (1996) argues, it is also necessary to think through how a market might respond to actions designed to retain existing customers and win new business, while outflanking and outperforming competitors. One of the reasons for Canon's continued success has been its ability to spot new market opportunities for its advanced technologies and exploit them early. Canon is also adept at reducing its dependency on products/markets as competition intensifies and demand plateaus. In the 1970s, for example, Canon successfully and systematically switched emphasis away from cameras (while remaining active and innovatory in the market) to photocopiers, and then to computer printers and facsimile machines, always adopting the same focus principles.

In order to become and remain strategically successful, organizations must create and sustain competitive advantage. They must continue to enjoy E–V–R (environment–values–resources) congruence, frequently in a dynamic and turbulent environment. To achieve this, information must be gathered and shared, but this is not merely a question of designing a new information system.

Day (1996) contends that many organizations 'do not know what they know' either because data and signals are misinterpreted or because the flows are inadequate. Decision makers do not receive the information that they need, or they fail to learn about things that might prove useful. Organizations that prioritize vertical channels and ignore horizontal flows are the ones most likely to fail to learn. The important elements for strategic success are:

- tracking events in the market and the environment, choosing responses (both proactively and reactively) and monitoring the outcomes of the actions which follow. Competitor initiatives must be dealt with; benchmarking best practices and general awareness can suggest new ideas
- making sure that important information from the questioning and learning from these emergent changes is disseminated effectively
- reflecting upon outcomes in the context of E–V–R congruence to ensure that the organization can sustain an effective match with its environment
- where appropriate, adapting policies and procedures better to guide future decisions.

The implication is a constant willingness to be flexible and to change as necessary. Companies must work from the twin perspectives of opportunity and threat. First, a willingness to learn and grow and, secondly, a realization that without appropriate and timely change a company is likely to face a crisis. Gilbert (1995) further argues that strategically successful organizations leverage their innovative competitive ideas with speed and act quickly.

They obtain market feedback continuously and rapidly and adapt to the feedback ahead of their rivals. They exploit the potential of strategic as well as competitive and operating information systems.

Three levels of information

- *Operating information systems* – Cost accounting systems, sales analyses and production schedules are essential for efficiency and control. Used creatively as, for example, is the case with airline reservation systems, they can create competitive advantage, but they are not designed to drive strategic change.
- *Competitive information systems* – Important elements of the various operating systems need to be integrated and synthesized to ensure that the organization is using its resources both efficiently and effectively. Specifically, it is meeting the needs and expectations of important external stakeholders. Competitive information systems, therefore, relate to competitive advantage and E–V–R congruence. They require managers to think and work across functional boundaries and consider the total service package provided to customers, encapsulating all the ways in which an organization can add value in a co-ordinated way.

  However, Gilbert (1995) argues that managers will not always be aware of the information they have used in arriving at a competitively successful formula. Where organizations do not fully understand why they are successful, that success may be fragile.

- *Strategic information systems* – While competitive information systems will typically focus on existing competition, organizations must also be able to learn about the business environment in order that they can anticipate change and design future strategies. Marchand (1995a) stresses that strategic information management should not be confined to the level of the strategic leader, but rather dispersed throughout the whole organization. This implies an innovative culture and an organization structure which facilitates the sharing of information – one essential element of a learning organization. A learning organization requires considerable decentralization and empowerment, which must not be at the expense of control. Centralized systems are often required for sound control and effective co-ordination, thus presenting organizations with the dilemma of how to obtain the speed and flexibility benefits of decentralization without sacrificing control.

Hence, as one moves up these three levels of decision making, the contribution of IT and information systems to decision making changes. Once operating systems are established, they can be used to make a number of decisions and drive the operations. By measuring performance, the systems can again make a valuable contribution and highlight when things are going wrong. For strategic decisions, however, IT is primarily an aid to decision making. Systems cannot realistically make the decisions, and consequently interpretation and meaning systems are particularly important. For such decisions the systems should be designed to provide information in a form that is useful to decision makers.

Information uses

Expanding this point, Marchand (1995b) distinguishes among four important and distinct uses for information at the operating, competitive and strategic decision-making levels.

- *Command and control* – The formal gathering of information to allow centralized control and decentralized accountability. Budgeting and resource allocations will typically be included. Command and control is valuable for managing resources efficiently but, used in isolation, it does not drive rapid change. Many organizations use tight financial targeting and monitoring as an essential driver of their competitiveness. Command and control invariably requires an organization to be broken down into subunits, such as independent businesses, divisions or functional departments.
- *Improvement* – Here the emphasis is on integrating the functions to improve both efficiency and effectiveness through better all-round service. Processes that link the functions are often the focus of attention, and initiatives such as total quality management and business process improvement will be integral.
- *Opportunities for organizational synergy* – If complex multibusiness organizations can find new opportunities for internal synergy, sharing and interdependency, they can clearly benefit. Teamworking and special project teams are one way of doing this. This can be particularly important if the organization acquires another business which needs to be integrated.
- *Environmental opportunities* – Market intelligence, competitor monitoring and benchmarking best practice can generate new ideas and opportunities, as we have seen. This requires that managers are vigilant and enquiring. Critically, ideas spotted by one part of an organization, and of no discernible use to that business, might be valuable for another business or division, and consequently the ability to share – based on an understanding of needs and a willingness to trust and co-operate – is essential.

Figure 10.5 illustrates that an organization must be able to manage all four information needs simultaneously and harmoniously if it is to benefit from improved efficiencies and manage change both continuously and discontinuously. Herein lies the real strategic information challenge. The deployment of organizational resources, the corresponding style of management and the cultural implications vary between the four information needs and the decision-making processes that

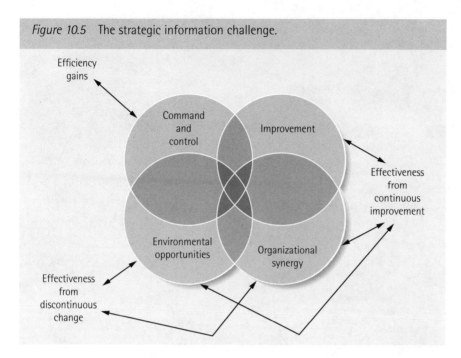

Figure 10.5 The strategic information challenge.

they support. Command and control management requires the organization to be separated into functions, businesses and/or divisions for clarity; the others demand different forms of integration, both formal and informal, to share both information and learning.

Figure 10.6 illustrates how organizations need first to develop a perspective on how they can add value and create competitive advantage. Through monitoring, measurement, continuous improvement and innovation they should seek to become increasingly efficient and effective. This continual process represents single-loop learning and it is essential if competitive advantage is to be sustained in a dynamic environment. This requires sound operating and competitive information systems. However, over time, on its own, this will not be enough. Organizations must always be looking for new competitive paradigms, really new ways of adding different values, ahead of competitors – both existing rivals and potential new entrants – looking for an opportunity to break into the market. Effective strategic information systems, relying on informality, networking and learning, are required for this double-loop learning.

Fostering a culture of improvement and single-loop learning in an organization is more straightforward than the challenge of double-loop learning. Organizations that invest in strategic planning, research and development and new product/service programmes are locked into the process, but the real benefits

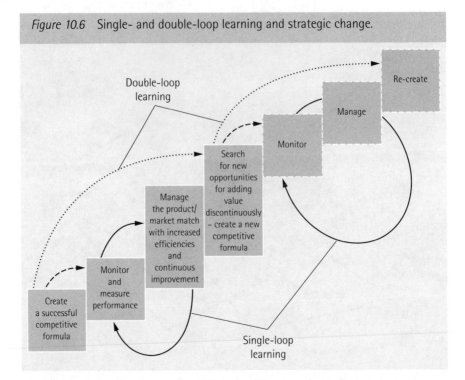

Figure 10.6   Single- and double-loop learning and strategic change.

cannot be gained if these activities and the requisite learning are confined to head-office departments and specialist functions. They must permeate the whole organization and become embedded in the culture. This reflects a key organizational tension and dilemma – the paradox of stability and instability. Stability concerns running existing businesses efficiently and effectively, exploiting strategic abilities and continually looking to create higher returns from the committed resources. Instability refers to the search for the new competitive high ground ahead of one's rivals.

Information, however, as well as being a vital element in decision making, can also be a source of competitive advantage, as shown in the next section.

Information, Information Technology and Competitive Advantage

It is clear that IT offers many potential strategic opportunities which go beyond the notion of faster data processing, but that harnessing these opportunities involves changes in attitude and culture among managers. McFarlan (1984) claims that IT strategies should relate to two criteria:

- How dependent is the organization on IT systems which are reliable 24 hours a day, seven days a week? International banks and stock and currency dealers who trade around the clock, and who use IT to monitor price movements and record their transactions, need their systems to be wholly reliable.
- Is IT crucial if the organization is to meet key success factors? If it is, there is an implication that companies can benefit from harnessing the latest technological developments. An obvious example is the airline industry.

Rayport and Sviokla (1995) argue that competition is now based on two dimensions: the physical world of resources and a virtual world of information. Information clearly supports and enhances every activity in an organization, but it can itself be a source of added value and consequently competitive advantage as long as organizations are able to extract that value.

Michael Porter (1985) had earlier suggested that technological change, and in particular IT, is among the most prominent forces that can alter the rules of competition. This is because most activities in an organization create and use information. Porter and Millar (1985) contend that IT could affect competition in three ways:

- IT can change the structure of an industry, and in so doing alter the rules of competition
- IT can be used to create sustainable competitive advantage by providing companies with new competitive weapons
- as a result of IT new businesses can be developed from within a company's existing activities.

These three themes are examined in greater detail below.

Industry structure

As shown in Chapter 6, according to Porter (1980), the structure of an industry can be analysed in terms of five competitive forces: the threat of new entrants; the bargaining power of suppliers; the bargaining power of buyers; the threat of substitute products and services; and rivalry amongst existing competitors. Porter and Millar (1985) suggested that IT could influence the nature of these forces, and thereby change the attractiveness and profitability of an industry. This is particularly applicable where the industry has a high information content, such as airlines, and financial and distribution services. Moreover, firms that were either slow or reluctant to introduce IT might well be driven out of the industry, because they would be unable to offer a competitive service. Where the cost of the necessary IT, both hardware and software systems, is high it can increase the barriers to entry for potential new firms.

UK holiday companies have made use of IT to lower costs and allow them to compete more aggressively on pricing. The result of the competitive activity has been an increase in concentration, with the largest companies gaining market share at the expense of smaller rivals, many of whom have left the industry.

Porter and Millar show that IT can both improve and reduce the attractiveness and profitability of an industry, and that as a consequence manufacturers should analyse the potential implications of change very carefully.

IT and the Internet – which is discussed below – have transformed such financial services as banking, enabling customers to carry out many of their financial transactions by telephone or personal computer without needing to queue for a cashier. However, there is the disadvantage that certain aspects of banking are being made more impersonal, and the personal service aspect is being reduced.

The creation of competitive advantage

Lower costs

If costs are reduced to a level below competitors' costs and this advantage is maintained, above-average profits and an increased market share can result. Porter and Millar suggest that while the impact of IT on lower costs has historically been confined to activities where repetitive information processing has been important, such restraints no longer apply. IT can lead to lower labour costs by reducing the need for certain production and clerical staff. As a result, there should be both lower direct production costs and reduced overheads. IT applied to production systems can improve scheduling, thereby increasing the utilization of assets and reducing stocks, and in turn lowering production costs.

Enhancing differentiation

Differentiation can be created in a number of ways, including quality, design features, availability and special services that offer added value to the end consumer. McFarlan *et al.* (1983) contend that IT offers scope for differentiation where:

- IT is a significant cost component in the provision of the product or service, as in banking, insurance and credit-card operations
- IT is able to affect substantially the lead time for developing, producing or delivering the product (CAD/CAM systems play an important role in this)
- IT allows products or services to be specially customized to appeal to customers individually
- IT enables a visibly higher level of service to customers, say through regular and accurate progress and delivery information, which might be charged for
- more and better product information can be provided to consumers.

Most insurance companies quote rates for insuring property and cars partially based on specified postcode districts. To achieve this they need accurate information on the risks involved in different areas and how these are changing. This in turn requires close liaison and information exchanges with brokers. The insurers, brokers and ultimately customers can all benefit as premiums more accurately reflect risks.

Supermarkets began to use hand-held computers several years ago, and these allowed staff to record the current stock levels each evening. Shelves could then be replenished overnight or the next day from regional warehouses. Sales representatives from, say, food manufacturers who sell extensively to small outlets were able to use similar hand-held computers for entering their orders. The computer could price the order immediately and a confirmation was then printed out. Further cost savings were possible where computer systems could be networked. Tesco also sought to establish closer linkages with its suppliers. Orders for immediate delivery were transmitted electronically, although projections based on the latest sales analyses would have been provided some weeks earlier. If supplier delivery notes were sent ahead of the actual delivery these were then used to check the accuracy of the shipment and a confirmation was returned. This represents a promissory note to pay by an agreed date, and no further invoicing is required. These linkages made use of electronic data interchange systems to exchange information. More recently, using the Internet, e-markets have begun to appear and these are discussed later. These developments clearly saved costs and allowed for lower prices, but they also streamlined the distribution network. Fast replenishment meant that customers should not find that stores have run out of an item; moreover, fresh produce could easily be replenished daily. Overall, the level of service was improved.

New competitive opportunities

IT has resulted in the creation of new businesses in three distinct ways.

- New businesses have been made technologically feasible. Telecommunications technology, for example, led to the development of facsimile services and organizations that provide fax services. In a similar way microelectronics developments made personal computing possible.
- IT created demand for new products such as high-speed data communications networks that were unavailable before IT caused the demand.
- New businesses have been created within established ones. Several organizations have diversified into software provision stemming from the development of packages for their own use.

There are numerous examples of how competitive advantage has been derived specifically from IT. Debit cards, such as Barclay's Connect, have replaced cash and cheques for many customers; similar to credit cards in format, they allow money to be debited immediately from a bank account. Because computers can store and process information very quickly, they allow the banks and building societies to offer rates of interest which increase and decrease directly in line with the size of a customer's deposit.

The US company McKesson, which supplies over-the-counter pharmaceuticals to retail chemists, used its salesforce to record on a computer the counter and shelf layouts of their customers. This allowed McKesson to pack orders in such a way that customers could unpack them and display them quickly and sequentially.

Most newspapers now enjoy cost and differentiation benefits from computerized typesetting, whereby type is set directly by a journalist typing at a keyboard. The files can now be transmitted electronically via the Internet so the journalist need not be located in the newspaper building. In the case of UK national daily newspapers, and against some trade union resistance, computerized typesetting was pioneered by Eddie Shah, when he established the *Today* newspaper which, after changes of ownership, has now been closed down. For the *Financial Times*, IT supports all the share prices, charts and other information included every day.

Most large hotel chains, including Sheraton and Marriott, operate clubs or programmes for their regular visitors. Participants receive such benefits as free upgrades and free meals as well as the programme points which they can exchange later for free stays or air miles. It is quite normal for travellers to prioritize a particular chain because of the perceived benefits of programme membership. These hotel chains typically cover much of the world, and often include independent hotels in franchise arrangements. Loyalty programmes would simply not be feasible without IT.

The US retailer Wal-Mart issues pagers to customers waiting for prescriptions so that they can continue shopping rather than either wait in line or come back speculatively to check whether their package is ready.

In summary, implementing IT for competitive advantage requires:

- an awareness of customer and consumer needs, changing needs, and how IT can improve the product's performance or create new services
- an awareness of operational opportunities to reduce costs and improve quality through IT
- an appreciation of how the organization could be more effective with improved information provision, and how any changes might be implemented. The impact upon people is very significant.

The argument is that competitive advantage can stem from any area of the organization.

The Impact of the Internet

The emergence and rapid growth of the Internet and the World Wide Web during the 1990s spawned a number of new and very entrepreneurial businesses. It is easy to be seduced by Internet possibilities and, supported by venture capital, many new Internet companies have grown rapidly. Few, however, have turned growing revenues into profits. At the same time, it has also demanded that every organization develop a strategy for harnessing its potential: it will 'not go away' and, for some, will completely transform their ways of operating and doing business. This section briefly explores some of these issues.

The Internet:

- provides information – which can make decision making much easier, but is potentially in quantities so great that it is hard to assimilate
- allows a company to advertise and promote itself and its products and services
- speeds up communication by replacing printed memos and telephone calls
- enables electronic trading. This again can take several forms. For consumer sales, information on a product (such as a book) can very readily be provided, along with reviews; moreover, in the case of a compact disc, sample tracks can be played. Virtual reality can be employed to move people around either a shopping mall or a supermarket.

Case Study 3 showed how certain organizations have been able to secure very large amounts of capital to pursue an apparent good idea for an e-commerce business. However, it also showed how volatile the traded shares of these businesses can be as they grow in size but fail to post any profits.

The fundamental principle behind many new *e-commerce businesses* is trading without either manufacture or long-term inventory. E-commerce cuts out the retail store element. New organizations dedicated to e-commerce are similar in principle yet distinctly different from the situation where established organizations (for example, Tesco and Waterstone's) sell via the web as well as through their own high-street outlets. The large retailers are increasingly moving in this direction because of the impact of the specialist e-commerce companies on customer buying habits. While the new businesses may own warehouses for collecting stock for onward transmission and holding limited numbers of fast-moving items, there will rarely be any need for them to employ either sales or production staff, and this element can be outsourced to specialists in logistics, leaving the e-commerce company to focus on creating and maintaining a successful website once the supply chain is set up. Simply, they are a virtual company.

The transaction begins when a potential customer uses a home computer to check out the website of the e-commerce business, selects an item and places an order electronically. Typically, credit-card information will be requested, and an instant credit check will be carried out by contacting the computer system of the relevant credit-card company. Once the payment details have been confirmed, an order is transmitted to the manufacturer of the product in question. If the e-commerce company is holding the product in stock, this would be replaced by an order to the company's own warehouse, who will later reorder from the manufacturer. Delivery to the customer can be direct from the manufacturer or via the e-commerce business who will receive bulk supplies and post out individual parcels.

Their fundamental advantage is their ability to reach a wide customer audience at low cost, as long as they can be attracted in the first place and then retained as a regular customer. Relatively specialist items can thus be made available to people who find it difficult to visit the shops that sell them directly. One key disadvantage is that the goods cannot be touched and inspected, which matters more for some customers and products than it does for others. The main infrastructure requirements for a successful e-commerce business are appropriate managerial and technical skills, venture capital to set up a sophisticated supply chain and secure payment systems. They also need customers who can and do access their site, recognize the convenience and benefits being offered, and believe that the payment systems are private and secure.

Every business needs an Internet strategy; it has to decide upon the extent to which it intends to use the Internet for promotion and for commercial transactions. For many organizations, it is far more important for business-to-business transactions than it is for direct sales to customers.

The ultimate popularity of Internet trading for consumer products remains difficult to predict for a number of reasons. More and more households are 'on-line' but the penetration is uneven. While all age groups are involved, younger people are more likely to use the Internet than older generations. Men seem more comfortable with the technology than women in many cases, and there is a greater incidence when people have enjoyed higher education and have above-average earnings. The geographical coverage in the UK is biased to the southern counties. But this is 'now'. Various predictions for future take-up have been offered and they are not all in accord. Some customers are keen to use the Internet for information gathering but stop short of buying electronically. This is partly linked to a reluctance to input credit-card details into a personal computer.

However, the potential of the Internet to link business with business is enormous and it offers both cost savings and service improvements. The term *e-markets* is normally used for this linkage. E-markets:

- link computers and databases
- constitute virtual and private networks where companies and their suppliers can share vital information
- allow easy and fast transfer of up-to-date information on current orders, contracts, prices, inventory, deliveries and so on – access can be controlled through passwords
- monitor and analyse activities
- have a facility for transactions
- enable cost reductions together with better information and a faster response time
- allow suppliers to auction any surplus stock, and
- allow buyers to ask for bidders against a special or an emergency need.

Conclusion: Information, Knowledge and Corporate Capital

Information, then, is required to support the decision-making processes related to strategic change – both formally planned changes and emergent, adaptive, incremental change – at all levels of the organization. Figure 10.7 summarizes

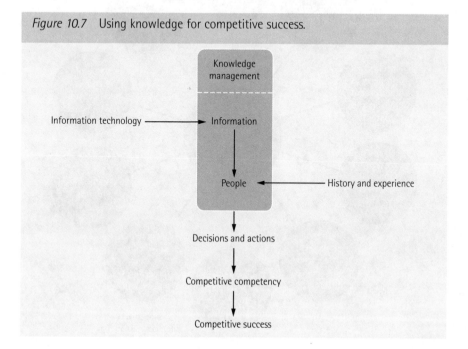

Figure 10.7 Using knowledge for competitive success.

the key points. Information, itself supported by IT, is used by people to help them to make decisions. History and experience qualify the information and analysis. The information, and the way in which people use it, comprises the organization's knowledge.

Figure 10.8 attempts to draw together those elements and resources which comprise the organization's corporate capital. It is a summary of many of the points and issues raised and discussed in previous chapters. Earlier we distinguished between opportunity-driven and resource-based strategy. Figure 10.8 is a comprehensive summary of all the resources that an organization possesses and which it should lever and exploit to create and sustain competitive advantage and strategic success. Logically, it can be argued that a company which aims to build and sustain competitiveness and success will audit these elements and use this analysis as a source of ideas for attention and improvement.

Figure 10.8 Corporate capital. Developed from ideas contained in the 1994 and 1995 Annual Reports of Skandia.

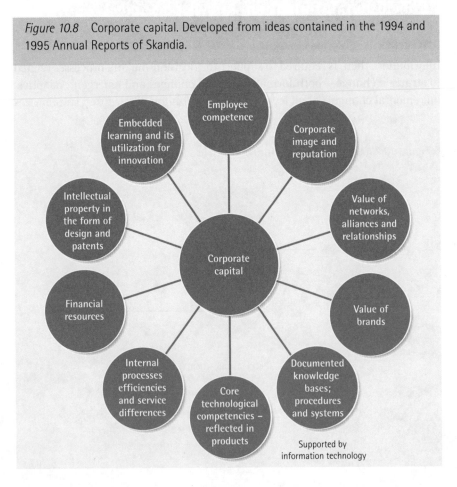

Summary

Emergent strategy creation takes two forms. *Incremental* changes happen as intended strategies are implemented and managers learn from their ongoing experiences. *Adaptive* strategies happen when managers, with delegated authority, respond to opportunities and threats in the environment.

Emergent strategies are a reflection and an outcome of *decision making* in the organization. Who makes them? How? Decision making involves two key themes: people and information. Information matters, but it must be harnessed as knowledge.

Emergent strategies imply learning and change in a dynamic environment. Consequently, *innovation* is a fundamental element.

Innovation by managers who accept delegated responsibility represents *intrapreneurship*, with the relevant managers acting as internal entrepreneurs. Here power has been released from the centre and effective control is based on information gathering and synthesis rather than instruction.

Innovation can happen at the product, service or process level. They are all important and capable of improvement. Innovation happens when someone builds value from a creative idea.

However, ideas with potential may look relatively unproven at the outset. As a consequence some large organizations will see the idea as potentially disruptive and thereby open a gap for the smaller business, if it can find the resources to exploit the idea and the opportunity.

People who contribute as innovators and intrapreneurs must be in a position where they feel stretched and rewarded. For some organizations, *empowerment* is a wonderful idea but no more. They find it difficult to create the appropriate climate and culture; their employees may not wish to be empowered to some considerable degree.

Emergent strategy possibilities are enhanced where people work well together and collectively. There is a team spirit, sharing and learning. *Synergy* is the outcome. Extended to the level of the organization, this constitutes a learning organization. Like empowerment, this can seem attractive as a theoretical idea and ideal but be difficult to implement effectively.

The information that feeds the whole process of decision making comes from a variety of internal and external sources, both formal and informal. Formal information systems and *information technology* can both make a valuable input, but information is more than information technology.

However much information they have, managers are still not 'seeing reality', rather they are put in position where their perception of events can be more informed and hopefully more insightful. Because issues of meaning are crucial, it is possible that decisions lead to counterintuitive behaviour with unanticipated outcomes.

Nevertheless, as well as informing decision making, information and information technology can be a source of competitive advantage in its own right.

The emergence of the *Internet* has spawned a host of new businesses. It has also required every company to formulate a strategy for harnessing its potential effectively.

References

Ackoff, RL (1967) Management misinformation systems, *Management Science* (14), December.

Belbin, RM (1981) *Management Teams: Why They Succeed or Fail*, Heinemann.

Bridge, S, O'Neill, K and Cromie, S (1998) *Understanding Enterprise, Entrepreneurship and Small Business*, Macmillan.

Capelli, P and Crocker-Hefter, A (1995) HRM: The key to competitive advantage, *Financial Times Mastering Management Series*, No 6, 1 December.

Christensen, CM (1998) *The Innovator's Dilemma*, Harvard Business School Press.

Churchill, NC (1997) Breaking down the wall, scaling the ladder. In *Mastering Enterprise* (eds S Birley and D Muzyka), Financial Times/Pitman.

Coulson-Thomas, C and Brown, R (1989) *The Responsive Organization. People Management: The Challenge of the 1990s*, British Institute of Management.

Cummings, TG (1981) Designing effective work groups. In *Handbook of Organizational Design* (eds PC Nystrom and WH Starbuck), Oxford University Press.

Day, G (1996) How to learn about markets, *Financial Times Mastering Management Series*, No. 12, 26 January.

de Geus, A (1997) The living company, *Harvard Business Review*, March–April.

Drucker, PF (1985) *Innovation and Entrepreneurship*, Heinemann.

Earl, MJ and Hopwood, AG (1980) From management information to information management. In *The Information Systems Environment* (eds HC Lucas, FF Land, JJ Lincoln and K Supper), North-Holland.

Forrester, J (1969) *Urban Dynamics*, MIT Press.

Fradette, M and Michaud, S (1998) *The Power of Corporate Kinetics – Create the Self-adapting, Self-renewing, Instant Action Enterprise*, Simon and Schuster.

Gilbert, X (1995) It's strategy that counts, *Financial Times Mastering Management Series*, No. 7, 8 December.

Handy, C (1989) *The Age of Unreason*, Hutchinson.

Hersey, P and Blanchard, K (1982) *The Management of Organisational Behaviour*, 4th edn, Prentice-Hall.

Hertzberg, F (1968) One more time how do you motivate employees? *Harvard Business Review*, January–February.

Horovitz, J (1997) Growth without losing the entrepreneurial spirit. In *Mastering Enterprise* (eds S Birley and D Muzyka), Financial Times/Pitman.

Hurst, DK (1995) *Crisis and Renewal – Meeting the Challenge of Organizational Change*, Harvard Business School Press.

Kanter, RM (1983) *The Change Masters – Innovation and Entrepreneurship in the American Corporation*, Simon and Schuster.

Kanter, RM (1989) *When Giants Learn to Dance*, Simon and Schuster.

Kotter, JP and Heskett, JL (1992) *Corporate Culture and Performance*, Free Press.

Lucas, H (1976) *The Analysis, Design and Implementation of Information Systems*, McGraw-Hill

Maitland, A (1999) Strategy for creativity, *Financial Times*, 11 November.

Marchand, DA (1995a) Managing strategic intelligence, *Financial Times Mastering Management Series*, No. 4, 17 November.

Marchand, DA (1995b) What is your company's information culture? *Financial Times Mastering Management Series*, No. 7, 8 December.

McClelland, D and Winter, D (1971) *Motivating Economic Achievement*, Free Press.

McFarlan, FW (1984) Information technology changes the way you compete, *Harvard Business Review*, May–June.

McFarlan, FW, McKenney, JL and Pyburn, P (1983) The information archipelago – plotting a course, *Harvard Business Review*, January–February.

McGregor, DM (1960) *The Human Side of Enterprise*, McGraw-Hill.

Pais, A (1982) *Subtle is the Lord – The Science and the Life of Albert Einstein*, Oxford University Press.

Pinchot, G III (1985) *Intrapreneuring*, Harper and Row.

Porter, LW, Lawler, EE and Hackman, JR (1975) *Behaviour in Organizations*, McGraw-Hill.

Porter, ME (1980) *Competitive Strategy: Techniques for Analysing Industries and Competition*, Free Press.

Porter, ME (1985) *Competitive Advantage: Creating and Sustaining Superior Performance*, Free Press.

Porter, ME and Millar, VE (1985) How information gives you a competitive advantage, *Harvard Business Review*, July–August.

Quinn, JB (1980) *Strategies for Change: Logical Incrementalism*, Irwin.

Rayport, JF and Sviokla, JJ (1995) Exploiting the virtual value chain, *Harvard Business Review*, November–December.

Roffey Park Management Centre (1995) *Career Development in Flatter Structures*, Research report.

Schein, EH (1983) The role of the founder in creating organizational culture, *Organisational Dynamics*, Summer.

Senge, P (1991) *The Fifth Discipline – The Art and Practice of the Learning Organization*, Doubleday.

Spear, R (1980) *Systems Organization: The Management of Complexity*, Unit 8, *Information*, The Open University, T243.

Terazano, E (1999) Fresh impetus from the need to innovate, *Financial Times*, 25 June.

Additional material on the website.

In 1988 Peter Drucker wrote an insightful paper on the link between people and information in organizations. The reference is:

Drucker, PF (1988) The coming of the new organization, *Harvard Business Review*, January–February.

For those who do not want to read the complete paper, a short summary is included on the website.

Test your knowledge of this chapter with our online quiz at: http://www.thomsonlearning.co.uk

Explore Emergent Strategy and Intrapreneurship further at:

FT Mastering Management online   http://www.ftmastering.com

Management Science   http://www.informs.org/Pubs/Mansci

Questions and Research Assignments

TEXT RELATED

1. Think of any example of an emergent strategy with which you have been involved and consider how people and information were contributory to the decision. What were the outcomes? What can you learn from this experience?

2. Consider how strategic changes in one retail sector, from an emphasis on hardware stores that specialize in personal service and expert advice

to customers from all employees, to a predominance of do-it-yourself supermarkets and warehouses, might have affected issues of staff motivation, personal development needs and appropriate reward systems.

3. Albeit by rule of thumb, take a team of people with whom you associate closely and evaluate their behaviour characteristics. Where is the team strong? Weak? Do you believe that it is balanced? If not, what might be done to change things?

4. Consider how the increasing utilization of information technology in retailing has affected you as a customer. Do you feel that the major retail organizations which have introduced and benefited from the greater utilization of IT have attempted to ensure that the customer has also benefited and not suffered?

5. Consider why it is argued that the increasing utilization of IT by organizations is a cultural issue. How might managers be encouraged to make greater use of the available technology?

6. How do you personally use the Internet? Do you feel that you are exploiting its potential?

Internet and Library Projects

1. Take an industry of your choice, ideally one with which you have some personal experience or insight, and determine the main innovations (product, service, process) in the last five years (ten years if you wish). How much of a difference has each major innovation made, and how? How and where did each one start?

2. For an organization of your choice ascertain the range of products and services offered and answer the following questions:
   - What are essential information needs from outside the organization (the environment) for managing these products and services both now and in the future?
   - Where are the limitations in availability?
   - What role might IT play in improving availability?

3. By visiting and talking to staff at an appropriate level and with several years' work experience in that environment, in both a travel agency and a retail store which makes extensive use of an EPOS (electronic point of sale) system, ascertain the effect that IT has had on their decision making. Do the staff feel that they are more aware strategically? If so, has this proved valuable?

11

Strategic Alternatives and Market Entry Strategies

This chapter outlines the various strategic alternatives that might be available to an organization in thinking and deciding where it wants to go, and for helping to close the planning gap. The attractiveness of particular alternatives will be affected by the objectives of the organization. While a whole range of options is discussed, it does not follow that they will all be available to an organization at the same time. Because of the costs or risks involved, particular alternatives might be quickly rejected. The appropriate strategy always matches the environment, values and resources congruently.

For many organizations the appropriate strategies will have a global dimension, and consequently a section on international issues is included in this chapter.

Organizations change their strategies over time, and the corporate profile takes a new shape.

In their consideration of strategic alternatives, some organizations will be entrepreneurial and actively search for opportunities for change. Others will only consider change if circumstances dictate a need. Some organizations will already have sound and effective strategies that are producing results with which they are satisfied. Others may ignore the need to change. Some texts have quoted the example of the typewriter companies who knew instinctively that electric typewriters, let alone word processors, would never catch on.

Case Study 11: Lego

In a volatile and competitive environment we have concentrated and used our strength to go deeper into what we know about.

(Kjeld Kirk Kristiansen, President)

Lego, the brightly coloured plastic building bricks, was launched in 1949, and has always proved popular in an industry renowned for changing tastes and preferences and for innovation. On the strength of this one product Lego has become the world's fifth largest toy maker. Lego is Danish, family owned and historically has been relatively secretive, hiding its actual sales and profit figures. The company admits to sales of 10 billion Danish Kroner (£830 million) in 1999.

The basic strategy is one of product development, with Lego developing an enormous number of variations on its basic product theme. By the mid-1990s some 300 different kits (at a wide range of prices) were available worldwide. There were 1700 different parts, including bricks, shapes and miniature people, and children could use them to make almost anything from small cars to large, complex, working space stations with battery-operated space trains. Brick colours were selected to appeal to both boys and girls; and the more complex Lego Technic sets were branded and promoted specially to make them attractive to the young teenage market. Over 200 billion plastic bricks and pieces have been produced since Lego was introduced.

In a typical year Lego has replaced one-third of its product range, with many items having only a short lifespan. New ideas are developed over a two- to three-year period and backed by international consumer research and test marketing. Lego concentrates on global tastes and buying habits. The Pacific Rim was perceived to offer the highest growth potential during the 1990s. 'If you differentiate too much you start to make difficulties for yourself, especially in manufacturing.' Competition has forced Lego to act internationally and aggressively. One US company, Tyco, markets products that are almost indistinguishable from Lego. Lego has attempted unsuccessfully to sue for patent infringement and now views this competition as undesirable but stimulating. More recently new competition has come from another rival construction product, K'Nex, again American.

In the mid-1990s sales were being affected adversely by changing tastes and by the growing popularity of computer games. In 1997 Lego opted for a new range extension. A new kit, especially for girls, was launched – a doll's house series complete with miniature dolls and furniture. Lego also began to market construction kits with microchips and instructions on CD-ROMs. In 1998 the company introduced a new Mindstorms range, built around a brick powered by AA batteries, which could be incorporated into a variety of different models that could then be instructed to move with the aid of an infra-red transmitter and a typical personal computer. Lego had had the technology for a while but had been waiting until it could reduce costs to a realistic level. More recently, Lego has ventured into the computer games market with CD-based products enabling users to 'build' train sets, vehicles, etc., on screen.

Lego manufactures in Switzerland, Germany, Brazil, South Korea and the USA as well as Denmark, making its own tools for the plastic injection moulding machines. Tool making could easily be concentrated in one plant, but takes place in three to engender competition and to emphasize quality. Lego deliberately maintains strong links with its machinery suppliers. In this and other respects Lego sees itself as being closer culturally to a Japanese company than a US one. Investments in production and improvements are thought to be in the region of at least £100 million per year.

Some years ago Lego diversified with a theme park, featuring rides and displays built with Lego bricks, in Denmark. This has been followed with a similar development on the site of the old Windsor Safari Park in the UK and followed by a third in San Diego, USA. In the late 1990s the UK park was attracting 1.5 million visitors every year.

QUESTION: Is Lego poised for further growth and prosperity with its focused strategy or is it still vulnerable to competitive threats?

Lego   http://www.lego.com

Introduction

Figure 11.1 provides a summary of the main strategic alternatives, which are separated into three clusters: limited growth, substantive growth and retrenchment. In addition, an organization can opt to do nothing; and on occasions the whole business will be sold or liquidated.

From origins in a single business concept, market penetration and product and market development are shown as limited growth strategies as they mainly affect competitive strategies rather than imply major corporate change. Invariably they involve innovation. The substantive growth strategies imply more ambitious and higher risk expansion which is likely to change the corporate perspective or strategy. These options, explained below, may involve either a strategic alliance or an acquisition, and these *strategic means* are discussed later in the chapter. It was established in Chapter 1 that it is important for organizations to seek competitive advantage for each business in the portfolio. Consequently, once an organization has diversified, it will be necessary to look for new competitive opportunities, or limited growth strategies, for the various individual businesses.

The bottom section of Figure 11.1 shows the main strategies for corporate reduction, namely turnaround and divestment.

Figure 11.2, market entry strategies, summarizes the various ways in which an organization might implement its chosen strategies. It should be appreciated that any strategic alternative can be international in scope, rather than focused on a

Figure 11.1   Strategic alternatives.

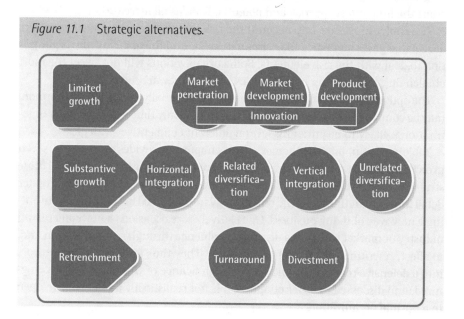

Understanding Corporate Strategy

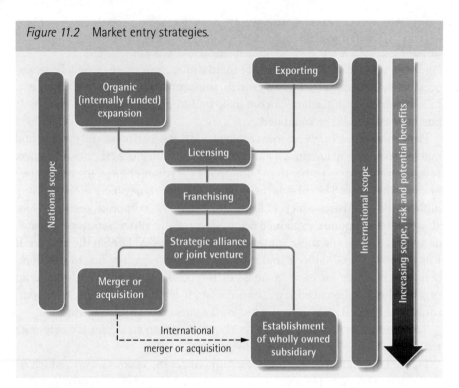

Figure 11.2   Market entry strategies.

single country or market, and that as we move from the top to the bottom of the chart the inherent scope, risk and potential benefits all increase.

The choice must take into account the risk that the strategic leader considers acceptable given any particular circumstances, and the ability of the organization to deal with the risk elements. Some organizations will not select the most challenging and exciting opportunities because they are too risky.

The options should not be thought of as being mutually exclusive – two or more may be combined into a composite strategy, and at any time a multiproduct organization is likely to be pursuing several different competitive strategies.

Table 11.1 combines the themes of this chapter. It provides examples of seven growth directions related to three alternative means of pursuing each of these strategic alternatives. Many of the examples included are discussed in greater detail throughout the book. The one strategy not discussed in detail here is inventing a new way of doing business. On relatively rare occasions a newcomer to an industry or market will have a disruptive influence through real innovation and, in effect, rewriting the rules of competition. They thus force other competitors into a defensive reaction. While the real significance of this possibility is recognized, and discussed in other chapters, it is not realistically an alternative open to a normal organization.

Table 11.1 Examples of strategic growth and change

		Direction of growth					
Means of growth	Inventing a new way of doing business	Market penetration/ development	Globalization	Vertical integration/ diversification	Related diversification	Unrelated diversification	Focus by divestment
Organic/ internal	Southwest Air Amazon.com Hotmail	Toyota (with Lexus)	McDonald's Canon	Exxon (with refineries) Disney (with stores)	Sony Disney (with cruise ships)	Tata* (India) Virgin Atlantic Airways	Hanson Burton/ Debenhams
Strategic alliance	Benetton and IKEA (with their supply chains)	General Motors and Saab	Star Alliance⁺ Coca-Cola and its bottlers	MBNA/Co-op Bank credit cards	Nokia and 3 Com (internet mobile phones)	Siam Cement‡ (Thailand)	Yorkshire Water's onion outsourcing strategy
Merger, acquisition take-over	Royal Bank/ Direct Line	Ford with Jaguar, Land Rover, Volvo, Daewoo	Astra/Zeneca	Merck with Medco, a distributor	Disney/ABC Television Wal-Mart and ASDA	General Electric (GE) and NBC Television	ICI's sale of non-core businesses after splitting from Zeneca

*Tata: construction machinery, engineering, locomotives; Tea (where it has global leadership).

⁺ Airline code sharing alliance: includes United Airlines, Air Canada, Air New Zealand, British Midland, Lufthansa, SAS.

‡ Siam Cement: also pulp and paper, construction materials, machinery and electrical products, marketing and trading.

Limited Growth Strategies

The do-nothing alternative

This do-nothing alternative is a continuation of the existing corporate and competitive strategies, whatever they might be, and however unsuccessful the company might be. The decision to do nothing might be highly appropriate and justified, and the result of very careful thought and evaluation. However, it can also be the result of managers lacking awareness, being lazy or complacent, or deluding themselves into believing that things are going well when in fact the company is in difficulties. Doing nothing when change is required is a dangerous strategy.

A company might appear to an outsider to be doing nothing when in reality it is very active. Some companies, for example, prefer not to be the first to launch new product developments, especially if they know that their competitors are innovating along similar lines. A product may be developed and ready to launch but be held back while another company introduces its version into the market. This allows the initial reaction of consumers to be monitored and evaluated, and competitive and functional strategies reviewed before eventual launch. Timing is the key to success with this strategy. A company will want sufficient time to be sure that its approach is likely to prove successful; at the same time it must react sufficiently quickly that it is not perceived to be copying a competitor when that competitor has become firmly established. In general, the rather more theoretical than realistic do-nothing alternative could conceivably be viable in the short term but is unlikely to prove beneficial or plausible in the long term as environmental factors change.

We next discuss internal growth strategies – market penetration, market development, product development (all of them dependent upon innovation) and combination strategies. It should be appreciated that the strategies described are typically organic in nature (namely, growth from within) and they are not fully discrete and independent of each other. The ideas behind them are closely linked, and it may be very difficult to classify a particular strategic change as one of these strategies rather than another. They can all be linked to the idea of the product lifecycle for they provide suitable means of extending the lifecycle once it reaches a stage of maturity and potential decline. It will also be appreciated that they are the key elements of the Ansoff grid introduced in the discussion of the planning gap (Chapter 9). At the heart of all these competitive strategies are customers. It is essential that organizations develop strategies for:

- simply retaining existing customers, which may itself require innovation in a competitive market or industry

- expanding the relationship with existing customers by providing them with additional products or services. Direct Line began with car insurance, but soon realized that there was an opportunity to provide home and contents insurance for its existing client base. Kwik Fit also realized that it had a valuable database of motorists and diversified into providing them with insurance as well as tyre and exhaust services. Sometimes the relationship can be expanded by providing more specialized product and service alternatives to target quite narrow niches
- winning new customers (and hence market share) from competitors.

Consequently, the important issue is the line of thought and the reasoning behind the strategy in question, and the objectives.

Market penetration

This strategy can have one of two broad objectives. First, to seek assertively to increase market share; and secondly, and more defensively, to hang on to existing customers by concentrating, specializing and consolidating, which implies what Peters and Waterman (1982) designate 'sticking to the knitting' in their book *In Search of Excellence*, which was discussed in Chapter 2.

It involves concentrating on doing better what one is already doing well, and quite frequently involves an investment in brands and brand identity. Although it may seem similar to doing nothing, growth is an objective and there is an implicit search for ways of doing things more effectively. In this respect, and because market environments are invariably dynamic, it overlaps with the ideas of market and product development described below.

Resources are directed towards the continued and profitable growth of a 'single' product in a 'single' market, using a 'single' technology. This is accomplished by attracting new users or consumers, increasing the consumption rate of existing users and, wherever possible, stealing consumers and market share from competitors. The word 'single' needs careful interpretation, in the context of the limited growth strategies, as companies such as Kellogg (breakfast cereals) and Timex (watches) would be classified as organizations which have succeeded with specialization strategies based around a core brand identity. An extensive product line of differentiated brands designed to appeal to specific market segments would periodically have new additions and withdrawals.

At the same time, productivity and more effective cost management can make significant contributions. Sometimes this will be achieved by investing in new technology at the expense of labour.

The two main advantages are, first, that the strategy is based on known skills and capabilities and in this respect it is generally low risk. Secondly, because the organization's production and marketing skills are concentrated on specialized products and related consumers, and not diversified, these skills can be developed and improved to create competitive advantage. The company has the opportunity to be sensitive to consumer needs by being close to them, and may build a reputation for this.

Market penetration strategies generally have a high likelihood of success, greater in fact than most other alternatives. There are important limitations, however. Alone they may be inadequate for closing an identified planning gap.

While market penetration is a growth strategy, the long-term growth is likely to be gradual rather than explosive. This should not be seen as a disadvantage, because steady growth can be more straightforward in managerial terms. Any firm pursuing this strategy is susceptible to changes in the growth rate or attractiveness of the industry in which it competes, and therefore the strategy can become high risk if the industry goes into recession. There is also a constant need to monitor competitors and ensure that any innovations do not constitute a major threat.

This strategic alternative is particularly applicable to small businesses which concentrate their efforts on specific market niches.

Market development

Market development, together with product development which is considered next, is very closely related to a strategy of specialization. All of these strategies build on existing strengths, skills, competencies and capabilities. Market development is generally another relatively low-risk strategy; and the idea behind it is to market present products, with possible modifications and range increases, to customers in related market areas. This may imply broadening a product range to increase its attractiveness to different customers in different market segments or niches. Clearly, therefore, this strategy is about modifications to strategic positioning. Changes in distribution and advertising will also typically support this strategy.

In summary, the key themes are:

- modifications to increase attractiveness to new segments or niches
- new uses for a product or service
- appropriateness for different countries with particular tastes or requirements.

One example of a market development strategy, then, would be a firm which decided to modify its product in some minor way to make it attractive to selected export markets where tastes and preferences are different. This would be supported by advertising and require the opening of new channels of distribution.

Product development

Product development implies substantial modifications or additions to present products in order to increase their market penetration within existing customer groups. It is often linked to an attempt to extend or prolong the product lifecycle, and typical examples would include the second and revised edition of a successful textbook, or the relaunch of a range of cosmetics with built-in improvements which add value. As product lifecycles contract and time becomes an increasingly important competitive issue, this strategy becomes more significant. Case Study 11 looks at how Lego has built its success around constant product development.

This strategy is customer driven. Another example would be a retailer such as WH Smith which relatively frequently changes its product ranges and offerings to provide a suitable and profitable package for its regular customer base. As new retail competitors threaten the viability of certain products, making them less attractive for WH Smith, Smith's looks for other alternatives which will be relevant for its customers. Toys are less prominent than in the past; in-store travel agencies have disappeared; stationery has been increased; and the ranges of books, music and video have been adapted. Sometimes, as we shall see later, these product line changes constitute a strategy of diversification, highlighting again the fact that these alternatives are not mutually exclusive and some changes are hard to categorize.

Innovation

Innovation is linked to the three strategies described above but it often involves more significant changes to the product or service. As a strategy it can imply the replacement of existing products with ones which are really new, as opposed to modified, and which imply a new product lifecycle. The line which differentiates a really new product from a modification is extremely difficult to quantify. In the case of cars such as the Ford Escort or Ford Fiesta, for example, which appeared in new forms every few years, the changes for each new model were typically marked differences rather than essentially cosmetic. Each new model was very different from the existing model, simply the name was the same.

Similarly, it is important to consider which product lifecycle is being addressed. The Sony Walkman and similar personal cassette players have enjoyed their own successful lifecycle; at the same time they have extended the product lifecycle of cassette players in general. As shown in Table 11.1, innovation can be behind the invention of a new way of doing business.

It can be risky not to innovate in certain industries as a barrier against competition. Innovatory companies can stay ahead by introducing new products ahead of their rivals and concentrating on production and marketing to establish and consolidate a strong market position. All the time they will search for new opportunities to innovate and gain further advantage. Several food manufacturers have utilized innovation to consolidate their market positions as the major food-retail chains have increased in size and power. Not only were the retailers in an increasingly strong negotiating position concerning prices and trading arrangements, they were also beginning to market their own-brand alternatives at very competitive prices. Astute manufacturers have innovated and maintained a flow of new products to retain a competitive advantage by limiting the market potential for retailer own-brands.

Constant innovation is likely to prove expensive, and will require other products and strategies to be successful in order to provide the funding.

Combination strategies

A firm with a number of products or business units will typically pursue a number of different competitive strategies at any time. Product development, market development and innovation may all be taking place.

The internal growth strategies discussed in this section are primarily concerned with improving competitive strategies for existing businesses. Such changes may not prove adequate for closing the planning gap, and consequently higher risk external growth strategies may also be considered. Such changes are likely to involve a new strategic perspective.

Substantive Growth Strategies

This section provides an overview of four substantive growth strategies – horizontal integration, vertical integration, related and unrelated diversification. Substantive growth strategies are frequently implemented through acquisition, merger or joint venture rather than organic growth. Franchising can provide another means of generating external growth, but it is only likely to be applicable for certain types of business.

External growth can involve the purchase of, or an arrangement with, firms that are behind or ahead of a business in the added value channel, which spans raw material to ultimate consumption. Similarly, it can involve firms or activities that are indirectly related businesses or industries, those which are tangentially related through either technology or markets, and basically unrelated businesses. The key objectives are additional market share and the search for opportunities that can generate synergy. The outcome from this will be larger size and increased power, and ideally improved profitability from the synergy. In reality, the outcome is more likely to be increased size and power than improved profitability. Synergy often proves to be elusive.

Proposed acquisitions of organizations which would result in substantial market share, and possible domination may well be subject to reference to either the UK or European Competition Commission, or both, which, as discussed earlier (Chapter 5), may act as a restraint on proposed corporate development. Certain avenues for growth may in effect be closed to an organization.

Horizontal integration

Horizontal integration occurs when a firm acquires or merges with a major competitor, or at least another firm operating at the same stage in the added value chain. The two organizations may well appeal to different market segments rather than compete directly. Market share will increase, and pooled skills and capabilities should generate synergy. Horizontal integration is, therefore, concerned with issues of critical mass.

Numerous examples exist. Rover Cars, recently part of BMW and previously known as Austin Rover, and before that British Leyland, was the result of a series of amalgamations over many years. Such brand names as Austin, Morris, MG, Wolsley, Standard, Triumph and Rover, which were all originally independent car producers, became combined. Jaguar was also included until it was refloated as an independent company in the mid-1980s and later bought by Ford. The new owners of Rover, a financial consortium, are anxious to resurrect some of the older brand names.

In 1998 Enso (Finland) merged with Stora (Sweden) to create the world's largest forest products (paper making) company. Interestingly, the company enjoyed only a 4% share of the global market, although holding strong positions in certain segments, particularly newsprint, fine paper and liquid-beverage packaging board. The aim was to provide a stronger base for expansion in South-East Asia where wood fibre is cheaper than it is in Europe.

In the financial services sector, the National Westminster Bank was created by the merger of the National Provincial Bank and Westminster Bank. In early 2000 NatWest was itself acquired by the Royal Bank of Scotland, but this was a hostile take-over in competition with the Bank of Scotland. NatWest had failed to implement a number of strategies over a period of years and had become vulnerable. Shareholders were promised cost savings and profit increases from the larger group, which would be in a position to close some branches and consolidate overlapping activities. The new group, although operating as independent banks at the moment, is second in the UK for current accounts, sixth for mortgages and the leading lender to small and large businesses. Similarly, a number of building society mergers has taken place. The Alliance and Leicester and Nationwide Anglia are typical examples.

Insurance has also been affected. In 1998 Commercial Union and General Accident merged; two years later the new CGU merged with the floated Norwich Union. In 1997 BAT (British American Tobacco) merged its insurance activities (Eagle Star and Allied Dunbar in the UK, Farmers in the USA) with Zurich of Switzerland. Two years later, BAT's residual tobacco interests were merged with Rothman's to create a company large enough to compete seriously with global market leader, Philip Morris. The larger company might also be in a stronger position to deal with the increasing litigation resulting from tobacco-related illnesses. Also in 1999, the French insurer Axa (which already owned Sun Life) merged with Guardian Royal Exchange, itself an earlier merger.

Vertical integration

Vertical integration is the term used to describe the acquisition of a company which supplies a firm with inputs of raw materials or components, or serves as a customer for the firm's products or services (a distributor or assembler). If a shirt manufacturer acquired a cotton textile supplier this would be known as backward vertical integration; if the supplier bought the shirt manufacturer, its customer, this would constitute forward vertical integration.

At times firms will reduce the extent to which they are vertically integrated if they are failing to obtain the appropriate benefits and synergy from the fusion of two sets of skills and capabilities. Early in 1988, for example, the UK clothing retailer Burton Group sold the last of its suitmaking factories in order to concentrate on retailing. At one time Burton had been one of the leading clothing manufacturers in Europe, but that was before made-to-measure suits were substantially replaced in popularity by ready-made suits.

Backward vertical integration aims to secure supplies at a lower cost than competitors, but after the merger or acquisition it becomes crucial to keep pace with technological developments and innovation on the supply side, or competitive advantage may be lost.

In 1987 Rover divested its parts distribution business, Unipart – an example of vertical disintegration. Eight years later, after its acquisition by BMW, Rover sought unsuccessfully to buy Unipart back, arguing that it needed to control its parts distribution to support its increasingly international role.

Forward vertical integration secures customers or outlets and guarantees product preference, and it can give a firm much greater control over its total marketing effort. At the consumer end of the chain, retailers generally are free to decide at what final price they sell particular products or services, and their views may not always accord with those of the manufacturer. However, greater control over distribution might mean complacency and a loss of competitive edge through less effective marketing overall. In addition, manufacturing and retailing, if these are the two activities involved, require separate and different skills, and for this reason synergy may again prove elusive.

With vertical integration there will always be uncertainty as the system of relationships among a group of suppliers and manufacturers, or a group of manufacturers and distributors, is changed. It is generally argued that if there are only a few suppliers and several buyers vertical integration can have significant effects. Figure 11.3 features a system comprising three suppliers, five manufacturers and four retailers, all of whom are independent. The lines joining the boxes show the trading relationships. If supplier C acquired, or was acquired by, manufacturer 5 (option 1) then a number of issues has to be resolved. Currently manufacturer 5 relies exclusively on supplier C. Does it make sense for this to continue, or might it be useful to establish a trading relationship with another supplier (also now a competitor) to hedge against future possible difficulties such as technological change and innovation? At the moment, also, competing manufacturers 2, 3 and 4 all buy some of their supplies from supplier C. Will they continue to do so? If not, supplier C is likely to have substantial spare capacity. Similar issues would be raised by option 2, integration between manufacturer 1 and retailer W.

Many of the benefits of vertical integration can be achieved without merger or acquisition. Joint ventures, discussed later, are one option. In addition, there

Figure 11.3 Vertical integration.

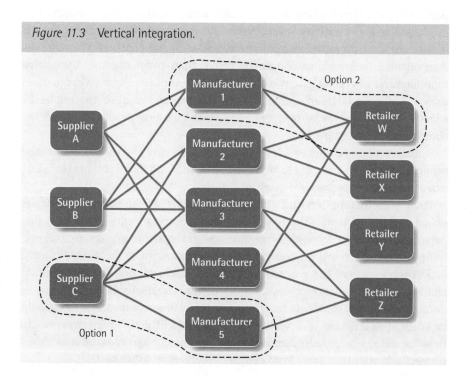

may simply be agreements between companies who appreciate that there can be substantial gains from proper co-operation. Marks and Spencer (Case Study 1) provide an excellent example historically. Marks and Spencer has benefited from long-term agreements with their suppliers with whom they have worked closely. Many suppliers of a wide variety of products sold by Marks and Spencer rely very heavily upon them, as they are their major customer. At the same time Marks and Spencer sets exacting standards for cost, quality and delivery, and guarantee to buy only when these standards are met continuously; and there will always be competitors who would like them as a customer.

The effect of vertical integration can be created organically, without merger or acquisition, but this is likely to be more risky. New skills have to be developed from scratch. Examples of this would be a manufacturer deciding to make components rather than buying them from specialist suppliers, or starting to distribute independently rather than relying on external distributors.

Because new and different skills are involved, vertical integration really implies diversification, but normally these strategic change options are considered separately.

Related (or concentric) diversification

Any form of diversification involves a departure from existing products and markets. The new products or services involved may relate to existing products or services through either technology or marketing; where this is the case, the diversification is known as concentric rather than conglomerate. A specialist manufacturer of ski clothing who diversified into summer leisure wear to offset seasonal sales would be an example. Potential consumers may or may not be the same; distribution may or may not change; the existing production expertise should prove beneficial.

Similarly, when retailers such as WH Smith add new and different lines and products, they are seeking to exploit their resources and their retailing skills and expertise (core competencies) more effectively.

There is an assumption that synergy can be created from the two businesses or activities; and ideally the new, diversified, company enjoys strengths and opportunities which decrease its weaknesses and exposure to risks.

Any organization seeking concentric diversification will look for companies or opportunities where there are clearly related products, markets, distribution channels, technologies or resource requirements. The related benefits should be clear and genuinely capable of generating synergy. However, diversification might be adopted as a means of covering up weaknesses or previous poor decisions. Benefits will not be expected immediately, and the change involved may divert interest and attention away from existing problems or difficulties.

Unrelated (or conglomerate) diversification

In the case of conglomerate diversification there is no discernible relationship between existing and new products, services and markets. The diversification is justified as a promising investment opportunity. Financial benefits and profits should be available from the new investment, and any costs incurred will be more than offset. Financial synergy might be obtained in the form of greater borrowing capacity or acquired tax credits.

The strategy is regarded as high risk because the new technologies, new skills and new markets involved constitute unknowns and uncertainties. Moreover, because the change is uncertain and challenging, it can be tempting to switch resources and efforts away from existing businesses and areas of strength, and this compounds the element of risk involved.

Conglomerate diversification is often linked to portfolio analysis, and sometimes the search for businesses which might remedy any perceived strategic weaknesses. A company with reserves of cash to invest, because it has a number of cash cow businesses, might seek to buy businesses with growth potential in new industries. Some acquisitive and financially orientated companies diversify in this way with a view to rationalizing the businesses that they buy. Parts will be retained if they feel they can add value and benefit accordingly; other parts will be divested. In such cases, the critical issue should be the opportunity-cost of the money involved. In other words, the long-term return on capital employed should exceed alternative uses for the money, including simply keeping it banked! While some companies build up substantial capital reserves to ensure that they have the resources to manage during the recessionary stage of a business cycle – as was the case with GEC under Arnold (Lord) Weinstock – others will use the cash to buy back equity. Shareholders will like to see a company enjoying sound financial health but may well feel that a 'cash mountain' should be used for something! It can be a difficult balance. Referring to points made earlier, where a company is anxious to grow, it might initially look for closely related acquisitions but find such routes blocked by competition authorities who feel that customers might be disadvantaged. When such companies opt for unrelated acquisitions they are very likely to argue that there is more relatedness than in reality there is!

Unrelated diversification became less popular in the 1990s. The real issue concerns whether the strategic leadership can deliver value for all key stakeholders from the diversification. Certain conglomerates such as Hanson were successful because they targeted underperforming companies and turned them around – linkages and synergies were not high on the agenda. Such strategies are only feasible when sleepy companies are there to be acquired, and this is less likely in a strong economy. Hanson, as a consequence, was ultimately split into five parts. At the same time General Electric (GE) remains a highly successful diversified conglomerate which achieves synergies across unrelated businesses through its ability to operate as a 'learning organization' which exchanges skills and ideas.

Some companies diversify to build a bigger business and thus reduce the likelihood of being acquired by an unwelcome outsider. The argument is, the bigger they become, the fewer companies can afford to buy them. Paradoxically, if they fail to achieve synergy, they may look attractive to an outside bidder who sees value in buying them to split them up. We return to the subject of diversification later in the chapter.

After considering both internal and external growth strategies, we look at a number of consolidation and reductionist strategies, primarily for companies experiencing difficulties. Quite often the problems arise because previous growth, diversification and acquisition strategies have been either poorly conceived or poorly implemented.

Disinvestiment clearly relates to business failure situations and consequently a short commentary on failure is included.

Business Failure

Ultimate business failure happens when a business is liquidated or sold. Its managers have made strategic errors or misjudgements; maybe they simply avoided the need to change in a dynamic environment. However, a business can similarly fail to meet the needs and expectations of key stakeholders, experience financial difficulties but be 'saved'. In this latter case, one or more factors might be involved. A new strategic leader might be appointed who succeeds in turning the company around. Part, or all, of the business might be sold.

There are several signals of a company in difficulty – these constitute symptoms of the failing situation. These should normally be easily discerned by vigilant managers who are tracking a company's performance although, on occasions, circumstances can change quickly. It is the actions which follow that are critical.

Companies fail for a variety of reasons, and normally more than one factor is in evidence. The main ones are:

- *Poor management* – either at strategic leader level, or through the heart of the organization. The latter is also indicative of weak leadership.
- *Poor financial control* – weak budgeting and cost management; an inability to cover overheads.
- *Competition* – the company has become relatively weak in comparison to its competitors.
- *Decline in profits* – meaning that there is inadequate funding to meet the business' commitments (suppliers' bills and interest on loans, for example), let alone

reinvest in the business. This can be the outcome of lost competitiveness or poor financial management.

- *Decline in demand for the product or service* – which implies a need to change and suggests an inadequate response by the company's managers.
  These last three factors all imply *poor marketing*.
- *Misjudged acquisitions or other changes in corporate strategy* – implying that the company's resources have been overstretched and attention has been diverted away from the needs of existing products and services.

Disinvestment Strategies

The term 'disinvestment' is an umbrella term which encompasses retrenchment (consolidation), turnaround and divestment. It is used to represent strategic alternatives where money is not invested for growth purposes. However, the sale of assets or businesses may be involved and money raised from this may well be reinvested to develop or enhance competitive advantage and support those remaining areas of the business which are seen as essential. Where disinvestment strategies are successful, and businesses in difficulty are turned around, money may then be invested for future growth.

In 1990 ACT, at the time UK manufacturers of Apricot computers, were in financial difficulties. The hardware business was sold to Mitsubishi, leaving ACT to focus on their remaining core competence: computer services. Some of the money from the sale was used to acquire a related financial services software company. Rappaport and Halevi (1991) defended this strategy, arguing that at that time the best opportunities for adding value in computing lay in applications. Existing technology had created powerful machines whose potential consumers had yet to exploit.

Disinvestment strategies involve consolidation and repositioning strategies as well as the sale or closure of one or more parts of a business. They are applicable in certain circumstances, including:

- where a firm is overextended in a particular market
- where it experiences an economic reversal because of competitor or other pressures
- when demand declines
- where the opportunity cost of resources being used is such that better returns could be earned elsewhere
- when the synergy expected from an acquisition proves elusive.

Disinvestment can be accomplished through retrenchment, turnaround, divestment or liquidation, and the choice from these particular alternatives determines whether the changes relate to functional, competitive or corporate strategies. Sometimes the term 'turnaround' is used to represent both the re trenchment and the turnaround strategies described in this section; and the expression 'recovery strategies' is also synonymous with both. Where part of a firm is sold to generate funds which can be channelled into areas or business units which are regarded as good future prospects, this too would be categorized as a recovery strategy.

Retrenchment

Remedial action is required when a company experiences declining profits as a result of economic recession, production inefficiency or competitor innovation. In such circumstances efforts should be concentrated on those activities and areas in which the company has distinctive competence or a superior competitive position. The assumption would be that the firm can survive.

In order to improve efficiency three aspects are involved, either individually or in combination:

- *cost reduction* through redundancies, leasing rather than buying new assets, not replacing machinery or reducing expenditure on such things as maintenance or training – the danger lies in cutting spending in areas where competitive advantage might be generated
- *asset reduction* – selling anything which is not essential
- *revenue generation* – by working on the debtor and stock turnover ratios.

Essentially, the aim is to reduce the scale of operations to a position where the company has a solid, consolidated and competitive base. The key issue concerns how much reduction is needed, whether it is minor or drastic, and how quickly the company must act. It is all too easy to cut back and slim down an organization to a size where is does not have the solid base required for later expansion. It has been downsized but not 'rightsized'. Where any changes are regarded as temporary, it is important to ensure that there is the necessary flexibility to allow for renewal and growth.

Turnaround strategies

Turnaround strategies involve the adoption of a new strategic position for a product or service, and typically lead on from retrenchment. Resources that are freed up are re-allocated from one strategic thrust to another; particularly significant here is the re-allocation of managerial talent, which can lead to an input of fresh ideas. Revenue-generating strategies, such as product modifications, advertising or lower prices designed to generate sales, are often involved; and in addition products and services may well be refocused into the niches that are thought to be most lucrative or defensible.

Retrenchment, cutting back, is accomplished relatively easily as long as managers are willing to take the necessary steps. As suggested above, the three key issues are:

- cutting in the 'right' areas and not destroying important competencies
- cutting back to a carefully determined core, and then
- creating new competitive advantages to build upon this core and generate new growth.

In 1990 Tony O'Reilly, the Irish businessman and entrepreneur who was, at that time, chief executive of Heinz in the USA, formed a group of investors to buy the struggling Waterford Wedgwood crystal and ceramic products group. Three years of further losses in the early 1990s then preceded years of profit once the business was rationalized with the loss of 3000 jobs. In the mid-1990s O'Reilly felt that he was in a position to set ambitious targets for doubling the size of the reduced business in the next five years. Strategies, which were typical for a situation like this, put forward included:

- expanding core businesses by targeting new markets. Younger buyers, attracted by lower price points, were seen as one possible opportunity, and a new brand, Marquis, was developed to exploit it
- diversification into loosely related areas such as linen and leather products to exploit the company's competency in brand management
- developing the collectability of products such as Coalport figurines. This strategy opened international opportunities in the USA and the Far East
- increasing product availability through more specialist gift boutiques in large stores and mail order
- infill acquisitions such as the purchase of Stuart Crystal in 1995.

Divestment

Divestment can be proactive, from a company that chooses to follow this route but is not under real pressure necessarily to do so. A successful company may decide that both it, as a parent, and the, possibly very successful, subsidiary would simply be better off if the subsidiary were sold to another company or to its managers. There is no synergy from the linkage.

It can also be more essential and reactive. Where retrenchment fails, or is not regarded as feasible, a part of the business may have to be sold. Basically the organization is hoping to create a more effective and profitable portfolio of products and services. The key problem is finding a buyer if the business in question is in difficulties, and particularly a buyer who is willing to pay a premium price for the assets. This can happen where a prospective buyer feels that he or she has the appropriate skills to manage the business more effectively, or where there is potential synergy with the activities already managed by the acquirer. Management buy-outs relate to the first of these issues. Existing managers often feel that they could manage their business more profitably if they were freed from any constraints imposed by the parent organization and were completely free to try out their ideas for change.

Divestment often happens, then, when a company needs to raise money quickly, or when a business is seen as having a poor strategic fit with the rest of the portfolio and, as a result, is holding back the whole organization. Divestments of parts of a business often follow an acquisition. This could be the sale of parts that do not appear to fit strategically. However, it is sometimes a key requirement for the acquisition imposed after an investigation by the Competition Commission.

Where a business is not contributing strategically to a parent organization, but there is no urgent need for cash, it may be floated off as an independent company rather than sold. Existing shareholders are simply given separate shares in the newly formed company, which needs to be strong enough to survive on its own. Organizations adopting this strategy hope to see the market value of their shares improve as the more concentrated business is perceived to be stronger.

Sometimes companies will swap assets with other organizations. In 1992 ICI swapped its fibres operations for the acrylics businesses of Du Pont, the US chemicals company. This was just one aspect of ICI's strategy of specializing in activities where it could achieve a strong global presence, and divesting others. Du Pont benefited by becoming the leading supplier of nylon in Europe, an area that they had targeted for expansion; ICI moved from third place to world leadership in acrylics, which are used, for example, in windows and bathroom furniture.

Liquidation

Liquidation involves the sale of a complete business, either as a single going concern or piecemeal to different buyers, or sometimes by auctioning the assets. It is generally regarded as an unpopular choice as it appears to represent an admission of failure by the present management team, but it may well be in the best long-term interests of the stakeholders as a whole. However, there are also instances where a successful entrepreneur, whose business has grown to a size where he or she has obtained all the benefits that they sought, is seeking to sell out. This can be linked to a situation where there is no natural successor to the entrepreneur who simply wants to capitalize on his or her investment.

This section concludes by emphasizing that organizations change their strategies, either regularly or occasionally, to pursue different alternatives at different

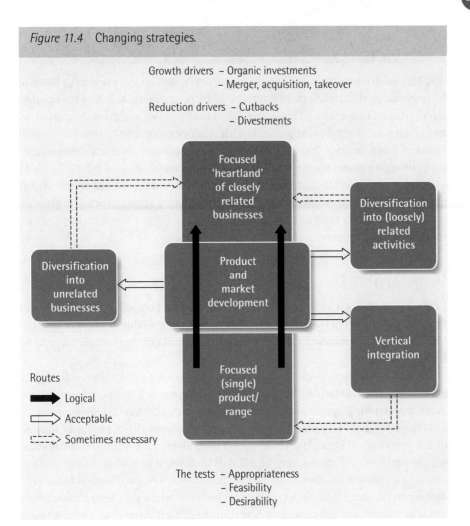

Figure 11.4 Changing strategies.

Growth drivers – Organic investments
– Merger, acquisition, takeover

Reduction drivers – Cutbacks
– Divestments

Focused 'heartland' of closely related businesses

Diversification into (loosely) related activities

Diversification into unrelated businesses

Product and market development

Vertical integration

Focused (single) product/range

Routes

➡ Logical

⇨ Acceptable

⇢ Sometimes necessary

The tests – Appropriateness
– Feasibility
– Desirability

times. Figure 11.4 tracks a range of possible moves. For many, the most logical strategic choices are built around relatedness and the consequent synergy. The central spine of the chart shows that product and market development are used to extend a single product range while retaining a clear focus. Chapter 13 looks in greater detail at the idea of a 'heartland' of related businesses which all benefit from belonging to one particular parent organization. On occasions acceptable diversification strategies will also be followed, but sometimes these will later be reversed as the organization returns to a more focused alternative. The three tests – appropriateness, feasibility and desirability – listed at the bottom of the chart for completeness, are the subject of Chapter 12.

Strategic Means

The limited growth strategies described earlier in this chapter are most likely to be implemented through the reinvestment of past profits, building on existing strengths and capabilities. This is generally known as organic growth, and it does not involve any formal arrangements with other organizations. However, certain forms of joint venture, together with franchise arrangements, can also be useful in bringing about market and product development.

Substantive growth strategies, particularly concentric diversification which exploits existing competencies, could also be achieved through organic growth, but for the reasons outlined below, they are more likely to involve acquisition, merger or joint venture.

Organic growth

Organic growth is an attractive option in that it can be controlled and the changes need not be sudden or traumatic as is typical of an acquisition or merger. In addition, there is no problem of different organizational cultures which have to be harmonized.

However, if organic growth is used to implement an external growth strategy, it may take considerable time; and while it is happening competitors may have more than enough opportunity to prepare their defences and possibly introduce strategies designed to create barriers to entry and thwart the potential success of the proposed changes. If diversification is involved, new skills and capabilities will be required, and these may be difficult to develop to a stage where there is competitive advantage. If existing management resources are allocated to the new development, there is an opportunity cost involved when they are removed from areas in which they are currently contributing. Finally, it may be easier to raise money for an acquisition, as it happens more quickly and consequently the money invested starts to earn returns sooner.

Acquisition, merger and joint venture

An acquisition, merger or joint venture is likely to take place when an organization lacks a key success factor for a particular market. In this book the term acquisition is used for the friendly purchase of one business by another, the outcome being that one is subsumed in the other and over time its name largely disappears. When it was still a building society, the Halifax acquired the Leeds Permanent, and the name of the latter has disappeared from the high street. Where the two businesses in effect pool their assets and retain their individual identities afterwards, the term merger is used. Take-overs are when one company acquires another acrimoniously and often, as a result of resistance on the part of the business being bought, pays a premium price. Joint ventures (jointly owned independent companies set up by other organizations) and strategic alliances (partnerships) are particularly useful where there are strong reasons against a full merger or acquisition. Joint ventures and strategic alliances can take a number of forms. When a group of oil companies collaborated in the development of the Alaskan pipeline to transport oil from the wells in the north of Alaska to the unfrozen ports in the south, it amounted to joint ownership. The strategy was logical: the pipeline was prohibitively expensive for one company alone, and the appropriate capacity was far in excess of the demand from any single company involved. Agreements could concern collaboration on design or rights to manufacture products designed by other companies. These types of joint venture are particularly popular with companies in different countries. Finally, if a manufacturer acquired a minority shareholding in a supplier, this would also constitute a form of joint venture aimed at achieving the advantages of vertical integration without a full merger and the need to fuse two cultures and sets of skills.

Joint ventures with local companies are essential for strategic development and growth in many developing countries, which wish to limit foreign ownership, promote domestic employment and obtain some involvement in industries that operate multinationally.

Whatever the strategic means selected, there are likely to be problems in bringing together the interests, skills and managers of two companies and cultures. The managerial time required to make it work can compromise the value added and reduce profitability, and divert attention away from other important issues within existing businesses.

Issues in diversification and acquisition

Periodically, organizations must make decisions about how focused and how diversified they wish to be. Horizontal integration, such as acquiring or merging with a competitor, will engender critical mass but may be restrained by the relevant competition authorities.

Where a company does choose to diversify it is more likely to implement this strategy through acquisition (friendly purchase), merger (bringing together the assets of two businesses) or take-over (hostile purchase) than it is through organic growth.

Unrelated diversification is invariably high risk, but it may be justified or chosen for one of the following reasons:

- weakness of the present businesses
- existing businesses having strengths and competencies that could be exploited in other industries
- the ambitions of the strategic leader.

Research in both the UK and US consistently indicates that diversification through acquisition has only a 50% likelihood of success, specifically delivering the hoped-for benefits. The typical reasons for failure are:

- the synergy potential is overestimated
- managerial problems and issues are underestimated
- key managers leave after the acquisition
- hidden weaknesses are not spotted until it is too late
- too much money is paid and the premium cannot be recovered.

The companies that succeed with this strategy tend to follow a number of simple rules:

- they carefully target their acquisitions
- they learn from previous experiences and become 'professional acquirers'
- they avoid paying too high a premium
- they adopt an appropriate post-acquisition structure and style and ensure that the businesses are integrated effectively
- corporately, they add value.

Where two companies choose to merge there is the opportunity for a reasonably comprehensive assessment of relative strengths and weaknesses, although it does not follow that one or both will not choose to hide certain significant weaknesses. In the case of a contested take-over less information will be available. UK take-over law requires that once a company has built up a shareholding of a particular size in another company it must offer to buy the remaining shares,[1] at which stage, the targeted company must make certain information available through the process of due diligence. Crucially, however, the information that will affect the ease or difficulty of merging the two cultures and organizations, and implementing the changes, is less freely available than financial data. It is never easy to determine from outside an organization what the style of man-

---

[1]Since 1989 one company must inform another if it builds up a share of 3% or more. When the ownership reaches 10% a company has to declare its intent – preparation for a later bid or a mere investment. Companies will be held to this declaration. If one says that it is merely investing it will not then be able to launch a bid for at least one year. A company can own up to 29.9% without making a bid for the remainder, but once this figure is exceeded a bid for the rest must follow.

agement is, its managers' attitude to risks, how decisions are made and whether managers are largely self-reliant. In the final analysis, the success of an acquisition or merger will be influenced markedly by the way the companies fit (or do not fit) together as well as by the logic used to justify the strategy (see Figure 11.5). As a result financial analysis may be used to justify the acquisition, but it will not answer questions relating to implementation. Table 11.2 highlights the significant information that is unlikely to be available until after the acquisition.

The following list of questions and issues indicates the key considerations which should be addressed by a company before it acquires another:

- how the acquiring company should restructure itself in order to absorb the new purchase, and what implications this will have for existing businesses and people
- what acceptable minimum and maximum sizes are for proposed diversifications in relation to present activities
- what degree of risk it is appropriate for the company to take
- how to value a proposed acquisition and how much to pay
- how to maintain good relationships with key managers during negotiations to try to ensure that they stay afterwards
- how to maintain momentum and interest in both companies after a successful offer

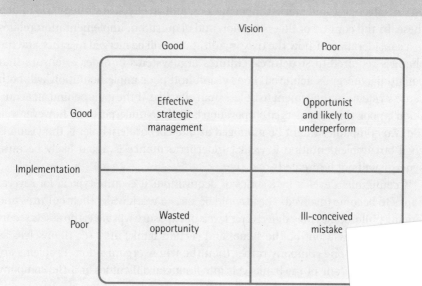

Figure 11.5 Strategy creation and implementation. Based on a matrix devised by Booz, Allen and Hamilton.

Table 11.2   Information available before and after an acquisition

Before	After
Organization charts	Inner philosophy and culture
Data on salaries of top management	Real quality of staff in decision roles
Reasonably detailed information on board members and key executives – but only brief details on middle management	Salary and reward structures and systems
	Decision processes
	Interrelationships, power bases, hidden conflicts and organizational politics
Products	Individual objectives being pursued
Plants	
Corporate identity, image and reputation	
Past record, especially financial	

- how quickly to move in merging organizational parts and sorting out problems
- reporting relationships and the degree of independence allowed to the acquired company, particularly where the business is unrelated
- whether and how to send in a new management team.

Figure 11.5 illustrates that an effective strategy is one that is based upon good vision and sound implementation prospects. Vision is in relation to the organization's strengths and market opportunities, and an effective strategy will match these. In the context of diversification and acquisition, implementation relates to a consideration of how the two organizations will be merged together and the changes required to structures, cultures and systems in order to ensure that potential synergy is achieved. Poor vision and poor implementation will both cause strategic management to be less than effective. If the logic behind an acquisition is poor, then the merged corporation is likely to underperform, however well the two companies might be managed as one corporate whole. If the vision is good but implementation is weak, underperformance is again likely because synergy will not be created.

If companies develop by a series of acquisitions it is quite typical for several banks to become involved. These could be spread worldwide; their cultures and lending philosophies may differ; their levels of exposure will vary; the assets securing the loans will not be the same; and certain banks may see themselves as lenders to just one company rather than the whole organization. Problems are likely to arise if one of the banks gets into financial difficulties or if the company seeks to extend a loan or adjust the terms.

Issues in strategic alliances and joint ventures

Strategic alliances and joint ventures (a stronger type of alliance where shares are exchanged or an independent company is set up) provide an alternative to an acquisition or merger. While they are designed to deliver synergy, cost savings and access to either technology or markets, they are not without their own implementation challenges.

It is generally acknowledged that the Japanese in particular have developed real capabilities in alliance management and that many Western companies have looked upon them from a more defensive perspective. For example, they are an alternative when an acquisition is not feasible for whatever reason.

There are three main reasons behind this strategy:

* to gain access to new markets and technologies
* to share expensive research and development costs
* to manage innovation more effectively.

Clearly these reasons overlap.

There are six particular, and again overlapping, forms of alliance and joint venture:

1. the merging of component parts of two or more businesses
2. companies joining forces to develop a new project
3. companies joining forces to develop a new business together
4. agreements between partners in the same supply chain
5. where companies purchase a stake in another business for strategic, rather than purely financial, reasons
6. international trading partnerships.

For alliances and joint ventures to work successfully, commitment from all parties is required. Everyone must appreciate that they can benefit and commit accordingly. Trust, sharing and collaboration become essential, even though different cultures and languages might be involved.

Franchising

Franchising again takes many forms, and it provides an opportunity for rapid growth for established businesses and a relatively low-risk means of starting a small business. Service businesses are more common than manufacturing in franchising, and as the UK continues to switch from a manufacturing to a service economy they may become increasingly important. Tie Rack is one example of a retail organization which has concentrated on specific market segments and grown rapidly with franchising. Thornton's chocolate shops, Fastframe picture framing, Prontaprint printing and copying shops, The Body Shop and the British School of Motoring are other examples. Although McDonald's is franchised throughout the USA, many restaurants in Britain are owned by the company. Kentucky Fried Chicken, Burger King and Spud-U-Like, however, are franchised.

A company which chooses franchising as a means of strategic growth enters into contractual arrangements with a number of small businesses, usually one in each selected geographical area. In return for a lump sum initial investment and ongoing royalties, the typical franchiser provides exclusive rights to supply a product or service under the franchiser's name in a designated area, know-how, equipment, materials, training, advice and national support advertising. This allows the business in question to grow rapidly in a number of locations without the investment capital that would be required to fund organic growth of the same magnitude. Another advantage for the franchiser is the alleviation of some of the need for the development of the managers, skills and capabilities required to control a large, growing and dispersed organization. Instead, efforts can be concentrated on expanding market share. It is essential, though, to establish effective monitoring and control systems to ensure that franchisees are providing the necessary level of quality and service.

The small business franchisee needs sufficient capital to buy into the franchise, but the risk is lower than for most independent starts because the business is already established. As a result several small, independent businesses operate as part of a chain and can compete against larger organizations.

Licensing

Licensing is an arrangement whereby a company is allowed to manufacture a product or service which has been designed by someone else and is protected by a patent. Companies in different countries are often involved. Pilkington, for example, patented float glass and then licensed its production throughout the world. Pilkington earned money from the arrangements and established world leadership; they would not have been able to afford to establish production plants around the world. In contrast, Mary Quant, designer of cosmetics, tights, footwear, beds and bed linen, never manufactured the products that she designed. They were all licensed; and some were marketed under the Quant name and some under the manufacturer's name (Myers beds and Dorma bed linen, for example). Licensing also provides an ideal opportunity for the owners of valuable intellectual capital (such as Disney with their characters) to earn revenues from their knowledge-based resource without having to invest in manufacturing. One argument in favour of this arrangement has been that production and labour relations problems are avoided, enabling the business to concentrate on the areas in which it has expertise and competitive advantage.

Globalization is now no longer an objective, but an imperative, as markets open and geographical barriers become increasingly blurred and even irrelevant. Corporate alliances, whether joint ventures or acquisitions, will increasingly be driven by competitive pressures and strategies rather than financial structuring.

John F Welch, Chairman and CEO, General Electric, quoted in Fortune,
26 March 1990

In future we will have local [retail] companies and global companies and not much in-between. Globalization pressures will lead to those who are not in the first division and those who are purely national to make alliances.

David Bernard, Chairman,
Carrefour (hypermarkets)

International Strategies

Internal growth, external growth and disinvestment strategies may all involve an international dimension with special complexities. Countries differ economically (variable growth rates), culturally (behaviours, tastes and preferences) and politically. National politics can dictate the appropriate strategy – some markets cannot be penetrated effectively without joint ventures with local companies.

Internal growth might involve exporting to new markets overseas and the development of special varieties of a product or service in order to target it to the specific needs and requirements of overseas customers. External growth can range from the creation of distribution or assembly bases abroad, to joint ventures and licensing agreements with foreign companies, to the establishment of a comprehensive global organization. The latter can be accomplished through both acquisition and strategic alliances.

Kay (1990) recommends that organizations should seek to determine the smallest area within which they can be a viable competitor. While a retail newsagent can still succeed by concentrating on a local catchment area, most car manufacturers, in common with many other industries and service businesses, now see their relevant market as a global one. Diageo (previously Grand Metropolitan) is illustrative of a company which chose to concentrate on products or services (in food and drinks) where it was able to be an internationally strong competitor. Such companies are hoping to create synergy by specializing in core skills and competencies and exploiting these as widely as possible. The term 'multinational' is generally applied to any company that produces and distributes in two or more countries; a transnational, global, corporation is one that has a large proportion of its sales, assets and employees outside its home base. Using these criteria, Nestlé is the most global business in the world.

Organizations that develop their corporate strategy internationally have to consider in particular:

- marketing and financial strategies
- the structure of the organization
- cultural and people issues.

Before discussing these factors individually, Figure 11.6 endeavours to link them together and implicitly reinforce the notion of E–V–R (environment–values–resources) congruence. The situational factors have to be 'right' for an international strategy to make sense. Specifically, the returns must exceed the investment. This is illustrated in Figure 11.7.

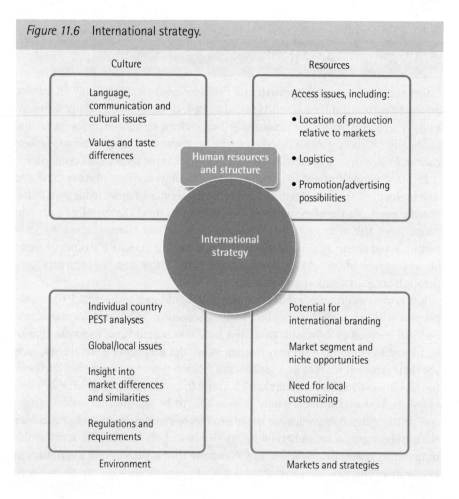

Figure 11.6   International strategy.

Culture

Language, communication and cultural issues

Values and taste differences

Human resources and structure

International strategy

Resources

Access issues, including:

- Location of production relative to markets
- Logistics
- Promotion/advertising possibilities

Individual country PEST analyses

Global/local issues

Insight into market differences and similarities

Regulations and requirements

Potential for international branding

Market segment and niche opportunities

Need for local customizing

Environment

Markets and strategies

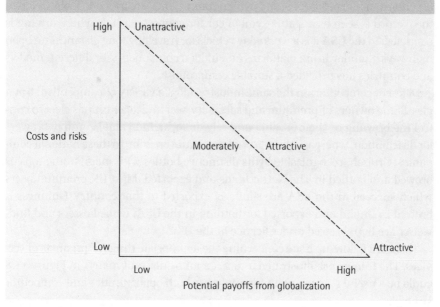

Figure 11.7 The attractiveness of the international opportunity. The costs and risks (vertical axis) refer to entry barriers, local regulations, e.g. need for a local partner, and extent of investment to make products/services suitable for individual markets.

Gupta and Govindarajan (1998) argue that the potential payoff can be assessed by addressing a number of obvious questions:

- Which product lines are (most) suitable for internationalization?
- Which markets should be targeted – and in what order of priority?
- What are the most appropriate ways of entering these target markets?
- How rapidly does it make sense to expand? Does a fast-track approach (such as Glaxo licensing Zantac for production in various countries simultaneously) make more sense than a slower approach (IKEA deliberately restricting the number of new branch openings every year to retain tight control)?

Marketing

The issue of how global products and services can be made, and the extent to which they have to be tailored to appeal to different markets is critical. Markets vary from those termed multidomestic (where the competitive dynamics of each separate country market are distinctive and idiosyncratic) to global (where competitive strategies are transferable across frontiers). Coca-Cola, Levi jeans and the expensive perfumes and leather goods marketed by LVMH, Moët Hennessy Louis Vuitton, attract a global consumer with identical tastes, but they are more exceptional than normal. The challenge to design the 'world car', for example, remains unresolved. Honda initially hoped to achieve this when it began redesigning its Accord range in the mid-1980s, but concluded that international performance expectations, and in turn components, are irreconcilable. In Japan the Accord is seen as a status-symbol car for congested roads where driving is restricted; in the USA it is a workaday vehicle for travelling long distances on open highways. Standardizing platforms and hidden components for different models and countries has provided a suitable compromise.

Different competitors in the same industry adopt a variety of competitive strategies. Some owners of premium and speciality beer and lager brands elect to control the brewing of their product and rely on local, individual country brewers for distribution, whereas others license the actual brewing to these national companies. Grolsch, recognizable by its distinctive bottles with metal frame tops, is brewed and bottled in The Netherlands and exported. Most UK premium beers which succeed in the USA are similarly exported to that country. Guinness is brewed in Dublin and exported for bottling in the USA, while Fosters and Budweiser are both brewed under licence in the UK.

There is a follow-up issue concerning the appropriate range of products or services. The framework illustrated as a 2 × 2 four-quadrant matrix in Figure 11.8 could be a useful starting point for analysing both opportunities and competitor strategies.

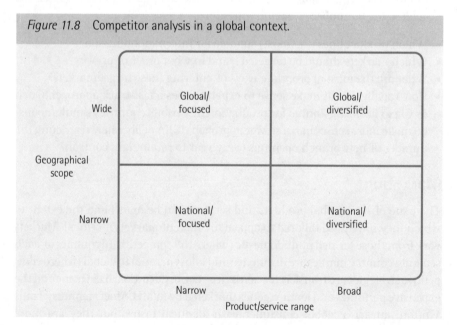

Figure 11.8   Competitor analysis in a global context.

Where organizations find it necessary to be located close to customers in order to provide the delivery and other services demanded, this can be achieved with strategic stockholding rather than manufacturing.

Finance

The management of currency transfers and exchange rates adds complexity. Floating exchange rates imply uncertainty, although companies can, and do, reduce their risk by buying ahead. The European Exchange Rate Mechanism (superseded by the single European currency, the Euro) was originally designed to minimize currency fluctuations, but economic pressures still cause periodic devaluations. Predictable or fixed rates benefit, for example, a car manufacturer which produces engines and transmission systems in one country, transfers them to assembly plants in a second and third country, each specializing in different cars, and then finally sells them throughout Europe. Costs and estimated profits must be based on predicted currency movements, and any incorrect forecasting could result in either extra or lost profits.

Where such an organization structure is created, transfer pricing arrangements are required. If managers of the various divisions or business units are motivated or measured by their profitability figures there will be some disagreement about transfer prices which affect their value-added figures. Equally, the organization may be seeking to manage transfer arrangements for tax purposes, seeking to show most profit where taxes are lowest.

Companies with a main base in a country whose currency is strong and appreciating may find their international competitiveness weakened. Exported products will become relatively expensive and competing imports cheaper. Such companies may be tempted to invest and relocate elsewhere. In 1995, for example, Toyota, which already had a number of manufacturing plants around the world, began seriously to consider closing down plants in Japan because of the high yen. Companies must also see financial markets as global, seeking to borrow where loans are cheapest, as long as the source is not too risky.

While both governments and companies would ideally like a strong local currency and to be able to export at high prices to earn substantial wealth internationally, this may not be practical. It certainly requires high added value and very clear differentiation.

Structure, culture and people

The two key questions are:

1. Where to make the various products and services to obtain the necessary people and other resources required, to be as close as appropriate to each defined geographical market, and to manage costs efficiently; and

2. How best to structure the organization in order to control it effectively but, at the same time, ensure that it is sufficiently responsive to changing environments. The speed and nature of change pressures may be uneven. IT increasingly offers opportunities for more effective control of globally dispersed businesses.

The alternatives are:

- a globally centralized organization, remote from markets, and relying on exporting. This is likely to prove cost-efficient but possibly out-of-touch
- manufacturing plants located close to markets in order to satisfy local needs and preferences. This structure, known as both international and multidomestic, could still be controlled centrally, or substantially decentralized into fully autonomous units, in which case the plants may be independent or co-operate in some way. This is a more expensive structure, but one that can offer higher levels of service. Unilever, which relies on localized manufacturing and marketing, is an example. While cement is an international commodity product, companies are structured in this way because there is no benefit to be gained from transporting cement across frontiers
- centralized manufacture of key components, possibly in a low-wage country, with final assembly or finishing nearer to markets. Caterpillar Tractor utilizes this strategy
- an integrated global structure with production locations chosen on resource or cost grounds. Finished goods will be transported to markets. In this structure the organization will have an international presence, but in say country X its sales could consist mainly of products imported from other locations, while most of country X's production is exported. Marketing, production control, purchasing and research and development will all be co-ordinated globally if they are not centralized
- a global network via strategic alliances.

Centres of excellence may be established where cultural values and behaviours are most appropriate. Philips chose to concentrate technology development in the Far East, where a long-term perspective is natural, whereas IBM has established R&D facilities in Italy, which it regards as suitably intuitive and innovative. However, if national preferences and requirements are markedly different, there is an argument in favour of establishing dedicated R&D facilities in several countries. ICI established a technical centre in Japan for developing special chemicals and materials in collaboration with the major car and electronics manufacturers. The intention was to sell their products to Japanese plants throughout the world. 'Japanese companies prefer to collaborate with chemicals suppliers which have scientists and engineers in Japan, and a factory to produce material locally.' General Motors strengthened its Opel technical development centre in Frankfurt to spearhead its expansion in all international markets outside the USA. Eastern Europe and the Pacific Rim are targets for growth in respect of both production and sales. Meanwhile, Ford has sought to integrate product development globally in its search for a range of world cars.

This alternative has many strategic advantages, but it can be complex to control and costly in overheads. Typical companies are Sony and Coca-Cola (Case Study 6). Coca-Cola, based in Atlanta, USA, commands 50% of the world's soft drinks market and 44% of the US domestic market. The key success factor is obtaining distribution and access to markets, and because Coca-Cola is mostly water this is decentralized. Branding and marketing are global and centralized. The strategy is to sell concentrate or syrup to local bottlers, be they independent businesses or joint venture partners. Pricing is based on what can be afforded locally, and a variety of support mechanisms is offered. Coke is frequently promoted with local endorsements, but marketing and advertising also feature sponsorship of international sporting events.

The international location decision is affected by a number of key issues, including:

- the existence of any national resources that influence competitive advantage in any significant way. Nike and Reebok have built factories in China, Thailand and the Philippines for labour-cost savings. A number of leading computer and semiconductor businesses is located in California's Silicon Valley because of the pool of skilled labour and acquired expertise to support research and development. Consumer electronics and pharmaceuticals are further examples of industries where the headquarters of the leading companies are concentrated in one or a few countries
- scale economies from key resources in, say, production or technology. Toyota, Honda and Nissan preferred to produce in Japan and export for many years, but the strong yen eventually encouraged them to locate abroad
- transport considerations
- the availability of a suitable supply chain
- political issues.

Whatever the structural format, a truly international business must develop a global mission and core values (such as consistent quality worldwide), and achieve integration through effective communications. The corporate strategy must be centralized even if the company has a number of independent subsidiaries and operates in several multidomestic markets. However, the organization must be able to embrace the different national cultural traits and behaviours, and this presents an important managerial challenge. Decisions have to be made concerning the balance of local managers and mobile 'international' managers who are easily transferable between divisions and countries.

Bartlett and Ghoshal (1989) summarized the above points as three potentially conflicting issues which must be reconciled. These are:

- the need for efficiency through global centralization
- the need to respond locally through decentralization
- the need to innovate and transfer learning internationally.

Bartlett and Ghoshal (1992) also reached the following conclusions.

- There can be no such thing as a 'universal international manager'. Large global companies will need functional specialists (such as production experts) and national managers (committed to one country and most familiar with that culture) as well as those executives who are able to switch readily between divisions and countries. International managers are responsible for corporate and competitive strategies within the organization, while national managers ensure that the needs of local customers, host governments and employees are satisfied effectively. The organizational challenge in respect of functional managers is to ensure that best practices are learned and spread throughout the organization.
- The attempts to integrate all of the global operations (products, plants and countries) should be concentrated towards the top of the organizational hierarchy. At lower levels managers should have clear, single-line, responsibilities and reporting relationships.

One benefit of adopting these recommendations is a limited requirement for international managers who, inevitably, are in short supply because of the qualities that they are required to have. Some industrialists would argue that this supply constraint is the deciding force, and that a successful global matrix structure would be preferable.

Contrasting views on international strategy

Porter (1990) believes that global strategies essentially supplement the competitive advantage created in the home market. Firms must retain their national strengths when they cross over borders. Ohmae (1990) disagrees and argues that global firms should shake off their origins. Managers must take on an international perspective, avoiding the near-sightedness that often characterizes companies with centralized and powerful global headquarters. Markets, he says, are driven by the needs and desires of customers around the world, and managers must act as if they are equidistant from all of these customers, wherever they might be located.

Ohmae is perhaps presenting a futuristic vision of how he believes things will be as global forces strengthen. At the moment, while world leaders such as IBM,

Sony and Nestlé are spread around the world, and substantially dependent on non-domestic customers, their underlying cultures and competitiveness remain rooted in the USA, Japan and Switzerland, respectively.

Chandler (1990) stresses the continuing importance of economies of scale (cost advantages with large-scale production) and economies of scope (the use of common materials and processes to make a variety of different products profitably). This implies carefully targeted investment in large-scale operations and a search for international marketing opportunities.

The Selection of a Strategy

The issue of what constitutes a good strategic choice is the subject of Chapter 12, but it is important here to emphasize that the strategic choices described above may not be real options for an organization at any given time. Theoretically, they may exist as alternatives; realistically, they could not be implemented. Equally, certain alternatives may be forced on organizations.

While internal or external growth strategies might be preferred to fulfil objectives and fill the planning gap, disinvestment strategies may be required because of competitor or other environmental pressures. Strategies are only feasible if they can be implemented; a desire to grow through horizontal or vertical integration, concentric or conglomerate diversification may require a suitable acquisition to be available at a price the company can afford to pay. An inability to raise money for any reason can act as a constraint on a particular choice. If management skills are not available to manage a merger or acquisition it may prove sensible to avoid or delay such a choice, however desirable it might be. Penrose's (1959) argument that growth is limited by the organization's spare resources, particularly management, was discussed in Chapter 2. The ability to succeed with product or market development will be dependent on the firm's relative strength and power in relation to competition; there may be competitive barriers to successful implementation.

Whichever strategy is selected, issues of competitive advantage and implementation become paramount. Chances of success increase if there is an opportunity to create and sustain competitive advantage.

The influence and preference of the strategic leader will be a major determinant of the strategy selected. The strategic leader will also build the organization structure, and ideally the strategy and structure will mould together to generate synergy from the various activities. This in turn will depend upon the organization culture. Hence there is a relationship between strategy, structure, leadership and culture. When there is a change of leadership there may well be a change of strategy and in turn of structure and culture; when strategies fail to meet up to expectations, there may be a change of leadership.

Summary

There is a range of strategic alternatives and strategic means that organizations might review and possibly choose at any time. Organizations will change their directions and strategies and they do not always pursue the same strategy in the same way. Normally, they will aim to be proactive and purposeful about this. Sometimes, however, they are constrained: an option that they would like to pursue is unrealistic. This would be the case if a proposed acquisition was blocked by the Competition Commission. Similarly, the Commission might insist on a particular divestment in return for permission to proceed with a merger.

Over time, the corporate portfolio migrates. It should be built around a defensible heartland of related businesses, accepting that at times there will be diversification into related and unrelated activities. We cannot finally judge the worthiness of a particular choice until we take account of the organization's ability to implement the strategy that it has chosen.

The key strategic alternatives are limited growth, substantive growth or retrenchment.

Limited growth:
- market penetration, either in a deliberate attempt to build market share or as a form of consolidation to protect a customer base
- market development – opening up new opportunities with different customers, possibly in overseas markets
- product development – extending the range in order to expand the level of business with existing customers.

Substantive growth:
- horizontal integration – generally merging with a direct or indirect competitor, again to increase market share
- vertical integration – linking with another company in the same supply chain
- related diversification – moving into an area where either marketing or technology issues are similar, often by acquisition, merger or strategic alliance
- unrelated diversification – the higher risk strategy involving new markets, new products and new technologies.

Retrenchment – beginning with ideas of consolidation either:
- as a basis for turnaround of a company experiencing difficulties, or
- linked to the divestment of non-core activities.

The key strategic means are:
- organic growth – internal investment to develop new competencies
- acquisition (friendly purchase), merger (two companies simply joining together) and take-over (hostile purchase)

- strategic alliances (partnerships, whatever the form) and joint ventures (alliances which involve a major financial investment by the parties concerned)
- franchising and licensing – two alternative forms for exploiting intellectual capital while minimizing the financial outlays.

Certain of these strategies can have an important international dimension, which brings its own special complexities and impacts upon the structure of the organization in conjunction with the strategy.

References

Bartlett, C and Ghoshal, S (1989) *Managing Across Borders: The Transnational Solution*, Harvard Business School Press.

Bartlett, C and Ghoshal, S (1992) What is a global manager? *Harvard Business Review*, September–October.

Chandler, AD (1990) The enduring logic of industrial success, *Harvard Business Review*, March–April.

Gupta, A and Govindarajan, V (1998) How to build a global presence, *Financial Times Mastering Global Business*, No 1.

Kay, JA (1990) Identifying the strategic market, *Business Strategy Review*, Spring.

Ohmae, K (1990) *The Borderless World*, Harper.

Penrose, E (1959) *The Theory of the Growth of the Firm*, Blackwell.

Peters, TJ and Waterman, RH Jr (1982) *In Search of Excellence: Lessons from America's Best Run Companies*, Harper and Row.

Porter, ME (1990) *The Competitive Advantage of Nations*, Free Press.

Rappaport, AS and Halevi, S (1991) The computerless computer company, *Harvard Business Review*, July– August.

Test your knowledge of this chapter with our online quiz at:
http://www.thomsonlearning.co.uk

Explore Strategic Alternatives and MArket Strategy Selection further at:

Business Strategy Review   http://www.blackwellpublishers.co.uk/journals/BSR

Questions and Research Assignments

TEXT RELATED

1. For each of the following strategic alternatives, list why you think an organization might select this particular strategy, what they would expect to gain, and where the problems and limitations are. If you can, think of an example of each one from your own experience:

   - do nothing; no change
   - market penetration
   - market development
   - product development
   - innovation
   - horizontal integration
   - vertical integration

- concentric diversification
- conglomerate diversification
- retrenchment
- turnaround
- divestment
- liquidation.

2. What are the relative advantages and disadvantages of organic growth as opposed to external growth strategies?

Internet and Library Projects

1. What has happened to ACT since Apricot Computers were divested? Was the argument that the future lay in specialist software a robust one?

2. What has happened to Waterford Wedgwood? Was the ambitious growth objective to double the size of the business between 1995 and 2000 realistic? Has it been achieved? What strategic changes – both corporate and competitive – have been employed?

Waterford Wedgewood   http://www.waterford-usa.com

3. (a) What are the essential differences between an export, an international and a global organization?

   (b) Consider the most appropriate strategy for a sizeable UK-based company with international ambitions in the following industries (assume that your choice could be implemented):
   - steel
   - pharmaceuticals
   - civil aircraft
   - ladies' cosmetics/fragrances.

4. For an organization of your choice, trace the changes of strategy and strategic direction over a period of time. Relate these changes to any changes in strategic leadership, structure and, wherever possible, culture.

5. Sony is renowned as an innovative company within the consumer electronics industry, and its success has depended substantially on televisions, videos and hi-fi equipment. In recent years Sony has followed a strategy of globalization and diversification, arguably in related product areas. The international strategy has been called global localization; Sony aims to be a global company presented locally, and this involves devolving authority away from Tokyo and expanding manufacturing and R&D around the world.

   How does Sony achieve this?

Sony   http://www.sony.com

12

Strategy Evaluation

Introducing Strategy Evaluation

Criteria for Effective Strategies

Summary

Finance in Action: Financial Management

We might like to think that strategic decisions would be taken objectively rather than subjectively. After all, there is a host of useful techniques available to decision makers – if only they always had the time to use them! Then again, it does not follow that using a selection of these techniques would provide consistent answers or priorities, leaving the manager(s) concerned to exercise judgement.

Some of the relevant issues have been discussed in earlier chapters. The issue of 'who' chooses was discussed briefly in Chapters 8 and 10. Some strategic leaders are particularly concerned with the size of the organization, together with the power and status that size can bring, and individual managers sometimes have personal agendas that can conflict with the objectives of other people and the organization as a whole. Several techniques were described in Chapter 9 which are useful for strategic analysis and which contribute to the 'what' element of strategic choices.

This chapter pulls together the strands of the 'what' element and provides a comprehensive evaluation framework for strategic decisions.

A sound choice will always address four issues:

1. *competitiveness and competitive advantage*
2. *strategic logic and synergy*
3. *the financial returns, which should normally exceed the cost of capital*
4. *the ability to implement.*

The opening case on Walt Disney considers issues 1, 2 and 4.

Case Study 12: Walt Disney Corporation

Walt Disney's fame and initial success was based substantially upon films, books and comics featuring cartoon characters such as Mickey Mouse and Donald Duck. Walt Disney was an entrepreneur and cartoonist who eventually found his fortune in the moving picture industry of the 1930s. He was not, however an 'overnight' success. To utilize these characters further, which Disney saw as resources, and to capitalize upon increased leisure spending (a window of opportunity) the first Disneyland theme park was later opened in 1955 in Anaheim, California. Within one year Disneyland contributed 30% of the company's revenue. The success of the theme-park strategy must be attributed to Walt personally, as others in the corporation, including his brother, Roy, were against the development.

Although Walt Disney died in 1966 his strategies were continued. The Magic Kingdom Park was opened in Florida in 1971, followed 11 years later by Epcot. These have proved immensely successful, but were not seen as 'really new'. In the 1980s the environment for leisure businesses was perceived to be changing dramatically, but Disney was no longer regarded as a trendsetter. Revenues, profits and stock prices all fell.

Disney Corporation appointed a new strategic leader, Michael Eisner, in 1984, and he successfully opened several new windows of opportunity for the corporation. He introduced more aggressive marketing (together with price increases) at the theme parks, and throughout the 1980s the numbers of visitors, including foreigners, grew steadily. Additional attractions, including the Disney-MGM studios in 1989, were added, together with a support infrastructure including Disney resort hotels. Eisner found hundreds of cartoons not previously syndicated to television. New marketing and licensing opportunities for Disney characters have always been sought. Disney established a new film company, Touchstone Pictures, to enable it to make movies with more adult themes for restricted audiences without affecting the Disney name and family image. They also invested in videos and satellite television. One key theme pervades most of the developments – the hidden wealth of the Disney name and characters. Disney has been a successful, growing, profitable company, partially thanks to recent films such as Aladdin, The Lion King, Pocahontas, Toy Story and Hercules.

Simply, Disney had developed distinctive competencies in storytelling and 'set' management and continually sought, and found, new ways of exploiting these competencies. Of course, over time it also strengthened its competency in these key areas.

Five strategic developments

In 1992 Disney opened EuroDisney, its new theme park outside Paris – the concept had already been moved successfully to Japan. However, the initial visitor, revenue and profit targets had to be revised downwards after the first trading year. Drastic refinancing of the project was required. While attendance levels were disappointing, the key problem was that visitors, affected by the recession, were not spending liberally. The recession was also affecting Disney's ability to sell associated properties in the theme park; the projected cash flows needed this extra income. High French interest rates then compounded the difficulties. However, it was also apparent that European employees were initially unable to replicate the enthusiasm of their US counterparts, and the overall service package was not the same. EuroDisney [now Disneyland Paris Resort] has since established itself and become profitable, but there was a steep learning curve, which involved the need to bring in outside partners to help to finance overseas developments of this magnitude. In 1999 Disney announced that it would build a second park outside Paris – Disney Studios should open in 2002.

In 1994, environmentalist opponents forced Disney to abandon plans for a new park in Virginia (near Washington DC) which would have celebrated the main events in US history. Disney concluded it had 'lost the perception game'. Arguably, Disney perceived itself as a 'guardian of wholesome American values', but to its opponents it came over as an 'outsize entertainment company with a penchant for sugar-coating'. Disney has not confirmed that the idea has been shelved permanently!

One year later, in 1995, and following a gradual downward trend in theme-park attendances in Florida, Disney began to construct a new attraction – Disney's Animal Kingdom, its biggest so far – which it billed as 'a celebration of all animals that ever or never existed'. The live animals would (unusually) be presented in 'true-life adventure stories of mystery, danger and humour' rather than in zoo or safari park settings. Mechanical, mythical animals will be featured alongside the live ones.

Also in 1995 Disney paid the equivalent of £12 billion to acquire Capital Cities/ABC, owner of ABC Television in America, to create the world's largest entertainment company. A major *content* company, Disney, was merging with a leading *distribution* company. The deal was justified with two arguments. One, Disney's valuable intellectual property would enjoy enhanced media access – ABC owned eight television stations, ESPN cable TV and an extensive radio network. ABC also published newspapers, books and magazines. Two, Disney's existing distribution network was ideally placed to exploit and syndicate ABC's programmes. However, having mainly concentrated on content and intellectual property, Disney was now diversifying into a new area with new strategic demands. It was moving away from direct competition with focused companies such as Viacom to rival communications giants such as Time Warner.

In 1998 Disney launched its first cruise ships, named *Disney Magic* and *Disney Wonder*. These identical ships can carry 1750 passengers and they sail on short cruises between Florida and the Bahamas all through the year. They are designed for families, but adults who wish to be kept apart from children can achieve this aim. The lounges are, inevitably, Disney themed, and the shows are 'unlike any other in the cruise industry'. Disney invested in 1000 seat theatres with state-of-the-art acoustics. Naturally, there are also cinemas on board the ships. Externally, the ships look like other cruise liners, but internally they incorporate the latest in technology.

QUESTION: How would you evaluate these five strategic developments?

Walt Disney Company   http://disney.go.com

Introducing Strategy Evaluation

There is no single evaluation technique or framework as such that will provide a definite answer to which strategy or strategies a company should select or follow at any given time. Particular techniques will prove helpful in particular circumstances. Several frameworks and techniques which are often classified as means of evaluating strategy have been discussed in earlier chapters and are listed in Box 12.1, together with a number of additional financial considerations which are explained and discussed in a Finance in Action supplement ti this chapter.

STRATEGY IN ACTION – Box 12.1
Strategy Evaluation Techniques

SWOT analysis

E–V–R congruence
Planning gap analysis
Porter's industry analysis and competitive advantage frameworks
Break-even analysis
Sensitivity analysis
Portfolio analyses
Scenario modelling
Simulations of future possibilities using PIMS

Investment appraisal techniques using discounted cash flows
Net present value
Internal rate of return
Payback
Cash-flow implications
(The public sector often also uses cost–benefit analysis)

Certain essential criteria, however, should be considered in assessing the merits and viability of existing strategies and alternatives for future change. This chapter considers how one might assess whether or not a corporate, competitive or functional strategy is effective or likely to be effective. The issues concern *appropriateness, feasibility* and *desirability*. Some of the considerations are likely to conflict with each other, and consequently an element of judgement is required in making a choice. The most appropriate or feasible option for the firm may not be the one that its managers regard as most desirable, for example.

In many respects the key aspects of any proposed changes concern the *strategic logic*, basically the subject of this book so far, and the *ability to implement*. Implementation and change are the subject of the final chapters.

Strategic logic relates to:

- the relationship and fit between the strategies and the mission or purpose of the organization; and the current appropriateness of the mission, objectives and the strategies being pursued (synergy is an important concept in this)
- the ability of the organization to match and influence changes in the environment
- competitive advantage and distinctiveness
- the availability of the necessary resources.

Understanding Corporate Strategy

Figure 12.1, which recrafts the earlier model of E–V–R (environment–values–resources) congruence, shows that organizations must seek and exploit opportunities for adding value in ways that are attractive to customers. This can be at both the corporate and competitive strategy levels. At the corporate level, the organization is looking to establish a heartland of related businesses and activities; at the competitive level, the challenge is to create and sustain competitive advantage. Resources must be deployed to exploit the new opportunities, and this is driven or, in some cases, frustrated by strategic leadership and the culture of the organization.

Implementation concerns the management of the resources to satisfy the needs of the organization's stakeholders. Implicit in this is the ability to satisfy customers better than competitors are able to do. Matching resources and environmental needs involves the culture and values of the organization, and decisions about future changes involve an assessment of risk. Relevant to both implementation and strategic logic is the role and preference of the strategic leader and other key decision makers in the organization.

This chapter addresses the following questions:

- What constitutes a good strategic choice?
- What can the organization do and what can it not do?
- What should the organization seek to do and what should it not seek to do?

The last question should not be treated lightly. There will always be options available which are not appropriate for the organization as a whole, even though they might be attractive to some managers and could be readily implemented.

Figure 12.1 E-V-R congruence restated.

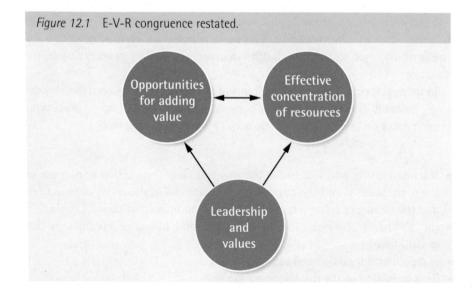

STRATEGY IN ACTION – Box 12.2
Ten Principles of Strategy

1. Market orientation and customer relevance
2. Innovation
3. Distinctiveness – relating to differentiation and competitive advantage
4. Timeliness (appropriate for the current situation) and
5. Flexibility (capable of change)
6. Efficiency – relating to cost control and cost efficiency, particularly in production and operations
7. Building on strengths and competencies
8. Concentration and co-ordination of resources (rather than spreading them too widely) to achieve synergy
9. Harmonization of strategy creation and implementation
10. Understanding – remembering that if a strategy is to be supported by employees who are motivated and enthusiastic it must be communicated and understood.

When evaluating any corporate, competitive or functional strategy it is worth considering ten strategic principles, all of which are discussed in detail elsewhere in the book. Where these principles, which are listed in Box 12.2, are evident, and particularly where they are strong and powerful forces, the likelihood of strategic success and effectiveness is enhanced. In addition, the financial returns should always exceed the costs involved, unless there is a defensible strategic reason for cross-subsidization.

Corporate strategy evaluation

Rumelt (1980) argues that corporate strategy evaluation at the widest level involves seeking answers to three questions:

- Are the current objectives of the organization appropriate?
- Are the strategies created previously, and which are currently being implemented to achieve these objectives, still appropriate?
- Do current results confirm or refute previous assumptions about the feasibility of achieving the objectives and the ability of the chosen strategies to achieve the desired results?

It is therefore important to look back and evaluate the outcomes and relative success of previous decisions, and also to look ahead at future opportunities and threats. In both cases strategies should be evaluated in relation to the objectives that they are designed to achieve. A quantitative chart along the lines of Table 12.1 could be devised to facilitate this. In this illustration, and in order to evaluate current and possible future strategies and help to select alternatives for the future, the objectives are listed at the top of a series of columns. It will be appreciated from the sample objectives provided that some can have clear and objective measurement criteria while others are more subjective in nature. The alternatives, listed down the left-hand side, could be ranked in order of first to last preference in each column, or given a numerical score. In making a final decision based on the rankings or aggregate marks it may well prove appropriate to weight the objectives in the light of their relative importance. This table could simply be used as a framework for discussion without any scoring or ranking, if this approach is preferred.

In terms of assessing the suitability of strategic alternatives in particular circumstances Thompson and Strickland (1980) suggest that market growth and competitive position are important elements. Table 12.2 summarizes their argument. Concentration, for example, is seen as an appropriate strategy where market growth is high and the existing competitive position is strong. By contrast, where market growth is slow and the competitive position is weak, retrenchment is likely to be the most suitable strategy for the organization. Where 'not material' is listed in a column, the contention is that the strategy is appropriate for either high or low growth or strong or weak competitive positions.

Table 12.1 Evaluating strategies in terms of objectives

Strategic alternative	Objectives*					
	Ability to achieve specific revenue or growth targets	Ability to return specific profitability targets	Ability to create and sustain competitive advantage	Synergy potential – relationship with other activities	Ability to utilize existing (spare) resources and skills	and so on
Existing competitive strategies for products, services, business units	Score out of say 10					
and	or					
Possible changes to corporate and competitive strategies	rank in order of preference					

*For evaluation purposes, each objective could be given a relative weighting.

Table 12.2   Strategic alternatives: their appropriateness in terms of market growth and competitive position

Strategy	Market growth	Competitive position
Concentration	High	Strong
Horizontal integration	High	Weak
Vertical integration	High	Strong
Concentric diversification	Not material	Not material
Conglomerate diversification	Low	Not material
Joint ventures into new areas	Low	Not material
Retrenchment	Low	Weak
Turnaround	High	Weak
Divestment	Not material	Weak
Liquidation	Not material	Weak

Developed from ideas in Thompson, AA and Strickland, AJ (1980) *Strategy Formulation and Implementation*, Irwin.

Criteria for Effective Strategies

When assessing current strategies, and evaluating possible changes, it is important to emphasize that there is no such thing as a right or wrong strategy or choice in absolute terms. However, certain factors will influence the effectiveness of strategies and the wisdom of following certain courses of action. Several authors, including Tilles (1963) and Hofer and Schendel (1978), have discussed the factors that determine the current and future possible effectiveness of particular strategies.

The factors that they suggest, and others, are considered in this chapter in three sections: appropriateness, feasibility and desirability. This categorization has been selected for convenience, and it will be appreciated that there is some overlap between the sections.

The major issues are summarized in Figure 12.2 and are discussed in the following text.

Appropriateness

In reviewing current strategies, assessing the impact of adaptive incremental changes that have taken place and considering strategic alternatives for the future it is important to check that strategies are consistent with the needs of the environment, the resources and values of the organization, and its current mission.

Figure 12.2   Criteria for effective strategies.

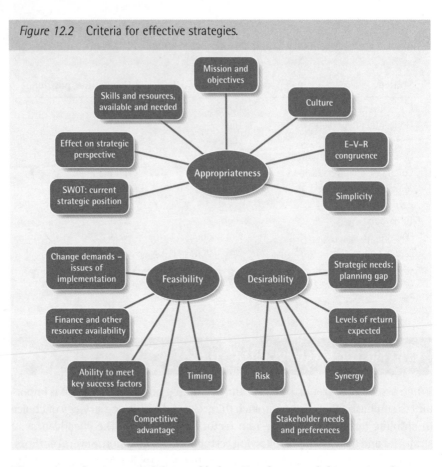

These general points are elaborated below. For the rest of this section the term 'the strategy' is used to refer to each particular strategy being considered, be it a current one or a proposed change or addition.

Mission and objectives

Does the strategy fit the current mission and objectives of the organization? Is it acceptable to the strategic leader and other influential stakeholders? (This issue is developed further in the Desirability section below.)

Effect on the strategic perspective

Does the strategy proposed have the potential for improving the strategic perspective and general competitive position of the organization? In other words, will the individual business not only have a strong competitive position (possibly drawing upon strengths and competencies from elsewhere in the organization) but also be able to make a positive and synergistic contribution to the whole organization?

The company, then, must be responsive to changes in the environment and it may wish to be proactive and influence its market and industry. All the time it should seek to become and remain an effective competitor.

SWOT; current strategic position

Is the strategy appropriate for the current economic and competitive environment?

Is the strategy able to capitalize and build on current strengths, competencies and opportunities, and avoid weaknesses and potential threats?

To what extent is the strategy able to take advantage of emerging trends in the environment, the market and the industry?

Skills, competencies and resources: available and needed

Are the strategies being pursued and considered sufficiently consistent that skills, competencies and resources are not spread or stretched in any disadvantageous way?

Does any new proposal exploit key organizational competencies? For current businesses and strategies: can the organization effectively add value, or would a divestment strategy be more appropriate?

It will be appreciated that this consideration embraces both the opportunity-driven and resource-based perspectives on strategy.

Culture

Does the strategy fit the culture and values of the organization? If not, what are the implications of going ahead?

E–V–R congruence

Summarizing the above points, is there congruence between the environment, values and resources?

Simplicity

Is the strategy simple and understandable? Is the strategy one which could be communicated easily, and about which people are likely to be enthusiastic? These factors are also aspects of desirability.

Feasibility

Change demands – issues of implementation

Is the strategy feasible in resource terms? Can it be implemented effectively? Is it capable of achieving the objectives that it addresses?

Can the organization cope with the extent and challenge of the change implied by the option?

Finance and other resource availability

A lack of any key resource can place a constraint on certain possible developments. The cost of capital is explained in the Finance in Action supplement at
the end of this chapter.

The ability to meet key success factors

A strategic alternative is not feasible if the key success factors dictated by the
industry and customer demand, such as quality, price and service level, cannot
be met.

Competitive advantage

The effectiveness of a strategy will be influenced by the ability of the organization to create and sustain competitive advantage. When formulating a strategy
it is important to consider the likely response of existing competitors in order to
ensure that the necessary flexibility is incorporated into the implementation plans.
A company which breaks into a currently stable industry or market may well
threaten the market shares and profitability of other companies and force them
to respond with, say, price cuts, product improvements or aggressive promotion
campaigns. The new entrant should be prepared for this and ready to
counter it.

Timing

Timing is related to opportunity on the one hand and risk and vulnerability on
the other. It may be important for an organization to act quickly and decisively
once an opening window of opportunity is spotted. Competitors may attempt to
seize the same opportunity.

At the same time managers should make sure that they allow themselves
enough time to consider the implications of their actions and organize their
resources properly. Adaptive incremental change in the implementation of
strategy can be valuable here. An organization may look to pursue a new
strategy, learn by experience and improve by modification once they have gone
ahead.

Strategic leadership and the structure, culture and values of the organization
are therefore important.

This theme also relates to the theory of growth and the existence of the
receding managerial limit suggested by Edith Penrose (1959), which was discussed
in Chapter 2.

Resources must be stretched if they are to achieve their full potential, but if the
targets set for them imply a 'bridge too far' there is a real danger of both underachievement and damage to the rest of the organization. Here, resources might have

to be redeployed, which will have consequences for the business from which they are taken. The reputation of the organization might easily be tarnished. Clearly, the decisions reached will reflect the risk perspective of the managers concerned.

Desirability

Strategic needs; the planning gap

The ability of the strategy to satisfy the objectives of the organization and help to close any identified planning gap are important considerations. Timing may again be an important issue. The ability of the strategy to produce results in either the short term or the longer term should be assessed in the light of the needs and priorities of the firm.

The level of returns expected

Decisions concerning where a company's financial resources should be allocated are known as investment or capital budgeting decisions. The decision might concern the purchase of new technology or new plant, the acquisition of another company, or financing the development and launch of a new product.

Competitive advantage and corporate strategic change are both relevant issues.

The ability to raise money, and the cost involved, are key influences, and should be considered alongside two other strategic issues:

- Does the proposed investment make sense strategically, given present objectives and strategies?
- Will the investment provide an adequate financial return?

The latter question is partly answered by the company's cost of capital and the whole topic of investment decisions is explored in the Finance in Action supplement to this chapter. Strategic fit is a broad issue and is addressed in the main part of the chapter.

Synergy

Effective synergy should lead ideally to a superior concentration of resources in relation to competitors. The prospects for synergy should be evaluated alongside the implications for the firm's strategic perspective and culture, which were included in the section on appropriateness. These factors in combination affect the strategic fit of the proposal and its ability to complement existing strategies and bring an all-round improvement to the organization. Diversification into products and markets with which the organization has no experience, and which may require different skills, may fit poorly alongside existing strategies and fail to provide synergy.

Risk

It has already been pointed out that risk, vulnerability, opportunity and timing are linked. Where organizations, having spotted an opportunity, act quickly, there is always a danger that some important consideration will be overlooked. The risk lies in these other factors, many of which are discussed elsewhere, which need careful attention in strategy formulation:

- the likely effect on competition
- the technology and production risks, linked to skills and key success factors. Can the organization cope with the production demands and meet market requirements profitably? Innovation often implies higher risks in this area, but offers higher rewards for success
- the product/market diversification risk – the risk involved in overstretching resources through diversification has been considered earlier in this chapter
- the financial risk – the cash flow and the firm's borrowing requirements are sensitive to the ability of the firm to forecast demand accurately and predict competitor responses
- managerial ability and competence – the risk here involves issues of whether skills can be transferred from one business to another when a firm diversifies, and whether key people stay or go after a take-over
- environmental risks – it is also important to ensure that possible adverse effects or hostile public opinion are evaluated.

Many of these issues are qualitative rather than finite, and judgement will be required. The ability of the organization to harness and evaluate the appropriate information is crucial, but again there is a trade-off. The longer the time that the organization spends in considering the implications and assessing the risks, the greater the chance it has of reducing and controlling the risks. However, if managers take too long, the opportunity or the initiative may be lost to a competitor who is more willing to accept the risk.

In my experience those who manage change most successfully are those who welcome it in their own lives and see it as an opportunity for stimulation and learning new things. Implicit is the willingness to take risks, including making intelligent mistakes. I am much more interested in important failures that prepare the way for future success than I am in cautious competence and maintaining the status quo.

Robert Fitzpatrick, when President
Directeur Général, Euro Disneyland SA

Stakeholder needs and preferences

This relates to the expectations and hopes of key stakeholders, the ability of the organization to implement the strategy and achieve the desired results, and the willingness of stakeholders to accept the inherent risks in a particular strategy.

Strategic changes may affect existing resources and the strategies to which they are committed, gearing, liquidity and organization structures, including management roles, functions and systems. Shareholders, bankers, managers, employees and customers can all be affected; and their relative power and influence will prove significant. The willingness of each party to accept particular risks may vary. Trade-offs may be required. The power and influence of the strategic leader will be very important in the choice of major strategic changes, and his or her ability to convince other stakeholders will be crucial.

Using the evaluation criteria

The criteria can be used in a number of ways in the search for an appropriate balance and trade-off; it is rare that one strategic option will be the most appropriate, most desirable and completely feasible. For example:

- A company might well discern just which option or options are highly appropriate and desirable and then evaluate or test their feasibility.
- An objective review of internal resources and relative strengths and competencies could flag options which are appropriate and internally feasible. These can then be evaluated for external feasibility and desirability. Is there a real market opportunity? Does it accord with the ambitions and preferences of the strategic leader?
- Environmental scanning can be used to highlight opportunities which would be appropriate and externally feasible. These then need testing for internal feasibility and desirability, taking into account the risk element.

Sometimes a new window of opportunity will be spotted and all of the criteria will need to be applied, possibly quite quickly. The final choices and prioritization may be difficult. There might be two feasible alternatives, one of which is highly desirable to certain stakeholders but logically less appropriate than the other for the organization's overall strategy. Some organizations, particularly small companies and ones dominated by powerful, idiosyncratic leaders, may be tempted to place desirability first. A strategic leader may have personal ambitions to develop the organization in particular directions and in terms of growth targets. If the preferred strategy is implemented successfully, it will later be rationalized as highly appropriate.

Conversely, a risk-averse company may have an acquisition opportunity which is strategically appropriate and feasible, but for cultural reasons is seen as undesirable.

It is important to stress again that a strategy must be implemented before it can be considered effective. The formulation may be both analytical and creative, and the strategy may seem excellent on paper, but the organization must then activate it. The value of commitment and support from the strategic leader, managers and other employees should not be underestimated.

It would be appropriate at this stage to return to Case Study 12 (Walt Disney) and reconsider the relative merits of the five strategies which are described.

While evaluation techniques can assist in strategic decision making, individual subjectivity and judgement will also be involved.

The decision-making processes used will inevitably have elements of subjectivity. Judgement will have to be applied alongside any technique-driven strategic analyses. Decision making, therefore, must embrace issues of intuition and political reality alongside the available information and analyses. There is a number of explanations – all easily appreciated – for 'poor' decision making.

Judgement comprises three key elements (see Vickers, 1965):

- a reality judgement of the situation and the implied problem
- an action judgement about what to do.
- value judgements concerning expected and desired outcomes.

Summary

It is important for organizations to address the following questions:

- What constitutes a good strategic choice?
- What can the organization do and what can it not do?
- What should the organization seek to do and what should it not seek to do?

An effective strategy is one that meets the needs and preferences of the organization, its key decision makers and influencers – ideally better than any alternatives – and can be implemented successfully.

The techniques introduced in earlier parts of the book can all make a contribution, but there are likely to be subjective elements as well.

There are three broad criteria for evaluating strategies:

Appropriateness

- Does the proposal fit – and strengthen – the existing portfolio of activities?
- Is it compatible with the mission of the organization?
- Does it address any targeted opportunities or help redress any critical weaknesses?
- What impact would the change have on E–V–R congruence?
- Is this an opportunity for stretching the organization's resources and exploiting core competencies further? Or does it imply diversification?

Feasibility

- Can the strategic change be implemented successfully – and without any detrimental impact upon present activities?
- Does the organization possess the skills and competencies required? If not, can they be acquired in a relevant timescale?
- Can the implied costs be met?
- Is there an opportunity to build and sustain a strong competitive position?

Desirability

- Does the option truly help to close the planning gap?
- Is the organization comfortable with the risks implied?
- Is this a justifiable (and, in certain cases, the most profitable) use of organizational effort and resources?
- Is there potential synergy?
- Which stakeholder needs will be met and satisfied?

When reviewing options, it is unlikely that one will turn out to be the most appropriate, the most feasible and the most desirable. Trade-offs will have to be made.

References

Hofer, CW and Schendel, D (1978) *Strategy Evaluation: Analytical Concepts*, West.

Penrose, E (1959) *The Theory of the Growth of the Firm*, Blackwell.

Rumelt, R (1980) The evaluation of business strategy. In *Business Policy and Strategic Management* (ed. WF Glueck), McGraw-Hill.

Thompson, AA and Strickland, AJ (1980) *Strategy Formulation and Implementation*, Richard D Irwin.

Tilles, S (1963) How to evaluate corporate strategy, *Harvard Business Review*, July–August.

Vickers, G (1965) *The Art of Judgement: A Study of Policy Making*, Chapman & Hall.

Test your knowledge of this chapter with our online quiz at:
http://www.thomsonlearning.co.uk

Explore Strategy Evaluation further at:

Learning Organization Journal   http://www.mcb.co.uk/tlo.html

Public Administration Review   http://par.csuohio.edu

Questions and Research Assignments

TEXT RELATED

1. Which of the evaluation techniques listed at the beginning of the chapter (Box 12.1) do you feel are most useful? Why? How would you use them? What are their limitations?

2. From your experience and reading, which evaluation criteria do you think are most significant in determining the effectiveness of strategies?

List examples of cases where the absence of these factors, or the wrong assessment of their importance, has led to problems.

Internet and Library Projects

1. In 1996 Walt Disney Corporation was thought by analysts to be a prospective buyer for EMI Music after its split from the Thorn Rentals part of Thorn-EMI. Would 'music' have been an appropriate and desirable addition to the Disney portfolio? Do you think that the acquisition of an essentially British company would have been difficult for Disney to absorb?

What in fact has happened with EMI Music? Was the actual outcome more appropriate, feasible and desirable for EMI?

Walt Disney Company   http://www.disney.go.com
EMI Group   http://www.emigroup.com

2. In 1983 Tottenham Hotspur became the first English football club to be listed on the Stock Exchange. Subsequently, the club diversified, acquiring a number of related leisure companies. The intention was to subsidize the football club with profits from the new businesses. Initially this happened, but in the recession of the late 1980s football had to prop up the other activities. Businesses were closed or divested, and the ownership of Tottenham Hotspur changed hands in 1991. Research the various changes and evaluate the strategies. Was it appropriate and desirable for Tottenham to become a public limited company?

How different was the approach taken some years later by Manchester United? What strategies have made Manchester United the richest football club in the world?

Tottenham Hotspur plc   http://www.spurs.co.uk/corporatenew/index.html
Manchester United FC   http://www.manutd.com

Finance in Action

Financial Management

Financing the Business

Sources of funds

Most funds used by established UK organizations are normally generated internally through retained profits, but from time to time it is necessary to raise funds externally. This conclusion applies to both the public and the private sectors. In general, loan capital or borrowing has been used more extensively than equity, which might take the form of new equity issued openly or rights issues to existing shareholders.

At present in the UK and USA, equity funding is proving more significant than borrowing; the reverse is the case for Germany, France and Japan, partially the result of different regulations. In the 1990s some UK companies used new equity to compensate for reduced cash flows and retained earnings, and US companies bought back shares and returned funds to their shareholders. This strategy is a form of defence against possible unwelcome bids. Regulations reduce the likelihood of German, French and Japanese companies being acquired by unwelcome predators.

Investment funding, then, is available through borrowing or increased equity, but assets can be increased without investing to the same extent. This is accomplished by leasing them rather than purchasing them.

Equity capital

In general, equity capital would be increased by a rights issue of ordinary shares to existing shareholders. As an example, holders of ordinary shares might be offered one new share for every two or three that they already own, at a price equal to or below the current market price. At a higher price people would be unlikely to purchase. If all shareholders take up the offer then the percentage breakdown of the shareholders' register will remain the same; if they are not taken up by existing shareholders they will be offered to the market by the institutional underwriters, and the share register profile may change. Blocks of shares could be built up quite readily, and at a price below the current market price; and depending upon who was buying them threats to the organization from powerful shareholders could emerge.

Rights issues will not be successful without the support of institutional shareholders. This requires investor confidence in the company's strategy and strategic leadership.

Although many shareholders buy and retain shares with a view to a long-term capital gain, resulting from their sale at a price higher than the one at which they were bought, dividend policy is important. Dividends represent a rate of return on shareholders' investments. Although dividends are not fixed and can theoretically be raised or lowered freely and in relation to increases or decreases in profits, and to any changing need for retained earnings for investment, companies generally seek stability.

Loan capital

There are various forms of loan capital, but they all have one essential characteristic. They do not carry ownership, which ordinary shares do. Loans might well be for a definite period, after which they are repayable, and with a fixed rate of interest for each year of the loan. Hence, interest payments come out of profits, but they cannot be reduced if profits decline through unfavourable trading conditions. Overdrafts provide flexible short-term funding up to an agreed limit, and their cost will vary both up and down as the prevailing market rate of interest changes. Loans are invariably secured against assets, which reduces the risk for the lender. If interest payments are not met, the bank, or whoever has loaned the money, is free to appoint a receiver and effectively take over day-to-day control of the company. Interest is paid out of profits before they are assessed for taxation, and they can thereby reduce the company's tax burden; dividends for ordinary shareholders are paid after tax.

Generalizing, the cost of borrowing can be expected to rise as the degree of risk for the lender increases. Lenders will expect higher returns from higher risk investments. Government securities are considered very safe, for example, and consequently the anticipated rate of return will typically be lower than for other investments. Secured loans are safer than ordinary shares, as mentioned above, and therefore borrowing should normally prove cheaper than equity.

The ability to obtain either – and the cost – are likely to be dependent on how well the company has been performing, and how well it has been perceived by the market to have been performing. Opportunity, ability and cost are therefore essential criteria in deciding upon a preference between equity and loan funding, but this decision should be related to the decision concerning whether to invest at all. Investments, which are discussed later in this Appendix, should be analysed by comparing their returns, discounted for the period they are earned, with the cost of financing them, or the opportunity cost of the money being used. The viability of an investment is therefore dependent upon the cost of the capital used. The cheaper the cost of capital, the more likely it is that an investment is viable and profitable. Hence if the cost of obtaining investment funding is high, opportunities might be lost.

Moreover, the capital structure of the company determines the impact of profit fluctuations on the money available after tax for paying dividends and for reinvestment. Large loans and high interest payments absorb profits, and this can be crucial if profits fluctuate significantly for any reason. The more is paid out in dividends, the less is available for reinvesting, and vice versa. In turn, dividend payments are likely to affect the view held by shareholders and the market of the company's performance, and this will affect their willingness to lend more.

Leasing

In many cases organizations are more concerned with using assets than actually owning them. Leasing assets is one way of acquiring them without paying their full price at any one time; the popularity of leasing has grown since the late 1970s.

When an asset is leased there will normally be an agreed annual charge for a fixed number of years, and possibly there will be an arrangement whereby the company obtains ownership of the asset for a residual price at the end of the period of the lease. In aggregate terms leasing is unlikely to be cheap, but it can have a significant effect on cash flow. In addition, there have been advantageous tax regulations. Leasing is generally low risk for the lessor, who retains legal ownership of the asset and can reclaim it if the lease payments are not met.

Leasing has offered strategic opportunities, as well as financial benefits, for certain organizations. Some companies have chosen to sell and lease back property that they owned, for example, finding willing partners in property companies and institutional investors. The funds released have then been available for other investments.

The cost of capital

The optimal capital structure

In theory there is an *optimal capital structure* (OCS) in terms of debt and equity for any firm, and it will depend on:

- the amount of risk in the industry
- the riskiness of the company's corporate and competitive strategies, and their potential impact on profits
- the typical capital structure for the industry, and what competitors are doing
  – the cost of funding can provide competitive advantage

- management's ability to pay interest without too serious an impact on dividends and future investment
- both the owners' and the strategic leader's preference for risk, or aversion to it.

The weighted average cost of capital

In considering, or attempting to decide, the OCS it is important to evaluate the *weighted average cost of capital* (WACC). The WACC, again in theory, is the average rate of return that investors expect the company to earn. In practice it is the average cost of raising additional investment funding. If a company used only loan funding the WACC would be the after-tax cost of borrowing more; but most organizations have a complex structure of debt and equity, each of which carries a different cost. The WACC is therefore an attempt to approximate what more funding would cost if it were raised proportionately to the percentages of debt and equity in the OCS. In practice it will relate to the current capital structure.

Determining the weighted average cost of capital

The formula is:

WACC = (Percentage of long-term debt in the OCS × After-tax cost of debt)

plus

(Percentage of ordinary shares in the OCS × After-tax cost of equity)

As mentioned above, the WACC will normally be calculated in terms of the firm's current capital structure rather than the theoretical OCS.

The *cost of long-term debt* is the weighted average of the various interest rates incurred on existing loans, after accounting for tax. Hence, for a company which pays 10% interest on 40% of its loans, 12% on the other 60% and tax at an effective rate of 30%, the cost of long-term debt is:

$$((10\% \times 40) + (12\% \times 60)) \times (1 - 0.3) = 7.84\%$$

The *cost of equity* is more difficult to calculate. One popular model for estimating it is the capital asset pricing model (CAPM), which is described here only in outline.

The capital asset pricing model

In theory the cost of equity for an individual company should equal the rate of return that shareholders expect to gain from investing in that company. This is based on their perception of the amount of risk involved. The CAPM attempts to capture this. The formula is:

$$R = F + beta(M - F)$$

Source of funding	Total £ million	Percentage of total	Cost %	Weighted cost
Equity	1.2	60	16	9.6
Loans	0.8	40	8	3.2

R is the expected earnings or return on a particular share and F represents the risk-free rate of return expected from the most secure investments such as government securities, where the likelihood of default is considered negligible. The expected risk-free rate is determined by the current interest rate on these securities and expected inflation. M is the average rate of return expected from all securities traded in the market and beta is a measure of risk based on the volatility of an individual company's shares compared with the market as a whole. A beta of 1.6 (empirically high) means that a company's share price fluctuates by 1.6 times the market average. In other words, if the market average rises or falls by 10%, the company's share price increases or decreases by 16%. A low beta might be 0.3. Low beta shares in a portfolio reduce risk, but in general high beta shares do little to reduce risk.

Research at London Business School yielded the following betas in the mid-1990s:

Hong Kong and Shanghai Bank (includes Midland Bank)	1.6
J. Sainsbury	0.6
Manchester United Football Club	0.4

As an example, assume that the risk-free rate is 10%, the market as a whole is returning 18% and a company's beta is 1.2:

$$R = 10 + 1.2(18 - 10) = 19.6\%$$

In other words, the market would be expecting the company to achieve 19.6% earnings on shareholders' funds. This is earnings after interest and tax divided by total shareholders' funds, including reserves.

By contrast, if a company's beta was 0.5:

$$R = 10 + 0.5(18 - 10) = 14\%$$

The CAPM is useful for estimating the cost of equity but there are certain problems in implementing it. Primarily, all of the data will be adjusted and extrapolated historical data, when really it is realistic forecasts of future earnings and returns that matter. F and M theoretically represent expected future returns, and beta should be based on expected future fluctuations, but normally historical data will be used in the model on the assumption that trends continue. The prevailing and predicted rates of interest in the economy will be used to increase or decrease past return figures.

The WACC can now be calculated – see p. 545. Assume that a company has £1.2 million equity funding and £800,000 in long-term debt, and that the relative costs of each are 16% and 8%, respectively:

Thus WACC = 12.8%.

Of course, retained earnings that can be reinvested in the company could alternatively be paid out as dividends, which shareholders could themselves invest wherever they chose. Consequently, the return on such reinvestments in the company should be at least the same as that which investors expect from their existing shares. Given that all shareholders' funds are incorporated in the CAPM, this is taken into account.

This whole area is extremely complex, but nevertheless the cost of capital is an important consideration alongside availability. The cost of capital can affect the viability of a proposed investment, and it can affect the overall costs of producing a product or service and thereby influence competitive advantage. Investments, and how they might be evaluated, are the subject of the next section.

Investments and Capital Budgeting

In simple terms, an investment represents the commitment of money now for gains or returns in the future. The financial returns are therefore measured over an appropriate period. Estimating these returns relies substantially on forecasts of demand in terms of both amount and timing; and generating the returns further relies upon the ability of managers to manage resources in such a way that the forecasts are met. Uncertainty is therefore an issue.

In general, any investment should be evaluated financially on at least the following two criteria:

- Individually, is it worth proceeding with?
- Is it the best alternative from the options the company has, or if money is reasonably freely available to the company, how does the proposal rank alongside other possibilities?

In the financial evaluation of a proposed investment which produces a cash flow over a period of time, it is necessary to incorporate some qualification for the fact that inflation and other factors generally ensure that a 'pound tomorrow' is worth less than its current value. This is achieved by discounting the cash flow.

Analysing proposed investments

The background to **discounted cash flows**

If the prevailing rate of interest on bank deposit or building society accounts is 10% an individual or organization with money to invest could save and earn compound interest with relatively little risk. If the rate stayed constant, £100 today would be worth £110 next year and £121 the year after if the interest was not withdrawn annually. To calculate future values simply multiply by $1 + r$ each year, where r is the rate of interest. Therefore, in ten years' time £100 is worth $£100(1 + r)^{10}$.

Reversing the process enables a consideration of what money earned in the future is worth in today's terms. In other words, if a company invests now, at today's value of the pound, it is important to analyse the returns from the investment also in today's terms, although most if not all of the returns from the investment will be earned in the future when the value of the pound has fallen. This is known as *discounting future values*. So £100 earned next year is worth $£100/(1 + r)$ today, i.e. £90.90.

Similarly, £100 earned ten years' hence would be worth in today's terms $£100/(1 + r)^{10}$. This is known as *net present value*.

In discounting cash flows and calculating net present value discount tables are used for simplicity.

An example

Assume that a company invests £1 million today and in return earns £250,000 each year for five years, starting next year. Earnings in total amount to £1.25 million, but they are spread over five years. The company's estimated cost of capital is 10%:

Year	Cash-flow receipts £ thousand	Discount factor at 10%	Net present value £ thousand
1	250	0.909	227
2	250	0.826	206
3	250	0.751	188
4	250	0.683	171
5	250	0.621	153
			945

Hence £1 million is invested to earn £945,000 in today's terms – a loss of £55,000. Logically, a positive figure is sought; and if the investment is required to show a return which is higher than the cost of capital, this target return rather than the cost of capital should be used as the discount rate and a positive net present value should be sought at this level.

Financially, this investment would only be viable with a lower cost of capital. Logically, all projects look increasingly viable with lower capital costs. The calculation which follows is of the cost of capital at which this particular project becomes viable.

The internal rate of return

The next step would be to discount at a lower rate, say 5%:

Year	Cash-flow receipts £ thousand	Discount factor at 5%	Net present value £ thousand
I	250	0.952	238
2	250	0.907	227
3	250	0.864	216
4	250	0.823	206
5	250	0.784	196
			1083

This time a positive net present value of £83,000 is obtained.

The following formula is used to calculate the internal rate of return:

$$\frac{83,000}{138,000} \times \frac{5}{100} = 3\%$$

(£83,000 is the positive net present value at a 5% cost of capital, £138,000 is the difference in net present value between the 5% and 10% rates, and the 5/100 represents the percentage difference between the 5 and 10).

This 3% is added to the 5% to give 8%, which is the yield or internal rate of return from this investment.

Check:

Year	Cash-flow receipts £ thousand	Discount factor at 8%	Net present value £ thousand
I	250	0.926	232
2	250	0.857	214
3	250	0.794	198
4	250	0.735	184
5	250	0.681	170
			998

In other words, this investment gives a yield of 8%. This is also known as the internal rate of return, the discount rate which makes the net present value of the receipts exactly equal to the cost of the investment. In the same way that one might look for a positive net present value, one would be looking for an internal rate of return that exceeded the cost of capital.

Payback

Payback is simply the length of time it takes to earn back the outlay; and obviously one can look at either absolute or discounted cash flows, normally the former. In the example above the payback is four years exactly. The outlay was £1 million, and the receipts amounted to £250,000 each year.

Payback is quite useful. For one thing it is relatively simple. For another it takes some account of the timing of returns, for returns can be reinvested in some way as soon as they are to hand.

Evaluating proposed investments

If an organization wishes to be thorough and objective, investments could usefully be analysed against the six criteria listed below. The first three of these are essentially quantitative; the second three incorporate qualitative issues. Sometimes the strategic importance of a particular proposal may mean that, first, the most financially rewarding option is not selected or that, secondly, an investment is not necessarily timed for when the cost of capital would be lowest. As an example of the first point consider a firm in a growing industry which feels that it has to invest in order not to lose market share, although the current cost of capital may mean that the returns from the investment are less than it would wish for or that it could earn with a strategically less important option. An example of the second point would be a firm whose industry is in recession but predicted to grow, and where investment in capital in readiness for the upturn might result in future competitive advantage. At the moment the cost of capital might be relatively high, but the strategic significance of the investment might outweigh this.

The six criteria for evaluating a proposed investment are as follows:

- the discounted present value of all returns through the productive life of the investment
- the expected rate of return, which should exceed both the cost of capital (the cost of financing the investment) and the opportunity cost for the money (returns that might otherwise be earned with an alternative proposal)
- payback – the payout period and the investment's expected productive life – which is a very popular measure as it is relatively easily calculated
- the risk involved in not making the investment or deferring it

- the cost and risk if it fails
- the opportunity cost – specifically, the potential gains from alternative uses of the money.

Discounting techniques are theoretically attractive and used in many organizations, although more in the USA than Europe, and particularly where the proposal is capital intensive. However, the technique must involve uncertainty if the cash flows cannot be forecast accurately, as is often the case. In addition, the net present value is dependent on the discount rate used, and this should relate to the weighted average cost of capital, which again may be uncertain.

There will always be some important element of managerial judgement, and one might argue that this managerial intuition will be preferred in some smaller firms which place less emphasis on planning than do larger firms and in those companies that are more entrepreneurial and risk orientated. However, if the decision maker really understands the market and the strategic implications of the proposed investment, this may not be detrimental.

Large organizations evaluating possible investments for different divisions or business units should consider the estimated rate of return from each proposal, the current returns being obtained in each division and the company's average cost of capital, as well as any strategic issues. Take the following two possibilities:

	Division A	Division B
Rate of return on proposal	20%	13%
Current returns	25%	9%

Division A's proposal could seem unattractive as it offers a lower return than existing projects, while B's investment offers an improvement to current returns. If the company's cost of capital is 15%, A's proposal is profitable and B's proposal is not.

Questions

1. Calculate the weighted average cost of capital given the following information:

   Optimal capital structure 50:50

   Debt funding: half is at 10% interest, half at 12%

   Effective tax rate 30%

   Risk-free rate 8%

   Return expected in the stock market 12%

   Company's beta 1.2.

2. A firm has two investment opportunities, each costing £100,000 and each having the expected net cash flows shown in the table below. While the cost of each project is certain, the cash-flow projections for project B are more uncertain than those for A because of additional inherent risks. Those shown in both cases can be assumed to be maxima. It has therefore been suggested that while the company's cost of capital is of the order of 10%, B might usefully be discounted at 15%.

   (a) For each alternative calculate the net present value, the internal rate of return and the payback.
   (b) On the data available what would you advise the firm to do?
   (c) How limited do you feel this analysis is?

| | Expected cash flows | |
	Project A (£)	Project B (£)
Year 1	50,000	20,000
Year 2	40,000	40,000
Year 3	30,000	50,000
Year 4	10,000	60,000

13

Strategy Implementation

Strategy > Structure or Structure > Strategy

Structural Issues

Structural Alternatives

Styles of Corporate Management

Corporate Parenting

Contemporary Organizations

Strategic Success and Changes

Summary

Successful implementation is critical for strategic success. It was emphasized in the previous chapter that to be considered effective a chosen, intended strategy must be implemented successfully. The prospects for effective implementation are clearly dependent on the appropriateness, feasibility and desirability of the strategy. Some strategies are not capable of implementation. At the same time, competency in implementation – the ability to translate ideas into actions and generate positive outcomes – can itself be a source of competitive advantage. Internal processes can add value by creating high levels of customer service and/or saving on costs by, say, removing any unnecessary delays or duplication of activities. In this final chapter of the book therefore we consider issues of strategy implementation. We begin by explaining how strategy and structure are interdependent – successful strategy implementation requires an appropriate structure; decisions taken by managers within the structure affect emergent strategy creation. We look at a number of key structural issues – centralization yields control, but decentralization is required for flexibility.

We describe six identifiable structural formats briefly and then consider the style, role and contribution of corporate headquarters, a key issue for large corporations. We conclude with a brief introduction to aspects of strategic change.

The case study looks at how a series of strategic, structural and leadership changes at Apple Computers. The case charts the story of Apple over some 20 years and shows how the company has enjoyed mixed fortunes. Sometimes highly innovative and successful, Apple has also been affected by competitor initiatives which have changed the personal computer industry in dramatic ways. Some of the changes documented were therefore reactive while others were more proactive.

Case Study 13: Apple Computers

Apple was started in 1976 by a young entrepreneur, Steven Jobs, and his partner, computer nerd Stephen Wozniak. They began by making personal computers (PCs) in a garage. In 1983 the company's turnover, from essentially one model – the distinctive Apple computer – was approaching $1 billion. At this stage in the company's development Wozniak had already left and Jobs had been quoted as saying that he was no longer able to do what he most enjoyed, working with a small group of talented designers to create new innovative products. To overcome his frustration with an increasingly bureaucratic organization Jobs had formed a new team of designers and set about developing the company's second major product, the Apple Macintosh, away from corporate headquarters and the production plant. The Macintosh was regarded as very user friendly and featured an illustrated screen menu and a hand-held mouse unit for giving instructions. It was launched in 1984 and sold immediately. However, it was launched at a premium price, which remained high as sales took off. This niche-marketing approach left a wide-open gap which was ultimately filled by Microsoft.

Jobs had actually seen the first graphic-user interface being demonstrated at Xerox PARC (Palo Alto Research Center) where it had been developed by a Xerox scientist in the 1970s. At this stage, Xerox failed to appreciate the value of the idea they had; Jobs immediately saw the potential of this new technology and set about developing a PC which used it. Jobs used Bill Gates to help with some of the development work – and this was the birth of *Windows*. Had Xerox executives been more visionary, they would probably have driven the PC industry instead of . Microsoft.

John Sculley, previously CEO of PepsiCo, was recruited by Jobs to be Apple president in 1983 and he took over executive control. Sculley reports that Jobs challenged him: 'Do you want to spend the rest of your life selling sugared water or do you want a chance to change the world?' His initial priorities were to co-ordinate product development activities, which he felt were fragmented, and to integrate these developments with existing programmes. To achieve this, power was centralized more than it had been in the past and was supported by formalized reporting procedures and new financial control systems.

Sculley was regarded as being more marketing orientated than Jobs, and their business philosophies clashed. Jobs resigned in 1985, together with a number of other key employees, deciding to concentrate his efforts on the development of sophisticated PCs for university students in a small, entrepreneurial organization environment.

Despite the increased business discipline, Sculley attempted to preserve important aspects of the original Apple culture. Informal dress codes, a 'fun working environment' and elaborate celebrations when targeted milestones are reached were all considered important. Apple retained a structure with few layers of management, few perks and few status-carrying job titles.

Sculley's challenge was to move the company away from an informal and entrepreneurial management style to a more functional and later (1988) a divisionalized structure, while retaining the important aspects of the culture. In addition, Sculley felt that Apple needed to be repositioned in the market in order to overcome the competitive threats from the Far East.

With new versions of the Macintosh, Apple moved from an education and home computer base into a business computer company which also sold to schools and universities. Apple was a major innovator in desk-top publishing, pioneering the market in advance of competition from IBM and Xerox.

Apple prospered in the late 1980s, but its strategy began to appear inappropriate for the recession and the 1990s. Apple had concentrated on, and succeeded with, high-margin products which were substantially differentiated. However, Sculley claimed that Apple's ideas were being copied and used in cheaper rival products – Apple began a legal action against Microsoft, alleging that its Windows software used ideas from the Macintosh. Moreover, PCs have become more of a commodity product in a maturing market. Although Apple had sold 22 million Macintosh computers at this time, the continued success of Microsoft has been very damaging to the company.

In 1991 Apple agreed a series of strategic alliances, mostly with IBM, historically its main rival. The alliances concentrated on areas where Apple lacked either development skills or the ability to fund the research and development independently. New PC technology and operating systems software were key areas. Cultural and other differences between Apple and IBM have led to their alliances being relatively unsuccessful.

Coincidental with its agreements with the global IBM, Apple's culture had actually been changing. Empowerment, flexibility and freedom remained important, but 'there had to be more discipline. Our cost structure was out of line. We did not know how to meet schedules. We were a benevolent company that sponsored people to work on things they were interested in' (Sculley).

Apple reduced the prices of its existing products, hoping for higher volumes which would more than compensate for the lower margins, and introduced a range of cheaper, lower-performance Macintosh computers. In terms of new products Apple was arguably two years late with its lap-top computer. Other new products concentrated on personal electronics devices and included electronic books and a notebook computer. In 1993 Apple launched *Newton*, a $7 \times 4\frac{1}{2}$ inches black box with a 5×3 inches screen; users could jot down ideas on the screen and draw sketches as they talked and thought, and record notes and appointments. The machine could translate the images, store and organize. In addition, electronic data, such as a map, could be input. Sales of the Newton were disappointing and it failed to live up to Apple's early expectations.

As market shares and gross margins fell during the early 1990s, Apple's pre-tax profits and share price were both erratic. Sculley, the Newton product champion, was accused of neglecting the main hardware products to push the new idea, and his position was threatened. Sculley was in fact replaced by Michael Spindler in 1993, an internal promotion but, three years later, Spindler also left. Another new strategic leader, Gil Amelio, joined Apple from National Semiconductor in 1996. After his own departure Sculley commented: 'I don't think anyone can manage Apple'.

Amelio decided to halve the Macintosh product range (responsible for 80% of Apple's revenue) in order to reduce costs and help to restore profitability. This controversial cut radically affected Apple's strategy of market segmentation. In addition, six varieties of its software operating system were consolidated into one, which Apple would also seek to license to other manufacturers. Allied with Adobe – which could put on to a laser printer what was appearing on a screen – Apple pioneered desk-top publishing. The Macintosh has always been the preferred machine for designers.

The company was also restructured into seven profit-centre divisions: four for different hardware products, plus software, service and Internet –

the Macintosh has always been an ideal machine for creating Internet products.

Amelio recognized that cultural change was again an issue – he believed from one where 'employees felt free to question, and even defy, management decisions' to a more conventional style. Product managers would no longer be 'free to veto the strategic leader'.

Apple's core competency was still its ability to make technology easy to use and Amelio argued that it needed to exploit this in ways that allowed it to move further away from the cut-throat PC market and capitalize upon the new opportunities that were emerging as more and more people worldwide gained access to computers. Currently just 9% of the world's population had access.

Apple's new Macintosh operating system, called Copland, and due around the end of 1996, was being predicted 'to make Windows 95 seem as quaint and feeble as DOS' because of its radical new ability to organize, track and retrieve stored data and files. However, in 1996 Steve Jobs stated:

> *'If I were running Apple I would milk the Macintosh for all its worth – and get busy on the next great thing. The PC wars are over. Done. Microsoft won a long time ago'.*

Declining sales and falling profits were a feature of 1996, and Amelio had to shoulder some of the blame. The new Macintosh operating system, Copland, was not launched on time; the development team had been depleted too much by redundancies and resignations. However, in December 1996, Apple attempted to help rectify these weaknesses by acquiring NeXT Software, the company formed by Apple cofounder Steven Jobs after he was ousted by John Sculley in 1985. The assumption was that Apple should now get the new technology it required for updating the Macintosh. In addition, though, it would obtain the part-time consultancy services of Steven Jobs, who would advise on product strategy.

Jobs commented: 'For the past ten years the PC industry has been slowly copying the Mac's revolutionary graphical user interface. Now the time has come for new innovation . . .'. The key relationships lay with other software developers who typically produced a Windows version first, and only released Macintosh versions some months later.

NeXT's software had generally been highly acclaimed, but it had enjoyed only limited commercial success. Jobs meanwhile had been more successful with his other company venture, Pixar. Pixar is the film animation company which worked with Disney on *Toy Story* and had a ten-year partnership deal with the Walt Disney Corporation. Jobs quickly began to make an impact. Executives from NeXT took over senior positions at Apple and a close colleague of Amelio was demoted. Jobs' cofounder at Apple, Steven Wozniak, was also brought back as a consultant. Costs and employees continued to be cut back, however. The workforce of 13,000 was reduced to between 10,000 and 11,000. Product development, sales and marketing were streamlined. It was quickly speculated that the Apple Newton would be floated off as a separate business.

Once Amelio had left it was also speculated that Jobs would take over full-time, although he continually denied any interest in the challenge, emphasizing his commitment to Pixar. While some assumed that he would be able to rejuvenate Apple with his renowned entrepreneurial flair, one analyst was sceptical: 'The idea that they are going to go back to the past to hit a big home run to beat Microsoft is delusional'. In addition, there were fresh rumours that the NeXT software was after all proving to be inappropriate for Macintosh.

So, two questions arose. One, where did Apple currently fit in the PC industry? And two, could it continue to survive in its present form? Sales of Macintosh had declined to a level where Apple had less than a 5% share of the US PC market; just two years ago it had an 11% share. The odds on Apple being taken over began to shorten. After all, IBM had already made two unsuccessful offers (in 1994 and 1995) and Sun Microsystems one (in 1996).

Early in August 1997 Steve Jobs announced that Microsoft was to invest $150 million in Apple and the two companies were forming a partnership. The key terms of the agreement were as follows:

- Microsoft would develop and distribute office applications for the Apple Macintosh
- Apple would bundle Microsoft's Internet browser software, Internet Explorer, in future Macintosh products.

For Apple, the alliance clearly provided a positive new lease of life. For Bill Gates and Microsoft, it was more of a defensive strategy. If Apple collapsed, Microsoft would be a monopoly supplier – between them, Apple and Microsoft accounted for virtually all the sales of PC operating systems software around the world – and this might raise issues for the US anti-trust authorities. Moreover, Microsoft's real competitive threat at this time did not come from Apple's software and PCs, but rather from Netscape's rival Internet browser and Oracle's network computer which could grow at the expense of independent PCs. Consequently, this deal was designed to strengthen its overall position.

Early in 1998 Apple became profitable again. A new range of PCs was beating sales forecasts – the latest G3 version of the Mac was faster and cheaper than equivalent Windows-based PCs, a very different situation from the earlier years. Jobs, now firmly in control again, took the credit. Newton was abandoned. One lingering concern, though, was that sales were still to committed Mac users, who were updating, rather than to new buyers.

In May 1998 Apple announced its radical new iMac, an integrated computer and monitor in a single unit and in a bright, translucent housing. A keyboard and mouse could be attached in an instant. The keyboard was also translucent and the mouse lit up. At its launch in August it 'flew off the shelves'. In 1999 Apple launched a new range of notebook computers in a similar style and packaging to the iMac. Jobs appeared to have tapped into a new market segment – 'the Generation Y buyer that likes individuality'.

QUESTIONS: Do you think Apple's latest turnaround might be real and sustainable?

What would be required for sustainability?

In the context of Apple, do you agree with the view that 'the right strategy depends upon personal vision, and personal vision depends upon having the right person'?

Apple computers   http://www.apple.com

Strategy > Structure or Structure > Strategy

The structure of an organization is designed to break down the work to be carried out, the tasks, into discrete components, which might comprise individual businesses, divisions and functional departments. People work within these divisions and functions, and their actions take place within a defined framework of objectives, plans and policies which are designed to direct and control their efforts. In designing the structure and making it operational it is important to consider the key aspects of empowerment, employee motivation and reward. Information and communication systems within the organization should ensure that efforts are co-ordinated to the appropriate and desired extent and that the strategic leader and other senior managers are aware of progress and results.

We have already established that in a competitively chaotic environment one essential contribution of the strategic leader is to provide and share a clear vision, direction and purpose for the organization (see Figure 13.1). From this, and taking into account the various ways in which strategies might be created (incorporating the themes of vision, planning and emergence), actions and action plans need

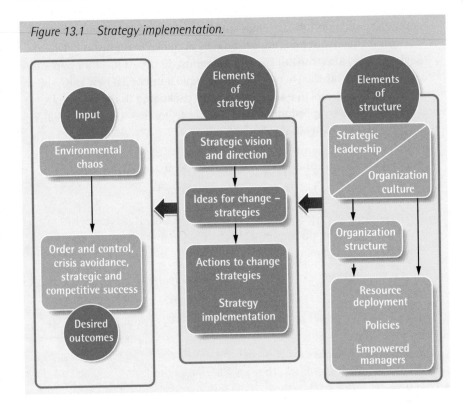

Figure 13.1 *Strategy implementation.*

to be formalized – the middle column in the figure. These strategies and proposals for change cannot be divorced from the implementation implications, which are shown in the right-hand column. Is the structure capable of implementing the ideas? Are resources deployed effectively? Are managers suitably empowered? Do organizational policies support the strategies? If the answers to these questions contain negatives, then either the strategic ideas themselves, the structure, organizational policies or aspects of resource management will need to be reviewed and rethought. The final decisions will be either determined or strongly influenced by the strategic leader, and affected by the culture of the organization. Amstrad, for example, a company which has made a wide range of innovatory electronics products available to the mass consumer market, has always been strategically creative, but it has sometimes been constrained by implementation difficulties which have constituted important setbacks.

If appropriate, feasible and desirable strategies which are capable of effective implementation are selected and pursued, the organization should be able to establish some order and control in the environmental chaos and avoid major crises – the left-hand column of Figure 13.1. This still requires that strategies, products and services are managed efficiently and effectively at the operational level. Responsibility for operations will normally be delegated, and consequently, to ensure that performance and outcomes are satisfactory, sound monitoring and control systems are essential.

It is important to appreciate that while structures are designed initially – and probably changed later at various times – to ensure that *determined or intended* strategies can be implemented, it is the day-to-day decisions, actions and behaviours of people within the structure which lead to important *emergent* strategies. There is, therefore, a continual circular process in operation:

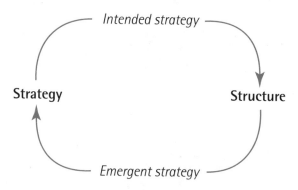

Consequently, while issues of structure and implementation are being considered at the end of this book, they should not be thought of as the end-point in the strategy process. They may be the source of strategic change.

Understanding Corporate Strategy

Figure 13.2 explains the implementation of intended strategies in more detail. The strategic leader is charged with ensuring that there are appropriate targets and milestones, establishing a suitable organization structure and securing and allocating the relevant strategic resources such as people and money. People then use the other strategic resources, working within the structure, to carry out the tasks that they have been allocated – and their actions should be monitored and evaluated to check that targets and objectives are being achieved.

Figure 13.3 summarizes the emergent strategy process, which, clearly, is less prescriptive. The strategic leader this time provides a broad strategic direction. Empowered managers work within a decentralized structure, but they are constrained by any relevant rules, policies and procedures. The strategies that emerge are affected by the constraints, the extent to which managers accept empowerment and the accumulation, sharing and exploitation of organizational

Figure 13.2 Intended strategy implementation.

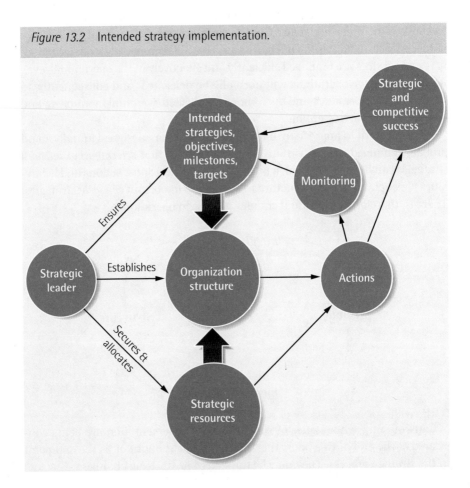

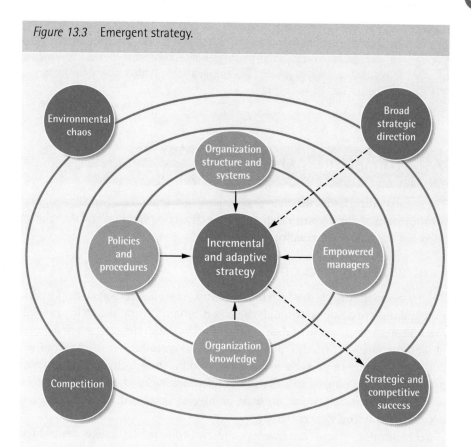

Figure 13.3 Emergent strategy.

knowledge. The outcome of the strategies is related to the extent to which they deal with the competitive and environmental pressures with which the organization must deal.

To summarize, the outcome, in terms of strategic management and organizational success, is dependent on:

- the direction provided by the strategic leader
- the culture of the organization
- the extent to which managers throughout the organization understand, support and own the mission and corporate strategy, and appreciate the significance of their individual contribution
- the willingness and ability of suitably empowered managers to be innovative, add value and take measured risks to deal with environmental opportunities and competitive surprises
- the effectiveness of the information sharing, monitoring and control systems.

> The holistic planner overlooks the fact that it is easy to centralize power, but impossible to centralize all that knowledge ... necessary for the wise yielding of that centralized power ... [so] the greater the gain in power, the greater will be the loss of knowledge.
>
> *Sir Karl Popper (philosopher)*

Structural Issues

The key structural issues which impact on strategy creation and implementation are the extent of any decentralization, the need for co-ordination and the relative degree of formality–informality.

Centralization–decentralization

This relates to the degree to which the authority, power and responsibility for decision making are devolved through the organization. Centralization is where all *major* strategic decisions are taken at head office by the strategic leader or a group of senior strategists. Strictly enforced policies and procedures constrain the freedom of managers responsible for divisions and business units to change competitive and functional strategies without reference back to head office. As more and more responsibility for strategic change is delegated, the organization becomes increasingly decentralized.

Centralization brings consistency and control; unfortunately, centralized organizations may be slow to change in a dynamic environment, and ambitious, entrepreneurial managers may feel constrained and demotivated.

Decentralization allows for competitive and functional strategies to be changed more quickly by managers who are in close touch with the competitive environment and who will also be responsible for implementing any changes. In addition, it can improve motivation. However, information networks must ensure that the whole organization is able to stay strategically aware or control is inevitably sacrificed. Individual parts of the organization can easily make changes which impact unfavourably on other parts, neglecting synergies and interdependencies.

Co-ordination

Organization structures and charts represent the way in which the activities to be carried out have been divided up among functions, businesses and divisions. Clear delineation allows for clarity of purpose and prioritization. It is also necessary for the organization to incorporate mechanisms for integrating these contributions – internal architecture – if synergies are to be achieved.

Formality–informality

Restrictive policies, procedures and reporting systems represent formality. More informality is required if managers and other employees are to use their initiative, innovate change and share their knowledge and learning.

Decentralization and informality both imply empowerment.

Four structural types

Small firms often have a powerful central figure who relies on informal communications to lead the business entrepreneurially. A more formal structure is required when the size and complexity grow.

Centralized, formal organizations tend to be bureaucratic and slow to change, but efficient in stable circumstances. Historically, much of the public sector has adopted this model, but has seen a relaxation on both dimensions in recent years as the environment has become much less certain.

Decentralized, formal organizations are typically large businesses which have been divided up into divisions and business units. Some power is devolved to allow adaptive and incremental change, with formal communications systems and performance measures used for co-ordination. Informal communications will operate alongside the formal channels; without these co-operation would prove impossible.

Decentralized, informal 'organizations' are often seen in the form of temporary project groups and task teams existing inside a more formal structure. The individual businesses within Richard Branson's Virgin Group, though, operate with both decentralization and informal communications, but within a framework of centralized *corporate* strategy creation.

Quite simply, in a centralized organization, planned activities and intended strategies – which may, of course, be out of date – are controlled. Decentralization means that dynamic external links are controlled more effectively. The situation is often unstable as companies attempt to find an appropriate balance, and trade-off growth with stability.

We saw above that as small companies succeed they switch from formal to informal communications to enable further growth. Centralization maintains control. Companies later tend to decentralize when they want to continue growing and need to be able to implement changes quickly. Any loss of control, and especially if the organization's financial performance deteriorates, will lead to a desire to restore stability and a temptation to recentralize decision making. Eventually decentralization will again be used to fuel renewed growth.

Morgan (1993) uses the analogy of a spider plant, with a number of small, growing offshoots, to examine linkages in complex, multiactivity organizations. As the plant grows the offshoots can be retained with a permanent link back to the mother plant, or they can be severed and given independence. Without independence, their growth will be limited; with freedom they can easily grow larger than the mother plant, which is now likely to produce more new offshoots. Organizations can be similarly 'severed' through extensive decentralization and large numbers of relatively independent divisions, business units and profit centres enjoying a degree of independence and autonomy. It is also possible for non-core businesses to be sold off, but with links retained.

The lines of communication which need addressing, and establishing as either tight controlling feeders or less formal linkages, are:

- values, purpose and objectives
- information flows
- resources and dependencies
- accountability
- rewards.

Where growing organizations are put together for financial rather than synergistic reasons we can expect tight controls and a strong focus on resource efficiency. Where synergies and interdependency are critical, performance measurement needs to be more creative. Similarly, where people work in teams and depend on each other it is important to ensure that reward systems reflect this.

Although we often use diagrammatic charts to illustrate the structure of an organization, it is important to recognize that charts are static and unable to explain the processes and interactions which determine how the structure actually works.

In the following sections we look at how these issues impact on:

- the type of structure adopted
- the style of strategic control and
- the contribution of head offices.

Structural Alternatives

Organization structures are unique to individual firms, but they are likely to relate to one of the forms discussed in this section. The six alternative forms are illustrated in Figure 13.4, where they are shown in a hierarchy and linked to growth strategies. As organizations grow, and new strategies are developed, it is normal for an organization to adopt or change its structure in some logical way.

The entrepreneurial structure

This is a typical small organization structure built like a web around the owner/manager, who retains control of all important decisions. It is heavily

Figure 13.4 Growth strategies and related structural formats.

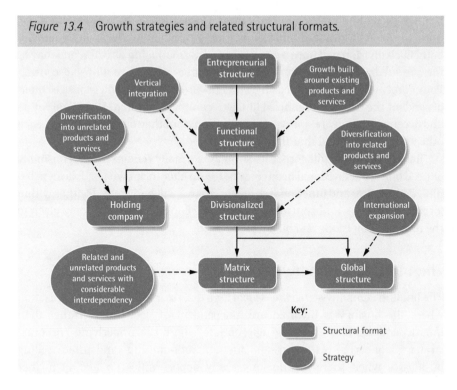

Key:

Structural format

Strategy

centralized and features informal channels of communication, and in some respects it is not really a 'structure' at all. While the organization remains small it is very flexible, but it is inappropriate beyond a certain size if only one person is deciding all major issues.

The functional structure

A functional structure is appropriate when businesses have outgrown the entrepreneurial structure but remain focused on a limited range of clearly related products and services. Given this qualification it can work for both small/medium and much larger organizations. The business is built around functional activities – production, marketing, sales, personnel, finance, research and development and information management are all examples – each of which is headed by a manager with some delegated authority. Success is very dependent on the ability of the managers to work as a team.

The divisionalized structure

When the number and diversity of the products and services increases, the simple functional structure is inadequate. Individual products and services cannot be championed and prioritized effectively. Consequently, the organization will normally be split into a number of divisions, based on products, geography or both. Each division will have a general manager/managing director, and may be further subdivided into individual business units which are all profit centres. Power and authority are increasingly decentralized, but if the divisions are inter-dependent the need for organized linkages cannot be ignored. Divisionalization and decentralization are not synonymous terms, but they often accompany each other. It is not essential that they do.

Changes to the overall corporate strategy normally remain the responsibility of head office, but divisional heads may be free to alter their own portfolio of activities. Competitive and functional strategic change will be devolved, either within formalized policies and controls, or with some considerable autonomy given to the respective divisions and businesses.

The holding company structure

The holding company structure is ideal for a diverse, multiproduct organization where the businesses involved are independent of each other, rather than interdependent. It is especially appropriate where the underlying corporate strategy concerns restructuring: buying, rationalizing and then selling businesses when there are no longer any opportunities for adding further value.

Each business is run as an individual company, but controlled by tight financial management. Budgets, which must be achieved, and regular formal reporting are essential features. Head office will retain responsibility for, say, buying and selling businesses, and the overall corporate portfolio, delegating the strategic responsibility for each business to its own managers. Subsidiaries are more likely to benefit from low-cost head-office financing than they are from links with other businesses in the holding company.

The matrix structure

Matrix structures are an attempt to combine the benefits of decentralization (motivation of identifiable management teams; closeness to markets; speedy decision making and implementation) with those of co-ordination (achieving economies and synergies across the business units, territories and products). This structural form is, however, complex and difficult to implement; managers often have dual reporting relationships. A typical example would be an organization comprising divisions based on product groups, and responsible for co-ordinating the production and marketing of a number of products manufactured in several plants, alongside geographical divisions responsible for co-ordinating the sales, marketing and distribution of all the corporation's products, regardless of where they are produced, within their territorial area.

Managers in divisionalized organizations may be members of ad hoc project teams, which cut across several businesses or divisions and are charged with carrying out a specific task, at the same time as they continue in their normal roles. This overlay represents a temporary form of the matrix structure.

The global structure

The challenge for large, diverse, international businesses lies in:
- *exercising control and containing structural costs through decentralization whilst*
- *remaining sensitive to varying customer tastes and expectations in different geographic markets and*
- *innovating and transferring learning internationally.*

Bartlett and Ghoshal (1989)

Production may be in selected locations to achieve scale economies; equally it may be dispersed and closer to the markets where the products are sold. Marketing and sales efforts can be handled for the whole world from a central location; again they can be localized and dispersed. If the organization is divisionalized, and it almost certainly will be, all the divisional head offices can be located in one single corporate headquarters or spread around the world. When they are dispersed the activities of each business are likely to be markedly different, with only limited interdependency.

Clearly, the organization needs a global mission and core values, such as consistent quality worldwide, and Bartlett and Ghoshal (1992) recommend that regardless of the structural format, *integration* is co-ordinated centrally at the top of the corporation, with individual businesses and countries given clear sets of expectations. This would appear to suggest that it is probably unimportant whether *production* is essentially centralized or decentralized. The real issue concerns the location of 'future focus' activities such as research and development and product design and development and whether these are centralized or decentralized. The normal tendency will be centralization.

We have seen how the basic structure can relate to the corporate strategy. It is now important to consider how strategic change is managed within the structure. The relationship between head office and the individual businesses and divisions in a large complex organization is critically important. This is reflected in the size, scope and role of the corporate headquarters, and the way in which the centre seeks to control strategy creation. Control is vital, but it should not be achieved by over-elaborate reporting, which slows down strategic change, or by expensively duplicating activities at head office and in the divisions and businesses.

Styles of Corporate Management

Goold and Campbell (1988, 1993) have researched in depth how head offices advise, control and add value to their constituent businesses. They categorize three distinct styles – described below – and conclude that all the styles can work successfully; the secret lies in adopting the style which is appropriate for the range and diversity of the businesses in the group. The culture and the preferred approach of the strategic leader are also important influences.

Financial control

- An ideal approach for a holding company where the businesses are seen as independent and unrelated. Hanson and BTR historically provide excellent examples.
- Strategy creation is heavily decentralized to business unit managers. Within their agreed financial targets they are free to develop and change their competitive and functional strategies.
- Budgets and targets – and their achievement – are critically important control mechanisms.
- Head office monitors financial returns closely and regularly, intervening when targets are missed.
- Head office also acts as a corporate investment banker for investment capital.
- Achievement is rewarded, and units are encouraged to put forward and chase ambitious targets. Underperforming managers are likely to be removed.
- The head office *adds value* by acquiring and improving underperforming businesses; if additional value cannot be added it may well sell off businesses.
- Growth is more likely to be by acquisition than organic investment, with many financial control companies taking a short-term view of each business and being reluctant to invest in speculative research and the development of longer term strategies.

Strategic planning

- Strategic planning tends to be adopted in organizations which focus on only a few, and preferably related, core businesses. Examples include Cadbury Schweppes and BP. Historically, it has been the favoured approach for most public-sector organizations.
- Strategic plans are developed jointly by head office and the business units, with head office retaining the final say. Strategic planning is centralized.
- Day-to-day operations only are wholly decentralized.

- Head office sets priorities and co-ordinates strategies throughout the organization, possibly initiating cross-business strategies.
- A long-term perspective is realistic, and the search for opportunities for linkages and sharing resources and best practice can be prioritized. This normally requires central control. Individually the businesses would tend to operate more independently; organization-wide synergies may involve sacrifices by individual businesses.

    Goold and Campbell conclude there are co-ordination problems if this approach is used in truly diversified organizations.
- Budgets are again used for measuring performance.
- The tight central control can become bureaucratic and demotivate managers, who may not feel ownership of their strategies.

Other dangers are: first, thinking may become too focused at the centre, with the potential contributions of divisional managers underutilized, and second, the organization may be slow to change in response to competitive pressures. Value can be added successfully if corporate managers stay aware and expert in the core businesses and if the competitive environment allows this style to work.

Strategic control

Financial planning and strategic planning are appropriate for particular types of organization, but both styles, while having very positive advantages, also feature drawbacks. The strategic control style is an attempt to obtain the major benefits of the other two styles for organizations which are clearly diversified but with linkages and interdependencies. Value is added by balancing strategic and financial controls.

- Strategy creation involves decentralization to the business units, although head office still controls the overall corporate strategy.
- The role of head office is to review divisional and business plans, and approve strategic objectives and financial targets, accepting that they may need to be changed in a competitive environment.
- Strategy creation and budgetary control can be separated, allowing for more creative performance measurement.
- Sometimes competitive pressures and misjudgements mean that strategies have to be changed, and hoped-for financial targets may be missed. A strategic control style can recognize this and deal with the implications.
- Head office does, however, monitor and control financial performance and success against strategic milestones and objectives.

Although decentralization is a feature, head office still requires considerable detail about the various businesses if it is to ensure that synergy potential is achieved and very short-term thinking is avoided. Political activity will be prevalent as individual businesses compete with each other for scarce corporate resources.

Two leading organizations which utilized this style, ICI and Courtaulds,, both concluded that they were overdiversified. They had ended up with numerous businesses and some were clearly interlinked. At the same time, however, these 'clusters' of linked businesses were not linked themselves. They had little in common and featured different strategic needs and cultures. Because of these differences, and the inevitable complexity, corporate headquarters could not add value with a single entity. Both companies split into two distinct parts to enable a stronger focus on core competencies and strategic capabilities and to release trapped value. ICI was split into a new ICI and Zeneca, a largely pharmaceuticals business. Since the split, ICI has struggled and it has been transformed from a bulk chemicals business to one focusing on consumer products. Zeneca, in contrast, has prospered and has merged with the Swedish company Astra. Courtaulds, meanwhile, split itself into a textiles and a chemicals business, both of which have since been acquired by new parents.

Corporate Parenting

Goold *et al.* (1994) reinforce Porter's arguments when they contend that acquisitions can be justified where the corporation can add value to the business, generating either synergy or valuable emergent properties. Any business must add value to its parent corporation; in turn, the corporation must add value to the subsidiary. The company is better off with its existing parent than it would be with another parent or on its own. Parenting skills, therefore, relate to the ability of a head office and strategic leadership to manage a portfolio of businesses efficiently and effectively and to change the portfolio as and when it is necessary. It is, in fact, quite conceivable for head offices to destroy value if a subsidiary simply does not fit with the rest of the portfolio and is consequently held back.

Parenting skills vary between countries and cultures. In Japan, for example, the most successful companies are skilled at:

- securing and sustaining access to government, power and influence
- accessing investment capital and
- retaining skilled managers.

Much of this is facilitated by the *keiretsu*, families of companies interlinked by share ownership and characterized by intertrading, regular meetings of senior executives and sometimes geographical proximity in a single 'corporate village'. Interestingly, and significantly, these companies are interwoven but there are no corporate headquarters.

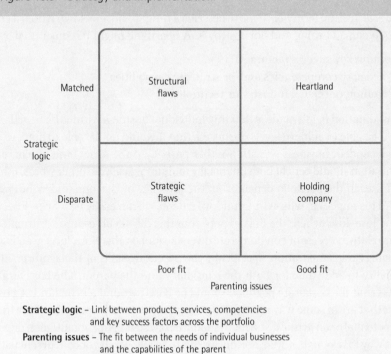

Figure 13.5   Strategy and implementation.

Strategic logic – Link between products, services, competencies
and key success factors across the portfolio

Parenting issues – The fit between the needs of individual businesses
and the capabilities of the parent

Figure 13.5 builds on Goold *et al's* arguments and draws these points together. On one axis we have strategic logic, the link between products, services, competencies and key success factors across the corporate portfolio. On the other axis we have the parenting issues, the fit between the needs of individual businesses and the corresponding capabilities of the parent organization. Where they fit together well, we have a *'heartland'* of related businesses, which we explain below. Where there is no natural synergy between the businesses, the organization can be successful to some degree if the parent company uses a *holding company* structure. Here we imply strong individual companies which could survive elsewhere, but which are managed in a 'hands-off' way. In this respect it is interesting that both Lord Hanson and Lord Weinstock had a reputation for rarely visiting the subsidiary businesses in the conglomerates they ran.

Where the parenting issues are not addressed properly we will see evidence of either strategic or structural flaws and the consequent underperformance. Here *strategic flaws* again imply fragmented businesses with no real synergy potential but this time linked to an inappropriate structure and style. There is a real likelihood of poor performance. *Structural flaws* reflect a potential for synergy but a potential that is not being realized because of structural and stylistic weaknesses.

The notion of a 'heartland'

Goold *et al.* use the term heartland to describe a range of businesses to which a corporation can add value and not destroy it. A heartland might be constituted by:

- common key success factors
- related core competencies and/or strategic capabilities
- a common or related industry or technology.

The assumption being made is that any individual business within the heartland should be able to achieve levels of success that it would not be able to achieve as an independent business or with another parent. At the same time, the parent organization should benefit both financially and strategically; in other words, other businesses in the portfolio benefit from the presence of the 'one under the spotlight'. This implies a 'win–win' situation, whereas it can easily be a 'win–lose' or even a 'lose–lose' where the fit is so poor that there is a real resource distraction.

The relative success of conglomerate diversification is, therefore, largely an issue of strategy implementation, specifically the parenting skills of the acquirer, and the ability to add value for both the subsidiary and the parent. The basic argument is that the corporate portfolio should be based around a heartland of businesses that are in some way related. Any which are not, and especially where they are a potential or an actual distraction, should be divested. As an organization divests in this way to refocus it is quite normal for this to be followed by, or concurrent with, acquisitions of related businesses to strengthen the core of the new focus.

Determining the heartland

The issues concern:

- first, whether the parent is able to provide, and is actually providing, the services and support that the individual businesses need, and
- second, whether the businesses have the people and competencies to fulfil the expectations of the parent.

Goold *et al.* offer the following framework as a starting point for assessing the existence of, or potential for, a heartland.

1. Mental maps (or philosophies) of the parent, incorporating issues of culture and values and broad policies for dealing with events and opportunities.
2. Issues of structure, systems and processes – incorporating the style of corporate management. This would include: procedures for appointing, promoting and rewarding people; the relative significance of budgeting and financial reporting; strategic planning systems; and capital allocation procedures.
3. Central services and resources – what is provided centrally and what is devolved.

4. Key people throughout the organization; key functions; key skills and competencies.
5. The nature of any decentralization 'contracts' and expectations – linked to issues of power, responsibility and accountability; reward and sanction systems; and the expectations that subsidiaries can have for the support they receive from corporate headquarters.

The role and contribution of corporate headquarters

There are two fundamental purposes of corporate headquarters:

- serving the global legal and financial needs of the business and
- supporting strategy making.

Many head offices have historically provided a more extensive range of services to their constituent businesses, including, for example:

- marketing
- management development and personnel
- property management
- centralized research and development
- corporate public relations
- industrial relations.

There is a clear need for head offices to add value to the corporation and not simply 'spend the money earned by the businesses'.

The recent trend has been for organizations to slim down the size and scope of head offices, and some centres have seen the bulk of their previous activities devolved to the individual businesses. Only corporate strategy, financial reporting and control and secretarial/legal services are centralized. Some head offices retain a responsibility for *policies* but not the activities.

Summarizing points made earlier, large centralized head offices where all the key business heads are located in one place – Unilever has been an example of this, but changes have been made – can control the corporation *efficiently*, but strategies can easily become top–down and slow to change. Decentralized organizations push profit responsibility down to the businesses and empower managers. The head office provides more of a support role with few discrete functions. The challenge is one of co-ordination.

In considering how head offices can best add value to the business as a whole, three issues must be addressed:

- how to control and co-ordinate the constituent businesses
- how to advise the strategic leader and keep him or her strategically aware
- which activities should be:

(i)   provided from head office – for which a fee should be levied
(ii)   devolved to the individual businesses
(iii) bought-in from outside specialists?

Contemporary Organizations

Rosabeth Moss Kanter (1990) offered a view on how the competitively successful organization in the 1990s would evolve. She argued that competitive success would lie in the capability to change and to accomplish key tasks by using resources more efficiently and more effectively. Organizations must be innovative and, at the same time, control their costs. Sustainable competitive advantage, however, does not come from either low costs, or differentiation, or innovation alone. It needs the whole organization to be *focused, fast, flexible and friendly.*

Being focused requires investment in core skills and competencies, together with a search for new opportunities for applying the skills. Intrapreneurship should be fostered constantly to improve the skills; and managers throughout the organization should be strategically aware and innovative. They should own the organization's mission, which, by necessity, must be communicated widely and understood.

Fast companies move at the right time, and are not caught out by competitors. New ideas and opportunities from the environment will be seized first. Ideally they will be innovating constantly to open up and sustain a competitive gap, because gradual improvements are likely to be more popular with customers than are radical changes. But 'instant success takes time' and the organization culture must be appropriate.

Flexibility concerns the search for continual improvement. The implication is a 'learning organization' where ideas are shared and collaboration between functions and divisions generates internal synergy. This, in turn, suggests that performance and effectiveness measures – and rewards – concentrate on outcomes.

Internal synergy can be achieved with cross-functional teams and special projects, and by moving people around the organization in order to spread the best practices.

It is important that internal constraints (imposed by other functions and divisions) and which restrain performance are highlighted and confronted. To be effective this requires a clear and shared vision and purpose for the organization, decentralization and empowerment.

Friendly organizations are closely linked to their suppliers and customers to generate synergy through the added value chain. Such external collaboration may be in the form of strategic alliances.

Handy (1994) contended that in order for companies to remain competitive internationally they must rethink their basic structures: 'Fewer key people, paid very well, producing far more value.' Companies in the future will be smaller, focused and closely networked to their suppliers and customers. More activities and components will be bough in from specialists than is the case at the moment (*external architecture*). Internally they will also comprise networks, with the 'centre' (as distinct from a traditional head office) doing only what the parts cannot do themselves. The real power will switch from the top of the organization to the businesses, and consequently a co-ordinating mission and purpose will be essential.

Supported by sophisticated information technology and systems, people will become the most important strategic resource, and, because their expertise and intelligence are intangible assets, largely unquantifiable, it will become harder to value the real assets of a business. Consequently, the appropriate measures of performance must be carefully evaluated; and reward systems will have to be derived which motivate and keep those managers who are potentially the most mobile. They will not all be at the most senior levels. Moreover, the strategic competencies required if an organization is to be competitive and successful will depend heavily on people. One dilemma concerns whether any new competencies that must be acquired should be developed internally with existing managers or 'bought in' by recruiting new people with the necessary skills and competencies. Whichever strategy is adopted, but especially with the second approach, there are likely to be cultural changes.

Handy's argument implies major changes to strategies, structures and styles of management. Where these are simultaneous – and amount to *strategic regeneration* – the changes are dramatic, painful and often difficult to carry through.

Strategic Success and Changes

The E–V–R (environment–values–resources) congruence framework was introduced in Chapter 1 to explain that effective strategic management requires an organization to manage the matching of its resources with its environment, when both E and R are subject to change pressures. Throughout the book we have discussed those strategic skills and competencies which are most likely to be needed for creating and maintaining an effective E and R match. We have also looked sequentially at how strategies can be created, evaluated and changed with these needs in mind. In this final chapter we attempt to draw these themes together.

There is no single recipe for creating long-term strategic success. We have seen that 'what works today' is unlikely to remain appropriate for a changing future, a principle which can apply to strategies, organization structures and approaches to managing circumstances and change. We have seen how there are a number of important ideas which underpin this ideal and which will contribute towards its achievement. These are:

Understanding Corporate Strategy

- the ability to add value – and innovatively create new values – for customers in ways which separate the organization from its competitors. Linked directly to this is
- the ability to create and sustain competitive advantage through cost leadership, differentiation and speed of change
- core competencies and strategic capabilities. The ability to exploit the organization's most critical resources to create and add value and, in turn, generate competitive advantage. *Synergies* should be sought and resources, including people, should be *stretched* to higher levels of achievement. People must be able to learn and willing to change

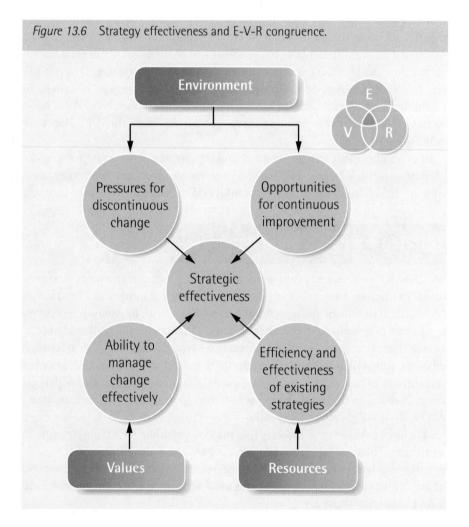

Figure 13.6   Strategy effectiveness and E-V-R congruence.

- internal and external architecture and linkages. To enjoy the benefits of synergy, organizations must be able to create and sustain internal cohesion: people must adopt supportive, teamworking behaviours, learning and sharing best practices. Further benefits are possible if the organization can ally itself more closely with the other organizations in its supply chain, particularly its suppliers and distributors, to create a 'continuous value stream'. Effective communications networks, trust and sharing are at the heart of this.

In summary, strategic success requires the organization to develop and retain a wide range of competencies which enable it to outperform its competitors and deal with the pressures of increasingly dynamic and turbulent business environments.

The theme of strategic change is central to all our arguments concerning strategic success. Figure 13.6 takes the concept of E–V–R congruence and restates the idea from the perspective of effective change management. The environment provides opportunities for organizations to benefit from innovation and continuous improvement; on other occasions the environment will encourage more dramatic, discontinuous change. This pressure can take the form of a threat (major environmental disturbance) or an opportunity (an ability to see the future ahead of competitors). The relative strength of the organization's resources is reflected in the success of existing strategies; values dictate the ability of the organization to manage change effectively. Strategic effectiveness demands congruency.

Strategic learning

The relationship between an organization and its environment is based on a perpetual circular relationship:

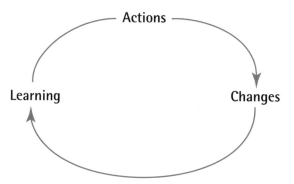

An organization will learn about the need to change from its observations and interpretation of events in the environment, often events created by the actions of other companies. As a result, managers decide on the actions they should take,

In this race ... you run the first four laps as fast as you can – and then you gradually increase the speed.

William Weiss, CEO, Ameritech

and they implement the necessary changes. These changes affect other organizations (competitors, suppliers, customers) in what we have termed an environment of competitive chaos. In turn, they react, and the organization is again able to learn about the impact and outcome of its decisions.

There is an important double-loop matching process. The organization is attempting to match its strategies with a changing environment; at the same time, it is attempting to shape and manage its environment in order best to exploit its strategic abilities and resources.

Internal and external architecture, which we have stressed throughout the book, are central to an organization's attempts to manage its environment. Externally, mutual trust and interdependencies must be built and nurtured with suppliers, distributors and customers; internally, alliances constitute an attempt to generate synergies and maximize the returns from resources. We have also discussed how powerful stakeholders – employees, suppliers and customers, for example – can, like competitors, spring surprises. There is, therefore, always the likelihood of corporate, structural or architectural chaos in addition to competitive chaos. No strategy or alliance should be seen as safe, certain and perpetual. The fifteen year alliance between Rover and Honda, for example, was effectively destroyed when British Aerospace sold Rover to BMW in 1994. In the same way, key employees can resign, important suppliers might go out of business and major customers can change their requirements.

A fast reaction and an ability to deal with change pressures, ideally changing a threat into an opportunity, will always be required alongside proactive endeavours to shape and manage the environment.

The challenge of strategic change

Effective change management requires:

- A clear perception of need, or dissatisfaction with the existing status quo. A recognition that current strategies, however successful they might be at the moment, will be inadequate for achieving future objectives and expectations.

Sometimes the need for change will be obvious: reduced profits, falling market share, operating problems. On other occasions nothing will *seem* to be fundamentally wrong – at the moment. The challenge is one of timing and, as we said earlier, changing while the organization is still successful. In the latter case, persuading people of the need to change will clearly be more difficult. Open communication is essential; people must be given both information and reasons.

- A way forward – a vision of a better future, a new direction or a perceived opportunity. Implicit are a clear and shared mission and environmental awareness.
- The capability to change – the necessary resources and strategies which are capable of implementation. This requires clear targets or definable 'winning posts' and suitable rewards for success.
- Commitment – change needs managing. There should be a commitment to both the continual improvement of existing strategies and genuinely new directions.

Change is ongoing.

Managing change and a culture of change

In Chapter 4 we looked at a number of important issues involved in attempting to change the culture of an organization. Whilst change can be required and implemented at several levels, namely:

(i)   the corporate culture
(ii) the organizational mission
(iii) corporate strategies
(iv) organization structures, systems and processes
(v)   competitive strategies and
(vi) operational tasks and functional strategies,

with the complexity and difficulty of the challenge increasing as we ascend this hierarchy of six levels, the basic principles discussed are relevant for every occasion.

The management of a change programme requires, first, that existing behaviours are *unfrozen*. People must be convinced about the need for change. Behaviours must be *changed* to a better way; and, last, these new ways must be *refrozen* and seen as normal. Championing and persistence are essential. Kurt Lewin, who introduced this description of the change process, also emphasized the importance of *force field analysis* (Lewin, 1951).

Change pressures are constant, especially at the competitive and functional strategy levels. Customers provide new opportunities and active competitors constitute an ever-present threat, for example. As we have already seen, markets represent a form of *competitive chaos*. These are our pressures, or forces, for change. The survival and economic prosperity of the business demand that these are dealt with.

People driving the changes will encounter *resistance* in the form of countervailing pressures or forces. Crucially, the reasons for the resistance are more concerned with the social implications than with the economic logic, highlighting the importance of effective management if desirable or necessary changes are to be implemented successfully. People often feel threatened by change and by the unknown; they are concerned about the possibility of losing their jobs or status. They worry about whether they will be able to cope with the new pressures that the change will place on them. People have often become both comfortable with, and expert at, the existing ways. It is not unnatural that they should feel personally threatened. They are really being asked to question their existing beliefs.

Ideally, the organization will seek to develop a culture where people do not feel threatened when they are constantly asked to question and challenge existing behaviours and acknowledged ways of doing things – and change them: a culture which sees innovation and change as normal; a culture that is ideal for dealing with the competitive chaos which characterizes many industries and markets. This cannot happen without strong strategic leadership which fosters, encourages and rewards intrapreneurial and innovative contributions from managers and other employees throughout the organization.

A culture such as this will frequently be based around a working atmosphere of creativity and fun; people must enjoy doing things differently and originally, actively looking for new competitive opportunities, instead of simply copying others. A change culture is highly desirable for many organizations but very difficult to achieve.

Discontinuous change and strategic regeneration

We have seen how powerful environmental issues such as deregulation, globalization, lower trade barriers and economic recessions have combined in the 1990s to place enormous change pressures on companies. The individual significance of these issues will vary from year to year but, in aggregate terms, the outcome is an increasingly turbulent and uncertain business environment for most organizations, private and public sector, manufacturing and service, large and small, profit-seeking and not-for-profit.

Companies have responded. Many have sought to manage their assets and strategic resources more efficiently and effectively – again levels (v) and (vi), the lowest two levels of the change hierarchy. Some have restructured; others have radically changed their processes through business process re-engineering. This implies level (iv) change. The need for innovation has been accepted.

However, continuous improvement to an organization's *competitive* capabilities, essential as it is, will not always be sufficient to meet these pressures.

Tom Peters (1992) argued that for some companies the challenge is 'not just about a *programme* of change ... strategies and structures need to change perpetually'. Peter Drucker (1993) agreed and contended that 'every organization must prepare to abandon everything it does'. Both authors are implying wholesale corporate renewal or reinvention, which we have earlier termed strategic regeneration

Successful regeneration requires both an external and an internal focus. Externally, organizations must search for new product, new service and new market opportunities, working with suppliers, distributors and customers to redefine markets and industries. Internally, structures, management styles and cultures must be capable of creating and delivering these products and services. Innovation is dependent upon processes and people. Strategic awareness, information management and change are critically important if the organization is to outperform its competitors.

Summary

Strategic management comprises analysis, choice and implementation. Strategies are implemented through the organization structure. However, the structural processes are the determinants of adaptive and incremental changes. As a result there is a circular relationship between strategy and structure.

Effective control is achieved when strategy and structure are matched and are also congruent with the style of corporate management. Simultaneous change to these three, what we have earlier termed strategic regeneration, is difficult, but sometimes necessary for organizations.

Structures are designed , first, to split up and separate the key activities and tasks which the organization must carry out, and second, to integrate and coordinate efforts to achieve synergies. In relation to this, organizations must decide how much responsibility should be centralized and how much can be effectively decentralized and devolved to divisions and business units.

Centralization yields control. Decentralization may be required for growth and flexibility. It is also more likely to motivate managers.

Organizations are likely to conform, either closely or loosely, to one of six identifiable structural forms: the entrepreneurial structure, the functional structure, the divisionalized corporation, the holding company, the matrix structure or the global organization.

Head office will look to exercise both strategic and financial control over the business. When the organization is multiproduct or multiservice, and possibly diversified, control is likely to be exercised in one of three ways. Financial control is ideal for an organization which comprises independent, unrelated businesses in a holding company structure. Strategic planning reflects centralization. It is most appropriate when there is a limited range of possibly related core businesses. Strategic control is most likely to be found when there is a diverse group of businesses which are related in some way.

Goold *et al* highlighted the importance of corporate parenting – essentially the fit between a head office and the subsidiary businesses in an organization and the opportunities for two-way benefits. Where each business can benefit from being part of an organization, and at the same time make a positive contribution to the whole organization, we have what Goold *et al.* call a heartland of related businesses. Businesses should be acquired and divested to strengthen the heartland.

The corporate headquarters drives the strategy of the business and provides the structural framework. The range of services which remain centralized is a reflection of the adopted style of corporate management. Head offices should add value and not merely spend money earned by the subsidiaries. In recent years, head offices have been slimmed down.

Not only must companies be able to manage a programme of change, they should also look to develop a culture which is responsive to perpetual change pressures.

Strategic change can be categorized in six layers: corporate culture; organizational mission; corporate strategies; structure, systems and processes; competitive strategies; and functional strategies. These six layers can be seen as a hierarchy of complexity. Competitive and functional strategies can be changed far more easily than the corporate culture, for example.

Resistance to change can always be expected.

References

Bartlett, C and Ghoshal, S (1989) *Managing Across Borders: The Transnational Solution,* Harvard Business School Press.

Bartlett, C and Ghoshal, S (1992) What is a global manager? *Harvard Business Review,* September–October.

Drucker, PF (1993) *Managing in Turbulent Times,* Butterworth-Heinemann.

Goold, M and Campbell, A (1988) *Strategies and Styles,* Blackwell.

Goold, M, Campbell, A and Luchs, K (1993) Strategies and styles revisited: strategic planning and financial control, *Long Range Planning,* 26, 5.

Goold, M, Campbell, A and Luchs, K (1993) Strategies and styles revisited: strategic control – is it tenable? *Long Range Planning,* 26, 6.

Goold, M, Campbell, A and Alexander, M (1994) *Corporate Level Strategy,* John Wiley.

Greiner, LE (1972) Evolution and revolution as organizations grow, *Harvard Business Review,* July–August. Provides real insight into how structures change when strategies develop.

Handy, C (1994) *The Empty Raincoat,* Hutchinson.

Kanter, R M (1990) *Honouring the Business Experts, Economist* Conference, London (March).

Lewin, K (1951) *Field Theory in Social Sciences,* Harper and Row.

Mintzberg, H (1993) *Structure in Fives: Designing Effective Organizations,* Prentice-Hall. Gives a different perspective on structural forms.

Morgan, G (1993) *Imaginization,* Sage.

Peters, T (1992) *Liberation Management – Disorganization for the Nanosecond Nineties,* Macmillan.

Questions and Research Projects

TEXT RELATED

1. It was stated in the text that decentralization and divisionalization are not synonymous. What factors determine the degree of decentralization in a divisionalized organization?

2. For which (general) corporate strategies are the financial control, strategic planning and strategic control styles of corporate management most appropriate?

3. For an organization with which you are familiar, obtain or draft the organization structure. How does it accord with the structural forms described in the text? Given your knowledge of the company's strategies and people, is the structure appropriate? Why? Why not? If not, in what way would you change it?

4. Describe an event where you have personally experienced forces for change, and discuss any forces which were used to resist the change. What tactics were adopted on both sides?

Internet and Library Projects

1. Evaluate the divisionalized or holding company structure of a large diverse multiproduct multinational, considering the main board status of the key general managers. Does this suggest centralization or decentralization? If you are familiar with the company, do your findings accord with your knowledge of management styles within the organization?

2. It was commented in the text that Amstrad is an innovative company which has sometimes experienced setbacks with strategy implementation. What setbacks can you identify and how significant do you think their impact was?

3. Mention was made in this chapter of the splitting of ICI into the new ICI and Zeneca. What has happened to the two companies since the split? With hindsight, did the split make sense?

4. Investigate the changes made by Lord Simpson at GEC since he replaced Lord Weinstock. What is GEC's new heartland? What has happened with joint ventures and strategic alliances?

Long case: Amazon.com

Amazon.com is the story of an amazing company, led by a true entrepreneur, at the forefront of e-commerce and online retailing. Its growth rate has been astounding but it has yet to make a profit. This case study looks at the growth of Amazon.com and its impact on bookselling, the business where it began, and at its further expansion and diversification. Several key strategic issues in e-commerce are discussed.

This version of the case was written by John L Thompson in 2000. It is for classroom discussion and should not be taken to reflect either effective or ineffective management.

An alternative version appears in Bolton, WK and Thompson, JL (2000) *Entrepreneurs: Talent, Temperament, Technique*, Butterworth-Heinemann.

Introduction

Amazon.com, the 'Earth's largest bookstore', pioneered bookselling via the Internet and, in the process, changed consumer buying habits and forced the existing major booksellers to react and also offer electronic sales and postal deliveries. It has also become the world's largest, and probably the best-known, online retailer. Paradoxically, this has happened in an environment where – and in parallel – 'good bookstores have become the community centres of the late twentieth century' by providing comfortable seats, staying open late and incorporating good coffee bars.

The Amazon site allows bibliophiles to exchange views and reviews as well as place orders – and some browsers apparently spend hours searching through the catalogues for titles that they think will interest them. Amazon.com can never replace the hands-on element of a physical bookshop, nor engage authors for meet-the-customer signing sessions, but it can, and does, offer a far wider choice. The number of people around the world who are connected to the Internet – and buying goods electronically – is now growing rapidly. And the number of people who buy at least one book a year is huge. Many of them are willing to buy on the strength of an author's reputation or a good review of the content and style, sacrificing an insistence to inspect the book beforehand. Because of the different time zones around the world, Amazon.com can sell 24 hours every day.

However, Amazon.com is now far more than an online bookstore, having diversified into a much wider and diverse range of products and activities. Its premise or 'business model' relies on a difficult balance between short- and long-term issues. Internet retailers such as Amazon.com must grow quickly to claim a substantial slice of a developing market, and for this they have to be able to raise funds for continued investment.

However, they are unlikely to be profitable in their early years and argue that short-term profits do not matter as long as the company is growing and establishing a strong reputation. Inevitably, this is an uncertain world and adverse publicity can be one factor behind the associated volatility in the trading prices of any shares in these businesses. Not unexpectedly, their book value tends to rise and fall very steeply.

Bookselling

Books are bought and read all round the world and they are published in various languages. The UK market is worth some £2 billion per year, but the American market is about ten times this size. Sales of best-selling paperback fiction titles can be huge, but other more specialized books may only sell a few hundred copies during the time they are in print. While many people buy books regularly, others rely more on libraries. The industry risk lies with the publishers, who pay royalties to their authors on confirmed sales and who accept unsold books back from their wholesalers and retailers. Publishers can reprint books which sell consistently well, but generally they will always carry surplus stock because of time lags. Final returns of 30% are not exceptional, but the average is something below 20%.

Distribution is fragmented and comprises the following channels:

- specialist book 'superstores', which often also sell music. The largest chains are Barnes & Noble and Borders, American-based businesses which are now expanding into the UK. Waterstone's/ Dillons is the market leader in the UK. All of these are still growing in size and opening new stores. WH Smith has the second largest market share in the UK and is the leading travel (airports and railway stations) bookstore
- smaller independent bookshops, both single outlets and small chains. These are generally served by wholesalers as well as directly by publishers
- supermarkets, who typically sell only a limited range at discounted prices
- book clubs
- supplies to libraries, sometimes via specialist library wholesalers
- sales through university bookshops and to schools. In the UK, Waterstone's is a leading university campus retailer
- virtual bookstores. As well as Amazon.com, Barnes & Noble, Borders, Waterstone's and WH Smith all sell electronically via the web, and there are several other specialist e-commerce booksellers.

Since the abolition of the NBA (the net book agreement, which allowed publishers to set prices and reduced the incidence of discounting) in the UK in the mid-1990s, price discounting has been a major feature of the industry, as it is in the USA. The scope for this is significant as full retail prices are often twice the amount that the publisher receives. This latter amount typically breaks down as follows:

Direct manufacturing costs	20%
Overheads (including marketing)	30%
Returns and allowances	25%
Author royalties	10–20%
Operating profit	5–15%.

The market overall grew throughout the 1990s, but some forecasters predict that it will be more stagnant in the early years of the new millennium.

Jeff Bezos – the entrepreneur

Amazon.com was founded in 1994 by Jeff Bezos. The son of a Cuban immigrant, Bezos once dreamt of being an astronaut and consequently went on to graduate in electrical engineering and computer science from Princeton. While a teenager, a paper he wrote on the effect of zero gravity on the common housefly won him a trip to the Marshall Space Flight Center in Alabama. After Princeton he became a successful investment banker on Wall Street. He was the youngest senior vice president ever at D.E. Shaw, which he joined from Bankers Trust. Intrigued by the speed of growth of the Internet in the early 1990s, he decided to 'seize the moment'. He had experienced his trigger and he left the bank with the straightforward intention of starting an e-commerce business.

At this stage he had no specific product or service in mind, and so he began by drawing up a list of possible activities. He narrowed down his first list of 20 to two – music and books – before choosing books. In both cases, the range of titles available was far in excess of the number that any physical store could realistically stock. In 1994 there were 1.5 million English-language books in print, and another 1.5 million in other languages, yet the largest bookstore carried only 175,000 titles. Moreover, Bezos appreciated that the distribution was fragmented. He believed that there was scope to offer books at discounted prices and wafer-thin margins to seize sales from existing retailers, while also boosting the overall size of the market.

His second decision was location. He quickly narrowed the field to Boulder, Portland and Seattle before selecting Seattle. In theory, he could have picked anywhere, but he believed that a number of important criteria had to be met. A ready supply of people with technical ability was essential, and other key members of his management team would need to find it an attractive place to live and work. As the firm has grown, several experienced people have been recruited from nearby Microsoft. In addition, it had to be a relatively small state. Bezos would have to charge a relevant sales tax to residents of any state where Amazon.com had a physical presence, but others would be exempt.

He rented a house and started in the garage, using the coffee shop in the nearby Barnes and Noble bookstore to interview potential staff. He personally made the first desks they used from old, recycled doors. After raising several million dollars from venture capitalists and private investors whom he knew, he moved into a 400 square foot (40 square metre) office and began trading on the Internet in July 1995. Bezos is adamant that he warned his investors of the inherent risks in his ambitious venture. Sales began immediately, and within six weeks he moved to a 2000 square foot (200 square metre) warehouse. Six months later he moved again. This time he set up Amazon's headquarters in a 12-storey former hospital.

Within its first year, Amazon.com earned revenues of $5 million, equivalent to a large Barnes and Noble superstore. Sales have since grown dramatically as the company has expanded rapidly, but so too have the costs. After five years the company is still trading at a loss, and profits are not in the forecast time horizon. The company went public in May 1997. Not unexpectedly, its share price and market valuation are very volatile, but

Amazon has been valued at $27 billion, some $2 billion more than Wal-Mart. Bezos remains infectiously enthusiastic. He is noted for two personal quirks: his loud and frequent laugh and his tendency to always have to hand a small camera. His closest colleagues confirm that he is 'sometimes goofy'. Bezos is married to a novelist who has occasionally been involved in his business. She was, for example, instrumental in negotiating his first freight contract.

The virtual bookstore

There are four value propositions to Amazon.com: convenience, selection, service and price.

Clearly, there are no books to touch, open and read. All communications are through the world wide website pages or via e-mail. The website allows customers to search the extensive (one million plus titles) book catalogue by topic and author, to read explanations and summaries from authors as well as reviews from other readers, specialist reviewers and Amazon's own staff, and to order with a credit card. Those who prefer can reserve books via the web and then telephone Amazon with their credit card details. Orders are processed immediately. Amazon holds limited stocks of its best-selling titles, which it can post out immediately when it receives an on-line order from a customer and credit card details have been confirmed. Otherwise, the customer order triggers an order to the relevant publisher or a specialist wholesaler. These books are redespatched very quickly after Amazon receives them into stock. Delivery to the customer of a non-bestseller, therefore, is normally around a week, with more unusual titles taking longer.

The site can also provide information on any books which are similar to any title a customer nominates, and Amazon.com will also keep customers up to date with new publications from selected authors. Readers are encouraged to post their own book reviews and, if they wish, they can communicate electronically with any other readers looking at the same book or topic at the same time. This allows an instantaneous exchange of views and opinions.

All books are discounted: bestsellers typically by 30% and others by at least 10% of the jacket price. For special promotions, and to compete with the websites of Barnes and Noble and Borders, bestselling titles have occasionally been discounted by as much as 50%. Amazon.com can do this because a book is held in stock for just two days; a high-street bookseller is holding the equivalent of at least three months sales in stock at any time. Increased marketing expenditure (mostly on the Internet) for a virtual bookstore partially offsets this relative cost advantage. Moreover, the price gap is narrowed again when packing, postage and administrative charges are added back to the discounted price. These vary and depend on the point of delivery. There are no salespeople. The 'store' is open 24 hours every day and is accessible from anywhere in the world.

The combination of price and service is instrumental in attempting to persuade customers to return to the website and to Amazon.com. After all, the most committed book-buyers buy several titles at different times through the year. Finally, there is an element of fun and irreverence. Every week Amazon makes an award for the most amusing and obscure book on order at the time. Past winners include *Training Goldfish Using Dolphin Training Techniques* and *How to Start Your Own Country*. Bezos, however, maintains that:

people don't understand how hard it is to be an electronic merchant . . . most correspondence is by e-mail . . . some people do nothing but answer customer e-mails . . . we have to develop our own technologies . . . no-one sells software for managing e-mail centres. There are lots of barriers to entry.

Behind the success

We always wanted to build something the world has never seen.

Bezos is allegedly obsessed by customers and service. 'The Internet is this big, huge hurricane . . . the only constant in that storm is the customers'. Bezos was not the first Internet bookseller, but he was always determined to be the most customer friendly. When interviewed, he talks about his customers constantly; they have clearly been a major focus for the business. In many respects, this view contradicts a belief held by many that there is no customer loyalty on the Internet. His efforts have paid off: 70% of Amazon shoppers are regular customers.

In reality, Amazon.com should not be seen as a bookselling operation but as an 'e-commerce customer relationship business' because it has successfully used its website, its image and reputation and its network to expand into other areas such as electronic greeting cards, music, videos, pharmaceuticals and pet supplies. Amazon.com also hosts Internet auctions. Some of this diversification has been achieved by the acquisition and absorption of other e-commerce businesses. Amazon's core competencies are in generating site traffic and potential customers, persuading them to order and then satisfying them with excellent service. An innovative and robust website, and a distinctive brand, have always been critical elements of the Amazon strategy. The company has been at the forefront in a number of ways, many of which have been copied by other Internet businesses. It pioneered numbered steps in the purchasing operation, proactive order confirmations, credit cards sales and the single-click transaction. In the case of the single-click transaction Amazon obtained a temporary injunction against Barnes and Noble for copyright infringement.

Bezos clearly understands web technology and knew the type of people to recruit to build a strong central team. As an organization, Amazon.com is structured into five divisions: marketing, operations (order processing and warehousing), business expansion (new products and services), development (software innovations) and editorial (website design and content). He was willing to offer generous stock options. There are five vice presidents (VPs) who report directly to Bezos. The marketing VP was recruited from Cinnabon World Famous Cinnamon Rolls, and prior to this he had several years' experience in a variety of fast-moving consumer goods businesses and an MBA degree. The operations VP came from Black and Decker. The business expansion VP was experienced in book retailing. Originally the founder of a software business, Omni Information systems, he was working for Barnes and Noble before he joined Amazon. The development VP was a mathematics graduate with over 20 years' experience in designing both hardware and software systems. The executive editor, the fifth VP, was a PhD graduate who had had a similar post at PC Magazine, which he had also launched on the web. Clearly, Bezos wanted a team that was both intellectually strong and experienced in areas which would be critical for the success of the business. The team remained intact until summer 2000 when the operations VP resigned. His resignation prompted analysts to query the real value of stock options when share prices are extremely volatile.

Bezos always recognized the importance of the supply chain. His second and third warehouses in Delaware and Nevada were again located to reduce the impact of sales tax on purchases. At the end of 1999 there were five warehouses in the USA and one in the UK. Specialist websites in the UK (Amazon.co.uk) and Germany supplement the main website.

Growth and success

Without question, Amazon.com has grown dramatically to become the world's third largest bookseller through constant change and innovation. But with 12 million customer accounts and a brand name recognized by 118 million adults in America (1999) it is far more than a bookseller. Bezos maintains that he now offers 'the earth's biggest selection of goods'.

Sales began by doubling in size every ten weeks. In 1996, revenues amounted to $16 million, by 1997 they had increased to $150 million, and in 1998 they almost quadrupled again. The 1999 figures were $1.64 billion sales and $390 million losses. In comparison, the leading players in bookselling, Barnes & Noble and Borders, earn approximately $3 billion and $2.5 billion, respectively. Tables 1 and 2 use indices to illustrate the costs, profits and losses as a percentage of sales revenue for Amazon over a period of five years

Table 1   Amazon profitability shown as an index of revenues

	1995 Part-year	1996	1997	1998	1999
Indices for					
Revenue	100.0	100.0	100.0	100.0	100.0
Cost of goods sold	80.4	77.8	80.5	77.1	79.0
Gross margin	19.6	22.2	19.5	22.9	21.0
Overheads	80.4	59.9	39.3	40.3	45.0*
Loss as %	(60.8)	(37.7)	(19.8)	(17.4)	(24)

* Increasing because of new developments requiring additional investments.

Table 2   Amazon compared with Borders and Barnes & Noble, 1997

	Amazon.com	Borders	Barnes & Noble
Revenue	100.0	100.0	100.0
Cost of goods sold	80.5	72.1	72.2
Gross margin %	19.5	27.9	27.8
Overheads*	39.3	24.3	22.0
Profit/(Loss) %	(19.8)	3.6	5.8

* Mainly marketing and product development.

and for Amazon compared with its two main competitors in 1997. When it was launched, it was thought that Amazon.com could be profitable within five years, but this milestone has been abandoned. Towards the end of the 1990s Bezos commented: 'If we are profitable anytime in the short term it will just be an accident'.

The total Amazon.com trading volume and revenues in the first six months of 2000 were recorded as almost double those for the comparable first half of 1999. However, two points were worthy of mention. First, the second quarter (April–June) was no higher than the first quarter, implying some flattening, when a year earlier there had been growth over the same period. Secondly, although overall sales were up nearly 100%, sales of the core books, music and video had increased by 38%. Analysts wondered whether the current Internet market for these products might be nearing saturation, and that the rate of growth enjoyed in the past would require a substantial increase in Internet shoppers.

Throughout the 1990s Jeff Bezos was able to raise the investment funding he needed to fuel the company's rapid growth. The public offering of shares in May 1997 was followed by three separate bond issues, two of which were convertible bonds. These are exchangeable for stock at a prescribed later date. The Appendix tracks how Amazon was financed until 1999. However, in summer 2000 the shares were trading at a price which represented a 70% discount on the all-time high and which was lower than the initial offer price in 1997. Bonds could be bought at 60% of their original price and the convertibility element did not look attractive. Could Bezos continue to raise funding and grow, and ignore the need to bring Amazon.com into profits, or would the business model have to change?

The shares had fallen by 20% in June 2000 when a report from Lehman Brothers suggested that Amazon.com was indeed running out of cash – something that Bezos quickly denied. The report also implied that cost cutting was not a realistic option for Amazon.com and that aspects of the strategy needed rethinking.

Strategic developments

The key people at Amazon realized some years ago that the Internet would generate a proliferation of new enterprises, many of them small and specialist, and that a network would offer enhanced distribution and selling opportunities. Consequently, in 1996 Amazon.com pioneered the idea of strategic alliances with other websites. Visitors to the sites of any Amazon Associate company can hyperlink and buy relevant books from the Amazon catalogue. There are now over 60,000 Associate companies. Typical examples would include a food-orientated site linked to cookery books, and a horticulture site and gardening books, and an outdoor clothing site and guide books. Amazon pays a referral fee of between 5 and 15% of sales revenues for the introduction and sales. The Amazon site is set up to provide a unique, customized collection of relevant titles for each Associate.

Music and video were added to books on the website after Amazon bought Junglee Corporation in 1998, a company which had developed innovative comparison shopping technologies. Consumer electronics, games, toys and pharmaceuticals – a market six times as big as books – have followed at various times. Simply, Amazon.com became increasingly concerned with lucrative electronic sales of almost anything to a vast number of customers rather than specializing as a bookseller. It is a brand.

The next step from this was almost inevitable. Late in 1999 Amazon opened its site and customers to products being sold by other companies, for whom it essentially provides an electronic shopfront. Amazon charges a small monthly fee and a percentage of sales revenue, in the region of 2–5%. Beauty products, pet foods, branded sports wear and antiquarian books were early subscribers to this opportunity. Amazon bought equity stakes in most of these partner businesses to strengthen the alliance. In 1999 Amazon also entered the electronic auction market, another area of rapid growth, in a further attempt to exploit its customer base. Simply, it provides access to its site for companies who want to auction goods over the Internet. To support these strategic developments, Amazon earlier (1998) bought PlanetAll, a business that had built a site which allows people to maintain their personal calendars and web directories. The intention was to use it to develop a reminder service to prompt people to buy birthday and other presents.

In August 2000 Amazon.com announced a ten-year strategic alliance with Toys R Us, the world's largest toy-store chain. Amazon would link its toy business with the on-line subsidiary of Toys R Us. Toys are a very seasonal product with the bulk of the year's sales coming in the run up to Christmas. In this period in 1999 Amazon.com had been left with considerable unsold merchandise – it had bought in too many items which simply did not sell. In contrast, Toys R Us had been unable to fill all the orders it had received as its distribution network was inadequate. Clearly there was an opportunity to generate synergy from an alliance.

Amazon.com would provide:

- the electronic shop window for the combined businesses
- the distribution network – including the warehousing of the inventory
- customer service

and Toys R Us would contribute the merchandising – the selection, purchasing and management of the inventory. Toys R Us will finance the stock in Amazon's warehouses and collect the revenues from sales and then pay Amazon a fee.

Later the same month another alliance with Microsoft was announced. With this agreement, Microsoft's Reader software would be used by Amazon.com to distribute electronic books, which people could download onto their personal computers or hand-held devices. Reader enables large amounts of text to be read easily on a computer screen. At this time the market for electronic books was uncertain and still emerging. Interestingly, Stephen King, popular author of bestselling horror stories, had begun to put his latest novel on the Internet, releasing it chapter by chapter. Readers can access the material completely free but are asked to contribute $1 for each chapter they read. The next chapter is only released when King has received a level of contributions with which he is happy.

Challenges and risks

Amazon.com is a pioneer and 'the quintessential Internet company'. Its customer base and its range of products continue to grow and diversify. But each new development appears to require additional investment. In the end, Amazon may be profitable, but it might also be a disaster waiting to happen.

There is no shortage of direct competition to its main business from other Internet book retailers, which keeps margins very low. Establishing an efficient, effective supply chain is a barrier to entry, but setting up a website is relatively easy. As the range of activities becomes more extensive, and the company's site becomes more diverse, it is conceivable that the more serious book buyers will select a more focused competitor such as Barnes & Noble, Borders, Waterstone's or WH Smith, all recognized brands with an e-commerce presence. This switching could even be encouraged if Amazon is too aggressive at targeting its promotions of non-book products and services at customers whose buying profile has been tracked and analysed, or if it allows other partner companies access to this information. After all, Jeff Bezos has said: 'customers are loyal right up to the point somebody offers them a better service'. Although books are a reducing proportion of Amazon's business, they are where the company started and they are the product upon which its reputation has been built.

Although Amazon invests considerably in developing and improving its site, it is not inconceivable in this dynamic and turbulent industry that some form of technological breakthrough by a rival could make Amazon appear much less attractive and innovative.

Amazon.com   http://www.amazon.com

Questions

1. How would you define and justify the Amazon.com 'business model'?

2. How significant is reputation for Amazon.com – in relation to both customers and potential investors? Is there a link between reputation and the share price volatility? How might Amazon.com attempt to reduce this volatility?

3. How might the alliance with Toys R Us affect both the business model and Amazon's reputation?

4. Does Amazon.com have a distinctive competitive advantage? If so, what is it – and how might it be sustained? If not, how might it achieve one?

5. Evaluate the challenges listed at the end of the case. Can you think of additional issues?

6. What is the contribution of Jeff Bezos to Amazon.com and to e-commerce generally?

Long case: C & J Clark

C&J Clark ('Clarks') is a long-established family company, based in the UK but well-known in the shoe industry around the world. By the late 1980s the company was in decline but has since been turned around with new strategic leadership. Both marketing and operational issues have been addressed. This case contains sufficient information for analysing and evaluating the relevant strategic issues, but readers are also encouraged to visit Clarks and rival shoe retailers to check out the latest designs and marketing strategies.

This case is copyright John L Thompson, 2000. It is for classroom discussion and should not be taken to reflect either effective or ineffective management.

Introduction–the footwear market in the UK

At the end of the 1990s Clarks was UK market leader for shoes. Well-known as both a manufacturer and a retailer, the name Clarks is typically associated with children's shoes, especially among the older generations who 'grew up in Clark's sandals'. Now, of course, children are more keen to wear designer-name trainers. Over many years the company had become associated with sturdy and sensible shoes for adults as well as children, rather than high fashion shoes, although these are also included in the range. Sturdy, sensible shoes are still manufactured, but they have been relaunched with a different image and appeal. Clarks shoes are sold widely overseas, and increasingly they are made overseas. The company wants to be recognized as an 'international casual shoe company'.

The footwear market in the UK exceeded £5 billion annual sales for the first time in 1999. During the mid-late 1990s the growth rate had exceeded the prevailing rate of inflation. The highest growth was in children's shoes of all types, although these account for less than one-fifth of the market overall. Women's shoes account for 43% of sales revenue but 50% of the number of pairs bought. However, 75% of the shoes involved had been manufactured outside the UK, in both the Far East and other countries with relatively low labour costs.

In 2000 C&J Clark was 175 years old and still controlled by descendants of the founding family. A Clark has been strategic leader for most of the company's history, although this situation has changed in recent years. Eighty per cent of the shares are owned by 500 family members and descendants, some of whom have a direct involvement with the company. Staff own a further 10% and institutional shareholders the remainder.

Table 1 shows market shares by manufacturer in 1999 and Table 2 provides details of retail distribution. Small, sometimes independent, businesses play a major role, as evidenced by the fact that the leading seven retailers account for just one-third of the market. Specialist manufacturers vary from those making high-quality shoes for adults

Table 1 Shoe sales by type of outlet, 1999

Outlet	%
Specialist stores (both chains and independents)	44
Sports shops	20
Home shopping	11
Clothing stores (e.g. Next)	8
General stores	7
Department stores (including concessions)	5

Table 2 Market shares, 1999 (Source: *Euromonitor*)

Manufacturer	%
C&J Clark	10.0
Nike	6.0
Reebok	5.0
Marks and Spencer	5.0
Stylo	4.5
British Shoe Corporation	2.0
Adidas	2.0

(such as Charles Church) to those making rugged, waterproof outdoor footwear (Timberland) and children's wear (Start-rite). Most towns have at least one local independent store, often with a loyal customer trade. During the 1990s the popularity of trainers and other sports shoes, backed by heavy brand advertising, has grown dramatically, as has the popularity of shoes associated with designer names.

Taste and fashion changes have meant that the relative fortunes of different shoe retailers have changed. Some have improved, while others have declined markedly. However, at the same time, shoe manufacture in the UK has declined sharply. Some companies, like Clarks, have reduced their dependency on manufacture; others have simply closed down. One family company, based in Northamptonshire, home at one time to countless small and medium-sized manufacturers, has diversified imaginatively. When he inherited the family boot business, Steve Pateman realized that it was in long-term decline. Its fortunes have been changed dramatically as it has become one of the UK's leading manufacturers of boots and kinky leather products for the fetish-wear market.

The growth of C&J Clark

The business began in 1825 when the founder, Cyrus Clark, began trading in sheepskin rugs in Street, Somerset, which remains home to the business to this day. The Clarks are a Quaker family and the business has always been paternalistic and, in some ways, benevolent to its workforce.

In 1828 Cyrus' brother, James, became an apprentice in the business and it was he who later used cut-offs from the rugs to make sheepskin slippers, which they called 'Brown Peters'. James became a full partner in 1833, hence the name C&J Clark. By this time socks and welted boots had been added to the product range. Together with the slippers they generated 30% of the company's revenue – until 1920 they were sold as Torbrand products. Most of the trade had grown by word of mouth.

In 1849 the company was experiencing trading difficulties and it began to use posters for advertising its products. On the verge of bankruptcy, Clarks exhibited at Prince Albert's Great Exhibition at Crystal Palace, where two prizes temporarily restored prosperity to the business. By the 1860s the company was once more nearly insolvent. Cyrus and James retired and William Stephens Clark took over as chairman. His contribution was to transform the company from a cottage industry to a mass-market shoemaker.

After the later death of Cyrus Clark the sheepskin business was moved to a separate company in nearby Glastonbury. New ranges and types of shoe followed, including (in 1893) a special range of hygienic boots and shoes, which followed the natural lines and shape of people's feet. Clarks was, by this time, the dominant employer in Street and the town was dependent upon its success. Interestingly, a coffee house, established earlier to dissuade workers from drinking, was turned into an inn which served beer. In 1903 Clarks opened a London showroom in Shaftesbury Avenue; the shoes were still made to order at this time. Five years later the family business was turned into a limited liability company.

Between 1900 and 1940 new materials and technologies were embraced and the manufacturing activities were able to benefit from economies of mass production. In 1920 a new production and distribution system allowed Clarks to despatch from stock upon receipt of an order. In 1920 the company used the brand name Clarks for the first time on its shoes, and soon afterwards began to produce women's fashion shoes which did not cover the whole ankle. Success throughout this period led to press advertising (1934) and to a number of small retail outlets, named Peter Lord (1937).

During World War II the factory switched over to the manufacture of aircraft components and torpedo parts. In 1942 Bancroft Clark succeeded his father, Roger, as chairman and, as soon as the war was over, declared that expansion would follow. One notable contribution from Bancroft, who remained in charge for 25 years, was the renowned foot gauge which measured both the width and length of the foot. This gave the company pre-eminence in children's shoes. In the 1950s Clarks introduced their casual but smart Desert Boot, made out of soft suede leather, and then, in the 1960s, the Wallabee moccasin shoe, again in suede. Both of these designs are still popular today. In 1952 the name Clarks was used on retail outlets for the first time.

During the 1970s Clarks pioneered their cushioned polyurethane soles and spawned a range of shoes which again remains popular today – lightweight but strong, casual and semiformal shoes with springy soles which are both comfortable and shock absorbent. In 1967 Clarks bought Ravel, which made and sold fashionable shoes; and in 1980 also acquired K Shoes, based in Kendal, Cumbria, which remains as an independent label famous today for formal men's and women's shoes and lightweight casual shoes for women, known as Springers.

The situation in 1990

C&J Clark prospered through the early 1980s and earned a record £35.7 million in pre-tax profits from sales of £604 million in 1986. The company was now established in Europe, America and Australia, where its products were popular. Some 60% of the shoes were manufactured in the UK; 40% were produced in Portugal, Italy and Brazil. The main brands were Clarks (mostly associated with children's and comfortable semiformal shoes), K (targeted at mature adults) and Ravel (high fashion shoes). But its fortunes then changed very quickly and both sales and profits fell towards the end of the decade.

As shown in Figure 1, the market leader at this time was British Shoe Corporation (BSC, owned by Sears) with a range of distinctive (but sometimes competing) retail outlets, including Curtess, Manfield, Saxone, Freeman Hardy Willis, Dolcis (good-quality, medium-priced stylish shoes for fashion-conscious youngsters) and Shoe City (a new warehouse-type operation in out-of-town shopping centres). BSC overall had a dominant position for low- and medium-price shoes for people up to middle age. High-price shoes for all ages were supplied by a host of independents including Ravel (owned by Clarks) and Cable and Co. (a new brand name invented by BSC in 1988 to gain introduction to this sector). Marks and Spencer was dominant with low-priced shoes for older people, leaving Clarks in a strong position with medium-priced shoes for a number of age groups.

However, the retail environment had been changing during the latter years of the 1980s:

- Sales had fallen as an economic recession took hold, but high-street property rents remained high.
- The market was much more competitive as an increasing number of imported brands was introduced and gained popularity.
- Customer tastes were changing, with casual shoes and trainers becoming increasingly popular.
- Market demographics were also changing, with fewer people in the younger age groups.

A concerned BSC introduced a number of strategic changes, designed in part to strengthen their position in the sector dominated by Clarks. Among other changes, the Manfield brand was consciously repositioned in the medium-priced older age groups. This required new store layouts and fittings, different ranges of shoes and a higher level of customer service. Thirty new outlets were opened in 1990 to complement the existing 850 concessions in department and fashion stores.

Family squabbles broke out inside Clarks as the company struggled to clarify a new strategic response. The company appeared to have 'boxed itself into a corner'. Its manufacturing costs were relatively expensive, making it relatively vulnerable to cheaper imports. As sales declined the company had to reduce its costs. Still with its Quaker traditions and still the dominant employer in Street, the company was reluctant to go down the redundancy route. Instead, the company sought to reduce its costs by using cheaper leathers and introducing simpler (easier-to-make) styles. The company, already with a 'traditional' image, was now seen as both dull and relatively expensive by many customers. The Danish company Ecco, which manufactured strong, comfortable, semiformal shoes in countries such as Portugal, was one new competitor which would take sales from Clarks during the 1990s.

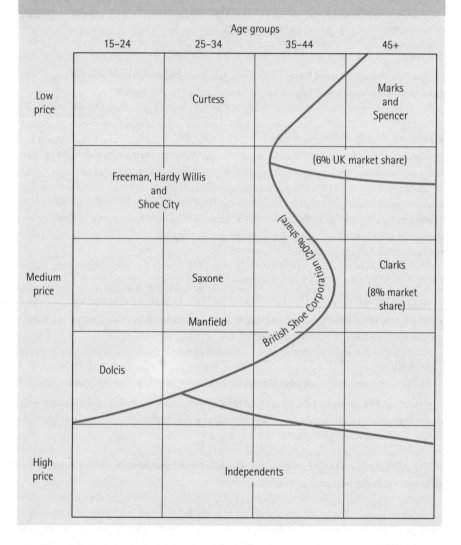

Figure 1 Shoe retailing in the UK, late 1980s-segment domination. (Developed with the co-operation of British Shoe Corporation.)

In 1990 a new, external chairman, the first non-Clark, was recruited. Walter Dickson had been a former chairman of Mars Europe and was recognized as a marketing expert. Two years later some of the Clark family board members attempted to oust Dickson, but he survived and the company put itself up for sale.

The bid from Berisford

Analysts were divided over the proposal. Some believed that Clarks was a strong company at heart, while others felt that it had lost its way and was unsure whether it was really a manufacturer or a retailer. There were, in the end, three serious bidders in spring 1993: rival shoe manufacturer FII, a venture capital bid put together by Electra, and Berisford, the successful commodities business which had earlier bought and turned around RHP Bearings. Berisford, offering £184 million, became the preferred bidder – but the family was divided. While seven out of the 11 board members were in favour, four were vehemently opposed. They argued that Berisford had no experience in shoes. Analysts generally seemed to believe that had Clarks been a publicly owned company the bid would have succeeded easily, as the institutions which owned most of the shares that were outside the family's control were certainly all supportive of the sale. One commented wryly that experience in shoes was an irrelevant issue, Clarks was far too introspective and 'Troubleshooter' Sir John Harvey Jones (so-named because of the successful BBC television series) should have been called in some years ago.

Bersiford stated that should its bid succeed it would make a number of key changes:

- The lead-time between new shoe designs and their availability in stores would be shortened dramatically.
- In part to achieve this, production in the UK would be increased, against the current trend.
- New designs would exploit Clarks' technical and manufacturing competencies more effectively, especially its expertise with cushioned soles.
- The brand would be invigorated to widen its appeal – there was a real need to persuade teenagers that Clarks was not just for young children, for example.

In the end the bid failed and the board opted to remain independent. Dickson resigned shortly after this and was replaced by Roger Pedder. Pedder, then in his early 50s, had worked for Clarks in the past. He had joined the company in 1963, where he soon became personal assistant to the chairman, who at that time was still Bancroft Clark. In 1968 Pedder married Bancroft's daughter and then left the company. He stayed in retailing and worked for BHS, Burton, Halford's and Harris Queensway before becoming a joint founder of Pet City. He had rejoined as a non-executive director in 1988.

Pedder quickly established a Shareholder Council, a body which would look after the interests of the family shareholders in the future. Three years later Pedder head-hunted Tim Parker as chief executive. Parker had no connections with the family or the business. A graduate of the London Business School, he had been credited with turning around Kenwood, manufacturer of kitchen appliances. Pedder had read an article about his success here and felt that he might be the person who could restore prosperity to Clarks.

Turnaround

Parker has introduced a number of strategic changes since his arrival in 1996. Table 3 shows how pre-tax profits had collapsed just before the Berisford bid and how, after a three-year revival, they had collapsed again in 1996. In year ended 31 January 2001 both sales and profits were at record highs. In this year 38 million pairs of shoes were sold; the company was growing in a static market. However, the number of employees had declined as the proportion manufactured overseas had been increased.

Table 3 C&J Clark

Year ending 31 January	No. of employees	Turnover £'000	Pre-tax profits £'000
1990	20,835	599,927	30,317
1991	19,538	605,793	30,117
1992	19,550	594,223	20,389
1993	18,416	624,572	1687
1994	17,913	655,314	20,761
1995	18,631	684,318	19,623
1996	18,251	721,630	24,806
1997	17,405	727,345	(3200)
1998	16,620	743,141	35,003
1999	16,426	792,210	6261
2000	15,561	831,614	39,235

Specifically:

- Parker reduced, arguably culled, the existing team of managers. As well as taking out a complete layer, newcomers have been recruited to replace some of the others who left. There have also been internal promotions.
- He reduced the workforce worldwide. This included 25% of the workforce at the Street factory in Somerset. Parker dedicated some considerable time to visiting the factories and explaining what was happening.
- Some factories were shut completely and sold to the company which manufactures Doc Martens shoes and boots.
- The number of retail outlets was increased from 550 to 650 and every one was restyled with Clarks' new logo and new colours. The stores now have a different ambience – they no longer feel like an 'older person's store'. Worldwide there are almost 800 shops.
- Manufacturing in the UK has been reduced to just 25% of the total sold. Clarks was becoming more of a designer, wholesaler and retailer at the expense of manufacturing its own shoes. Clarks now owns eight factories, three in southwest England, three in northwest England and two in Portugal. Working conditions have been improved by Parker. Imported shoes are manufactured in Brazil, India, China, Romania and Vietnam.
- New designs have been introduced while older designs have been revamped and relaunched.
- New advertisements take a more 'tongue-in-cheek' approach. A typical magazine advertisement for ladies' boots features a large picture of the boots lying flat in their box. The main headline says: 'New boots and why you just have to have them'. Smaller illustrations are accompanied by the following copy: 'They'll keep your ankles warm', 'A box that big has to come in handy' and 'You won't have to shave your legs.'
- There is a website and on-line sales of selected products are planned for 2001. Clarks believes that there is a market for trainers but not shoes. People are less concerned about

exact fit with trainers and are willing to adjust the thickness of the socks worn with them; in the case of shoes the issue of fit is much more critical.

- A shopping village outlet opened in the 1980s was sold to raise cash.

The situation in 2000

Clarks is world leader for 'brown shoes' and shoe-care products and a major player in children's shoes. Table 2 showed that Clarks is overall market leader in the UK with 10% of sales – up 2% from 1990. The term 'brown shoes' represents casual shoes and loafers in the shoe industry; formal shoes are known as 'black' and trainers are 'white shoes'. The industry remains very fragmented and globally static. Sales are strong in the USA where the Clarks and Bostonian (men's fashion shoes) brands turn over £200 million a year and contribute 25% of the total profits – some 95% of the shoes sold in America are imported. The company is also particularly successful in Japan where its range of men's originals is very popular.

Clarks has a very wide range of practical (work) shoes, casuals, sandals and children's wear. They are not the highest price, but they are certainly not the cheapest. Of generally high quality, they represent value for money. The new image is focused on shoes that are fashionable and casual. The company claims that it offers individual designs, exceptional comfort, premium quality and expert service. Clarks' shoes are focused mainly on the 35–45 age group and the K brand on the over 50s.

There are five distinct ranges of women's shoes: formal, smart (with thicker soles), casual, boots, and Springers – semiformal casual shoes with soft soles sold under the K brand.

There are also five men's ranges: formal, smart, casual, originals, and waterproof (walking boots). The originals range includes designs from years ago which have been successfully relaunched. The Desert Boot (a lightweight lace-up boot made with thin, rugged suede leather and with crêpe soles) has become a fashion product, sported by media figures such as Oasis' Gallagher brothers. The Wallabee (a luxury soft suede lace-up moccasin shoe, again with a crêpe sole) was first introduced in the 1960s, a decade after the Desert Boot. The third main original is the Millcreek, another suede shoe with a crêpe sole, but this time a slip-on. The range competes effectively with designer fashion brands but sells at much lower prices – the first time that Clarks has been able to compete successfully in this particular sector.

There are separate children's ranges for boys and girls. These ranges comprise four age groups: first shoes, 2–4, 5–7, and 8 years and over, as well as a range of trainers with their own brand identity, Cica.

Excluding Nike and Reebok – manufacturers of trainers and sports shoes and which together with Adidas account for 13% of the UK market – *Marks and Spencer* follows Clarks with a 5% share, 1% less than its share in 1990. In 1999 the M&S profit margin on shoes was reported to be 6.6%, whereas a year earlier it had been 14.1%. The company had lost some of its international sales as a result of the high pound. It still retained a value-for-money image but it was introducing new designs for more fashion-conscious customers. *Stylo*, with 4.5% of the UK market, sells mainly through its chain of 250 Barratt stores and 350 ladies' shoe concessions in department stores.

The once-dominant British Shoe Corporation has seen its share tumble from 20% to 2% as Sears has divested brand after brand. Freeman Hardy Willis was sold in 1995, followed a year later by Saxone and Curtess and in 1997 by Shoe City and Dolcis. BSC had been overdependent upon that part of the market most affected by the growth and popularity of sportswear chains and clothing retailers such as Next and River Island, which have systematically added shoes to their range of products. BSC is now primarily the repositioned Manfield and its newer self-service format, Shoe Express, designed to provide convenience at low prices.

New retail names such as *Shoe* (targeted at young people) and *Dune* (high-fashion shoes at premium prices) have made an impact recently. Top (clothes) designer names are being attached to ranges of shoes, which are available in selected outlets and department store concessions. These include Pierce Fionda, DKNY, Patrick Cox and LK Bennett.

The future

After the failed bid by Berisford and the formation of the Shareholder Council it was thought that the company might seek a flotation, but the family shareholders appear to have no inclination to relinquish their control at the moment. There is no longer any need to raise capital to fund expansion plans. There is, however, a rumour that Clarks might seek to acquire Shoe City from the Belgian retail group, Brantano, which bought it from BSC.

C&J Clark: http://www.clarks.co.uk

Questions

1. Using Porter's five-forces model, how attractive do you think the shoe industry is? Apply the model to both manufacturing and retailing.

2. How does Clarks add value? How would you summarize the company's strategic (competitive) position in 1990? In 2000? Do you believe that Clarks is now in a much stronger position than it was ten years ago?

3. Evaluate the changes introduced by Parker in the last five years. To what extent do you think the current results can be attributed to these changes, and to what extent might they be the result of external circumstances?

4. If you were Tim Parker, what future strategies would you be considering? Is the family ownership a relative strength or a relative drawback?

Index